Called by the Gospel

An Introduction to the New Testament

(revised edition)

Called by the Gospel

Introductions to Christian History and Thought
From a Distinctly Lutheran Perspective

Volume 1
Called to be God's People: An Introduction to the Old Testament
Andrew E. Steinmann, editor

Volume 2
Called by the Gospel: An Introduction to the New Testament
Michael P. Middendorf and Mark Schuler

Volume 3
Called to Believe, Teach, and Confess:
An Introduction to Doctrinal Theology
Steven P. Mueller, editor

Volume 4
Called to be Holy in the World: An Introduction to Christian History
Timothy H. Maschke, editor

Called by the Gospel

An Introduction to the New Testament

Michael P. Middendorf

Mark Schuler

with editorial assistance from
Rhoda Schuler

CALLED BY THE GOSPEL
An Introduction to the New Testament
(revised edition)

ISBN: 978-1-55635-526-4

This book is dedicated to
those who serve the church
with faith and fervor
professionally or simply out of love
past, present, and future
because they are
called by the Gospel.

Contents

Acknowledgments

Michael P. Middendorf wishes to thank the following:

- My co-author, editor, and archaeology mentor, Mark Schuler;
- The Harry and Caroline Trembath family for establishing the Chair of Confessional Theology at Concordia University, Irvine. I was able to complete a substantial portion of this book while occupying the Chair in 2003–2004;
- President J.A.O. Preus, former Provost Kurt Krueger, Dean James Bachman, and all the members of the School of Theology at Concordia University, Irvine for their insights and support;
- Professor Rachel Soo and David Rueter for assistance with maps, graphics and pictures;
- Jaclyn Gibson for proofreading my portions of this textbook;
- The Fall 2004 and 2005 New Testament Honors classes at Concordia University, Irvine who gave valuable feedback on draft sections of this work;
- All the students I have been privileged to interact with at Concordia University, Austin (1992–2001) and Concordia University, Irvine (2001–present). I hope I have been able to teach you even a small portion of what I have learned in the process; and
- Above all, "the name that is above every name," our Lord Jesus Christ (Philippians 2:9, 11).

Mark Schuler wishes to thank the following:

- Dr. Rhoda Schuler, my wife and best friend, whose editorial work on this project saved us from biblical, theological, and grammatical gaffes too numerous to mention;
- Dr. Erich Kiehl, professor emeritus from Concordia Seminary, Saint Louis, who introduced me to the world behind the text;
- The late Professor Yizhar Hirshfeld, from Hebrew University, Jerusalem, who invited me into the work of archaeological research;
- Concordia University, Saint Paul for research time on sabbatical;
- Luther Seminary, Saint Paul, who welcomed me as a scholar-in-residence during the writing of significant portions of this work;
- Students from Concordia University, Saint Paul, who for thirteen years have explored the New Testament with me;
- My co-author, Mike Middendorf, whose work on Paul complements my work on the gospels and who is a very lucky amateur archaeologist;
- Colleagues Steve Mueller, Andy Steinman, and Tim Maschke, who helped birth this textbook project; and
- The one who is the Alpha and the Omega (Revelation 21:13), whose final word (*tetelestai*) is most appropriate at this moment … and always.

1

Approaching the New Testament

Introduction

"Sometimes it is hard to see the forest for the trees." This saying suggests that when people get too focused on one or two specific issues, they tend to lose sight of the overall significance of what is happening or may overlook the most important things. For example, an army general may expend too many resources in order to win one battle and, thereby, end up losing the war. A university student may devote all her time and attention to one class or assignment and, as a result, neglect her overall progress toward a degree. Before we look at the individual books or "trees" in the New Testament, it will be helpful to have a view of the larger "forest" in mind. In order to accomplish this "in the beginning," the next section of this book provides an overall summary of the entire Bible. These Holy Scriptures are an extensive, all-encompassing narrative that is nevertheless unified by the person and work of Jesus Christ.

The rest of chapter one addresses a number of introductory questions related to the New Testament: Where did the New Testament come from and how? In what ways is it properly studied, interpreted and understood? Is it really the word of God? If so, what exactly does this mean? What effect did the New Testament's message have upon people two thousand years ago? How does it apply today? What role should it have in the Christian life?

Chapter Outline

The Message of the New Testament
The Written Word of God
Lutheran Hermeneutics
The Text of the New Testament
Key Tools

The Message of the New Testament

When students contemplate reading through the New Testament, they probably approach the task with a certain level of anxiety. After all, the Bible is often depicted as a deep, complex, and imposing book that is difficult to understand. Yet the New Testament is basically trying to answer three simple questions:

- Who is Jesus?
- What has he done?
- What effect should the answers to these first two questions have on those who read the New Testament or hear its message?

Although these are simple questions, the answers to them may be very complex. If so, apprehensions about entering the New Testament would logically resurface. In addition, striving to understand the New Testament more fully, we will encounter a number of other difficult issues, and our attempts to resolve them may seem to be less than satisfactory or even elusive.

Our hope is that wrestling with these essential questions will not cause us to lose sight of the basic answers to them, since the three questions above focus our attention on the vital core of the New Testament—the person of Jesus of Nazareth and his birth, life, teaching, ministry, death, resurrection, ascension, and reign. That is to say, the New Testament is **christocentric** or Christ-centered. It answers questions about who Jesus is and what he has done. To stress this point, our presentation of each New Testament book will conclude with a discussion of how Jesus is portrayed in that particular document.

But what about the third question? What significance do the answers to those first two questions intend to have for those who read the New Testament? While the New Testament has much to say about how we are to respond to its message, the Bible's main interest is **soteriological**. That is to say, the primary aim of the message of Jesus is to give people salvation. This is the Gospel or "good news" Jesus proclaimed. For example, Jesus says he "came to seek and to save the lost" (Luke 19:10) and to give abundant, eternal life (John 5:25; 10:10). Through faith in what Jesus accomplished, people receive those gifts of salvation and eternal life; they are rescued from their "lost" condition.

Jerusalem's Dome of the Rock from the *Dominus Flevit* Church

The New Testament certainly has a lot more to say in response to that third question. It contains numerous instructions regarding how those who receive and believe the message of Jesus should live in response to it, but these instructions are not the main point. Rather, central to the New Testament are the two fundamental characteristics identified above—it is christocentric and soteriological. Together, these two characteristics explain the title of the book you are now reading. *Called by the Gospel* expresses the truth that the good news about Jesus Christ calls us into a saving relationship with the one, true God.

These famous passages from the New Testament illustrate what it means to be "called by the Gospel":

- What is the New Testament all about? John 3:16 provides this commonly quoted *christocentric* response: "For God so loved the world that he gave his only Son, that whoever believes in him should not perish but have eternal life."
- Another well-known summary that emphasizes the *soteriological* aspect of the New Testament is Ephesians 2:8–9: "For by grace you have been saved through faith. And this is not your own doing; it is the gift of God, not a result of works, so that no one may boast."
- Romans 10 is *both christocentric and soteriological* when it simply asserts, "If you confess with your mouth that Jesus is Lord and believe in your heart that God raised him from the dead, you will be saved" (Romans 10:9). St. Paul goes on to say that this belief or "faith comes from hearing, and hearing through the word of Christ" (Romans 10:17).

The Bible: One Book or Two?

The New Testament normally comes or is "packaged" as the second part of a larger book called the Bible. It is significant that the Bible is the single best selling book in the United States year after year. The Bible, however, is really made up of two distinct sections called the "Old Testament" and the "New Testament." By one word count, over seventy-five percent of the words in the Bible are contained in the Old Testament. So perhaps we should say that only the last fourth of the Bible is the New Testament.

To even speak of the Bible as a "book" is somewhat misleading. The Bible is actually more like a library, a collection of documents. In English Bibles, the Old Testament contains thirty-nine documents in its library; the New Testament has twenty-seven. We will talk more about how those twenty-seven documents were collected into the New Testament later (see the discussion of the canon below). Our concern here is with why those two collections have been collected into one "book." What is the relationship between them?

The Christian church has asserted what the New Testament itself asserts. The "New" Testament is not a new story at all, but a continuation of the narrative which began in the Old Testament. In this sense, the Bible is rightly considered one book, for it is one story. In fact, the phrase "New Testament" (or Covenant) was first used by an Old Testament Prophet named Jeremiah. The Hebrew word translated "new" in Jeremiah 31:31 (*chadash*) does not convey the idea of something totally new and different. It is used, for example, to refer to a "new" moon. Each month, however, does not welcome a different moon. Instead, it is the same moon renewed once again. That is the sense in which the New Testament is "new." At the same time, the New Testament announces that in Jesus the Old Testament is brought to its culmination or fulfillment.

Is the Bible one book, or two books, or sixty-six books? The New Testament emphatically declares that the answer is "one." The Bible is a collection of documents, which contains one continuous narrative about God's interaction with humanity.

The Whole Story: The Bow-Tie Diagram

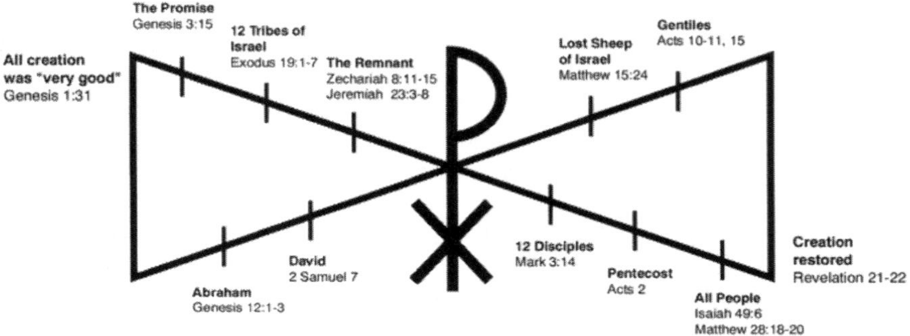

This diagram provides a framework for understanding the essential message of the entire Bible. It also illustrates the main points we have discussed so far. First, it is shaped like a bow-tie whose center expresses the christocentric point of the Bible. The symbol in the middle is a chi-rho. It is comprised of the first two Greek letters in the word for **Christ**. The Greek term *christos* translates the Hebrew title **Messiah**.

In addition, this diagram unites the Old and New Testaments into one continuous account of God acting in history to save his people. As we work our way across the diagram, please refer to the passages listed on it. The left edge portrays where the Bible begins. In Genesis God created everything that exists and it was "very good" (Genesis 1:31). The Fall into sin, however, disrupted that goodness and brought rebellion, suffering, and death. Yet God immediately made a promise to restore his fallen creation through the offspring of a woman (3:15). The left side of the diagram shows how that promise was narrowed down through a number of Old Testament people until it was eventually fulfilled in the birth of Jesus. This promise was more fully expressed to Abraham beginning in Genesis 12. God promised Abraham that he would become a great nation, that his descendents would receive the promised land, and that in him "all the families of the earth will be blessed" (12:3). God reaffirmed these promises to Abraham's son, Isaac, and his grandson, Jacob. Jacob's name was changed to Israel. The descendents of his twelve sons comprised the twelve tribes of Israel. They were freed from slavery in Egypt through Moses. After the Exodus they journeyed to Mount Sinai and, forty years later, entered the promised land of Canaan under Joshua's leadership.

Around 1000 B.C. King David came to the throne from the tribe of Judah. In 2 Samuel 7 God promised to build David a royal house or dynasty. He then spoke of one of David's offspring and pledged, "I will establish the throne of his kingdom forever" (2 Samuel 7:12–13). David's son, Solomon, ruled after him and built a magnificent temple in Jerusalem. But the Babylonians destroyed Jerusalem and that temple in 586 B.C. They also carried the people of Judah and their king into exile. Yet God fulfilled the promise he made through his prophets to bring a remnant of the people back to their land. All of this is illustrated on the left or Old Testament side of the diagram.

At the center point of the bow-tie diagram is a symbol for Christ; according to the New Testament, the point of the whole Old Testament is a narrowing down, leading up to, and looking ahead toward the coming of the Christ or Messiah in whom God's promises to his people would be fulfilled. The New Testament begins by identifying Jesus of Nazareth as the "Christ, the son of David, the son of Abraham" (Matthew 1:1). The rest of the New Testament goes on to assert that Jesus is the goal and fulfillment of the entire Old Testament.

Jesus himself claimed to be the focal point of it all. During his ministry, Jesus said this to his fellow Jews: "You search the Scriptures because you think that in them you have eternal life; and it is they that bear witness about me" (John 5:39). After his death and resurrection, Jesus referred to the three main sections of the Old Testament when he told his disciples,

> These are my words that I spoke to you while I was still with you, that everything written about me in the Law of Moses and the Prophets and the Psalms must be fulfilled.... Thus it is written, that the Christ should suffer and on the third day rise from the dead, and that repentance and forgiveness of sins should be proclaimed in his name to all nations (Luke 24:44, 46–47).

Jesus' reference to "all nations" explains the right side of the diagram. The New Testament begins with the birth, life, ministry, suffering, death, and resurrection of Jesus. The New Testament side of the story shows how Jesus, during his ministry, reached out to include his twelve Jewish disciples and "the lost sheep of Israel" (Matthew 15:24). On the day of Pentecost, the message of Jesus expands to include thousands of Jews who had been scattered throughout the Mediterranean world among his people (the **Diaspora**; see Acts 2). Then the good news of Jesus branches out further to non-Jews or **Gentiles** as it strives to encompass all peoples and nations.

God's Old Testament people waited for the coming of the Messiah; God's New Testament people similarly anticipate the end of the story. Jesus Christ will come again to restore God's creation and to bring his people into the eternal promised land of heaven. Then, as depicted on the right edge of the diagram, all things will be made "new" and "very good" once again (Revelation 21–22; see especially 21:5).

This bow-tie diagram helps to illustrate what the Scriptures do with a number of significant, unifying themes that run throughout the Old and New Testaments. Notice how each of the items listed below is prominent on the left/Old Testament side. The New Testament then declares that they have all come to fulfillment in Jesus, the center point of the diagram and the Scriptures. But this christocentric focus is not the end of the story. All of them continue to be used to describe God's people in a transformed way on the right/New Testament side.

- One of the foundational elements in the Old Testament is God's repeated promise to bless *Abraham and his offspring* (for example, Genesis 12:2–3, 7; 13:15–16; 17:8; 24:7). In identifying the recipient of these promises, St. Paul asserts that the Scripture "does not say 'And to offsprings,' referring to many, but referring to one, 'And to your offspring,' who is Christ" (Galatians 3:16). Yet later in the same chapter of Galatians, Paul declares that all those who belong to Christ "are Abraham's offspring, heirs according to the promise" (Galatians 3:29).
- As indicated above, the title *christos* is Greek for the Hebrew "messiah." Both terms mean "anointed one." Many people and things were anointed throughout the Old Testament (for example, priests, kings, prophets, and furnishings for the tabernacle and temple). All these pointed toward *the* anointed one, Jesus. In a discussion about antichrists and *the* Christ, 1 John reminds his readers that you all "have been anointed by the Holy One, … [and] the anointing (*chrisma*) you have received from him abides in you" (1 John 2:20, 27).
- There are many *sacrifices* described and required throughout the Old Testament. The New Testament book of Hebrews repeatedly insists that they are all fulfilled in Christ who was sacrificed "once for all" (for example, Hebrews 9:28; 10:10, 12; also Romans 6:10). There is no need for further sacrifices (Hebrews 10:18). Yet Hebrews later calls believers in Jesus to offer sacrifices of praise and good works to God (13:15–16). In his letter to the Romans, Paul urges those who have received God's mercy in Christ to offer their "bodies as a living sacrifice, holy and acceptable to God" (Romans 12:1).
- In the Old Testament, the descendents of Aaron, Moses' brother, served as *priests* to God. The New Testament identifies Jesus Christ as our great High Priest (Hebrews 4:14). Yet, in him, Peter declares, "You are a chosen race, a royal priesthood" (1 Peter 2:9). The book of Revelation concludes that Jesus' death has "made us a kingdom, priests to his God and Father" (Revelation 1:6).
- Those Old Testament priests served at the *tabernacle* and, then, the Jerusalem *temple* where God dwelled in the midst of his people. The opening chapter of John's Gospel says that Jesus came and "tabernacled" or "dwelled" among us (John 1:14). When Jesus predicts, "Destroy this temple and in three days I will raise it up" (2:19), John 2:21 concludes, "He was speaking about the temple of his body." Later, Paul reminds the Corinthian Christians, "Do you not know that your body is

a temple of the Holy Spirit within you, whom you have from God?" (1 Corinthians 6:19; see also 3:16 and 2 Corinthians 6:16).

Peter utilizes the last three bullet points within two verses when he tells believers, "You yourselves like living stones are being built up as a spiritual house, to be a holy priesthood, to offer spiritual sacrifices acceptable to God through Jesus Christ" (1 Peter 2:5–6).

This discussion has introduced the field of **Biblical Theology**. It is a discipline that demonstrates how consistent themes run throughout and unite the Old and New Testaments into one, unified whole.

Conclusion

We hope this introduction will help the readers to keep the big picture in mind. The overall framework of the bow-tie diagram also provides a tool for understanding and interpreting the New Testament, as well as the entire Bible. Finally, it should be evident by now that the essential background for understanding the New Testament comes from the Old Testament. At times this is clearly stated in the New, but more often the Old Testament is there by implication. Its influence is always present, even if it lies just beneath the surface. As a result, the New Testament generally presumes a certain degree of familiarity with Old Testament events, persons, and theology. If New Testament readers have not had much exposure to the Old Testament, this will often be a significant obstacle to understand properly the New Testament. While there is no substitute for studying the Old Testament itself, one purpose of this book is to fill in some of its background.

The Written Word of God

What is the New Testament? Is it just like other books? Does the New Testament merely contain great literature from the past? Is it simply recounting history? If so, are its historical accounts pious fictions or verified fact? Is the New Testament on the same level as other religious literature such as the Koran or the Talmud, or does it stand out even among those other "holy" books? If so, how? Does it glow in the dark or have other magical qualities that prove its distinctiveness?

Before answering those questions, it is significant to note that within the New Testament there are any number of paradoxes which, at first glance, may appear to be contradictions. For example, was Jesus Christ human or divine? Are his followers sinners or saints? Is the kingdom of God present in Jesus' ministry or do his followers still await its coming? As we will see, the New Testament's answer to all of these questions is, "both!"

Here is the paradox we consider now: Is the Bible human words *or* the word of God? Many people have concluded that the Bible is comprised of human words that convey stories from the past, along with myths, legends, and fables created and told by human beings. On the other hand, Christians often view their Holy Scriptures as a divine book dropped straight out of heaven from God. In reality, the Bible is *both* a human *and* a divine book. It was written by and through human beings. At the same time, God's Holy Spirit was working in and through those people so that the product is not simply human, but also, and primarily, from the hand of God himself.

Inspiration

First of all, the New Testament clearly regards what we call the Old Testament as the written word of God. Second Timothy 3:16 concisely states, "All Scripture is breathed out by God." Here Paul is referring specifically to the Old Testament since the New Testament was not yet all written or collected in his day. The phrase "breathed out" has also been translated "inspired." As a result, **inspiration** is the technical term used to explain how the Bible is, in fact, the word of God. It is also important to notice that the word for "breath" or "wind" in Greek and Hebrew is the same as the word used for "spirit" and the Holy "Spirit." A connection between the Holy Spirit and inspiration is, at least, implied in this verse. Paul is saying that God breathed or God "spirited" the Scriptures.

The term "Scripture" in this passage literally means "writing." As a result, inspiration does not apply merely to the thoughts or ideas conveyed, but to what was literally "written," the very words themselves. This is expressed by the phrase "**verbal inspiration**." Finally, Paul's use of the word "all" is significant. The term "**plenary**," when used of inspiration, means everything in the written Scriptures comes fully from the breath of God; nothing is excluded.

Second Peter 1:20–21 similarly asserts, "No prophecy of Scripture comes from someone's own interpretation. For no prophecy was ever produced by the will of man, but men spoke from God as they were carried along by the Holy Spirit." At the time Peter is writing, he, like Paul, is referring to the entire Old Testament. People usually misunderstand "prophecy" to "mean predicting the future." The definition of "prophecy" in the Scriptures is much broader. It means speaking and applying God's will in a variety of different settings. In fact, Moses was the greatest prophet of the Old Testament and its first five books (Genesis through Deuteronomy; called the Torah or Pentateuch) were given through him. In the Hebrew Bible, Moses' writings are followed by the Former Prophets (Joshua through Kings) and then, the Latter Prophets (Isaiah, Jeremiah, and so forth). Rather than simply predicting the future, these biblical prophets used the vast majority (over 90 percent) of their words to speak of the past and present. Prophecy, then, is speaking for God and is God speaking. Notice again the exclusive terminology Peter uses to express plenary inspiration as discussed above ("no prophecy"; "ever").

On the one hand, this passage from 2 Peter excludes the view that the Scriptures are merely a human product. It clearly expresses the role of the Holy Spirit in carrying along those who were inspired to speak "from God." On the other hand, 2 Peter 1:21 also rejects what is called the "dictation theory." The latter implies the authors were passive and uninvolved in the process as is conveyed by terms like "robotic," "automatic," or "mechanical." The origin of Scripture is clearly God; yet, at the same time, "*men* spoke from God" (v. 21).

This understanding of the Old Testament Scriptures as the written word of God is ultimately applied to the New Testament as well. Note the following steps:

- In John 6:63, Jesus declares that the words he speaks are from the Spirit of God (compare 2 Peter 1:21 above). They also have the power to give life.
- In 1 Corinthians 11:23 and 15:3, Paul speaks of "receiving from the Lord" and "delivering" or "passing on." These are technical rabbinic words for accurately and authoritatively receiving words directly or indirectly from the source and then faithfully passing them on just as received. Thus Paul here implies he is *quoting* the actual, Spirit-filled and empowered words of the Lord Jesus.
- Galatians 1:1–2 and 1:11–12 show that the Apostle Paul based the authenticity of his Gospel message on the fact that it did not come from any human source, but rather by *direct revelation* from Jesus himself.
- As a result, when St. Paul taught in Thessalonica, the believers there did not simply hear the words of Paul. Rather, as 1 Thessalonians 2:13 makes clear, they comprehended that Paul actually *spoke* "the word of God" to them as he proclaimed Jesus to be the Christ (see Acts 17:3).
- In 1 Corinthians 14:37 Paul explicitly asserts that what he *writes* is also "a command of the Lord."
- Finally, the New Testament itself begins to place its own words on the same level as the Old Testament. 1 Timothy 5:18 quotes Deuteronomy 5:24 and then the words of Jesus recorded in Luke 10:7. Both quotations are introduced with the phrase, "For the Scripture says." This reveals that as Paul wrote to Timothy around A.D. 65, Jesus' words were already equated with the Old Testament written word of God.
- In a similar manner, 2 Peter 3:15–16, written about the same time, acknowledges that the writings of Paul were being collected, studied, misunderstood, and distorted shortly after they were written! Even more important, the end of verse 16 explicitly groups Paul's writings together with "the other Scriptures." This verse places his letters on the same level as the Old Testament as well.

How do we explain all of this? How can the Bible be both human and divine words? Ultimately, inspiration is a miracle that defies human explanation. The New Testament, however, does give glimpses into how this happened. In John chapters 14 and 16 Jesus establishes further connections between the Holy Spirit and the word of the Lord. In John 14:25–26 Jesus describes how the Holy Spirit will teach the disciples "all things" and remind them of everything he said.

These words explain how we received accurate and reliable written gospels. Two of them have traditionally been attributed to the disciples Matthew and John. In addition, Mark's Gospel is associated with the disciple Peter. The author of Luke states that he received his information from those "who from the beginning were eyewitnesses and ministers of the word" (Luke 1:2). However, this understanding of inspiration does not apply merely to direct quotations from the Jesus in "Red-Letter" Bibles. It includes all the words of the Lord. John 16:13–14 describes how the Holy Spirit guides people "into all truth" by hearing from Jesus and then speaking his words and will to us.

Source and Norm

Since the Bible is God's word and is inspired by his Spirit, it maintains a unique role in the life of God's people. The Lutheran Reformation centered on these three *solas* (Latin for "only" or "alone"): we are saved by God's *grace alone*, through *faith alone*, as revealed in *Scripture alone*. While the New Testament affirms we can know some things about God apart from his revealed word (see Romans 1:19–20), our sure and certain knowledge of God, as well as about ourselves and this world, comes from Scripture alone. The Old and New Testaments, then, are our solid and certain source for understanding who God is and how he relates to people. Theologians use the phrase **formal principle** to describe this. The form of God's revelation to us is his own word.

To assert *Scripture alone* means that traditions of the church, our human reason, and our own experiences are not authoritative sources for truth about God. While we can learn some things about God from each of these areas, none of them is on the level of God's word. In a qualitative sense, the Scriptures stand alone and above all other sources of knowledge. As a result, theologians also speak of the Scriptures as being a **norm**. This term simply means that whatever we hear, learn or experience about God must always be gauged by or measured against what God's own word says. Other human sources of knowledge are not in the same category as God's word, but, rather, are "normed" by it. If tradition, reason or experience contradicts God's word, those sources of truth are in error and ought to be changed. As Jesus said to his Father, "Your word is truth" (John17:17).

Law and Gospel

What message does God speak to us in his word? People react to the New Testament in a variety of different ways. Some are confused about what the message of the New Testament is; others are perplexed by the God revealed therein. This is understandable. After all, the Bible declares, "God is love" (1 John 4:16). Yet it also speaks of the coming day of his wrath (Revelation 6:16–17). Jesus assures us of his gentle care, compassion and self-giving love (Matthew 11:28–20; 20:28), yet he also pronounces harsh "woes" upon cities and Pharisees (Matthew 11:20–24; 23:1–36). Jesus describes a time when people will be cast out into the darkness, where there will be weeping and gnashing of teeth (see Matthew 8:12; 13:42, 50; 22:13; 24:51; 25:30). So is Jesus kind, compassionate, and accepting, or is he harsh and judgmental? Is the God of the Bible consistent or capricious? Does he play favorites, or have "mood swings," or what? Here again, we run into a paradox that many people find perplexing and even troubling.

One key insight for understanding these apparent contradictions comes from a nineteenth-century Lutheran theologian named C. F. W. Walther. Based upon Martin Luther's understanding of the God who speaks in the Scriptures, Walther wrote a book titled *The Proper Distinction Between Law and Gospel* (St. Louis: Concordia, 1986). There he makes the following points:

- Thesis 1. The doctrinal contents of the entire Holy Scriptures, both of the Old and the New Testaments, are made up of two doctrines differing fundamentally from each other, namely, the Law and the Gospel.
- Thesis 4. The true knowledge of the distinction between the Law and the Gospel is not only a glorious light, affording the correct understanding of the entire Holy Scriptures, but without this knowledge Scripture is and remains a sealed book.

What Luther and Walther recognized is that God's word is intended to impact people in two different ways. There is a dual, paradoxical, or *both/and* character to God's message. For example, the Bible speaks of God being *both* a God of justice *and* of mercy; God's word proclaims a message about *both* sin *and* forgiveness; the New Testament talks *both* of the works God requires from us *and* of his grace which freely gives sinners what we could never accomplish by our own deeds.

Lutherans use the term **Law** to describe those parts of God's word that tell us what to do or not do. The Law proclaims how we are to live according to God's will. But, because we all fall short, the Law identifies our sins and shortcomings, and then pronounces God's judgment upon all who disobey his commands. The term **Gospel** comes from the Greek word that means "good news." In the Bible the good news is what God has done for us in Jesus Christ. All his promises of grace, mercy, and eternal life are freely given to us through faith in Jesus. As St. Paul wrote, "For all the promises of God find their Yes in him" (2 Corinthians 1:20).

The messages of both Law and Gospel must be heard and held in tension with each other. The tendency to resolve them into one or the other should be resisted, because the Scriptures themselves do not resolve the paradox. Finally, it should be stressed that the Gospel is the dominant expression of God's will. As James puts it, "Mercy triumphs over judgment" (2:17).

Jesus, for example, proclaims both Law and Gospel in the Sermon on the Mount (Matthew 5–7). He asserts the continuing validity of the demands of God's Law, as well as the harsh consequences of disobedience (5:17–20). Indeed, he even appears to expand the scope of God's commands (5:21–37) and finally asserts, "You, therefore, must be perfect as your heavenly Father is perfect" (5:48; compare Leviticus 19:2). Yet, in the same sermon, Jesus announces that he fulfills God's Law for us (Matthew 5:17; compare 3:15). Elsewhere he says he came "to give his life as a ransom for many" (Matthew 20:28) and, thereby, to freely grant eternal life to us (John 10:28).

St. Paul occasionally uses the structure of his letters to distinguish carefully between Law and Gospel. For example, in Romans 1:18–3:20 Paul stresses the works required by God's Law, the inability of all humanity to live up to the demands of his commandments, and the serious consequences of human failure. Paul concludes that all people "are under the power of sin" (3:9). At Romans 3:21, Paul switches to the Gospel. He declares that we are "justified by [God's] grace as a gift, through the redemption that is in Christ Jesus, ... For we hold that one is justified by faith apart from works of the law" (3:24, 28). A final, very concise illustration of both Law and Gospel is given in Romans 6:23: "For the wages of sin is death, but the free gift of God is eternal life in Christ Jesus our Lord."

While "Law and Gospel" terminology is distinctively Lutheran, this insight into the God who speaks to us in the Scriptures is shared by many other Christians. Whenever the contrast is made between God's message of sin and grace or between God's justice and his mercy, a similar point is being made.

Conclusion

One final overarching truth about the word of God as portrayed in the New Testament concludes our discussion. God's word is not merely verbiage; it is also God in action. When God speaks in Genesis 1, all creation comes into existence. God's word, therefore, is not *merely* word; it is also an event, a proclamation, an action. When the Lord prophesies in the Old Testament, what he states is as good as done. The only question is how long people will wait to experience the actual fulfillment of his words. When Jesus speaks words of forgiveness, healing, or cursing, what he says happens; word and action are combined (see, for example, Luke 5:17–26; John 4:46–53; Mark 11:12–14, 20–21). The same thing can be said about all of God's New Testament words. The book of Hebrews states it this way: "For the word of God is living and active" (Hebrews 4:12).

Even more profoundly, the New Testament announces that God's word is embodied in the person of Jesus. This is particularly the language of John who begins his Gospel with these words: "In the beginning was the Word, and the Word was with God, and the Word was God.... And the Word became flesh and dwelt among us" (John 1:1, 14; see also 1 John 1:1–2; Revelation 19:13). As a result, our discussion about the word of God is not simply about spoken words or printed words on a page; this topic is not some philosophical abstract concept. Rather, the very speaking of God which was active at creation and throughout the Old Testament became a human being in the womb of the Virgin Mary. Yes, Jesus did speak God's word, but he *is* even more. He is the word of God incarnate as a physical human being. God's word is ultimately and climactically a person, Jesus Christ himself.

Lutheran Hermeneutics

Hermeneutics is a technical word for how one interprets Scripture. While a number of more specific issues will be addressed below, this chapter has already laid out the fundamental interpretive principles which will be utilized in this textbook. First, the New Testament is Christ-centered, and its main focus is on the salvation which comes to people in and through him. Second, the New Testament is the continuation and fulfillment of the Old Testament. Third, the words which make up the New Testament are the word of God given through Spirit-inspired human authors. As a result, the Bible is the authoritative source and norm for teaching about God. Finally, when interpreting and applying the New Testament, one must distinguish between God's message of Law and of Gospel.

The field of hermeneutics provides much more for us to consider. Traditionally, hermeneutics has dealt with the text under consideration. Recent studies, however, contend that interpreting a text is a complicated process which involves more than just the text itself. In *What Does This Mean?* (St. Louis: Concordia, 1995, 16–19), James Voelz stresses that we need to be cognizant of the significant roles played by all three of these overlapping areas: 1) the source/author of the text and his/her world, 2) the text itself, and 3) the receptor/hearer/reader.

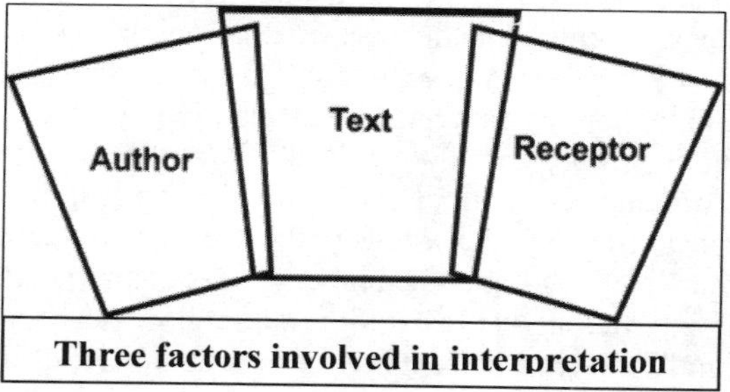

Three factors involved in interpretation

Source/Author

When reading a text, one needs to understand the author and the world in which he or she lived. The New Testament did not drop down to us out of thin air. The New Testament was written within a specific linguistic, geographical, political, social, and religious context. Its authors were real people who lived in a world different from our own in many ways. As a result, there is a whole world behind the text. Yet the New Testament does not always tell us things in the background which were assumed by the authors and by the original readers as well. In order to interpret a text effectively, it is important to learn all we can about the author and his setting.

For example, when Paul wrote the letter we call 1 Corinthians, there was much in the background. The influence of each of the following should be considered

- The personality of Paul and his apostolic calling (Acts 9);
- Paul's prior ministry in Corinth (Acts 18);
- Paul's location and situation as he writes the letter;
- the verbal and written communication that occurred between Paul and the Corinthians after he left their city; and
- the first-century, Graeco-Roman culture within which both Paul and the Corinthians lived.

We are much better equipped to understand the letter properly if we know more information about each of these factors from a variety of sources outside the text itself (for example, the New Testament book of Acts, archaeological findings, sociological studies). In order to enhance understanding, this textbook provides information that will help us see into the world behind the text of the New Testament.

Text

One also needs to deal with the text itself. Here careful study is given to the words, their precise forms, and their specific meaning in context. We should note that the New Testament was written in Greek. Anyone who reads the New Testament in English or any language other than Greek needs to be aware that he or she is reading a translation. As a result, the reader is already at some distance from the original text of the New Testament. To help bridge that gap, insights related to significant Greek words will occasionally be provided here.

Bible scholars have identified a number of specific hermeneutical principles to be utilized in interpreting the texts of Scripture. Previously, we mentioned the importance of understanding it in terms of Law and Gospel. Furthermore, the view that the entire Scriptures are the word of God leads to the conclusion that "Scripture interprets Scripture." This adage means difficult or unclear passages are to be interpreted in light of other passages whose meaning is more evident. Some other principles include

- Interpreting the words of Scripture according to their grammatical form and historical context.
- Identifing the literary form or genre and its significance (for example, parables).

- Being aware of the use of figurative and symbolic language (for example, the book of Revelation).
- Concentrating on the common, literal meaning of the text. One dictum asserts that the authors of Scripture had only "one literal sense" in mind when they wrote. Generally, this is sound advice and keeps interpretation from becoming allegorical. Yet the New Testament at times sees a fuller meaning in Old Testament passages. Note, for instance, the use of Hosea 11:1 in Matthew 2:15 and Jeremiah 31:15 in Matthew 2:18.

Hearer/Reader

A recent insight from the field of hermeneutics recognizes that all people approach a text from a certain viewpoint and that this affects how they understand that text. Their perspective may be atheism, or the Apostles' Creed, or a personal spiritual journey; it might also be the tradition of the Roman Catholic Church, or the faith of Islam, or a specific denomination's beliefs, such as those expressed in the Lutheran Confession. In reality, a complex combination of backgrounds and perspectives is involved whenever someone reads a text. This means no one who reads the New Testament is completely impartial or objective.

On the one hand, this helps to explain why there are so many different interpretations of the Bible around today (for example, feminist readings, African-American perspectives, religious or denominational interpretations, and so on). On the other hand, it is exciting that we are included in the process! Our upbringings and experiences, as well as our spiritual backgrounds and perspectives, all play a part in how we understand the text.

Remember that everyone approaches the New Testament from a given perspective or perspectives. Each one of us should acknowledge the influence of our own context and seek to identify what we bring to the text. Then it is crucial to discern the ways in which our background affects what we get out of the New Testament and how we react to it.

The Hermeneutical Circle

The Lutheran tradition has, in a sense, always recognized and admitted that it approaches the texts of the Bible from a specific perspective. In the sixteenth century, Martin Luther and his followers made a number of formal declarations about what they believed the Bible taught. Some of these topics were rather general statements about the Christian faith; others addressed more specific issues related to the situation of the church in Luther's day. In 1580 these documents, along with the three great ecumenical creeds of the church (the Apostles', Nicene and Athanasian), were collected into the ***Book of Concord***, which is also referred to as the **Lutheran Confessions**.

While many people think the term "confession" has to do with admitting you did something wrong, the Greek word literally means "to say the same thing." Lutherans affirmed that God had spoken first in his word. The Lutheran Confessions then testify to the truth of the Holy Scriptures and declare the one scriptural faith. As a result, the Lutheran Reformers asserted that these documents were drawn from the Scriptures and simply "confessed" the Bible's message on a variety of topics. In this way, the Scriptures produced the Confessions. Lutherans then hold that they read and interpret the texts of Scripture in light of the doctrinal statements of these Confessions. The figure below illustrates that there is something of a circular argument here. In fact, Lutherans speak of this as the hermeneutical circle.

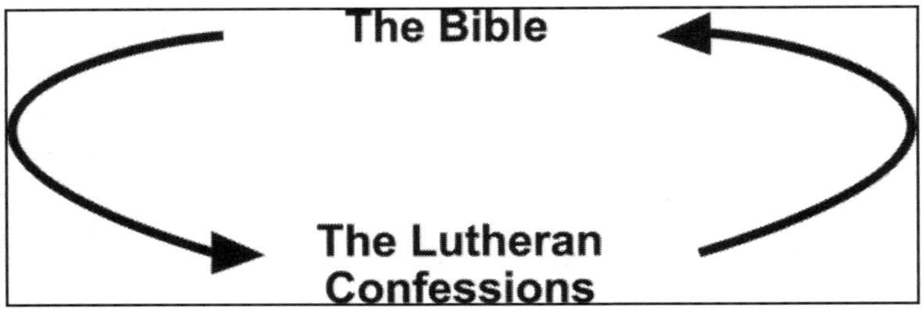

The key point, however, is where the circle starts. It begins with the Bible, with God speaking. The Bible produced the Confessions; one then reads the Bible based upon those Confessions.

In light of our discussion above, we need to consider a number of other hermeneutical circles. Any time a person encounters a text, a circle involving interaction between those two elements is immediately present. Indeed, it is improper to leave the reader out of the circle. As noted previously, a number of additional elements are also "in the loop" and affect one's interpretation of a given text. The integration of all of these factors is what makes the interpretive process dynamic and complex.

Finally, the New Testament claims an even more profound hermeneutical circle is involved when we read the Scriptures. This circle involves a connection between the reader and Jesus Christ himself. Jesus, who is God's word made flesh (John 1:14), speaks to us through these texts and these texts lead us to faith in Jesus.

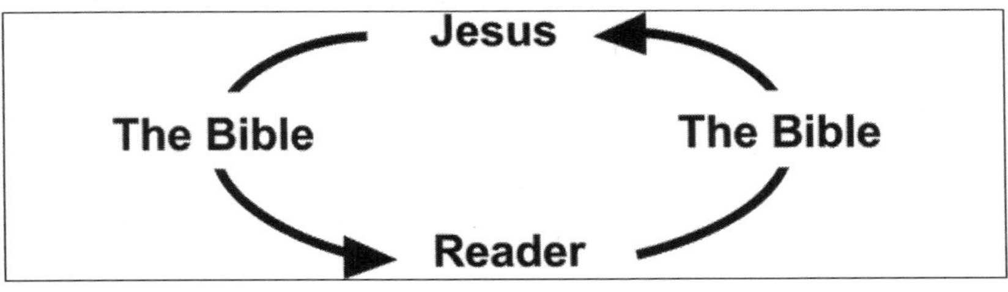

The Text of the New Testament

It may be a surprise to hear that we do not actually possess any of the original texts of the New Testament. Nor did the New Testament simply drop out of the sky directly from God. The section above on inspiration noted that God used human authors to produce the texts of the New Testament in the first century. Our discussion of hermeneutics pointed out that when speaking of the New Testament, we are actually talking about texts written in Greek. The style of Greek used in the New Testament is called ***koine*** which means "common." In other words, the New Testament is not highly sophisticated literature written for the learned, upper class. Rather, it employs the language of the common people and is written so they could comprehend the message being conveyed. After the New Testament was first written, God continued to use humans in an extensive process of copying, collecting, caring for, preserving, handing on, and translating those texts so that we have the New Testament available to us today. This section explains how that happened.

Transmission

Today's era is often called the Information Age. So much data is available to us in books and magazines, by radio and television, via computers and the internet that we can only grasp a small portion of it. But think back to a time when none of those existed, when even "paper" for writing on was expensive and scarce. How would one receive and pass on information? The term **transmission** is used to describe the process by which the texts of the New Testament were copied, dispersed, and preserved so that early copies of those texts are still available in large numbers today.

Various fields of research into the New Testament have concluded that Jesus' teachings were passed on orally at first, and then, perhaps, circulated in small written segments. Complete gospels were not composed until decades after Jesus' death and resurrection. The other documents in the New Testament were probably written between A.D. 45–100.

The authors of the New Testament most likely wrote on papyrus scrolls. Papyrus is made from reeds that grow in marshy areas. Strips of them are laid upon each other in a crisscross fashion and glued together to make sheets; these can then be attached to other sheets in order to form scrolls of various lengths. One estimate is that a scroll of Paul's letter to the Romans would be approximately eighteen feet long. Other first-century materials used for writing included animal skins, called parchment or vellum. Beginning around the second century, written materials were also assembled together in a book-like format called a codex. For writing instruments, the authors used a sharpened piece of reed or, perhaps, some type of quill.

For a number of centuries these same materials were used to copy the texts of the New Testament by hand. These copies were disseminated throughout the Mediterranean world. Through this process of transmission, it is clear the early church deemed the words of Jesus, Paul, and the other New Testament authors to be of great significance. Consider the number of texts of the New Testament that have been found in contrast to other writings from the ancient world (based upon F. F. Bruce, *Are the New Testament Documents Reliable?* Downers Grover, IL: InterVarsity Press, 1990; c. means "approximately"):

Work	Written	Earliest Copies	Time Span in Years	Number of Copies
Herodotus	488–428 B.C.	A.D. 900	1300	8
Thucydides	c. 460–400 B.C.	c. A.D. 900	1300	8
Tacitus' *Histories*	A.D. 100	A.D. 900–1100	800–1000	2
Caesar's *Gallic War*	58–50 B.C.	A.D. 900	900	9–10
New Testament	A.D. 40–100	A.D. 350 for complete manuscripts; portions from A.D. 130	300	5000 in Greek

While these copies were made with great care and dedication, the New Testament texts which we have are not always complete or identical. At times, only small fragments or incomplete portions survive. In addition, the texts we have are not all the same. Some copies have a word, phrase, or section that differs from other copies of the same passage. How should one respond to this? Does it affect the doctrine of verbal inspiration or the "source and norm" character of the New Testament itself?

The good news is that the overall evidence from the abundant manuscripts we do have leads to the conclusion that these surviving texts are remarkably accurate. Where there are differences, the best we can do is to try to discern the original text by examining the various copies and readings available to us. This field of study is called **textual criticism**. It tries to resolve the discrepancies between these **variant readings** of Scripture passages.

In making judgment calls about which reading was most likely original, textual criticism normally distinguishes between external and internal evidence. External evidence evaluates variant readings based upon the quality of the manuscripts in which they occur. Which reading is supported by the best and most widespread manuscripts? Scholars also use internal evidence in seeking to determine which changes could have come about as a result of human error. At times these errors were intentional, such as, when a text was deliberately altered to match another text of Scripture, to give added explanation, or to better support one's doctrinal position. Other times, these errors were unintentional, such as, when copyists confused similar words, skipped a line, or lost their concentration for a moment.

The fascinating field of textual criticism is like detective work that involves part art and part science. The number of manuscripts available to us today has increased dramatically from centuries ago. As a result, scholars working in this field have more and more evidence on which to make sound judgments.

Canonization

God did not send down the Bible or even the New Testament in one complete package. To produce the New Testament he used over a dozen authors writing in various places around the Mediterranean world over a period of approximately fifty years. Nor did God provide an authorized list of which books were to be included in the Scriptures. So how did the twenty-seven documents that comprise the New Testament library get assembled together?

In past years, it has been difficult to get students interested in this topic. However, the challenges recently presented by *The Da Vinci Code*, a fictional novel by Dan Brown, have raised this issue to prominence and highlighted its significance. What are reliable sources that give us solid information about who Jesus is and what he has done?

The technical term used to refer to the authoritative collection of New Testament books is the **canon**, which comes from a Greek word for a "reed" or "rod" used as a measuring stick. The documents in the canon provide the authoritative measuring stick by which teachings are to be compared and judged.

The process by which books were included in or excluded from the canon is a fairly extensive one. Initially, the early church simply used the writings of the apostles and the gospels in worship together with readings from the Old Testament Scriptures. At the same time, the documents which came to be included in the New Testament were distinguished from other early Christian writings (for example, works by Clement, Ignatius, and Polycarp). Therefore, it is fair to say that the New Testament was received and recognized as the word of God by the Christian church from the beginning. It took a number of centuries, however, for the full extent of the canon, as well as its limits, to be formally acknowledged.

In the mid-second century, a teacher named Marcion asserted that the canon of the Christian church consisted of Luke's Gospel and ten letters by Paul. In his view, the Old Testament revealed a wrathful God of vengeance. As a result, Marcion rejected the entire Old Testament and ended up with only those eleven books in his "bible." His position forced the church to come to terms with the issue and to define the canon.

First of all, the church reasserted that the Old Testament was the word of the very same God who had come to his people in Jesus Christ. Second, around the end of the second century, the church came to substantial agreement on twenty documents which it asserted were also the word of God to his New Testament people. The Muratorian Canon (c. A.D. 200), an early list of books, and church fathers such as Irenaeus (c. A.D. 130–200), Tertullian (c. A.D. 160–225), and Clement of Alexandria (c. A.D. 150-215) bear witness to this agreement. In contrast to claims in *The Da Vinci Code*, the church's acceptance of the four canonical gospels, as well as over two-thirds of the New Testament, was well established by the end of the second century.

During the third and fourth centuries, the church debated the place of other documents, seven of which were eventually included in the New Testament (Hebrews, James, 2 Peter, 2 and 3 John, Jude, and Revelation). Some Christians in certain places had questions about one or more of these. Other Christians regarded those same books as part of God's word to his people and continued to use them in worship. Around A.D. 325 the church historian Eusebius distinguished between "recognized" and "disputed" books within the canon; he also identified other writings as books which the church was to exclude from the canon. In A.D. 386 Athanasius listed all twenty-seven books of our New Testament and identified them as "the fountains of salvation." The wider church recognized the same list formally at the Council of Carthage in A.D. 397. This did not settle every issue regarding the extent of the canon, but it did bring substantial unanimity.

Two concluding points should be made in reference to the terms ***homolegoumena*** and ***antilegomena***. The former refers to the twenty books which were "spoken of the same." That is, they were widely recognized by the church almost immediately as belonging in the canon and, for all practical purposes, universally acknowledged as such by the third century. The other seven were identified as antilegomena because their place in the canon was "spoken against" or disputed by someone somewhere in the church. While all seven of these books were eventually included in the canon, a compromise accepted that no doctrine could be based solely upon a book from among the antilegomena.

Second, this process was not simply one of inclusion, but also of exclusion. There are many writings from the early church (for example, the Gnostic Gospels) which were not included in the canon. Reasons for excluding such works involved their non-authoritative character, incorrect doctrinal content, uncertain authorship, and lack of credible sources. Some scholars suggest that the power structure of the early church selected only those books that agreed with its positions and, therefore, excluded and marginalized other voices. According to this view, the church produced the canon. On the other hand, many Christians assume the manner in which the New Testament was brought together was simple, immediate, and unanimous, as if today's Christian Bible existed as an assembled unit by the end of the first century. Neither view is correct. God had spoken to his people through these writings which claim to be the word of God. Ultimately, the church recognized God's word for what it was. Instead of saying that the church formed the canon, it is more accurate to acknowledge the extent to which the canon formed the church from its infancy and produced the church's teachings about God, Jesus, and salvation. At the same time, we should be cognizant of the historical reality that this process of recognition involved discussion and debate, inclusion and exclusion, and took approximately three hundred years to resolve.

Translation

Under the section on hermeneutics, we noted that the original text of the New Testament was written in Greek. As a result, unless someone has studied that language, his or her only access to the New Testament is in translation. There is a famous saying that "all translators are liars." This claim acknowledges that language is a complex thing, and, no matter how fine the effort, one always loses a little in the translation. A more appropriate phrase might be that "every translation is an interpretation." Any attempt to reproduce what is expressed in one language into a different one via translation is inherently complicated and somewhat imprecise. Since translation is always imprecise, one might wonder whether it is legitimate to "alter" God's word, at least to some degree, by translating it at all. The New Testament implies the affirmative.

In the years before Christ, many adherents to the faith of the Old Testament were no longer proficient in Hebrew. As a result, their Scriptures were translated into Greek, the common language of the Mediterranean world since the days of Alexander the Great. This Greek translation is called the **Septuagint**, and it contains minor differences when compared to the Hebrew Old Testament. When the New Testament quotes from the Old, it regularly takes the language directly from the Septuagint rather than re-translating the Hebrew text into Greek. In this way, the New Testament sanctions the practice of translation. Through it, God's word reaches people of "every nation, tribe, people and language" (Revelation 7:9).

What is the best way to translate? There are a range of options which can be expressed in terms of a spectrum from literal to dynamic-equivalent to free/paraphrase. Literal translations give more of a "word-for-word" feel and also stay closer to the sentence structure of the original language. While technically more accurate, these translations also tend to be rather difficult to read and understand. Dynamic-equivalent translations strive to put thoughts or phrases into the modern, spoken language. Free translations are really less of an actual translation than an attempt to paraphrase the thoughts, ideas and idioms of the original text as they are transformed into another language. As one moves further on the spectrum, translations tend to get more expansive and interpretive. Sometimes this is a help; at other times it is a hindrance.

What, then, is the "best" translation? The answer is determined by the way in which the translation is used. For careful, in-depth, word-for-word study, a literal translation like the *New American Standard Bible* (*NASB*) is a wise choice. But it is not the best translation for public reading. For that purpose, one would do well to choose a dynamic-equivalent translation like the *New International Version* (*NIV*). Free translations are really paraphrases like *The Message*. These are well-suited for settings where one is working with children, teenagers, those for whom English is a second language, or people who are not familiar with the Bible and its vocabulary.

Unless indicated otherwise, this textbook utilizes the *English Standard Version* of the Bible in its scriptural quotations (Crossway Bibles, 2001). This translation is an update of the *Revised Standard Version*. It falls somewhere in between a literal and a dynamic-equivalent translation.

Key Tools

We began with the observation that many people view the Bible as an imposing book to study. As a result, it is no surprise that many and various tools have been produced to assist readers in understanding Scripture. This section introduces various types of resources that are available. Some of these cover the whole Bible; others deal only with the New Testament. In addition, there are many more advanced tools available for graduate and seminary level study. Most of these utilize Greek extensively. We are assuming most of our readers are not (yet) able to use that language, and therefore, we have generally omitted those resources from the examples listed below.

Study Bible

Many Bibles simply contain the text of Scripture. However, more Bibles are including additional materials along with the actual text of Scripture in order to provide explanatory detail. Often included within these Bibles are introductions to each book, notes at the bottom of the page for interpreting passages, maps, limited concordances, cross/linked/chain references, and informative articles.

Hoerber, Robert, ed. *Concordia Self-Study Bible: New International Version*. St. Louis: Concordia Publishing House, 1986. This is a Lutheran adaptation of Barker, Kenneth, ed. *The NIV Study Bible.* Grand Rapids: Zondervan, 1985.

Thompson, Frank, ed. *The Thompson Chain-Reference Bible: New International Version*. Grand Rapids: Zondervan, 1983.

Handbook

Bible handbooks generally provide materials similar to that of a Study Bible. Since they are separate books, they usually contain more extensive information. Handbooks normally proceed book by book in the same order as in the Bible.

Alexander, David, and Patricia Alexander, eds. *Eerdmans' Handbook to the Bible*. Grand Rapids: Eerdmans, 1973.

Halley, Henry. *Halley's Bible Handbook: An Abbreviated Bible Commentary by Henry H. Halley*. Grand Rapids: Zondervan Publishing, 1965.

Concordance/Topical Bible

Concordances provide an alphabetical listing of words with references to Scripture passages that use those words. Some "exhaustive" concordances include every time each word is used in a particular Bible. Others will include only a selective list of words. Concordances can be produced in Greek, English, or any other translated language. Those cited below are based upon English translations.

Goodrick, Edward and John Kohlenberger. *The NIV Complete Concordance*. Grand Rapids: Zondervan, 1981.

Strong, James. *Strong's Exhaustive Concordance of the Bible: King James Version*. Nashville: Thomas Nelson Publishers, 1996.

Whitaker, Richard, ed. *The Eerdmans Analytical Concordance to the New International Version of the Bible*. Grand Rapids: Eerdmans, 1988.

A Topical Bible is similar to a Concordance, but organized around a more limited number of "topics" of interest. Each entry provides a certain number of biblical references most directly related to that topic.

Nave, Orville. *The New Nave's Topical Bible*. Regency Reference Library. Grand Rapids: Zondervan, 1969.

Nelson's Quick Reference Topical Bible Index. Nashville: Thomas Nelson, 1995.

Dictionary

Bible dictionaries arrange topics of interest alphabetically. This enables one to look up people, places, events, teachings, and so forth in order to find an explanation or article on the topic. Since these dictionaries give much more information than simple definitions for words, they are really more like an encyclopedia. Once again, you will notice that some of the resources listed below cover the whole Bible, some just deal with the New Testament, and others are more narrowly focused on specific areas of the New Testament and/or its theology.

Achtemeier, Paul, ed. *Harper's Bible Dictionary*. San Francisco: Harper and Row, 1985.

Alexander, Desmond and Brian Rosner, eds. *New Dictionary of Biblical Theology*. Downers Grove, IL: InterVarsity Press, 2000.

Brown, Colin, ed. *Dictionary of New Testament Theology*. Grand Rapids: Zondervan, 1975.

Douglas, J. D., ed. The *New International Dictionary of the Bible*. Grand Rapids: Zondervan, 1987.

Douglas, J. D. and Merril Tenney, eds. *New International Bible Dictionary: Based on the NIV*. Grand Rapids: Zondervan Publishing, 1987.

Elwell, Walter, ed. *Evangelical Dictionary of Biblical Theology*. Grand Rapids: Baker Books, 1996.

Evans, Craig and Stanley Porter, eds. *The Dictionary of New Testament Background*. Downers Grove, IL: InterVarsity, 2000.

Freedman, David Noel, ed. *The Anchor Bible Dictionary*. 6 volumes. New York: Doubleday, 1992.

Green, Joel and Scott McKinght, eds. *Dictionary of Jesus and the Gospels*. Downers Grove, IL: InterVarsity, 1992.

Guthrie, Donald. *New Testament Theology: A Thematic Study*. Grand Rapids: InterVarsity Press, 1981.

Hawthorne, Gerald and Ralph Martin, eds. *Dictionary of Paul and His Letters*. Downers Grove, IL: InterVarsity, 1993.

Martin, Ralph and Peter Davids, eds. *Dictionary of the Later New Testament and Its Developments*. Downers Grove, IL: InterVarsity, 1997.

Myers, Allen, ed. *The Eerdmans Bible Dictionary*. Rev. ed. Grand Rapids: Eerdmans, 1987.

Tenney, Merril, ed. *The Zondervan Pictorial Encyclopedia of the Bible*. 5 volumes. Grand Rapids: Zondervan, 1975.

Commentary

One of the best ways to do an in-depth study of a particular book of the Bible is to use one or more commentaries. These resources give running "comments" or interpretations of the Bible. They may go verse by verse, or handle small groups of verses together. Commentaries provide the author's interpretation, but the best ones will also provide a range of other interpretations of difficult passages so the reader can make an informed choice from among them. There are commentary series that cover and commentary series that address only one testament. A commentary series typically has a separate volume for each book or, at times, for two to three smaller books that have been grouped together.

Clements, Ronald and Matthew Black, eds. *New Century Bible Commentary*. 22 volumes. Grand Rapids: Eerdmans, 1980-1996.

Gaebelein, Frank and J. Douglas, eds. *The Expositor's Bible Commentary with the New International Version of the Holy Bible*. 12 volumes. Grand Rapids: Zondervan, 1976-1992.

Guthrie, Donald and J. Motyer, eds. *Eerdmans' Bible Commentary*. Grand Rapids: Eerdmans, 1987.

Hubbard, David and Glenn Barker, eds. *Word Biblical Commentary*. 52 volumes. Dallas: Word Books, 1982-1997.

Harrisville, Roy, Jack Kingsbury, and Gerhard Krodel, eds. *Augsburg Commentary on the New Testament*. 15 volumes. Minneapolis: Augsburg/Fortress, 1980-1990.

Keck, Leander, ed. *The New Interpreter's Bible*. 12 volumes. Nashville: Abingdon, 1994-2004.

Keener, Craig S., ed. *The IVP Bible Background Commentary: New Testament*. Downers Grove, IL: InterVarsity Press, 1993.

Mays, James L., ed. *HarperCollins Bible Commentary*. San Francisco: HarperSanFrancisco, 2000.

The New International Commentary on the New Testament. 30 volumes. Grand Rapids: Eerdmans, 1951-2006.

Concordia Commentary: A Theological Exposition of Sacred Scripture. 13 volumes. St. Louis: Concordia, 1996-2007.

Software

Bible software programs generally contain numerous versions of the Bible in various languages and translations. Packaged together with them are handbooks, concordances, dictionaries, commentaries, maps, and other resources. As a result, many of the resources cited above are available on CD Rom. Having the biblical texts on computer enables one to perform a wide variety of searches and linguistic analyses. Comparisons among various translations are easy as well.

Bible Works for Windows, Bible Works LLC.

Logos Bible Software, Logos Research Systems, Inc.

Internet

The Internet provides access to an enormous amount of information related to the New Testament, yet it does present both significant advantages and disadvantages. The main advantages are ease of accessibility and cost. The major disadvantage is a lack of quality control. Generally, for a book to be published, the material has been edited and deemed worthy of publication. With the internet, no such controls necessarily exist. As a result, one should exercise caution and always consider the source of the material before relying upon it. As URLs frequently change, use a reputable search engine to find these resources.

Bible Gateway

Crosswalk Bible Study Tools

New Testament Gateway

Resource Page for Biblical Studies

Travel

An expression commonly used when trying to describe an event is, "You just had to be there!" Various study trips, tours, archaeological digs and programs that involve travel to the lands of the Bible are available. It is true that visiting the Holy Land does not make a person holy. Nor does it automatically put someone into closer contact with Jesus. However, his earthly life did take place in a specific area of the world, and a trip there is bound to be an enlightening experience. It is one of the best ways to get a feel for the land of the Bible and to absorb a great deal of information related to the land in a relatively short amount of time. In addition, being there enables one to visualize and

The Acropolis in Athens seen from Mars Hill where Paul preached (Acts 17)

comprehend better the settings and images used in the New Testament. Finally, these learning experiences can greatly enhance what we learn about the Bible from books and other resources after returning home.

For Further Discussion

1. Imagine you are Jesus' mother, Mary, or Peter living in the first century. Write a paragraph explaining to your fellow Jews why you believe Jesus is the Messiah and the fulfillment of God's plan.

2. Do you consider the Old Testament and the New Testament to be separate books or one? Is it necessary to understand the Old Testament before one can truly understand the New?

3. Explain your interpretation of the bow-tie diagram. Can you think of a better illustration that unifies the message of the Bible?

4. What are some of the factors, influences or experiences which impact your interaction with and interpretation of Scripture?

5. How was the New Testament written, and on what basis were certain documents included in or excluded from it? Was this a human or a divine project?

6. Describe the three different types of translations which were discussed. Which one is best?

For Further Reading

Drane, John. *Introducing the New Testament*. Revised and updated. Minneapolis: Fortress, 1999.

Elwell, Walter and Robert Yarbrough. *Encountering the New Testament: A Historical and Theological Survey*. Grand Rapids: Baker, 1998.

Fee, Gordon and Douglas Stuart. *How to Read the Bible for All It's Worth*. 3rd ed. Grand Rapids: Zondervan, 2003.

Gundry, Robert. *A Survey of the New Testament*. 3rd edition. Grand Rapids: Zondervan, 1994.

Kolb, Robert and Timothy Wengert, eds. *The Book of Concord: The Confessions of the Evangelical Lutheran Church*. Minneapolis: Fortress, 2000.

Middendorf, Michael. *God's Word.* The Lutheran Difference. St. Louis: Concordia, 2004.

Stott, John. *The Story of the New Testament.* Rev. by Stephen Motyer. Grand Rapids: Baker, 2001.

Voelz, James. *What Does This Mean?: Principles of Biblical Interpretation in the Post-Modern World.* St. Louis: Concordia: 1995.

C. F. W. Walther. *The Proper Distinction Between Law and Gospel.* St. Louis: Concordia, 1986.

2

The World of the New Testament

Introduction

The previous chapter concluded with an invitation to travel to the Holy Lands. Both of us writing this textbook have done so and frequently. We invite you to join us on future trips! But for this course, you are in a classroom or an online environment. Travel is not possible at the moment. Nevertheless, we must explore this world into which Jesus came and within which the Gospel was first spread, for that world provides the context for understanding the stories and teaching of the New Testament.

Our exploration will focus in four areas. Initially, we will examine the geography of the eastern Mediterranean and of the land of Jesus in particular. A sense of place and relationship will emerge. Second, we will enter into the Graeco-Roman world of politics, religion, and economics. A new form of the Roman Empire is emerging at the time of New Testament events. A sense of that world will give greater perspective to New Testament stories. What we often call Palestine was on the far eastern frontier of the empire. In that remote locale the story of Jesus played out. The history and culture of the late Second Temple period provide a third topic. Finally, the Jewish religious world will be the focus of our attention. Jesus lived and died as a Jew. The term "Christian" does not arise until later (Acts 11:26).

As we take this journey into the world of the New Testament, we will pause along the way to indicate how particular details can make New Testament stories come alive. We encourage readers to think along similar lines. The world of the New Testament provides rich opportunities for biblical students to gain new insight into the Word of God!

Chapter Outline

Geography
Graeco-Roman World
Late Second Temple Period
Jewish Religion in the Second Temple Period

Geography

The stories of Jesus and Paul take place in the eastern half of the Mediterranean, and area about half the size of the lower forty-eight states of the United States of America. A third of that expanse is covered by Paul's shipwreck and voyage to Rome. Most of Paul's work occurs in and around the Aegean Sea. Jesus frequented only limited areas of Galilee and Judea on the eastern edge of the Mediterranean

Topography of the Eastern Mediterranean

Three land masses jut into the Mediterranean—the modern countries of Italy, Greece, and Turkey. Rome, the power center of the ancient world, is centrally located on the west side of the Italian peninsula. Blocked to the east by a range of hills, Roman was initially oriented to the west and south toward the Tyrrhenian Sea. Rome's great rival was Carthage (modern Tunis) on the north African coast. Three Punic wars were fought between 264 and 146 B.C. (the Latin term for Carthaginians was *Punici*) after which Rome stood as the dominant power in the western Mediterranean.

To the east is the Greek peninsula with its irregular coastline of nine thousand miles. The peninsula is divided in half by the Gulf of Corinth with the Peloponnesian peninsula to the south. A narrow land bridge (four miles wide) connects the Peloponnesian peninsula with the mainland of Greece, near the city of Corinth. Corinth was a major trade center, as shipping interests preferred to transit their cargo across the isthmus rather than risking the dangerous route around the southern Peloponnesus. The sirens of ancient myth were thought to lure ships to wreck on the rocks. The ports of Corinth—Cenchreae to the east and Lechaeum to the west—enabled the transit, while the city lured waiting merchants and sailors. Corinth was also the capital of the Roman province of Achaia. Paul made three visits and spent a year and a half at Corinth.

Mountains cover more than three-quarters of surface area of Greece. The mountains and the valleys between them form barriers to movement across the peninsula. Thus, in Greece's early history, individual cities developed traditions of independence. Most famous of these cities was Athens, forty miles east of Corinth. Although its political power had waned in the New Testament era, Athens was still a center of learning and culture and hosted the youth of many of Rome's finest families.

To the east of Greece is the Aegean Sea with more than two thousand islands. The seafaring traditions and dangers immortalized in Homer's *Odyssey* sprang from the difficult trek across this sea to Troy. Virgil's *Aeneid* would employ elements of Homeric myth, in particular the wanderings of Aeneas, to spin a founding epic for Rome and to legitimate the Julio-Claudian dynasty that ruled during the time of Jesus. Paul's travels would take him across and around this same sea.

North of the Aegean was the Roman province of Macedonia from which had come Alexander the Great. Its capital, Thessalonica, was a major port and sat astride the major land route from Italy to the east called the *Via Egnatia*. Seventy-five miles to the east northeast on the *Via Egnatia* was the Roman colony of Philippi, enlarged after the battle of Philippi in 42 B.C. Paul would stop briefly and found house churches at both Philippi and Thessalonica on the second mission journey.

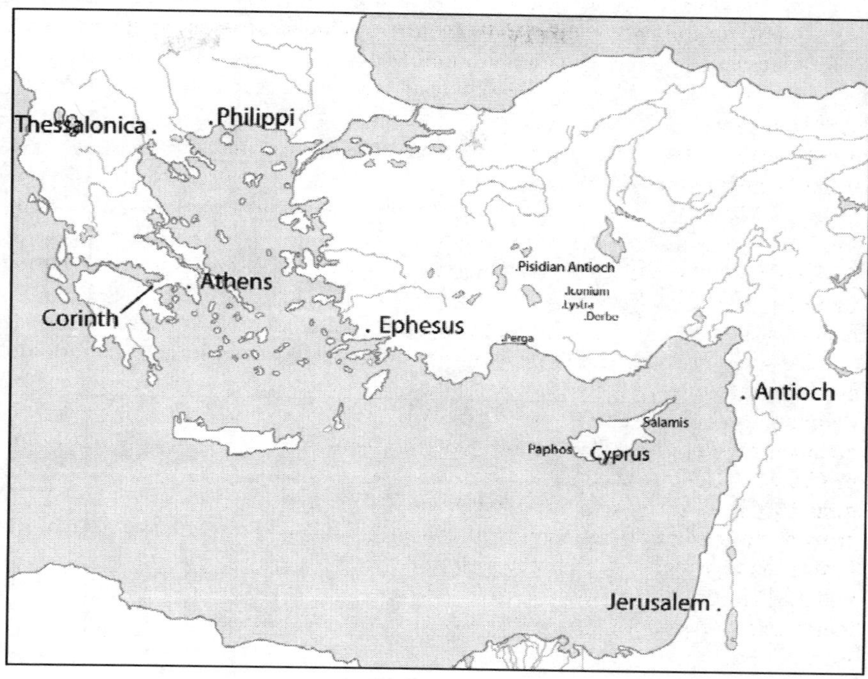

Modern Turkey is the easterly-most land mass in the northeast corner of the Mediterranean. It is a land bridge between the continents of Europe, Asia and Africa. Its peninsula that juts into the Aegean was called Anatolia by the Greeks and Asia Minor by the Romans. Turkey is more mountainous than Greece with major ranges running parallel to the north and south coasts. Its highest peak in the east is Mount Ararat.

Travel and trade in Greece centered in coastal cities and routes following the major rivers inland. The principal city of the Roman province of Asia was Ephesus, on its west coast. The seven cities mentioned in Revelation formed an arc of satellites centers. Rome divided Anatolia into several provinces. Galatia and Asia feature prominently in the story of Acts.

At the northeast corner of the Mediterranean was Antioch of Syria, the third largest city in the empire and the gateway to the trade route to the east. According to Acts, this Antioch was the center of the Gentile mission. Eighty-five miles to the northwest is Tarsus, the hometown of Saul, who would become the great missionary Paul. It is the story of his travels along trade routes and to major cities that makes the topography of the eastern Mediterranean important to the geography of the New Testament world. Attention to that topography enlivens the story.

The Topography of the Land of Jesus

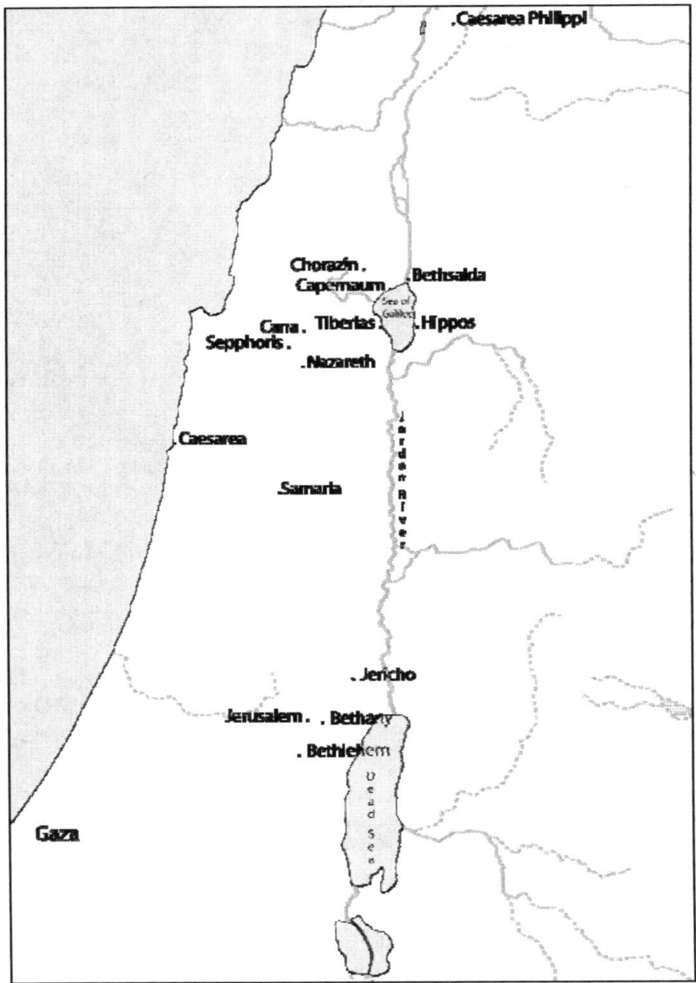

Quite commonly, Christians refer to the land of Jesus as Palestine. The name may derive from the Philistines and was used by Greek writers for the area from Phoenicia to Egypt. In contemporary times political overtones are attached to the term as a product of the intractable Arab-Israeli conflict. Indeed, when Emperor Hadrian renamed the province of Judea to *Provincia Syria Palaestina* after the second Jewish revolt against Rome, he did so as part of an effort to drive a wedge between the Jewish people and the land. The shortened *Palaestina* of the Byzantine period is the origin of the modern "Palestine." Equally problematic is the designation "land of Israel." Although used once in the New Testament (Matthew 2:20), modern usage of the phrase often carries the implication that all the land belongs exclusively to the Jewish people. The term "Holy Land" is no better, as the Crusades were started to recover the "Holy Land" for the religion of the New Testament. Therefore, we will use the designation "land of Jesus" for the area encompassed by Galilee, Samaria, and Judea.

The land of Jesus is quite small compared to the area traversed by Paul. It is a mere eighty miles from the north shore of the Sea of Galilee to Jerusalem. The entire modern state of Israel would fit inside Lake Michigan. Although Jesus did travel somewhat more broadly, including the regions of Tyre and Sidon and the Decapolis, the extent would be at most 150 miles (not including the escape to Egypt during his infancy).

Geologically, the most prominent feature of the land of Jesus is the Jordan rift valley, with the Sea of Galilee to the North and the Dead Sea to the south. The two "seas" are connected by the Jordan River. The rift valley actually runs some 3700 miles from northern Syria to central Mozambique in East Africa. It is the meeting point of several tectonic plates and is still quite active geologically.

The Jordan River has its origins in run-off from the Hermon range and springs fed by aquifers. These waters coalesced at the swamps around Lake Huleh (disastrously drained by the Israelis in the 1950s). From there the Jordan flows south to the Sea of Galilee, which sits about 640 feet below sea level.

The small dimensions hardly merit the designation "sea." In modern times it is 12.6 by 7.8 miles, although its northeast section seems to be partially filled with debris. In parts the Sea of Galilee is over 150 feet deep. In the New Testament era, it also went by the names Lake of Gennesaret (Luke 5:1), Sea of Tiberias (John 6:1), and Gennesar (Josephus, *Jewish War* 2.573).

To the east, the Sea of Galilee is bounded by the Golan Heights, to the north and west by the hills of lower Galilee. The Sea of Galilee sits down in a bowl. Winds prevail from the west and can be quite brisk later in the day. During the rainy season, strong winds off the Syrian steppe rush down valleys from the Golan and cause dangerous conditions in localized areas. The former winds may have been those of the "sea walking" (Matthew 14:24) and the latter winds may provide the context for the "stilling of the storm" (Matthew 8:24).

To the west is the Galilee, an area of low hills and fertile valleys. It is bounded to the north by a heavily forested area of higher hills and to the south by the plain of Esdraelon. Several valleys run from east to west thought the hill country and provide access from the Sea of Galilee to the coastal plain. The most prominent is the Beit Netofa valley overlooked by Sepphoris, the capital of the Galilee and in which Cana is located.

The region around the Sea of Galilee was the center of Jesus' public ministry and had a significant population during the time of Jesus. After the Hasmonean annexation of the Galilee in the century before Jesus, many Judeans moved north and settled the area. It was an agrarian and fishing economy within which were Jewish villages and several Graeco-Roman urban centers.

Ruins of Capernaum

The small fishing village of Capernaum on the north shore of the Sea of Galilee was the center of Jesus' public ministry. Cana, recently identified on the north side of the Beit Netofa valley, was an agrarian center with some light industry. Both wealthy and poor neighborhoods have been located. Chorazin has been excavated north of the Sea of Galilee, and Bethsaida emerges at a site about 1.5 miles from the northeast shore.

The archaeology of these Jewish villages in the Galilee points to relatively self-sufficient agricultural and fishing-based economies. Economic differentiation is present in the larger towns. Religiously, there seems to be a common Judaism implied in the **material remains**, including use of a communal meeting place and both public and private ritual baths. Some used stoneware, as appear in the story of the wedding at Cana (John 2:6). Jewish burial customs and dietary concerns likely prevailed.

Also present in and around the Galilee were several centers of Graeco-Roman power and culture. A mere five miles from the little village of Nazareth was Sepphoris, the capital of the Galilee. It was rebuilt by Herod Antipas during Jesus' youth. Beginning in A.D. 20, Herod built a new capital on the western shore of the Sea of Galilee and named it in honor of the emperor Tiberius. Although it certainly was a factor in the economic and political world of the Galilee, Jesus seems never to have gone there. Directly across the Sea of Galilee on a hill above the eastern shore was Hippos. It was one of ten Graeco-Roman cultural outposts generally east and south of the Sea of Galilee called the Decapolis. It has a large limestone temple that dated to the time before Jesus. Likely, it is the "city set on a hill" to which Jesus referred in the Sermon on the Mount (Matthew 5:14).

These Roman centers presented a stark economic and cultural contrast to the Jewish villages of the Galilee. While their economies seemed to have intertwined, cultural tensions may have been present as well.

The Jordan River meanders south for some sixty-five miles to the Dead Sea. The river's actual route is closer to 120 miles. The Yarmuk and Jabbok rivers along with a number of seasonal streams increase the flow of the Jordan en route. Nevertheless, the Jordan River hardly merits the description "deep and wide, milk and honey on the other side." It would take the Jordan River more than one thousand years to deliver the flow of the Mississippi River in just one year.

The Dead Sea is at the southern end of the Jordan River. It is at the lowest place on earth at 1300 feet below sea level. The Dead Sea is fifty miles from north to south and ten miles across. In places the Dead Sea is over 1400 feet deep. As the rate of evaporation is so great due to high temperature and lack of rainfall, the inflow of the Jordan and a few other streams kept the level relatively constant until modern times. As there is no outlet to the ocean, the salt solution of the Dead Sea is about 33 percent, making the human body buoyant. The Dead Sea and its environs have a unique but harsh beauty.

The Jordan Rift Valley may be the most prominent feature of the land of Jesus, but there are other geological zones. Along the Mediterranean is a coastal plain. To its east is a ridge of hills running from Hebron in the south through Jerusalem and Samaria. The ridge then veers to the northwest as the Carmel Range to the coast. This central hill country consists of hills roughly two thousand to 2700 feet above sea level. From the Mount of Olives on the east side of Jerusalem, the topography drops some four thousand feet in just fourteen miles to the Dead Sea. As the prevailing weather patterns are from the west, this dramatic drop off creates a unique desert climate called the Judean wilderness. This wilderness was from ancient times considered a place of testing. It is the place of the temptation of Jesus (Matthew 4:1), the Samaritan helping the wounded traveler (Luke 10:30), and the shepherd seeking the lost sheep (Luke 15:4).

South of this central hill country is the Negev desert. Part of this desert region was Idumea. Other parts were controlled by the Nabateans. To the north and separating the Carmel Range from the Galilean hill country is the great Esdraelon Plain. At its eastern ends was Scythopolis, another Decapolis city that included the ancient tel of Bethshean.

In the time of Jesus the land was divided into a number of political entities. Judea in the south and the central area of Samaria were together the Roman province of Judea. To the north was the Galilee; to the east across the Jordan was Perea. These two comprised the tetrarchy of Herod Antipas. To the north and east of the Sea of Galilee was the tetrarchy of Philip, essentially from Mount Hermon to the Yarmuk River. South and east of the Sea of Galilee was the region of the **Decapolis**.

Central to the final events in the story of Jesus is the city of Jerusalem. Originally, the small Jerusalem of David and Solomon sat on a narrow ridge west of the Mount of Olives between the Kidron and Tyropoean valleys. The Gihon spring provided the water source for the city with its temple complex to the north. In New Testament times the city had spread across the Tyropoean valley to include the westerly hill (Mount Zion) and was bounded on the south by the Hinnom valley. Recently discovered in the southern part of the lower city is the majestic Siloam Pool. The upper city on Mount. Zion housed the city's elite and was the location of the palace of Herod the Great. The temple complex, expanded extensively at the direction of Herod, dominated the city. The city's weakness was to its northwest. In the time of Jesus, two walls defended that part of the city. A third wall was added by Herod's grandson Agrippa I.

About five miles south of Jerusalem on the central ridge of the Judean hill country is the small but ancient village of Bethlehem. About three miles east of Jerusalem on the road to Jericho is Bethany, the village of Mary, Martha, and Lazarus. Further to the east the topography drops precipitously to the ancient oasis of Jericho and the Dead Sea. The beginning and end of the story of Jesus are set in this small area in and around Jerusalem.

Graeco-Roman World

Rome ruled the civilized world from Britain and Spain in the west to Syria in the east. Its power and cultural influence were everywhere. Even as American cultural weight and political power breed envy and hatred today, so Rome was viewed by those it dominated in the first century. But just as American culture is a product of earlier European influences, so we must properly speak of the Graeco-Roman world. From Greek antecedents came culture, language, art, and architecture. Rome assimilated these and dominated the world through its political power and economic prowess.

When Alexander the Great set out from Macedonia in 334 B.C., not only did he extend his conquests as far as India in 325 B.C., he also brought to the east the Greek language, culture, religion, and architecture. Rome may have come to control the eastern Mediterranean through the conquests of Pompey in 63 B.C., but Greek influence remained strong. The common language of the Roman Empire was not Latin, but Koine ("common") Greek. As English is the second language of much of the world today, so was Koine Greek in the time of Jesus. This common tongue would be the original language of the New Testament. When Jesus was crucified, the charge was published "in Aramaic, in Latin, and in Greek" (John 19:20).

Zeus/Jupiter

Rome assimilated the Greek pantheon of Homeric legend; Zeus became Jupiter, for instance. Public buildings in Roman cities developed Greek architectural styles. Temples, theatres, and bath houses— typical Greek structures— were constructed throughout the empire. Plato and Aristotle would continue to influence Roman thinkers, and their dualism would be embraced by many philosophic schools.

To grasp Rome's political place in the world, we must step back to the century before Jesus. The Roman republic was troubled. Expansion through the conquests of Pompey in the east (63 B.C.) and the campaign of Julius Caesar in Gaul (57–56 B.C.) set the stage for civil war between ambitious and powerful men in 49 B.C. Caesar emerged victorious, only to be assassinated in 44 B.C. Civil strife continued. Octavian, great-nephew and adopted heir of Julius Caesar, together with Mark Anthony defeated Brutus and Cassius at the battle of Philippi in 42 B.C. That same year the Roman senate declared the murdered Julius to be a god of the Roman state (*Divus Julius*), allowing Octavian to claim himself as son of God (*Divi filius*). Octavian returned to Rome and Anthony went to Egypt where he allied himself with Rome's enemy and Ceasar's lover Cleopatra. In 31 B.C. Octavian would defeat Anthony and Cleopatra at the battle of Actium and remain the sole surviving force. The senate bestowed on Octavian the title *princes* (first citizen) and Octavian cleverly "restored the republic" by turning his powers back to the senate. As he was the one who brought to an end the civil wars and had returned peace to the state, the senate in turn granted him the title Augustus. In subsequent years in part due to his astute treatment of the senate, Augustus was made the religious head of state (*pontifex maximus*) in 12 B.C. and father of the country (*pater patriae*) in 2 B.C. Over time, Augustus demobilized armies into colonies, revived the state religion (along with protecting ancient shrines), and consolidated the empire through the use of census. Augustus ruled the emerging Roman Empire for forty-one years (27 B.C. to A.D. 14). During his reign, Jesus was born (Luke 2:1).

The Julio-Claudian dynasty has passed from Julius Caesar to his adopted heir Octavian. Similiarly, Augustus adopted his step son Tiberius as his own son and made him co-regent in A.D. 13. Tiberius succeeded his adoptive father and proved himself an able administrator. Herod Antipas named the new capital of Galilee in his honor. Tiberius appointed Pontius Pilate as prefect of Judea in A.D. 26. In that same year, Tiberius withdrew to Capri where he lived as a recluse until his death in A.D. 37.

Divus Augustus
"Divine Augustus"

Tiberius was succeeded by a great nephew Gaius Julius (Caligula) whose bizarre reign was ended when his bodyguard stabbed him to death in A.D. 41. The Praetorian Guard forced the senate to accept Gaius' uncle Claudius as emperor under the presumption that they could control him, since his handicaps had isolated him from imperial corridors of power. By orchestrating an invasion of Britain and reorganizing the imperial bureaucracy, Claudius proved himself to be an able emperor. According to Acts, Claudius expelled Jews from Rome. As a result, Aquila and Priscilla meet up with Paul at Corinth (Acts 18:2). Claudius' private life was his undoing. He was likely poisoned by his fourth wife Agrippina in A.D. 54, so that her son Nero might grab the throne.

As Nero was only sixteen when he became emperor, he took guidance from Burrus the Praetorian prefect and from Seneca, a stoic philosopher. His early years were enlightened and the empire prospered. Seneca's brother Gallio was the proconsul at Corinth who dealt positively with Paul (Acts 18:14–15). Perhaps for this reason, Paul was confident to appeal his case to the emperor (Acts 25:11). But in A.D. 59 Nero disposed of his dominating mother by murdering Agrippina. Subsequently, he stayed away from Rome for a year and a half, perhaps explaining why Paul has to wait for two years in Rome to have his case heard (Acts 28:30). With his mother out of the way, little restrained Nero. He fancied himself a performing artist and arranged to win every contest he entered. After a massive fire in Rome in A.D. 64, he built an enormous palace on the ruins. To deflect rumors that he was responsible for the fire, Nero blamed the Christian community in Rome. Many met gruesome deaths for the entertainment of Roman crowds in subsequent years. Later tradition places the deaths of Peter and Paul in this period. When parts of the army finally revolted, Nero committed suicide (A.D. 68). The Julio-Claudian dynasty came to an end.

Nero

Subsequent emperors only impact the story of the New Testament tangentially. The army put up several leaders who ruled briefly. It was Vespasian, having left his son Titus to finish off the Jewish revolt, who became the first of the Flavian emperors. The Flavians were considered outsiders by the elites of Rome. Their power rested with the army. Vespasian (A.D. 69–79) was energetic, restoring the fortunes of the empire and discipline in the army. The Colosseum was built during his reign. His sons Titus (A.D. 79–81) and Domitian (A.D. 81–96) would succeed him and work to stabilize the frontiers of the empire. Domitian was more severe and insisted on observance of the imperial cult, bringing his reign into conflict with both Jewish and Christian sensibilities. His reign could provide the context for the book of Revelation. Domitian was murdered in A.D. 96.

The emperors dominated the Roman political system that emerged in the first century. It was an aristocratic empire where those with wealth and military might prevailed. These elites—at most two or three percent of the population—extracted product and labor from a populace of slaves and non-elites through ownership of land and through burdensome debt, taxation, and coercion. Local elites were often enlisted by Roman rulers in this process. Where opposition arose, the army brought and enforced the *Pax Romana*, the Roman peace.

The Roman provincial system exemplified this control. By A.D. 120, the Roman Empire consisted of fifty-four provinces. Senatorial provinces were relatively peaceful and were governed by a proconsul appointed by the senate for one year; sometimes the term could be renewed for a second year. Sergius Paulus, the proconsul of Cyprus, and Gallio, the proconsul of Achaea, are characters from the stories of Paul's mission journeys (Acts 13:7–12; 18:12–17). Imperial provinces were under the direct control of the emperor and served as a primary source of his power. As more restive locales, such provinces were governed by a legate appointed by the emperor. In such provinces, a **legion** was garrisoned. Augustus believed that twenty-eight legions were sufficient for defending the empire without becoming a political threat.

At the outskirts of the empire, governance was not so neatly categorized. Sometimes Rome would form alliances with local elites who would rule on Rome's behalf. The Herodian family, featured prominently in the New Testament, is an example. The Galilee during Jesus' ministry was ruled by Herod Antipas. It was not a province. Even the province of Judea was somewhat irregular. Although under the control of the emperor, no legion was garrisoned there. Pontius Pilate, appointed by Tiberius, was not of consular rank, but was an equestrian. His technical title was prefect. Imperial niceties did not hold in Judea. Pilate's soldiers were for the most part regional mercenaries (John 19:24). Their treatment of the populace would have been brutal.

Pilate Inscription

Another technique used to maintain control of the vast empire was the establishment of **colonies**. Originally, colonies were military outposts constructed in newly conquered territories. In the imperial period, the emperor attained sole right to found colonies. Sometimes—after the battle of Philippi, for instance—victorious soldiers were settled locally as part of such colonies. Colonies also enjoyed special status. Citizens of colonies were counted as part of the populace of Rome. Colonies functioned as little Romes scattered about the empire. Their loyalty was to Rome and the emperor rather than the local province. As Philippi was such a colony, Paul wrote provocatively to the community there, "Our citizenship is in heaven ..." (Philippians 3:20).

The Graeco-Roman world was one where the elites ruled, often in collusion with local aristocracies. Military might upheld their rule. The wealth to fund the empire came through control of the land. Although the glory of Rome was on display in cities, ninety percent of the population lived in agrarian contexts. Most toiled in difficult circumstances as slaves or tenant farmers. Sixty to seventy percent of the land was held by the elites, much by the imperial household. From this land and from taxes imposed on other lands and laborers, significant wealth was extracted for the benefit of the few. When Jesus spoke of debt, his hearers understood (Matthew 6:12; 18:27–34; Luke 7:41–43).

To convey this wealth to the elites, to provide quick movement of military forces, and to foster economic prosperity, Rome built a network of roads, cleared the sea lanes of pirates, and provided a common currency that served as well to unite the empire and spread Roman civilization. The basic silver coin of the realm was the **denarius**. On its obverse (front side) was the bust of the emperor. It was the standard payment for a day's labor (Matthew 20:2).

Roman cities and especially Rome itself were the visible symbol of the rule of the elites. There conspicuous consumption and civic display trumpeted Roman values. Feasts, games, statues, buildings—these were the glory of Rome. Roman cities were typically orthogonal (laid out on a grid) with accommodation to topography. A city would be surrounded by walls and entered through majestic gates. The main streets would be flanked with colonnades. The major street usually ran from north to south and was called a cardo. The major perpendicular street was a decumanus. At the center of the city would be a forum—an open square surrounded by colonnades and public buildings. Many of the public buildings would be temples; other civic structures were basilical in form. Theatres, circuses, and amphitheatres provided entertainment for the masses and opportunities for the elites to parade their wealth and prestige. Public bath houses with an attendant gymnasium were places of exercise, commerce, and pleasure. Power, display, consumption, and superiority—these Roman values are preserved for posterity in the grandeur of Roman cities. The coming of such Romanization to the Galilee at Sepphoris and to the Sea of Galilee at Tiberias may have been a point of tension with the Jewish population during the time of Jesus.

Rome dominated the Mediterranean world through its emperor and elites and through its army and extractive economic system. Rome also had the gods on its side. According to the Augustan poet Virgil, Jupiter gave to Rome an *imperium sine fine* (Aeneid 1.279), an "empire without end." Romans were quite religious. Polytheistic practices restored by August, himself the religious head of state, sanctioned the empire. Participation in the public rituals was the means by which one demonstrated loyalty to empire and emperor. The Jewish belief in monotheism (one God) made no sense to the Romans. And so Romans paraded utensils from the Jewish temple in Rome after Jerusalem was destroyed (see photo, right).

From the Arch of Titus

The political elements of such religious practice seem to have been of greater significance than any serious belief, especially on the part of the elites. This reality is doubly true of the imperial cult. With its origins in the "deification" of Julius Caesar, the cult grew through the dedication of temples for and to the emperor, the multiplication of rituals and festivals invoking divine sanction of the emperor, prayers and sacrifice for and even to emperors, dead and living. Such practices, often funded by the elites, affirmed divine rule through the emperor and those in the emperor's circle.

But for the ninety-seven percent of the empire who were not in elite circles, such practices meant little. Life was brutal, harsh, and short. The fates were cruel. Manipulating or controlling **fate** was the only hope. Astrology had its followers (Matthew 2:1); amulets and magical superstitions abounded (Acts 19:13–20); and **mystery religions** gained fanatic followings. The dying and rising cult of Dionysus was popular. Among the military, Mithraism found many practitioners. The cult centers of Mithra often display the deity slaying a bull. Rather than some sort of blood rite, the cult seems to have developed subsequent to the startling discover of Hipparchus in 128 B.C. that the spring equinox had moved in the zodiac from Taurus the bull to Ares the ram. If Mithra could cause the stars to shift (by slaying Taurus the bull), Mithra could certainly shift the fate of the god's adherents. Soldiers going into battle often consulted the stars and auguries.

Formal religious practice in the Roman Empire sanctioned and favored the elites. It was more political than religious. Among the masses fate ruled mercilessly and could be at best manipulated briefly. Even the popular philosophy of stoicism emphasized the acceptance of fate. There was little in the religious world of Rome for the "least of these" (Matthew 25:40), and certainly no one came to "seek and save the lost" (Luke 19:10).

Into a remote corner of this Graeco-Roman world, Jesus was born in the days of Caesar Augustus. And he would die at the hands of a minor prefect, Pontius Pilate. Seemingly, Jesus was just another victim of the elites of Rome. How Roman rule came to the land of Jesus and how the Jews responded to this occupying power are also part of the context of the New Testament.

Late Second Temple Period

The **Second Temple period** refers to the history of the Jewish people from the rebuilding of the temple at Jerusalem following the Babylonian exile (514 B.C.) until the destruction of that temple by the Romans in A.D. 70. Roman rule came and Jesus lived in the last century of this period. Although the period began after the exile with the formation of the Persian province of Yehud, the land of Jesus came under Greek rule with the conquest of Alexander the Great. This Hellenistic period gets its name from *hellenikos*, the Greek word for Greek.

With Alexander's death in 323 B.C., the empire was divided up by his generals, and the land of Judah came under the control of Ptolemy and his descendants who ruled from Egypt. The Ptolemaic period saw the translation of the Hebrew Bible into a Greek version call the **Septuagint** (abbreviated LXX). During that same period, the Jewish population of Alexandria swelled. When the land came under Seleucid control in 198 B.C., significant cultural tensions arose over a policy of enforced **Hellenization**. The Maccabean revolt of 168 B.C. drove out the Seleucids from Jerusalem and its environs and allowed the cleansing and rededication of the temple in 164 B.C. These events are still celebrated in the Jewish festival of Hanukah.

Also arising from the revolt was a brief period of Jewish independence under the Hasmoneans. Simon, the brother of Judas Maccabaeus, was the first to rule from 142–135 B.C. But during the next century there was much palace intrigue among the Hasmoneans over control of the throne and the high priesthood. As a consequence of this intrigue, part of the family formed an alliance with Rome in 139 B.C. After Pompey conquered the region in 63 B.C., he deposed Aristobulus II and installed his brother and rival, the high priest John Hyrcanus II. Finally Rome had enough of Hasmonean squabbles and named Herod of Idumea as King of the Jews (40 B.C.). In the midst of all the Hasmonean struggles, the conquest of the Galilee by Alexander Janaeus (83–80 B.C.) was significant. As a result, many Jews migrated north to settle the Galilee. Jesus would carry out the bulk of his ministry among their descendants. This settlement might also explain why Joseph was living in Nazareth, although his family was from Bethlehem (Luke 2:4).

The Roman senate may have named Herod as king of the Jews, and Herod may have taken a Hasmonean (Mariamne) as one of his wives, but his appointment was not well received. It took Herod three years, plus the help of Mark Anthony, to fight his way into Jerusalem. In gratitude Herod gave the name Fortress Antonia to the structure defending the temple. But Herod was also quite shrewd when it came to Roman politics. When Octavian defeated Anthony and Cleopatra six years later, Herod traveled to Rhodes to pledge his loyalty to Octavian. He was reaffirmed as king, would loyally serve and honor Augustus, and would reward him greatly in his will.

Herod ruled the Jews from 37–4 B.C. He was suspicious and cruel—as rivals, family members, and even his own children discovered. The slaughter of the innocents in Bethlehem (Matthew 2:16) was very much in character with a man who would execute his most beloved wife Mariamne and later her sons. Nevertheless, Herod is remembered as "Great" because of his massive building projects.

Herod constructed for himself lavish palaces. On the western (and most defensible) height of Jerusalem was his royal palace. It was guarded by three towers, the base of one being still visible. He had a lavish winter palace at Jericho and, at a plateau called Masada near the southern end of the Dead Sea, Herod constructed a lavish three-tiered palace with majestic view of the sea and Judean wilderness.

Herod was an urban architect. On the Mediterranean coast he constructed a royal city, Caesarea. His engineers built an artificial port, the entrance of which was guarded by a lighthouse similar to the one at Alexandria. Fresh water was brought in by aqueducts from the north. Caesarea was a city of pleasure and entertainment. Next to the sea a theatre and hippodrome can be seen. Herod's palace juts out into the sea with a colonnaded pool. Crowning the city was a temple for his patron Augustus, one of three such temples built in Herod's realm. The second was at Samaria, a city that Herod renamed Sebaste. Sebaste is the Greek form of the Latin Augustus. The third temple for Augustus was in the north at Caesarea Philippi.

Herod's greatest architectural achievement still shapes the urban fabric of Jerusalem. For Herod expanded and rebuilt the temple complex in Jerusalem, making it the largest sacred precinct in the entire ancient world (compare Matthew 24:1). The platform itself was expanded dramatically to a slightly irregular rectangle (the walls are 1038 ft. on the north, 1590 ft. on the west, 914 ft. on the south, and 1530 ft. on the east, enclosing an area of 172,000 square yards). Majestic staircases provided access. Aqueducts brought water. The platform was surrounded by colonnades. Capping the southern wall was a royal stoa—a large basilica. The temple itself stood in the center of the platform. Herod's project put the mark of Roman architecture (and power!) onto the central shine of Judaism, even as Augustan law specifically protected such ancient shrines. Perceived violation of that law may have been behind the charge of the false witnesses against Jesus (Matthew 26:61).

Herod's paranoia may have been behind a third type of building project—a series of desert fortresses. They protected his realm to the east and south and provided for Herod a place of retreat should a significant personal threat arise. The Herodium, Herod's fortress outside of Bethlehem is the most stunning. Herod built this round fortress, defended by four towers, on top of a hill and almost doubling its height. On the plain below is a more typical palace structure with pools, gardens, colonnades, and possibly a hippodrome. According to the Jewish historian Josephus (A.D. 37–c. 100), when Herod died in 4 B.C., his body was carried in regal procession from Jericho to the Herodium for burial. The foundation for his mausoleum and fragments of his sarcophagus may have been recently discovered near the top of a staircase ascending to the fortress between the east and north towers. If confirmed, this discovery would solve one of the great mysteries of the archaeology of the Second Temple period.

After the death of Herod, Augustus executed his will. The kingdom of Herod was divided among three of his remaining sons. The situation is somewhat confusing, since Herod had five wives and some names are repeated. Archelaus, son of Herod and Malthrace, was named ethnarch of Judea, Samaria, and Idumea. Antipas, also from Herod via Malthrace, was made tetrarch of Galilee and Perea. Philip, son of Herod and Cleopatra, was crowned as tetrarch of areas east and north of the Sea of Galilee (Gaulanitis, Batanea, Trachonitis, Autanitis, and portions of Iturea; Luke 3:1). Some cities, such as Hippos, were given independence from the Herodians.

The competence of Archelaus was questioned from the beginning. His rule motivated Joseph to take Mary and the infant Jesus back to the north (Matthew 2:22). He was deposed in A.D. 6, and Judea came under direct Roman rule through prefects. After the death of Herod the Great, the people of Sepphoris revolted. The legate of Syria re-conquered the city. So Herod Antipas had to rebuild his capital when he took up the tetrarchy of Galilee and Perea. Antipas was the most competent of Herod's sons, ruling until A.D. 39. He imitated his father's great city of Caesarea by building a new capital on the Sea of Galilee in honor of the emperor Tiberius. Philip his brother, son of Herod and Mariamne II, was married to Herodias and with her had a daughter Salome. Herodias left Philip and took up with Antipas. As a consequence, the behavior of Antipas was condemned by the popular preacher John the Baptist (Mark 6:18). When the daughter of Herodias danced for Antipas on his birthday, she asked for the head of the Baptist in response to Antipas' foolish pledge (Mark 6:25). Later, Jesus would be sent to Antipas as part of his Roman trial (Luke 23:7–12).

A different Philip, the son of Herod and Cleopatra, ruled an ethnically mixed area east and north of the Galilee until A.D. 34. He rebuilt his capital and named it in honor of the emperor and himself: Caesarea Philippi. He later married Salome, his niece and the daughter of Herodias and his other brother, also named Phillip. Some excavators believe he also built a small temple at Bethsaida in honor of Livia-Julia, wife of Augustus and mother of Tiberius, and renamed the town in her honor (Bethsaida-Julia). This example of the imperial cult may provide some of the background for the request of the Greeks from Bethsaida to Philip, "Sir, we wish to see Jesus" (John 12:21).

From A.D. 6–44, Rome ruled Judea directly through seven different prefects. Pontius Pilate served the longest term from A.D. 26–36. If we only had the gospels as our guide, Pilate would seem to be a weak and equivocating character. But there are also hints of a violent streak in Pilate (Luke 13:1; Mark 15:7; Luke 23:19). Philo of Alexandria (c. 20 B.C.–A.D. 50) and Josephus portray him a capricious and cruel. Both report him introducing into Jerusalem honorific items of the emperor (images or shields) that offended the Jews. Use of temple funds to construct an aqueduct without attention to ritual purity was the cause of a riot that left many dead. A massacre of Samaritans led to his recall. Although his rule corresponded roughly with the high priesthood of Caiaphas (A.D. 18–36), and Caiaphas only continued in office with the approval of Pilate, Caiaphas still had good reason to fear violence from Pilate (John 11:50).

After Pilate, Judea may have been attached to Syria for a time. In A.D. 41, Herod Agrippa I, grandson of Herod the Great, assumed the throne in Jerusalem, having helped Claudius come to power in Rome. Agrippa expanded Jerusalem to the northwest (the third wall) and is known for executing James, the brother of John and the first apostle to die for the faith (Acts 12:2). After Agrippa's death in A.D. 44, Claudius appointed a procurator to rule Judea (procurators were also of equestrian rank).

Two subsequent procurators appear in New Testament accounts. Felix (A.D. 52–59) tried the case against Paul and kept him in prison for two years at Caesarea while awaiting a bribe (Acts 24). Felix was married to Drusilla, the daughter of Agrippa. Felix was replaced by Porcius Festus (A.D. 59–61) who forwarded Paul's case to the emperor at Paul's request. During this incident Paul also had an opportunity to address Herod Agrippa II and his sister Bernice who affirmed his innocence (Acts 26). Bernice, whose relationship with Agrippa II was subject to rumor, later became the mistress of Titus, who sent her away from Rome when he became emperor in A.D. 79.

In the time of Jesus and the apostolic church, Rome ruled directly or indirectly. As an aristocratic empire, Roman power was exercised often in conjunction with local elites, as the Herodian dynasty demonstrates. But the New Testament also mentions another local power center—the **Sanhedrin**. It shows up occasionally in stories from Jerusalem and seems to consist of Jewish religious elites including the high priest. Later rabbinic writing would speak of a council of seventy-one members that met in the temple and was headed by the high priest. Some even liken the Sanhedrin to a Jewish supreme court.

Such descriptions seem unlikely in a time of Roman occupation. If we limit ourselves to material from the first century (the gospels and Josephus), the Sanhedrin only appears in capital cases when the outcome seems to have been previously determined. The Sanhedrin serves as an ad hoc assembly meant to involve a larger group of elites in carrying out the sentence. Given the volatile nature of relations with Rome and a restive populace under hostile occupation, niceties implied by the designation "supreme court" were lacking. Elites in collusion with and yet resistant to Rome did what they had to do under the circumstances. The fate of Jesus was determined well before he appeared in front of the Sanhedrin (John 11:53).

The Second Temple period came to an end with the Jewish revolt (A.D. 66–72). The origins of the revolt can be traced to decades of tension, cultural conflict, and a weakening of Roman power. Josephus points to an incident in A.D. 66 when Greeks sacrificed birds in front of a local synagogue. Probably of greater significance was the action of the procurator Florus who, in a dispute over the tax burden imposed as of the result of a new census, extracted the deficit from the temple treasury. In Florus' view Rome, as the protector of the temple, had a right to its wealth. Subsequently, prayers and sacrifices for emperor Nero ceased at the temple. The revolt had begun. The Roman garrison in Jerusalem was defeated. When Cestius Gallus, the legate of Syria, brought in the Legio XII Fulminata to restore order, he was beaten at the Battle of Beth Horon.

Even the weakened Nero recognized the significance of the defeat of a legion. He named Vespasian to crush the rebellion. Vespasian and his son Titus along with the Legio X Fretensis and the Legio V Macedonica systematically crushed Jewish resistance beginning in the north. Agrippa II and Bernice quickly sided with Rome. Josephus, commander of the Jewish forces in the north, surrendered. Some communities, such as Sepphoris, did not even resist Rome. Others, such as Gamla, were completely wiped out. The conflict in the north was over by A.D. 68.

In A.D. 69, Vespasian was proclaimed emperor after the death of Nero. He returned to Rome and within a year defeated his rivals. Titus finished the work in Judea. The siege of Jerusalem turned ugly in A.D. 70. Thousands of escapees were crucified on crosses surrounding the city. Other defenders starved as the siege wore on. In early summer the third and second walls were breached and the temple fell at the end of August in A.D. 70. The Romans systematically destroyed the city's fortifications

Destruction of Jerusalem

and the temple itself, "not ... one stone upon another" (Luke 19:44). So intent were the Romans on quelling the rebellion that the new legate of the Roman imperial province of Judea, Lucilius Brassus, spent two years chasing down the last of the Zealots. Lucius Flavius Silva replaced him and besieged the final group of holdouts at Masada, Herod's fortress palace overlooking the Dead Sea. Silva encircled the fortress with walls and built a siege rank to its height (both still visible today). When the Romans breached the walls, Josephus reports, they found that the final defenders had committed mass suicide. More likely, the suicide is a mythic invention of Josephus who attempted to rehabilitate the Jews in the eyes of the Roman world by writing of their history and wars. The defenders of Masada met the same brutal demise as other rebels against Rome. In the early 130s, the Jews would revolt again, at which point Hadrian drove them from Judea, rebuilt Jerusalem as a pagan city (Aelia Capitolina), and renamed the province as Palaestina.

Although Rome prevailed and brought the Second Temple period to a close, more than a million people lost their lives in a century of brutal conflict. Interestingly, Titus at his triumph at Rome refused to accept the wreath of victory, since he saw no glory in destroying a people forsaken by their own God. Nevertheless, before the fall of Jerusalem a Pharisaic rabbi, Yohanan ben Zakkai, received permission to establish a school at Yavne; and the Christian followers of another rabbi named Jesus fled to Pella. From this century of conflict came two of the west's great religions.

Jewish Religion in the Second Temple Period

The Jewish religious world was quite complex at the time of Jesus. Many Jews were scattered throughout the Graeco-Roman world and so were influenced by Greek culture and local conditions. Within Judea and Galilee, diversity of belief and practice was a hallmark, even though there were a number of religious characteristics commonly held. As Jesus grew up within this milieu, lived and died as Jew, and was one of its distinct voices, we now turn to Jewish religion in the Second Temple period to consider its commonalities and its diversity.

Jewish religion before the destruction of the second temple was marked by at least six distinct commonalities: the temple in Jerusalem, the role of the local synagogue, the festival cycle, the significance of the Torah, the theology of monotheism, and a concern for ritual purity. The diverse groups, discussed below, all interacted with or related to these commonalities, for the common characteristics helped to establish Jewish religious identity.

The temple in Jerusalem was the cultic and physical center of Jewish religion. It was on a par with the rival Samaritan sanctuary (John 4:20) until Herod the Great dramatically doubled the size of the complex. The temple also served as a rallying locale for national identity and resistance against Rome. For that very reason, the religious authorities were most disturbed by Jesus' triumphal entry into Jerusalem and the temple (Matthew 21:15–17). The temple was a place of prayer and sacrifice, on both annual and daily cycles. The temple was also a place of pilgrimage, drawing to Jerusalem over a million people each year. It was a place of piety, noise, smells, and passion. Those who controlled the temple controlled the Jewish religious world.

Model of the Temple

The temple displayed a unique hierarchical geography that bluntly identified personal proximity to God. The outer courts of the temple plaza, including the Royal Stoa, were public spaces open to all. Sacrificial animals were sold and money exchanges in there areas. Roman coins had on them images of the emperor. These needed to be exchanged for Tryian shekels, to avoid the sacrilege of bringing the image of a god into holy areas (Matthew 22:20–21). These public places may also have been places for rendering religious rulings, prayer, and some teaching.

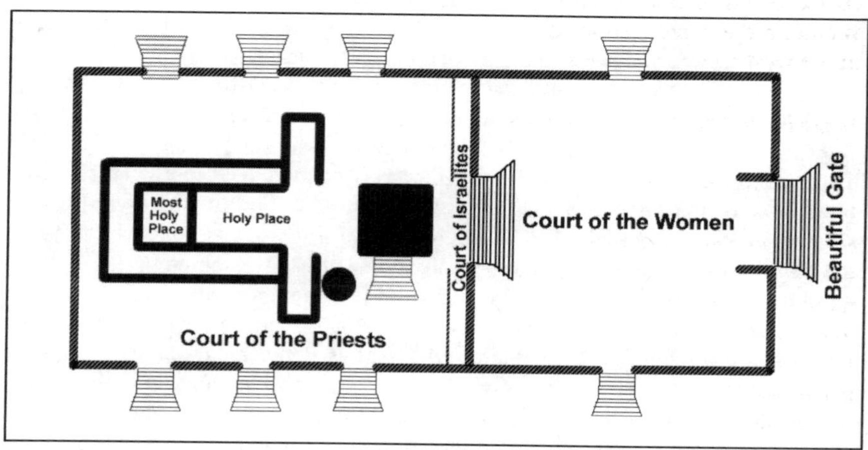

As one approached the temple proper, a low wall or balustrade (*soreg*) marked off the area restricted to Jews only. Warning signs threatened death to those who violated these restrictions. A riot broke out when some thought Paul had brought a Gentile into these precincts (Acts 21:27–28). In the temple proper itself, the easterly court was the court of the women. It was an open court that served as a place of prayer for all Jews. Males wishing to offer sacrifices would climb stairs to the west and pass through the Nicanor Gate into the court of the Israelites. In that court, males would present their offerings to the priests to be burned on the altar of burnt offerings in front of the main door of the temple. The temple proper stood to the west of the altar and consisted of two rooms: the holy place into which a priest entered daily (Luke 1:8–23), and behind it, the holy of holies into which the high priest entered once a year on the Day of Atonement.

Even as the temple in Jerusalem was the visible sign of religion and national identity for Jews, the **synagogue** functioned in local communities as a weekly gathering place. Although the word "synagogue" typically evokes the idea of a building, better would be to read the word as referring to the "gathering" rather than the physical place. Only three synagogue buildings have been firmly dated to the Second Temple period: at Gamla, Masada, and the Herodium. These likely come from the time of the revolt against Rome and may not even have existed in Jesus' day. More likely, public buildings or even private homes were reconfigured for the use of the synagogue assembly on the Sabbath. During the week, these spaces served the community in one way; on the Sabbath they served as the synagogue. Thus, the synagogue derived from the city gate or village square, and it remained a community center even as one room took on the form of a diminished sanctuary after the destruction of the temple.

Ten men were required to hold a synagogue assembly. A prominent member of the community served as the ruler of the synagogue (*nasi)*. Rabbis were not leaders of synagogues, as is popularly perceived today; rather, prominent rabbis might be associated with a house of studies. The pattern of the rite followed in the synagogues (**Shema**, blessings, prayers, readings from the Torah and Prophets, comment on their application, and blessing) would be copied in subsequent Christians assemblies to which a meal was added.

The Jewish religion had its public space in temple and synagogue. The Jewish religion marked time with a cyclical series of sacred days or festivals. The weekly celebration was the Sabbath, a day of mandated rest from sundown on Friday to sundown on Saturday (Jews began their days at sundown; Romans began their days at midnight). The chief annual festival was **Passover**. It fell at the beginning of the wheat harvest (usually April) and commemorated deliverance from slavery in Egypt. It was also one of the chief pilgrimage festivals. The Feast of Weeks came seven weeks later at the end of the wheat harvest. Christians have come to celebrate that festival as Pentecost (Acts 2). The third pilgrimage festival was the Feast of Booths. While commemorating the wandering in the wilderness, its themes of light and water may have provided a counterpoint to Jesus' self-identification as the light of the world and as living water (John 7:37–39; 8:12). The feast of the Dedication (Hanukah) and the Day of Atonement also receive passing reference (John 10:22; Romans 3:25; Hebrews 2:17). Although different subgroups within the Jewish religion may have used slightly different calendars (the Synoptic Gospels place the crucifixion on the day after the Passover sacrifice while John puts it on the same day), marking of the week and of annual festivals was a common characteristic among the diverse elements of Judaism.

The fourth commonality of the Jewish religion in the Second Temple period was the primary place of the Torah—the five books of Moses (Genesis, Exodus, Leviticus, Numbers, and Deuteronomy). The Torah contained the central story and teaching of the Jewish religion. The covenantal regulations conveyed by the Torah were the fabric of Jewish life. Sometimes Christians simplistically portray Torah observance as an attempt to earn God's favor and merit salvation. Paul correctly states that no human being will be justified in God's sight by deeds prescribed by the Torah (Romans 3:20). But Torah observance was only possible for Jews as a result of God's choice and saving act in the Exodus. Since God had saved the Jews, Torah observance was their life. As a result, the Jewish religion of the Second Temple period was quite concerned with the application of the Torah to daily life. Indeed, Jesus took that very approach in the Sermon on the Mount (Matthew 5:21-48).

Since the Torah was the central and authoritative teaching of the Jewish religion, other sacred writings were commentary, comparable to layers around a central core. The Prophets and Writings of the Hebrew Bible explicated the Torah. An oral tradition of the elders provided another layer of commentary meant to guide the observant in keeping the Torah. This tradition would become a source of tension between Jesus and other religious authorities (Matthew 15:2–6; Mark 7:3–13). But this tradition would also enliven the rabbinic Judaism that survived the destruction of the temple. It would be codified around A.D. 200 in the **Mishnah**, to which would be added another layer of commentary called the **Talmud**. These layers—the Prophets and Writings, the tradition of the elders, the Mishnah, and the Talmud—have at their core and seek to uphold the Torah. The Torah was a commonality of the Jewish religion in the Second Temple period.

A fifth commonality to the Jewish religious world was strict monotheism. The creed is simple: "Hear, O Israel: The Lord our God, the Lord is one" (Deuteronomy 6:4). For the Jews, God alone is God—a teaching that was received sympathetically by some in the Roman world. Nevertheless, the religious world of Rome was polytheistic and syncretistic. Even emperors could be gods, and one displayed loyalty to Rome by participating in the rites of Roman religion. So the exclusive claim of the Jews seemed odd if not subversive to Romans. When Pompey entered Jerusalem in 63 B.C., he was surprised to find the holy of holies to be an empty room.

From the Jewish perspective, the world consisted of two types of people, Jews and non-Jews (**Gentiles**). This fundamental theological distinction was at the root of Roman/Jewish tension. So when the Jews revolted, part of the means by which Rome put down the revolt was to destroy the Jewish temple. This departure from the standard practice of treating ancient sanctuaries as inviolable is noteworthy. For Rome, the gods abandoned the Jews in part because the Jews did not worship the gods properly. Nevertheless, Jews held to monotheism tenaciously, even without a temple.

A sixth common characteristic of the Jewish religious world was a practice with which Jesus often came into conflict—strict observance of ritual purity. According to the Tosefta, "purity broke out among Israel" in the Second Temple period (Tractate Shabbat. 13b). Observance of ritual purity may be traced back to the destruction of the first temple, for which failure of Torah observance was a perceived cause. Ritual purity marked Jewish life from the days when Ezra called on Israel to separate itself from foreigners and to divorce foreign wives (Ezra 10:10–11). This "dividing wall of hostility" (Ephesians 2:14) was manifested in the *soreg* wall of the temple, separating Jews from Gentiles. Ritual bathing prepared one for entry to the temple and marked the lives of the observant. In Jewish villages both public and private ritual baths called ***mikva'ot*** are frequently discovered. Jars and cups carved from soft stone were thought to prevent the transference of impurity. Pork avoidance was characteristic of Jewish dietary practices. But in practice rites of ritual purification were observed primarily by those with the leisure and wealth to do so. From the beginning of his ministry, Jesus collided with this common practice. There is no little irony in his first miracle: turning into wine the water for ritual purification stored in stone jars (John 2:6–9).

Ritual bath near the temple

These commonalities of Jewish religion in the Second Temple period—temple, synagogue, the festival cycle, Torah, monotheism, and purity—forged Jewish identity amidst the diversity of other beliefs and practices. That diversity is characterized by the sects, literature, and expectations of Jews in this period. To that diversity we now turn.

Prominent in the circles of Jerusalem were the **Sadducees**. They were the elites of the Jewish world, many descending from Hasmonean families. They controlled the high priesthood and ran the temple. As such they had to collude with the Romans to a degree. Religiously, the Sadducees were quite conservative, accepting only the Torah as authoritative. Since the Torah contains the temple regulations, it was seen to uphold their practices and position. The Sadducees rejected popular beliefs in angels, spirits, and the general resurrection of the dead at the end of time. Zechariah's angelic experience in the temple would not have been well received by the Sadducees (Luke 1:11–22).

In the story of Jesus, the **Pharisees** play a significant role, often questioning or opposing him. But in the late Second Temple period, the actual influence of the Pharisees was minimal, although Josephus claims otherwise. Their numbers were small, perhaps five or six thousand. Their origins are unclear, possibly emerging after the Maccabean revolt. But they did provide a popular oral interpretation of the Torah. They were concerned with purity and tithing. They believed in an afterlife following a general resurrection. They spoke of a complex spirit world. Closer to the masses than the Sadducees, they were perceived as particularly pious. In Pharisaic tradition there is a precision in applying the Torah that borders on legalism, and yet there is a practicality in helping people to follow the Torah. Interestingly, the apostle Paul was himself a Pharisee (Philippians 3:5). Moreover, the rabbinic Judaism that arose from the ashes of the destruction of Jerusalem would point in its documents to prominent Pharisees as giving it foundation (Gamaliel, Hillel, and Shammai).

Occasionally in the New Testament we meet the Herodians (Matthew 22:16; Mark 3:6; 12:13). These seem to be Jews, as they appear with the Pharisees in the temple (Matthew 22:16). The same story suggests they have a positive disposition toward the Romans. If they are small in number, they may be part of the Herodian household, or the designation could be a generic identifier of Jews who were pro-Roman. We have little data on the basis of which to decide. The existence of the Herodians does however point to the diversity in beliefs and practices among the Jews of the Second Temple period.

The **Zealots** would play a significant role in the revolt against Rome all the way to the final stand at Masada. One of the disciples of Jesus is identified as a Zealot (Luke 6:16). Although zeal is a characteristic attributed to Jesus in some of his more provocative political actions (cleansing the temple in John 2:17), Jesus is clearly distinguished from such groups. The Zealots opposed the occupation by Rome and worked to overthrow Roman rule. Some refused to pay taxes; others were part of assassination squads called *sicarii* for the small swords they used. Romans often identified such insurrection with banditry. Pilate may have been trying to so smear the reputation of Jesus by crucifying him between two bandits (Matthew 27:38; Luke 23:32, 39–43).

Josephus tells of another group not mentioned in the New Testament—the Essenes. These people withdraw from society during the time of the Hasmoneans because of they were convinced that the Hasmoneans had defiled ritual practice in the temple. They were a holiness sect—concerned with purity and awaiting the final battle of the sons of light against the sons of darkness. The Dead Sea Scrolls, dramatically discovered in caves near the Dead Sea between 1947 and 1956, belonged to participants in this sect and give much detail about their beliefs, practices, and expectations. Most of the scrolls were found near Khirbet Qumran. But identification of the sect with the ruins at the site is doubtful. It is popular to suggest that John the Baptist or even Jesus had direct connections with this sect, although evidence for the connection is at best circumstantial.

In addition to the above sects that are identifiable from literature of the time, several broader and more generic terms attest to diversity in the Jewish religious world. In the Fourth Gospel, Jesus' opponents are often called "Jews." But a careful reading of the text clarifies that a better translation for the designation is "Judeans." While the writer does at times seem to be speaking of all Jewish people (John 2:13; 4:22), the opponents of Jesus are from the south part of the country in and around Jerusalem (John 5:16; 7:13; 9:22; 10:31; 18:31; 19:7, 31). To blame all Jews for the death of Jesus is wrong both historically as well as theologically.

If the Judeans opposed Jesus, Galileans are positively disposed toward Jesus, although confused by him. Historically, the Galileans of the New Testament are descendants of Judeans who populated the north after the Hasmoneans annexed the Galilee. Their distinctive material culture is quite similar to that found in the south. Yet distance from Jerusalem is bound to have an impact on their practice of the Jewish religion, even as many in the north would later refuse to participate in the revolt against Rome.

Between the Galileans and the Judeans were the **Samaritans**. On the margins of Jewish religion, these people had their own version of the Torah, a different sacred mountain (John 4:20), a separate temple and sacrificial system, and even their own expectations of the Messiah. The Samaritans likely descended from remnants of the northern tribes who had intermarried with the local populace. Often disparaged by other Jews (Luke 9:54), the conversion of some of them to Christianity through the preaching of Philip was a cause for concern in the early Christian community (Acts 8:14). But Jesus has positive relations with Samaritans and used them as examples of faithfulness (John 4; Luke 10:33; 17:16). A small number of Samaritans still populate the area around Mount Gerazim and continue their sacrifices.

A fourth grouping, although far less distinct, is the **Diaspora** (1 Peter 1:1). The term means "dispersion" and refers to the scattering of Jews throughout the Roman world. The population of Jews in Judea and Galilee at the time of Jesus was about one million. A similar number of Jews may have lived in and around Alexandria in Egypt. And there were Jewish populations in Persia and most other major imperial cities, including Rome. Strabo is quoted by Josephus as describing the Jews, "This people has already made its way into every city, and it is not easy to find any place in the habitable world which had not received this nation and in which it has not made its power felt" (*Antiquities* 14.7.2). With scattering would come a diversity of practice. There were at least two recensions of the Hebrew Bible (Palestinian and Babylonian) along with the Septuagint, which may represent a third textual tradition. In addition to the temple in Jerusalem, temples at Elephantine and Samaria pointed to rival sacred locales. And as synagogues developed as miniature sacred places (without sacrifices), even more diversity would be expected.

The primary piece of evidence pointing to diversity in Jewish religious practice was the existence of a variety of sects and subgroupings within Jewish religion. Variations in the sacred text allude to a second indicator—the wide variety of secondary religious literature that circulated, portions of which functioned in some authoritative way for various Jewish communities.

The **Apocrypha** are those intertestamental writings in the Septuagint that do not have a known Hebrew antecedent. As the Apocrypha were included in the Vulgate, they are part of the Bible for most Christians in the Catholic and Orthodox traditions. They include history and legend (1 and 2 Maccabees), pious fiction (Tobit and Suzanna), psalms, hymns, and wisdom material (Wisdom of Solomon and Eccelsiasticus). Their value lies in showing respect for temple and Torah, the importance of legal requirements and personal piety, and an understanding of eschatology as national triumph with little personal salvation.

A second class of writings from the Second Temple period is **Pseudepigrapha.** These writings are primarily apocalyptic or contain major **apocalyptic** sections. That is, through symbolic language (some quite strange) and pictures of violence and destruction, they portray the ultimate victory of God. These works are attributed to ancient heroes of the faith (for example, the *Testament of Adam*), although they could not have been written by them—thus the designation pseudepigraphic. Some seem to have been authored in and around Judea; others come from Hellenistic contexts.

A third class of writings illustrating the diversity of Jewish religion is the Dead Sea Scrolls. Over two hundred of the eight hundred scrolls recovered were biblical texts. Previously, the oldest extant texts of the Hebrew Bible were from the ninth century. As important as these texts are for the demonstration of the integrity of the Hebrew Bible, they do show that variant forms were circulating and, most importantly, that Judaism was a pluriform phenomenon. For in the Dead Sea collection are documents that for the first time give detail about one Jewish sect—the Essene movement. Led by a teacher of righteousness, possibly a priest, this group withdrew from Jerusalem during the Hasmonean period over Hasmonean handling of the priesthood. In the wilderness they sought to prepare the way of the Lord through an ascetic lifestyle. They considered themselves to be the sons of light, a remnant of the true Israel. They followed a rule of the community; their war scroll anticipated the final conflict between the sons of light and the sons of darkness. Based on the Dead Sea Scrolls, more now is known of the Essene movement than of the particular teachings of the Sadducees or the Pharisees.

Diverse groups and assorted texts point to a Jewish religion that was quite variegated in the Second Temple period. We ought not to be surprised that Jewish expectations for the future were quite varied. Some, such as the Herodians, had sided with Rome and looked to the west for their national destiny. Others, such as the Zealots, brutally resisted Rome and became instrumental in a national tragedy. Still others looked to God to rescue the nation, in particular through the coming of the Messiah. But again teachings were quite disparate. Some, such as the Essenes, believed that the death of the Teacher of Righteousness would usher in a new age. Others anticipated some sort of political Messiah who would restore the fortunes of Israel (Acts 1:6). Some looked for a prophet, others a Messiah of Aaron, and still others a Messiah of Israel. For one group the Messiah would function in a priestly way; for another the Messiah would be royal. The Samaritans even expected a leader who would deliver called the Taheb. We should not be surprised that such dissimilar perspectives swirled around Jesus, too (Matthew 16:14).

Assorted groups, varied sacred texts, and distinct Messianic perspectives were all part of the rich fabric of Jewish religion in the Second Temple period. This religion had its common markers in temple, synagogue, festival cycles, Torah, monotheism, and purity. But there was no normative Judaism. The priests may have held the greatest power by virtue of their elite status in the hierarchy of the Roman world. But even in Jerusalem varied, if not distinct, practices were followed. In this religious world Jesus moved. Pointedly, those who adhered to his teachings after his resurrection were call followers of "the Way" (Acts 9:2).

Conclusion

A critical context for understanding the stories and teachings of the New Testament is the geographical, cultural, political, and religious world in which the material was set. We have examined the geography of the eastern Mediterranean and of the land of Jesus in particular, a small and somewhat isolated place from which the story went out. We have entered into the Graeco-Roman world of politics, religion, and economics. The Roman Empire was emerging at the time of New Testament events. Its power and politics are behind many stories. The history and culture of the late Second Temple period provided a third topic. A tragic collision was coming in the imperial period. Jesus provided another way. Lastly, we discovered some of the diversity of the Jewish religious world. Jesus lived and died as a Jew. Christianity came from this pluriform context. Its distinct message and exclusive claims have this richness as its background. We are now ready to move from the context to the story itself.

For Further Discussion

1. Business leaders have a mantra that has yet to be overturned by globalization—location, location, location. Pick several stories from the gospels that mention a specific location. Find that location on a map. How might the location play a part in the story? You might do the same with one of Paul's letters to a community in a city or with the opening section of Revelation. What does a map teach you in each of these cases?
2. The coming of the Roman Empire is the genesis for many stories of power gone wrong. For instance, the *Star Wars* saga has many affinities with the rise of the Roman Empire. How does *Star Wars* offer an anti-imperial perspective? Paul seems to do something similar with his letter to the Philippians. How might a Roman official react to that work?
3. Jewish people in Judea and Galilee lived under Roman occupation either directly or indirectly during the days of Jesus. How did Jesus, as a religious leader, react to this occupation? For a comparison, discuss the religious and nationalistic reaction to the entrance into Iraq by U.S. forces.
4. How would you compare the diversity of global Christianity today to the diversity present in the Jewish religious world in the Second Temple period? What characteristics are similar? Which are different? What are the implications of this comparison?
5. Does it matter in what political or cultural context a story is told or a teaching is given? Why do you say so? What difference might the context make?

For Further Reading

Arnold, Clinton E., editor. *Zondervan Illustrated Bible Background Commentary*. 4 volumes. Grand Rapids: Zondervan, 2002.

Carter, Warren. *The Roman Empire and the New Testament*. Nashville: Abingdon Press, 2006.

Hansom, K. C. and Oakman, Douglas E. *Palestine in the Time of Jesus*. Minneapolis: Fortress, 1998.

Jeffers, James S. *The Graeco-Roman World of the New Testament Era*. Downers Grove, IL: InterVarsity Press, 1999.

Neusner, Jacob. *Judaism When Christianity Began.* Louisville: Westminster John Knox Press, 2002.

Rousseau, John J. and Arav, Rami. *Jesus and His World*. Minneapolis: Fortress Press, 1995.

3

The Story of the New Testament

Introduction

There is something about a story. In the story of the New Testament we Christians hear information, receive instruction, and are drawn into ancient times and places inhabited by heroes, villains, and lots of ordinary folk. But the story does even more. This story changes our world, shapes our being, and shows us the Father in his son Jesus. It reveals God's saving purpose in Jesus Christ. However, when we speak of "the story," we must identify which story we are talking about.

The New Testament contains not one story but many stories, not the whole story but select stories. Four gospels convey the story of Jesus. As we will discover later, each gospel is trying to answer the question, "Who is Jesus?" Each answer is particular to the audience being addressed. The story of the earliest Christian communities is told by Acts, but the bulk of that work focuses on one apostle (Paul) and only part of his work. Paul's own writings and the known spread of Christianity suggest that there are many untold stories. Later New Testament works only hint at the stories behind them. So, to speak of "the story" of the New Testament, as if it were a singular tale, is a misnomer.

Yet, this chapter will trace "the story" of the New Testament. I placed the words "the story" in quotes because this chapter is actually a plausible reconstruction of the story behind the New Testament. Do not confuse this reconstruction with the inspired stories of the New Testament! Other reconstructions are possible, and none are as authoritative as the New Testament itself. Nevertheless, reconstructions have value because they help illumine the biblical stories, place them in larger contexts, and suggest connections among the stories. This chapter is meant to enrich your understanding of the sacred text, so that the story of Jesus and the first Christians might shape your story, too.

Chapter Outline

- Jesus of Nazareth
    - Birth
    - Public Ministry
    - Passion and Resurrection
    - Searching for Jesus
- The First Century
    - In Jerusalem
    - Crossing Cultural Boundaries

The Gentile Mission of Paul
Untold Stories

Jesus of Nazareth

Two of the four gospels (Matthew and Luke) start their respective stories of Jesus with birth narratives. The Fourth Gospel speaks of the "Word" becoming "flesh" (John 1:14) from which comes the doctrinal term **incarnation** (in flesh), but does not narrate details. Mark begins his story with the work of John the Baptizer (Mark 1:4). Notable are the differing emphases of the two birth narratives.

Birth

The earlier of the two accounts is from the Gospel according to Matthew. There the birth of Jesus is told as part of a larger story of "righteous" Joseph. The genealogy with which the gospel opens is actually the genealogy of "Joseph, the husband of Mary, of whom Jesus was born" (Matthew 1:16). It is stylized in three blocks of fourteen and contains the names of the famous and infamous, including women. When Joseph names Jesus (1:25), Jesus becomes Joseph's legal heir and the genealogy applies to him as well, affirming several Matthean themes (see the section on Matthew below).

The birth of Jesus is narrated in the context of a struggle of the observant Joseph with the seeming infidelity of Mary. The betrothal period was meant to assure Mary's purity at the beginning of the marriage and the legitimacy of any children born of the marriage. In the Jewish religious world of the first century, purity was a dominant theme. According to the Torah, infidelity demanded punishment (Deuteronomy 22:20–21). Matthew labels Joseph as "righteous" (Matthew 1:19), suggesting that Joseph was careful to observe the Torah. According to the second-century *Protoevangelium of James*, Joseph worries, "If I hide her sin, I am fighting the Law of God" (14.1). But Joseph tempered his observance with mercy, a theme in the teaching of Jesus as well (Matthew 5:7). Joseph resolved to send Mary away. However, an angelic message in a dream would reveal the Lord's intent for Jesus and for Joseph. Joseph discovers a greater righteousness in the prophetic promises of God. Matthew's birth narrative does assert the divine origin of Jesus. Jesus is "from the Holy Spirit" (1:18) and is "God with us" (1:23). Details about the place and time of birth are only noted in passing during the subsequent story of the magi.

By contrast, Luke places his birth narrative at a particular time and place. Jesus is born during an empire-wide census ordered by Caesar Augustus and executed by Quirinius, the legate of Syria (Luke 2:1–2). This census requires Joseph to return to his ancestral home in Bethlehem. As part of the process of consolidating imperial power, Augustus did use the census in various provinces. Unfortunately, history lacks record of one census that covered the whole empire; the only known census conducted by Quirinius was in A.D. 6–7; and it was held in Judea only after the chaotic rule of Archelaus. While attempts to reconcile the historical record with the details of Luke are problematic at best, Luke's theological point is clear. At a time of universal rule came a Savior who is indeed for all (see the discussion of Lucan Christology below).

Of greater note in the Lucan story is the focus on the female characters. If Matthew's story is about Joseph, Luke's story is about two insignificant women to whom sons are born in miraculous fashion. The first is Elizabeth, the wife of a minor priest, whose insignificance is affirmed by her barrenness (Luke 1:7). As the annunciation of the birth of a child to Elizabeth and her husband Zechariah left him mute during his temple service (Luke 1:20), Elizabeth comes into prominence, expressing the joy of this most impossible pregnancy (Luke 1:25). More prominent in the story is a second woman, Mary of Nazareth, who receives a direct angelic visitation announcing an even more miraculous pregnancy. She then visits her relative Elizabeth whose greeting is filled with the Holy Spirit. Their encounter and Mary's song, reflecting the prayer of Hannah (1 Samuel 2:1–10), bring the two into prominence. Elizabeth even acts in the place of her mute husband by giving the name of John to her son.

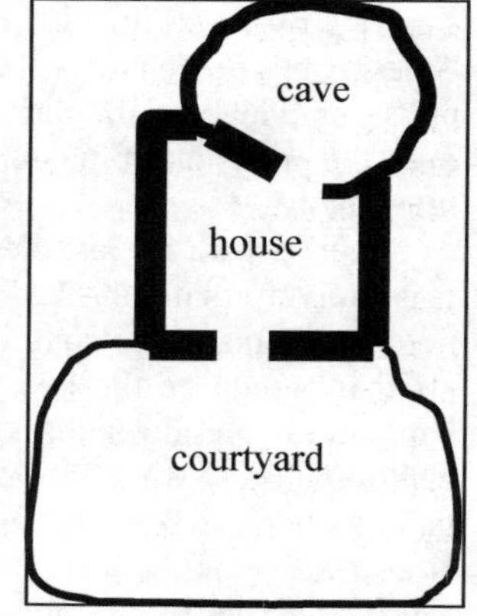

For most of us, annual re-enactments of the Lucan birth account during Christmas festivities provide a familiarity with the story that is not always true to the account. Depictions of the birth in a stable or barn of north European construction do not accord with known construction techniques of the Judean hill country. In these limestone hills, even into the twentieth century, homes of the poor consisted of a courtyard and a single enclosed room built of stone behind which may have been a cave. At night, the family would sleep in the room and any family animals would be herded into the cave (Luke 13:25; Matthew 6:6). The "place for guests" (the correct meaning of the word often translated "inn") would have been in the main room; the cave would be a more private place to deliver a child. Such an understanding fits better with near eastern concepts of hospitality (no one would turn away a pregnant woman), with the Matthean reference to a house (Matthew 2:11), and with the fact that a small village would be a most unlikely place for a caravanserai (the ancient version of a Motel 6). The nearness of shepherds would suggest that Jesus was born sometime in the dry season.

Hinted at by the difference in focus of the two accounts are various points that the respective gospel writers make by selecting and presenting their material. One other difference surfaces in the stories of those who visited the infant Jesus. In Matthew the visitors are astrologers from "the east" (Matthew 2:1). In Luke, shepherds come. While both are led to the scene by phenomena in the heavens, Matthew's magi foreshadow the Matthean emphasis on making disciples of all nations (Matthew 28:19). Luke's shepherds are of marginal social standing and continue a theme of the gospel's import for the poor and marginalized (Luke would also include the story of Simeon and Anna in the temple in the block of infancy materials). Together the narratives further the universal appeal of the incarnate one.

Public Ministry

The opening scene of the second gospel—the appearance of John the Baptist—is the common starting point in all four gospels for the public ministry of Jesus. John's clothing identifies him as a prophet and his diet (locusts and wild honey) are those of a desert dweller. In the theological background of these stories is the formation of Israel in a wilderness experience (the exodus). Isaianic prophecy is also in the background (Matthew 3:3; Mark 1:2–3; Luke 3:4).

Luke dates the beginning to the "the fifteenth year of the reign of Tiberius Caesar" (Luke 3:1) and names other regional rulers of the time. Precise dating is complicated by several factors: whether Luke begins with the co-regency of Tiberius over certain provinces, the death of Augustus, or the acclamation of Tiberius by the Senate; whether Luke counts the accession year as the first regnal year; which of the various contemporary calendars Luke has in mind; and even the precision of the number fifteen (a decade and a half). A.D. 27 or 28 are most likely.

John's work is characterized by baptism and a call to repentance. Although it is unlikely that John had a relationship with the **Essene** community (despite popular claims to the contrary!), his washings are more akin to purification rituals than would be the later initiation ritual of early Christianity. Notably, the baptism of John does not convey the Holy Spirit (the baptism of Jesus is an exception). There were political overtones to the preaching of John. The New Testament characterizes his basic message as, "Repent, for the kingdom of heaven is at hand" (Matthew 3:2). We tend to hear these words strictly in a religious sense, because in our culture religion and politics are separate. In the world of Roman Palestine, religion and politics were intimately connected. Rome was ruled by a son of a god; to announce the nearness of a different reign—the reign of the Jewish God—was insurrection and eventually led to John's execution by Herod Antipas. The nearness of God's reign, a surprising claim in view of Roman domination of the land, would also be at the core of the ministry of Jesus (Matthew 4:17; John 1:15).

The story of the New Testament ends the ministry of John with the baptism of Jesus in the Jordan, probably near Jericho. All four gospels point to the baptism and bestowal of God's Spirit as the inauguration of the public ministry of Jesus. With the gift of the Spirit comes the authority for the work. In the **synoptic** tradition, a voice from heaven identifies Jesus as "my beloved Son" (Matthew 3:17; Mark 1:11; Luke 3:22). In the Fourth Gospel, John the Baptist bears witness that "this is the Son of God" (John 1:34). There is a continuity between John and Jesus, but it is between a lesser and a greater.

In the first three gospels, conflict between Jesus and the authorities will be a major theme and a precipitating factor in the move to execute Jesus. That conflict is given a cosmic dimension in one final inaugural story—the temptation of Jesus. The temptation is attributed at least in part to the working of the Spirit (Matthew 4:1; Mark 1:12) and so serves as a test of the faithfulness of Jesus. Testing and temptation are part of the same conceptual world. These forty days would be for Jesus as were the forty years for Israel. In this contest, Satan is vanquished "until an opportune time" (Luke 4:13). Jesus is truly ready to start his ministry of proclamation, parables, and miracles.

The Sea from Galilee

Were we restricted to the Synoptic Gospels, the public ministry of Jesus would open in the Galilee after the arrest of John the Baptist. After a period of time, Jesus would travel south (Mark 10; Luke 9:51–19:28). Then a tumultuous week would lead to his crucifixion. There are few chronological indicators in the synoptic tradition. If we follow Mark's story, the disciples are plucking grain in chapter 2 (dry season). In chapter 6, those present at the feeding of the five thousand sit on green grass (rainy season). And the story comes to a culmination at the **Passover** (chapter 14). Since the rainy season is December through February and Passover corresponds with the start of the harvest season, the synoptic narrative seems to span but one year. The Fourth Gospel speaks of at least three Passovers (John 2:13, 23; 6:4; 18:28, 39; 19:14), implying a three-year public ministry. Although merging synoptic and Johannine chronologies is a tenuous activity, a ministry of several years is a plausible reconstruction leading up to his crucifixion in A.D. 30 (or even perhaps A.D. 33). Luke says he was "about thirty" when he began his work (Luke 3:23).

In continuity with John the Baptist, Jesus began his ministry proclaiming, "Repent, for the kingdom of heaven has come near" (Matthew 4:17). Matthew uses "kingdom of heaven" for the more common "kingdom of God" out of deference for Jewish readers who might have been offended by the use of the divine name. Of greater import is the political context for Jesus' words. After a period of freedom under the Hasmoneans, onerous Roman rule expressed through the Herodian family and the prefects of Judea had raised an **apocalyptic** hope of the coming of God's kingdom. That hope would then turn into violent revolt against Rome in the mid sixties.

In such a charged context, Jesus preached often of the **kingdom**, using language with political overtones. What Jesus announced is probably better understood as "rule" rather than "kingdom," as Jesus incorporated into his teaching the eternal rule of God over creation, God's rule on earth in the lives of the faithful, and God's future rule at the end of the age. The use of parable and metaphor solicits proper behavior and relationships in light of the nearness of God's rule. At the same time his kingdom is not of this world (John 18:36). Through proclamation, parable, and even miracle, Jesus would draw his followers into the mystery of the reign of God.

Torah observance was one of the defining characteristics across the range of Judaism in the first century. So, even the poor were concerned with keeping the Law, in so far as they could. The proclamation of Jesus must be read in this context.

Jesus is often called by the title **rabbi** in Matthew, Mark, and John. Luke prefers a different title meaning "school master." In the first century, "rabbi" was a title of respect meaning "teacher." But before the revolt in the late sixties, it had not yet become an official term for an ordained scholar. After the revolt, only rabbinic forms of Judaism survived. Yet, even in the time of Jesus, the Jewish teaching implied by the term "rabbi" was concerned with application of the Torah to daily life. The "tradition of the elders" (Matthew 15.2; Mark 7:3–5) seems to be an oral form of such teaching. This oral tradition would later be redacted by Rabbi Yehuda Ha-nasi into the **Mishnah** around A.D. 200.

While the Mishnah was codified later, it does quote sages from before the revolt, and so may reflect the typical teachings of a rabbi. The Mishnah organizes the legal material of the **Pentateuch** into six broad orders, which are subdivided into tractates. The tractates are further subdivided into chapters, which are composed of individual teachings. The teachings report the accepted decisions of the sages and the major dissents. So when an individual rabbi taught legal material, he (there were no women in this role) would report decisions and dissents, "The school of Gamaliel says . . . , but the school of Hillel says . . ."

In some ways, the proclamation of Jesus was similar; but in other ways his words were unique. Jesus taught in ways similar to other rabbis by helping people apply the Torah to their daily lives. For example, he will quote a commandment of the **Decalogue**, and then talk about its implications (Matthew 5:21–48). A section of the **Sermon on the Mount** is devoted to the three great acts of Jewish piety: Prayer, almsgiving, and fasting (Matthew 6:1–18). But Jesus was markedly different in his teaching: "You have heard that it was said to those of old, … But I say to you …" (Matthew 5:21–22). Jesus did not quote the traditions or the sages, he spoke on his own authority—a fact recognized by those who heard him. "And they were astonished at his teaching, for he taught them as one who had authority, and not as the scribes" (Mark 1:22).

His announcement of the nearness of the reign of God also distinguished his teaching. According to Mark, the coming reign of God is good news or Gospel (Mark 1:15). The Sermon on the Mount opens with acclamations popularly called beatitudes. Jesus proclaims, "Blessed are you …." The translation "happy" misses the Gospel point and reduces the good news to an attitude. In fact, those who are "blessed" would under normal circumstances hardly consider themselves so, for those who mourn or hunger and thirst for righteousness or are persecuted might wonder whether the curse of God is upon them. Even peacemakers often get bloodied in the process! But for Jesus, the nearness of the reign of God means unexpected blessing, that is, good news even in difficult times. This gospel provides the context for the ethical teaching to follow. Jesus taught on his own authority, and at the heart of his message was the good news of the imminent reign of God.

The teaching of Jesus is recorded in several forms. We have already mentioned the Sermon on the Mount. It is one of five major "discourses" in Matthew that some suggest parallel the five books of Moses. "Discourses" may be a somewhat deceptive description, as the Gospel writers are likely collecting various teachings of Jesus into larger blocks. The collection in Matthew 5–7 has been given the title the Sermon on the Mount. But the title is an extra biblical addition. The collection of sayings is followed by a collection of miracle stories in Matthew 8–9. The shorter Sermon on the Plain in Luke 6 is similar. Large blocks of speech are also characteristic of the Fourth Gospel. The so-called Upper Room discourse meanders (literally!) from John 13:31 to John 17:26. Whether these blocks of proclamation were delivered at once or are collections that sample the proclamation of Jesus, one form of his proclamation seems to be sermonic.

By contrast, the gospel writers also note that Jesus could convey his teaching is short and pithy statements. "Repent for the reign of God is at hand" is the best known example. There are others: "So the last will be first, and the first last" (Matthew 20:16). "He who has ears, let him hear" (Matthew 13:9). "The spirit indeed is willing, but the flesh is weak" (Mark 14:38). "For the Son of Man came to seek and to save the lost" (Luke 19:10). These aphorisms put Jesus in the wisdom tradition of Proverbs.

The best-known form of Jesus' proclamation is his **parables**. The parables use metaphors drawn from daily life in Roman agrarian Palestine to illustrate the reign of God. At times a parable begins with such characteristic words, "What is the kingdom of God like? And to what shall I compare it?" (Luke 13:18). The parables serve a revelatory function. Through them we get a glimpse of the reign of God.

It is critical when working with parables not to interpret them excessively. In a parable, there is generally a single point of comparison, unless the Scripture indicates otherwise. For example, Jesus tells "a parable to the effect that they ought always to pray and not lose heart" (Luke 18:1). In the parable, a widow persistently calls for justice from a judge, as an illustration of "God giv[ing] justice to his elect, who cry to him day and night?" (18:7) The widow's actions are the point of comparison, not the judge who is described as one who "neither feared God nor respected man" (18:4). God is not like that judge! On the other hand, many details in the parable of the sower are pertinent to its interpretation. We know that because Jesus says so (Mark 4:13–20).

As parables are drawn from the daily life of the hearers, we modern readers must enter that world to grasp the parable, for sometimes simple details are key to the parable's revelation of the surprising nature of the reign of God. The parable of the mustard seed is well known: a small seed that grows to become a tree where the birds of the air make nests in its branches. However, this parable is about more than growth, for the black mustard grown in Palestine is a shrub, not a tree with branches for nests. The miraculous growth of the kingdom shows the surprising nature of the reign of God—a shrub become a tree. Likewise, in the parable of the sower, the key point is not the good soil, but the miraculous growth of seeds (called “the word” in Mark 4:14). The yield is “thirtyfold and sixtyfold and a hundredfold" (Mark 4:8), far beyond what one would expect of a typical harvest (compare Genesis 26.12).

Parables illustrate the reign of God, especially its surprising nature. They have a revelatory nature (Matthew 13:11). But, for the opponent, parables hinder understanding: “This is why I speak to them in parables, because seeing they do not see, and hearing they do not hear, nor do they understand” (Matthew 13:13). The frequency of parable telling increases as Jesus approaches Jerusalem and in the temple controversy Jesus speaks parables “against” the chief priests and **Pharisees** (Matthew 21:45). Parables reveal, but they also hide.

Interestingly, no parables are recorded in the Fourth Gospel. Parables are unique to the synoptic tradition about Jesus. In John’s Gospel the use of metaphorical language is much more stylized. Seven times Jesus speaks in metaphors mostly drawn from daily life. But in this gospel “the kingdom of God is like” is replaced by “I am.” Metaphors invoking the bread of life, the light of the world, the door of the fold, the good shepherd, the way, truth, and life, and the vine (John 6:35; 8:12; 9:5; 10:7, 11, 14; 14:6; 15:1) function like parables to illustrate the reign of God in the one who is “I am.”

The ministry of Jesus has at its center the imminent reign of God. It is the core of his teaching, and it is illustrated in his use of metaphorical language in the parables. The third characteristic of Jesus’ public ministry is his working of mighty deeds. These, too, are finally about the coming reign of God.

Those deeds we call miracles are never so labeled in the New Testament. The Greek word for miracle is not used. Instead, the surprising acts of Jesus are called “works” or “mighty deeds” or “signs and wonders.” When approaching the miracles of Jesus, the first problem is one of definition. What is a miracle? We should avoid modernist descriptions such as a “violation of the laws of nature,” for the ancients did not so construe their world. Realms that we might call miraculous or even spiritual were considered indistinguishable from the world of observation. At the same time, those who witnessed the works of Jesus could exclaim, "We never saw anything like this!" (Mark 2:12) There was something of note about the actions of Jesus.

Perhaps a better way to approach the actions of Jesus would be to name descriptive classes of noteworthy acts. Predominant among the actions of Jesus were exorcisms. Mark summarizes the ministry of Jesus as “preaching in their synagogues and casting out demons” (Mark 1:39). In a way the ministry of Jesus could be understood as a contest between Jesus and the demonic. Again, we must be cautious about applying modern conceptions of illness both physical and mental to the ancient world, even as we must remember that the physical and spiritual worlds were one to the ancients. However we may look at our world, the world of Jesus was one in which he silenced and cast out demons.

A second class of noteworthy acts involved healing of the sick. In the ministry of Jesus, healing was often more than the skilled practice of medicine. Healing and salvation were aspects of the same event. The same word is at times used for both. When a paralytic is brought in, Jesus first announces. "My son, your sins are forgiven" (Mark 2:5). Only later does he say, "Rise, pick up your bed, and go home" (Mark 2:11). To a Canaanite woman pleading for her daughter, Jesus declares, "O woman, great is your faith! Be it done for you as you desire." And her daughter was healed instantly (Matthew 15:28). This theological side of healing is also a sign of the messianic age. When John the Baptist questioned whether Jesus was the messiah, Jesus answered his followers, "Go and tell John what you hear and see: the blind receive their sight and the lame walk, lepers are cleansed and the deaf hear, and the dead are raised up, and the poor have good news preached to them" (Matthew 11:4–5; compare Isaiah 29:18–19, 35:5–6; 61:1).

In several instances, the healing acts of Jesus included the restoration of life to those who had died. Out of pity, Jesus raised the son of the widow of Nain (Luke 7:11–17). The raising of Jairus' daughter was the occasion for Jesus to speak of death as "sleep" (Luke 8:41–56). But the raising of Lazarus (John 11) is the culmination of the actions of Jesus in the Fourth Gospel and anticipates his own resurrection.

A third class of noteworthy acts occurs in the natural world, when Jesus stills storms, walks on the sea, or feeds the multitudes. The stilling of the storm in Mark is told with language reminiscent of an exorcism ("rebuked … 'Be still!'" Mark 4:39). The sea walking is an **epiphany**. And the feedings anticipate the eschatological banquet.

A calm Sea of Galilee

The ministry of Jesus is punctuated by many noteworthy acts: demons are silenced, maladies healed, lives are spared. But these acts of Jesus are more than noteworthy. They are illustrative of a greater struggle between the divine and the demonic. Their context is one of faith and salvation.

Some complexity of the miracle stories surfaces when we compare the telling of the same story in different gospels. For example, the story of Jesus walking on the sea has common components in the three gospels (Matthew, Mark, and John) that recount the event. The story follows immediately after the feeding of the five thousand. The disciples start to cross the sea in a boat while Jesus dismisses the crowds. A strong wind opposes their progress. In the middle of the night, Jesus comes walking on the sea. They are frightened, supposing him to be a ghost, and cry out for fear. Jesus answers with the same words in all three versions, "It is I; don't be afraid" (Matthew 14:27; Mark 6:50; John 6:20).

"Don't be afraid" is standard biblical language at the appearance of God or God's messenger. In Greek, "It is I" is the same as "I am," the divine name given to Moses at the burning bush (Exodus 3:14). The use of both phrases informs the reader that the one walking on the sea is God. The miracle is an epiphany—an appearance of God.

But miracles are not simple and easily understood. In John, "they were glad to take him into the boat" (John 6:21). By contrast, Mark says, "They were utterly astounded, for they did not understand about the loaves, but their hearts were hardened" (Mark 6:51–52). The act of Jesus elicited a broad range of response. At this point in the story, Matthew includes a longer narrative centered on Peter. The extension begins with Peter displaying lack of faith. "If it is you …" Not only did Peter doubt the divine identification, he asked for proof. He wanted to be like God and walk on the sea. Peter repeated the fatal mistake first made by Adam and Eve (Genesis 3:5). But the Matthean narrator exposes Peter's flawed thinking. For Peter asks to come to Jesus on the "water" not the "sea." Peter's demand is defective from the beginning. Only God comes on the sea. Foolish it is for a mortal like Peter to want to walk on water. And of course, he begins to sink.

At this point the narrative takes an important turn. Peter cries out, "Lord, save me" (Matthew 14:30). Rescue comes at once, and those in the boat "worshiped him, saying, 'Truly you are the Son of God'" (Matthew 14:33). Peter's failure turns into a liturgical cry of the church, assuring us that no matter the trouble into which we sink, rescue by Jesus is at hand. In the midst of his troubles, Peter becomes a positive example of a believer calling out to God (Psalm 6:4). The complexity of responses to this epiphany, along with the varying emphases of the gospel writers, suggests that miracle stories function in several ways. For some they elicit faith; for others they are the occasion for doubt.

Feeding the 5000

In the Fourth Gospel, the deeds of Jesus assume a particular theological purpose. Seven such events are narrated, all in the first half of the work, and all are identified as "signs." As such, these signs point beyond the actual event to something ahead. Just as a "stop" sign is not as important as the upcoming reason for commanding a driver to stop (for example, the cross traffic of a highway), so these signs point beyond themselves to the imminent reign of God. To quote the gospel writer, "Now Jesus did many other signs in the presence of the disciples, which are not written in this book; but these are written so that you may [continue to] believe that Jesus is the Christ, the Son of God, and that by believing you may have life in his name" (John 20:30–31). The sign is a momentary encounter of that ultimate life in his name experienced now in part but coming fully at the end of time.

So the mighty works of Jesus are like a visible word (Matthew 9:8, 33). For some they are revelatory of the coming messianic age (Matthew 8:17). For others, the miracles hide and lead to false conclusions (Matthew 9:34). Such deeds are part of the "proclamation of the good news of the kingdom" (Matthew 9:35). The teaching of Jesus, his parables, and his miracles ought to be viewed together as various forms of proclamation. In his teaching Jesus announced the imminent reign of God. In his parables, he illustrated that reign by drawing on metaphors from daily life to show what the reign of God is like. In his miracles, the proclamation becomes concrete; the reign of God is visible and experienced in a specific place for a specific moment. One gets a taste of what ultimately is to come. Teaching, parable, and miracle are simply different facets of the public ministry of Jesus.

When the gospel writers tell the story of Jesus, central to their stories are those with whom Jesus comes into contact. Although the characters are many, both named and unnamed, they fall into four classes: the disciples, the crowds, the religious leaders, and people on the margins of society.

Best known are the disciples, those who went with Jesus in his public ministry. Closest to Jesus were three: Peter, James and John. They accompanied him on key occasions (the raising of Jairus' daughter, the transfiguration, and at Gethsemane). Of the three, Peter held a central position (Matthew 16:18–19). These three were part of a larger group called the Twelve, although the listing of names shows some variation (Matthew 10:2–4; Mark 3:16–19; Luke 6:13–16; Acts 1:13). Sometimes the term "disciple" seems to be limited to this group. Accompanying Jesus and the twelve was a somewhat larger group, including some women who were patrons of the group and well as followers (Luke 8:1–3).

The disciples are loyal followers of Jesus. They respond to his call (Matthew 4:18–22), are sent out as his representatives (Matthew 10:1–4), and are instructed in the mysteries of the kingdom (Matthew 13:11). But they also show persistent lack of understanding (Mark 4:13), are resistant to Jesus' purpose (Matthew 16:22), and at the most critical moment, they forsake him and flee (Mark 14:50), denying that the ever knew him (Mark 14:72). Even after his resurrection, they are slow to respond (John 20:9).

The constant opponent of Jesus is the religious and political establishment. Various subgroups may be identified (scribes, Pharisees, priests, **Sadducees**, the Herodians, Pilate), but they function as one character. They raise questions of Jesus (Mark 2:6), identify him with the working of Beelzebub (Luke 11:15), plot against him (Matthew 12:14), and finally condemn him to death (Matthew 26:66). They are his implacable enemy. Conflict with them drives many narratives.

The crowds fill a medial place between the disciples and the establishment. They are attracted to Jesus, astounded by this words and works (Mark 2:12), and bring to him their sick and demon-possessed (Mark 1:22). But they are also confused by him, identify him with a range of religious and political hopes (Mark 8:28), and those from Jerusalem in the end join in his demise (Luke 23:23).

A fourth character grouping in the story of Jesus is the little people—those on the margins of religious and economic life whom Jesus meets once and who experience the mercy of God in a unique way. These marginal people (the Canaanite woman, the woman with the flow of blood, a little child, a blind man, a tax collector, even a thief on a cross are examples) provide a contrast to the lack of commitment by the crowds or the slow understanding of the disciples. These little people are the ones with great faith worthy of emulation (Matthew 15:28).

The public ministry of Jesus may be characterized as proclamation of the reign of God in the form of teaching, parables, and miracles. Conducted primarily in the Galilee, the ministry attracted crowds, gathered disciples, inspired great faith, and contested with those in authority. Tension and conflict grew. It would be resolved at Jerusalem in one great week.

The Life of Jesus according to Paul

Paul writes at length about the implications of the death and resurrection of Jesus for Christians and for all creation. But Paul does not provide any narrative of earlier parts of the life of Jesus. The only references are in passing. In Galatians, Paul notes that Jesus was born of a woman and lived under the law (Galatians 4:4). In Romans, Paul mentions the Davidic lineage of Jesus (Romans 1:3) and that he "confirm[ed] the promises given to the patriarchs" (Romans 15:8). Other allusions to the public ministry are rare.

Paul does claim to have received commands from the Lord (1 Corinthians 7:10). The attitude of Paul toward enemies (Romans 12:14, 1 Corinthians 4:12–13; 1 Thessalonians 5:15) probably derives from the Sermon on the Mount. Paul's use of "Abba, Father" in prayer (Romans 8:15; Galatians 4:6) reflects the way Jesus addressed God (Matthew 6:9; Mark 14:36; John 12:27–28). Paul apparently knew such material. But he was so focused on the passion and resurrection that the rest received at best slight mention.

Passion and Resurrection

According to the synoptic tradition, a significant transition in the public ministry of Jesus happened after Jesus predicted the events to come in Jerusalem. In sharp contrast with Jewish messianic expectation, "he began to teach them that the Son of Man must suffer many things and be rejected by the elders and the chief priests and the scribes and be killed, and after three days rise again" (Mark 8:31; compare 9:30–32; 10:33–34). Jesus then set his face to go to Jerusalem (Luke 9:51).

Jesus arrived at Jerusalem for the Passover celebration. This festival was a tense time in Jerusalem. The festival commemorated God's miraculous deliverance from foreign oppression and raised expectations of imminent deliverance from Roman occupation. Passover was the chief pilgrimage festival, and so Jerusalem swelled in population from sixty- to as many as three hundred-thousand. The prefect Pontius Pilate also came to Jerusalem at this time to maintain order. Pilate was hardly sensitive to Jewish concerns. He was the first Roman ruler to display images of the emperor on Roman standards in the city. After he robbed the temple fund to build an aqueduct, protests led to riots and many Jewish deaths. Caiaphas, who served as high priest with the permission of Pilate, would have been quite concerned to keep a lid on things.

Jesus likely arrived several days early with other Galilean pilgrims to undergo ritual purification in anticipation of the festival. During this purification period, several events occur, some with purity overtones, which heighten the conflict and anticipate later happenings. Jesus is anointed at Bethany, but none understand it as preparation for burial (Matthew 26:12; Mark 14:8).

The first critical event was the entry of Jesus into the city. Although he rode a donkey, chosen to recall Zechariah 9:9, his entry was a triumph with distinct political overtones. The one who rides the donkey in Zechariah is a king (Matthew 21:5). The spreading of coats recalls the greeting of Jehu after the Lord had made him king to drive out the house of Ahab and Jezebel (2 Kings 9:13). The waving of palm branches recalled the "removal of the yoke of the Gentiles" when Judea gained independence under Simon (1 Maccabees 13:41, 51). The pilgrims may have been singing the **Hosanna** from Psalm 118:25–26, as singing Psalms on the way up to the temple seems to have been a common practice (Psalm 122). But greeting Jesus as "the son of David" (Matthew 21:9) and "the one who comes in the name of the Lord" (Mark 11:9) had political overtones, earned a rebuke for Jesus (Matthew 21:16; Luke 19:39), and troubled the city (Matthew 21:10). But the entry was likely a small event. A major disturbance would have brought the Romans and immediate arrest.

The second critical event was the cleansing of the temple. Although placed early in the Gospel according to John, the Synoptic Gospels list it in the complex of events leading to Jesus' crucifixion. Mark frames it with the story of the cursing of the fig tree to symbolize the desolate nature of the temple and its leadership. That Jesus would cleanse the temple when pilgrims are cleansing themselves to enter the temple highlights the conflict. To label the exchange of money and selling of sacrificial animals as making the temple a "den of robbers" is the same as saying that the temple leaders were insurrectionists against God. As a result, the chief priests and scribes and principal men of the people sought to destroy Jesus (Mark 11:18; Luke 19:47), a move that would lead somewhat ironically and perhaps intentionally to the crucifixion of Jesus between two robbers.

The third critical event was a running exchange between Jesus and various religious authorities as Jesus taught in the temple. Matthew devotes three chapters (21–23) to the contest. Each group has their turn at Jesus, confronting him and trying to trap him. It was a contest of honor with the goal of turning the crowds against Jesus. First the chief priests and elders (Matthew 21:23–44), then the chief priests and Pharisees (Matthew 21:45–22:14), then the Pharisees and the Herodians (Matthew 22:15–22), then the Sadducees (Matthew 22:23–33), and finally an expert in the Torah (Matthew 22:34–45) take Jesus on with the result that "no one was able to answer him a word, nor from that day did anyone dare to ask him any more questions" (Matthew 22:46).

Typical was the contest involving the Pharisees and the Herodians. Tensions were already high as the religious authorities perceived that Jesus was directing his parables against them (Matthew 21:45), so two opposing groups worked to set the perfect trap. The Pharisees represented the conservative religious perspective calling for strict Torah observance. The Herodians apparently represented a liberal Judaism welcoming of Hellenistic and Roman influences and at home in that world. Their trap was perfect, "Is it lawful [read: proper according to the Torah] to pay taxes to Caesar, or not?" (Matthew 22:17) For an affirmative answer would give the Pharisees an opening to use the Torah against Jesus; a negative answer could be chargeable offense with Pilate in town. Jesus asked to see the coin for the tax, and one in the group, presumably a Herodian, brings out a denarius.

Denarius of Tiberius

A **denarius** was a Roman coin with the image of the emperor on it, Tiberius in this case. Jews exchanged such coins for Tyrian shekels prior to entering the temple, so as to avoid defiling the place with the image of a god (Exodus 20:4–6). Recall the offense when Pilate brought standards with the image of the emperor to the city a few years earlier. The Passover crowd in the temple that day would have been aghast, as Jesus asked pointedly, "Whose likeness and inscription is this?" (Matthew 22:20) The lack of Herodian sensitivity condemned the Pharisee partner as well. When Jesus added, "Therefore render to Caesar the things that are Caesar's, and to God the things that are God's" (Matthew 22:21), he allowed a shameful retreat for his opponents while defusing a potentially violent situation. The winner of the contest was clear.

The final word in the long-running contest belongs to Jesus. It is a caustic diatribe against the scribes and Pharisees as "hypocrites," "fools," "blind guides," and "white-washed tombs." The die is cast between Jesus and the authorities when Jesus declares, "For I tell you, you will not see me again, until you say, 'Blessed is he who comes in the name of the Lord'" (Matthew 23:39). Only one outcome is now possible; the authorities must respond.

As if the above were not enough, both Matthew and Mark highlight the crisis with teaching of Jesus about the end (Matthew 24–25; Mark 13). More is at stake than Jewish politics, Roman power, or the fate of a Galilean preacher. The events about to unfold are about the destiny of the cosmos, the inauguration of a new creation. Faithfulness and endurance are required (Matthew 24:13). But only one will endure to the end.

Jesus had arranged somewhat secretly to eat the Passover meal with his disciples in Jerusalem. As the place was a large and furnished second-story room

(Mark 14:15), the home was likely in the upper city and belonged to a wealthy individual. Later tradition would suggest it was the home of Mary of Jerusalem (Acts 12:12).

Within the context of the rituals of the Passover meal, Jesus performed two important actions. According to the Fourth Gospel, he washed the feet of his disciples (John 13:1–20) and gave them the new commandment to love one another (John 13:34). From the Latin word *mandatum* ("commandment") comes the liturgical designation of the day as Maundy Thursday. The Fourth Gospel also recounts much teaching of Jesus (John 14–17) but makes little mention of the meal. In the synoptic tradition (and 1 Corinthians) elements of the Passover meal are given new meaning. Before the main course, Jesus declares over the unleavened bread, "This is my body" (Matthew 26:26). After the main course, in similar fashion he announces over the third cup of blessing (1 Corinthians 10:16), "This is my blood of the covenant" (Matthew 26:28; Mark 14:24) or "the new covenant in my blood" (Luke 22:20; 1 Corinthians 11:25). The festivities take on a dark tone when Jesus warns that one would betray him (Matthew 26:21–25; Mark 14:18–21; Luke 22:21–23; John 13:21–30).

Olive grove at Gethsemane

Following the meal, Jesus takes his followers out of the city, across the Kidron, to the Mount of Olives to a place called Gethsemane ("oil press"). It was likely a cave used for pressing olives. At least one such cave is known from the Second Temple period. Although John calls it a "garden" (John 18:1), the name Garden of Gethsemane does not occur in the New Testament. There Jesus withdraws with Peter, James, and John, and then goes further alone to pray. The Synoptic Gospels stress his torment: "Abba, Father, all things are possible for you. Remove this cup from me. Yet not what I will, but what you will" (Mark 14:36). The Fourth Gospel does not record this prayer, but offers an earlier one: "Now is my soul troubled. And what shall I say? 'Father, save me from this hour'? But for this purpose I have come to this hour. Father, glorify your name" (John 12:27–28). A similar contrast occurs in the narratives when Judas arrives with armed men from the religious authorities to arrest Jesus. In Mark, the scene is violent (Mark 14:43–49). But in John, Jesus has to go out and identify himself twice to his befuddled captors (John 18:4–9). While some might see irreconcilable variation among the accounts, taken together these gospel stories draw us into the mystery of the sacrifice of Jesus, who is at the same time fully human and fully divine. In Mark, the human is central; in John, the divine.

When Jesus is arrested, the disciples forsake him and flee. Their failure was anticipated at the meal in the notice that one would betray him. The inability of disciples to watch and pray with Jesus (Matthew 26:40) is a second indicator. Although Peter struck out with a sword (John 18:10), Jesus stopped him (Matthew 26:52). The scattering of the disciples is highlighted in Mark by a young man in the group dressed in a linen cloth. When seized, he leaves behind the linen cloth and runs away naked (Mark 14:52). He is a symbol of the shame of the forsaking. In Mark, the disciples never appear again as a group.

A religious trial of sorts takes place back in the upper city at the home of Caiaphas. After a brief appearance before Annas, the father-in-law of Caiaphas (John 18:13), Jesus is brought before the **Sanhedrin**, consisting of chief priests, elders, and scribes (Mark 14:53–55). Modern conceptions of jurisprudence and even the idealized portrayals of the Sanhedrin in the Mishnah ought to be set aside at this point. During Roman occupation, the Sanhedrin was hardly a regularly-meeting supreme court. In evidence from the first century (Josephus and the New Testament), the assembly is mentioned only in capital cases when the outcome is predetermined. Pilate was a bloody man, given to wanton executions (Philo, *Exposition of the Laws of Moses* 38.302) and eventually recalled for executing a group of Samaritans (Josephus, *Antiquities* 18.4.1–2). He would tolerate no challenge from a restive population, which may help explain Caiaphas' advice that "one man should die for the people" (John 18:14). Jesus was both a religious and political threat. In the chaos of the occupation, Caiaphas assembled others to support his predetermined plan.

During the assembly, testimony is sought against Jesus. Matthew and Mark label it as "false testimony" (Matthew 26:60; Mark 16:55). Some charged Jesus as threatening the temple, an offense on the basis of which Jesus could be handed over to Pilate. Since the time of Augustus, ancient shrines had come under imperial protection. The second temple had been expanded and rebuilt into the grandest shrine in the Roman world by Herod the Great, who had orchestrated a close relationship with Augustus. But agreement on the charge could not be found. Caiaphas then put Jesus under oath, demanding a clear answer, "Are you the Christ, the Son of the Blessed?" (Mark 14:61) Although a variety of answers are reported ("You have said so" [Matthew 26:64]; "I am" [Mark 14:62]; "If I tell you, you will not believe" [Luke 22:67]), those present understood the words of Jesus affirmatively and condemned him to death for blasphemy. In tragic parallel, Jesus' closest follower Peter denied three times and with an oath that he ever knew Jesus.

Early the next morning, the religious authorities take Jesus to the Roman prefect Pontius Pilate. Religious charges have been replaced by political ones that Pilate takes to be a royal claim on Jesus' part. "Are you the king of the Jews?" (Matthew 27:11; Mark 15:2; Luke 23:3; John 18:33). The New Testament writers paint the trial and Pilate in a rather positive light. It is understandable that they do so, for early Christianity had to negotiate its place in the Roman world from a position of weakness. So in Luke, Pilate three times declares Jesus innocent and even sends him to Herod Antipas. Matthew and Mark have Pilate playing Jesus off against a man ironically named Barabbas ("son of the Father"). And all three Synoptic Gospels show Pilate wavering before the crowd (Matthew 27:22–23; Mark 15:12–15; Luke 23:20–22). Nevertheless, it is Pilate who gives the order for crucifixion (Matthew 27:26; Mark 15:15; Luke 23:25; John 19:16). The charge is insurrection (Matthew 27:37; Mark 15:26; Luke 23:38; John 19:19). Pilate would be ever remembered for this deed in the creedal statements of the church; but it is doubtful if Pilate remembered Jesus a week later. Execution was Pilate's way of dealing with troublemakers.

As early Christians were solicitous to Roman authority in their writings, they also increasingly distinguished their identity from Judaism, especially the Judaism of Jerusalem that would eventually revolt against Rome. Thus, the religious authorities are particularly vicious in their plotting and words, and even the crowds of Jerusalem call for the death of Jesus. Most notorious is the quote: "His blood be on us and on our children!" (Matthew 27:25) Subsequent generations of Christians have used these words as an excuse to condemn all Jews as Christ-killers, the most notorious example of which is the Holocaust. No early Christian would so understand these words! The Jerusalem elites were blamed (Acts 2:23), especially in the early decades when Christians did not fully appreciate the significance of the cross (Paul would provide the important corrective). But Jews as a race were never so blamed. Anti-Semitism is not Christian teaching but a perspective read into the texts much later with tragic consequences.

Crucifixion is called by Josephus "the most wretched of deaths" (Josephus, *War* 7.203). In the Roman period crucifixion was practiced widely, most famously the crucifixion of some six thousand followers of Spartacus after the slave revolt in 71 B.C. Normally crucifixion was reserved for criminals and people of the slave class. Stoning was the Jewish method of capital punishment, although Alexander Janneus did have eight hundred Pharisees crucified in 267 B.C.

In 1968, a Jewish ossuary inscribed with the name Jehohanan was discovered north of Jerusalem. It contained the remains of a man in his twenties who had been crucified. His right heel bone had been penetrated by a 4.5 inch nail. Remains of wood between the head of the nail and the heel bone suggest that the nail was driven through a piece of wood to make it difficult for the victim to free his leg. As there was no trauma to the arms, he had probably been tied to the cross.

The relative paucity of archaeological evidence for crucifixion may suggest that most victims were tied to the cross, although Josephus notes that the Roman soldiers used "nailing" to affix survivors of the fall of Jerusalem to crosses (Josephus, *War* 5.11). Death by crucifixion was gruesome. Depending on how the victim was affixed to the cross, death could come quickly or take days. Asphyxiation, suffocation, hypovolemic shock, and blood loss could all be factors. Crucifixion was a public event meant as a deterrent, so crowded locations were chosen and sadistic practice was common. Proper burial rarely followed crucifixion. Victims were simply cut down and thrown in a dump or left on the cross to be devoured by animals and birds.

The crucifixion and death of Jesus took just a few hours and so was relatively brief. Jesus had been scourged beforehand (Matthew 27:26; Mark 15:15), a brutal beating that would quickly remove the skin and could leave one near death. The Roman scourge, also called a *flagellum*, was a short whip made of two or three leather thongs connected to a handle. The leather thongs were knotted with several small pieces of metal, usually zinc and iron, attached at various intervals. As Jesus could not carry his own cross, Simon of Cyrene was compelled to do so.

The place of crucifixion is identified as **Golgotha**, the place of the skull (Matthew 27:33; Mark 15:22; Luke 23:33; John 19:17). Although General Charles Gordon in 1884 noticed a rock outcropping near the Damascus gate that looked to him like it could be the "place of the skull," the ancient rock quarry over which the Basilica of the Holy Sepulchre has been built is a more probable location. The site was outside the wall of the city prior to the expansion of Jerusalem in the time of Herod Agrippa I (A.D. 40–44). Excavations in the area have shown no occupation prior to the re-founding of Jerusalem as Aelia Capitolina in A.D. 135.

Christian commemorations of Good Friday tend to combine the four gospel accounts of the crucifixion. Tre Ore services and collections of the "seven last words of Christ" tend to deprive the individual gospels of their unique perspective on the crucifixion. Matthew and Mark stress the violence of the event and the abandonment Jesus experienced. After refusing a mixture of wine and gall/myrrh, Jesus is crucified under a sign naming the charge, and his executioners cast lots for his clothing (Matthew 27:33–37; Mark 15:22–26). In a subsequent scene, two robbers are crucified with Jesus while passersby and religious authorities mock him (Matthew 27:38–43; Mark 15:27–32). After a period of darkness, Jesus cries out, "My God, my God, why have you forsaken me?" (Mark 15:34). With a subsequent anguished cry, he dies, his death attended by ominous symbolic signs (Matthew 27:50–53; Mark 15:37–38).

Luke's account lacks the darkness and dereliction. The death is no less horrid, but Jesus forgives those who do not know what they are doing (Luke 23:34, omitted in some ancient manuscripts), welcomes to Paradise a thief who pleads for remembrance (Luke 23:43), and at the point of death commends his spirit into the hands of his Father (Luke 23:46). John portrays the death of Jesus as part of his glorification. Jesus seems in control to the end and conveys no sense of abandonment. Jesus commends his mother to the beloved disciple (John 19:25–27), and in the end asserts, "It is finished" (John 19:30).

As at Gethsemane, so at Golgotha, we encounter a mystery. Jesus, fully God and fully human, dies for us and for the world. We lose some of the mystery when we deprive the depictions of some of their tension by creating a single harmonized version. Jesus was abandoned—a darkness we cannot begin to grasp. Jesus forgave executioners and even a condemned criminal—a mercy that sustains us at the point when we must commend ourselves into the hands of the Father. Jesus willingly and purposefully went to the cross to glorify the Father, accomplishing all for all. Only as separate narratives can the sacred words speak most effectively.

In subsequent Christian reflection an almost morbid fascination with the crucifixion developed. Christian art, especially of the medieval period, stresses the agony and suffering. In recent times, that emphasis has been fostered by Mel Gibson's *The Passion of the Christ* in which Jesus is tormented in excruciating detail (and slow motion!). We should recall that Jesus' time on the cross was relatively brief. Many others suffered far worse and for a more extended period. As is implied by the selection of stories we call gospels, the point is not how much Jesus suffered, but who suffered and to what end. "When the centurion and those who were with him, keeping watch over Jesus, saw the earthquake and what took place, they were filled with awe and said, 'Truly this was the Son of God!'" (Matthew 27:54)

Ossuaries and Loculi

Joseph of Arimathea arranged a hasty burial for Jesus in "a tomb cut in stone, where no one had ever yet been laid" (Luke 23:53). Roman execution did not preclude proper Jewish burial. During the late Second Temple period, wealthy Jews of the Jerusalem area developed a method of burial reflecting strong Hellenistic influence. These tombs had a porch in front of the entrance and a burial chamber with benches for the newly deceased. The tombs were not for individuals but for families; so after an additional death the bones of the previously deceased would be placed into loculi cut into the walls. The Hebrew word for these loculi is *kokhim*, and such tombs are sometimes called by that name. Later some kind of column or pyramid would be built over the tomb. As Joseph's tomb was new, porch, loculi, and column were probably not present. The entrance of the tomb would have been blocked by a large stone fashioned as a plug. The use of such a plug fits well the description: "an angel of the Lord descended from heaven and came and rolled back the stone and sat on it" (Matthew 28:2). The oft-pictured round stone disk in a channel (rolling stone tomb) was only used by the wealthiest families. Of some seven hundred Second Temple-era tombs that have been discovered, only four have rolling stone closures.

The resurrection of Jesus is the pivotal narrative of Christianity. Paul would later write: "If Christ has not been raised, then our preaching is in vain and your faith is in vain" (1 Corinthians 15:14). Therefore, all four gospels end with resurrection accounts and appearances. The resurrected Jesus meets with his disciples in the opening scenes of Acts. When Paul discusses the resurrection, he includes a list of appearances (1 Corinthians 15:3–9). The central proclamation of the first Christians was the resurrection: "God raised him up, loosing the pangs of death, because it was not possible for him to be held by it" (Acts 2:24).

When turning to the stories themselves, the modern reader may be put off by the seeming inconsistencies. In Matthew, "an angel of the Lord" rolls back the stone and sits on it (Matthew 28:2). In Mark, the women meet a "young man" dressed in white sitting inside the tomb on the right side (Mark 16:5). In Luke, there are "two men" standing next to the women in the tomb (Luke 24:4). In John, Mary sees "two angels" sitting where the body of Jesus had lain, but she does not seem to recognize them as such (John 20:12). Were the early Christians making up a story after stealing the body (Matthew 28:13), they certainly couldn't keep their story straight! A number of details are simply uncertain in the resurrection narratives. Some of this variance may be due to points being made by the gospel writers. Mark, for instance, may use the description "young man" to draw a contrast with the "young man" who epitomized the desertion of the disciples at Gethsemane (Mark 14:51–52). The heavenly "young man" is the first to bear witness, even as the "young man" with the disciples was the last to flee. The stories in John about Thomas are selected to demonstrate the necessary move from doubt to faith (compare also the footrace of Peter and the beloved disciple and the tender story of Jesus and Mary.).

But more is involved here than the varying approaches of the gospel writers. As we noted with events at Gethsemane and at the cross, the resurrection is also a mystery. It cannot be proven; it can only be accepted by faith. The resurrection of Jesus is something beyond our rational and modernistic understandings. Human language fails before such mysteries. Could that failure explain some of the uncertainties? Nevertheless, the stories are clear on the central point: the risen Jesus is not a ghost, not someone recovering from nearly fatal wounds, and not a corpse haunting his followers in some grade-B, drive-in thriller. "But in fact Christ has been raised from the dead, the firstfruits of those who have fallen asleep" (1 Corinthians 15:20). For us who are Christians, our hope rests here.

Searching for Jesus

When Mary Magdalene recognized that Jesus had risen from the dead, she called out to him, "Rabbouni" (John 20:16). From the moment of the resurrection, the key question for Christians became, "Who is Jesus?" Paul will call him "Lord" (Phil. 2:11). The gospel writers will use "Messiah/Christ," "Son of God," and "Savior." Other New Testament writers expand the list. (This textbook devotes many pages to Christology.) **Gnosticism** and Arianism will raise questions about Jesus eventually answered in the Nicene Creed, which confesses belief in "one Lord, Jesus Christ, the only Son of God, eternally begotten of the Father, God from God, Light from Light, true God from true God, begotten, not made, of one Being with the Father. Through him all things were made."

Although Christianity retained a degree of diversity in its christological assertions, the belief in Jesus as Lord and Savior and acceptance of biblical narratives continued without challenge until the seventeenth century. Then, because of the Enlightment, the rise of rationalism, and scientific ways of viewing the universe, scholars attempted to approach Jesus using historical research unfettered by dogmatic considerations or ecclesiastical control. An early example was H. S. Reimarus (1694–1768), who wanted to discover who Jesus was by entirely rational means. David Friedrich Strauss, author of *The Life of Jesus Critically Examined* (1835), denied most miracles. Albert Schweitzer in the *Quest of the Historical Jesus* (1909) gave a name to this secular movement and showed conclusively that the "Jesus" so reconstructed would have been at home in the liberal thought world of the nineteenth century. The first quest for the historical Jesus has remade Jesus in the image of these authors.

In the early part of the twentieth century Rudolf Bultmann in *The History of the Synoptic Tradition* (1921) and other influential works argued that it is impossible for scholars to come to know much about the Jesus of history. They could only uncover the Christ of faith reflected by early Christian writings.

After the trauma of the Second World War, a new quest for the historical Jesus began, under the influence of such scholars as Ernst Käsemann, Günther Bornkamm, and James M. Robinson. Its work faded until a third quest began involving such figures as Robert Funk, Marcus Borg, John Dominic Crossan, Burton Mack, and the members of the Jesus Seminar. They took their work into the public, meeting and voting with colored marbles on that which could be proven historically. In their *The Five Gospels* (1993; including the Gospel of Thomas) they offer an answer to the question: What did Jesus really say? By way of example, their historical reason and research leave a Lord's Prayer in which only the words "Our Father" can be authentically traced to Jesus. Another group of contemporary scholars has taken a less radical approach. Martin Hengel, John Meier, E. P. Sanders, Ben Witherington, and N. T. Wright stress the Jewishness of Jesus. They consider him an apocalyptic prophet who announced the coming of the Kingdom of God. They all stress the importance of the death of Jesus by asking: What was it about Jesus that caused him to be crucified?

Distinct to all these methods is the modernist attempt to view Jesus without the so-called encumbrances of theology or creed. But such an approach will necessarily come up short. Martin Luther wrote in an explanation to the Third Article of the Apostles' Creed: "I cannot by my own reason or strength believe in Jesus Christ my Lord or come to him." A strictly historical approach cannot produce the faith of Thomas who confessed of the risen Jesus, "My Lord and my God!" (John 20:28) Continuing Luther's words: "But the Holy Spirit calls me by the Gospel." Through the Gospel, we Christians are called to faith in Jesus. This faith leads us to trust in the words of Scripture that convey the Gospel. In these words, "God speaks to us though his son" (Hebrews 1:1). The study of history indeed illumines our examination of the story of the New Testament. But the study of history alone cannot lead us to Jesus. That is a matter for faith alone, and through faith we "see Jesus" (Hebrews 2:9).

The First Century

When piecing together the story of Jesus, we have the luxury and challenge of four gospels. For the story of the first Christian century, we have much less. Besides the Acts of the Apostles, the only other sources are inferences from other New Testament writings and hints from later non-biblical works. The task is limited and more challenging. We are limited because we have only one narrative—Acts. It starts with a tiny community in Jerusalem that is scattered by persecution, and the work then follows the travels of one missionary—Paul. As a result, we have but one narrow slice of earliest Christianity. Acts is silent on everything else. Our source is limited. But when we turn to other New Testament writings such as the letters of Paul, Hebrews, or Revelation, we discover though passing references that much was going on elsewhere. For example, Peter writes a letter to the "elect exiles of the dispersion in Pontus, Galatia, Cappadocia, Asia, and Bithynia" (1 Peter 1:1). We know of Paul's work in Asia and Galatia, but nothing of work in Pontus, Cappadocia, or Bithynia much less of work there by Peter. So we have a challenge as we assess the first Christian century.

Here we will first follow the storyline from Acts. (For a discussion of the themes and theology of Acts, turn to chapter five in this book.) Then we will point out other untold stories at which our materials hint before summarizing the status of Christianity at the start of the second century.

In Jerusalem

After the ascension of Jesus, the disciples were to wait in Jerusalem (Acts 1:4). The community was small, including the eleven, Matthias who replaced Judas, certain women, and Mary the mother of Jesus (Acts 1:14). The outpouring of the Holy Spirit marked a transitional point for the community. Three thousand were added to their number (Acts 2:41), but most of these likely were pilgrims who returned home after the festival (Acts 2:9–11). The focus of Acts stays on the Jerusalem community. The community is presented in idealistic terms. In their community gatherings are the origins of later Christian worship practice (Acts 2:42). Wonders and signs attend the apostolic work. Belongings are held in common (Acts 2:42–43), perhaps out of expectation of an imminent return of Jesus, even as those who joined the Essene community divested themselves of their possessions in preparation for the final conflict. At the same time, the Jesus movement in Jerusalem kept its connection to the temple and likely understood itself strictly within the confines of Judaism, not as a separate religion.

Idyllic times did not last, as tension arose with the religious authorities and even within the community. A healing in the temple and subsequent preaching about Jesus led to arrest by temple authorities and attempts to silence the new sect (Acts 4). Within the community, use of resources and cultural distinctions were a point of tension, as shown by the story of Ananias and Sapphira and complaints about the distribution for widows, especially among the Greek-speaking members of the community. Acts portrays the community as responding faithfully to outside threats (Acts 4:12, 20) and developing new leaders to help deal with internal tensions (Acts 6:1–6). With one of several summary statements, Acts states, "And the word of God continued to increase, and the number of the disciples multiplied greatly in Jerusalem, and a great many of the priests became obedient to the faith" (Acts 6:7).

The martyrdom of Stephen marks a major transition in the early Christian community and brings to a close the focus of Acts on the community in Jerusalem. The lynching of Stephen leads to a severe persecution that scattered the Jerusalem community. The story also introduces a character named Saul, who would become the prominent Paul in the last half of Acts. With the scattering from Jerusalem, earliest Christianity begins to spread out geographically and culturally.

Crossing Cultural Boundaries

Once the story leaves Jerusalem, it is no longer possible to narrate comprehensively the tale of early Christianity. Trajectories must be followed. Significantly, Acts takes up the crossing of cultural boundaries first. These boundaries are crossed within the Roman province of Judea.

There are three blocks of stories. The first block has as its protagonist a man named Philip, but more importantly the stories are concerned with those on the margins of Judaism. This Philip was not of the Twelve, but was one of the seven set aside to help with the distribution for the widows (Acts 6:5). He enters Samaria and proclaims Jesus as the Messiah. His work is confirmed by Peter and John and by an outpouring of the Holy Spirit similar to Pentecost (Acts 8:14–15). Samaritans, with their own Torah and temple, shared many common traditions with Jews. Yet the rift between the groups was significant. Bringing the "word of God" to Samaria (Acts 8:14) crossed a important cultural boundary.

The second story in this block involves an Ethiopian eunuch. He also would have been on the margins of Judaism, for his physical mutilation would keep him at a distance in temple and synagogue (Leviticus 21:17–23). That he came to Jerusalem "to worship" (Acts 8:27) and was bringing home an Isaiah scroll, likely to replace a worn one in his synagogue, says much of this person. The Ethiopian also hears the good news and is baptized. Another cultural taboo falls before the embrace of the Christian Gospel.

The second story block follows another trajectory. The Saul who has been involved in the lynching of Stephen is on his way to Damascus to arrest followers of the Way. "The Way" was an early designation for Christians. These followers were likely from Jerusalem and so were to be extradited by Saul. But on his way, a light from heaven strikes him blind, and he is addressed by Jesus (Acts 9:3–4). Then in Damascus his sight is restored, he is baptized, and he begins to proclaim Jesus as the Son of God (Acts 9:10–20). Often called a conversion, Saul's experience is more like a prophetic call (Acts 9:15–16; Jeremiah 1:5). In the story told by Acts, the event on the road to Damascus begins a story line that will become central in the last half of the work.

The third story block shatters the great cultural boundary between Jews and **Gentiles**, what Paul would call "the dividing wall of hostility" (Eph 2:14). Jewish identity as the chosen people of God led to a classification for the rest of humanity as Gentiles. The designation was more than ethnic or political; "Gentile" could be used in a negative way for those who do not properly worship God, even in a Christian Gospel (Matthew 18:17)! As Christianity came out of Judaism, this bias against Gentiles had to be overcome. It would not be easy.

The difficulty is illustrated by Peter's threefold dream: "What God has made clean, do not call common" (Acts 10:15). Peter then responds to an invitation (at the prompting of the Holy Spirit) and ventures to Caesarea with witnesses in tow (Acts 10:19, 23). There he meets Cornelius, a God-fearing centurion. Cornelius is a double challenge for Peter. He is a Gentile, and he is a representative of the occupying Roman power. But Peter has been led across cultural boundaries: "Truly I understand that God shows no partiality, but in every nation anyone who fears him and does what is right is acceptable to him" (Acts 10:34–35). To confirm the boundary crossing, there is another outpouring of the Holy Spirit as at Pentecost and as among the Samaritans (Acts 10:44). The household of Cornelius is baptized. So important is this boundary crossing that Peter must explain his actions step by step in Jerusalem. Acts summarizes the response: "When they heard these things they fell silent. And they glorified God, saying, 'Then to the Gentiles also God has granted repentance that leads to life'" (Acts 11:18). The Christian community would continue to struggle with this boundary, but in the telling of Acts, there is no going back. The word of God is for those on the margins, for the persecutor, and even for the Gentile. Jesus is savior of all (see chapter five).

The Gentile Mission of Paul

The trajectory of the story in Acts now narrows to accounts of work done in or launched to the west from Antioch of Syria. As we follow this story line, we ought to remember that the initial scattering from Jerusalem would have put Christians in other locales as well. By the second century there are Christian communities in eastern Syria, in Egypt, in North Africa, and certainly in other places. Their earliest stories are untold. As important as the rest of Acts may be, it is only one of many stories.

Antioch was the third largest city in the Roman Empire. As the capital of the eastern-most province that was governed by a legate, Antioch was the gateway to the orient and a terminus for the Silk Road. Antioch had been made a free city by Pompey in 64 B.C. and was religious center, with groves for Daphne and a sanctuary to Apollo. Some Christians scattered from Jerusalem ended up at Antioch. "There were some of them, men of Cyprus and Cyrene, who on coming to Antioch spoke to the Hellenists also, preaching the Lord Jesus" (Acts 11:20). Peter has witnessed the first Gentile conversion; but the conversion of Cornelius was more an act of God to which God brought Peter as a witness. Peter had not sought out Cornelius. In Antioch, the situation was different. So began the mission to the Gentiles.

The church at Antioch, likely comprising several house churches, was the mother of all Gentile churches. At Antioch the controversy over the status of Gentile Christians boiled over. The mission journeys narrated in Acts all had their starting point at Antioch. Barnabas was sent by the church in Jerusalem to Antioch. He found the work there so fruitful, that he went to Tarsus and recruited the convert Saul to help with the work. For a year the work progressed to the point that locals began to identify (or chide) them as "partisans of the Christ," in Latin "Christians" (Acts 11:19–26). So active was the community that they sent famine relief to the church in Jerusalem. Later evidence would note the popularity of the Gospel of Matthew in and around Antioch.

The church(es) in Jerusalem must have been hard pressed during the early forties. Not only did they need support during the famine, but Herod Agrippa I, who exercised royal rule in Judea on behalf of Rome, had both James (the brother of John) and Peter arrested at Passover time. James was executed, the first of the apostles to meet that fate; but Peter was miraculously released and escaped from the area (Acts 12).

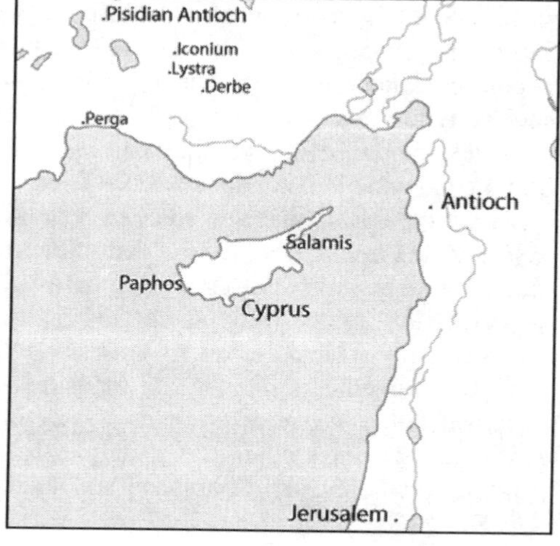

Back in Antioch, through promptings that Acts attributed to the Holy Spirit (Acts 13:2), Barnabas and Saul set out on what is popularly called the first mission journey. They took along John Mark, a relative of Barnabas. Their first work was on the island of Cyprus, starting in the east at Salamis and working through to the west at Paphos. Their method, which would become the norm for later, was to enter the local synagogues first. Synagogues gave an opportunity for proclamation, as it was customary to invite visitors to share their insights into the readings. Also, synagogues in the **Diaspora** attracted **proselytes** and **God-fearers.** God-fearers were Gentiles attracted by the morality and monotheism of Judaism, but who were unwilling to become fully Jews. Proselytes were Gentiles who underwent rituals to convert to Judaism. Both groups would have given entrée for Christian evangelists into Gentile communities.

Toward the end of their work on Cyprus, a Jewish magician named Elymas Bar Jesus (son of Joshua) tried to hamper contacts with a proconsul named Sergius Paulus. Saul, identified at this point also by the name Paul, struck him with blindness (Acts 13:6–11) even as Saul himself had been stopped from persecuting the Way by being struck blind. The missionaries, now called "Paul and his companions" (Acts 13:13) leave Cyprus for Perga in Pamphylia; but John Mark returns to Jerusalem.

Paul, formerly know as Saul, from this point on in Acts, leads the Gentile mission. The group travels to Antioch of Pisidia in the southern part of the Roman province of Galatia (Acts sometimes uses regional names rather than provincial names). The pattern of work in the synagogue followed by work among the Gentiles is repeated (Acts 13:14, 46). Travels next take Paul and Barnabas to Iconium, Lystra, and Derbe where signs and wonders attend their work. The group then backtracks to Perga before returning to Antioch of Syria. There is evidence of institutional forms beginning to emerge as "elders" are appointed for each church (Acts 14:23). The first mission journey confirms for the Antioch communities that God "had opened a door of faith to the Gentiles" (Acts 14:27).

Not everyone in the larger Christian community was so convinced. Paul's letter to the Galatians, written after this first journey, complains of those proclaiming a "different gospel" that required Torah observance of Gentiles (Galatians 2:16). At Antioch of Syria the same issue boiled over when "some men came down from Judea and were teaching the brothers, 'unless you are circumcised according to the custom of Moses, you cannot be saved'" (Acts 15:1). Galatians provides extra detail about the controversy. Those from Jerusalem represented James, the brother of Jesus, who was now the leader of the Jerusalem communities. And Peter, who had come to Antioch, withdrew from the Gentiles because of their influence. Paul "opposed him to his face, because he stood condemned" (Galatians 2:11).

"Paul and Barnabas and some of the others were appointed to go up to Jerusalem to the apostles and the elders about this question" (Acts 15:2). By the time they arrived at Jerusalem the controversy had grown beyond the ritual of **circumcision**. Some were now arguing: "It is necessary to circumcise them and to order them to keep the law of Moses" (Acts 15:5).

Acts describes a meeting of "apostles and the elders" (Acts 15:6). Peter, who had failed at Antioch, makes a forceful case based on his experience with Cornelius and cites again the principle that God makes "no distinction" (Acts 15:9; compare 10:34). "Barnabas and Paul" (note the change of order in the names when at Jerusalem) recount signs and wonders done among the Gentiles (Acts 15:12). James then quotes a combination of passages from Amos, Jeremiah, and, Isaiah announcing, "Therefore my judgment is that we should not trouble those of the Gentiles who turn to God, but should write to them to abstain from the things polluted by idols, and from sexual immorality, and from what has been strangled, and from blood" (Acts 15:19–20). His position offers something to both sides. It does not require circumcision or full Torah observance from the Gentiles, but it also observes the Torah by requiring of the Gentiles what Leviticus 17–18 requires of the alien living in the midst of Israel. Both sides could claim a victory of sorts. The decision James said he made was sent by way of letter with the opening words, "For it has seemed good to the Holy Spirit and to us to lay on you no greater burden than these requirements …" (Acts 15:28). Differing views of the authority behind the decision suggest that the issue is far from settled. Indeed, the issue continues to resurface is the writings of Paul and in Acts (Acts 21:18–22).

The focus of the story in Acts narrows again at the start of the second mission journey. There is a falling out between Paul and Barnabas over the continued participation of John Mark (Acts 15:37–39). Barnabas and John Mark return to Cyprus. Paul and Silas headed into Syria and Cilesia. We hear nothing more about Barnabas and John Mark. Theirs is one of many untold stories.

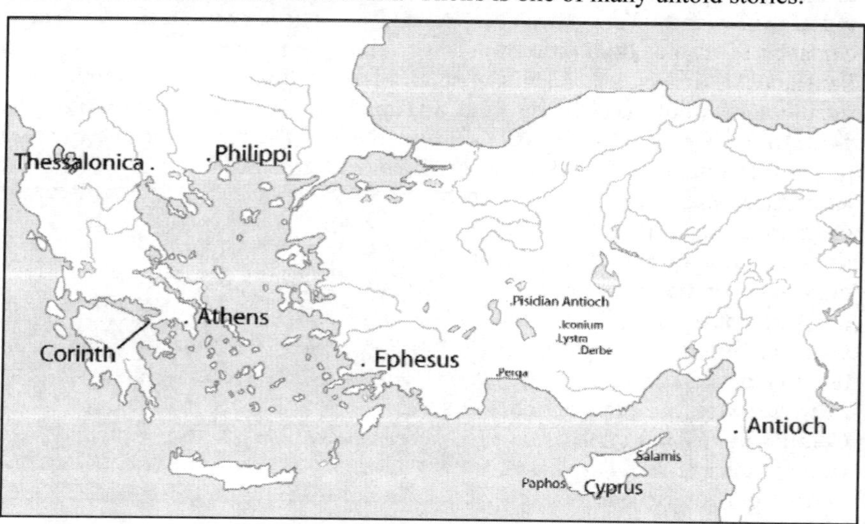

While Paul revisits the churches of southern Galatia, Timothy from Lystra joins the group. Timothy will become Paul's protégé. But their mission efforts start slowly. Attempts to go into the Roman province of Asia (western Turkey) and Bithynia (northern Turkey) are hindered by "the spirit of Jesus" (Acts 16:7). When the group finally arrives at Troas (ancient Troy), Paul has a vision: "a man of Macedonia was standing there, urging him and saying, 'Come over to Macedonia and help us'" (Acts 16:9). Apparently the author of Acts has joined the group at this time (or the author is using a first-person source) as "we" crossed over. Paul's group sets foot on European soil for the first time!

When the group landed at Neapolis and traveled toward Philippi, they followed the ***Via Egnatia***. The proconsul of Macedonia, Gnaeus Egnatius ordered its construction around 146 B.C. The road stretched across Illyria, Macedonia, and Thrace, running across modern Albania, the Republic of Macedonia, Greece, and Turkey. The route was of strategic importance both for trade and for the movement of military forces. Paul's group would found house churches in major communities along the route.

Their first stop was the Roman **colony** of Philippi where a woman named Lydia, a dealer in purple cloth and a God-fearer, welcomed them into her home. She was baptized and became the patron of the fledgling Christian community. Local difficulties over the exorcism of a slave girl caused the party to move on. The first-person discourse fades at this point, causing some to speculate that Luke may have stayed at Philippi. Paul would revisit the community at the end of his third journey. The community would be supportive of Paul during a time of imprisonment, sending support by Epaphroditus (Philippians 4:18).

Further west on the *Via Egnatia* was Thessalonica, the capital of Macedonia. As the city had a synagogue, Paul reverted to his practice of starting among the Jews. "Some of them were persuaded and joined Paul and Silas, as did a great many of the devout Greeks and not a few of the leading women" (Acts 17:4). Opposition arose from some said to be jealous of their success, so Paul and Silas departed, leaving Timothy behind (presumably). In the next months Paul would get reports from Silas and Timothy and would write back twice to the Thessalonians (1 & 2 Thessalonians). The pattern at Thessalonica repeated itself at Beroea, so Paul went on alone to Athens.

Parthenon at Athens

Athens had been the center of Greek culture in the fifth century B.C. Its power waned with the rise of Philip and Alexander in Macedonia, and it always seems to be to the losing side in the Roman civil wars. Politically, Athens was eclipsed by Corinth, the capital of the province of Achaia. But Rome continued to treat Athens deferentially as a center of culture. Many Roman youth were sent to study in the philosophical schools of the city.

Although Paul did engage with Jews and devout people in the synagogue at Athens, he also is portrayed by Acts as engaging in philosophic debate with Stoics and Epicureans (Acts 17:18). Paul appears as a putative Christian philosopher, uncharacteristically quoting Epimenides and Aratus before the assembly at the Areopagus, rather than the **Septuagint**. But mention of the resurrection of Jesus from the dead led to scoffing (Acts 17:32), as it conflicted with Greek dualism. Paul's minimal success at Athens is confirmed, as Athens receives no further mention in Christian materials from the first century. Just over a century later, Tertullian would exclaim, "What has Athens to do with Jerusalem? or the Academy with the Church?" (*De praescriptione*, 7)

Paul had only limited time at each major stop on his second journey. Wherever he went, trouble seemed to follow, although Acts makes the point that others caused the problems. With Paul's arrival at Corinth, he began work which would keep him in the city for a year and a half (Acts 18:11).

Corinth was the capital of the Roman province of Achaia. Previously it had been part of the Achaean League, but it was destroyed after the victory of Lucius Mummius over the League in 146 B.C. Julius Caesar formed a colony of veterans on the site in 44 B.C. It grew quickly into a major city in the province.

Corinth is situated on the isthmus between Greece proper to the north and the Peloponnese to the south. Seven miles to the east was the port of Cenchreae on the Aegean and to the west was the port of Lechaion on the Adriatic. Periander had built a *diolkos*, a paved slipway that allowed smaller ships to be the dragged across the isthmus. Even off-loading larger ships and reloading the cargo onto other vessels on the other side was safer than sailing south around the Peloponnese. As a result, Corinth was a major trade center with all the vices typical of such a crossroads.

Modern canal at Corinth

On arrival, Paul met up with "a Jew named Aquila, a native of Pontus, recently come from Italy with his wife Priscilla, because Claudius had commanded all the Jews to leave Rome" (Acts 18:2). There is a tantalizing section by the Roman historian Suetonius (born c. A.D. 69) mentioning the expulsion: "Since the Jews constantly made disturbance at the instigation of Chrestus, he expelled them from Rome" (*Life of Claudius* 25.4). Perhaps "Chrestus" refers to Christ, for the Christian theologian Tertullian (c. A.D. 160–c. 225) wrote that Romans sometimes mispronounced "Christianus" as "Chrestianus" (*Apology* 3.5). If Chrestus refers to Christ, then there might have been a large enough Christian community in Rome in A.D. 49 to create awkwardness in the Jewish community. Acts seems to suggest that Aquila and Priscilla, having been expelled from Rome, were already Christians. On the other hand, Suetonius identified by name the "Christians" in his *Life of Nero* (2.16). If he got the name right in that work, why would he use "Chrestus" in the *Life of Claudius*? The evidence is inconclusive. At most, we can say this text from Suetonius *may* be the first non-biblical reference to Jesus.

At Corinth Paul returned to his typical tactic of beginning in the synagogue. When opposition arose, he said "From now on I will go to the Gentiles" (Acts 18:6). Paul then set up a house church in the home of Titius Justus, a God-fearer. Setting up shop next door might sound to us like an aggressive move, but it was typical in ancient cities for a wide variety of religious buildings to co-exist in the same neighborhood, even next door to each other. After a vision, Paul commits himself to long-term work at Corinth (Acts 18:9–11).

Little else is mentioned of Paul's work at Corinth in Acts. But Paul's Corinthian correspondence suggests that the relationship between Paul and the Corinthians house churches was prone to strife. Paul wrote at least four times and visited the community at least two more times. At issue were moral and inter-personal problems to be expected as people moved from the polytheistic and brutal Roman world into a monotheistic and moral community where all are brothers and sisters in Christ.

Acts concludes its story of the Corinthian mission with Paul's appearance before the proconsul Gallio, brother of the famous Roman philosopher Seneca. To a charge of "persuading people to worship God contrary to [Roman] law" (Acts 18:13), Gallio responds: "If it were a matter of wrongdoing or vicious crime, O Jews, I would have reason to accept your complaint. But since it is a matter of questions about words and names and your own law, see to it your-selves. I refuse to be a judge of these things" (Acts 18:14–15). From the per-spective of Acts, the account is another example of a Roman official turning aside (trumped-up) charges against fledgling Christianity.

The story has importance for a second reason. From an inscription at the Temple of Apollo in Delphi, we can do a rough computation of the years during which Gallio was proconsul of Achaea. The inscription refers to the twenty-sixth acclamation of Claudius, which took place between January and August of A.D. 52. If Gallio served two years as proconsul, he assumed office no earlier than the spring of A.D. 50. As Paul arrived at Corinth after the expulsion of Jews from Rome in A.D. 49 and as he "stayed many days longer" after his case was rejected by Gallio (Acts 18:18), A.D. 50 or 51 seem the best dates for Paul's trial. The dating given by the Gallio inscription enables us to make reasonable guesses about the rest of New Testament chronology.

The second mission journey ends when Paul, Priscilla, and Aquila leave for Ephesus, where the couple stays while Paul travels on to Jerusalem and then back to Antioch of Syria (Acts 18:18–22).

Acts narrates a third journey, which is less a trip and more a mission to Ephesus, the capital of the Roman province of Asia. As Paul revisits the Gala-tian churches (Acts 18:23), the story opens at Ephesus by telling of a Jew from Alexandria in Egypt. He had been "instructed in the way of the Lord, … and taught accurately the things concerning Jesus, though he knew only the baptism of John" (Acts 18:25). Apollos is an example of some of the diversity that char-acterized earliest Christianity. We modern Christians look back after two thousand years and sometimes assume that the earliest followers converted completely to Christianity and had a fully integrated theology from the beginning. In fact, conversion was a process that took significant time, even as Christian expressions of the faith developed in their understanding over time. Jesus had so indicated when he promised to send the Spirit who "will guide you into all the truth" (John 16:13). Guiding involves a process over time. We see that process in the stories of early Christianity.

For example, Christianity started in Jerusalem as a sect of Judaism and only after some time came to recognize that God shows no partiality, that God's grace is for all. Then Christians had to figure out that Gentiles did not have to become Jews as part of becoming Christian. Or think about the crucifixion of Jesus. Peter preached that it was an evil done to Jesus. Not until the preaching of Paul did "Christ crucified" come to be seen as redemptive. Paul had to be called from persecutor to apostle. Apollos had only a limited understanding. "When Priscilla and Aquila heard him, they took him and explained to him the way of God more accurately" (Acts 18:26). When Paul arrived at Ephesus, there were still some who had been baptized only into the baptism of John, so Paul laid hands on them (Acts 19:1–6).

Theatre at Ephesus

Paul's work at Ephesus spanned two to three years (Acts 19:10; 20:31). But the book of Acts gives us only three glimpses of those years. We read of his initial work in the synagogue leading to a withdrawal to the lecture hall of the philosophical teacher Tyrannus (Acts 19:8–9). A second humorous story speaks of the indirect impact of Paul's work on the practice of magic (Acts 19:11–20). A third story points to the power of Paul's work, causing a decline in the local cult of Artemis (Acts 19:23–41). Hints from other New Testament works expand our view. According to the Corinthians correspondence, Paul had extensive dealings with the Corinthians from Ephesus involving at least four letters and an additional visit not narrated in Acts (2 Corinthians 2:1). In 1 Corinthians, Paul says he "fought with beasts at Ephesus" (1 Corinthians 15:32). Unless Paul is speaking metaphorically, the reference could imply a period of imprisonment while at Ephesus. Paul's letters to the Colossians and Philemon may come from this period, or at least suggest a ministry that had regional impact. Such regional impact may be the origin for churches in the area mentioned as active during the writing of Revelation (Revelation 1:4–3:22).

Of the two incidents in Acts, the first concerns some itinerant Jewish exorcists who tried to use the name of Jesus to cast out an evil spirit. As later magical writings have demonstrated, it was common to invoke the names of many deities, often one right after another, to bring about a cure. In a polytheistic magical context, a Jew calling on the "Jesus whom Paul preaches" (Acts 19:13) would not be surprising. Ephesus was a noted center for the practice of magic, and "Ephesians letters" was a popular designation for magical texts. Since the story ends with the burning of magical texts worth "fifty thousand pieces of silver" (Acts 19:19), the story declares the significant impact of Christianity on the community during Paul's time at Ephesus. The second story has a similar function. One of the seven wonders of the ancient world was the temple of Artemis at Ephesus. Apparently Paul's work at Ephesus was so influential that it had an effect on the trade associated with the Artemis cult.

Following the work at Ephesus, Acts mentions a brief tour of the Macedonian house churches to encourage them and to gather an offering for the community in Jerusalem (Acts 20:2; 2 Corinthians 8–9). As Paul returns to Jerusalem, we get two glimpses into the community life of early Christianity. At Troas, the community gathers on the first day of the week to break bread (Acts 20:7). At Miletus, Paul appoints elders to keep watch over the flock (Acts 20:28).

In Acts twenty, the story shifts away from tales about early Christianity to a story about Paul. He arrives in Jerusalem where issues of Torah observance are still in play (Acts 21:21). After being arrested to quell a riot of those who thought Paul brought a Gentile into the temple, Paul is transported to Caesarea Maritima. The Roman procurator Felix holds him there for two years awaiting a bribe (Acts 24:26–27). When Felix is replaced by Festus, Paul's case comes up again. Paul exercises the right of a Roman citizen to have his case heard by the emperor (Acts 25:11). Paul is sent as a prisoner to Rome, but on the way is shipwrecked on the Island of Malta (Acts 27–28). The final section of Acts fits well with the theory that the writing of Luke/Acts served—at least its initial form—as a defense document in the Roman trial of Paul.

The close of Acts does speak indirectly of Christianity in Rome. Paul is given a hearing by local leaders of the Jews who seemed to know nothing of his case (Acts 28:17–22). Some are persuaded by his preaching; others are not. Paul also seems to have had some audience among the Gentiles (Acts 28:28). We are not told the outcome of the trial, just that "he lived there two whole years at his own expense, and welcomed all who came to him, proclaiming the kingdom of God and teaching about the Lord Jesus Christ with all boldness and without hindrance" (Acts 28:30–31).

Untold Stories

The most baffling untold story of the New Testament is the outcome of Paul's trial, but there are many other untold stories. Some are suggested by New Testament writings. In four of Paul's letters he speaks of being in prison (Ephesians, Philippians, Colossians, and Philemon), but we do not know the exact circumstances. The Pastoral Epistles hint at mission work and circumstances beyond those narrated in Acts. Was Paul released in A.D. 62 (at the end of Acts) to do additional work before being arrested and losing his life (2 Timothy 4:6–8)? When was Peter active among the congregations addressed by his letters? What is the Roman persecution implied by Revelation? And we have not even begun to tackle the wild speculation about Jude!

In addition, two major events in the first century certainly had an impact on early Christianity. They are not addressed in the New Testament, although they occur at almost the same time. The first is the fire in Rome that occurred in the summer of A.D. 64. According to the Roman historian Tacitus (c. A.D. 56–c. 117), Nero accused Christians who were subsequently victimized in the *circus maximus* (*Annals of Imperial Rome* 15.44). Later traditions would place the deaths of Peter and Paul in this persecution, and we will suggest that the writing of Mark's Gospel took place in the aftermath of Nero's horrors. But surviving stories of these times are expansive, are from a much later period, and are likely more legendary than factual. The second major event is the Jewish revolt that culminated in the destruction of Jerusalem and the temple in A.D. 70. Acts would suggest that there was a large community of Jewish Christians in Jerusalem in the early sixties. According to the Jewish historian Josephus (A.D. 37–c. 100), their leader James was executed by religious authorities in A.D. 62 (*Antiquities* 20.9. 197–203). The community must have been large enough to be considered a problem. But for the impact of the destruction of the city on the Christian community, we have no direct evidence. We must presume that the community and its records were destroyed and scattered, as suggested by a later tradition that the leaders of the Jerusalem community fled to Pella. Little else is known.

A few other glimpses are available from written sources. Tacitus mentions a woman, Pomponia Graecina, who was arraigned for "alien superstition" (*Annals of Imperial Rome* 13.32). Some think the charge was the practice of Christianity, implying it had made inroads into the imperial hierarchy (Philippians 4:22). Clement, bishop of Rome, writing around A.D. 95, says Paul "reached the limits of the west" (1 Clement 5:1–7). It is uncertain whether this reference is a fulfilling of Paul's dream to reach Spain (Romans 15:28); but the existence of the letter points to a recovering Christian community in Rome. Portions of the *Didache*, also from the late first century, allude to a community whose beliefs and practices are close to Judaism, implying recovery among those scattered by the revolt. And we must presume that Christians may have been caught up in Domitian's persecution of the Jews (Suetonius, *Life of Domitian* 12.2; Cassius Dio, *Roman History* 67.14), even if we have serious questions about Christian historian Eusebius' later tales (*Ecclesiastic History* 3.19–20).

Two points are of note as we close our review of the first Christian century. Recorded in the New Testament and a few other documents are mere glimpses of early Christianity. First, most of the story is untold, and the story we have focuses on one person (Paul) and his particular work. As important as Paul may be, he is not the whole story. Second, by the end of the first Christian century, Christianity remains a small and insignificant phenomenon. Although Acts portrays great growth (Acts 2:47; 5:15; 6:7; 9:31), of the about sixty million people in the Roman Empire only ten to forty thousand were Christians. They were too few to be noticed. How affairs would change over the next two centuries!

For Further Discussion

1. Is there a hierarchy among the stories told by the New Testament? That is, are some stories of greater importance than others? Why? Why not? What different might a hierarchy make?

2. As we have tried to show, the stories of the New Testament are set in certain times and places. We live in very different times. What challenges and/or opportunities are present when telling the stories of the New Testament today? You might discuss how several of the recent "Jesus" movies have attempted to tell the story for a contemporary audience.

3. Stories tell us what happened. How do such descriptions shape the life of Christians and churches today? How are descriptions different from instructions given by Jesus and the Biblical writers? For example, Jesus says, "Love one another." That word is an instruction we can follow. Another example is the sharing of goods by the early church (Acts 2:44). Because the early Christians did so, should Christians today do likewise? Why or why not?

4. How important are stories, both biblical and otherwise, in the life of the church and in the experiences of Christians? Why have Christians always told stories? Why are stories so important?

For Further Reading

Bailey, Kenneth E. *Poet and Peasant: A Literary-Cultural Approach to the Parables in Luke*. Grand Rapids: Eerdmans, 1976.

Brown, Raymond E. *The Birth of the Messiah*. New York: Doubleday, 1977.

________. *The Death of the Messiah*. 2 volumes. New York: Doubleday, 1994.

Fitzmyer, Joseph A. *The Acts of the Apostles*. The Anchor Bible. Volume 31. New York: Doubleday, 1998.

Goppelt, Leonhard. *Apostolic and Post-Apostolic Times*. Translated by Robert A. Guelich. Grand Rapids: Baker, 1970.

Green, Joel B. et al., editors. *Dictionary of Jesus and the Gospels.* Downers Grove, IL: InterVarsity Press, 1992.

Johnson, Luke Timothy. *The Real Jesus: The Misguided Quest for the Historical Jesus and the Truth of the Traditional Gospels*. San Francisco: HarperSan-Francisco, 1996.

Wright, N. T. *Jesus and the Victory of God*. Minneapolis: Fortress Press, 1996.

4

The Writings of the New Testament: Confessing the Christ Boldly

Introduction

Our introduction to the New Testament now brings us to the texts themselves, those twenty-seven writings (sometimes called books) that have moved and guided Christian communities for two millennia. Although the background work we have done is necessary to read the texts in the context in which God inspired their writing, it is the texts themselves that have spoken and still speak God's Word. We now hear them—ancient human voices that are the Word of God for us today.

The writings of the New Testament in most modern Bibles are arranged roughly by content and author. So the gospels are listed first, followed by the writings of Paul, and then other authors and Revelation. The gospels appear in a possible order of authorship; Paul's letters are arranged (with one exception) by length. We, however, will not present the New Testament writings in that order. Since this textbook stresses the importance of reading texts in their context, we will look at the writings according to one possible chronological arrangement. Other reconstructions are possible, as the New Testament often only hints at authorship or date. But by paying attention to those hints and by considering plausible contexts, we will better hear those particular voices God moved to write about Jesus and the import of his good news. In this chapter, we hear from those first authors who boldly wrote of Jesus in Jewish and Graeco-Roman contexts.

Chapter Outline

Matthew
James and Galatians
1 and 2 Thessalonians
1 and 2 Corinthians
Colossians and Philemon
Romans

Matthew

What is a Gospel?

We Christians are quite familiar with the names of the four gospels in the New Testament, since the gospels recount the stories of Jesus. But, in reality, it is the individual stories that are familiar to us. Many of us can recount the details of the wedding at Cana or the parable of the Prodigal Son. But fewer of us could state that the former comes from John and the latter from Luke. We know the basic story of Jesus, a harmonization of the gospels. However, in the New Testament there are *four* gospels. The challenge for us is to learn to read each gospel on its own terms, to get each unique perspective on Jesus. That process begins by asking, "What is a **gospel**?"

Matthew calls his work, or at least the first part of it, a "book" (Matthew 1:1). Mark titles his a "gospel" (Mark 1:1). The Greek word means "good news." Luke calls his work "an orderly account" (Luke 1:3). John uses the same term as Matthew—a "book" (John 20:30). This diversity of terminology displays the conceptual range of the authors. They were doing something new. No commonly agreed term was yet in place to describe these writings about Jesus.

Significantly, biblical authors did not write in a vacuum. Others in the Graeco-Roman period wrote about famous individuals. Stories about goddesses and gods circulated, recounting their fame and foibles. But the distinct humanity of Jesus distinguished his stories from these.

Another class of stories, called **aretologies**, was popular in Roman and Egyptian circles and was used as religious propaganda. Aretologies told of individuals, at times born of the union of human and divine, who claimed divine power by means of their ability to do miracles. The popularity of the more outlandish aretologies evoked the scorn of the satirist Lucian of Samosata (c. 115–c. 200). While such aretologies display broad similarities and were part of the religious marketplace in which early Christianity competed, the gospels are of a markedly different form. In the gospels, the hero is crucified.

The writings of Roman historians Plutarch (born c. A.D. 50), Suetonius (born c. A.D. 69), and Tacitus (born c. A.D. 55) provide another genre of writings to which the gospels might be compared. These Graeco-Roman biographies differ from modern biographies in their focus. While modern historians use scientific methodologies in an attempt to write a relatively neutral account of what happened, ancient biographers primarily used oral sources about a person's life to detail the individual's character and personality traits. The intent of Graeco-Roman biographies was to extol the hero and to promote moral character in the reader. The gospels of the New Testament work in a somewhat similar way. They extol the characteristics of Jesus and promote his moral teachings. But there is also a sense in which Jesus is totally different from those who might try to emulate him. And the focus on his death at the hands of Roman power is unprecedented in Graeco-Roman biography.

The gospels are not aretologies, and they are not ancient biographies extolling the character of Jesus. Still, ancients familiar with such genres could relate to the character and identity of Jesus as recounted in the gospels. They would not be put off by miracles stories, as are modern readers. But the unique aspect of the gospels—the story of a crucified and risen Jesus—would change the way ancients might think about Jesus, even as it continues to challenge and inspire us today. To the gospel writers, this was "good news." Among the variety of designations for their works noted above, "gospel" is the one that came to embrace them all.

How Did the Gospels Come to Be?

The gospels have their origin in the words and deeds of Jesus and in what actually happened to him in Jerusalem. They are not myths—religious stories the details of which are unimportant. They are not fabrications—stories concocted to serve the needs of early Christian communities. There would be no gospels if there were no Jesus crucified and risen. But the gospel writers are not news reporters, filing their stories from the Holy Land.

Between the actual events and the writings of the gospels, the stories of Jesus circulated orally. Peter's sermon in Acts 2:22–24 is an example of a summary of those stories. Elsewhere, Paul recounts various appearances (1 Corinthians 15:5–8). Individual sayings of Jesus show up in other New Testament documents (Acts 20:35; Revelation 22), as well as documents such as the *Gospel of Thomas*. Oral proclamation continued even after the gospels were written. The story of the accused woman in John 8 was not part of the earliest manuscripts. It apparently circulated orally and was inserted later into the gospel. In examples that come from such sources, the words and deeds of Jesus are told to persuade (Acts 16:31). The stories are not told for antiquarian or entertainment purposes; rather, "these are written so that you may believe that Jesus is the Christ, the Son of God, and that by believing you may have life in his name" (John 20:31).

Out of this persuasive intent (compare Luke 1:1–4) and in view of the needs of the communities for which they were written, evangelists wrote gospels. The audiences to which they wrote knew stories of the divines and had heard biographies of the greats. The gospels appeal to such an audience. Second, the gospels advocate and reflect a theology drawn heavily from Israel's Scripture (especially the Septuagint) and from the reflections of Second Temple Judaisms on those writings. The words and deeds of Jesus parallel and fulfill that tradition. Third, the gospel writers have a closeness to Jesus and an experience of him and his Spirit that contribute a unique part to the composition of the works. These three characteristics make the gospels unique yet understandable in their time. The gospels are **narrative Christology**.

As much as the four gospels must be read in view of their antecedents and pagan competitors, they are themselves part of a larger set of writings from within early Christian communities that also bore the designation "gospel."

Gospels are attributed to Thomas, Peter, Mary, the Egyptians, the Hebrews—some fifteen works that are often called Christian apocrypha. These other gospels, some expansive, display the diversity among early communities as Christianity struggled with its public articulation of the faith. By the end of the second century, the four gospels became the standard or rule (**canon**) for early Christianity. The modern designation "canonical gospels" reflects this authority. The apocryphal gospels provide a comparative context.

A final question of gospel origins surfaces when we compare the narratives of the four canonical gospels to each other. Matthew and Luke start with the birth of Jesus; Mark opens with John the Baptist. Otherwise Matthew, Mark, and Luke follow the same storyline. After a ministry of word and deed in Galilee, Jesus travels to Jerusalem where he is crucified and raised. John has a different style and structure.

A closer look at the first three gospels shows at times a remarkable similarity in vocabulary. In the story of the healing of a leper (Matthew 8:1–4; Mark 1:40–44; Luke 5:12–16), the plea of the leper and the response of Jesus are identical. The similar story lines and use of identical phraseology are the basis for calling the first three gospels **synoptic**. The word "synoptic" refers to the common view these gospels have of the content, order, and telling of the story of Jesus.

On other occasions, the Synoptic Gospels display a confusing dissimilarity. Peter confesses in Matthew 16:16, "You are the Christ, the Son of the living God." In Mark 8:29, the confession is, "You are the Christ." In Luke 9:20, Peter answers, "The Christ of God." These variances raise at least two questions. What explains the remarkable verbal and structural similarity? What is behind the variances that are noticeable when the stories are placed side by side? These questions form the basis of the synoptic problem and offer an opportunity to explore how modern scholarship approaches the gospels.

The Gospels and Modern Scholarship

For centuries the gospels of the New Testament have inspired the faith and living of Christians. Within Christian communities the gospels have been heard, taught, preached, and believed. They were the church's Scriptures. They continue to be central to our common worship and teaching.

With the coming of modernity (the Reformation, the Enlightenment, rationalism, national independence, scientific advances, and industrialization), universities became a second center of biblical studies. As universities became increasingly secular, their approaches to the Christian Scriptures treated the gospels more as artifacts of the origin of a religion, as documents that could be studied like any other ancient religious text. The embrace of scientific historiography gave rise to the historical critical method, which still dominates modern biblical scholarship, especially in the solution it offers to the synoptic problem: the **Four Document Hypothesis**.

The Four Document Hypothesis begins with a proposition: the remarkable similarity among the Synoptic Gospels is best explained if gospel authors combined and edited written sources into the gospels as we know them. This approach is sometimes called source criticism. Second, the Four Document Hypothesis supposes that Mark was written first. Then Matthew and Luke used Mark as their primary source. The Four Document Hypothesis makes this argument based on the patterns of agreement in the stories that occur in all three gospels, the sequence of stories that are in Matthew and Luke but not in Mark, and the tendency for Matthew and Luke to have smoother readings for some texts that are difficult in Mark. Third, the Four Document Hypothesis proposes that Matthew and Luke had a second source (the **Q source**, from the German *Quelle*, meaning source). From Q comes material recounted in both Matthew and Luke that has no parallel in Mark. Finally, two additional source documents are proposed (M and L) from which Matthew and Luke respectively drew the material unique to each Gospel. Thus, four written documents—Mark, Q, M, L—are the sources for Matthew and Luke.

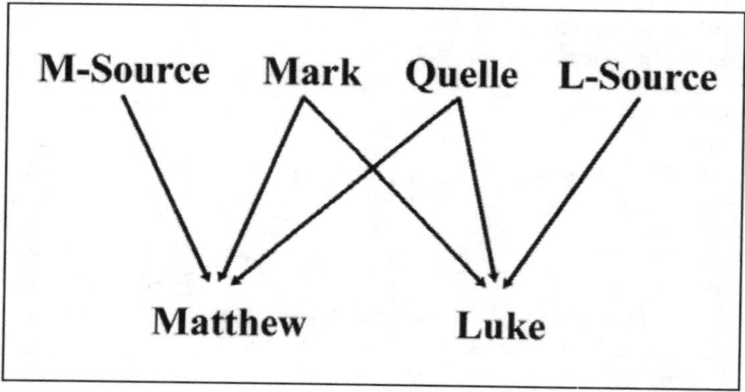

A documentary hypothesis is a plausible assumption, since Luke makes reference to other written narratives about Jesus (Luke 1:1). However, Luke does not claim to use such written documents. Rather, he cites the use of eyewitnesses (Luke 1:3). It is equally plausible to suggest that the commonality among the Synoptic Gospels derives from a common memory and oral telling of the stories about Jesus. Second, the assumption that the shorter and more difficult document must be earlier (Marcan priority) is at best a developmental hypothesis. Mark could be an abbreviation of longer documents or a basic summary of the common oral tradition. Most problematic are the hypothetical documents Q, M, and L, since no evidence for such documents comes from antiquity.

Barring a unexpected discovery, the exact relationship among the Synoptic Gospels will remain a mystery. But problematic are the following in explaining gospel origins: hypotheses based on evolutionary conceptions of development, skepticism about what actually happened, documents for which there is no physical evidence, and assumptions that early traditions about Jesus were manipulated to serve the needs of the first Christian communities. The skepticism and secular nature of modern scholarship require discerning use.

Faith in the Good News

How then did the gospels come to be? They began with the words and deeds of Jesus. They were anticipated by the preaching and witness of early Christians. They came into written form as four distinct portraits of Jesus, each for a particular audience. At least one author knew of others. The rest is hypothesis at best. Concurrently and subsequently others wrote. Harmonization was attempted (the *Diatessaron* of Tatian). But only these four came to be recognized universally as good news, as the gospels. Faith in the risen Jesus, faith to proclaim the good news, faith to write these works—all call for faith in the gospels. While this book does interact with and respond to the skepticism and secular nature of modern scholarship, my approach as an author and my invitation to you, the reader, is to hear these texts as Scripture—the Word of God in the words of human authors writing to inspire faith in their readers. I invite you to hear good news that is for you, too.

Matthew: the First Gospel

Its place of precedence among the books of the New Testament affirms the importance of the first gospel. Its well-known teachings—the Beatitudes, the Lord's Prayer, the golden rule, and the great commission—make the gospel a treasure. Its unique stories—the visit of the magi, the flight to Egypt, the Sermon on the Mount, the parables of the Ten Bridesmaids and the Sheep and the Goats—are favorites of many. More than any other gospel, Matthew connects Jesus to his Jewish roots and to the prophecies of the Old Testament. The Gospel according to St. Matthew is a majestic work. It is also a work, like the other gospels, shrouded in mystery.

The title of the gospel, familiar from modern translations, is an addition to the text from the late second century. No where does the text itself claim to be authored by Matthew, the tax collector and disciple. In contrast to the specific statements in the letters of Paul, the authorship and audience of this work are unknown. Attribution of the gospel to Matthew is a church tradition.

That church tradition is a strong one. Papias (c. A.D. 60–130), a bishop from Asia Minor, whose writings are preserved only in fragmentary form in quotes from others, attributes to Matthew the organization of the Lord's *logia* ("sayings") in Hebrew and notes that people interpreted the *logia* in various ways. Whether *logia* refer to the first gospel or to an earlier collection of the sayings of Jesus, two points are clear. According to Papias, Matthew wrote his initial work in **Aramaic** (a derivation of Hebrew spoken by Jesus and his first followers). Early church authors Irenaeus (c. A.D. 130–c. 200), Pantaenus (died c. A.D. 190), and Origen (c. A.D. 185–254) similarly attribute to Matthew a gospel written in Aramaic. Later, as the gospel was brought into the Graeco-Roman world, early Christianity used Greek, the common cultural language of the empire.

In addition, the church tradition has some internal support from the gospel. A tax collector called by Jesus is named Levi in Mark 2:14 and Luke 5:27. But in the first gospel his name is Matthew (9:9). Further, in the dispute about paying taxes to Caesar, only Matthew uses the technical term for the coin used by the state for tax payment.

Church tradition attributes the first gospel to Matthew and suggests that Matthew wrote originally in Aramaic before later composing a new work in Greek. Usage of the gospel by early Christian writers is also suggestive for the place and date of writing. Ignatius (c. A.D. 35–107), bishop of Antioch, and the *Didache* (an early Christian book of instruction associated with Antioch) both knew and used the gospel. The later *Gospel of the Nazoraeans*, which drew heavily from Matthew, also circulated in Syria. Therefore, it is plausible to suggest that Matthew's work was done in association with the mission at Antioch.

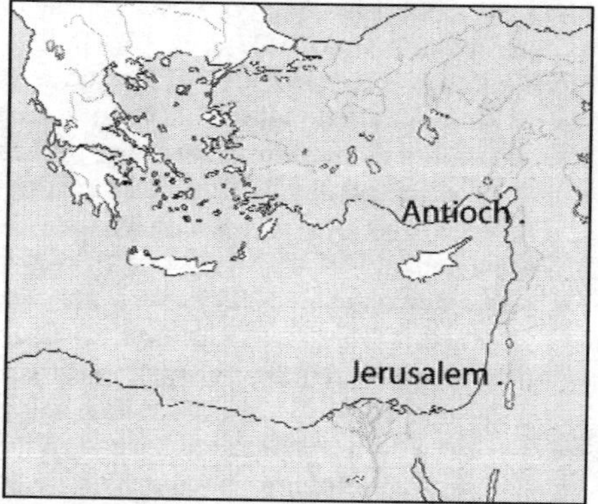

Jewish Christians from Jerusalem had come there after the death of Stephen and began to share the good news with Hellenists (Acts 11:20), that is, those who spoke Greek. At Antioch the followers of "the Way" became known as *Christians* for their cross-cultural work. From Antioch the mission journeys of Barnabas and Paul began. At Antioch, Christians debated the integration of Gentiles (a Jewish designation for those who are not Jews) into the community (Galatians 1–2). The first gospel anticipates the Gentile mission in the visit of the magi and the great commission of Jesus. At the same time, the first gospel is directly addressed to followers of Jewish background who were well grounded in the Old Testament. An early collection of the sayings of Jesus may have fostered this mission, even as the later gospel would confirm it. Matthew then began his written work in the forties, even if the gospel did not take its final Greek form until the sixties or seventies.

Admittedly, this theory is at best a hypothesis. It cannot be affirmed with certainty. But the reconstruction does provide a plausible context within which the gospel might be read and its original intent might be discerned.

Structure and Theme

The gospel opens with the words, "The book of the genealogy of Jesus Christ, the son of David, and son of Abraham" (Matthew 1:1). Matthew intends to talk about Jesus, to identify who he is. Because Matthew opens with references to Abraham, David, and the Messiah, Matthew asserts continuity between the hopes of the people of Israel and Jesus of Nazareth. In Jesus, the prophecies, laws, and hopes of the Old Testament are fulfilled.

In Matthew's Gospel Jesus is a teacher. As one would expect in a Jewish context, the teaching of Jesus expounds on the **Torah**, the books of Moses, and, in particular, their legal content. In the Second Temple period, observance of the Torah was a central concern. Jesus addresses that concern. Jesus teaches his followers how to live as a community. In Matthew 18, the Greek word for church even occurs.

Since there are five major sermonic blocks in Matthew (chapters 5–7, 10, 13, 18, 24–25), some suggest that Matthew portrays Jesus as a new Moses with his own five books for the new Israel. However, Jesus in Matthew (23:2) rejects that suggestion. Jesus came to fulfill the Torah (5:17), not to promulgate a new one.

Of greater import to Matthew is a move from particular to universal. In Matthew's opening chapters, Jesus repeatedly fulfills particular promises given to a particular people (1:23; 2:6, 15, 18, 23). In chapter ten, Jesus sends his disciples only "to the lost sheep of the house of Israel" (10:6). But by chapter 28, the mission is to "all nations" (28:19), a profound assertion for the followers of Jesus in Antioch, the third largest city of the Roman Empire. From Antioch, one could go west (as did Paul) or east to the region from which the magi came (2:1). Since most of us who read Matthew today come from European, African or Asian lineage, Matthew's move from particular to universal opens the door for us to receive the Gospel.

Bracketing Matthew's narrative about Jesus is a promise that would encourage the readers of this first gospel, even as it offers us hope today. The birth of Jesus to Mary fulfills a promise. His name is **Immanuel**, which Matthew translates, "God with us." At the other end of the gospel, the promise is more than a translation of an obscure passage. The final words of Jesus are, "I am with you always, to the end of the age" (28:20). The coming of Jesus was in continuity with the hopes of Israel; the commission of Jesus is in continuity with the work of the church.

Matthew presents Jesus as the principal character in the gospel. Many are attracted to Jesus—the magi, the disciples, the crowds. Others oppose Jesus—the Roman authorities and the religious leaders. These blocks of narrative characters appear together in one of the first stories in the gospel, a story that hints at the flow of the entire gospel.

In Matthew 2, Jesus has been born (2:1). The next character group to appear on Matthew's narrative stage is the magi. They follow a star looking for a king, even as the disciples and crowds would later follow Jesus wondering if he is the promised Messiah. The magi meet Herod, who is troubled along with all Jerusalem (2:3). Herod consults with religious authorities who are complicit in Herod's plot against Jesus. The Roman government, the religious leaders, and troubled Jerusalem are an opposing block of characters. In this opening story,

Jesus escapes (2:13–15), but blood is spilled violently (2:16–18). Matthew has set the stage for the rest of his narrative. Jesus appears; some follow, while others oppose. And in Jerusalem during a final conflict with the authorities, blood will be spilled again. Matthew's narrative flow is visible in the following outline of his work.

MATTHEW: JESUS THE MESSIAH AND SON OF GOD	
MATTHEW PRESENTS JESUS TO THE READER	1:1–4:16
JESUS PRESENTS HIMSELF TO HIS PEOPLE	4:17–11:1
PEOPLE FOLLOW OR REJECT JESUS	11:2–16:20
THE FINAL CONFLICT	16:21–28:20

Key Texts

1:1 Matthew opens by asserting that Jesus is the Messiah, the son of David. The word **messiah** derives from a Hebrew verb meaning "to anoint" and recalls the act of anointing a king (1 Samuel 10:1; 16:13). The English word **Christ** derives from the Greek word for the Messiah (*christos*).

By the Second Temple period, various groups were expecting a royal figure in the line of David (2 Samuel 7:10–14). He would be the Lord's anointed, addressed by the Lord as "my Son" (Psalm 2:2, 7). The *Psalms of Solomon*, possibly authored in Pharisaic circles, calls him, "the anointed of Israel," "the branch of David." In addition, this hoped-for king would deliver Israel from bondage to the Romans and set up a just and righteous kingdom. To call Jesus the Messiah was daring on the part of Matthew, for Jesus had been crucified by a Roman ruler, and Rome still ruled the promised land (along with the rest of the Mediterranean world). Matthew had to answer two questions: How could Jesus be the Messiah? and Where is the messianic kingdom?

1:2–17 To demonstrate that Jesus is the Messiah, Matthew offers a **genealogy**. Genealogies establish not only the descent but also the honor of the individual. The genealogy of Jesus is a literary perfection. There are three groups of fourteen generations. As numbers were often symbolic, the choice of a multiple of seven may hint at a doubling of the perfection of the original act of creation (six days plus a day of rest) that was itself tripled. There is a precision implied by Matthew's selection of fourteen names between Abraham and David, David and the exile, and the exile and Jesus. Interestingly, the last block of fourteen is actually thirteen. The pattern naming "the father of" is broken at the end to stress the miraculous conception of Jesus in the womb of Mary.

The famous and the infamous are named; patriarchs, kings, and unknowns are listed. Abraham, Isaac, Jacob, David, Solomon, Hezekiah, and Josiah impress. But Uzziah got mixed reviews (2 Kings 15:1–7); Ahaz "did not do what was right in the eyes of the Lord his God" (2 Kings 16:2); and Manasseh was worse (2 Kings 21:1–17). Four women are part of this messianic line. Three were Gentiles and one was married to a Gentile. If Jesus is the particular and perfect Messiah of Israel in the line of David, his genealogy hints at a universal reach of his kingdom. Matthew lays out the genealogy as he does in order to address both of the questions he faced. Jesus is the Messiah; but his messianic kingdom embraces more than just the righteous of Israel.

Matthew's genealogy ought not be confused with a modern family tree. It is intentionally selective, not inclusive. When we compare Matthew 1:8 to 1 Chronicles 3:10–12, Matthew lists Joram as the father of Uzziah. But the chronicler names Joram as the great-great-grandfather of Azariah, the given name of king Uzziah. Matthew organizes the data into a scheme of three sets of fourteen generations because his concern is not chronology but theology. He is not trying to list all of Jesus' ancestors. Rather he is asserting that, according to God's word of promise, the perfect son of David ushers in an expansive messianic kingdom. It is a new creation.

Matthew's presentation of a genealogy teaches an important lesson about the gospels. Each evangelist is selective in the material presented. One will include a story; another will not. One will tell only part of a story; another will give more detail or emphasize different points. This is not a process of later authors editing and combining documents. Rather, these variances point to the process by which evangelists selectively wrote in view of their larger theological task. "Jesus did many [things] … which are not written …, but these are written so that you may believe …" (John 20:30–31).

1:23 For the early Christian community, especially those of Jewish background, the Old Testament was a Christian book. When Paul wrote that "all Scripture is breathed out by God" (2 Timothy 3:16), he was referring to the Old Testament. For the early Christians, the Old Testament preaches Christ.

In Matthew's opening chapters, he frequently cites the Old Testament. The prophetic words are fulfilled even in the details of Jesus' coming. For example, Matthew's cites Isaiah 7:14 using the unambiguous language of the **Septuagint**. Although offensive to modernity, the church uses this passage to support its teaching of the virgin birth. Jesus had a human mother, but no biological father. Unfortunately, these modern debates often detract from the point Matthew is making with the citation. For Matthew, the virgin birth was a settled matter. The angel of the Lord, speaking for God, had so announced to Joseph. But that announcement also triggered in Matthew's mind the citation from Isaiah, due to its reference to a virgin. From the passage came a greater truth about the new-born son of David. He is Immanuel, "God with us" (1:23), a major point in Matthew's portrait of Jesus (28:20). The miracle of the birth is important; but as Matthew reads Isaiah, there is something more important. In this birth God is "with us." Jesus is the Messiah and Jesus is the Son of God "with us."

3:1–15 Matthew inaugurates the adult life of Jesus with the story of John the Baptist. John is in the wilderness of Judea, a narrow strip of desolate land between the Judean hills and the Dead Sea. In about twelve miles, the elevation of the land drops four thousand feet, causing severely dry conditions. The desert is a place of wandering and testing for people and prophets.

John calls out, "Repent, for the **kingdom of heaven** is at hand" (3:2). Repentance is more than being sorry. Repentance involves a reversal of mind and action. It bears fruit (3:8). This call to repentance has a basis—the surprising declaration that the kingdom or reign of God has drawn near. Matthew, a Jew writing to Jews, avoids using the divine name directly and so speaks of the kingdom of heaven. Repentance does not bring in the kingdom; rather it is our response to the coming of the kingdom. Matthew selects this story in order to address a key issue: How can Jesus be the Messiah since he did not bring in the expected messianic kingdom? John's preaching about repentance begins to reshape that expectation.

Judean Wilderness

John's call was accompanied by a **baptism** or washing symbolic of purification. Ritual washings were part of Jewish practice in the Second Temple period. A **mikveh** is a pool for such ceremonial bathing. These are found both in private residences, public places (for example, near the southern entrance to the temple), and in communal contexts. The Dead Sea scrolls speak of such washings as a regular part of the life of this pious community.

John's baptism is not for everyone. He warns away certain religious elites, calling them a brood of vipers (3:7). The basis for his warning is God's impending judgment (3:10) and the coming of the one who will baptize with the Holy Spirit and with fire (3:11). John also warns away Jesus (3:14), but for a different reason. If John's rhetoric reviled the religious elites with warnings about the judgment of the messianic age, by contrast, his rhetoric recognizes that Jesus is the agent of that age—the Messiah.

3:16–17 Matthew does not narrate the actual baptism of Jesus. Rather, his focus is on the signs that attend the baptism. An opened heaven, a dove descending and resting, and, most significantly, the voice from the heavens all affirm that Jesus is the Son of God and the Messiah on whom the Spirit would rest (Isaiah 42:1). These words of God that mark the beginning of the ministry of Jesus will also commission his final trip to Jerusalem (Matthew 17:5).

4:1–11 Matthew's opening presentation of Jesus concludes in dramatic form. Jesus the Messiah confronts the devil. The narrative also functions to define what type of Messiah Jesus is. The encounter of Jesus with the devil is brought about by the Spirit, whose active role Matthew stresses. Although the role of the Spirit echoes the prophecy of Isaiah (61:1), the encounter is often called a temptation. But the term also implies a testing. In this test, Jesus shows himself obedient to the One who just named him in baptism and demonstrates his superior power over the devil.

In the first temptation, physical hunger is the issue. According to popular expectation, the messianic age would be one of abundance with no more hunger. Jesus quotes Deuteronomy (8:3) to identify his reign as a spiritual one centered on the words that come from the mouth of God. In the second test, the devil quotes Psalm 91, arguing that the Messiah would be protected by God. By quoting a single verse, the devil invokes the message of the entire Psalm. Jesus again turns to Deuteronomy (6:16) to refute the tempter. For Jews, quotations from the Torah were of greater authority than those from the prophets or writings like the Psalms. Jesus appeals to a higher authority. In subtle fashion, Jesus also quotes from the instructions of Moses to the children of Israel prior to their entry into the Promised Land. Moses spoke (and wrote) these words, calling for faithfulness in view of the failure of the previous generation during forty years in the wilderness. Jesus is faithful where the generation with Moses in the wilderness had not been.

In a final test, the devil offers Jesus a reign far wider than that of his ancestors David and Solomon. Under Roman occupation, the Jews of the Second Temple period yearned for a Messiah who would restore the greatness of the rule of David. *Psalms of Solomon* 17:21–22 speaks of the son of David purging Jerusalem from Gentiles and driving out sinners from the inheritance. If he bowed before Satan, Jesus could give them even more. But Jesus passes the test by clinging to the creed of Israel—its commitment to one God (Deuteronomy 6:13). The devil leaves, and angels begin to minister to Jesus. As Jesus earlier escaped from Herod (Matthew 2:13–15), he bests Satan in the wilderness. But these two conflicts imply that more are to come.

4:13–25 By this point in the gospel, we readers have a clear idea about this Jesus. Matthew had presented him as the Messiah, the Son of God, who fulfills the prophetic Scriptures. Matthew next presents Jesus to his own people as one who teaches, preaches, and heals (4:23; 9:35; 11:1).

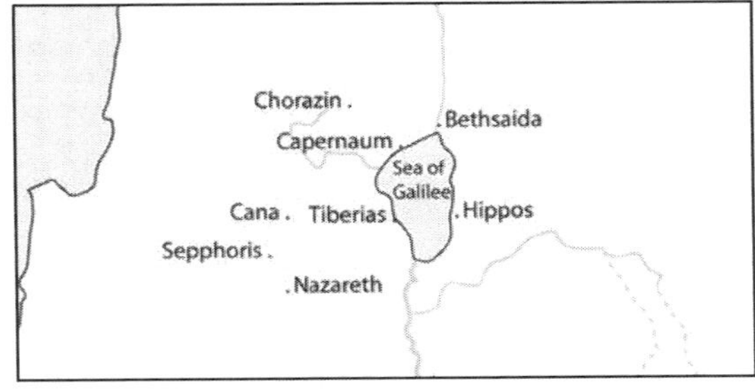

Jesus locates his ministry in Capernaum on the northern shore of the Sea of Galilee. Capernaum was a fishing village with significant local trade. Some modern writers mistakenly speak of a major trade route called the *via maris* passing nearby. No such route existed in this area in Jesus' time. Galilee was an area into which Gentiles were encroaching (4:15), and it would also become a great center of Jewish learning after the destruction of Jerusalem. But the center of

Jesus' ministry on the north shore of the Sea of Galilee was in his day rather isolated. Matthew notes with astonishment the large crowds who come to Jesus (4:25).

Matthew uses the same sentence to characterize the teaching of Jesus as he used to summarize the preaching of John: "Repent, for the kingdom of heaven is at hand" (4:17). Jesus is as unconventional as John. Normally, a student seeks out a **rabbi**. Jesus calls his own disciples. Peter, Andrew, James, and John are named. Matthew stresses that they left their nets and families to follow Jesus "immediately" (4:20, 22). Following Jesus is a topic to which Matthew will return often in the material he selects for his gospel.

Matthew summarizes the teaching of Jesus as "proclaiming the gospel of the kingdom." Only Matthew uses this phrase. What Jesus teaches is for Matthew "good news." It is news that rescues and delivers (and condemns; 21:45–46). It is news connected to the story about Jesus (26:13). It is good news for the lost sheep of the house of Israel (10:6) and for all nations (28:18). It is good news about the kingdom.

Assumed by the word *kingdom* is the phrase "kingdom of heaven," preferred by Matthew over the synonymous phrase "kingdom of God." Matthew, a former worker for the hated Romans who ruled most of the Mediterranean world, is asserting the rule or reign not of the Caesar but of God. In Jesus the rule of God has come near. It may not be the expected messianic kingdom, but for Matthew the coming of God's reign is good news.

5:1–7:29 In chapter three of this book, we spent significant time on the collection of the teachings of Jesus called the **Sermon on the Mount**. There we noted how the good news of the Beatitudes reversed the social order. We compared Jesus' comments on the Torah to those later recorded in rabbinic sources, noting that Jesus addressed similar topics but with a distinct personal authority (7:29). We also pointed out the use of a prayer as a significant tool to advance his message.

In terms of Matthew's Gospel, the so-called sermon of Jesus functions as a summation of his teaching to the crowds of Jews initially attracted to him (5:1). As Matthew's readers were likely Jewish Christians, the Jewish nature of the collection would speak in terms that are familiar to them as well as remind them of Jesus' unique authority. Other blocks of sermonic material (chapters 13 and 18) would broaden Jesus' appeal beyond strictly Jewish audiences and affirm his rejection of the religious establishments in Jerusalem (chapters 23–25). Matthew's Gospel moves from the ethnic particularity of Judaism to the universality of the Gentile world. The Sermon on the Mount is the starting point.

The Sermon on the Mount also serves Matthew's task of redefining contemporary expectations about the messianic kingdom. In God's kingdom, not only are the poor in spirit blessed, but the law of retaliation is transformed into a command to turn the other cheek (5:38–39). Love of enemies is the perfection God seeks (5:43–48). In marked contrast, the *War Rule* of the Qumran sectarians is full of descriptions of the coming destruction of enemies. According to the *Psalms of Solomon*, the heir of David would "shatter their substance with an iron rod, destroy unlawful nations" (17:24). The messianic kingdom brought near by Jesus would be very different from what was commonly expected.

That reign of God, although having come near, has an eschatological element. The word **eschatology** is a technical term describing those events that occur in the future at the end of time. Jesus does say much in the sermon about the present, but there is also a sense in which the fullness of the messianic age awaits the end of time. The plea of Jesus' prayer, "Your kingdom come" (Matthew 6:10), implies that the fullness of God's reign awaits the end. Instruction to "lay up for yourselves treasures in heaven" (6:20) is future oriented. The concluding texts of the collection caution about the future when the reign of God leads to judgment, for not everyone will enter (7:21); some who build are wise, but others are foolish (7:24–27).

8:1–9:38 Jesus, the Messiah of the word, is next presented as the Messiah in deed. Jesus acts with compassion, since the crowds are "like sheep without a shepherd" (9:36). Matthew gathers a series of nine miracle stories interspersed with narratives that are characteristic of the messianic age (8:17; 11:5). Healings, exorcisms, restoring sight, calming a storm, and resuscitating the dead elicit a variety of responses from people. The disciples wonder, "What sort of man is this?" (8:27). Others "begged him to leave their region" (8:34). The crowds "were afraid and glorified God" (9:7). But the Pharisees said, "He casts out demons by the prince of demons" (9:34). There is dissonance between the words and deeds of Jesus the Messiah and the expectations of many about the messianic age.

Of note in the narrative are two individuals who should have no part in the messianic age—a **centurion** (a Roman soldier in charge of one hundred men) and a tax collector. For the coming Messiah would "destroy the unrighteous rulers, … purge Jerusalem from Gentiles … [and] smash the arrogance of sinners like a potter's jar" (*Psalms of Solomon* 17:22–23). But when the centurion solicits Jesus' help for a servant, Jesus notes, "With no one in Israel have I found such faith" (9:10). Then Jesus assets the universal reach of his kingdom, "I tell you that many will come from east and west and recline at table with Abraham, Isaac, and Jacob in the kingdom of heaven" (9:11). Second, Jesus also calls a tax collector and reclines at his table with other tax collectors and sinners over the objections of the Pharisees (9:9–13). Just as the words of Jesus recounted by Matthew give a new understanding of the messianic kingdom, so do his deeds.

10:1–11:1 Matthew's presentation of Jesus to Israel concludes with instructions specifically for the disciples. The collection addresses a common theme—the mission of the disciples. The disciples are numbered as twelve, named, and for the first time called apostles—the sent ones. They are sent only to Israel and are warned away from Gentiles and Samaritans, a point recounted only by Matthew (10:5–6). They are to replicate the words and works of Jesus. Their message is the same, "The kingdom of heaven is at hand" (10:7). Their works are the same: heal the sick, raise the dead, cleanse the lepers, and cast out demons (10:8).

The mission will be a difficult one; the apostles will face many of the same challenges that Jesus faced. Their mission will require austerity (10:9–10), even as Jesus did not have a place to lay his head (8:20). Some will not listen (10:14), even as Jesus was questioned by religious sectarians (9:3, 11, 34). In harsh tones that will be repeated in Matthew 24, Jesus warns of persecutions to come (10:16–23) and of the divisions the mission will cause (10:34–39). Warnings are interspersed with words of encouragement (10:26–32) and promises of reward (10:40–42).

Interestingly, after recording these instructions, Matthew does not narrate the actual mission to Israel or its results. Matthew instead keeps the focus on Jesus who continues to teach and preach (11:1). As a result, the instruction to the Twelve takes on a timeless character. By the time Matthew is writing, the mission to Israel has been superseded by the great commission to all nations. As Matthew is heading to that point, he recounts only that aspect of the mission to Israel that has ongoing import for his readers—the real challenges and the promises of divine care that attend the mission. What Matthew preserves of the instruction to the Twelve still speaks to our contemporary mission efforts.

11:2–18 Matthew's narrative undergoes a dramatic shift in chapter 11. Having presented Jesus' messianic mission to Israel (4:12–11:1), Matthew next tells of increasing speculation about the identity of Jesus and the rejection of his messianic words and work. The first to raise questions is John the Baptist, held in prison by Herod Antipas. Perhaps even for him, the kingdom Jesus announced did not come about as he expected. John had spoken harshly of the judgment to be meted out by the one to come (3:12); but the judgment of Jesus was one of acceptance, even of tax collectors and soldiers. In Jesus' subsequent comments about John, it is clear that many reject the kingdom they both preached (11:18–19).

11:20–12:50 Skepticism about Jesus and rejection of his work are thematic for subsequent materials. Jesus denounces Chorazin, Bethsaida, and even Capernaum. Although Jesus did mighty works in their presence, they did not repent (11:20–24). The harsh rhetoric betrays the rising conflict in the narrative. The Pharisees question the behavior of the disciples of Jesus on the Sabbath (12:2) and plot to destroy Jesus after he heals on the Sabbath (12:14). Subsequent exchanges between Jesus and the Pharisees deteriorate further. Even while the people wonder if Jesus is the son of David (12:23), the Pharisees charge that Jesus is in league with Beelzebul, the prince of demons (11:24) and demand a sign to authenticate his teaching (12:38). Jesus in turn employs the judgmental rhetoric of the sin against the Holy Spirit (12:32) and the sign of Jonah (12:39). But even in the midst of such rising conflict, Matthew interjects a **fulfillment prophecy** that keeps the universal reach of the messianic kingdom before the readers then and us today. Some followed and were healed (12:15), so that "in his name the Gentiles will hope" (12:21; quoting Isaiah 42:4).

13:1–58 In chapter three, we discussed the role of **parables** in the ministry of Jesus. As we noted, the parables speak of the surprising nature of the reign of God and stand as a more concrete manifestation of the teaching of Jesus about the coming kingdom. Matthew waits until the point of rising conflict to introduce parables in his narrative. For Matthew, the parables are conflict discourse. Matthew reinforces this point by including a fulfillment prophecy (13:14–15) that speaks to the controversial nature of parables. Only Matthew has the portion of the quotation from Isaiah 6 that references the conflict. Luke 8 and Mark 4 have part of the quote. Conflict is the theme of the parable of the Weeds, a parable only Matthew recounts (13:24–30). Because of the confusion and conflict, Jesus speaks to the crowds in parables (13:34). At the end of the chapter, the people of his hometown misidentify him as "the carpenter's son" (13:55) and take offense at him (13:57). Their rejection stands in sharp contrast to Matthew's repeated identification of Jesus as the Messiah, the son of David. But to the disciples (and to us readers!) the secrets of the kingdom are given (13:11). The kingdom is like seed planted in good soil that produces an astonishing hundred- or sixty- or thirtyfold, like a mustard plant become a tree, like a hidden treasure, a pearl of great value, and a net that gathers fish of every kind.

14:1–12 Having been placed in league with Satan by the religious elites and called a mere carpenter's son by people from his home town, the misidentification of Jesus continues in the character of Herod Antipas. Haunted by his execution of John the Baptist, Antipas thinks that Jesus is the Baptist raised from the dead. Matthew proceeds to narrate the execution of John. Although the event occurred earlier, its placement at this point in the narrative recalls the blood spilled by Herod's father at the birth of Jesus and foreshadows the eventual execution of Jesus at the hand of the Jerusalem elites and the Romans. Matthew directly connects the death of John to the withdrawal of Jesus (14:13).

14:13–16:12 Matthew continues to narrate growing opposition to Jesus. In Matthew 15:1–9, Jesus has sharp exchanges with the Pharisees and scribes about the **tradition of the elders**—an oral tradition meant to help the people keep the Torah that would be later codified into the Mishnah. Jesus found the contemporary practice of this tradition hypocritical. In Matthew 15:10–20, the point of debate is purity and its corollary, **defilement**. The pursuit of ritual purity was a significant issue in the Second Temple period. It could even be a source of division in the Jewish religious practices of the day. According to Jesus, it missed the point. In Matthew 16:1–10, Pharisees and Sadducees test Jesus by seeking a sign. Jesus warns his followers against their teaching.

Interspersed amidst the controversy, Matthew narrates stories that confirm for his readers (and for us) Jesus' messianic identity. When the story of the feeding of the five thousand notes that all were satisfied (14:20), it echoes prophetic anticipation of the messianic banquet (Psalm 63:5; Isaiah 25:6). The theme re-echoes in the feeding of the four thousand (15:32–39). Messianic healing continues (15:21–31). In the central story of the unit, Jesus walks on the "sea," uses the language of divine self-identification (Exodus 3:14), and those in the boat worship him: "You are the Son of God" (Matthew 14:33). As Matthew presents Jesus, he is the Messiah and the Son of God.

Also interwoven in the controversy is material that teaches his readers about **discipleship** and broadens the concept of the community that will carry on the work of Jesus. In the story of Jesus walking on the sea, only Matthew narrates Peter's failed attempt. As we discovered earlier in chapter three, through the subtle use of language, Matthew describes Peter's attempt as defective from the start—merely walking on "water." Only God comes on the "sea." Yet, when in trouble, Peter cries, "Lord, save me" (14:30). This plea is a positive example for future followers and points to the rescue Jesus will affect for all those who seek his divine help. The story of Peter is a call to faithful discipleship. With similar language many of us today address our God at the beginning of the Divine Service, "Lord, have mercy on us."

Discipleship is also a subtle factor in the feeding narrative. Only Matthew points out that Jesus gave the broken loaves to the disciples, who then distributed them to the people (14:19). As with the mission to Israel, the disciples will carry on the work of Jesus. The story of the faith of a Canaanite woman extends that work beyond the confines of Israel (15:21–28). Although the story occurs in both Matthew and Mark, three additional details are included in Matthew. Those details support Matthew's fundamental theme: the community of disciples includes all nations.

In Matthew 10, the disciples were sent "only to the lost sheep of the house of Israel" (10:6). In Matthew 15, Jesus resists the cries of the Canaanite woman by saying, "I was sent only to the lost sheep of the house of Israel" (15:24). When the woman approaches Jesus, Matthew alone quotes her request, "Lord, help me" (15:25)—a plea almost identical to Peter's earlier cry, "Lord, save me" (14:30). Matthew stresses Jesus' response to her, "Woman, great is your faith" (15:28). In contrast, Matthew alone tells of Jesus' words to the Peter after the sea-walking, "O you of little faith, why did you doubt?" (14:31) By stressing these verbal parallels, Matthew affirms the place of this Gentile woman among those like the magi and even those of us who are disciples from all nations.

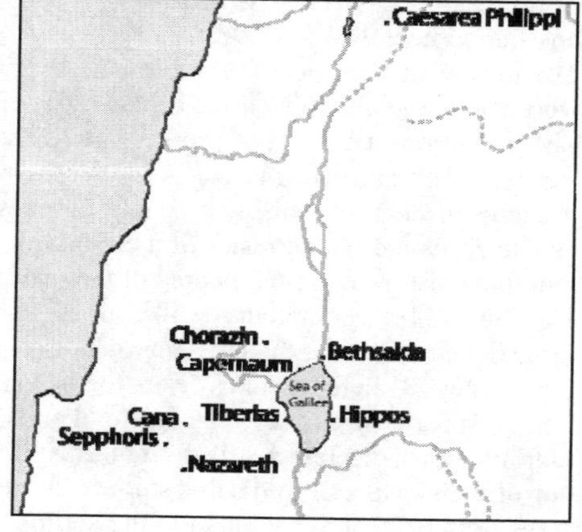

16:13–20 Controversy over the identity of Jesus reaches a point of clarification at Caesarea Philippi. It has been Matthew's program to identify Jesus as the Messiah, the Son of God. Religious elites have rejected such identification; crowds have wondered; the disciples have struggled to be faithful. After reviewing a diversity of responses, Peter provides what is for Matthew the correct identification: "You are the Christ, the Son of the living God" (16:16). The blessing that Jesus gives to Peter and the leadership role assigned to him (16:19) function to affirm the truth of his answer. However, two errors ought to be avoided when examining this story. The first is to read into the text a basis for the later hierarchical structure of the church. The second is to assert that Peter had a full and complete understanding of the person and work of Jesus already at this point. Matthew, writing later, affirms by these accolades the correctness of Peter's answer. But Matthew also shows in subsequent verses that Peter still had much to learn.

16:21 Matthew's narrative shifts direction as Jesus turns toward Jerusalem and predicts his coming execution and resurrection. It is the first of three such predictions (see also 17:22–23 and 20:18–19). The ministry in Galilee concludes as Jesus moves south. However, Matthew relates in his story more than chronological and geographical factors. Matthew's constant concern is identifying Jesus as the Messiah and Son of God. In so doing, Matthew is also redefining that identity over against the expectations of the times.

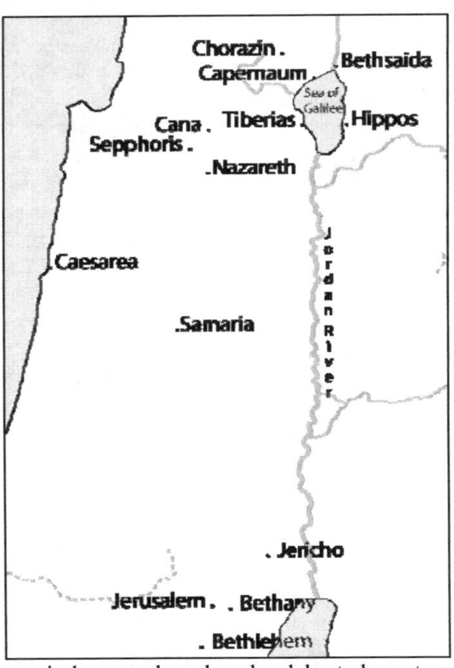

For Matthew, the messianic identity would involve suffering and violent death. Paul would later call the crucifixion of Jesus a stumbling block for Jews (1 Corinthians 1:23). The issue is not the violent death of Jesus. The people of the Second Temple period remembered and celebrated martyrs who endured violent death on behalf of Torah, temple, and the God of Israel. The execution of the seven brothers in 2 Maccabees 7:1–42 is the best-known example. The difference in the case of Jesus would be execution at the hands of religious leaders from his own people. Jesus would not die as a patriot of Israel. His death would be the result of a clash with the elites of Jerusalem and would redefine those who are the people of God and part of his kingdom. The death of Jesus would be redemptive for all nations. Who Jesus is and why he died are of far greater importance than the gory details of his suffering.

16:22–28 Peter rebukes Jesus for intending to die in Jerusalem. Although Peter had used the correct language to identify Jesus in the previous narrative, he (and the other disciples) still did not grasp the intent of Jesus' messianic work nor of their own call to discipleship. Jesus censures Peter with the same words Jesus used to send away Satan at the end of the third temptation (4:10). Linked to the censure of the chief disciple is a new definition of discipleship. Since his messianic role culminates in suffering, Jesus calls on his disciples to take up the cross and follow him (16:24). Having fully presented Jesus and discipleship, Matthew must now prepare his readers for their task as followers, even as he concludes the story of Jesus.

Although religious persecution is still experienced by some, modern life in the western world protects freedom of religion. Few of us will face the violence and persecution that awaited Jesus and his first followers. Pressures on our faithfulness tend to be more subtle. Yet the call to discipleship can be a costly one. We for whom life is now easy may not always have it so easy.

17:1–8 The sweep of Matthew's Gospel has looked back to the beginnings of God's people. The Jesus of this gospel has anchored his teachings in the words of the Torah. The gospel writer has repeatedly framed the words and deeds of Jesus as fulfillment of the Scriptures. At the opposite end of Matthew's narrative is the resurrection and the promise to be "with you always" (28:20). The **transfiguration** is a literary tool used by Matthew to tie together the entire gospel. In the appearance of Moses and Elijah, Jesus' messianic work is placed in continuity with Israel's past. The words from the cloud echo the words at Jesus' baptism that inaugurated his messianic work. The description of Jesus' appearance and his words to the disciples ("Rise and don't be afraid") foreshadow the language and descriptions of resurrection (28:3, 5). To lift up the eyes and see Jesus only (17:8) will be the fitting response of the faithful to the final promise of Jesus at the end of the gospel (28:20). Matthew chooses to include the story of the transfiguration since it looks both backward and forward at a critical point in the narrative.

18:1–35 In a sermonic collection, Matthew has gathered material spoken by Jesus to his disciples about life together. At Peter's confession, Jesus promised, "I will build my church" (16:18). In this collection, the Greek word for "church" occurs again (18:17). Here Jesus describes a community quite unlike other institutions. Matthew presents this material at this point for three reasons. First, it reinforces his identification of the new community of followers from all nations. Second, it further defines how this community lives together as the church. Finally, Matthew deems it important to his community as they try to live together as Christians after the resurrection of Jesus. In view of Matthew's intent, this collection of teachings is worthy of our particular attention today as we live and work together as Christians awaiting the return of Jesus.

Humility, not greatness, is the mark of those who enter the kingdom of heaven (18:1–6). Ethical discipline is called for (18:7–9). The perishing individual is of greater importance than the faithful majority (18:8–14). Restoring the sinner is the goal, pursuing them even as Jesus sought tax collectors and sinners (18:15–20). The new community is marked by forgiveness without limit—implied by the multiplication of seven, the symbolic number for perfection (18:22). Refusal to forgive is wickedness, if not absurd.

This final point is affirmed by a parable in which a servant, who has been forgiven a debt of ten thousand talents, refuses to forgive a debt of one hundred denarii. A **denarius** is the wage paid to a day laborer. A talent is roughly equivalent to the lifetime earnings of such a laborer. Although it is possible to calculate a comparison (one debt was some 600,000 times larger than the other), in a peasant, agrarian culture the refusal to forgive is ridiculous in view of what had been forgiven.

19:1–20:28 As Jesus approaches Jerusalem, Matthew repeats now familiar themes about discipleship and the new community. The kingdom belongs to children (19:14). "The first will be last and the last first" (19:30). The eleventh hour is not too late (20:12–15). Service and sacrifice mark the messianic community (20:28).

After presenting Jesus to Israel as the Messiah and Son of God in word and deed (4:12–11:1), Matthew has recounted growing opposition to and repudiation of Jesus by the religious elites (11:2–20:28). In parallel, Matthew has selected material that defines the members of Jesus' messianic kingdom and how we disciples can live together under God's reign. Matthew's narrative is reaching its climax.

20:29–21:10 Matthew makes the messianic identity of Jesus clear as Jesus approaches Jerusalem. Outside of Jericho, two blind men appeal to Jesus using the title, "Son of David" (21:31–31). Matthew had opened his gospel ascribing that title to Jesus (1:1). The Canaanite woman had used the same title in her appeal (15:22). As Matthew notes, the blind men receive their sight and follow Jesus (20:34), in sharp contrast to the opposition which Jesus later labels as "blind" (23:16).

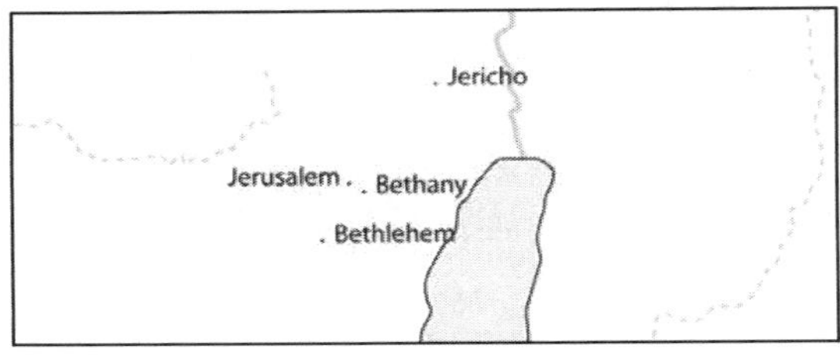

A messianic theme continues as Jesus enters the city. Although the event had political overtones, Matthew invokes a fulfillment prophecy from Zechariah. The arrival of "your king" was the awaited messianic moment (21:5). The city is "stirred up"—a word drawn from the same semantic domain as the city's reaction to the report of the birth of a king (2:3). Significantly, the crowds identify Jesus as "the prophet" (21:11). For Matthew, Jesus comes as the Messiah; for the crowds, he is only a prophet. Their failure to identify Jesus properly at this critical point may be an ominous indicator of what is to come.

21:12–22:46 The conflict swirling around Jesus from his birth and through his ministry comes to a head in the temple in Jerusalem. Words and actions clash. Exchanges are harsh. The cleansing of the temple was a direct challenge by Jesus to the authority of the religious elites. To call them "robbers" was an insult (21:13). Subsequently, Jesus healed the blind and the lame who came to him "in the temple" (21:14). Not only was the healing a characteristic of the messianic age, these people were kept out of the temple due to their imperfections. They now had full access. Finally, when children use a messianic title (son of David) with their hosannas, the elites react. The chief priests and scribes raise questions; Jesus retorts by quoting Psalm 8. Although Jesus retreats to Bethany for the evening, the stage is set for greater controversy.

In a series of clashes, Jesus confronts and silences all opposition: chief priests and elders (21:23), chief priests and Pharisees (21:45), Pharisees and Herodians (22:15–16), Sadducees (22:23), even a specialist in the Torah (22:35). Jesus does so with actions (such as, the cursing of the fig tree), sharp questions (about the baptism of John, taxes, and the identity of the Messiah), scriptural quotations, and parables (the Two Sons, the Tenants, and the Wedding Feast) told against them. In each case, Jesus displays mastery of the Scriptures, expertise in argument, and the ability to trap those who try to entrap him. His honor increases; his opponents are put to shame—silenced on their own turf before the crowds (22:46).

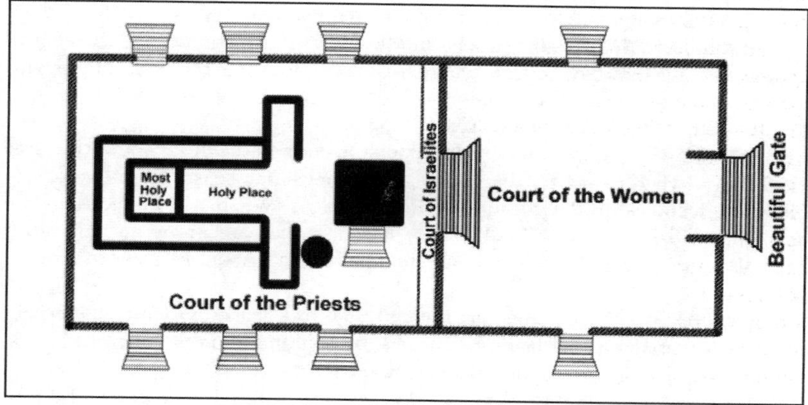

Each of the stories in this block of material is best understood within the context of controversy. The debate over paying taxes (22:15–22) is a typical example. The famous dictum, "Render to Caesar the things that are Caesar's and to God the things that are God's" (22:21), has little to do with duty to God and country. In the midst of a fierce controversy, representatives of two extremes (the Pharisees, representing a pious and observant Judaism, and the Herodians, representing secularized supporters of Rome) attempt to trap Jesus. If Jesus sides with Torah and temple, the authority of Rome can be brought against him. If Jesus sides with Caesar, the Pharisees could turn the pious faithful against Jesus, especially in the season of Passover, with its message of deliverance from oppressors.

At a moment of high drama within the courts of the temple, Jesus asks to see the coin for the tax. One of the challengers, likely a Herodian, produced a denarius. It would be struck with the image of Tiberius Caesar and the inscription, "Tiberius Caesar, son of the divine Augustus." When coming to the temple, devout Jews exchanged their Roman money for a type of shekel that lacked such an image. To bring such an image into the temple on a coin, especially at a politically charged festival, would shock the crowd. Just a few years earlier, Pontius Pilate provoked a violent confrontation by bringing images of the same emperor attached to his military standards into Jerusalem (Josephus, *Antiquities* 18.3.1). By producing a denarius, those attacking Jesus were defiling the temple! The offended crowd would have rioted against Pharisee and Herodian together, had not Jesus defused the moment with the words, "Render to Caesar … to God …" In this round of the conflict, Jesus is the winner; and the accusers withdraw.

Following the confrontations in the temple, Jesus denounced the religious elites and the city of Jerusalem (chapter 23). The rhetoric is fierce and unrelenting in a seven-part cycle, a symbolic number for completeness. The elites are condemned for words without actions and actions done from sinful motives. The speech echoes language from the charges of hypocrisy raised against Jesus during his ministry. It functions as an antithesis to the Beatitudes. After such a speech, we readers have every reason to expect that the religious elites will strike out against Jesus whose claim in verse 39 accords with Matthew's presentation of him as the Messiah and Son of God.

24:1–25:46 The fifth major sermonic collection in the gospel addresses eschatology—what happens at the close of the age. In one sense, these two chapters are a response to the question of the disciples, "When will these things be and what will be the sign?" (24:3) But placed as they are in the narrative just prior to Jesus' passion, they anticipate the final conflict about to occur in Jerusalem.

For those wishing to calculate the end time or at least to identify its onset, the sermonic material is frustrating. Instead of pointing to one sign, Jesus draws on common Jewish apocalyptic themes. **Apocalyptic** refers to a genre of literature that flourished roughly from 250 B.C. to A.D. 250. Using visions, symbolism, other-worldly creatures, cosmic struggles, violent imagery, and numeric codes, apocalyptic literature is a revelation or disclosure of what will happen at the end. Early forms exist in the books of Ezekiel, Zechariah, and Daniel. It is common in Second Temple literature. The classic Christian example is the book of Revelation.

Jesus warns of the signs of the end of the age, cites the abomination of desolation spoken of by Daniel (24:15) and announces the appearance of the Son of Man coming on the clouds. This sequence seems near (24:34), yet its time is unknown (24:36). The obscurity and imprecision of the imagery allows Jesus to direct his followers away from their specific speculation to his call for readiness and preparation.

That call for readiness is illustrated by three parables: the Ten Virgins, the Talents, and the Sheep and Goats. The first parable advocates watchfulness, and the second sharpens the judgment motif. In the third all are tested by a common standard reminiscent of the teaching of the Sermon on the Mount and quite different from the behavior of the religious elites whom Jesus attacked in chapter

24. The impending end calls for faithfulness, watchfulness, and preparation, not speculation. Jesus himself would soon be a living example of this call.

Often these parables are interpreted in a moralistic way, implying that divine judgment is based solely on our actions. Instead of being one who acts on our behalf to rescue and save, Jesus is reduced to a mere exemplar of faithfulness that we must try and imitate. Good news seems lacking in such interpretations. However, in each of these parables as Matthew recounts them, there is good news along with the call for watchfulness—an indicator that God's judgment is one of acceptance.

The first parable tells of ten virgins awaiting a bridegroom. If acceptance to the banquet were solely based on preparation, then those who get in are those who are selfish and do not share. Those who lack are lost. But these results are inconsistent with other teachings of Jesus recounted by Matthew (5:42). On the other hand, perhaps the five are called foolish for believing they had to go and buy more oil, rather than trusting that the bridegroom would welcome them even if their oil ran out. In the parable of the Talents, each is entrusted with a gift. As a talent is roughly equivalent to what one would earn in a lifetime, one was given enough for five lifetimes, another for two, and another for one. The question then becomes, "What are you going to do now that you don't have to do anything?" As to the separation of sheep from goats, those who tend flocks in the Middle East always mix goats with sheep because goats are intelligent. Goats will not run into a road in front of a truck. Sheep are simply followers. Goats do the right thing. The ones who should be at the "right hand" are the goats!

These parables do call on us to be prepared and watchful, to live an ethic concerned about the least. But God's ultimate judgment is one of acceptance—an acceptance that makes such faithfulness on our part possible and forgives us when we fail.

26:1–4 The narrative of Matthew's Gospel has marched relentlessly to this point. The final act of the conflict between Jesus and the religious leaders commences. Jesus speaks again of his impending crucifixion (26:2). The authorities, led by the high priest Caiaphas, plot the death of Jesus (26:4).

26:6–75 Matthew's narrative of what the church calls Holy Thursday follows the same sequence of stories as are recounted by Mark and Luke. Jesus is anointed in Bethany. Judas joins the plot. The disciples prepare and eat the Passover. Matthew alone makes reference to the thirty pieces of silver (26:15) and notes an exchange between Jesus and Judas in the upper room about his impending betrayal (26:25). Later Matthew will detail the suicide of Judas (27:3–10) and interpret it as a fulfillment of the prophecy of Jeremiah, although the words that Matthew quotes come from Zechariah (27:9). Jesus prays and is arrested at Gethsemane. When Peter cuts off the ear of the servant of the high priest, Matthew recounts more of the rebuke. Noteworthy is a reference to the Scriptures being fulfilled—a Matthean theme (26:54).

A religious trial takes place before Caiaphas. Again, Matthew is the writer who makes note of Caiaphas' name (26:57). At the trial's decisive moment,

Caiaphas challenges Jesus' identity as "the Christ, the Son of God" (26:63). An affirmative and defiant response from Jesus seals his fate. Matthew, having been reticent in the early part of his work to use the word "God," translates directly the implication of the question put to Jesus. The charge is the truth Matthew has been stating—Jesus is the Messiah and the Son of God. Only Matthew relates the use of the messianic title in the subsequent mockery of Jesus (26:68). Peter's public denial of any knowledge of Jesus provides the stunning contrast of a faithless disciple.

27:1–66 As foreshadowed in Matthew 2, Roman political authority, the Jerusalem religious hierarchy, and people from the city would together bring about the death of Jesus. For a Roman prefect, Pilate is a weak character in Matthew's telling. He is amazed that Jesus gives no answer to his questions (27:14), gives ear to a report of his wife's dream while sitting on the judgment seat (27:19), and, when a riot begins, washes his hands of the affair (27:24). So weak is Pilate that he can be bought off by those who wish to cover up the report of the guard after the resurrection (28:14). Nevertheless, Pilate is still the one responsible for the death of Jesus. Pilate gives the order for the execution (27:26).

Model of Herod's Palace – Trial before Pilate

The chief priests and elders are Jesus' prime opponents and the key instigators of his execution. They gather at first light and send his capital case to Pilate (27:1–2). They are merciless with Judas (27:4). They are the accusers before Pilate (27:12). They convince the crowd to ask for Barabbas instead of Jesus (27:20). Along with the scribes, they mock Jesus while he dies (27:41–43). With the Pharisees they set a guard at the tomb (27:62–66), and they spread disinformation about the resurrection (28:11–15).

In an infamous scene, the crowds present at the trial also assume responsibility for the execution of Jesus, "His blood be on us and on our children" (27:25). Much to the shame of future and present generations of Christians, this verse has been the basis for unspeakable violence against Jews, as if the whole Jewish race were responsible for the death of Jesus. But theologically, we all are responsible. We put Jesus on the cross. To quote from Isaiah, "Surely he has born *our* sins and carried *our* sorrows … He was wounded for *our* transgressions" (Isaiah 53:4–5). To blame a particular race for the death of Jesus is simply wrong. Therefore, anti-Semitism is a crime which we Christians must oppose and against which we must be on guard. Matthew is hardly anti-Semitic, for he, like Jesus, was a Jew and gives a most Jewish presentation of Jesus.

Throughout the gospel, Matthew has identified Jesus as the Messiah, the Son of God. That identity is at stake in the trial and execution of Jesus. Pilate asks, "Are you the king of the Jews?" (27:11) Twice he recognizes that Jesus is called the Messiah (27:17, 22). The battalion mocks him as the "king of the Jews" (27:29). The same phrase occurs in the charge placed over his cross (27:37). As death approaches, the religious authorities inveigh against him using both "king of Israel" (27:42) and "Son of God" (27:43). In contrast, the centurion invokes the title "Son of God" after witnessing the death of Jesus and the attendant signs (27:54).

28:1–20 Two sending scenes complete the gospel. In the first, an angel sends two women to tell the disciples that he is risen. They are to go to Galilee where they will see him. An appearance of Jesus reinforces their commission (28:1–10). In the second sending scene, the eleven meet Jesus at a designated mountain in Galilee. They are given the task toward which Matthew has been pointing—to disciple all nations. The prophetic promise of divine presence is reassured (28:16–20). This small group from this remote locale will continue the work of Jesus, baptizing in his name and teaching his words to the end of the age.

Matthew has presented Jesus. In his opening stories, Matthew lays out this identification for his first readers and for us. In a collection of sermonic material and mighty deeds, Jesus announces the reign of God to Israel. Many question and repudiate Jesus, especially the religious elites. In Jerusalem, the controversy over Jesus' identity culminates. The religious authorities orchestrate the execution of one they believe to be a messianic pretender. But in the resurrection, Jesus' ultimate authority (remember the third temptation) as Messiah is affirmed.

Jesus in Matthew

Earlier we stated that Matthew writes a narrative Christology. The gospel is an attempt to flesh out Peter's answer to Jesus' query, "Who do you say I am?" (16:15) Christology describes who Jesus is. For the gospel writers, their narratives and their titles for Jesus are chosen to convey to their particular audience their individual portrait of Jesus. Later in the history of the church, Christology would come to refer to doctrines concerning the person and nature of Christ and discuss how Jesus could be both God and human. At the stage of the gospels, later technical terms and the debates that elicited them are only implicit. By studying individual gospels on their own terms, the Christological portraits they narrate come into focus.

Matthew's two key Christological titles are Messiah and Son of God. As noted above, the titles occur repeatedly, are illustrated by the words and deeds of Jesus, and their veracity is debated by the opponents of Jesus. Matthew's readers, most being Jewish in background, had been awaiting the Messiah. For them Matthew portrays Jesus as the one expected by the prophets, even though his messianic kingdom differed from some popular expectations. But Matthew moves from the particular of Israel to the universal of all nations. In so doing, he welcomes into the community those who neither expected nor understood the messianic hopes of Israel. For these Gentile Christians, the prophetic identification of the Messiah as God's servant and Son provided language they could grasp. Jesus is the Messiah, the Son of God. Today we are the heirs of the faith of these Gentile believers.

In Matthew's narrative, Messiah and Son of God stand in close proximity. They are together in Peter's confession (16:16), together in the accusation of Caiaphas (26:63), together in the insults of those surrounding the cross (27:40–43). But in Matthew's opening chapters, he makes the identification with power and literary flourish. Matthew selects stories that rhythmically alternate between these two titles.

The genealogy is messianic. Jesus is the son of David (1:1). But according to the next narrative—the birth narrative—Jesus is also "God with us" (1:23). The magi come from the east seeking a king whom Matthew identifies as the Messiah (2:4–6). The consequent flight to Egypt fulfills the prophecy, "Out of Egypt I called my son" (2:15). The return to Nazareth fulfills an obscure messianic prophecy (2:23); at his baptism, the voice from heaven identifies Jesus as "my beloved Son" (3:17). In the final scene of this opening section—the temptation in the wilderness—messianic tests and divine titles play off each other (4:1–11). Matthew selects these opening scenes to paint a bold portrait for his readers: Jesus is the Messiah, the Son of God. This Christology is the chief contribution of the first gospel.

For Further Discussion

1. In some ways, Matthew presents the best of the Jewish religion along with the insights of Christianity. What do you think Matthew would identify as the common threads uniting the Jewish religion and Christianity?

2. As noted above, Matthew does much to help his Jewish Christian readers reach outside of their cultural enclaves into the Graeco-Roman world. How might Matthew's insights help Christians today to reach outside of their cultural comfort zones? What issues in particular are challenges for contemporary Christians?

3. How would Matthew describe discipleship? What does it mean to "follow Jesus" according to Matthew?

4. What is the kingdom of heaven, according to Matthew? What relevance does it have for daily life?

5. In the Sermon on the Mount, Jesus instructs his followers to turn the other cheek when an enemy strikes. How practical is such teaching in an age of religious terrorism?

For Further Reading

Carter, Warren. *Matthew and Empire: Initial Explorations*. Harrisburg, PA: Trinity Press International, 2002.

Garland, David E. *Reading Matthew: A Literary and Theological Commentary on the First Gospel.* New York: Crossroad, 1993.

Keener, Craig S. *A Commentary on the Gospel of Matthew*. Grand Rapids: Eerdmans, 1999.

Kingsbury, Jack Dean. *Matthew as Story*. Minneapolis: Fortress, 1989.

Overman, J. Andrew. *Matthew's Gospel and Formative Judaism*. Minneapolis: Fortress, 1990.

James and Galatians

The Form and Function of New Testament Letters

Human beings, it seems, have a natural desire to want to know what is going on in other people's lives. As a result, we might be tempted to listen in on someone's telephone conversation or to read their email. Normally, those are improper things to do. But the New Testament gives us just such an opportunity, a chance to read other people's mail! Most of the "books" in the New Testament are actually letters or, to use an older term, epistles. Sometimes these letters were written to individuals such as Philemon or Titus. Others, like Romans and Colossians, were addressed to groups of people. While it is probable that some of these documents were originally intended for a wider audience (for example, Luke/Acts, Ephesians), most of them are, in fact, other people's mail which has been preserved for us to read.

The New Testament was written in the language of the common people (*koine* Greek). New Testament letters also utilize an outline or format common to commercial or personal letters of the day. Today, our formal written correspondence utilizes envelopes with addresses, return addresses, and postmarks. In addition, information about dates and addresses is normally included on the inside as well. Unfortunately, first century letters normally did not contain such information. As a result, we often do not know when or where a New Testament letter was written. The normal outline of letters from that era, as evidenced by the New Testament, consists of five parts. Since the chapters are divided so well, the book of Ephesians is used as an example.

- Opening – See Ephesians 1:1–2. The opening usually began with the name of the author followed by the addressees and a common greeting (for example, "A to B, Greetings!"). In the New Testament the standard greeting of the day is often given a Christian focus with words like "grace and peace."
- Thanksgiving – See Ephesians 1:3–23. Typically, the thanksgiving praised the recipient of the letter, his family, the governing authorities or the gods. When present, New Testament thanksgivings turn the focus away from people and toward God who is thanked, praised, or blessed.
- Body – See Ephesians 2–3. This is the main focus or argument of the letter. In the New Testament the body of a letter contains doctrines or teachings regarding the Christian faith.
- Exhortation – See Ephesians 4:1–6:20. This section depicts the desired response from the recipients and applications to everyday life.
- Closing – See Ephesians 6:21–24. Here we find personal greetings and final words.

The traditional Christian view of New Testament letters has emphasized their universal nature. According to this approach, these letters are essentially addressed to all Christians of all times. This understanding flows from the doctrine of inspiration discussed in chapter one. It asserts that all the letters are consistent in their theological content and application, and tends to emphasize the general, overarching truths they present. Recently, however, scholars have tended to stress the **contextual** nature of these letters. After all, they were written by a number of authors and addressed to different individuals or groups of people in a wide variety of settings and circumstances. The view of some contextualists is that the teachings and applications of these letters vary as they strive to speak to the immediate and particular context being addressed. They say that there is, therefore, no coherent theology in the New Testament as a whole or even within Paul's thirteen letters.

While some of these scholars may ignore the unity of the Scriptures, Christians tend to overlook their contextual nature. Believers often speak of what the Bible or a particular passage "says to me." The fact is that these New Testament letters were not written directly to any of us today. At least initially, they were addressed to others a long time ago, and we are engaged in reading their mail. As a result, before asking what these words say to me, I should first consider what the author intended them to mean in the context of the people to whom they were originally addressed. It is also important to recognize that these different letters spoke to different people in vastly different situations. It is unwise to overlook this, and to read flatly through the New Testament as if each "book" or letter simply followed the one preceding it like the consecutive chapters of a modern novel.

To recognize the value of both of these positions and to strike a balance between them is wise. We should take into account the situation of the addressees and how that influenced the author to write what he did to a particular setting. For example, the situation in Corinth differed considerably from the setting of Philippians. As a result, the tone and content of the letters Paul wrote to those two places are quite different. In addition, it is logical that letters addressed to congregations would have a different style than those addressed to individuals, like Philemon, or to church leaders, such as Timothy. At the same time, it is important to acknowledge the unifying role of the Holy Spirit in inspiring the words that were written. While different topics are addressed and while applications may vary some based upon these and other factors, there is an overall theological unity and consistency throughout the New Testament. At least to some degree, some of its authors were cognizant of both their contemporary setting and the more universal application of their writings. One example of this is 1 Corinthians. The letter is addressed to "the church of God that is in Corinth … together with all those who in every place call upon the name of our Lord Jesus Christ, both their Lord and ours" (1:2).

In a similar fashion, some scholars speak of understanding both what the text meant back then and what it means as applied in our day. This distinction helps us understand the meaning of New Testament letters in their original setting before applying them to our own day and lives. It also acknowledges that different cultural contexts may lead to different applications of a specific theological principle. But it should not lead us to conclude these letters somehow mean something different now than they originally did. While the contemporary or contextual application of these texts may differ, their meaning does remain consistent.

Debate over the Law in Early Christianity

In this textbook we are studying the documents of the New Testament chronologically, that is, in the order in which they were likely written. It is probable that the letter of James was one of the first, if not the first, to be composed. It is also very likely that the earliest of Paul's letters is Galatians. It is striking that both of these early letters, like Matthew's Gospel, deal heavily with the Old Testament Law and its role within the Christian community. However, at first glance James and Galatians appear to have very different responses to this issue. A few introductory comments may be helpful before we deal with these two letters individually.

A common response in the face of change today is, "We have never done it that way before!" For early Jewish Christians, that reaction was certainly understandable. It is difficult for us to overestimate the impact the coming of Jesus had upon believers who had grown up living in adherence to the Scriptures of the Old Testament. Those who accepted Jesus as the promised Messiah were in a new situation, even a new age (1 Corinthians 10:11; Hebrews 1:1). The bow-tie diagram in chapter one illustrates this new reality. Instead of being on the left side of the center point looking ahead to the coming of the promised Messiah, these early believers had moved over to the right side. The Messiah had come, God's kingdom had, in some sense, arrived, and their hopes were fulfilled. But what did this mean for how they continued to relate to the theology and practices of their Scriptures? What effect did the Messiah's coming have on over a thousand years of practices and beliefs based upon the Law or Torah of the Old Testament?

Part of the complexity in resolving this issue stems from the use of the term "law" both in a broad and narrow sense in the New Testament. In its broad sense Law represents the Hebrew word *torah* which means "revelation" or "instruction." In Jewish tradition, the **Torah** is a term for the first five books of the Old Testament (Genesis through Deuteronomy). In this broad sense, the New Testament speaks of "the Law of Moses" (Luke 24:44). Translating *torah* with the Greek word *nomos* probably indicates a focus on the laws or commands of God as the essence of those Old Testament books. God revealed the Law (Torah in broad sense) to Israel so that it would know God's laws (Torah in the narrow sense) and live in obedience to them. While a Pharisee tended to view the books of Moses in the narrow sense, the Torah contains much more than laws. There are genealogies, extensive historical narratives, promises, law codes, songs, and prophecies. At times, these are all included when the New Testament speaks about "the law" in this broad use of the term (Matthew 22:40; the second occurrence in Romans 3:21).

The New Testament also uses the Greek word *nomos* in a narrow sense to describe the commandments, rules, and regulations contained in Genesis through Deuteronomy. Paul most commonly speaks of the Law in this way (Romans 3:19; 3:20; the first occurrence in 3:21). It is comprised of the "thou shalts" and "thou shalt nots" that God wants obeyed. The Pharisees counted all these "laws" and came up with 613 "dos and "don'ts" in those five books of Moses. As a result, there are 613 laws (that is, commands) within the five-part Law (that is, the Torah) of Moses. The latter encompasses the former, but is not equal to it. As this distinction can be complicated and confusing, our textbook will usually use the term "Law" in the narrow sense. But we will indicate to the reader when we are speaking of the Torah as a whole.

The early Jewish Christians had much to wrestle with in regard to their understanding of the Law and its ongoing application. These early New Testament books present the argument in its sharpest terms. Is the Law still in force? If so, how is it intended to function and why should its commands be obeyed? Chapter two noted that, even within the Judaisms of the first century, a variety of responses were being given to questions like these.

Is obedience to the Law the means by which one is to merit God's favor and, thereby, obtain eternal life (for example, Matthew 19:16–20; Luke 10:25–29)? If so, people should strive to earn their salvation by doing the works of the Law. This view has been described as **legalism** or works righteousness. Traditionally, many Christians have identified this as the dominant view of the Law's purpose and function within first-century Judaism. Those who advocated it in the Christian community are sometimes called **Judaizers**.

However, many modern scholars have countered that this understanding of first-century Judaism is an improper caricature that is not supported by the evidence as a whole. As an example, E. P. Sanders contends that most Jews would have acknowledged that they were chosen by God as his people and saved from Egypt purely on the basis of his mercy and apart from their works. God's actions got them "in" as his covenant people. However, obedience to the Law's commands was the necessary response in order to stay in the covenant or to maintain one's place among his people. He calls this schema **covenantal nomism** (E. P. Sanders, *Paul and Palestinian Judaism*, Philadelphia: Fortress, 1977).

However, in both of these cases—for getting into God's good graces or for staying there—obedience to the Law was viewed as a necessary requirement for all of God's people. For Jewish Christians, then, all of the Law's religious and moral demands still stand. Forgiveness for disobedience, which had been provided through the sacrificial system at the temple, was now available in Jesus Christ.

Another perspective is posited by James Dunn, who suggests that the Law's commands merely served to provide cultural boundary markers for Jewish identity as God's chosen people. Regulations regarding **circumcision**, worship, religious festivals, food laws, and ritual purity did not earn or maintain God's favor. Rather, they established Israel before God and before the world as his separate and distinct people. In this regard, it is significant that the root meaning of the Hebrew word normally translated "holy" means "to be set apart." If the Law was intended to provide identity markers for God's people, the critical issues for first-century Jewish Christians were: 1) whether the Law continued to perform that function after the coming of the Messiah; and 2) to what degree, if any, the Law's commands should now be imposed on non-Jewish (that is, Gentile) believers.

Finally, passages like Matthew 5:17 and Romans 10:4 led other Christians to argue that Jesus fulfilled and, thereby, abolished all the Old Testament laws of God. As a result, they no longer apply and none of them ought to be heeded in the present messianic age. Believers were now entirely free from the Law. This position is often called **antinomianism** or **libertinism**. Those who advocated it faced questions like this: "If the Old Testament laws are no longer in force, are there, in fact, any rules or commands which God requires or expects his New Testament people to obey?" After examining James and Galatians, some concluding comments about the Law will be made.

James

Introduction

The title given to James identifies the author of the letter. This James is not the disciple in the gospels who is the son of Zebedee and the brother of John.

That disciple was killed by Herod Agrippa I around A.D. 43 (Acts 12:2). Rather, this James is the half brother of Jesus. Passages like Matthew 13:55 strongly imply that Mary and Joseph had a number of children after the virgin birth of Jesus and identify James as the oldest among them. Apparently, James was not a believer in Jesus during his earthly ministry (John 7:2–5). But this changed when Jesus appeared to him after the resurrection (1 Corinthians 15:7). How intriguing then, that this James, who was not one of the twelve disciples, rose up to be the leader of the early church in Jerusalem (Acts 15:13; 21:18). The Jewish historian Josephus (A.D. 37–c. 100) tells us that James was killed for his faith around A.D. 62.

This letter is addressed by James to "the twelve tribes in the Dispersion" (James 1:1). The term **Diaspora** comes from the Greek word used here which means "scattered." It suggests the recipients are Jewish Christians scattered around and outside of Judea. A number of factors support an early date around A.D. 45 for this letter. These include

- the apparent absence of Gentiles within the community;
- the lack of any reference to the controversy surrounding whether such non-Jews could be included in the Jewish Christian community and the basis upon which they might be accepted (see Acts 15:1–5); and
- the use of the Greek word *synagoge* (James 2:2) to refer to a gathering of Christian believers.

Structure and Theme

James covers a variety of themes, most of which relate to encouraging his readers to an active, Christian lifestyle. In 108 verses there are fifty-four imperatives urging believers to respond in some manner. A good summary of James' practical **wisdom** from God states, "But be doers of the word, and not hearers only, deceiving yourselves" (1:22). This is reminiscent of Jesus, who urges us to hear God's word *and* to do what it says (Luke 6:47; 8:21; 11:28). In fact, much of James' teaching builds upon the practical guidance found in Old Testament wisdom literature and employs images used by Jesus himself (compare James 5:2–3 and 5:12 with Matthew 6:19–20 and 5:33–37, respectively). In like manner, James asserts that following this "wisdom from above" (James 3:17) leads to joy even in trials, refuses to show partiality to the wealthy, cares for the poor, and produces the good fruits of peace and righteousness. It does all of this while waiting patiently for the Lord who "opposes the proud, but gives grace to the humble" (4:6; quoting Proverbs 3:34).

Aside from the introduction, it is difficult to outline James' letter using the structure given above. After a typical opening, James launches into his words of exhortation on various topics in fairly distinct segments. While some themes do recur, there does not seem to be a logical progression from one topic to the next. This is similar to the Old Testament book of Proverbs. The end of the letter is also very abrupt.

Key Texts

1:13–18 At the beginning of the letter, the imagery of birth is used in a brief Law/Gospel illustration that states the source of good and evil as well as the basis of the community's identity as God's people. Today, when someone does something wrong, that person may attempt to shirk responsibility by using the trite phrase, "The devil made me do it." James asserts the opposite. God is never the source of temptations to sin, for God "himself tempts no one" (James 1:13), nor can the devil force anyone to do evil. Rather, evil desires come from within the person to tempt and entice. These desires give birth to sin, which grows up and leads to death.

In light of this assertion by James, consider the petition in the Lord's Prayer, "Lead us not into temptation" (Matthew 6:13). The request should not be understood as trying to talk God out of leading us toward sinful temptations. James assures us God never does that. Rather, the Greek word *peirasmos* can also refer to times of testing or trial (for example, Abraham in Genesis 22:1; Jesus in Matthew 4:1). While these trials can come from God and serve to strengthen a believer's faith (James 1:2–4), they are not pleasant to endure, so the petition asks to avoid them.

James then describes another birth that comes through God's word of truth. By virtue of this new birth, the community has a gracious heavenly Father who gives his children "every good gift and every perfect gift" (1:17). Later, this chapter again speaks of the Father's "implanted word which is able to save your souls" (1:21). People often attempt to draw a sharp contrast between James and Paul. However, James uses many Greek terms with the same theological force as Paul does. This section is a significant example (compare Romans 7:5–6).

2:8–24 God's Law insists upon holiness, and Jesus reaffirms the requirement of perfection (Leviticus 19:2; Matthew 6:48). Based upon that criterion James-—much like Paul in Galatians—asserts, people are either law-keepers or law-breakers. Any violation of God's Law places a person under judgment just as a single pin pops a balloon. Yet James' most glorious assertion is that God's "mercy triumphs over judgment" (James 2:13). God's word of Gospel overpowers the accusations of his Law.

James 2:14–26 is the most controversial section of the letter. On the one hand, the language James uses is very similar to Paul's vocabulary in Galatians and Romans (for example, faith, works, righteousness, justified). James even quotes Genesis 15:6 in reference to Abraham to support his point just as Paul does in Galatians 3:6 and Romans 4:3. In fact, James 2:24 is the only place in the New Testament which uses the phrase "faith alone." But James rejects "faith alone" as a basis for justification and stresses that Abraham was "justified by works" (2:21)! Passages like this led Martin Luther to call James "an epistle of straw" (*Luther's Works*, vol. 35, Philadelphia: Muhlenberg, 1960, 362). On the one hand, Luther's opinion was based partly upon the place of James among the disputed books of the New Testament canon (*antilegomenon*). It also reflected the misuse of sections of James by the church in Luther's day. What exactly is James saying?

First, faith without works is dead or worthless (James 2:14, 17, 20, 26). Good works are not optional. One who claims to have faith without deeds merely possesses a head knowledge such as exhibited even by demons (2:19; compare Mark 1:24, 34). The Greek language of the New Testament is able to formulate questions in a manner that tips off the expected answer to the reader. The format of James 2:14 implies the answer, "No." Such a faith is not able to save.

Second, there is a living and active interrelationship between faith and works. James cites Abraham as his primary example (James 2:20–24). Was Abraham saved or justified before God on the basis of his works? That is not exactly what James asserts. He quotes Genesis fifteen which affirms that Abraham was credited as righteous simply because he believed in God. Abraham's relationship with God as his "friend" (2:23) was established on the basis of his faith (Genesis 15:6) long before Isaac was even born in Genesis twenty-one. The evidence of that righteousness which James cites—Abraham offering up Isaac on the altar—did not occur until many years later in Genesis twenty-two. But Abraham's faith and actions were working together. His faith showed itself by his works and, thereby, declared that righteousness outwardly (James 2:18).

Third, Abraham's faith was brought to completion, maturity or fruition by what he did (2:23). The translation "fruition" is helpful here because it recalls Jesus' words: "Make the tree good and its fruit [will be] good … ; for the tree is known by its fruit" (Matthew 12:33). Abraham was made a good tree through faith in God's promise (Genesis 15). His faith then produced good fruit which could be recognized by others (Genesis 22). James emphasizes the critical interconnection between Abraham's faith and his works. James' other Old Testament example is almost shocking—Rahab, the Canaanite prostitute from Jericho (Joshua 2). Surely, she was not righteous before God on the basis of her immoral works! But her new-found faith in Israel's God was evident in her actions which followed.

Finally, James asserts that for those with faith, good works are not simply one choice among a number of different spiritual gifts (James 2:18). Indeed, they are necessary.

3:1–12 Lest anyone think one's works are ever good enough to fulfill God's Law (James 2:8), James uses the example of the tongue to demonstrate that "we all stumble in many ways" (3:2), for "no human being can tame the tongue" (3:8). With the same tongue people bless their Lord and Father, and then curse others made in God's likeness (3:9). Words have a lot of power, both for good and for evil (for example, 3:5–6). James asserts that the tongue, like a rudder on a ship, often guides the direction of Christians' lives (3:4). In addition, people often judge others by what they say. Even God will judge teachers "with greater strictness" based upon the words of instruction they speak (3:1). With many vivid images James illustrates the significance of words and the ongoing disconnect between who God's people are and what they should and should not be saying.

4:13–18 What is life? The Old Testament book of Ecclesiastes deprecates those who seek to exist apart from a relationship with God. James similarly asserts that such a life is brief and without substance, like "a mist that appears for a little time and then vanishes" (James 4:14). Instead, James challenges the community to live life and make plans toward the future in accordance with the Lord's will.

Jesus in James

Direct references to Jesus are rare in James. After the opening verse, the terms "Jesus" and "Christ" occur only once more in the letter (2:1; Jesus is referred to as "Lord" in 5:8 and, perhaps, in other places). As a result, some might say Jesus is not prominent in James and, therefore, conclude the letter lacks value.

However, Jesus lies behind the words of this epistle in a number of ways. First of all, Jesus is the author's half brother. More importantly, the book is full of wisdom. In the Old Testament, the most prominent human teacher of wisdom was King Solomon (1 Kings 3). He is the traditional author of Song of Songs, Ecclesiastes, and many of the Proverbs. But the letter of James affirms the truth of Jesus' own words in Matthew 12:42; in Jesus, someone "greater than Solomon is here." As noted in the discussion of James' structure and theme, Jesus gave much wise instruction, and many of his words are echoed throughout James. Jesus is often associated with wisdom elsewhere in the New Testament (1 Corinthians 1:30; Colossians 2:3; see also Proverbs 8). Ultimately, he is Wisdom Incarnate, the "wisdom that comes down from above" (James 3:15). As such, Jesus "is first pure, then peaceable, gentle, open to reason, full of mercy and good fruits, impartial and sincere" (3:17). By sowing peace he has produced "a harvest of righteousness" for all who believe in him (3:18).

Galatians

Introduction

Galatians is most likely the earliest of Paul's letters, though scholars have long debated its date and specific recipients. The term "Galatia" originally referred to the region of the Gauls that is north of the areas Paul visited on his first missionary journey (Acts 13–14, A.D. 46–48). However, the cities of Pisidian Antioch, Iconium, Lystra, and Derbe had been incorporated into the Roman province of Galatia in 25 B.C. (Ward Gasque, *Sir William M. Ramsay, Archaeologist and New Testament Scholar*, Grand Rapids: Baker, 1966, 421–26). The letter "to the churches of Galatia" is most likely addressed to believers in those cities (Galatians 1:2).

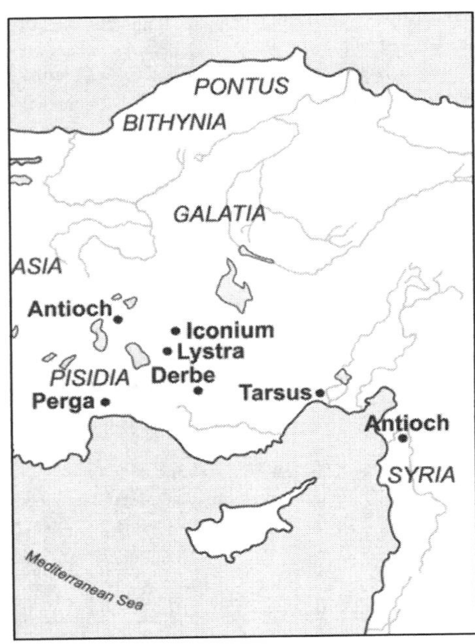

After Paul's first journey and his return to Syrian Antioch, a debate arose among the followers of Jesus about the role of the Law and, particularly, its application to Gentiles. The essence of the argument is recounted in Acts 15:1–2 and 5. Some teachers from among the believers in Jerusalem came and asserted that, in order to be saved, Gentile believers had to be circumcised and were required to follow the Law of Moses. According to the rest of Acts 15, James, Peter, and the other leaders of the church in Jerusalem rejected this teaching (Acts 15:10–11, 19). Since Paul does not appeal to the decision reached at the meeting, he most likely wrote Galatians after the debate had surfaced, but before his journey to Jerusalem. This position is called the southern Galatian theory.

Other scholars assert that the term "Galatia" referred only to areas north of those Paul visited on his first journey, that is, ethnic Galatia. This view is the northern Galatian theory. However, Acts does not record any details about Paul's activity in that region, even on his later journeys. Nevertheless, this view contends he did conduct missionary work there on his second and/or third journeys based upon references in Acts (16:6; 18:23; 19:1). He then wrote the letter afterward, sometime after A.D. 50. If so, it is odd that Paul does not refer to the decision of the Jerusalem church in Acts 15 to support the position he asserts in this letter.

In either case, Paul has clearly had a significant amount of personal interaction with the recipients of the letter. Galatians reflects an intimate relationship between author and addressees.

Structure and Theme

A careful examination of Galatians in light of the letter outline discussed above reveals that one part is missing. In fact, this is the only one of Paul's letters which does not contain all five of those sections. The missing component is the thanksgiving. Apparently, Paul is either so upset or in such a hurry to get to the heart of the matter, he omits it. Otherwise, an outline of Galatians follows:

GALATIANS	
OPENING	1:1–3
THE CRITICAL ISSUE—ANOTHER "GOSPEL"?	1:4–9
PAUL'S PERSONAL CREDENTIALS	1:10–2:21
BODY/DOCTRINE	3:1–4:31
EXHORTATION/PRACTICAL APPLICATION	5:1–6:10
CONCLUSION AND GREETINGS	6:10–14

The theme of Galatians centers on the basis of a person's relationship with God. From his own personal experience as well as through evidence from the Old Testament Scriptures, Paul asserts and defends the very heart of the Gospel. He proclaims: "A person is not justified by works of the Law, but through faith in [or "of"] Jesus Christ" (Galatians 2:16; see also Romans 3:28). In other words, he warns the Galatians that their standing before God is not and cannot be dependent upon how they live according to the Law. Rather, it is based on faith in who Jesus Christ is and what he has accomplished. The final two chapters of Galatians describe how believers live in response. They have not simply been freed *from* sin and death; they have also been freed *for* something, to serve one another in love (Galatians 5:13).

The structure of this letter introduces the three essential elements of St. Paul's theology that we will encounter repeatedly in his letters: *Law, Gospel, and response* (compare the outlines of Romans and Ephesians, below; see also the discussion of 1 Corinthians 6:9–12). The first two parts, Law and Gospel, deal with one's relationship with God. The third aspect describes how believers in Christ live in response to the good news of his grace.

Key Texts

1:6–12 Paul declares there is no other Gospel or "good news" than what he proclaimed to the Galatians. He here implies that some teachers have come and tried to convince the Galatians otherwise, as depicted in Acts 15:1–5. Both there and here Paul harshly rejects their teaching. Indeed, even if he himself were to change his tune, Paul insists he would also be condemned (1:8). The apostle sounds so confident regarding his position, as these verses explain. Paul received the Gospel directly from the source, "through a revelation of Jesus Christ" (1:12). As a result, Paul knows his message is correct; any other so-called "gospel" which deviates from it must be rejected.

> During World War II a newly commissioned officer took great pride in his assignment to captain a U.S. Navy ship. One dark night the captain saw faint lights moving in his direction. Immediately he told his signalman to send a message. "Alter your course 10 degrees to the south." He received a prompt reply. "Alter your course 10 degrees north." The captain was angered; his command had been ignored. So he sent a second message. "Alter your course 10 degrees south. I am the captain of United States Navy warship!" The response he received resolved the matter. "No, you alter your course 10 degrees north. I am the lighthouse."

Paul asserts he is the lighthouse. He knows he proclaimed the true Gospel to the Galatians because he received it from the light of the world himself, Jesus Christ (John 8:12). If any other gospel is being proclaimed, it is false. If the Galatians had listened to it, they now need to change course!

From Galatians 1:13–2:14 Paul refers to his own personal experience, his relationship with James and the Jerusalem church, and his interaction with Peter in Antioch. All of these support the authenticity of his teaching and the recognition of its validity by the "pillars" of the early church (2:9).

2:15–21 This section conveys a distinct summary of the good news Paul proclaimed. Galatians 2:15–16 lays out Law and Gospel in sharp contrast using legal terminology of the courtroom. Based upon Acts 15, it appears the teachers who visited Galatia asserted that the Gospel is a matter of *both/and.* Sure, they claimed, Gentile believers need to believe in Jesus, but they also must be circumcised and are required to obey the Law of Moses in order to be saved. Paul denounces this. It is not both/and, but *either/or*. A right relationship with God is not based upon *both* faith *and* works. Rather, one can try *either* faith *or* works in attempting to achieve a justified status before him. And any mingling of works and faith is fatal "because by works of the law no one will be justified" (2:16). In fact, "if **justification** were through the law, Christ died for no purpose" (2:21).

In verse 16 Paul says this righteousness comes "through" and then "from the **faith[fulness]** of Jesus Christ." The traditional understanding of this critical phrase is that it expresses our faith that is placed in and rests on Jesus Christ, as Paul specifically states later in verse 16. Recently, a number of scholars have espoused a different view. They suggest the phrase identifies the source of righteousness as "the faithfulness of Jesus Christ" in carrying out his mission. The christocentric focus of this interpretation is valuable and often makes good sense. Paul contends both are true. He tells the Galatians that their right standing before God is based upon Jesus' faithfulness to his Father's will to save *and* that they "also have believed in Christ Jesus" (2:16).

Paul applies both of these aspects to himself with some of his most profound words. He speaks of his relationship with God through Christ, as well as the life he lives in response. "For through the law I died to the Law, so that I might live to God. I have been crucified with Christ. It is no longer I who live, but Christ who lives in me. And the life I now live in the flesh I live by faith in the Son of God, who loved me and gave himself for me" (2:19–20).

3:6–14 To support his teaching on justification, Paul refers to Abraham, just as James did. In fact, Paul quotes the same verse from Genesis to support his argument. God counted Abraham as "righteous" because he believed (Genesis 15:6). Therefore, the same holds true for Abraham's children, who are defined by Paul in terms of faith, rather than physical lineage (Galatians 3:7). In fact, the Gospel spoken by God in Genesis 12:3 envisioned that Abraham's offspring would include Gentiles. It seeks to include those from "all nations" whom God justifies by faith, just as it was with Abraham (Galatians 3:8).

The Law, which was given 430 years later through Moses on Mount Sinai, could not and did not alter God's promises to Abraham and his **offspring/seed** (3:17). As Habakkuk 2:4 affirmed, the righteous live "by faith" (Galatians 3:11). According to Paul, God's people were never to rely on their observance of the Law as the basis of their relationship with God. Indeed, the Law itself said so! The Law requires doing (Galatians 3:12, citing Leviticus 18:5) and, unless one continually does everything written in the Law, they are cursed by it (Galatians 3:10, citing Deuteronomy 27:26). All people would be placed under God's **curse** were it not for this: Christ became "a curse for us" (Galatians 3:13). Again, the Law declared that anyone who was hung on a tree was cursed (3:13 citing Deuteronomy 21:23). On the tree of the cross, Jesus endured the consequences of that curse in the place of all those who fail to do the Law. The result is that, rather than a curse, the blessing given to Abraham now comes to those from any nation who are in Christ (Galatians 3:14).

The many references from the Old Testament cited make a point that cannot be overemphasized. In Galatians and throughout his letters Paul vehemently insists that what he writes is in no way different from what God had already spoken and promised in the Scriptures which we now call the Old Testament. We tend to separate the Old and New Testaments. Paul insists upon the unity between what he writes and what God had previously spoken. Galatians 3:6–14 supports this assertion. In addition, note the prominence of the Old Testament in sections that will not be covered here in detail (3:15–20; 4:21–31).

3:21–4:7 In these verses Paul universalizes his argument. All people are already prisoners of sin; the Law simply serves to lock them up (3:22–23). But God's purpose in declaring this truth in his Scriptures is to lead people to Christ. In verses 24–25 Paul uses the picture of a *paidagogos*, a slave who was in charge of the children of his master; he directed, led, accompanied, and disciplined the children to go where their parents wished. In line with this image, Paul may be saying that the Old Testament Scriptures lead people to Christ through the promises spoken about him to Abraham and his offspring (the Torah, or Law, in its broad sense; see 3:7–8). But here it is more likely a reference to the negative effects of the Law's commands. They set a standard of obedience which is impossible for us to fulfill due to sin. As a result, we are led to despair of our own righteousness, ability, and works, and are driven to seek a right relationship with God through faith in his promises now fulfilled in Christ (as in 3:10–12).

Verses 26–29 give clear expression to the Gospel and its impact. Paul specifically ties the relationship that believers have with God through faith to their baptism. In chapter one, we used the reference to Abraham's seed/offspring to illustrate the bow-tie diagram. Abraham's seed/offspring narrows down to a single person, "who is Christ" (3:16). But as many as are baptized into Christ now belong to Christ. They are Abraham's seed/offspring and inheritors of the promise (3:27, 29).

Here and in 3:7, Abraham's seed/offspring is not defined in terms of race or genealogy. Rather, the heirs of God's promises are those who are justified through faith in Christ Jesus (3:26). In the New Testament era, the removal of any distinction between Jew and Gentile had an enormous impact. Indeed, some would argue that Paul is radically altering the definition of who God's people are. However, Paul contends his definition is consistent with the Old Testament itself (see Romans 9–11). Paul declares that as people stand before God in Christ, there is no difference among them in terms of ethnic origin, social and economic status, or gender. At the same time, as those first-century Christians in Galatia lived out their lives, from a worldly point of view they continued to be either Jew or Greek, slave or free, male or female. As such, their roles in life varied. Yet for all those in Christ, these distinctions are without any ultimate difference. Paul declares that all who belong to Christ have the same value, essence, or worth in God's sight.

A young child lived under the *paidagogos* and the rules established by his father until the time when the father allowed the heir to actually live out what he always was by birth. Paul tells the Galatians that they also lived in slavery until the time set by the heavenly Father arrived. Then he "sent forth his Son, born of woman, born under the Law, to **redeem** those who were under the Law" (4:4–5). Earlier Paul said Christ passively suffered the curse resulting from disobedience of the Law while on the tree of the cross (3:13). Here Paul stresses that Christ also actively lived in obedience "under the law" and so fulfilled its requirements for all people. In this way people are redeemed, bought back, and brought back to God.

By virtue of their adoption as God's sons, the Galatian Christians are no longer slaves to sin and the Law (3:25–26; 4:3–4). Some people may think Paul's use of the term "sons" rather than "sons and daughters" or "children" sounds sexist. However, in Paul's culture the heir was normally the firstborn son. As a result, Paul brings all those who belong to God's Son, whether Jew or Greek, slave or free, male or female, into the position of those who have inherited an equal place in God's family and kingdom. The fact that the Father sent the Spirit of his Son into their hearts assures them that they have the same relationship with God as Jesus Christ (4:6).

5:1, 13–26; 6:1–2 The preceding section leads into these words: "For freedom Christ has set us free" (5:1). The false teachers in Galatia were demanding that these early Christians submit to the burden of circumcision and, thereby, the obligation to obey the entire Law (5:3). Paul warns the Galatians that the consequences of bringing the Law back into the equation of justification are harsh. "You are severed from Christ … ; you have fallen away from grace" (5:4). Yet, in this very context, Paul also declares that in Christ Jesus neither circumcision nor uncircumcision matters (5:6; restated in 6:15). So which is it?

The crucial point involves understanding what equation he is talking about. Acts 15:1 states: "But some men came down from Judea and were teaching the brothers, 'Unless you are circumcised according to the custom of Moses, you cannot be saved.'" If circumcision and the resulting obligation to obey the Law are brought into the equation of salvation and the basis of a relationship with God, they must be rejected in the harshest of terms (Galatians 5:12). But once that relationship is established on the basis of faith, there is great freedom in regard to circumcision, the Law, and all other areas of life. The question Paul now addresses concerns how this freedom in Christ should be expressed.

> Picture entering a university class in which there was a total of seven hundred possible points. In order to pass the class you had to earn all seven hundred, a perfect score on everything, 100 percent all the time. Imagine that on the first day of class, the professor announced that everyone in the class was given seven hundred points. Unless you dropped the course, nothing could or would change your grade. How would you act the rest of the semester? Would you go to class or do the assignments or study for the exams? Perhaps not. This may be wishful thinking on the part of a professor, but maybe you would say something like this: "I am a 'seven hundred-point, straight A' student because of this professor's gift. So, yes, I am free to do whatever I want. All the pressure is off. But out of my gratitude for that gift, I am going to act like a 'straight A' student the rest of the semester. 'Straight A' students attend class, do their homework and study hard for exams. That's what I am going to do, not to prove anything, not to earn anything, but just because that's who I am by grace, 'a seven hundred-point, straight A' student.

Paul tells the Galatians that God deals with people in a similar way. Thus far in this letter, he has declared that we are justified through faith in Christ, redeemed from slavery to sin, baptized into Christ and brought into God's family where we have the full rights of sons. All of this was accomplished by God in Christ. Beginning in Galatians 5:13, Paul describes the resulting God-given freedom. Freedom in Christ is not a license to indulge the sinful nature. We who have been baptized into Christ and received the Holy Spirit still have a sinful nature. Even in us, the Spirit and the sinful nature "are opposed to each other, to keep you from doing the things you want to do" (5:17). The sinful nature pulls us toward the acts described in verses 19–21. Note the presence of some culturally "acceptable" vices like jealousy, selfish ambition and envy. If we are engaging in those kinds of things, the sinful nature is at work.

But the fruit of the Spirit is "love, joy, peace, patience, kindness, goodness, faithfulness, gentleness and self-control" (5:22). Christian freedom exhibits itself through such fruit. Christ not only freed believers *from* slavery to sin, the Law, and death, he also freed us *for* something. Paul urges the Galatians to use their freedom "through love [to] serve one another" (5:13).

"The law of Christ" in 6:2 probably refers to Jesus' "new" commandment "that you love one another just as I have loved you" (John 15:12, 17). Yet Paul says the most extraordinary thing about this commandment. It is not contrary to the Law; it does not displace the Law. Instead, "the whole law is fulfilled in one word, 'You shall love your neighbor as yourself'" (Galatians 5:14, citing Leviticus 19:18). Paul calls the Galatians to use their freedom to love, and love is what the Law is all about. The key question then is, "Why?" Do they have to obey the Law in order to be right with God and acceptable to him? No. They cannot and are not supposed to obey the Law in order to earn this freedom by their works. Rather, it is because they have already been justified through faith in Christ and set free. As a result, they "get to" serve one another in love and, in so doing, end up fulfilling the Law after all.

6:11–18 Since this is the first of Paul's letters covered here, it is helpful to note a few things in his closing.

- It is likely that Paul did not actually write his letters. Rather, an **amanuensis**, a type of scribe or secretary, wrote the letter as Paul dictated it (for example, Tertius in Romans 16:22). At the end of Galatians, Paul picks up the pen himself to write the conclusion in his own hand (Galatians 6:11).
- Paul used to boast about his zeal for the Law and "the traditions of my fathers" (1:13–14). Now he declares, "But far be it from me to boast except in the cross of our Lord Jesus Christ" (6:14).
- Paul prays for peace and mercy upon all who follow his teaching and "upon the Israel of God" (6:16). This phrase describes those who are Abraham's seed and inheritors of God's promise. Based upon what Paul has written in Galatians, "the Israel of God" may now refer to those who are in Christ Jesus.
- Every one of Paul's letters begins and ends with a reference to God's grace. Even this hotly written letter to the Galatians is no exception (1:3; 6:18).

Jesus in Galatians

As Paul lays out and defends the basic Gospel he proclaims, Jesus stands at the very forefront of this letter. Jesus reveals the Gospel to his people in person, through his messengers, and by his Spirit (1:6, 12; 3:5–6). The essence of the good news is that Christ, the promised seed of Abraham, became "a curse for us" on the cross (3:1, 13, 16). As a result of his faithfulness, a right relationship with God is possible for all those who believe. In other words, Jesus is the one who justifies us through faith (2:15–21). As many as are baptized into Christ are also adopted into the family of God's Son, where we live in and through Christ

(2:20; 3:26–39; 4:4–5). In all this, Jesus is the great liberator. He has freed us from the curse of sin and the Law (4:23–25), and freed us to love and serve each other (5:1, 13).

Debate Over the Law in Early Christianity Resolved?

Faith and Works

Many people have concluded that the words of James and Paul about obedience to the Law contradict one another. Others have tried to reconcile the statements of James and Paul regarding the Law in a variety of different ways. It is probably best to acknowledge there is a tension between the two, but not one that is mutually contradictory. What follows are ways that explain the relationship between faith and works as espoused by Jesus, James and Paul:

1) In introducing New Testament letters, we discussed that one should be aware of both the overarching truths consistently present throughout the inspired word of God and the contextual nature of the individual letters. There is probably no better example than to compare the context of James with that of Galatians. James speaks to those who have been Christians for some time. They have grown lazy in their faith and are not putting it to work for the praise of God and the benefit of others. James challenges this view of cheap grace and warns his readers about its severe consequences. His diagnosis is that faith without works is dead and, therefore, cannot save (James 2:14, 17, 26). Instead, the faith they have as a result of their new birth from above (1:17–18) needs to be integrated into the horizontal relationships they have with others as they live out God's very practical "wisdom from above" (3:17).

Paul, on the other hand, addresses believers at a very different stage of development. These new Gentile converts are struggling with their vertical relationship with God. Apparently, they have adopted or are being coerced to accept the assertion that their works are necessary as a requirement for justification before God. Perhaps they have become convinced that circumcision, Sabbath worship, the observance of food laws, and other regulations are necessary markers in order to establish their identity before God and/or for acceptance into the community of his people.

In response to such notions, Paul writes Galatians to stress the vertical dimension of the Christian life, justification before God through faith in Christ. It is not at all based upon "works of the Law" (Galatians 2:16; 3:5). By that phrase Paul refers to works done in obedience to the Torah's commands that, in some way, affect a person's relationship with God. It is significant that James never uses the phrase "the words of the Law" as he urges the community to practical Christian living.

Because James and Paul are writing to different people in different contexts facing radically different challenges, they do say different things. But this does not mean they contradict each another. In fact, there are significant points of commonality. James makes the basis of identity as God's children clear at the beginning of his letter (1:17–18). Paul addresses the topic that James emphasizes, the significance of living out one's faith in relationships with other people (Galatians 5:13–6:10; this is called the doctrine of **sanctification**).

2) Paul certainly stresses that the basis of a person's relationship with God is a matter of faith or works. Those who asserted the necessity of faith *and* works for attaining salvation and/or a righteousness before God are teaching "a different gospel" which must be rejected. However, in the whole of Galatians, Paul speaks both about justifying faith *and* about works of love done in response. In Galatians 2–4 Paul contends that in justification, faith in Christ is the only thing that counts. Yet in Galatians 5 and 6 Paul acknowledges that justification is not the only thing! The manner in which believers live out their lives as Christ's freed people is also of great importance. Paul himself asserts that in Christ Jesus the only thing that counts for anything is "faith working through love" (Galatians 5:6). James would certainly agree.

Paul emphasizes faith, *then* works. James stresses the necessity of a faith *that* works. Paul asserts that faith in Christ alone saves and justifies totally apart from works. James would respond, "True enough. But faith is never alone!"

3) "Make the tree good and its fruit [will be] good" (Matthew 12:33). The analogy of a tree and its fruit, used by Jesus in Matthew 7 and 12, fits both letters. Paul speaks more about how God declares believers to be "good trees" in Christ. James stresses that, unless something is seriously wrong, good trees will produce good fruit. James 3:17–18 uses the language of "good fruit" to describe "the wisdom that comes from above." His list resembles the lifestyle Jesus depicts in the Beatitudes (Matthew 5:1–12) and corresponds closely to "the fruit of the Spirit" named by Paul in Galatians 5:22–23. Both James and Paul contend that this good fruit is aligned with and is an expression of the good works described in God's Law (James 1:25; 2:8; Galatians 5:13–14, 23).

The Law in the Old Testament

Israel's relationship with God was never intended to be based upon their works of the Law. In Galatians 3, as discussed above, Paul repeatedly uses passages from the Law itself to make this point. James quotes God's declaration that Abraham's faith was credited to him as righteousness in Genesis 15 many years before Abraham demonstrated that righteousness by the work of offering up Isaac (James 2:21–24; see also Genesis 22). In a similar temporal argument, Paul points out that God's promises to Abraham were granted long before the Law was even revealed on Mount Sinai. As a result, the Law could not set aside or nullify what God promised to Abraham (Galatians 3:15–18). The fulfillment of that promise, therefore, was not in any way dependent upon Israel's obedience to the Law (Romans 4:13–16).

Even for those Israelites who received the Law at Sinai, their obedience to its commands was not intended to be the basis of their relationship with God. To illustrate, God did not give his laws to helpless slaves in Egypt and say, "If you keep these commandments, I will deliver you from slavery." On the contrary, because of the promises God had spoken to Abraham (Exodus 6:2–8), God rescued the Israelites in the Exodus by his own might and power. Only afterward did God give Israel the Law on Mount Sinai (Exodus 20–24). The most famous part of the Law is called the **Ten Commandments**. Yet the Old Testament never calls them the "Ten Commandments," only the "Ten Words" (the meaning of *Decalogue* in Greek; Exodus 34:28; Deuteronomy 4:13; 10:4). In fact, according to Old Testament, the first word was not even a command. Instead it simply reaffirmed these words of Gospel to Israel: "I am Yahweh, your God, who brought you out of the Egypt, out of the land of slavery" (Exodus 20:2; compare Deuteronomy 5:6). The other nine "Words," and all the commandments which followed, expressed how they could live faithfully in response to the God who saved them from Egypt and in a loving relationship with one another. As people liberated by God, they were now free to live within the boundaries established by the Law (compare James 1:25; 2:12; Galatians 5:1, 13). Passages such as Deuteronomy 9 served to remind Israel that God did not choose them or bring them to the promised land because of their righteousness.

The Law in the New Testament

Are the Old Testament commandments still in force in the New Testament or not? In terms of establishing a right relationship with God, the answer was always "No." Because of our sinful nature, James and Paul contend that no one is able to keep the Law (James 2:10; 3:2; Romans 3:9, 23; Galatians 3:10). As a result, the Law has always had a negative effect. Paul says the Law "was added on account of transgressions" (Galatians 3:19); the Law makes people conscious of sin (Romans 3:20), brings wrath (Romans 4:15), increases trespasses (Romans 5:20), and locks up the whole world as a prisoner of sin (Galatians 3:22–23). While the Law is powerless to overcome human's sinful nature (Romans 8:3), these negative consequences are not the Law's fault, and they do not make the Law evil. Rather, they are intended to lead people to Christ (Galatians 3:24).

Since no one is able to obey the Law perfectly, the most severe problems with the Law occur whenever it is brought into the arena of justification—when it becomes a factor in establishing or maintaining a relationship with God. This was just as much an issue for "Old Testament" Israel as it was for the Galatians in the first century, and as it is for Christians today. A righteous standing before God has always been attained through faith in his gracious promise now fulfilled in Jesus Christ. Bringing "works of the Law" into the "righteousness" arena is like trying to use the rules of football to play basketball on a basketball court with basketball equipment. Those rules just do not belong in that arena and will not work there. Yet, that is what happens whenever obedience to the Law is used to try to establish or maintain a righteous standing before God. Although some Pharisees in Jesus' day, the false teachers in Galatia, and legalists throughout time have all advocated this use of God's Law, it is a misuse and misapplication of it.

The New Testament announces that the Law's demands have all been fulfilled by Christ. Jesus himself says he came "to fulfill" the Law and the Prophets (Matthew 5:17). He "became under the Law in order that he might redeem those who were under the Law" (Galatians 4:5). He also endured all the punishment which disobedience of the Law rightly deserves by "becoming a curse in our behalf" (Galatians 3:13). In this sense, Christ is the end, goal, or fulfillment of the Law (Romans 10:4).

In addition, the New Testament declares that the person and work of Jesus Christ make at least some of the Old Testament laws obsolete (Hebrews 8:13). For example, since Christ was sacrificed once for all, there is no need for further sacrifices (Romans 6:10; Hebrews 10:10, 12, 18). Christ embodied and fulfilled in himself the role of priest and temple (Hebrews 4:14; John 2:21). Jesus also freed his people from rigid Sabbath day rules (Matthew 12:1–8) and regulations about clean and unclean foods contained in the Law (Mark 7:19; Acts 10:15). Other laws were relevant to the political, military, and social nature of God's Old Testament people as the nation of Israel. Since the New Testament church no longer has a specific national identity, those commands no longer apply.

But, apart from such instances, the New Testament does not abolish or get rid of the Law. Jesus declares just the opposite. "Until heaven and earth pass away, not an iota, not a dot, will pass from the Law until all is accomplished" (Matthew 5:18). Is the Law, then, still an expression of God's will for believers in Christ? In Romans Paul describes the Law as "the embodiment of knowledge and truth" (2:20). Later he asserts, "The law is holy, and the commandment is holy and righteous and good" (Romans 7:12). In Matthew 22:37–40 Jesus says all the Law and the Prophets hang together in these two commandments: "You shall love the Lord your God with all your heart and with all your soul and with all your mind" (Deuteronomy 6:5) and "You shall love your neighbor as yourself" (Leviticus 19:18; compare Luke 10:25–28). Jesus also calls his disciples to love one another (John 15:12, 17). Paul says the command to "love your neighbor" fulfills the Law and then calls believers to "fulfill the law of Christ" (Galatians 5:14; 6:2). In summary, Romans 13:10 states, "Love is the fulfilling of the law."

Christians are called to love God and to love one another; the Law continues to inform their mind and will about the ways in which this love can be expressed. In this sense, they can join Paul in saying, "I delight in the law of God" (Romans 7:22). In response to God's promised goodness to Israel of old and to the whole world in Christ, the Law shows his people how to live in ways pleasing to him. In its proper arena of sanctification, God's Law continues to point out how Christians can and should love him and one another. This is what Jesus, Paul, and James all affirm.

For Further Discussion

1. Compare the format of letters in our day with the typical outline of New Testament letters.

2. Have you resolved the tension between faith and works? Is faith apart from works really dead as James asserts (James 2:14–17)? How does James support his position from the Old Testament (2:18–23)? Is "faith alone" really worthless (2:24)?

3. James' letter only mentions Jesus a few times, while Paul's letter to the Galatians is full of references to Jesus Christ. Why do you think this is so?

4. Paul writes with such certainty and authority. How can he be so certain his view is correct?

5. If you were a student in a class which was given all the possible points on the first day of class, how would you act the rest of the semester? Is this a fair comparison with the way God treats us in Jesus Christ?

6. Do you believe that circumcision was worth fighting over in the context of Galatians? Explain why or why not. Are any contemporary issues similar?

7. Is God's Law good or bad? Answer in terms of its source, content, and effect(s).

8. Which does the Christian church today need to hear more, the message of James or Galatians? Why? What about yourself personally? Which do you need to hear more?

9. Which is a greater danger among Christians today: legalism or libertinism? Why? What is the proper response to each?

For Further Reading

James

Johnson, Luke Timothy. *Brother of Jesus, Friend of God: Studies in the Letter of James*. Grand Rapids: Eerdmans, 2004.

Martin, Ralph P. *James*. Word Biblical Commentary. Waco, TX: Word, 1988.

Maynard-Reid, Pedrito. *Poverty and Wealth in James*. Maryknoll, NY: Orbis, 1987.

Moo, Douglas. *The Letter of James*. Tyndale New Testament Commentaries. Grand Rapids: Eerdmans, 1987.

Scaer, David. *James, The Apostle of Faith: A Primary Christological Epistle for the Persecuted Church*. St. Louis: Concordia: 1983.

Stulac, James. *The Letter of James*. Downers Grove, IL: InterVarsity, 1993.

General Works on Paul

Barclay, William. *The Mind of St. Paul*. San Francisco, Harper Collins, 1986.

Bruce, F. F. *Paul: Apostle of the Heart Set Free*. Grand Rapids, Eerdmans, 1977.

Donfried, Karl P., and I. Howard Marshall. *The Theology of the Shorter Pauline Epistles*. Cambridge: Cambridge University Press, 1993.

Dunn, James D. G. *The Theology of Paul the Apostle*. Grand Rapids: Eerdmans, 1998.

Furnish, Victor Paul. *Theology and Ethics in Paul*. Nashville: Abingdon, 1968.

Hawthorne, Gerald, Ralph P. Martin and Daniel Reid, eds. *Dictionary of Paul and His Letters*. Downers Grove, IL: InterVarsity, 1993.

Moe, Olaf. *The Apostle Paul*. 2 vols. Translated by L.A. Vigness. Minneapolis: Augsburg, 1954.

Pate, C. Marvin. *The End of the Age Has Come: The Theology of Paul*. Grand Rapids: Zondervan, 1995.

Ramsay, William M. *St. Paul: The Traveller and the Roman Citizen*. 3rd ed. Grand Rapids: Baker, 1962.

Schreiner, Thomas. *Interpreting the Pauline Epistles*. Grand Rapids: Baker, 1990.

Galatians

Cole, R. Alan. *The Letter of Paul to the Galatians*. Tyndale New Testament Commentaries. Grand Rapids: Eerdmans, 1989.

Gieschen, Charles., ed. *The Law in Holy Scripture*. St. Louis: Concordia, 2004.

Das, A. Andrew. *Paul, the Law and the Covenant*. Peabody, MA: Hendrickson, 2001.

Dunn, James D. G. *The Theology of Paul's Letter to the Galatians*. Cambridge: Cambridge University, 1993.

Hanson, G. Walter. *Galatians*. The IVP New Testament Commentary Series. Downers Grove, IL: InterVarsity, 1994.

Kim, Seyoon. *Paul and the New Perspective: Second Thoughts on the Origin of Paul's Gospel*. Grand Rapids: Eerdmans, 1992.

Luther, Martin. *Lectures on Galatians*. Edited and translated by Jaroslav Pelikan. Vol. 26–27 of *Luther's Works*. St. Louis: Concordia, 1962–63.

Panning, Armin. *Galatians/Ephesians*. People's Bible Commentary. St. Louis: Concordia, 1997.

Sanders, E. P. *Paul and Palestinian Judaism*. Philadelphia: Fortress, 1977.

Schreiner, Thomas. *The Law and Its Fulfillment*. Grand Rapids: Baker, 1993.

Stott, John. *Only One Way: The Message of Galatians*. The Bible Speaks Today. Downers Grove, IL: InterVarsity, 1992.

1 and 2 Thessalonians

Introduction: Placing the Letters in Paul's Second Missionary Journey

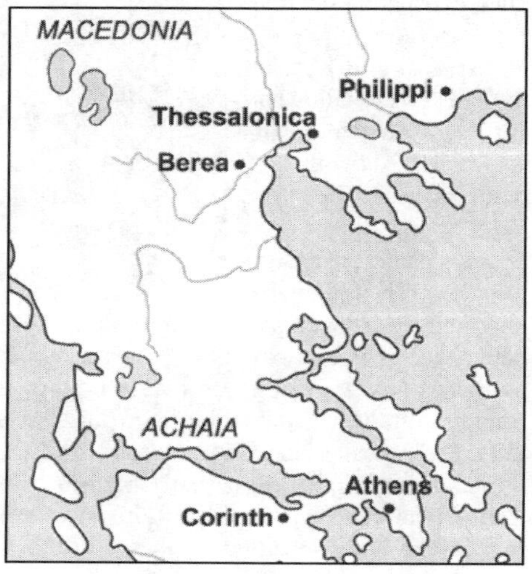

Chapter three overviewed the spread of Christianity from Jerusalem to Rome. On his first missionary journey, Paul visited Cyprus and Asia Minor in present-day Turkey (Acts 13–14). Then he wrote Galatians back to those believers and met with the leaders of the church in Jerusalem (Acts 15). Under the prompting of the Holy Spirit, he continued moving further west during his second missionary journey (Acts 16:9). In fact, he made a dramatic continental shift when he crossed from Asia Minor into the Greek provinces of Macedonia and Achaia. After his momentous visit to Philippi, Paul, along with his missionary team of Silas and Timothy, arrived in the commercial trade center of Thessalonica. The city was located on a significant trade route called the ***Via Egnatia*** and remains an important seaport to this day. The estimated population in the first century was 200,000.

Paul began, as usual, in the Jewish synagogue. He used the Old Testament to demonstrate "that it was necessary for the Christ to suffer and to rise from the dead" (Acts 17:3). He then concluded, "This Jesus, whom I proclaim to you, is the Christ" (17:3). Paul received the typical mixed reaction. Some Jews and Greeks believed Jesus was the promised Christ/Messiah. Other Jews responded violently against Paul and his message. As a result, after three short weeks the believers in Thessalonica sent Paul and Silas away to Berea. After some time in Berea, the Jews who opposed Paul in Thessalonica came there also. Fearing for his safety, the believers then sent Paul further away and on to Athens. When Timothy rejoined Paul, Paul sent him back to Thessalonica to check on the believers there (1 Thessalonians 3:1–2). Paul then moved on to Corinth where he stayed for at least eighteen months (Acts 18:11). There he received a positive report from Timothy and sent 1 Thessalonians from himself, Silas and Timothy back to them around A.D. 51. After hearing further reports and about some confusion among the Thessalonians, Paul and his team sent 2 Thessalonians from Corinth in A.D. 51 or 52.

Structure and Theme

The Parthenon on the Acropolis in Athens

Both 1 and 2 Thessalonians follow the letter structure introduced earlier. After the opening greetings and an expression of thanks to God (1 Thessalonians 1:1–2), 1 Thessalonians basically deals with two main issues. The first half of the letter recounts Paul's ministry to the Thessalonians and their positive response to it in spite of severe opposition and Paul's sudden departure (1 Thessalonians 1–3). At the beginning of 1 Thessalonians 4, Paul addresses how they ought to live in light of the coming of the Lord. Issues surrounding the **Parousia** or the return of Christ then dominate the last half of the letter (1 Thessalonians 4–5).

2 Thessalonians essentially revisits the topic of the second coming of Christ. The first two chapters of this brief letter strive to correct misunderstandings which have unsettled or alarmed the believers (2 Thessalonians 2:2). Paul

concludes by again encouraging them to live godly lives, to pray for Paul, and to avoid those who are idle.

1 Thessalonians	
Greeting	1:1–2
Explanation of Departure	1:3–3:13
Living in Anticipation of Jesus' Return	4:1–5:28
2 Thessalonians	
Misunderstandings	1:1–2:17
Exhortation to a Godly Life	3:1–18

In these two short letters, Paul covers two major themes. First, he expresses gratitude to God for the Thessalonians positive response to the Gospel and their continuing faithfulness in spite of Paul's absence and in the midst of trials. In short, God's messengers and his message met with success! Second, Paul encourages them to conduct their lives in a godly, responsible manner while waiting for the glorious return of Christ. He goes into quite a bit of detail concerning what will happen on the last day and discusses issues related to when it will occur. In fact, his letters to the Thessalonians include some of the most detailed information about the end times in the entire New Testament (this field of study is called **eschatology**; see Chapter 23: The Last Things in volume 3 of this series).

Key Texts

2:10–13 These verses provide a good basis upon which to discuss Paul's interaction with the Thessalonians. In those days there were many traveling religious teachers who came into town with some new message. Many of these charlatans tried to take advantage of people by their false teachings in order to draw attention and money to themselves (compare 1 Thessalonians 2:5). They were something like con artists or corrupt televangelists in our own day. In contrast, Paul, Silas and Timothy carried out their ministry in a holy, righteous and blameless manner (2:10). Elsewhere in the letter Paul points to a number of specific examples which illustrate this.

- The Gospel they together proclaimed did not come from error, deceit, or greed, but "in power and in the Holy Spirit, and with full conviction" (1:5; compare 2:3–5).
- The missionary team was not about pleasing men, but God (2:4). As a result, they dared to proclaim this good news even "in the midst of much conflict" (2:2).
- Paul and his team provided for themselves financially so that they were not a burden to the believers (2:6).

At the same time, Paul, Silas and Timothy developed a dear and intimate relationship with the Thessalonians. As a result, when persecution separated Paul's team from them, he declares, "We endeavored the more eagerly and with great desire to see you face to face" (2:17). Their gentle conduct among the Thessalonians was "like a nursing mother taking care of her own children" (2:7). They also behaved like a kind father as they "exhorted each one of you and charged you to walk in a manner worthy of God, who calls you into his own kingdom and glory" (2:12). Notice the theological significance of this verse. God first called the Thessalonians into his kingdom purely by his own word of grace apart from any worthiness or work on their part (justification). In response, God's word through Paul urges them to live a life worthy of that calling (sanctification).

The final passage cited above turns our attention to the Thessalonians' response to the message Paul, Silas and Timothy proclaimed. The Thessalonians "accepted it not as the word of men but as what it really is, the word of God, which is at work in you believers" (2:13). God spoke his word through Paul and that word acted powerfully, calling and bringing the Thessalonians into God's kingdom. God's word then continued to work in the lives of the believers. Paul identifies ways in which this was evident. After turning away from idols, their faith and desire to spread the Lord's message "sounded forth" from them so that it is well known throughout the region (1:8–9). Just as with Paul and his team, this bold proclamation of the Gospel has caused them to endure "much affliction" (1:6; compare 2:14; 3:3–4). But they have been faithful and Paul rejoices in the positive report Timothy has brought to him.

First Thessalonians 4 details some of what living a life "worthy of God" entails (2:12). It means a holy and honorable lifestyle, particularly avoiding sexual immorality and passionate lust (4:3, 5). While the Graeco-Roman world generally looked down on manual labor, Paul urges the Thessalonians to follow his example, to provide for themselves in a manner which gives a positive witness to the unbelieving world. Paul urges them "to mind your own affairs, and to work with your hands . . . so that you may live properly before outsiders and be dependent on no one" (4:11–12). It is possible that these two verses also serve as a transition into the second major topic of this letter.

Think about how most people would respond to a man carrying a sign that announced, "The End is Near!" The Thessalonians appropriately believed the return of Jesus could occur at any moment. But this may have become something of an obsession that led them to neglect their daily responsibilities. Paul has just tried to correct that incorrect response to the awareness of Jesus' imminent return (4:11–12).

4:13–18 This section is Paul's most detailed description of what will happen at the second coming of Christ. What he speaks is "by a word from the Lord" (4:15). This may refer to the Old Testament and/or to a revelation received by Paul from Jesus himself, whether directly or indirectly. But notice that Paul's concern is pastoral. Apparently the Thessalonians are worried that believers who have died will in some way miss out on Jesus' return (4:13). Instead of feeling grief over loved ones who have died, Paul wants them to be encouraged (v. 18). So Paul brings them back to the basic Gospel message and its ramifications: "For since we believe that Jesus died and rose, even so, through Jesus, God will bring back with him those who have fallen asleep" (2:14; note that those believers are now "with Jesus").

What will happen on the last day? The Lord Jesus will come down from heaven with great public fanfare. The key point addressed here is that "the dead in Christ will rise first" (v. 16). Then those believers who are still alive on earth will "be caught up together with them in the clouds" (4:17). The Latin translation of "caught up" is *rapiemur*, from which we get the word "**rapture**." Many Christians today believe Christ will return and secretly rapture up the believing church from this world. Then the world will continue on into a period of tribulation followed by another return of Christ to rule over a millennial kingdom here on earth (see figure below; advocated, for example, by the *Left Behind* series). The very public return of Christ described here, however, seems to speak against that view. His coming is accompanied by a loud command, the voice of an archangel and the trumpet call of God (4:16).

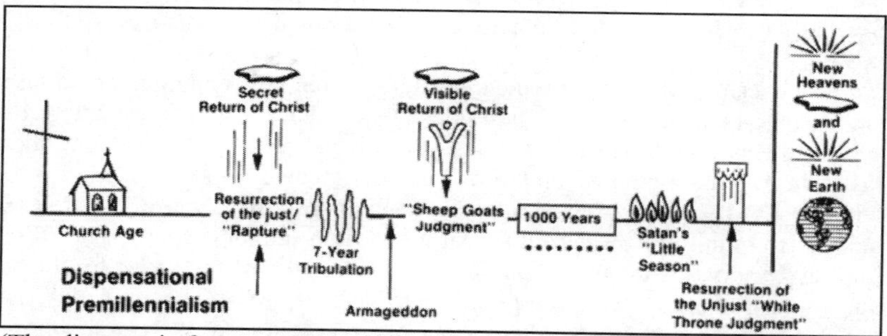

(The diagram is from page 45 of *The "End Times,"* A Report of the Commission on Theology and Church Relations of the Lutheran Church– Missouri Synod, September 1989; used by permission.)

More importantly, Paul declares that the dead in Christ will be raised at the coming described in 1 Thessalonians 4. Jesus repeatedly assures those who believe in him that he will raise them up "on the last day" (for example, John 6:39, 40, 54). The rapture of Christ's people depicted here occurs only after the dead in Christ are raised first (4:16). Since the dead in Christ are raised on the last day, it seems evident Paul is describing the events of that last day.

Those who assert that the world continues on after the rapture of the church described in 1 Thessalonians 4 point out that Paul does not say anything about unbelievers being raised or judged here. He does not, therefore, appear to be speaking about the final judgment day. In response, it is always important to keep in mind that Paul is not writing a complete treatment on the end times as would be found in a doctrine textbook. Instead, in interpreting Paul's letters, one should pay careful attention to identify the specific issue at hand. In this context, the question addressed is, "Will those *believers* who have died miss out on Jesus' coming?" Paul assures the grieving Thessalonians that they will not. The fate of *unbelievers* is simply not relevant to the specific topic being addressed.

Paul does speak about unbelievers in 2 Thessalonians. There he writes of the Lord Jesus being revealed from heaven and "inflicting vengeance on those who do not know God and on those who do not obey the gospel of our Lord Jesus Christ. They will suffer the punishment of eternal destruction, away from the presence of the Lord" (2 Thessalonians 1:8–9). Words like these are similar to numerous statements from the mouth of Jesus, yet their harshness continues to cause controversy (see Matthew 11:21–24; 13:42, 49–50; 22:7, 13; 24:51). Nevertheless, they speak the message of the Law in its ultimate finality.

In addition, the content of 1 Thessalonians 5 need not imply that the world continues on after the coming of Christ described at the end of 1 Thessalonians 4. Instead, Paul simply shifts his focus from what will happen to believers who have already died at Christ's return to a discussion of when those events will occur. The answer to the "when" question is simply that no one knows. The last day will come at an unexpected moment, "like a thief in the night" (5:2; compare Matthew 24:36, 42–44). As a result Christ's people should always be ready for that day when they will "obtain salvation through our Lord Jesus Christ" (5:9).

While many Christians dispute this interpretation, it is important not to lose sight of the main focus. In 1 Thessalonians 4:14 Paul begins by pointing the Thessalonians back to our belief in Jesus' death and resurrection. He concludes the section by assuring them and us of the final outcome. "So we will always be with the Lord. Therefore encourage one another with these words" (4:17–18). With this in mind, some of Paul's final instructions are most appropriate: "Rejoice always, pray without ceasing, give thanks in all circumstances; for this is the will of God in Christ Jesus for you" (5:16–18).

2 Thessalonians 2:1–8 The content of 2 Thessalonians is very similar to the last half of 1 Thessalonians. Paul again deals with the "coming of our Lord Jesus Christ" and how the Thessalonians should live as they wait for that day (2 Thessalonians 2:1). Why the repetition? The believers in Thessalonica have been "disturbed either by a spirit, message or letter alleged to be from us to the effect that the day of the Lord has come" (2:2). Perhaps they misunderstood something from 1 Thessalonians or, more likely, some false teaching about

Christ's return has been mistakenly attributed to Paul whether in writing or by word of mouth.

In response to the specific concern, Paul stresses that the end is not yet! In fact, one particular event has to happen before the day of the Lord comes. "For that day will not come, unless the rebellion [*apostasia* in Greek] comes first, and the **man of lawlessness** is revealed, the son of destruction" (2:3). Precisely what and whom Paul describes here have been a matter of continuous debate. Later he speaks of someone or something which restrains him and also says "the mystery of lawlessness is already at work" (2:6, 7). Suggested identifications of the rebellion, the man of lawlessness, and that which now restrains have included the Roman Empire, various emperors, emperor worship, the papacy, and a world ruler who will arise during a time of tribulation before the final end. The latter ruler is commonly identified as the **antichrist**. But it is important to note that Paul never uses that specific term. In the entire New Testament, it occurs only in 1 John. There it is used in the plural as John warns his first-century addressees that, even then, "many antichrists have come" (1 John 2:18).

The identification of this man of lawlessness remains a mystery. It may have been clearer to the Thessalonians as Paul chides them, "Do you not remember that when I was still with you I told you these things?" (2:5). Unfortunately, the specific things he told them in person are not available to us. This remains one of those things in Paul's letters that is "hard to understand" (2 Peter 3:16). In any event the final outcome is clear: "And then the lawless one will be revealed, whom the Lord Jesus will kill with the breath of his mouth" (2 Thessalonians 2:8).

Jesus in Thessalonians

Jesus Christ is present in the initial chapters of 1 Thessalonians as the one who sends his apostles and messengers to call people to faith in him (1 Thessalonians 2:6; 3:2). He is active in and through their message (2:13). Jesus was also persecuted and rejected, a pattern being emulated by Paul and the Thessalonians (2:14–15). However, the dominant picture of Jesus in Paul's letters to the Thessalonians is as the Coming One who will return and bring salvation to his people (1 Thessalonians 5:9; compare Matthew 11:3). At his second coming, Christ will raise the dead (1 Thessalonians 4:14, 16), gather believers into his eternal presence (1 Thessalonians 4:17; 2 Thessalonians 2:1) and judge all evil and wickedness (2 Thessalonians 1:7–9).

For Further Discussion

1. Compare and contrast the conduct of Paul's missionary team in Thessalonica with that of modern day (tele-)evangelists and missionaries.

2. Pretend that you knew Jesus would return within the next year. How would you respond? Would this be good news or bad news for you? Would you live your life differently from then on? How?

3. Write a narrative based upon your understanding of what will happen at the return of Christ and the end of this world as we know it.

4. Imagine that you and some of your friends hear the Rapture, the Tribulation, the Antichrist and the Millennium described in great detail by a speaker or see them portrayed in movie. How would you discuss these topics with your friends afterward?

For Further Reading

Bruce, F. F. *1 and 2 Thessalonians.* Word Biblical Commentary. Waco, TX: Word, 1982.

The End Times: A Study on Eschatology and Millennialism. A Report of the Commission on Theology and Church Relations of the Lutheran Church-Missouri Synod. St. Louis: Concordia, 1989.

Kuske, David. *Thessalonians.* People's Bible Commentary. St. Louis: Concordia, 1994.

Marshall, I Howard. *1 and 2 Thessalonians.* The New Century Bible Commentary. Grand Rapids: Eerdmans, 1983.

Morris, Leon. *1 and 2 Thessalonians.* Tyndale New Testament Commentaries. Grand Rapids: Eerdmans, 1984.

Wanamaker, C. A. *The Epistles to the Thessalonians.* Grand Rapids: Eerdmans, 1990.

1 and 2 Corinthians

Paul and the Corinthians

There are a number of connections between the Thessalonian correspondence we just studied and Paul's letters to the Corinthians. Paul made his first visits to both Thessalonica and Corinth during his second missionary journey. After leaving Thessalonica, Paul went to Berea and Athens before arriving at Corinth. It was during his stay in Corinth that Paul received information about the Thessalonians and wrote both letters back to them. Later, he sent at least two letters to the Corinthians as well.

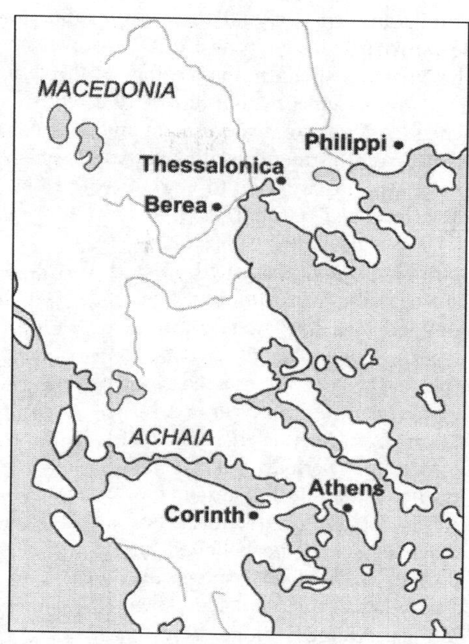

There are also differences. Paul stayed at Corinth much longer than the few weeks he spent in Thessalonica. As a result, we have more information about Paul's initial work in Corinth, the Christian community there, and his interaction with them. Acts 18:1–18 reveals that the basic pattern of events common to Paul's missionary journeys played itself out in Corinth. Paul began, as usual, at the synagogue and tried to convince both Jews and Greeks there that Jesus was the Messiah. After opposition from some of the Jews, Paul left the synagogue, along with Crispus, the synagogue ruler. He then began worshipping right next door at the home of a convert named Titius Justus. Paul also began reaching out directly to Gentiles outside the synagogue "and many of the Corinthians hearing Paul believed and were baptized" (Acts 18:8). In a vision, Jesus encouraged Paul's continuing work in Corinth and assured Paul of his protection. In response, "he stayed a year and six months, teaching the word of God among them" (Acts 18:11).

Then some Jews brought charges against Paul before Gallio, the proconsul of Achaia. An inscription found at the Greek city of Delphi tells us Gallio was in this position from A.D. 51–52. This is a key factor in dating Paul's visit to Corinth. From this fixed date, scholars also work backward and forward to determine the broader chronology of Paul's missionary journeys and his letters. Gallio told the Jews that the charges leveled against Paul involved "your own Law" (Acts 18:15). He then dismissed their accusations from his court. From a legal standpoint, Gallio recognized the faith Paul proclaimed was a part of the Jewish religion, which the Roman Empire allowed to be practiced openly (***religio licita***). From a theological perspective, Gallio unwittingly made an even more astute observation about the Old Testament basis of Christianity. As a result, Paul's mission work was allowed to continue without interference by Roman authorities. The Jews who opposed Paul responded to the dismissal by beating their current synagogue ruler, Sosthenes. Paul remained in Corinth for "many days" after his acquittal (Acts 18:18).

In Corinth Paul met two of his most faithful co-workers, Aquila and Priscilla. Paul stayed with them, and they all worked together making tents.

Aquila and Priscilla had come from Rome after the Emperor Claudius expelled Jews from that city (Acts 18:2). This event is corroborated by evidence outside the New Testament in the writings of the Roman historian, Suetonius (*Claudius*, 25). Aquila and Priscilla left Corinth with Paul, but they remained in Ephesus when Paul went on to Jerusalem and Syrian Antioch. A learned Jewish Christian named Apollos met Priscilla and Aquila in Ephesus. After some instruction from them, Apollos went on to Corinth where "he greatly helped those who through grace believed" (Acts 18:27).

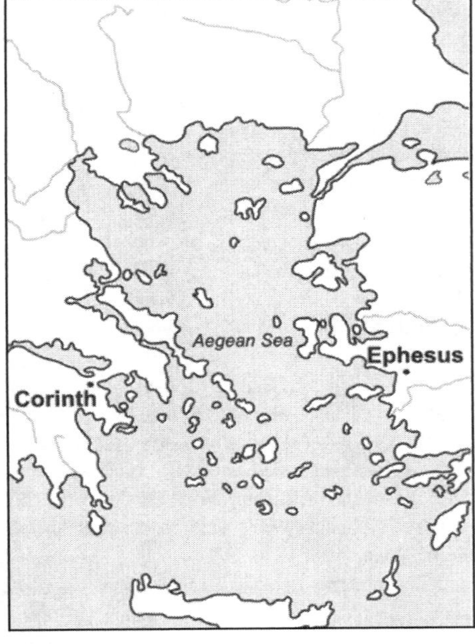

On his third missionary journey, Paul revisited the churches of Asia Minor that he founded on his first journey (Acts 18:23). Then he went to Ephesus where he stayed for approximately three years (A.D. 52–55; see Acts 19:10; 20:31). During this period, a fairly extensive amount of communication went back and forth between Paul and the believers in Corinth. It involved written correspondence and personal delegations. Although impossible to pin down the exact details, a plausible sequence of events goes something like this:

- It seems likely that the letter we call 1 Corinthians was not Paul's first letter to them after all. First Corinthians 5:9 implies Paul had written to them earlier.
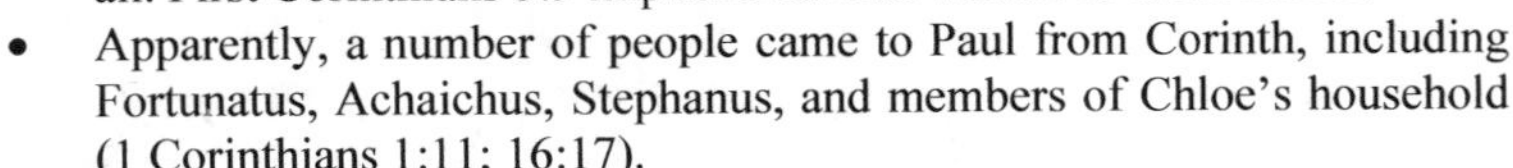
- Apparently, a number of people came to Paul from Corinth, including Fortunatus, Achaichus, Stephanus, and members of Chloe's household (1 Corinthians 1:11; 16:17).
- Some of these people probably delivered correspondence to Paul. In 1 Corinthians Paul responds to a number of matters about which they had written to him (1 Corinthians 7:1; 8:1; 12:1).
- Paul wrote 1 Corinthians from Ephesus early in A.D. 55 to address a number of these concerns.
- Some scholars speculate that, after sending Timothy to check on the Corinthians, Paul himself made a painful visit to Corinth from Ephesus (2 Corinthians 2:1). This is supported by his intention to come a "third time" later (2 Corinthians 12:14; see below).

- Paul wrote them a letter "out of much affliction and anguish of heart and with many tears" (2 Corinthians 2:4). While this sorrowful letter may be our 1 Corinthians, it could also refer to a letter written between 1 and 2 Corinthians.
- After leaving Ephesus and receiving a good report from Titus (2 Corinthians 7:6–7), Paul wrote 2 Corinthians, a letter of comfort to them (1:3–4), from Macedonia in northern Greece toward the end of A.D. 56.
- Paul spent three months in or near Corinth during his "third visit" there on his third missionary journey (2 Corinthians 12:14; see also 13:1; Acts 20:2–3).

If this sequence of events is what happened, it is intriguing to realize that the New Testament actually contains Paul's second and fourth letters to the Corinthians. His first and third letters have been lost. But in any case, we have what we have, and we now move on to study the two letters which have been preserved for us.

Introduction

First and Second Corinthians are perhaps the most contextual of Paul's letters. That is to say, they address specific issues of concern to a specific group of people in a specific setting. This is not to diminish the ongoing theological significance of Paul's words. But it recognizes that those of us who read his letters today must, at least initially, grasp the issues and Paul's response to them within the context of first-century Corinth.

The modern canal at Corinth

The city of Corinth provided a challenging atmosphere for these new Christians! It was a major commercial center with a population of well over half a million people steeped in Greco-Roman culture. The city's significance depended largely upon its strategic location near the Isthmus of Corinth. Six miles to the east was the seaport of Cenchrea on the Saronic Gulf. Less than two miles west lay the harbor of Lechaeium and the Gulf of Corinth. In order to save time and avoid danger, the cargo of ships, and even entire ships, were moved back and forth across this narrow isthmus. Corinth was, therefore, a seaport town something like New Orleans with the resultant reputation for immoral conduct.

At least twelve pagan temples were present in Corinth. The most famous was the temple to Aphrodite, the goddess of love. Up to one thousand prostitutes engaged in the immoral conduct associated with the worship of Aphrodite. There were also significant temples dedicated to Apollo and to Asclepius, a god of healing.

All of these cultural aspects exerted a significant influence upon the first Corinthian Christians. While Paul addresses issues that were, in many ways, specific to that day and society, these letters remain very helpful. They illustrate how believers always need to struggle with the influences their own culture exerts upon their faith and lifestyle.

Structure and Theme

The structure of 1 Corinthians allows Paul to address the numerous church problems which were challenging the believers there.

1 Corinthians	
Opening	1:1–3
Thanksgiving	1:4–9
Body/Exhortation	1:10–16:18
Divisions in the congregation	1:10–4:21
Immorality and lawsuits	5:1–6:20
Responses to Questions	7:1–14:40
Marriage	7:1–40
Eating meat offered to idols	8:1–11:1
Conduct when the community gathers/ worship and spiritual gifts	11:2–14:40
The Resurrection	15:1–15:57
Final Instructions	15:58–16:18
Closing	16:19–24

One should not overlook that the framework and outline of the letter convey a significant theological truth. As Paul speaks to the problem of divisions, he emphasizes the message of Christ crucified (1:18–25). Addressing their denial of the resurrection would seem to be next, both in terms of logical sequence and theological importance. Yet Paul holds off on responding to that critical issue until 1 Corinthians 15, just before the letter ends. Those two issues, Christ crucified and Christ raised from the dead, form the heart and center of the Christian faith. In this letter, those events of "first importance" also serve as a frame or bookends within which Paul handles all of the Corinthians' church problems (15:3). In so doing, he addresses and attempts to resolve those problems in the context of the Gospel, Christ crucified and Christ risen.

Aside from that overall frame, there is no unifying theme in 1 Corinthians other than Paul's personal and apostolic concern for his children in the faith (4:15). After assuring them of the grace they have received in Christ which enriches them in every way (1:4–5), Paul deals with their church problems in a direct and forceful manner. Yet, to borrow a thought from his letter to the Ephesians, he does speak even the harshest truth in the most excellent way, the way of ***agape*** love (Ephesians 4:15; 1 Corinthians 12:31–13:13).

On the surface, 1 Corinthians is a very practical letter, because it deals with everyday issues in the life of the church. However, the manner in which Paul speaks to those issues makes 1 Corinthians deeply theological in a most profound way. This is illustrated by the outline of the letter above; in it the Body and Exhortation sections are so intermingled they are collapsed into one inseparable unit. The supposed divide between theology and practice is here shown to be an intricate interrelationship.

Second Corinthians is, in part, a "letter of comfort" (1:3–7), because of the positive response of the Corinthians to Paul's previous admonitions. However, the dominant topic of the letter is an explanation and defense of Paul's apostolic ministry. There seem to have been some rivals who claimed to be apostles superior to Paul (11:5). Although Paul spends a lot of time describing his apostleship, this should not divert our attention from the central theme of his ministry. "For what we proclaim is not ourselves, but Jesus Christ as Lord, with ourselves as your servants for Jesus' sake" (4:5).

During this stage of his third missionary journey, Paul is gathering a collection for believers in Jerusalem. Various congregations are making contributions and, to insure the proper handling of the funds, are sending personal delegates along with Paul. Second Corinthians eight and nine serve as an excellent summary of the theology of Christian thankful giving.

An outline of 2 Corinthians is fairly simple.

2 Corinthians	
Opening	1:1–2
Thanksgiving	1:3–11
Body/Exhortation	1:12–13:10
Paul's apostolic ministry and conduct	1:12–7:16

THE COLLECTION FOR BELIEVERS IN JERUSALEM	8:1–9:15
A DEFENSE OF PAUL'S APOSTLESHIP	10:1–13:10
CLOSING	13:11–14

Key Texts

Ancient graffiti found in Rome

1 Corinthians 1:18–31 The practice of graffiti has a long history. One of the earliest pieces of anti-Christian graffiti was found on the walls of the *Domus Gelotiana* on the Palatine in Rome. It pictures a man before a cross. On the cross is a figure with a donkey's head. The inscription is this taunt: "Alexamenos worships God." The depiction of Christ as a crucified ass shows how the unbelieving world viewed the Christian faith in ancient times; such a response is common in our day as well. Paul begins by admitting that the message of the cross is folly or foolishness to those who are perishing in unbelief (1 Corinthians 1:18, 21). The Greek word for foolishness here is *moria*, from which we get the word "moronic." In short, believers in Christ seem like morons!

This misunderstanding is partly due to people's expectations. A number of times during Jesus' ministry, he was asked to perform a miraculous sign to authenticate who he was and what he said (Matthew 12:38; John 2:18). Paul characterizes Jewish people as "demand[ing] signs," before they would believe, because of their messianic expectations. Based upon those expectations, the specter of a crucified messiah caused them to stumble. Greeks, on the other hand, believed human intellect and philosophical wisdom held the answers to life's meaning and purpose. To those with such an attitude, the cross seemed "moronic."

Nevertheless, the message of Christ crucified reveals God's power and wisdom at work to save those who believe (1 Corinthians 1:18, 22, 24). On its surface, this appears to be an odd kind of power. To human eyes, it looks scandalous, foolish, and weak. Yet that is how God worked his salvation and, Paul reminds the Corinthians, that is how God *continues* to work. He chooses the poor and lowly in the eyes of this world to be his own (1:27). In so doing, he shames those with worldly wisdom, as well as the things the world views as strong. This reminder to the Corinthians serves to put their focus on Christ. If they want to see God's wisdom, it is Jesus. So also, their righteousness, holiness, and redemption are all Christ. Lutheranism has emphasized the theology of the cross. This section powerfully expresses that view.

4:6–7 The topic which dominates 1 Corinthians 1–4 is the factions within the Christian community at Corinth. Paul received a delegation from Chloe's household which informed him of the strife. Essentially, the Corinthians were dividing themselves in terms of allegiance to various teachers, namely Paul, Peter/Cephas, and Apollos (1:10–11). One party even allied themselves with Christ. That is certainly never wrong in and of itself. However, if being in the "Christ party" is an attempt to separate oneself from others in the believing community, it, too, is divisive. As indicated in the previous section, Paul's initial tactic is to place all the attention on Christ the crucified. That was Paul's sole message in Corinth (2:2). In fact, he admits that his own demeanor and presentation were not all that impressive, so that people would not cling to him, but to Christ alone. A natural person cannot grasp these spiritual truths apart from God's Spirit (2:14). But through the power of the freely given Spirit, believers know the mind of Christ, the Lord himself (2:16).

Chapter 3 uses two basic illustrations. The first is from agriculture (3:5–9). It was as if Paul planted seeds in the field of Corinth; Apollos came along later and watered. But it is God who owns the farm and causes things to grow. Then Paul switches to an architectural metaphor. He and Apollos helped build up "God's temple" of believers (3:9–12). But, as the hymn puts it, "The Church's one foundation is Jesus Christ, her Lord."

By the time we get to chapter 4, these analogies are all applied to Paul and Apollos. They are merely servants of God through whom the Corinthians came to believe. The Corinthians, therefore, should not take pride in one person over against another (4:6). Elevating one person to a position of honor has been a temptation in the church ever since. Allegiance is given to Peter or Paul, to the Pope, Martin Luther or John Calvin, or to a certain pastor. One is then played off against the other. In those situations, Paul here reminds the Corinthians and us of these three things: 1) do not go beyond what is written in God's Word; 2) keep human ministers in their proper perspective; and 3) focus upon the true source of every received gift, God's grace in Christ Jesus.

6:9–12, 19–20 Paul's entire theology of Law, Gospel, and response is powerfully encapsulated in these verses. Who will not inherit the kingdom of God? Paul gives quite a list which would exclude from heaven those who practice adultery, idolatry, and homosexuality. Yet his list also includes the more "mundane" vices committed by thieves, the greedy, drunkards, and slanderers. Who has not, at one time or another, been guilty of at least one of these things? This list represents violations of the moral demands of God's Law. Under it, all people are excluded from God's kingdom.

The key to note is the tense in verse 11. "And such were some of you." What changed? Paul does not say the Corinthians changed or even that they quit doing those things. Rather, they were passive as God changed them. He washed them up, made them holy, and declared them to be "just-as-if-I'd" never sinned.

How did this happen? In the name of Christ and by the Spirit of God. This is the good news of the Gospel expressed in baptismal language. The picture is of sin as dirt, dirt that God washes away in the name of Christ.

What is a proper response to such grace? A video entitled *Martin Luther: Heretic* (BBC TV production by William Nicholson in association with Concordia Family Films, 1984) contains this exchange between Dr. Luther, a professor at Wittenberg University, and his class:

> A student challenges Dr. Luther, "Man can do nothing about his sinfulness?" Luther answers, "Yes." The student responds, "God is to do everything?" Dr. Luther simply replies, "Yes." The student concludes, "Then I may do as I please. I can sin as much as I want. It makes no difference." Luther says, "Yes. You may do as you please. Now tell me what pleases you? . . . . Imagine it. No more laws. No more punishments. What do you do? Drink yourself senseless, make faces at the Duke, spend the rest of the week in a whorehouse? . . . . If you're a good man, you'll do good works, not to prove anything, not to gain anything, [but] just because that's how you are, how you are in your heart." The incredulous student asks, "Then what does it take to be a good man?" Luther answers with one word, "Faith."

St. Paul moves the issue in the same direction. First Corinthian 6:9–10 describes what the Corinthians were. But, according to verse 11, God has washed them clean. Then verse 12 asserts, "All things are lawful for me." Some interpreters think Paul is being ironic and using the slogan of some "free in Christ" libertines who improperly thought it was now alright to engage in the conduct depicted in verses 9–10. If so, Paul is sarcastically using their own words against them. However, later in the letter Paul uses the exact same phrase to conclude his discussion about eating meat offered to idols (10:23). There is no sense of sarcasm there. The same, then, is true here. The heart of the Gospel is that *God does everything* to make us clean, holy, and righteous. In reality, therefore, we can do whatever we please.

The question, though, is no longer merely about what is permissible, but what is beneficial or helpful for self and others (6:12). Yes, believers can do whatever, but they also must be careful not to be mastered by things like food, sex, and alcohol (6:12–13). And why not? Paul's reason drives right back to the Gospel. The assertion that "you are not your own" (6:19) may seem oppressive to people preoccupied with their own independence. But it is certainly far better to belong to God than to live apart from him! Paul reminds the Corinthians that God bought them at a tremendously high price, the death of his Son (6:20). In addition, his Spirit now resides within them, making their bodies his own holy temple. Therefore, Paul calls the Corinthians to honor God with their bodies instead of dragging Christ's holy temple into sexual immorality and other vices (6:20).

Consider a traffic signal. Up to this point in 1 Corinthians, Paul has discussed issues which are clearly displeasing to God (for example, divisions, lawsuits among the believers, immorality, and all the items listed in 6:9–10). You may think of them as a red light. God's word says, "Stop! Do not go there." At the same time, there are green lights, areas into which God clearly desires for his people to proceed (for example, unity around the message of Christ crucified, giving up one's rights for the benefit of others, living to the glory of God, gathering for worship).

But God's Word leaves a lot undefined. In and of themselves, these issues are like "yellow lights." They are neither strictly in accordance with God's will or opposed to it. Their propriety depends upon the person, the situation and how they are used. Too many drivers react to a yellow light by stomping down on the accelerator. Perhaps the Corinthians were doing something like that. In the "yellow light" areas discussed in 1 Corinthians 7–14, Paul certainly allows believers to proceed, but he urges them to do so with caution. The specific topics addressed by Paul include whether to marry, eating meat offered to idols in most contexts, and conduct in worship. Each of these can be done in a manner pleasing to God (green). They can also be abused to the detriment of self and others (red). But, in and of themselves, God does not specifically approve of or condemn them (yellow).

Many areas of life are in the "yellow" category. For example, God gives us freedom in regard to where we live, how we dress, what we eat, the vehicle we drive, our choice of vocation and recreation, where and when we worship, and so forth. But remember, proceed with caution!

7:1–17 The topic of 1 Corinthians 7 flows logically from the discussion at the end of chapter six. There Paul addressed the improper use of God's gift of sex through prostitution and immorality. At the same time, chapter seven inaugurates a new section of the letter in which Paul responds to questions the Corinthians had written to him (7:1; 8:1; 12:1). This chapter is an extensive discussion of marriage. Paul makes three essential points: marriage is a gift; a single life lived in devotion to God is a gift; and different people have different gifts (7:7; compare Jesus' words in Matthew 19:10:12). Paul does not denigrate marriage as some have charged. But, in light of the end of the world that Paul believed to be imminent as well as the added responsibilities of married life, Paul does point out the advantages of staying single and being wholly devoted to the Lord. The key point is stated repeatedly: Each person should live as the Lord has called him (7:17, 20, 24). This could mean singleness or marriage, even slavery or freedom (7:21–24).

Paul has words of the Lord Jesus which identify divorce as contrary to God's will (7:10–11; Matthew 19:1–9; compare Malachi 2:16). Divorce is certainly not an "unforgivable sin" (Matthew 12:31–32). But, as with all other sins, its guilt does need to be washed away. Paul then uses his own apostolic authority to address previously married believers whose spouse did not accept the faith together with them (1 Corinthians 7:12–14). Inasmuch as it depends on the believer, Paul encourages them to remain in the marriage.

10:23–11:1 All of chapters eight through ten address the issue of eating meat offered to idols. This seems like an odd issue in our day. However, in first-century Corinth the only fresh meat available had likely been ceremonially dedicated to pagan idols. Those with mature Christian knowledge were aware that such "gods" were fictitious. Since they do not exist, offering meat to them was ultimately meaningless and believers were free to eat the meat (8:4–6, 8; a "yellow light"). True enough, Paul responds, but not every one knows this (8:7). Some of the Corinthian believers were still troubled by the existence of the so-called gods they previously worshipped. If eating the meat knowingly causes such a fellow believer to stumble in his or her faith, the one who eats it sins against Christ (8:11–12). The principle at work here is that it is more important to act with love and concern for others for whom Christ also died, than to selfishly exhibit or even flaunt one's personal freedoms. The loving tactic is to give up one's freedoms willing them up if doing so will benefit or avoid causing harm to others.

The Temple of Apollo at Corinth

In chapter nine Paul points out that he himself provided that example while in Corinth. He was entitled to wages from the Corinthians for his work among them. The leaders who care for God's people spiritually should be provided for materially by them (9:14). However, Paul boasts he gave up that to which he was properly entitled. He also willingly adapted his own outward conduct in order to reach different groups of unbelieving people. A wonderful summary of Paul's attitude toward his entire ministry is in 9:19–23; he declares, "I have become all things to all people that by all means I might save some" (9:22).

Believers need to be careful how they handle these "yellow light" issues. Paul uses the analogy of athlete training for a race (9:24–25). Even Paul had to discipline his own body continually (9:26–27). As a further example or **type**, Paul notes that the vast majority of the Israelites who were rescued from Egypt did not make it to the promised land (10:6). Our freedom as God's people should not cause us to become complacent in times of temptation but to take the way out provided by God himself (10:13).

The specific issue at hand in Corinth had created a fine line between eating meat dedicated to an idol, even in the home of a guest, and engaging in worship of the idol to whom it was offered. If one's participation in a meal crosses over the line into worship of pagan gods, the conduct is in fact demonic and must be avoided (10:20; "red light").

In his summation at the end of 1 Corinthians 10, Paul returns to the words of chapter 6. Yes, everything is permissible, but that is not the only, or even the main, issue. The more critical matter concerns what is constructive for one's own faith walk and, just as importantly, for the good of others. Based on Psalm 24 Paul, in effect, says something like this:

> Everything is God's creation, so enjoy the meat; eat and drink to his glory. But if someone makes a point about the meat having been offered to an idol, refrain from eating it so as not to offend the other person. Yes, you are free to eat the meat and should not be condemned for it, but your greater concern for a fellow believer should cause you to focus on others rather than self.

Paul concludes by urging the Corinthians to imitate him because he has followed the example of Christ (11:1).

It is true that 1 Corinthians 8–10 addresses an obscure and outmoded topic. But the principles Paul lays out here apply very well to many contemporary issues. These chapters provide a model for dealing with any number of "yellow light" issues that are not right or wrong in and of themselves—issues that are neither specifically pleasing nor displeasing to God. Examples today include dancing, music, movies, clothing, the use of alcohol by those of legal age to consume it, and many more. Christians are generally free to engage in or abstain from such activities. Yet many of these same things can be abused to the harm of self and/or cause stumbling to the faith of others. Their propriety largely depends upon how they are used.

Dancing serves as a good illustration. One the one hand, there are certainly many kinds of "dirty dancing" which displease God, cause people to stumble, and inevitably lead to sin. These are "red lights." On the other hand, the Bible often calls God's people to dance for joy before the Lord in worship (Psalm 149:3; 150:4). This is a "green light." But dancing, in and of itself, is neutral. Most dancing probably lies between those two and fits in the "yellow light" category introduced above. Believers are free to engage in it without sin, but must also watch how their conduct is affecting themselves and others.

11:17–30 This is Paul's only discussion of the Lord's Supper in all his letters. The topic arises because of its abuse in Corinth. Jesus instituted the Lord's Supper during the celebration of a Passover meal. The early believers appropriately continued to share the Lord's Supper in the context of a larger meal, sometimes called an **agape feast** (Jude 12). However, in Corinth they are doing so inappropriately. The problem of divisions addressed in the first four chapters resurfaces here, but now in terms of the rich and the poor (1 Corinthians 11:18). According to I Corinthians 11:20–22, during the meal the rich are overindulging themselves while excluding the poor but then sharing with the poor in the Lord's Supper. Such conduct shames the poor and despises the community of believers.

The consequences of mishandling the Lord's Supper are severe: many are weak and ill, and a few have even died (1 Corinthians 11:30).

Paul returns, once again, to Jesus and his own words (11:24–25). The effect is to ask the Corinthians a question something like this: "Would you treat each other like that if Jesus was here?" According to the words faithfully received and handed down from the Lord himself, Jesus is indeed present in this meal of his body and blood. As the believers receive the Lord's Supper together, they are to be cognizant of his real presence, as well as the presence of those around them. In other words, there is both a vertical and a horizontal dimension involved.

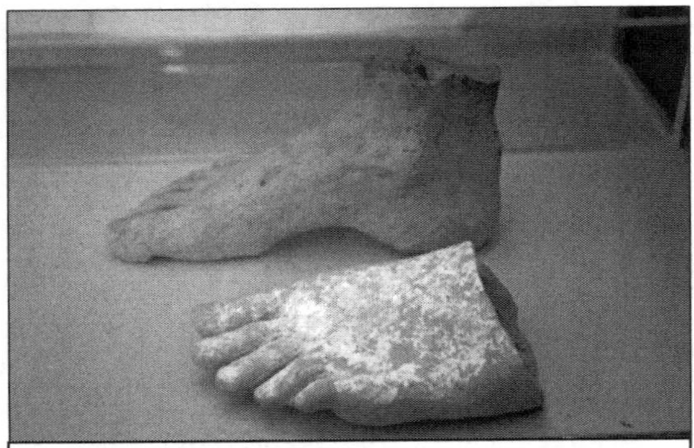

Body parts from the temple of Asclepius

Paul makes this point by utilizing the word "body" in a two different but interrelated ways. Earlier in chapter ten Paul stated, "The bread that we break, is it not a participation in the body of Christ? Because there is one bread, we who are many are one body" (10:16–17). In those two sentences Paul uses the term "body" in two senses. The first refers to the body of Christ in the Lord's Supper; the second describes the many who share together as one body in that meal. In 11:27 Paul speaks of sinning against "the body and blood of the Lord." This refers to a misuse of Christ's body in the Lord's Supper. But, as 1 Corinthians 12 makes clear, he also envisions the believers in Corinth as one body of Christ with many members. In the context of chapter 11, the problem identified by Paul is more relational than doctrinal. Thus, their failure to "discern or recognize the body" in verse 29 likely denotes their lack of regard for one another within the body of believers as they come to share in the body and blood of the Lord. In fact, the same Greek word for "discerning" or recognizing the body in verse 29 is used in a parallel sense in verse 31 where the Corinthians are called to "judge" themselves.

As a result, what we see in our Bibles as a new chapter, 1 Corinthians 12, flows very logically from the discussion which concludes chapter 11 (remember, chapter divisions were added long after Paul wrote; compare the transition between chapters 6 and 7 referred to above). In response to a question about spiritual gifts, Paul uses the analogy of a human body to describe the body of believers in Corinth (12:1, 12–27). The background for this metaphor may have been the temple of Asclepius in Corinth. It is described by Pausanius in a travel journal written in the second century (*The Description of Greece*, Book 2). When people received healing there, they responded by placing a terra cotta figure of the particular body part which was healed on a wall dedicated to the god. In Paul's day the wall was probably full of dismembered body parts. Perhaps Paul had this negative example in mind when he tells the believers, "For in one Spirit we were all baptized into one body.... Now you are the body of Christ and individually members of it" (12:13, 27). As the human body has many different parts, so individual believers have a variety of spiritual gifts (12:11–12). But each one is needed for the body to be whole and healthy. Individual believers should not look down on others (12:21), nor should they deprecate or exclude themselves (12:15–16).

Mirror from the Roman era

The best way to use any and all of these gifts is the way of love (12:31). Paul describes agape love in chapter 13 both in terms of what it is and what it is not (13:4–8). This kind of love focuses on others, not self ("does not insist on its own way"; 13:5). It is shown in actions, not merely feeling ("rejoices with the truth"; 13:6). It involves a conscious decision and commitment to be "patient and kind" (13:4). Love is also the greatest abiding gift of God (13:13). In this present era, God's people "know in part.... We see in a mirror dimly" (13:12). In heaven we will know God fully by sight and all our hopes will be realized. Then faith and hope will no longer be needed, but agape love will continue into all eternity.

14:1–4, 18–20 All of this discussion related to spiritual gifts is now focused upon a particular gift which has become problematic in Corinth, the gift of **tongues**. Unfortunately, it has disrupted the church in recent years as well. What is this gift? In Corinth it seems as though it was an ecstatic language in which the spirit prayed to God, while the mind was unfruitful (14:14). This ecstatic speech stands in contrast to the gift of speaking in human languages exhibited on Pentecost Day (Acts 2:8). Perhaps many in Corinth were attracted to this spirit language because it was more demonstrable and grabbed people's attention. Maybe those who displayed the gift felt themselves to be more spiritually mature than others. In any event, Paul downplays the gift of tongues and highlights the benefits of the gift of prophecy. Tongues are focused on self in relation to God (14:2, 4). **Prophecy**, on the other hand, is able to strengthen, build up, encourage, and console others (14:3). Therefore, it more effectively exhibits the love just depicted so beautifully in chapter 13.

What is the gift of prophecy? A popular misconception is that it mainly involves predicting the future. Such an understanding is biblically inadequate. According to Gordon Fee and Douglas Stuart, only eight percent of the material in the Old Testament Prophets is predictive of the Messiah or remains unfulfilled in our day (*How to Read the Bible for All Its Worth*, Zondervan, 1993, pp. 165–66). The vast majority of their prophecy spoke of God's words and actions in the past, of his will for Israel's present or of events fulfilled long before the time of the New Testament. In a more general sense, prophecy takes God's revealed will and applies it to people in their particular context. According to 1 Corinthians 14, this type of prophecy instructs and edifies.

How should these gifts be used? Paul had and cherished the gift of tongues (14:18), but when the community of believers gathers in Corinth, he places much greater value on prophecy. In fact, Paul says, "You can all prophesy one by one, so that all may learn and be encouraged" (14:31). Tongues, on the other hand, were to be utilized in a very limited manner in public worship. Only two or three people should speak in tongues, one at a time, and the content must be interpreted so that all can benefit (14:27). Otherwise, the one who speaks in tongues should "keep silent in church and speak to himself and to God" (14:28). The overriding principle is that everything be done decently and in order, because God is not a God of confusion but of peace (14:40, 33).

Women/Wives in Worship according to 1 Corinthians

Something that was a relatively minor issue in Corinth has become a major issue of debate within the church today. What is Paul saying about the role of women/wives in worship? Problems arise because the same words used in Hebrew and Greek for men and women in general are also used more specifically to refer to husbands and wives. So we can never tell for certain if Paul is addressing all women or, more narrowly, wives in relation to their husbands. In chapter 11 Paul asserts that it is wrong for women/wives to pray and prophesy in worship with their heads uncovered, or unveiled (11:5–6). Yes, Christian women/wives are free in Christ to appear unveiled (see 6:12; 10:23). However, to men in first-century Corinth who were not used to seeing unveiled women in public, the practice was disruptive. It also gave a bad impression to the unbelieving community. In that culture, unveiled women were normally prostitutes or other women of low reputation. This is why an unveiled woman/wife in worship "dishonors her head" (in all likelihood, her husband; 11:5). Following Paul's example in 1 Corinthians 9, women/wives should willingly give up their freedom and voluntarily return to wearing veils in worship (compare 11:1). Paul roots his argument in the creation of man first, followed by woman (11:8–9).

The majority of Christians view Paul's treatment of this issue as illustrative of an ongoing principle *based on creation (women/wives should not shame their head/husbands), which had a particular cultural* application *in first-century Corinth (they should wear veils). Although the principle remains the same, the specific application in various cultures may well differ. Two additional points should be noted. First, Paul's words imply that it is appropriate for veiled women/wives to pray and prophesy in worship. Second, since Eve was created after Adam, Paul asserts an ongoing order of "headship" (11:3, 8; see the discussion of Ephesians 5 below). But, in the Lord, the relationship is one of mutual interdependence. Indeed, "for as woman was made from man, so man is now born of woman. And all things are from God" (11:12; compare 7:2).*

In a very brief remark in chapter 14, Paul asserts that women/wives should "keep silent in the churches. For they are not permitted to speak but should be in submission, as the Law also says" (14:34). The interpretation of this verse is largely dependent upon identifying the specific problem Paul is seeking to correct. Almost no one takes the verse literally and concludes women cannot utter anything at all. That would contradict the argument of chapter 11 and passages such as 1 Corinthians 14:31. The major interpretations conclude women/wives are improperly engaged in 1) disruptive speaking; 2) uneducated questioning that has become disruptive; or 3) authoritative speaking. In each case Paul is not commanding total silence, but attempting to stop the conduct he considers shameful (14:35; compare 14:27–28). Since he refers to, but does not cite, a specific passage in verse 34, the Old Testament basis for his assertion is also unclear.

In both chapters Paul asserts a wider context than Corinth. The discussion about women being unveiled in chapter 11 concludes, "We have no such practice, nor do the churches of God" (11:16). In chapter 14 he states, "The things I am writing to you are a command of the Lord" (14:37). Paul's words certainly had an authoritative influence in first-century Corinth and they still do speak the word of God today. However, the church continues to wrestle with determining the specific, contextual application of these words was then, as well as how to apply them properly in various contemporary cultures (for further information, see the discussion of 1 Timothy 2:9–15 below).

15:1–8, 17–24, 50–58 In our discussion of the structure of 1 Corinthians, we noted the significant place of chapters 1 and 15. Chapter 1 emphasizes "Christ crucified." In chapter 15 Paul begins to wrap up the letter by stressing the resurrection of Jesus. He specifically identifies Christ's death, burial, and resurrection as being of "first importance" to the proclamation and acceptance of the Gospel (1 Corinthians 15:3). As a result, Paul is astonished that some in Corinth are claiming there is no resurrection of the dead (15:12). What were they thinking? Greek thought was heavily influenced by Plato and his distinction between lower, earthly, material things and a higher-level, spiritual plane. Once one escaped the physical, weak shell of an earthly body, the person ascended to a loftier realm of existence. To such thinking, any return to the earthly body was a step back. But one consequence of denying the bodily resurrection in general is to deny the resurrection of Christ (15:13). The ramifications of that denial are spelled out in verses 12–18:

- Paul's preaching is useless and he is a false witness about God.
- The faith of the Corinthians is worthless; they are still in their sins and to be greatly pitied.
- Those who have died in Christ are lost.

"But in fact Christ has been raised from the dead" (15:20). The evidence Paul cites in support of this fact has been authoritatively received by him and faithfully delivered to those in Corinth (15:1, 3; compare 11:23). It includes the manifold testimony of the (Old Testament) Scriptures and the numerous appearances of the risen Christ to Peter, the disciples, to more than five hundred believers on one occasion, to his half-brother James, and, finally, to Paul himself on the Damascus Road.

Whereas Adam fell into sin and brought death, Christ makes us alive through his resurrection (15:21–22). To deny the bodily resurrection is to deny Christ's resurrection, which is a denial of the faith. But the fact that Christ was raised proves that all will be raised. His resurrection is the **firstfruits**, guaranteeing the resurrection of all when the last enemy, death, is finally destroyed at the end of time (15:23–28).

The second major topic, beginning at verse 35, discusses what the resurrected body will be like. Paul distinguishes between "a natural body" and "a spiritual body" (15:44, 46). For a number of reasons, the term "spiritual" here does not imply an immaterial existence as a platonic thinker might assume.

- Paul still describes it as a body.
- Jesus, the last Adam, is called "a life-giving spirit" (15:45). But Jesus clearly had a physical body even after the resurrection (Luke 24:39–43).
- In Genesis 1 Adam was "a living being" in the fullest, created sense (1 Corinthians 15:45). The Hebrew word *nephesh*, often translated "soul," refers to the whole, complete person God had made. Jesus is not the antithesis of this; rather, he is a life-giver.
- Earlier in chapter ten Paul spoke of the "spiritual food" and drink given to the Israelites during their wilderness wanderings (10:3–4). The manna and water were not immaterial.

All these points lead to the conclusion that the term "spiritual body" here means something like a "Spirit-filled physical body." As a result, believers will not leave their bodies behind at the resurrection. Instead, God will raise the bodies of those who have died and change those who are still alive so that "we shall also bear the image of the man from heaven," Jesus himself (15:49, 51–52).

What will that changed body be like? Paul's analogies in verses 36–41 make the point that it will be the same, yet different. The contrasts are mostly negative. Our bodies are now weak, dishonored by sin, and, therefore, subject to death (perishable, mortal). But they will be changed to powerful, glorious, imperishable and immortal bodies (15:42–43, 52–54). This will happen "in the twinkling of an eye" when the last enemy, "death, is swallowed up in victory" (15:52, 54; quoting Hosea 25:8).

The climactic, final verses of chapter 15 lay out Paul's theology of Law, Gospel, and response in a profound manner. Sin and death, empowered by the Law, are on one side (15:56). But victory (*nikos*) over them is given freely by God through Jesus Christ (15:57). In response, Paul calls believers to stand firm in that faith and to give themselves fully to the work of the Lord (15:58).

Greek goddess *Nike* with victory

2 Corinthians 1:3–4 In light of all of the church problems addressed in 1 Corinthians, as well as other possible letters and the sorrowful visit referred to above, the opening verses of 2 Corinthians strike a refreshing change of tone. These verses also illustrate the Law, Gospel, and response format. The believers in Corinth experienced troubles and suffering. God, in Christ, comforted them in the midst of those. In response, they are called to pass that comfort on to others (see also 2 Corinthians 7:6–7, 13).

One matter of contention involved Paul's travel plans to and from Corinth (1:15–2:4). Another matter related to a fellow Christian who had been punished by them (2:5–11; see also 7:10–12). This was probably the man who was sleeping with his "father's wife" (probably his stepmother) in 1 Corinthians 5:1–5. Paul's harsh words there called for the Corinthians to expel him from their community and to hand him over to Satan. This seemingly cruel treatment was in order that he would ultimately be saved. Once the person had repented, the Corinthians were to forgive and restore him into their fellowship.

5:14–6:2 Beginning at 2 Corinthians 2:12 and running through chapter 7, Paul turns his attention to an exposition of the content and character of his apostolic ministry. Whether this is in response to specific challenges or simply a rehearsal of Paul's motives and methods in his relationship with the Corinthians is unclear. But this section contains many significant theological statements. In 2 Corinthians 4:5–7 Paul reaches back to Genesis 1 when God first spoke at creation, "Let there be light" (Genesis 1:3). This same God has made his light shine into our hearts through Jesus Christ. That is the precious message. Those who proclaim it are like crude, clay jars; they are vessels and servants used by God. Together with all those who receive that message, they long to be home with the Lord. Until then, "we walk by faith, not by sight" (2 Corinthians 5:7).

2 Corinthians 5:14 has been translated to say that the love of Christ "controls us" or "compels us" (NIV). This sounds like "Law" talk. Does our love for Christ force us to do certain things? No, the context of the passage is all about the love of Christ for us (5:14–15). He died for all and rose again so that we might be changed and motivated to live for others as he did. More literally, Paul here speaks about Christ's love "having its way" with us—his way, the way of the Gospel.

When God changes people, everything changes. There is, in fact, "a new creation" (5:17). A believer views Christ and others from a completely different perspective. Instead of living for themselves, they live for Christ and for others. This is quite a change from the way of the world! Paul utilizes the language of friendship to speak of this change as a reconciliation (5:18–20). A relationship that had been fractured by sin has been restored. But the estranged parties did not compromise and meet in the middle. Rather, God did all the reconciling and he did it for the whole world (5:19). God accomplished this by what Martin Luther called "The Blessed Exchange." God made Jesus Christ, who had no sin, to become sin for us on the cross. There the sin of all people was placed upon him. In exchange, sinners who are in Christ get righteousness from God (2 Corinthians 5:21).

God entrusts this message of reconciliation to human messengers like Paul. They serve as ambassadors, God's personal representatives (5:20). They are also fellow workers with God himself in their own time and place (6:1). As they are used to deliver the message of reconciliation in Christ, Isaiah 49:8 is fulfilled. The "favorable time" of God's grace has arrived; the day of his salvation is now present (2 Corinthians 6:2).

8:8–15; 9:6–15 These two chapters discuss an offering Paul is gathering for poor believers in Jerusalem (see Acts 20:1–6). 1 Corinthians 16:1–4 had already introduced the issue. Two significant points were made there about Christian giving. The gift is to be set aside for God first, at the beginning of the week, and the appropriate amount is proportional to what God has entrusted to the person. After leaving Ephesus, Paul intended to travel through Macedonia and Achaia. Along the way, he would pick up the offerings as well as a delegation to participate in and to ensure its proper delivery. In preparation for that mission, 2 Corinthians 8–9 expands upon the theology of giving and provides the following guidelines:

- Christian giving is rooted in the Gospel by which another "blessed exchange" occurs. Christ, the wealthy and powerful Lord of all creation, became a poor baby laid in a manger. He lived an impoverished life and died a pauper's death so that "poor miserable sinners" might become rich in him (2 Corinthians 8:8–9). All giving is to be a response of thanks to God for *his* inexpressible gift (9:15).
- Giving of one's own self to the Lord comes first (8:5).

- Giving is not to be coerced. "Each one must give as he has made up his mind, not reluctantly or under compulsion, for God loves a cheerful giver" (9:7).
- God is the ultimate source of everything we need (9:8–9). He desires that believers willingly and eagerly share what they have been given, proportionally and in relation to the needs of others. His desire is for equality (8:11–14).
- Giving is a sign of the obedience that accompanies confessing the Gospel (9:13). It is *a* (not *the*) valid test of the sincerity of one's love. Comparisons with the giving of others are also a legitimate indication of one's zeal (8:8).
- The ultimate goal of this giving is for those who receive it, or hear about it, to join in giving their thanks and praise to God (9:13).

11:21–12:10 While the earlier chapters of 2 Corinthians discussed Paul's ministry in a general sense, chapters 10–13 have a much more confrontational edge to them. They are a defense in light of challenges being directed against Paul. One charge was this: "His letters are weighty and strong, but his bodily presence is weak and his speech of no account" (10:10). Perhaps Paul's opponents also pointed out that he was not a trained speaker and that he did not even receive payment for his ministry in Corinth as others did (see 1 Corinthians 2:1–5; 9). In response, Paul sarcastically calls his opponents "super-apostles" (12:11), but he also makes clear that they are, in reality, false apostles and deceitful workers, who are merely masquerading as Satan himself does (11:13). They have a different Spirit, proclaim another Jesus, and teach a different gospel (11:4).

Since Paul's opponents initiated the tactic of making comparisons, Paul reluctantly engages in boasting about himself (10:12; 11:16–21; 12:1, 11). He lays out his background, upbringing, and the "signs and wonders and mighty works" that marked Paul as an apostle (12:12). But Paul spends most of his time laying out an impressive list of the suffering he has endured in his ministry up to this point (11:23–33). Additional information about the specific setting of some of these is given in Acts (for example, his stoning in Lystra and flogging in Philippi; see Acts 14:19; 16:22–23). In regard to others, we cannot identify the precise details, and the events remain a mystery (for example, shipwreck). Acts, however, records even more of the suffering Paul endured for Christ's name (for example, a later shipwreck; see Acts 27:27–44).

Then, in somewhat obscure fashion, Paul reveals a vision he experienced fourteen years earlier when he was "caught up to the third heaven" or "paradise" (2 Corinthians 12:2, 4). Further details about Paul's "visit" there would be most interesting. However, he is not permitted to relate them. Additionally, in order to keep Paul from becoming puffed up by the "surpassing greatness of the revelations," he was given a stake or "thorn in the flesh" (12:7). The precise nature of this affliction also remains a mystery, but the phrase seems to point to a physical ailment. Proposed identifications include poor eyesight, malaria, severe headaches, and epileptic seizures. Whatever it was, the fact that Paul calls it "a messenger of Satan to harass me" (12:7) makes its source and intended effect on him clear. Paul asked the Lord to remove it three times, but his request was not granted.

Nevertheless, this thorn, as well as all his other sufferings, drove Paul to a profound conclusion: "I will boast all the more gladly about my weaknesses ... For when I am weak, then I am strong" (12:9, 10). The insight which led to this realization came from the Lord himself who personally told Paul, "My grace is sufficient for you, for my power is made perfect in weakness" (12:9). God allows us to endure weakness, insults, hardships, persecutions, and difficulties in order that we, like Paul, might rely more completely on the power of his grace (see Romans 8:28). After discussing his travel plans and how the Corinthians should respond to the evidence authenticating Paul's apostolic ministry, he concludes the letter with a beautiful Trinitarian blessing. It begins by emphasizing, once again, "the grace of the Lord Jesus Christ" (2 Corinthians 13:14).

Jesus in Corinthians

Paul almost says it all in the first chapter of 1 Corinthians when he identifies Christ Jesus as the one "whom God made our wisdom and our righteousness and sanctification and redemption" (1 Corinthians 1:30). This is true, first of all, because Jesus is the Crucified Christ (1:18–25). Although the world cannot grasp it, the message of Christ crucified is God's power to save those who believe (1:21). As a result, Paul "decided to know nothing among [the Corinthians] except Jesus Christ and him crucified" (1 Corinthians 2:2). The cross of Christ is also God's wisdom revealed (1:21–25). In fact, the Spirit reveals so much about God to us that the unfathomable mind of the Lord is now made known—"we have the mind of Christ" (2:15–16; compare Isaiah 40:13). But Christ is just as certainly risen from the dead (15:1–11, 20). By these two actions of "first importance," we are declared righteous and holy in Jesus' name (15:3; 6:11). God even "gives us the victory" over sin, death, and the Law "through our Lord Jesus Christ" (15:56–57). When death is finally destroyed at Jesus' coming, he is the "life-giving spirit," who will change our bodies to be like his resurrected body (15:23, 26, 45, 49, 52).

Yet, even now, all who are baptized have been brought into Christ's body, the church (12:13). He is its one and only foundation (3:11). His members gather to receive his body and blood, and then live together as his body (11:17–34; 12:12–27). They are to love one another in the name of him who embodies the profound description of love given in 1 Corinthians 13.

Second Corinthians ties Jesus directly to the ministry of his chosen apostles and ambassadors. They "are commissioned by God" and, as "ministers of a new covenant," even "speak in Christ" (2 Corinthians 2:17; 3:6; compare 13:3). Their message is one of reconciliation in Jesus who "though he was rich, yet ... became poor" (2 Corinthians 8:9). He did this so that a relationship between God and humanity that was full of enmity and strife might be restored to one of friendship. In order to accomplish this, an even more startling thing happened; God made Jesus "to be sin" (2 Corinthians 5:21). This happened on the cross, so that we could receive his righteousness (5:18–21).

As a result, "if anyone is in Christ, he is a new creation" (5:17). Christ makes us a sweet-smelling aroma to God and gives us confidence to stand before him (2:14; 3:4). In Christ God "always leads us in triumphal procession" (2:14). In the context of Paul's travel plans, he profoundly summarizes the impact which Jesus has: "For all the promises of God find their Yes in him" (1:20). He truly is God's "inexpressible gift" (9:15).

For Further Discussion

1. Many people are dissatisfied with the Christian church today because of all of its problems. Are problems within the church anything new? Explain why or why not. What is a proper response to such people?

2. A number of the issues Paul addresses in 1 Corinthians continue to be problems which face God's people today. What are some of these issues? How can we use Paul's words to help us deal with them?

3. In 1 Corinthians 1–4 Paul writes about divisions in the church at Corinth. How do you think Paul would respond to all the divisions in the Christian church today?

4. Three times in 1 Corinthians Paul asserts that everything is lawful or permissible (1 Corinthians 6:12 twice; 10:23). What exactly does he mean by this? Do you agree?

5. If you were in first-century Corinth, would you have eaten meat that was offered to idols (1 Corinthians 8–10)? Why or why not? What do you think Jesus would have done?

6. Explain the analogy of the traffic signal. Is it accurate and helpful? Why or why not? Give two or three contemporary examples that fit into each category (red, yellow and green).

7. How does Paul describe the Lord's Supper in 1 Corinthians 10–11? What is it exactly? What was problematic about the Lord's Supper in Corinth? How is it intended to be beneficial for those who receive it? Can it be harmful as well? How and why?

8. What do you think our resurrected or "changed" bodies will be like in heaven (see 1 Corinthians 15:35–57)?

9. Why is there such a difference between the tone of 1 and 2 Corinthians?

10. Evaluate each of the bullet points about Christian giving which were drawn from 2 Corinthians 8 and 9. Which points do you think are most persuasive? Why?

For Further Reading

Barrett, C. K. *The First Epistle to the Corinthians*. Harper's New Testament Commentaries. New York: Harper and Row, 1968.

Bruce, F. F. *1 and 2 Corinthians*. The New Century Bible Commentary. Grand Rapids: Eerdmans, 1971.

Carson, D. A. *Showing the Spirit: A Theological Exposition of 1 Corinthians 12–14*. Grand Rapids: Baker, 1987.

Fee, Gordon. *The First Epistle to the Corinthians*. The New International Commentary. Grand Rapids: Eerdmans, 1987.

Hughes, Philip. *The Second Epistle to the Corinthians*. The New International Commentary on the New Testament. Grand Rapids: Eerdmans, 1962.

Lockwood, Gregory. *1 Corinthians*. Concordia Commentary. St. Louis: Concordia, 2000.

Murphy-O'Connor, Jerome. *St. Paul's Corinth: Text and Archaeology*. Collegeville, MN: Liturgical, 2003.

Scott, James. *2 Corinthians*. New International Biblical Commentary. Peabody, MA: Hendrickson, 1998.

Smedes, Lewis. *Love within Limits: A Realist's View of 1 Corinthians 13*. Grand Rapids: Eerdmans, 1978.

Toppe, Carleton. *First Corinthians*. People's Bible Commentary. St. Louis: Concordia, 1992.

Witherington, Ben, III. *Conflict and Community in Corinth*. Grand Rapids: Eerdmans, 1995.

Women in the Church. A Report of the Commission on Theology and Church Relations of the Lutheran Church-Missouri Synod. St. Louis: Concordia, 1985.

Vallesky, David. *Second Corinthians*. People's Bible Commentary. St. Louis: Concordia, 1992.

Colossians and Philemon

Prison Epistles

In four of his letters Paul specifically says he is a prisoner or in chains (Colossians 4:18; Philemon 1, 10, 13; Philippians 1:13; Ephesians 3:1; 4:1). As a result, Colossians, Philemon, Philippians, and Ephesians are called the **Prison Epistles** or Captivity Letters. The question left unanswered by these letters is, "Where is Paul in prison and when?" Since the letters do not tells us directly, we are left to search for answers based on Acts and on indirect evidence drawn from the Prison Epistles and Paul's other letters. These sources tell us he was in prison or under house arrest the following times: 1) very briefly in *Philippi* (Acts 16:23; A.D. 50); 2) in *Caesarea*, where he waited two years for a hearing before Governor Felix (Acts 24:27; A.D. 56–58); 3) in *Rome*, waiting two years

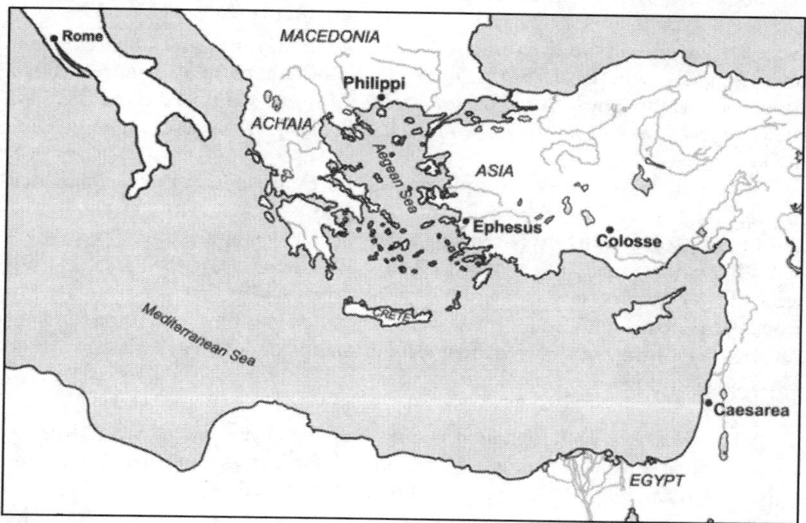

for his trial there at the end of Acts (28:30; A.D. 59–61); 4) Second Timothy speaks of a later imprisonment in *Rome* when Paul senses his death is near (2 Timothy 1:8; 4:6; A.D. 64). Regarding the second and third imprisonments, one should not envision Paul bound in chains in a dungeon. Rather, as a Roman citizen, he was placed under house arrest, able to receive guests, and able to write letters.

It is possible Paul was imprisoned at other times during his ministry, even though we do not have direct evidence indicating this. Second Corinthians 11:23–27 supports such an assumption. The passage suggests an additional imprisonment during his three-year stay in *Ephesus* on his third missionary journey (Acts 19:10; 20:31; A.D. 52–55). Although Acts does not refer to Paul being arrested at that time, the selective events it recounts from Paul's stay in Ephesus could fit within a month or less (Acts 19:1–41). As a result, an imprisonment, even a fairly lengthy one, is possible. There are numerous references to the hostility and suffering Paul endured while at Ephesus (Acts 19:9, 33; 20:19; 21:27; 1 Corinthians 16:9; 2 Corinthians 1:8; perhaps Romans 16:4); he even alludes to the possibility of facing imprisonment and death (2 Corinthians 1:9–10; 11:23). In 1 Corinthians 15:32 Paul refers to a time when he "fought with beasts at Ephesus." If these words are taken literally, they suggest Paul was in trouble with the authorities and, perhaps, imprisoned as well.

Theatre at Ephesus (see Acts 19: 29–41)

Where, then, do the Prison Epistles belong? Of the possibilities enumerated above, the first can be excluded since the imprisonment was too brief. The fourth also seems unlikely based upon the "last will and testament" tone of 2 Timothy, which stands in contrast to Paul's other letters. Scholars are basically left with these three options: Ephesus, Caesarea, or the first imprisonment in Rome. It is possible all four letters were written during the same imprisonment (in Rome?), or they are from different times and places. The available evidence leads to the following conclusions:

- *Colossians* and *Philemon* belong together. Both letters mention these same seven individuals in relation to the correspondence: Onesimus, Aristarchus, Mark, Epaphras, Luke, Demas, and Archippus.
- Despite the lack of concrete evidence for an imprisonment, geography favors Ephesus as the source of Colossians and Philemon. Ephesus is approximately 125 miles from Colosse.
- As a result, Paul's relationship with Onesimus, a runaway slave whom Paul met in prison and is sending back to his master, Philemon, seems most plausible. Caesarea is too distant for that relationship to have occurred, and Rome is less likely for the same reason. However, Rome is supported by the mention of Luke in both letters, since the author of

Acts was present during Paul's first Roman imprisonment (Acts 28:16). He is not, however, mentioned as being with Paul in Ephesus.

- References to the imperial guard and Caesar's household in *Philippians* favor Rome as the location from which that letter was written (Philippians 1:13; 4:22). However, these terms could apply to military or political entities in other cities as well. Philippians 1:20 indicates Paul is facing a possible death verdict as he writes. This is not likely away from Rome since a **Roman citizen** like Paul could always appeal his case to Caesar's court.
- The setting of *Ephesians* is even more uncertain due to the lack of personal references in the letter. Its content is similar enough to Colossians to suggest that it could have been written at the same time and served as a more general letter. In fact, some early texts do not contain the words "in Ephesus" at the opening of the letter (Ephesians 1:1). Perhaps Ephesians is a **circular letter** which Paul intends to be passed around or circulated among a number of different congregations (compare Revelation 1:11). If so, it may be the "letter from Laodicea" referred to in Colossians 4:16. In any event, the general content of Ephesians allows it to serve well as an over-arching summation of Paul's theology and practice.

Based upon our current evidence, the prospects for reaching a consensus about the setting of the Prison Epistles is unlikely and, ultimately, inconsequential. The content of the letters does not change based on the time and place of their writing. Nevertheless, they have to be put somewhere. In this book these four letters are arranged according to a plausible scenario based on the most reliable evidence available. Colossians and Philemon are located within the context of Paul's three-year stay in Ephesus. Philippians is identified with the setting of Paul's first Roman imprisonment. Ephesians, as its content is more generic, is placed at the beginning of our discussion of Paul's last letters addressed to Timothy and Titus.

Street in ancient Ephesus

Introduction

As illustrated above, Colossians and Philemon are integrally linked with each other. Yet one is addressed to a congregation, the other to an individual. Colossians is unique among the letters studied thus far, because Paul did not personally know the believers to whom he writes (Colossians 2:1). The congregation was founded by Epaphras. Paul speaks of him as a fellow prisoner, a fellow servant, and a faithful minister of Christ (Philemon 23; Colossians 1:7; 4:12). In light of the discussion above, it seems best to conclude that Epaphras was brought to Christ by Paul during his three years in Ephesus on his third journey. During that time, through the work of various missionaries trained by Paul, "all the residents of Asia heard the word of the Lord, both Jews and Greeks" (Acts 19:10). We know Epaphras did mission work in three cities east of Ephesus (Laodicea, Heirapolis and Colosse; see Colossians 4:13). Now, however, he is a fellow prisoner with Paul (Philemon 23).

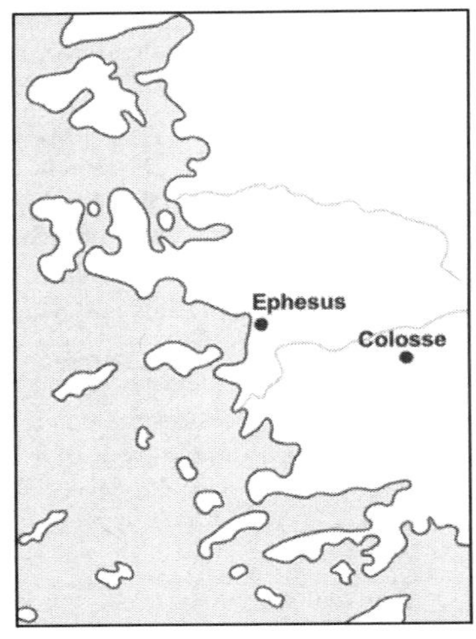

Colossians, like 1 Corinthians, is written in response to specific problems afflicting the Christian community. However, while the issues in Corinth are largely practical, Colossians is mainly striving to correct doctrinal problems. We do not have sources which provide specific details about the teachings being refuted. Rather, the false doctrines must be inferred from the corrective responses Paul directs toward the Colossians (see Colossians 2:20–23). Some problematic issues are related to controversies Paul regularly engaged in with his fellow Jews (for example, circumcision, observance of the Sabbath and other festivals; 2:11, 16). His reference to "the worship of angels" is probably directed against Jewish literature which had greatly expanded upon Scripture's teaching regarding angels during the intertestamental years (2:18). Other disputed issues seem to have a more **Hellenistic** basis (deceptive philosophy, fine-sounding arguments, ascetic practices; 2:4, 8, 20–21). Yet it is unwise to draw too sharp of a distinction between the two. There were streams of **Hellenistic Judaism** which tried to merge Old Testament teachings with Greek philosophies.

Many scholars identify the philosophic teachings being countered by Paul with **Gnosticism**, a heresy which came to prominence in the second century. It asserted that physical matter was evil and that salvation consisted in escaping the physical human body through the attainment of a secret *knowledge* (*gnosis* in Greek). For this reason, Colossians is often described as a document written long after Paul's death and attributed to him by a pseudonymous author. However, as the text stands, the letter is by the apostle. It is reasonable to conclude that an incipient form of Gnosticism was already developing in first-century Colosse and was opposed by Paul in this letter.

Closely related to Colossians is the story of Onesimus and Philemon. Onesimus was a slave who ran away from his master, Philemon. The runaway slave met Paul while in prison and became a believer as a result of his contact with Paul (Philemon 10). Master Philemon was also a believer as a result of Paul's work (19). Onesimus was sent back to his master along with a personal letter from the apostle. This letter written to Philemon is the first one we have studied that is addressed to a single individual. It is also the shortest of Paul's letters in the New Testament. (Their order in the Bible is roughly determined by length. Paul's longest letter, Romans, comes first. Philemon only has one chapter and is placed last.)

Structure and Theme

Colossians follows the regular pattern of Paul's letters that was identified at the beginning of this chapter.

COLOSSIANS	
OPENING	1:1–2
THANKSGIVING	1:3–14
BODY	1:15–2:23
EXHORTATION	3:1–4:6
CLOSING	4:7–18

In regard to theme, this textbook began with the assertion that the New Testament is really focused upon three fundamental questions. The first two were "Who is Jesus?" and "What has he done?" Consider the New Testament as we have studied it thus far. Which of those two questions has received the most attention? Certainly the second. Yet, from time to time, the New Testament reflects upon the enormous significance of how the first question is to be properly answered. Colossians is one book that does so (see also John 1:1–14; Philippians 2:6). As a result, its main theme focuses upon Christ as the head of his church.

Philemon is a personal letter and revolves around a single subject. It follows the typical letter structure, although the body is essentially an exhortation to Philemon to apply his faith to a specific issue. The subject at hand is a weighty and controversial one, slavery. It seems shocking to us that Paul would send a slave back into slavery. However, the penalty for a runaway slave could have been death. Onesimus is, in a sense, rescued from this fate by returning to a receptive master. That is what Paul encourages. Philemon should accept Onesimus back, not so much as a slave anymore, but as a dear brother in the Lord Jesus (Philemon 16).

This is an appropriate place to discuss the New Testament's attitude toward slavery. First of all, slavery is dealt with as a pre-existing condition. In other words, the New Testament does not inaugurate slavery; it is a reality already present in the Roman Empire when Christianity comes upon the scene. Second, the New Testament never suggests slavery is a good thing; neither does it encourage or promote slavery. Rather, it tolerates the presence of slavery within the culture of the day. But the New Testament profoundly transforms the relationship between slave and master. When Christ changes people, they behave in a radically different manner (2 Corinthians 5:17). For example, Philemon is to welcome and restore even a disobedient runaway like Onesimus because he is now "a beloved brother" in the Lord (Philemon 16). Ephesians 6:5–9 mentions that slaves are to obey their earthly masters with genuine respect as if serving Christ himself. But Paul then turns the tables and calls masters to treat their slaves in the same way. In reality, there is ultimately only one master or Lord, Jesus (compare Colossians 3:22–4:1).

Ancient slaves at work

Key Texts

Colossians 1:13–20 These verses conclude a prayer of thanks to God the Father who "has delivered us from the domain of darkness and transferred us to the kingdom of his beloved Son" (Colossians 1:13). Verse 14 equates this redemption with the forgiveness of sins. Paul then turns his attention from what Jesus accomplished "for us and for our salvation" (language from the Nicene Creed) to focus on who Jesus is.

What would it be like to see God? Paul says Jesus is the visible representation of God's character (2:15). Jesus' association with God is even closer. The Nicene Creed identifies God the Father as the "maker of heaven and earth." This often leads to the assumption that Jesus was not involved in creation. However, Paul clearly states Jesus is the firstborn over all creation; he existed before all things and "all things were created through him and for him" (Colossians 1:16). The personhood of Jesus is even more majestic. "For in him all the fullness of

God was pleased to dwell" (1:19). Jesus of Nazareth is fully God, the eternal Creator.

Verse 20 returns to speak about what Jesus has done. He reconciled and made peace for all through the blood he shed on the cross. As the firstborn from among the dead, he is also now the head of his body, the church. That is who Jesus is and what he has done.

2:6–17 The implications of the previous section are laid out here. Paul restates who Jesus is: "For in him the whole fullness of deity dwells bodily" (2:9). But Paul's even greater good news to the Colossians is this: "you have been filled in him" (2:10). As a result, they are called to live fully in Christ rather than being enticed by human traditions and philosophies. The implication of Paul's words is that some in Colosse are being drawn in those directions.

Verses 11–13 make a very significant connection between Old Testament circumcision and New Testament baptism. Paul equates uncircumcision with the sinful nature which was "cut off" when believers were buried with Christ and raised to new life in baptism. In baptism something of great significance happens. Those dead in sins are made alive with Christ! Baptism is also linked to "faith in the powerful working of God" (2:12). Now that Christ has come, circumcision done by human hands is no longer necessary. Baptism has rendered it obsolete (see the more complete discussion of baptism under Romans 6 below).

We can infer more about the false teachings being refuted by Paul in this letter from verses 16–17. Some were judging the Colossians based upon matters of food and drink and of holy days. The latter included Sabbath day observances, as well as other religious festivals and celebrations. As with circumcision, the basis for attempting to make a distinction between foods and days is clearly rooted in the Old Testament.

While the situation in Colosse does not seem quite as contentious as in Galatia, the implications are the same. Christ freed his New Testament people from rigid adherence to the Sabbath and other Old Testament festivals (Matthew 12:1–8). He also declared all foods clean (Mark 7:19). While continued acceptance of Old Testament food and festival regulations is permitted, they must not be a matter of judgment (Colossians 2:16). Paul describes them as a shadow which was created by something ahead. They were virtual reality, but the true substance is found in Christ (2:17).

The Application/Exhortation section of Colossians 3–4 is parallel to Ephesians 4–6. For example, compare Ephesians 5:18–6:9 with Colossians 3:16–4:2. To avoid repetition, the matters addressed in both letters will be discussed under Ephesians below.

Philemon 8–16 The name "Onesimus" means "useful." In verse 11 Paul puns on the meaning of the slave's name to make his point. Onesimus ran away from Philemon and became useless to him. Now, however, after encountering Paul while in prison and becoming a believer, he is useful both to Paul and Philemon. Paul sends Onesimus back for his own protection and to restore a wrong. Paul urges Philemon to accept him no longer as a slave, but as a dear brother in the Lord (Philemon 16). While their master/slave relationship may soon become a reality once again, it has been forever transformed for those who have together received the love of Christ (9).

Along with his direct appeal, Paul also uses some indirect means to encourage a new, reconciled relationship between master and slave. If Onesimus has robbed Philemon, Paul offers to repay the debt. But he reminds Philemon that he really owes Paul his very life in Christ (19). Paul also hints that he may come and visit soon (22). At least one aspect of that visit would certainly be to check on the treatment received by his "son" in the faith, Onesimus (10).

Jesus in Colossians and Philemon

In Colossians Paul speaks most directly concerning the person of Christ. All the fullness of God dwells in him (1:19; 2:9). He is the firstborn in these two ways: 1) of all creation; and 2) from the dead (1:15, 18). In regard to the former, he is, in fact, the creator and sustainer of all that exists (1:16–17). However, the Gospel message is encompassed in the latter. Jesus is the one through whom God reconciles and makes "peace by the blood of his cross" (1:20). Both of these aspects are then brought together under his all-encompassing dominion. As the firstborn of creation, all thrones, powers, rulers, and authorities exist in and through him (1:16); as the firstborn from the dead, he has triumphed over them all and, thereby, disarmed them (2:15).

But these are not merely ideas out there somewhere. God has made known "the riches of the glory of this mystery, which is Christ in you, the hope of glory" (1:27). Those of us in whom Christ lives "have been filled in him" (2:10). Our lives are also now "hidden with Christ in God" (3:3). Indeed, he is our very life (3:4). "The word of Christ" dwells richly within and among us (3:16). The true substance or reality of everything God has spoken is Jesus Christ (2:17).

The brief letter of Philemon makes few, if any, direct statements about the person and work of Christ. On the one hand, we can see Onesimus' freedom from slavery and gracious acceptance by his lord and master, Philemon, as a metaphor for what the Lord Jesus Christ has done for us. However, Jesus permeates the appeal of this letter in a much more direct and profound way. He is the basis upon which Paul urges Philemon to accept Onesimus back as a brother (8, 16). In other words, those who have "full knowledge of every good thing that is in us for the sake of Christ" (6) are, thereby, motivated and enabled to share those good things with others. As a result, Jesus is not only the source of our forgiveness and reconciliation with God, he also seeks to accomplish the same "good thing" among those of us who are now brothers and sisters "in the Lord" (6, 16).

For Further Discussion

1. Consider the setting of New Testament letters like the four Prison Epistles. Why is it helpful to know when and where these letters were written in order to understand them properly or fully? Why do you think God's inspired

word does not give us enough information to locate the context of these letters more precisely?

2. How does the New Testament respond to the issue of slavery in the Roman empire? Do you agree? What do you think Paul would say about slavery in the United States during the time of the Civil War and about slavery as it continues to exist in parts of the world today?

3. Most people accept that Jesus of Nazareth was a historical person, but do they view him as portrayed by Paul in Colossians? Why or why not? According to Colossians 1 and 2, who is Jesus? How long has he been around? What is his role now?

For Further Reading

Barclay, William. *The All-Sufficient Christ: Studies in Paul's Letter to the Colossians*. Philadelphia: Westminster, 1963.

Deterding, Paul. *Colossians*. Concordia Commentary. St. Louis: Concordia, 2003.

Nordling, John. *Philemon*. Concordia Commentary. St. Louis: Concordia, 2004.

O'Brien, Peter. *Colossians, Philemon*. Word Biblical Commentary. Waco, TX: Word, 1982.

Romans

The Romans Debate

In recent years there has been an ongoing debate surrounding how to relate the content of Romans to its origin, setting, and purpose (see Karl Donfried, ed., *The Romans Debate*, Peabody, MA: Hendrickson, 1991). Previously, it was noted that 1 and 2 Corinthians are perhaps the most contextual of Paul's letters. Romans has been regarded as the most generic. As we work through the letter, we will see that Paul often uses inclusive terminology and addresses issues with a universal scope in mind (Romans 2:9–10; 3:22–23, 29–20; 4:16; 5:18; 10:11–13). In fact, he does not mention any contemporary person by name until Romans 16, the final chapter of the letter.

As a result, some people contend that Paul could have written Romans to almost anyone, anywhere, at anytime. According to this analysis, the *content* of Romans is the determining factor for what Paul wrote, apart from any specific context in Rome or elsewhere. This "traditional" view is reflected in the appraisal of Philip Melanchthon, a sixteenth-century colleague of Martin Luther, who suggested Romans "contains the foremost and enduring topics of Christian doctrine" (*Commentary on Romans*, trans. F. Kramer, Concordia, 1992). Following Melanchthon's approach, a number of contemporary scholars emphasize the fact that Paul had not yet visited Rome. In most of his letters, what Paul writes is based upon the personal interaction he has already had with the addressees. However, the vast majority of believers in Rome have never heard the apostle teach in person. Therefore, he needs to cover the basics of the faith thoroughly. This helps explain the extensive treatment of a righteous relationship before God in Romans. Along similar lines, some suggest Paul is speaking in general terms about God's redemptive activity, dealing with issues surrounding Israel and the Law, and/or giving his summary of Christian teaching at a significant juncture in his missionary activity. If these all-encompassing evaluations are correct, it is curious that Romans never refers to the Lord's Supper, does not include a "table of duties" describing how believers should live out their lives in various roles (as in Ephesians 5–6 and Colossians 3), and makes only the briefest references to the return of Christ (see Romans 13:11–12; 14:10–12).

Others propose that the key factor is *Paul's situation* as he writes the letter. He is on his way to Jerusalem with an offering, and also aware of the dangers that await him there (15:25–27). Some who adopt this approach highlight the eschatological significance of the Gospel going out from the Jews to the nations, followed by the Gentiles bearing their gifts back to Jerusalem in fulfillment of the prophets (for example, Isaiah 60:5–9; 66:20; Haggai 2:7). The severity of the upcoming conflicts Paul is about to face in Jerusalem has led others to speak of Romans as Paul's "last will and testament" (see Acts 20:38; 21:10–13).

Forum at Rome

However, within the letter Paul is already looking beyond Jerusalem. He plans to visit Rome and, then to be sent by the believers there to do further mission work in Spain (Romans 15:24, 28). During his first three journeys Paul relied on the congregation in Antioch, Syria as the sponsor, supporter, and overseer of his mission work (Acts 13:1–3; 14:26–27; 18:22–23). As Paul moves far beyond them to the west, he is seeking another congregation to sponsor him. According to this approach, Paul's purpose is to lay out his teaching before asking for their approval and financial assistance. The word translated "helped" in Romans 15:27 is a technical term for such support (as in Acts 15:3; 1 Corinthians 16:6, 11).

Still others assert the content of Romans is Paul's response to information he has received about the believers in Rome. The problem here is our lack of specific evidence from Romans, Acts, or other sources regarding the origin, make-up, and current situation of the Christians in Rome. Aside from a reference to visitors from Rome being present at Pentecost (Acts 2:10), we are left to draw our own conclusions about these believers based on what Paul writes to them. However, it is difficult to tell from the letter if and how Paul speaks directly to their circumstances. Some scholars use the list of names in chapter 16 to try to draw a more complete picture of the Romans to whom Paul writes. More commonly, the attention given throughout the letter to issues surrounding the relationship between Jews and Gentiles is identified as key (Romans 1:16–17; 2:9–11; 3:9; 10:23). It is suggested that Romans 14:1–15:12, in particular, indicates there were either separate Jewish and Gentile house churches which needed to be united or conflicts among Jews and Gentiles within mixed congregations.

Each of these positions has some merit. However, the contextual nature of Romans, obscure as may be to us today, should not be underestimated. The emphasis Romans places upon the standing of Jews and Gentiles before God, as well as their relationship with each other, supports the validity of the last position cited. The extended discussion of the role of Israel in chapters 9–11 also adds credence to it. According to the Roman historian Suetonius, Emperor Claudius expelled all Jews from Rome in A.D. 49 because of their ongoing disputes about a certain "*Chrestus*" (*Claudius, 25*; see also Acts 18:2). It seems probable this is a misspelling of the Greek word *Christos*, that is, Christ. If so, this could be evidence that the sharp conflicts which arose throughout Paul's missionary journeys between Jews who had accepted Jesus as the Messiah and those who rejected him also occurred in Rome.

At the same time, the significance of Jew/Gentile issues would logically be prominent as Paul focuses on delivering an offering to Jerusalem from Gentiles who have accepted the Jewish Messiah. That Paul confronted issues related to Jews, Gentiles, and the Law throughout his ministry also lends support to the more generic view of Romans. Finally, the fact that Paul has not yet visited Rome buttresses the more general appraisal of the letter as an introductory overview of his teaching prior to seeking their support for his mission work. In conclusion, the interrelated facets involved in each of these positions shows how difficult it is to resolve the issues surrounding the content and purpose of this letter. The Romans debate continues.

Introduction

Despite our lack of information about the setting in Rome, we are able to identify fairly well the context from which Paul wrote the letter. On his third missionary journey, Paul left Ephesus after an extended stay. He then traveled through Macedonia and Achaia, revisiting many of the cities of his second journey. Paul was engaged in collecting an offering from the Gentile Christians to be given to the believers in Jerusalem (1 Corinthians 16:1–4; 2 Corinthians 8–9).

Acts 20:23 informs us that he stayed three months in Greece/Achaia. After delivering the offering, Paul planned to journey on to Rome (Acts 19:21).

This setting correlates well with a number of references from Romans. Romans 15:23–27 speaks of the offering being gathered for the poor believers in Jerusalem and of Paul's intention to visit Rome once this is completed. Romans 16 also contains a number of specific links to Corinth. Verse 1 identifies the bearer of the letter as Phoebe, the **deacon** (*diakonos* in Greek) of the church in Cenchrea which is the port just east of Corinth. Verse 23 mentions Erastus, the manager or treasurer of the city. An inscription found near the theatre in Corinth mentions an Erastus who occupied this same position. In addition, the same verse mentions Gaius. He is likely the person baptized by Paul in Corinth (1 Corinthians 1:14). He may also be the companion of Paul from Macedonia who is present with Paul in Ephesus according to Acts 19:29. Some suggest Gaius is another name for Titius Justus who is tied to Corinth in Acts 18:7. All this makes it safe to conclude Romans was written by Paul on his third missionary journey while at Corinth in A.D. 56.

Erastus Inscription at Corinth's theatre

Theme and Structure

Since Paul has not yet been in Rome to teach in person, he has much to write in this letter, which may account for the substantial length of Romans, as well as its comprehensive nature. People have long identified Romans as the most organized or systematic of Paul's letters. It has also been referred to as a summary of his entire theology.

We are used to books having titles. These New Testament letters have all had titles attached to them by later readers. With Paul's letters, the titles refer to the recipients. In other words, Paul did not title this letter "Romans" and it is misleading for us to speak of it in that manner. The theme of Romans is stated in 1:17 and borrowed from the Old Testament. Habakkuk 2:4 declared, "The righteous shall live by faith" (Romans 1:17). If Paul published this document as a book today, that would probably be its title for two important reasons.

First, it allows Paul to assert that his teaching concerning the righteousness of God is not something new. As he makes clear throughout the letter, it is drawn straight from the Old Testament. In this light, the quotation from Habakkuk in Romans 1:17 merely begins a long series of well over fifty Old Testament citations, far more than in any of Paul's other letters.

Second, Paul is using this prophetic verse something like a sermon text and unpacks all of its meaning as he proceeds. Some Jews of Paul's day interpreted Habakkuk 2:4 as prophetic of the Messiah. He would be *the Righteous One* who would live in faithfulness to God. Paul certainly identifies Jesus Christ as that Righteous One. But Romans illustrates that he sees much more in Habakkuk's words. Paul proceeds to announce that the faithfulness of Christ is now the source of *righteousness* for everyone who believes. Additionally, it is only by faith that people can be in a right relationship with God and, therefore, live before him. Finally, Paul expounds how those who are righteous by faith will live out their lives in response.

The outline of Romans follows the typical letter format of the day. But it also reflects the foundational nature of the quote from Habakkuk for the structure of the letter. It has been adapted from the *Commentary on Romans* by Anders Nygren (Muhlenberg Press, 1949).

ROMANS: THE RIGHTEOUS WILL LIVE BY FAITH (1:17)	
OPENING	1:1–7
THANKSGIVING AND THEME	1:8–17
BODY	1:18–11:36
RIGHTEOUSNESS IS BY FAITH	1:18–4:25
ALL ARE UNDER THE WRATH OF GOD	1:18–3:20
THE RIGHTEOUSNESS OF GOD IS FOR ALL WHO BELIEVE	3:21–4:25
THE ONE WHO IS RIGHTEOUS BY FAITH LIVES . . .	5:1–8:39
FREE FROM GOD'S COMING WRATH	5:1–21
FREE FROM SIN'S REIGN	6:1–23
FREE FROM THE LAW'S CONDEMNATION,	7:1–8:4
FREE FROM DEATH ETERNAL	8:4–39
THE RIGHTEOUSNESS OF FAITH IS NOT CONTRARY TO THE PROMISE OF GOD	9:1–11:36
THE PROMISE HAS ALWAYS BEEN ONLY TO BELIEVERS	9:6–29
AN ANALYSIS OF ISRAEL'S STUMBLING	9:30–10:21
ISRAEL'S REJECTION IS NOT FINAL	11:1–36
EXHORTATION/APPLICATION: HOW ONE WHO	

Is Righteous By Faith Can Live	12:1–15:13
As a living sacrifice and with sincere love	12:1–13:14
Relationships between the weak and the strong	14:1–15:13
Conclusion	15:14–16:27

After an extended opening in which Paul introduces the Gospel he proclaims, the apostle offers his typical thanksgiving to God. At the end of the introductory section, his theme from Habakkuk 2:4 is laid out, preceded by the famous words, "I am not ashamed of the gospel, for it is the power of God for salvation to everyone who believes" (1:16).

The rest of Romans 1–4 expounds on the theme "righteousness is by faith" by demonstrating that people are not righteous on their own, by their works, or through obedience to the Law. The demands of the Law are intended to drive all people toward the righteousness that comes through the faithfulness of and faith in Jesus Christ (3:22). This theme of righteousness by faith is consistent with the Old Testament's teaching as exemplified by Abraham, "the father of all who believe" (4:11).

The place of Romans 5–8 deserves further comment because it is critical to understanding Paul's theology. His theology has a **now/not yet** aspect to it. The Gospel announces and delivers many things through faith in Christ here and now. However, there are other aspects of the Gospel which are yet to be fully realized or experienced. Both facets are clearly expressed in Romans 5–8.

Chapter 5 declares that those who have been justified by faith are *now* at peace with God (5:1). Yet it is not until the future day of judgment that they *will be* saved from his wrath (5:9). According to Romans 6, those who have been baptized are raised to a new life in which they are no longer slaves to sin (6:4, 17). Yet believers are urged to continue in their ongoing struggle against sin (6:12–13). Romans 7 asserts that believers are no longer under the rule or condemnation of the Law (7:4, 6; 8:1). Yet they are still frustrated by their inability to live according to the Law's good, holy, and righteous commands (7:12–25). Finally, chapter 8 states that believers *now* possess the Spirit of Christ, but only as a kind of firstfruits (8:23). Since their sinful body is still mortal (8:10), they, like all of creation, groan in travail *waiting* to be finally delivered (8:22–23).

This now/not yet understanding of Paul's theology is summarized beautifully in Romans 6:8. Note the change in tenses when Paul writes, "If we died with him [past; baptism into Christ; 6:3–4] we believe [present] that we will also live with him [future]."

In Romans 9–11, Paul turns his attention to the people of Israel and assesses the impact of the Gospel on them. Although this section has sometimes been viewed as tangential to the main theme of the letter, that assertion is certainly a mistake. In many ways, these chapters drive home the central teachings Paul laid out earlier in Romans and anchors them securely within the Old Testament. Here again, paradox is present. Chapter 9 attributes salvation to the work of God alone (monergism), yet Romans 10 illustrates that God allows himself to be resisted.

In line with the Law, Gospel, and response structure of his theology, Paul uses the latter section of this letter to make applications based upon what he has taught thus far (Romans 12–15). In response to God's mercy in Christ, believers are to offer themselves as living sacrifices to God (12:1–2), by living a life of genuine love and of obedience to the governing authorities and by living in unity within the community of faith—a unity that can so easily be divided between weak and strong.

Romans 16 warrants some explanation. Before concluding the letter, Paul sends greetings to a long list of names (16:1–16). Why are these included in the Bible? Remember that Paul has not yet been in Rome to proclaim the Gospel himself. The people mentioned are already acquainted with him in some way and are aware of his teachings and reputation. They are probably intended to serve as his personal references to the rest of the believers there.

Key Texts

3:9–20 After boldly proclaiming the Gospel in his introduction (1:1–17), Paul sharply switches tone. At 1:18 he turns his focus to God's wrath. It is coming against all who have exchanged the clear evidence of God's existence and power which his creation provides (1:19–20; compare Psalm 19:1–6). They have turned away from worshipping him toward idolatry, homosexual activity, and a long list of other seemingly less serious vices, like gossiping and disobeying parents (Romans 1:21–31). Paul concludes, "Those who practice such things deserve to die" (1:32).

People tend to view some sins as worse than others and to look down in judgment on those who have committed what they consider to be the more heinous offenses. But any act of disobedience places us under God's judgment (2:3). This is true even for those who have not received the revealed will of God in the Scriptures. However, they will not be judged by the standard of God's written Law, but by "the work of the law" he has written on all people's heart and conscience (2:15). Humanity generally exhibits a knowledge of right and wrong even apart from God's special revelation, evidence that such a **natural knowledge of God** exists (2:12–16). Paul ominously concludes, "For all who have sinned without the law will also perish without the law" (2:12). On the other hand, those to whom the Law has been revealed have a good thing (3:1–2), but it also judges their failure to obey it fully (2:17–24). Apart from an inner relationship with God through faith, all stand under judgment.

Paul uses the legal language of the courtroom to pronounce his verdict in 3:9 and 19–20. The indictment encompasses all people; Jews and Gentiles alike "are under the power of sin" (3:9). Since God does not show favoritism (2:11), everyone is without excuse before his judgment seat. In 3:10–18 Paul supports the validity of his charge through a series of quotations from the written (Old Testament) word of God. The Law's role in this arena is negative. No one is righteous before God through the Law (3:19). Instead, its commands serve to make all people conscious of their sin and to leave them silent before God facing his impending wrath.

> A wealthy widow asked an artist to paint her portrait. It was to be hung prominently over the fireplace in her large living room. When the portrait was done, the artist unveiled the painting for her. The woman took one look at it and said, "I am not paying for that painting. It does not do me justice." To which the artist replied, "Ma'am, you don't want justice, you want mercy!" What do we want from God, justice or mercy? Justice is getting what we deserve based upon who we are and what we do. In Romans 1:18–3:20 Paul has demonstrated that all people justly deserve death and wrath. Thank goodness God is not fair with us; instead, he desires to "have mercy on all" (11:32).

3:21–28 This section marks a clear breaking point in Romans. Paul turns away from sin, judgment, wrath, and the Law to speak of a righteousness that comes from God through faith in Christ Jesus. A slogan on a t-shirt announced, "The righteousness he requires is the righteousness his righteousness requires him to require." Paul asserts something like this. God is not unjust; he does not simply ignore sin. Instead, God met his standard of righteousness through the sacrificial blood of Jesus. Paul uses language and imagery from the Old Testament to make his point. First, as Israel was ransomed or redeemed from slavery in Egypt, so Christ Jesus has bought us and brought us back to God (3:24; see Exodus 6:6; 15:13). Second, the atonement cover on the **Ark of the Covenant** foreshadowed Jesus' death. This image visualizes the accusations of the Law, whose tablets were contained in the Ark, being covered over with blood. So Jesus' death is the ultimate mercy seat, blood covering, or sacrifice of atonement for all who believe (3:25; see Leviticus 16:15–16; compare Hebrews 9:3–5).

Romans 3:28 is a key summary of Paul's teaching: "For we hold that one is justified by faith apart from works of the Law." This recalls the *either/or* argumentation of Galatians. There is no difference among people, for all have sinned and fallen far short of God's glory (3:23). Since all people fail to observe the Law, those who rely on "works of the Law" will also face wrath (2:17). But God justifies or declares righteous everyone who believes. They live in a right relationship with him through faith. Romans 4:4–5 explains these either/or opposites further. When someone works, they receive their wages as an obligation, not a gift. For Paul the opposite of "work" is faith, faith which trusts in a God who credits ungodly people as righteous (4:5). The fact that God regards or reckons wicked, godless people to be righteous reinforces the point that this is all the gracious work of God. Both aspects are concisely summarized at the end of chapter 6: "For the wages of sin is death, but the free gift of God is eternal life in Christ Jesus our Lord" (6:23).

In 3:29–30 Paul again asserts there is no difference or partiality with God. This righteousness is available to all who believe, whether Jew or Gentile. This teaching is consistent with the heart of the Old Testament faith, the ***Shema*** of

Deuteronomy 6:4, to which Paul alludes in these verses. The one, true God deals with all people in the same manner. The person Paul uses to make this point is Abraham, the father of the Jewish people.

4:20–5:1 In Romans 4:3 Paul quotes Genesis 15:6, as he did in Galatians, to assert that the basis of Abraham's relationship with God was faith. God credited his faith as righteousness. He did this long before the Law was given and even before Abraham was circumcised (Romans 4:9–11; see Genesis 17). His righteousness, therefore, was not dependent upon circumcision or the Law, but upon faith.

> In the late 1800s, a stuntman named Blondin announced in New York City that he would walk on a tightrope over Niagara Falls. A great crowd gathered to watch his death-defying feat. After Blondin walked carefully over and back, the crowd *knew* he was the greatest stuntman in the world. Then he grabbed a little wheelbarrow and walked back and forth again pushing the wheelbarrow in front of him. When he returned, the crowd *acknowledged* what they knew to be true. They burst into great applause, shouting, "You are the greatest stuntman in the world!" Blondin came up to one of the members of the wildly cheering crowd. He asked, "Do you really believe I am the greatest stuntman in the world?" "Yes," came the reply. "Good," he said. "Then get in the wheelbarrow and ride over with me next time." That is real *trust*!

This illustration defines faith. It involves knowing who God is, then acknowledging or confessing him as Lord, and, finally, trusting in him. That is how it was with Abraham. First, Abraham *knew* God because God came to him and spoke great words of promise (Genesis 12:1–3). Second, Abraham *acknowledged* God's word was true; in Paul's words, he "was fully convinced that God was able to do what he promised" (Romans 4:21). Finally, when God called Abraham to leave his homeland and his family, he got in the wheelbarrow and let God do the driving. Abraham *trusted* God, and his faith "was counted to him as righteousness" (4:3; quoting Genesis 15:6).

Yet the story of Abraham in the Old Testament also reveals that he doubted and struggled with how God would fulfill the promise to give him an heir (Genesis 16:1–6; 17:17–18). But Paul points out that Abraham did not waver into unbelief (Romans 4:20). Abraham never jumped ship. He always kept faith in God's word of promise even when he and Sarah were too old to have children. Eventually, God gave life to Sarah's "dead" womb (4:19). Later, when Abraham was asked to sacrifice Isaac, he was willing to obey because he knew God could give life to the dead (4:17; see also Hebrews 11:17–19). Now Abraham's offspring are his heirs by faith, and they similarly receive a promise that is guaranteed by God's power to do what he says (Romans 4:16, 21).

Paul concludes that Abraham's story is not told in the Scriptures just for him, but for all those who believe in the God who raised Jesus back to life from the dead (4:23–24). By his death and resurrection, we also receive forgiveness of sins and justification. All those who are justified through faith live in a right relationship of peace and wholeness with God (5:1; *shalom* in Hebrew). This is quite a change from the wrath all people were under earlier! Chapters 5–8 go on to describe the life of those who are righteous by faith.

5:12–14 These key verses explain the origin of death and the role of the Law. Apart from sin, there is no death. In Genesis 3 sin entered through Adam, and, as God had warned, sin brought death (Genesis 3:3). Paul then asserts that death has spread to all people because "all sinned" (Romans 5:12). People are not condemned for Adam's sin, but for their own. Adam, however, brought sin and the resulting death into the world.

What about the Law's role in this equation? Adam had one command which God revealed to him (Genesis 2:16–17). Ever since Moses and Mount Sinai, the commands of God's revealed Law have also been present. But what about those who lived between Adam and Moses? Since they had no revealed Law, could they have been guilty of sin? Paul says, "Yes," and the proof of his assertion is that they all paid the wages of sin; they all died (Romans 5:14; see 6:23). Sin is present and properly judged even apart from the revealed Law (compare 2:12–16).

6:1–4 At the end of Romans 5, Paul asserts that Adam's disobedience led to judgment and condemnation for all (5:16, 18). The Law came along and only made things worse. It posted clearly worded trespassing signs, violations of which added even more transgressions. But no matter how high sins are piled, God's grace in Christ supercedes all that Adam, sin, death, and the Law brought into the world (5:20–21).

If this is so, why not sin all we want? (6:1; compare 1 Corinthians 6:12). After all, this would provide a foil to show, by comparison, how righteous and gracious God truly is (see Romans 3:5–8). Paul emphatically rejects such a notion, and his reason is baptism. In baptism something of great importance happened. People died to sin and were buried with Christ as they went under the waters (6:2–3); then they were raised up with Christ so that they might live a renewed life, not a sin-filled one (6:4).

Notice that as Paul addresses the issue of sin in the believer's life, he switches his way of speaking. Earlier, Paul's used legal language to convict all of sin and to base the believer's righteousness on God's declaration of acquittal because of Christ's death *for* us. Now, when he addresses the believer's conduct in regard to sin, he uses the incorporation language of baptism; he speaks of us being joined *with* Christ. Both truths are expressed in verse 7: the one who has died the death of baptism has been and remains *justified from* sin (not "set free" as is often translated). Because of baptism, believers are freed from *slavery* to sin, but they still struggle against it (6:6, 17, 19). So Paul urges, "Therefore do not let sin reign in your mortal body so that you obey its evil desires" (6:12; NIV). Baptism ends the slavery (*now*), but begins the battle (*not yet*).

Baptism in the New Testament

Baptism is a controversial issue among Christians today. This is most unfortunate since it is a wonderful blessing. To us the word "baptism" is a technical term for a sacrament of God. In Greek, however, the verb baptizo *simply means "to wash, normally immerse." That it does not have to mean "immerse" is evident from Luke 11:38. There we are told that Jesus did not baptize himself before a meal at a Pharisee's house. In all likelihood, this indicates that he did not wash his hands and feet in preparation for table fellowship (compare John 13:4–11). In some manuscripts, Mark 7:3–4 similarly explains that the Pharisees do not eat unless they baptize their dishes and dining couches. Here also the word does not require the meaning "immerse." However, it should be noted that immersion was the preferred, though not required, method of baptism in the early church (***Didache*** *7:1–4).*

What happens in baptism? Here in Romans Paul speaks of being "baptized into Christ Jesus ... We were buried therefore with him by baptism into death" (Romans 6:3–4). Baptism is the means by which a person is incorporated "into Christ" and brought into the fellowship of believers. "For in one Spirit we were all baptized into one body" (1 Corinthians 12:13; see also Galatians 3:27). Acts regularly associates baptism with entrance into the Christian community (for example, Acts 2:38; 8:38; 9:47–48). The thematic passage of Acts 2:38 also links repentance, the forgiveness of sins, and the reception of the Holy Spirit with baptism. 1 Peter 3 refers to the water which held up Noah's ark, thereby saving those within it, and then concludes, "Baptism, which corresponds to this, now saves you" (1 Peter 3:21).

But the New Testament's teaching regarding baptism is broader than a single word. The Scriptures talk about baptism in a number of different ways without always using that specific term. A synonym of baptizo *is used to describe the act as a washing away or cleansing of sins. Ephesians 5:26 speaks of "the washing of water with the word" (also 1 Corinthians 6:11). Titus 3:5 similarly depicts baptism as a washing and, then, goes on to define it as "regeneration and renewal." This is the language of rebirth that Jesus also used when stating the necessity of being "born again" and "born of water and the Spirit" (John 3:3, 5; see also 1 Peter 1:3). While the person being baptized is normally passive, Paul does speak of baptism as putting on or clothing oneself with Christ (Galatians 3:27; compare Colossians 3:12; Romans 13:14). Finally, baptism is also described as "the circumcision of Christ" (Colossians 2:11–12).*

It is important to apply that last description to the question of who should be baptized. Abraham was circumcised as an adult along with his household (Genesis 17:23–24).

However, from then on God called Old Testament Israel to practice "infant circumcision" on the eighth day for all males born within the community of God's people (Genesis 17:11–14). If adults from other nations came to acknowledge Israel's God as the true God, they were to be circumcised as adults (Exodus 12:43–49).

Since Paul explicitly calls baptism "the circumcision of Christ" (Colossians 2:11), it is logical to assume that he intends the same pattern to follow. In the New Testament, we have the record of many adult baptisms received by those who had been brought to faith in Christ (Acts 2:41; 8:36–39; 1 Corinthians 1:14, 16). But what about the children of those believers? It is true that no passage in the New Testament explicitly mandates the baptism of infants. Yet it is implied in a number of instances (Matthew 28:19; Acts 10:24, 47–48; 16:33–34).

The link with circumcision, however, makes a more significant theological point. Just as eight-day old infants were brought into the community of faith in the Old Testament through circumcision, so babies are now able to receive a similar action of God on their behalf in baptism (compare Luke 18:16–17; Acts 16:34). In Old Testament times and now through Baptism, God incorporates children into the community of his people regardless of their ability to comprehend what is happening (1 Corinthians 12:13). Adoption is an earthly example where a child's relationship with his or her parents changes without regard to the baby's action or awareness. The New Testament uses that metaphor in order to speak of how we have been adopted into the family of our heavenly Father because of his action on our behalf (see the discussion of "Paul's Metaphors for the Gospel" below).

Finally, it is important to note that Paul describes all people as being "by nature children of wrath" (Ephesians 2:3; see also 2:1; Romans 5:15–19; 1 Corinthians 15:21–22). The need for baptism is a universal one (John 3:3, 5).

7:7–8:4 In Romans 7, the Law shows up alongside sin and death. Earlier, Paul asserted that the Law makes us conscious of sin (Romans 3:20), increases trespasses of a revealed Law (5:20), and brings God's wrath (4:15). Here Paul adds that the Law is used by sin to provoke further sin in people as well as to deceive and to kill (7:11). However, none of this is the Law's fault. The Law is holy and its commands are holy, righteous, and good (7:12; compare 2:20). The solution is to die to the Law that once bound us as captives and, thereby, to be freed from the obligation to obey it (7:1, 6; this language is reminiscent of baptism as discussed in 6:1–4).

In order to illustrate the Law's effects, Paul uses the first person singular throughout Romans 7:7–25 and, apparently, depicts his own personal experience. However, many scholars dispute whether this chapter is autobiographical. For example, it is difficult to understand precisely in what sense Paul once lived "apart from the Law" (7:9). Nevertheless, it seems verses 7–11 describe his life prior to his encounter with Jesus on the road to Damascus. Paul speaks in the past tense to describe how sin used the Law's commands to incite further sin and, ultimately, to deceive and kill "me" (7:11). Indeed, a self-righteous Pharisee, as Paul was, is just the kind of person whom he now recognizes is being deceived by sin into relying on his own supposed righteousness based upon obedience to the Law's commands (compare 2:17; 9:32; 10:3; Philippians 3:6, 9). Other interpretations conclude that the first person forms in these verses do not refer to Paul, but vividly portray the experience of Adam or Israel when the Law's commandment came (v. 9). It is difficult to proceed with either of these identifications of the "I" in verses 14–25.

Beginning in verse 14, the "I" speaks in the present tense. However, the starkness of the description has caused many to reject the possibility that the apostle here speaks of his own Christian life (for example, "of the flesh, sold under sin" in 7:14; "nothing good dwells in me" in 7:18). A dominant interpretation of verses 14–25 is that these verses do not describe any one person in particular. Rather, they portray any unbeliever who is struggling to live before God on the basis of doing the Law's commands. However, it is unlikely that an unbeliever despairing under bondage to the Law would admit that the Law is good and even delight in it (7:16, 22). On the other hand, no self-righteous Pharisee, including Saul, would admit that sin "dwells within me … making me captive to the Law of sin that dwells in my members" (7:17, 23). Once again, the other proposed interpretations cause more difficulties than reading the text in its most straightforward way. It seems best to conclude that the first person forms refer to Paul, the author, and verses 14–25 describe his present experience as he writes.

Earlier in the chapter, Paul spoke of those who have been "released from the Law," but who now serve "in the new life of the Spirit" (7:6). How do they serve? By rejoicing in and striving to fulfill the holy, righteous, and good commands of the Law (7:12). Yet, as they do, Paul illustrates that a now/not yet situation continues. Paul rejoices in the Law and strives to fulfill its commands. But there is a disconnect between will and action that is all too familiar to each one of us. The culprit that thwarts our resolve is identified as sin that still dwells in our flesh (7:17). As Paul writes in Galatians 5:17, "For the desires of the flesh are against the Spirit, and the desires of the Spirit are against the flesh, for these are opposed to each other, to keep you from doing the things you want to do." The continuing inability to live according to the Law prompts great frustration. "Who will deliver me from this body of death?" (7:24). Although Christ has done so, the present experience remains—a willing desire to serve God by obeying his Law that is repeatedly being disrupted by the sinful nature (7:25).

The reality and the solution to this predicament are laid out in the verses to follow. This is another place where the chapter division is unfortunate. Romans 8:1–4 provide something of resolution. The Law did not go away; "I" still do not fulfill the Law; the Law still condemns disobedience. The Law is able to inform the believer's mind about God's will, but it is unable to empower those still in sinful flesh to carry it out (8:3). As a result, righteousness is not attainable by works of the Law; neither can any believer, even St. Paul, maintain a righteous standing before God through obedience to the Law's commands (7:14–25; in contrast to covenantal nomism as discussed earlier in this chapter). Nevertheless, there is no condemnation for those in Christ Jesus (8:1). Why? Because he became a sin offering in our place so that "the righteous requirement of the Law might be fulfilled in us" (8:4; compare Matthew 5:17).

8:28–39 At first, Romans 8 seems to depict a new life in the Spirit that stands in sharp contrast to the old ways of the flesh (for example, Romans 8:5–8). But the situation is really another both/and. "Although the body is dead because of sin, the spirit is life because of righteousness" (8:10). Both are true. The Spirit of Christ *now* dwells within believers, *yet* we still await a day when Christ Jesus "will also give life to [our] mortal bodies" (6:11). In fact, all of God's creation now groans in travail like the "I" in 7:14–25 (see 8:19–23).

Yet God promises to work all things together for good for those who love him (8:28). This does not mean that all the things which happen to us are God's will or that all things are good. It does mean that God promises ultimately to work "good" out of each and every situation encountered by those who love God and are called by him. The Old Testament illustration of this is the life of Joseph. Although his brothers meant to harm him, God worked that evil out for good and used it to save many lives (Genesis 50:20).

God's call is so all-encompassing it began before time in his foreknowledge and predestination (Romans 8:29). It revealed itself in time when he called and justified those who are his own. So certain is a glorious future that Paul speaks of it in the past tense (8:30). How can anyone be so sure? Paul's answer is the culmination of Romans 1–8. Paul raises rhetorical questions and then answers them in a conversational style paraphrased below (as in 3:1–8):

Question: What should we say about all of this?
Answer: God is for us.

Question: Then who can be against us?
Answer: No one that matters.

Question: How do we know?
Answer: He gave his Son.

Question: If God declares us justified, who can make any charge against us hold?
Answer: Well, Jesus, who "will come again in glory to judge the living and the dead" (**Apostles' Creed**), could condemn us. But, instead, he died for us and now, like the Holy Spirit, intercedes in our behalf (8:27, 34). Nothing, even death, can separate us from God's love which is ours in Christ Jesus.

9:1–9 Romans 9–11 is one of the most disputed sections in the New Testament. A particular focus of debate is the assertion in 11:26 that "all Israel will be saved." What does this mean? Paul begins chapter 9 by expressing grief over his own race, the people of Israel (9:2–3). Why, one wonders, if they will all be saved? The answer to the "all Israel" question must be given within the context of chapters 9–11 and, really, the entirety of Romans. Additionally, there is an even wider context. Paul's argument in Romans 9–11 makes extensive use of the Old Testament for support (over thirty quotations in three chapters).

In 9:6–9 he makes two initial points: 1) "Not all descended from Israel belong to Israel" (9:6). In other words, it was never purely and simply a matter of race. Recall, for example, what happened to the vast majority of the Israelites who were rescued from Egypt (see 1 Corinthian 10:1–5). One should also note that Paul clearly uses "Israel" in two senses in this one verse. 2) The important matter is not being Israel in terms of natural or physical descent; rather, God counts *the children of the promise* as Abraham's offspring (9:8). In both cases Abraham is referred to as an example. This recalls chapter four, where Abraham is described as "the father of all who believe" (4:11).

A lot of ink has been spilled on chapter 9 regarding the issues of predestination and God's eternal election. Paul's fundamental point, based on the Old Testament experiences of Sarah, Isaac, Rebekah, Jacob, and Esau is that God's choosing and blessing are not based on who we are and what we do; it is "not because of works but because of his call" (9:11). But whom does God call? Paul will answer in Romans 10. First, he draws another significant conclusion: "So then [God] has mercy on whom he wills and he hardens whomever he wills" (9:18). Then which does he want to do? Harden or have mercy? That question is finally answered at the end of Romans 11.

9:30–10:17 This is a profound delineation between Law and Gospel, and their respective roles in the attaining of righteousness before God. The way of the Law strives to establish one's own righteousness by doing works (10:4–5; citing Leviticus 18:5). Israel is characterized as pursuing a "Law that would lead to righteousness," but not obtaining it (9:31). Instead of pursuing, Gentiles simply receive the gift of righteousness from God by faith (9:30). It is important to recognize that the terms "Israel" and "Gentiles" here serve as general, but not exclusive, characterizations. Indeed, Christ is the end, goal, or completion of the Law, so that there might be righteousness for *everyone* who believes, not simply every Jew or every Gentile (10:4; 1:16).

According to Romans 10:8–15, the righteousness of faith operates in this way: God's word comes near when those with beautiful feet are sent by God to proclaim the good news of the Messiah/Christ. That message is then heard with the ears, believed in the heart, and responded to with the confession. Romans 10:9 says it so simply, "If you confess with your mouth that Jesus is Lord and believe in your heart that God raised him from the dead, you will be saved" (10:9).

When this brief expression is expounded in its context, a number of significant theological conclusions emerge.

- Paul asserts it is "with the heart [that] one believes and is justified" (10:10). How, then, does one come to believe? Paul says that "faith comes from hearing" the good news, the word of Christ (10:17).
- Christians often and properly focus upon the cross, but note the centrality of the resurrection in 10:9. As with Abraham, it is faith in a God who *gives life to the dead* which justifies (4:17, 24–25; see also 1:4).
- The necessity of confession may sound like requiring a human work for salvation. However, the Greek word translated "confess" means "to say the same thing." God's word has come near and declares that Jesus is Lord. Those who believe simply repeat it back. In so doing, they confess or acknowledge that what God has first spoken is true (compare 1 John 1:8–10).
- The statement, "Jesus is Lord," formed the earliest Christian confession. It does not emphasize the lordship of Jesus in terms of him being like a master or boss. Rather, the language identifies Jesus with the LORD God of the Old Testament. LORD, in many English Bibles, translates the divine name **Yahweh**, a word that occurs over six thousand times in the Hebrew Old Testament. For example, Romans 10:13 quotes Joel 2:32 which promises that "everyone who calls on the name of Yahweh will be saved." In order to avoid misusing God's name, Yahweh was translated as *kurios* in Greek, the word for "lord" or "master." In the context of this Old Testament quotation, therefore, to confess "Jesus is *kurios*" or Lord is to confess that he is Yahweh God (as in Philippians 2:11 and Acts 2:36; compare Jesus' "I AM" statements in Mark 6:50; 14:62; John 8:24, 28, 58). Another conclusion is also clear: to "call on the name of the Lord" for salvation now means to call on the Lord Jesus (10:13).

Romans 9 asserts that the key is not our works, but God's call. Romans 10 declares that God, in fact, calls all who hear his word. Paul's key point is that this "good news," that is, the "word of Christ," is sent to all by the one who is Lord of all (10:12, 15, 17). The repeated use of "each," "every," "all" and "anyone" in verses 11–13 and 18 reaffirms a point Paul made previously. There is one God over all who shows no favoritism or partiality (Romans 2:11; 3:29–30). In Romans 3 there was no distinction or difference, for all have sinned and fallen short; Jews and Gentiles alike are all under sin (3:9, 20). In 10:12 there is once again "no distinction," for the same Lord bestows his riches upon all who call on him. Paul specifically obliterates the difference between Jew/Israel and Gentile, and by so doing, he reinforces the thematic verses of the letter. The good news is God's powerful call to save everyone who believes, first the Jew and also the Gentile (1:16–17). That salvation is for all reinforces the interpretation that the characterizations at the end of chapter 9 are generalities, not all-encompassing statements.

While the message is sent to all, God does not force people to believe it. He allows his saving work to be resisted and rejected, as is well illustrated by the life of Jesus. Many in Israel heard the good news of the Messiah, the Lord Jesus Christ, but they did not all accept it (10:16–18, citing Psalm 19:4). However, the fact that many in Israel rejected the message does not mean God has rejected Israel as a whole. In Romans 3, Paul had asked, "What if some [Jews] did not have faith? Will their lack of faith nullify the faithfulness of God? Not at all!" (3:3–4; NIV). Elijah was evidence for the existence of God's faithful remnant that numbered seven thousand in his day (11:2–4; 1 Kings 19:10, 14). As Paul writes he is a current example that there remains a remnant by grace, not by race or works (Romans 11:6). But, by definition, a remnant means some, not all. As Romans 9:6 stated, "Not all descended from Israel belong to Israel." Paul affirms this by citing Isaiah who announced, "Only a remnant of them will be saved" (9:27; Isaiah 10:22).

11:25–32 Nevertheless, the mystery remains. When those in Israel stumbled, God used it to send salvation out to the Gentiles (Romans 11:11). Notice that God did not trip Israel; they stumbled. Their stumbling was defined earlier as trying to attain their own righteousness by works (9:30–10:3) and, therefore, not accepting God's good news of righteousness through faith in Christ (10:16–17). God's response is to harden those who stumble over their own works. In this sense, Israel is in the place of Pharaoh from the Exodus story as cited in Romans 9:15–17. But Paul's hope is that Israel will be made envious by the inclusion of the Gentiles and that his ministry might "save *some* of them" (11:14).

This is the context in which Paul concludes, "And in this way all Israel will be saved" (11:26). Some have interpreted this phrase to mean that every Israelite will be saved, or that almost all Israelites will be saved even apart from believing in Jesus Christ (a **two covenant theory**), or that there will be a mass conversion of Jews to faith in Christ before the end.

However, the key to interpreting this statement is the overall context of Romans 9–11, along with the analogy of the olive tree which immediately precedes it (11:17–24; the analogy is like the bow-tie diagram from chapter one turned up on its Old Testament end). There is only one tree, one Israel. Israel is founded on the Old Testament patriarchs. They are the roots of the tree which support and sustain the whole. Those who are Israelites naturally belong to the tree, Abraham's family of faith. However, if they do not believe, they are cut out (11:20). This has allowed "wild" Gentiles to be grafted in by faith; it is also through faith that they remain standing in the tree (11:20).

But if unbelievers in Israel do not persist in their unbelief, they will be restored to the tree where they naturally belonged (11:23). God's call to Israel has not been revoked. Rather, his hands are still held out to the disobedient among them through the deliverer who has come from Zion (10:21, citing Isaiah 56:2; Romans 11:26). In the context of Romans, this deliverer must be Jesus Christ. His mission was to turn ungodliness away from Jacob (Israel) and to renew God's covenant of forgiveness with them (11:26–27).

The climactic conclusion of Romans 9–11 makes two essential points. First, we left the question from 9:18 unresolved. On whom does God want to have mercy and whom does he wish to harden? Romans11:32 answers, "For God has consigned all to disobedience, that he may have mercy on all." As 1:18–3:20 made clear, *all* people are disobedient. God hardens those who persist in obstinate disobedience. But God's ultimate purpose is to have mercy on *all* people. As Romans has made abundantly clear, this mercy is available through faith in Jesus Christ (3:22, 24; 5:1, 15, 17; 8:39). Second, Paul ends this section with a doxology of praise to God. His wisdom, knowledge, and ways are beyond ours, particularly in his desire to show mercy to all who are disobedient (11:33–34; compare Isaiah 55:6–9). The Gospel is that we cannot and do not have to repay God for anything he has done; all things are from God, through God and to God (11:35–36).

12:1–2 These verses serve as an important transition into the application section of the letter. However, unless one reinforces the basis for the exhortations to follow, they will be misapplied. Paul himself reminds his readers of this in 12:1 because he appeals to them "by the mercies of God." In other words, chapters 12–16 should not be read out of their context. Paul intends his hearers to listen to his entire letter. The motivation to exhibit the lifestyle described in Romans 12–16 is provided by chapters 1–11; there God's mercy in Christ Jesus is clearly in view.

The expected response in the rest of 12:1 is something of an oxymoron. In the Old Testament sacrifices were killed on the altar. Since Christ's death has paid the penalty "once for all" (6:10), there is no need for further blood to be shed. Thus believers can be this paradox: *living* sacrifices. Their lifestyle is then described in terms of worship. In the Old Testament, only the priests offered sacrifices during specific times at the tabernacle or temple. Now, all believers are called to offer themselves as sacrifices, and each and every moment that is lived according to God's good, pleasing and perfect will is, in fact, worship (12:1–2). Such a life ought not to be outwardly shaped according to the ways of this world. Rather, it is to exhibit outwardly the inner transformation God has already accomplished. This transformation is linked to the description of baptism in 6:1–4. The thematic characteristic of this lifestyle is given in 12:9, to love without hypocrisy. Paul proceeds to illustrate what genuine love is like in verses 10–21.

13:1–10 This is one of the few sections in the New Testament which speaks of a Christian's relationship to the governing authorities (see also 1 Peter 2:13–17). When asked about paying taxes to Rome, Jesus replied, "Render to Caesar the things that are Caesar's, and to God the things that are God's" (Matthew 22:21). It is proper to do the former, yet it is much more appropriate and difficult to accomplish the latter. The issue arises here because of Paul's discussion at the end of chapter 12. Believers are not supposed to take vengeance into their own hands; they are to leave room for God's wrath (Romans 12:19). His wrath will ultimately come on judgment day (see 2:5). In the meantime one way in which God already carries out his vengeance against evil is through the governing authorities. They are set in place as servants, ministers, or agents of God's wrath in order to punish evildoers (12:19; 13:4–6). Those who do what is good should not fear the authorities, but rather, receive their approval (13:3).

Because the governing authorities carry out their duties as ministers of God, Paul says believers should obey them, even if it is merely out of fear of punishment. Submitting to their authority includes paying taxes, as well as giving them respect and honor (13:6–7).

It is significant to read these verses in light of the Roman Empire of Paul's day. While people praise the overall law and order of the ***Pax Romana***, the Empire was, in many ways, a militaristic, expansionist, and totalitarian dictatorship. Still, Paul urges believers to live under the order of the day. What does this mean for us? On the one hand, no earthly government has been or ever will be perfect, yet many of them have been a positive force for maintaining good order. Then Christians are to obey. On the other hand, governments such as Nazi Germany, Stalinist Russia, and Saddam Hussein's Iraq were clearly evil. Does Paul order blind obedience even to governments like those?

Paul repeatedly asserts that these earthly authorities have been instituted or established by God (13:1). This means their authority is a *derived* one; God is the higher authority to whom they are accountable. The critical issue, then, is what they do with their God-given power. As ministers of God, they are set in place to carry out his vengeance upon evildoers and to give their approval to those who do what is right. When governments end up doing the opposite, praising evil and punishing those who do what is good, a believer is in a difficult situation. If a *Christian* is ordered to carry out evil actions, Paul would agree with Peter and John in protesting, "We must obey God rather than men" and be ready to suffer the consequences (Acts 5:29). But how should believers respond when they witness *others* doing evil at the command of those who are in authority? It is interesting that Paul calls for obedience both out of fear of punishment and because of conscience (Romans 13:5). The inclusion of conscience allows for the possibility that various believers may, in good conscience, come to different conclusions regarding how to respond to the perceived evils of the governments under which they live. Examples may include whether to join the military to fight in a war, or how to oppose abortion.

After urging believers to pay what is owed to those in authority, Paul asserts that we should leave no debts remaining except for the ongoing obligation to love one another (13:8). In negative terms, this means not harming one's neighbor by violating the commandments. On the positive side, it involves actively loving neighbor as self (13:9–10). In this context, the intended function of the Law's commands is not to condemn disobedience, increase trespasses or work wrath as is the case earlier in Romans. Here they serve as basic expressions of how God's people are to love one another. When believers love each other as God intends, they have, in fact, fulfilled the Law (13:10).

14:5–13 These verses may provide our best glimpse into the situation at Rome that Paul is addressing and striving to remedy. On its surface, chapter 14 may not appear to speak directly to issues related to Jews and Gentiles. But, in its first-century context, this is almost certainly the case. Paul speaks about "quarrels over opinions" (14:1). These are issues about which believers are free to disagree. In such matters, Paul's repeated theme is that they should not judge each other (14:4, 10, 13). In fact, all will have to give an account of themselves before God in regard to such judgmental conduct (14:11–12; citing Isaiah 45:23).

The disputable issues Paul deals with have to do with different views about days and foods (Romans 14:6; compare Colossians 2:16–17). Both flow out of the Old Testament and reflect the time of theological transition immediately following Jesus' death and resurrection. The weekly Sabbath and the other festivals were special days set aside by the command of God for rest, repentance, worship, and celebration. Similarly, the food laws of the Old Testament were established by God to set his people apart and, perhaps, for their physical health as well. But Jesus declared all foods clean, and the Lord of the Sabbath released his followers from rigid Sabbath regulations (see Mark 7:18–19; Matthew 12:1–14). As a result, Paul says first-century believers are now free to live either way, in continuing adherence to rules about food and worship or in freedom from them now that the kingdom has come in Christ (Romans 14:17).

When Paul later speaks of the weak and the strong, he includes himself among the strong who acknowledge that "nothing is unclean in itself" (14:14). On the other hand, the weak are unsure about whether there are still distinctions between foods and days. Yet, in either case, there should be acceptance rather than judgment. These matters of opinion are not that important. What really matters is our life together in God's kingdom (14:17). There, none of us lives to one's self alone, and none of us dies to one's self alone. No one in God's family lives in isolation, even at the most extreme moment of separation. Whether living or dying, we belong to the Lord Jesus (14:7–8).

15:7–8 These two verses wrap up the themes of Romans beautifully. *Romans 1–8* point out that, in spite of disobedience worthy of wrath from God, "Christ accepted you in order to bring praise to God" (15:7, NIV; compare 8:34). *Chapters 9–11* present how Christ became a servant to the Jews and, thereby, fulfilled God's Old Testament promises to the patriarchs (15:8). Romans 15:8 clearly states that God's promises to Israel are confirmed in Christ, not apart from him. One repeated component of those Old Testament promises was that Gentiles would also receive mercy from God and respond by giving glory to him. In 15:9–12 Paul quotes four Old Testament passages as evidence for this. These passages reinforce the point made beginning with the quote from Habakkuk in Romans 1 and running all the way through the letter. Paul is not writing something new; rather, the message of Romans marks the continuation and, indeed, the culmination of what God had already spoken in the Old Testament. Finally, Romans 12–15 discuss how believers should welcome each other in love in response to Christ, who first accepted them (15:7). This is possible because of the assurance that nothing "in all creation will be able to separate us from the love of God in Christ Jesus our Lord" (8:39).

Jesus in Romans

The opening verses of Romans contain an expanded introduction to the letter (1:1–7). These verses encapsulate the truth of the Gospel expounded by Paul in Romans and embodied in Jesus (1:1, 4). He "was descended from David according to the flesh" (1:3); this is shorthand for saying he is the fulfillment of all God "promised beforehand through his prophets in the holy Scriptures" (1:2). All of the Old Testament promises which permeate Romans are, therefore, focused upon Jesus, a human being from the lineage of King David (4:3, 23–25; 10:11, 13; 11:26–27; 15:9–12).

The beginning of this letter also announces that Jesus was "declared to be the Son of God in power … by his resurrection from the dead" (1:4). This phrase encapsulates all that Jesus accomplished. It encompasses the redemption that came by the shedding of his blood (3:24–25), the gracious overwhelming of all that sin and death brought into the world following Adam's transgression (5:12–21), as well as the completion or "end of the Law" (8:3–4; 10:4). He is the Son whom God did not spare; instead, God graciously gave him up for us all on the cross (8:32). At the outset of Romans, Paul asserts that Jesus' resurrection is the public declaration that all of this is true (1:4; compare 10:9; 1 Corinthians 15:12–22).

As Romans continues to give further details about this good news, it describes how "all of us who have been baptized into Christ Jesus" have become participants in those wondrous events (Romans 6:3). "We were buried … with him into death, in order that, just as Christ was raised from the dead by the glory of the Father, we too might walk in newness of life" (6:4). The "word of Christ" transforms all who hear and believe it (Romans 10:8–17). By this word we are justified through faith in his blood, freed from slavery to sin and the lordship of the Law, and assured that we will be saved from God's wrath on judgment day (5:1, 9; 6:22; 7:4). In the meantime, Christ himself intercedes on our behalf before God's throne (9:34). For those "in Christ Jesus" there is "no condemnation" (8:1).

"For to this end Christ died and lived, that he might be Lord both of the dead and of the living" (14:10). Here again we see Christ alive from the dead, and also Christ as Lord of all (10:9–13). Whether living or dying, we belong to him (14:9).

Paul's Metaphors for the Gospel

This textbook occasionally uses stories to illustrate and apply the truths presented in the New Testament. We recognize that all analogies are inadequate; they can also be misapplied or misunderstood. However, the use of stories has an important precedent in the New Testament, the parables of Jesus.

Paul's letters are often viewed as being very deep, theological, and abstract. They lack the concrete narrative of the gospels and do not appear to use many illustrations like the parables of Jesus. However, a close examination of Paul's language reveals a number of vibrant word pictures. He uses a wide variety of practical terminology in a metaphorical sense in order to convey important truths about God's relationship with people. On the surface this is less apparent to us today, especially as we read his letters in translation. But Paul's first-century readers would have readily connected his Greek words with the life experiences of their day.

What follows are a few examples which fit into one category, the different ways in which Paul communicates the Gospel. In fact, Paul rarely speaks of the good news in a purely straightforward manner. He regularly employs a number of comparisons or metaphors in order to express the fulness of what God has accomplished for us in Jesus Christ.

Legal *When Paul uses terms like "justified," "justification," and "righteousness," he is using the forensic language of the courtroom. Scholars have often spoken of justification as the center of Paul's entire theology. This is true when the category of justification is used in a broad sense to encompass all the metaphors used in Scripture to express the Gospel (as in the Lutheran Confessions). But, more narrowly, justification refers to Paul's actual use of legal terminology. The prominent role of the law in Graeco-Roman society enabled this language to communicate most effectively. It also functioned well as Paul strives to counter those who based their righteousness upon works of the Old Testament Law.*

This metaphor pictures God as a judge and the Law as prosecutor. All people are put on trial and the verdict against us is "guilty" for all have sinned. Our sentence is eternal death and separation from God. But Christ, our advocate and defender, endured that punishment in our behalf. As a result, a righteous judge can justly acquit us and declare *us "justified" or "righteous." Note that God has not yet* made *us righteous; we continue to sin. But in his sight we are most certainly what he declares us to be.*

Although brief references occur in a number of Paul's letters, the metaphor is developed by him only in Romans, Galatians, and Philippians (Romans 3:19–20,23–24, 28, 4:5, 5:1, 18–19; 9:30–10:4; Galatians 2:16, 21; 3:11; Philippians 3:9; Titus 3:5–7).

Sacrifice *This picture is very graphic, but also quite foreign; the vast majority of us have never witnessed, much less practiced, animal sacrifice. However, it was a prominent component in many religions of the ancient world, including those of Greece and Rome. Yet the dominant theological background for Paul was the Old Testament (Leviticus 1–7, 16).*

A key phrase which summarizes the significance of this metaphor is substitutionary atonement. Sin separates people from God and deserves the penalty of death. In the Old Testament God mercifully provided an animal substitute to shed its blood and suffer death in place of the sinner. The result was atonement, a relationship restored to being at-one.

Paul uses a variety of terms related to sacrifice which are translated in a number of ways ("blood," "sacrifice," "mercy-seat", "propitiation," "expiation," "atonement"). His point is that Jesus became the ultimate substitute whose blood was sacrificed as payment for sin. His death has made atonement for the whole world (Romans 3:25; 1 Corinthians 5:7; Ephesians 2:13; 5:2).

Slavery *Terms such as "redeem," "redemption," "ransom," "purchased," and "bought" come largely from the background of slavery. Estimates are that slaves comprised as much as one third of the population of the Roman Empire. While the American experience with slavery is a distant memory, it is still a painful one. Unfortunately, slavery continues to be practiced in much of the modern world. Slaves are owned and controlled by their masters unless some form of payment is made to set them free.*

For Paul all people are in bondage under sin, death, and the Law. But Christ's death and resurrection frees people from that slavery in order that they might willingly serve God and one another (Romans 3:24; 6:6–7, 16–17, 20, 22; 1 Corinthians 1:30; 6:20; 7:23; Galatians 3:13; 4:4–5; Ephesians 1:7; Colossians 1:14; 1 Timothy 2:6).

Adoption *Since we were all born into an earthly family, this metaphor is more familiar. It was also a very significant legal process in the Roman Empire. Sin has alienated us from God. Jesus, God's Son, died and rose again in order that we might be adopted into God's household. God has also brought his people together as brothers and sisters in Christ. As fellow members of his family, we are now heirs of all of the good gifts God has already granted, as well as those he will bestow upon his children in the future (Romans 8:15, 23; 9:4; Galatians 4:5; Ephesians 1:5).*

Friendship *Relationships that have been disrupted and need to be reconciled are also part of our normal experience. Our sin and rebellion have made us enemies of God; there is also a great deal of friction among people in our world. But in Christ Jesus, God has reconciled the whole world back to himself. Those who believe in Jesus are restored and now live in a relationship of peace and friendship with God. God has also reconciled us to one another so that we might live together in harmony (Romans 5:10; 11:15; 2 Corinthians 5:18, 20; Ephesians 2:16; Colossians 1:20–21).*

Gift *This is a most pleasing metaphor. We all like to receive gifts. "Gift" language stresses that everything God gives to us is totally undeserved. It comes as a gift of his grace to us in Jesus Chris (Romans 3:24; 6:23; Ephesians 2:8).*

Banking *For better or worse, this is a category most of us can relate to very well, because of an all-too-popular device, the credit card. Paul commonly expresses this metaphor by using a key Greek word,* logizomai. *Unfortunately, the connection is often lost because the term is translated in such a wide variety of ways ("credit," "reckon," "regard,"* *"consider," "count as," and "hold"). As a result, we will explain this metaphor in a little more detail.*

Paul's favorite example is Abraham. From the perspective of Abraham and the author of Genesis, Abraham does not appear to be righteous (see Genesis 12:10–29; 20:1–2). Nevertheless, reality is God's perspective on Abraham. In spite of his unrighteous conduct and even though the bill for his sins had not been paid, God counted *him as righteous (Genesis 15:6, cited in Romans 4:3; Galatians 3:6). Paul says God "passed over" the sins of Abraham and other Old Testament believers (Romans 3:25). In other words, he gave them credit until Jesus ultimately paid the bill for Abraham and for all who are "are* counted as *[his] offspring" (9:8).*

This financial metaphor profoundly expresses what reality is; it is God's perspective on us. God credits *the ungodly as righteous (4:5). Believers are similarly called to* consider *themselves as dead to sin (6:11), even though their present experience often appears to contradict that assertion. Why? That is the reality which took place in baptism (6:2–4, 7). In other words, reality is not always what Abraham, Israel, Paul or we perceive it to be. It is what God declares it is in his word. Thank God he gives us credit. Even though we do not deserve it, our debts have been erased and Christ's righteousness has been added to our account. (For additional references on this metaphor, see Romans 3:28; 4:6, 8, 9, 10, 11, 24; 8:18.)*

The key to each of these Gospel metaphors is that each one comes from outside of us. The judge declares us innocent; someone is sacrificed in our place; the price has been paid to free us from slavery; we have been adopted in God's family; our debt has been forgiven. These are all ways of speaking about God's gracious actions; together, they express his good news to us in Jesus Christ.

Many other metaphors are also used by Paul to communicate the Gospel. Some of these include light (Ephesians 5:8), new birth (Titus 3:5), cleansing (1 Corinthians 6:11; Ephesians 5:26), marriage (Ephesians 5:22–33) and victory (Romans 8:37; 1 Corinthians 15:57). For a more complete discussion, see J.A.O. Preus, Just Words *(St. Louis: Concordia, 2000) and William Barclay,* The Mind of St. Paul *(San Francisco: HarperCollins, 1986, pages 75–108).*

For Further Discussion

1. At the beginning of our section on Romans, a number of theories were introduced to explain the content of the letter. Which of those theories is most convincing? Why?

2. Paul proclaims, "I am not ashamed of the Gospel" (Romans 1:16). Why was Romans placed at the end of a chapter titled, "Confessing the Christ Boldly"? What other books in this section convey that same fervor? Explain.

3. Is Romans a complete statement of Christian doctrine? Why or why not?

4. What does Romans say about the relationship between Christianity and the faith of the Old Testament? What does this mean for Jews who did not believe in Jesus as the Messiah?

5. Which of Paul's metaphors for the Gospel is most meaningful to you? Think of and describe two modern metaphors which you could use to communicate the same message.

For Further Reading

Cranfield, C. E. B. *Romans*. International Critical Commentary. 2 vols. Edinburgh: T. & T. Clark, 1975–79.

Donfried, Karl P., ed. *The Romans Debate*. 2nd edition. Peabody, MA: Hendrickson, 1991.

Lucado, Max. *In the Grip of Grace*. Nashville: Word Publishing, 1999.

Middendorf, Michael. *The "I" in the Storm: A Study of Romans 7*. St. Louis: Concordia, 1997.

Moo, Douglas J. *Romans*. New International Commentary. Grand Rapids: Eerdmans, 1996.

Ortlund, Raymond. *A Passion for God: Prayers and Meditations on the Book of Romans*. Wheaton, IL: Crossways, 1994.

Schreiner, Thomas. *Romans*. Baker Exegetical Commentary on the New Testament. Grand Rapids: Baker, 1988.

Westerholm, Stephen. *Israel's Law and the Church's Faith*. Grand Rapids: Eerdmans, 1988.

5

The Writings of the New Testament: Confession in Conflict

Introduction

Toward the end of Paul's mission journeys, he has a strong awareness of approaching conflict. "I am going to Jerusalem, constrained by the Spirit, not knowing what will happen to me there, except that the Holy Spirit testifies to me in every city that imprisonments and afflictions await me" (Acts 20:22–23). Growing conflict with political and religious authorities along with internal divisions would challenge the infant church. And so Paul exhorts the Ephesians elders to "pay careful attention to yourselves and all the flock" (Acts 20:28). Likewise, Peter would warn, "Do not be surprised at the fiery trial when it comes upon you to test you" (1 Peter 4:12). His word of encouragement is similar to Paul's: "Shepherd the flock of God that is among you" (1 Peter 5:2). Jude would warn of those "who cause divisions, worldly people, devoid of the Spirit" (Jude 19). The vision of Revelation is equally urgent, "Do not fear what you are about to suffer…. Be faithful until death and I will give you the crown of life" (Revelation 2:10).

This chapter provides example upon example of faithful confession in times of conflict. Be they words of Paul from prison, a gospel likely composed at a time of persecution, or a vision of an earthly and heavenly conflict, all point to Jesus and urge "every tongue [to] confess that Jesus Christ is Lord, to the glory of God the Father" (Philippians 2:10).

Chapter Outline

Philippians
Luke/Acts
1 and 2 Peter
Mark
Hebrews
Revelation
Jude

Philippians

Paul at Rome: The Increasing Tension between Christianity and Rome

In chapter four, the four letters known as the Prison Epistles were introduced. That discussion placed Paul's letter to the Philippians during his first imprisonment in Rome. The arrest that led to that imprisonment occurred in Jerusalem during a riot provoked by Jewish religious leaders (Acts 21:27–36). That day, however, Paul became involved in an extended series of legal entanglements with the forces of the Roman Empire. By the time Paul reaches Rome, he has already been in the custody of various Roman officials for three years. The very end of Acts informs us that Paul waited under house arrest for at least two additional years until his hearing before Caesar occurred (28:30; A.D. 59–61). During that period we suggest Paul wrote to the Philippians.

In many ways, Paul's relationship with the Roman authorities can be seen as a microcosm of the relationship between Christianity and the Roman Empire. There is, for a time, peaceful and cordial coexistence interrupted only by brief skirmishes. In time, however, the exclusive claims of both entities produce more serious conflicts. Eventually, this leads to Paul's martyrdom under Nero and to the outright persecution of Christians by Roman authorities.

Introduction

The proud city of Philippi was named after the father of Alexander the Great. It was also a Roman **colony**, which meant its citizens were regarded as citizens of Rome itself (*jus italicum*; note Paul's words about the primacy of the believer's heavenly citizenship in Philippians 3:20–21; compare 1:27). Philippi was also a thriving commercial city located, along with Thessalonica, on the ***Via Egnatia***, the main east-west trade route in this part of the empire.

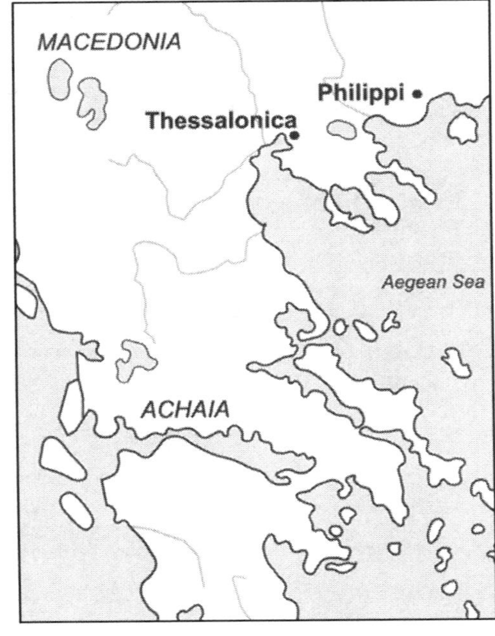

Paul first visited Philippi shortly after he entered Europe on his second missionary journey (Acts 16:11–40). He arrived along with Silas, Timothy, and Luke, the author of Acts. Apparently, there was no synagogue or sizable Jewish presence in the city, since Paul began his mission work among Gentile God-fearers at "a place of prayer" down by the riverside (16:13–14). A worshipper of God named Lydia invited Paul's team to her home and hosted the meetings of the Christian community.

After Paul drives a demon out of a fortune-telling slave girl, her owners, who had been exploiting the girl for profit, had Paul and Silas arrested. Paul and Silas were singing hymns in the middle of the night when an earthquake opened the jail doors. The jailer was afraid he had lost his prisoners and, therefore, would lose his life. He decided to commit suicide, but was stopped by Paul who assured him that none of the prisoners had escaped. The jailer responded with a profound question: "'Sirs, what must I do to be saved?' And they said, 'Believe in the Lord Jesus, and you will be saved, you and your household.'" (16:30–31). Paul was freed the next day and continued on his journey.

Almost immediately, the congregation sent a number of gifts to support Paul financially while he was in Thessalonica (Philippians 4:16). Apparently, they assisted him again during his stay at Corinth (2 Corinthians 11:9). Finally, yet another gift had recently been delivered by their emissary, Epaphroditus, who nearly died in the effort (Philippians 2:25–30; 4:18).

Where was Paul at the time of Ephaphroditus' visit, and when did it occur? Paul repeatedly says he is a prisoner (1:13, 14, 17). He describes his situation as "in chains." However, this could apply metaphorically to his two-year stay in a rented house in Rome at the end of Acts (Acts 28:30). In addition, reference to the imperial guard (Philippians 1:13) and Caesar's household (4:22) also make a Roman setting likely.

Forum at Rome

The congregation in Philippi is largely, if not exclusively, Gentile. It is also Paul's "joy and crown" (4:1). While Paul does send some words of instruction, he is writing to thank the Philippians for their ongoing support and, particularly, for their most recent gift. He is also giving them a report on his own circumstances and the health of Ephaphroditus, whom he is sending back along with the letter (2:25).

Structure and Theme

Philippians adheres to the basic letter structure of the New Testament.

Philippians	
Opening	1:1–2
Thanksgiving	1:3–11
Paul's Current Situation	1:12–26
Body/Exhortation	1:27–4:9
Thanksgiving for Gifts from Philippi	4:10–20
Closing	4:21–23

Because of the dear relationship that has developed between Paul and this church, the thanksgiving section is especially noteworthy. After his typical opening (1:1–2), Paul launches into a beautiful thanksgiving to God for the partnership he has experienced with this group of believers (1:3–11). Paul expresses joy and confidence that the Lord "who began a good work in [them] will carry it on to completion until the day of Christ Jesus" (1:6).

Prior to the main body of the letter, Paul gives an update on his circumstances (1:12–26; compare Galatians 1:11–2:21). Paul views his imprisonment as an opportunity to advance the Gospel. He is using it to make Christ known "throughout the whole imperial guard and to all the rest" (1:13). Paul seems to ponder the possibility that his current imprisonment could end in death (1:20). But whenever and wherever this occurs, his attitude is clear: "For me to live is Christ and to die is gain" (1:21). Paul reveals that when he departs this world he would, in some sense, be "with Christ" (1:23). But if it will benefit others, he will gladly remain in his present confinement. Either way, he is full of joy (1:18, 25–26).

The body of the letter runs from 1:27–4:9. Instead of one block of doctrine followed by a section of application, the two are interspersed. For example, the doctrinal content of 2:5–11 is surrounded by two sections of exhortation (1:27–2:4; 2:12–18; compare 1 Thessalonians and 1 Peter). Paul returns to the topic of the gifts he has received from the Philippians in 4:10–20 before his final greetings (4:21–23).

The theme which emerges from Philippians is this: ***Fellowship*** *in the Gospel gives joy in the Lord and leads to thinking like Jesus*. The Greek word usually translated "fellowship" (*koinonia*) is used six times in the letter. Philippians 1:5–8 illustrates four aspects of this *koinonia* in Christ.

- Through the word of the Gospel that Paul brought to them, the Philippians have become *fellow-receivers* of the grace of God (1:7).
- They have then shared in the joy of Jesus, together with each other and Paul "from the first day until now" (1:5); this *koinonia* produces a compassionate, emotional bond (1:8).
- The Philippians have been faithful in responding to the Gospel by becoming *partners* with Paul in his ministry (1:5; see 4:16; 2 Corinthians 11:6).
- Finally, Paul makes it clear that this *fellowship* was and remains God's work from beginning to end (Philippians 1:6).

Various forms of the word for "joy" (*chara*) occur sixteen times in the four chapters of Philippians. The discussion of 4:4–9 below will deal with this concept. The thematic Greek word *phroneo* occurs nine times in the letter; it is translated with various words or phrases such as "think," "attitude," "such a view" and "like-minded." It will also be explained below under 2:1–11.

Key Texts

2:1–11 Philippians 2:6–11 contains some of Paul's most profound words. These verses answer the two key questions which began this textbook: "Who is Jesus?" and "What has he done?" The answers are provided in a poetic format that is both beautiful and powerful. This poem may be an ancient Christian hymn either written by Paul or composed by someone else and incorporated by him into this letter. But these christological verses should be read in the context of verses 1–5. Note how the three thematic words identified above are all present here. "Fellowship" is in verse one; "joy" is in verse two; the word for "think" occurs twice in verse two and again in verse five.

The first two verses of chapter two are an extended conditional (if/then) sentence. However, the Greek implies that all the "ifs" are true. There is, in fact, fellowship (see 1:5, 7), affection (see 1:8), and so forth. As a result, the items laid out in verse two ought to follow. Notice that Paul does not say others are better, but that believers ought to count or regard them as such (2:3).

The lifestyle depicted in verses 3–4 runs counter to the materialistic culture in which so many of us live. Capitalism, in its extreme form, urges us to do everything out of selfish ambition and insists upon "looking out for number 1," namely, ourselves. Paul rejects such an attitude toward life, because that was not the way of Christ. In sharp contrast to the ways of the world, the *phroneo* of believers, that is, their thinking, mindset, or outlook should be that "which is yours in Christ Jesus" (2:5).

The poem or hymn in verses 6–11 has often been identified as laying out the humiliation (verses 6–8) and exaltation (verses 9–11) of Jesus. Verse six also speaks clearly to the issue of who Jesus is. The Greek states that he is in form or appearance God. This point is further interpreted in the same verse as "equality with God." In his character and nature, Jesus is fully God. In light of the exhortations of verses 1–5, the key point Paul makes here concerns Christ's attitude toward his own divinity and what he did with it. It was not something to be selfishly held on to or used for his own benefit. Just the opposite! "For us and for our salvation" he gave it all up (Nicene Creed).

The term translated "made himself nothing" in verse seven does not mean Jesus stopped being God. Rather, it stresses that Jesus gave up the use of many of his godly powers and, more importantly, poured himself out or gave his all. He did this by taking the nature of a servant. This involved becoming a human being, but it meant much more. His servanthood entailed obeying the will of his Father even though it meant his death (2:7–8).

In the poetic structure of these verses, all the lines are metrical in Greek except for one phrase that sticks out—"even death on a cross" (2:8). Structurally, the emphasis lies here. Paul's point is not merely that Jesus gave up the exercise of his divine glory in order to become human. He also humbled himself and became the **Suffering Servant** who poured out his life on the cross (compare Isaiah 52:13–53:12). Such was his humiliation. But Jesus is not most unlike God when dead on the cross. Rather, he there shows us most clearly what God is like!

In response, God graciously gifted Jesus with great exaltation (2:9). Even Jesus' death was not a matter of earning anything. Instead, Jesus is the ultimate illustration that the Lord exalts the humble because it is in his nature to do so (for example, see 1 Samuel 2:7–8; Proverbs 3:34; Luke 1:51–53; 18:4). Jesus is now highly exalted above every name and entity in existence. Note that the term "place," inserted in some translations, is not present in the Greek of 2:9; Jesus' exalted presence is not limited to a single location.

In this letter to a predominantly Gentile congregation, Paul never quotes the Old Testament directly. However, a key Old Testament text lies behind verses 9–11. In Isaiah 45:23 Yahweh declares, "By myself I have sworn; from my mouth has gone out in righteousness a word that shall not return: To me every knee shall bow, every tongue shall swear allegiance." Here Jesus receives the worship and honor due to "the name that is above every name" (Philippians 2:9). As a result, to "confess that Jesus Christ is Lord" (2:11) is not simply to acknowledge Jesus as master or boss. The text from Isaiah implies much more. He is Yahweh, equal to God in his very essence (as stated already in 2:6). Thus he receives the same glory.

This hymn marvelously proclaims who Jesus is and what he has done. Those who have heard this message are called to receive, acknowledge, believe, and repeat it. The word translated "confess" in verse eleven means in Greek, "to say the same thing." Indeed, in one way or another, all of creation will one day acknowledge Jesus' lordship or, better, his Yahweh-ness (2:10–11).

After the Gospel has been powerfully articulated, Paul returns to where he began. Jesus listened to and obeyed his Father's will, even to the point of death on the cross (2:8; compare Matthew 26:39). Believers are called to "have this mind among yourselves, which is yours in Christ Jesus" (*phroneo*; Philippians

2:5). Paul's dear friends in Christ are to live out the Christlike attitude depicted in 2:1–4. They should also listen and respond appropriately to the words that flow from verses 6–11. That is what the "therefore" that begins verse 12 is "there for."

Yet, it is dangerous to see what precedes and follows 2:6–11 merely in terms of depicting the humble servant-lifestyle of Christ as an example for others to emulate (Law). Such a narrow view sets all of us up for failure. After all, who can live up to his standard? The Gospel message of what Christ has done for us predominates. It then provides the basis and motivation for the attitude and lifestyle which flow from verses 6–11 and into the exhortations which surround them.

3:3–14 These verses reiterate Paul's theology concerning righteousness before God. While the language is similar to the general teaching of Romans on the subject, it is stated much more personally here. Paul uses himself as an example and speaks in the first person singular to illustrate the truth about one's relationship with God (as in Romans 7:7–25). There is a hint of the sharp polemic present when Paul debated this issue years earlier in Galatians; in Philippians 3:2 Paul warns the Philippians about "the dogs," false teachers who are insisting upon circumcision (compare Acts 15:1, 5; Galatians 5:10–12; 6:12–14). But then the opponents drop quickly from sight. Instead of engaging them, Paul proceeds to redefine circumcision. It is not something outward which enables one to put confidence in their own flesh. Instead, true circumcision involves worshipping God in the Spirit and glorying in Christ Jesus (Philippians 3:3; compare Romans 2:28–29).

The essence of the problem Paul is countering is the common attempt to base one's standing before God on "who I am and how I live." Paul asserts that if anyone had reason to place such confidence in the flesh, it was he. He lists his personal qualifications which, from a human perspective, would exceed those of any of the Philippians. In short, he had it all and had done it all in terms of striving for "a righteousness of my own that comes from the Law" (Philippians 3:9). But Paul has "suffered the loss" of all of this (3:7). It is "rubbish" (3:8; literally "dung") compared with receiving "that which comes through faith in [or "faithfulness of"] Christ, the righteousness from God that depends on faith" (3:9).

This Gospel message then motivates Paul to want to know Christ in a personal and intimate way (3:10–11), which involves experiencing the power of Jesus Christ's resurrection both now in baptism (Romans 6:3–4) and in the future bodily resurrection. But it also means sharing in his suffering and death (Philippians 3:11). In the present, Paul views his imprisonment as one aspect of this suffering. He struggles in other ways that reveal he is not "already perfect" (3:12); even Paul had not yet arrived. Yet, he pictures himself as a runner straining forward toward the finish line (3:13–14). Paul could forget what was past, even his zealous persecution of the church. Ever since Christ Jesus took hold of him, he keeps his focus on heaven where God has called and is bringing him in Christ (3:14).

While Paul has been speaking exclusively about himself since verse four, the intended impact of his words is clearly more than self-revelation. Verse fifteen makes clear that the Philippian believers are to "join in imitating" Paul's example. They are called to have the same attitude or outlook displayed by Paul with regard to righteousness and faith (3:7–9), self and Christ (2:1–11), the past and the future (3:12–14), and even life and death (1:21).

4:4–9 The letter to the Philippians displays how *fellowship in the Gospel leads to thinking like Jesus*, and to thinking like Paul. It also *gives great joy*! Paul expresses this beautifully in 4:4–9. In 4:4 Paul twice calls the Philippians to rejoice; he also expresses where true joy is found—"in the Lord." We can rejoice "always" if, like Paul, we have learned to be content in all situations (4:4, 11). Paul's joy or contentment did not depend on external circumstances, but upon the Lord. As a result, to "rejoice in the Lord always" is much deeper and more profound than simple, emotional happiness. Such joy is rooted in one's relationship with God in Christ (3:8–11). Paul confidently concludes, "I can do all things through him who strengthens me" (4:13).

The word often translated "meekness" or "gentleness" in verse five actually means to be strong enough in Christ to put up with injustice, poverty, persecution, imprisonment, and other mistreatment because one knows "the Lord is at hand" (4:5; compare 4:11–12). Jesus and Paul endured many of these things; the Philippians may be in the midst of them as well. Paul assures them that Jesus is near in terms of distance or time or, perhaps, both. Instead of being anxious (4:6; literally "split into parts"), the believer's focus is to be on the Lord through prayer. When this happens, God's peace is like a guard on duty watching over one's life (4:7).

In response, the Philippians are to set their minds and attitudes upon the lofty, noble, excellent, and praiseworthy things of life (4:8–9). And how do they know about these things? Certainly Christ exhibited them, but these early Philippian Christians had not met Jesus in person. In all likelihood, they did not even have access to written accounts about him. Rather, they had "learned and received and heard and seen" Jesus in Paul's words, demeanor, and activity (4:9). Their attitude and lifestyle should imitate Paul, who has modeled Christ to them (compare 1 Corinthians 11:1). Paul's joy-filled thinking sets a marvelous pattern for those leaders who follow him in the fellowship of Christ's church.

Jesus in Philippians

In recent years, a popular phrase among Christians has been to ask, "What would Jesus do?" (WWJD). Normally, this is applied to situations where believers are confronted with a decision in their lives. They should act as Jesus would (Philippians 2:5, 12; John 15:12). However, in Philippians Paul gives the more essential answer to the question, "What would Jesus do?" He would humble himself by becoming human; then, as the Suffering Servant, he would pour out his life unto death, even death on a cross (2:6–8). As a result, God has now given him the name above every name (2:9); every tongue will confess "Jesus Christ is Lord" (2:11). That is who Jesus is; that is what Jesus would do (WWJD). In fact, that is what he has already done.

In that message, we are forgiven and restored to fellowship with God and with each other. We are also enpowered to confront our own circumstances with the attitude of Christ (2:5). In Jesus we find our source and meaning for life (1:21); in him we are given joy and peace (4:4, 7).

For Further Discussion

1. What are the various aspects involved in Paul's use of the term *koinonia* in Philippians? Do you think there should be levels of fellowship or limits on the fellowship Christians express and experience with each other? Why or why not?

2. Does the description of Jesus in Philippians 2:5–11 serve as a role model for his followers? Why or why not? Consider the context of Philippians 2:1–4 and 2:12–18 in your response. Is the lifestyle described in Philippians 2:1–4 "the good life" according to our culture?

3. What does it mean to confess, "Jesus Christ is Lord" (2:11)?

4. Where does a Christian's joy come from? What is it? Is it present all the time, even in the midst of troubles and suffering? Why or why not?

For Further Reading

Fee, Gordon. *Paul's Letter to the Philippians*. The New International Commentary on the New Testament. Grand Rapids: Eerdmans, 1995.

Hawthorne, Gerald. *Philippians*. Word Biblical Commentary. Waco, TX: Word, 1983.

Martin, Ralph P. *A Hymn of Christ: Philippians 2:5–11 in Recent Interpretation and in the Setting of Early Christian Worship*. Downers Grove, IL: InterVarstiy, 1997.

________. *Philippians*. The New Century Bible Commentary. Grand Rapids: Eerdmans, 1976.

O'Brien, Peter. *The Epistle to the Philippians*. Grand Rapids: Eerdmans, 1991.

Luke/Acts

Typically, the books of Luke and Acts are treated separately, even as they are separated in the modern arrangement of the books of the New Testament. Here, we treat them together, as the second work (Acts) claims to be a continuation of the first (Acts 1:1). Common vocabulary, style, themes and purpose make Luke and Acts a unity.

Recall that many of the accounts from Luke and Acts have been treated above in chapter 3, which tells of the story of Jesus and early Christianity. In this section the focus will be on the themes and flow of the two works.

Author

As with other gospels, the author of the third gospel is not specifically named in the text. But from the late second century on, this gospel and Acts have been attributed to Luke, the companion of Paul mentioned in Colossians 4:14, Philemon 24, and 2 Timothy 4:11. The passage from Colossians says Luke was a physician and implies he was a **Gentile**. The argument for Lucan authorship may have some internal support from Acts. Four times in Acts (16:10–17; 20:5–15; 21:1–18; and 27:1–28:16) the discourse switches from the third person ("they…") to the first person plural ("we…"). If Luke is copying from a personal diary or using a form of self-reference, he would indeed be a companion of Paul and loyal until the end. Supposed allusions to technical medical vocabulary are less significant, since other ancient writers who were not physicians used similar references.

The identification of Paul's companion Luke as the author of the third gospel and Acts is not without problems. Any attempt to align the chronological references in Paul's letters with the narrative in Acts requires significant work. Was Galatians written after the first or the second journey? How do the pastorals fit? Greater challenges arise, since Acts does not mention or allude to the letters of Paul. On the other hand, reasonable chronological reconstructions are possible. As to Paul's letters, they were originally written to specific people or groups by a rather controversial leader in early Christianity. Only later were they universally recognized. It is plausible that Luke's audience did not know Paul's writings.

As with the other gospels, authorship of the third gospel and Acts will remain an open question. We will proceed under the hypothesis that Luke wrote these works, recognizing its tentative nature.

Audience and Purpose

Unlike the other gospels, Luke/Acts has an identified audience and purpose. In the opening verses of Luke (1:1–4) and Acts (1:1–2), the works are directed to Theophilus to the end "that you may have certainty concerning the things you have been taught" (Luke 1:4).

As the name "Theophilus" combines two Greek words, it could be a generic reference to one who is a "lover of God" or is "loved by God." But the name shows up in a range of literature from the third century B.C. "Theophilus" could equally refer to a particular person. The descriptor "most excellent" attached to the name may suggest that Theophilus was a person of note or even a Roman official. The procurators Felix and Festus are both called "most excellent" (Acts 24:3; 26:25). Other hints suggest more about the identity of Theophilus.

Theophilus may have been someone interested in Christianity or even a new convert to Christianity. As Luke mentions other gospel writings (Luke 1:1), Theophilus may have been acquainted with one or more. Of greater significance is Luke's reference to some earlier instruction that Theophilus had received (Luke 1:4). The Greek word for instruction is the same word that would later be used to describe formal instruction for new converts and from which comes the English word "catechism."

Another possibility may be inferred from the expense and resources necessary to produce such a work in antiquity. Writing was a rare skill; tools and papyrus were expensive; and Luke did not come from a wealthy class. The practice of medicine was more folk art than a profession. Most doctors in the Roman world were slaves. So an influential and wealthy patron would likely need to pay for Luke's work. Just as Josephus dedicated his *Antiquities* to his patron Epaphroditus, so Luke may be dedicating his works to Theophilus, his patron.

Forum at Rome

The content and the ending of Luke/Acts suggest a third intriguing possibility. Throughout the two works, Jesus and the Christian gospel are presented with a universal appeal. The good news is for all and spreads to the ends of the earth (Acts 1:8). In Luke's narrative, the protagonists of Christianity appear in a positive light before Roman officials. Pilate is persuaded of the innocence of Jesus and tries three times to release him. The proconsul Sergius Paulus seeks to hear the word of God (Acts 13:7). The proconsul Gallio declares Christianity a legal religion (Acts 18:14–15). The procurator Festus, King Agrippa II, and his wife Bernice find Paul innocent (Acts 26:31). Having presented this positive context, Luke builds slowly in the last chapters of Acts to Paul's trial before the emperor in Rome. But, like a television show that flashes "to be continued" at a critical moment, Acts never gives the outcome of the trial. Because of the unresolved ending of Acts, some have suggested that Luke/Acts was initially prepared as a defense document for Paul's trial. "Most excellent Theophilus" might then be the official who heard the case in Rome before any appearance before the emperor. In the early 60s, when Paul arrived in Rome to appear before Nero, the prefect of Rome was Titus Flavius Sabinus. If one takes the initial letters of his name, aspirates the "t", adds vowels, and transliterates from Latin the Greek, the result is Theophilus.

Although none of the above theories can be proven, the unresolved nature of the ending of Acts suggests that Luke/Acts had its origin in material gathered and organized to defend Paul at Rome (the final scenes of which are a "we"-section). That material would be the genesis for a fuller work with a broader audience, possibly prepared under the patronage of a Theophilus. Luke/Acts would then be dated in its early stage to 62.

A reworking of earlier material for a broader audience is likely for several other reasons. Although the work shows acquaintance with Greek rhetoric and Graeco-Roman historiography, the main literary influence on the writer is the **Septuagint**, the Greek version of the Old Testament. Not only does the author often cite from the Septuagint, but Luke also uses the literary style of the Septuagint in casting his narrative. Such careful writing would be lost in a document written for a Roman legal context. But, if the writer were addressing the final form of his work to a Christian audience to help them understand themselves and their faith, such nuances would be effective tools. Luke sees the history of the community in three eras. There is the time of promise, as reflected in the writings of the Old Testament (quoted from the Greek version). There followed the era of Jesus, whose saving work in Jerusalem was meant even for the ends of the earth (Acts 1:8). Finally, came the era of the church, a time when the Spirit of God empowered the spread of the good news and the welcome of the Gentiles (Acts 28:28). Those who might be unsure because they converted from a Judaism that fell to Roman power in A.D. 70 would see the old promises fulfilled in the new era of the church. Those who might be unsure because they converted from the religions of the Roman world to acclaim Jesus as Lord would gain new "certainty concerning the things you have been taught" (Luke 1:4). Luke/Acts is a writing about early Christianity to encourage new Christians, no matter their background.

Structure

In telling the story of Jesus, Luke/Acts follows the standard **synoptic** outline. After a public ministry in Galilee, Jesus travels to Jerusalem where he is executed. To that basic outline, Luke adds an extensive birth narrative (Luke 1:1–2:52), a lesser interpolation (Luke 6:20–8:3) that includes the Sermon on the Plain, a greater interpolation (Luke 9:51–18:30) during which Jesus travels to Jerusalem, and an epilogue (Luke 24:1–53) of resurrection appearances and an ascension story. In telling the story of early Christianity, Luke/Acts follows an outline suggested by Jesus' instruction to his disciples: "You will be my witnesses in Jerusalem, in all Judea and Samaria, and to the ends of the earth" (Acts 1:8). After work in Jerusalem (Acts 1:1–8:1a), the church spreads beyond its roots (Acts 8:1b–12:25). Then, following the mission work of Paul and his arrest and appeal to the emperor (Acts 13:1–28:31), Luke/Acts details one aspect of the spread of Christianity to the ends of the earth.

LUKE: JESUS AS SAVIOR OF ALL	
BIRTH STORIES	1:1–2:52
PUBLIC MINISTRY	3:1–9:50
LESSER INTERPOLATION	6:20–8:3
TRAVEL NARRATIVE	9:51–18:30
PASSION ACCOUNT	18:31–23:56
EPILOGUE	24:1–53

ACTS	
"YOU WILL BE WITNESSES"	1:1–1:11
IN JERUSALEM	1:12–8:3
CROSSING CULTURAL BOUNDARIES	8:4–11:18
MISSION TO THE GENTILES	11:19–15:35
TO EUROPE AND ASIA	15:36–21:16
TO ROME	21:17–28:31

Themes

As with the other evangelists, Luke presents to his readers a rich portrait of Jesus and the Gospel. To that portrait Luke appends a second narrative of the spread of the good news about Jesus. Unifying his writings are several themes that can be traced across the works.

Luke has a different *sense of time* from the other evangelists. Matthew portrays the story of Jesus as the fulfillment of the prophetic message. Jesus ushers in the end-time reign of God, the signs of which call for preparation (Matthew 24–25). The end is near. Likewise, Luke anchors his story in the hopes of Israel, but for Luke the coming of Jesus at the center of time ushers in a new age inaugurated when God pours out the Spirit (Acts 2). This age of the church is an extended time of mission to a broader world.

The role of the *Holy Spirit* is a second Lucan emphasis. The Holy Spirit is the means by which Mary conceives (Luke 1:35), helps Simeon identify the child (Luke 2:25–27), and marks the baptism, temptation, and beginning of Jesus' ministry (Luke 4:1–14). Jesus rejoices in the Spirit (Luke 10:21), promises the Spirit to those who ask (Luke 11:13), speaks of the Spirit's help (Luke 12:12), and at the end commends his spirit into the Father's hands (Luke 23:56). The Holy Spirit has an even more prominent role in Acts. After being poured out with attendant signs (Acts 2), the Spirit fills Peter (Acts 4:8), rests on Stephen (Acts 6:3–5), comes on the **Samaritans** (Acts 8:17), leads Philip (Acts 8:39), comes upon the Gentiles (Acts 10:44–47), fosters the mission journeys (Acts 13:2; 16:6–7; 19:21), shapes the church's stance toward the Gentiles (Acts 15:28), and sustains Paul as arrest drew near (Acts 20:22–23).

A third Lucan emphasis is on the role of *prayer*. The infancy narratives are full of prayer, including hymnic prayers by Mary and Zechariah. The Spirit comes on Jesus while he is praying (Luke 3:21) after the baptism. Jesus spends the night in prayer (Luke 6:12). The **transfiguration** occurs during a time when Jesus is at prayer (Luke 9:29). While Jesus prays, the disciples ask him to teach them to pray (Luke 11:1–2). Jesus tells **parables** about the need to pray (Luke 18:1) and about proper attitudes in prayer (Luke 18:9–14). In Acts, the early community devotes itself to prayer (Acts 1:14; 2:42; 4:31). While being stoned, Stephen prays (Acts 7:59). After the vision on the road to Damascus, Saul prays (Acts 9:11). After praying, Peter raises Tabitha to life (Acts 9:40). Peter's vision (Acts 10:9) and Cornelius' conversion (Acts 10:31) had a prayer context. While Peter was in prison, the church prays (Acts 12:5). Missionaries are sent off by prayer (Acts 13:3). Prayer is part of a rescue from prison (Acts 16:25) and survival of shipwreck (Acts 27:29). Prayer, a mark of piety in Judaism, is a major feature of the Lucan narrative.

Roman agrarian Palestine was a stratified and hierarchical society ordered by pyramids of power. With their emphasis on purity and their expectation that the **Messiah** would drive the Gentiles and the unrighteous from the land, the Judaisms of the **Second Temple period** sharply distinguished the faithful from the unrighteous. But the Jesus of Luke's portrayal "receives sinners and eats with them" (Luke 15:2). Noteworthy among the stories that occur only in the third gospel are: the shepherds worshipping the infant Jesus (Luke 2:8–20), the call of Simon Peter identified as "a sinful man" (Luke 5:8), the parable of the Good Samaritan (Luke 10:30–37), the parable of the Prodigal Son and his brother (15:11–32), the parable of the Rich Man and Lazarus (Luke 16:19–31), the call of the tax collector Zacchaeus (Luke 19:1–9), and the blessing of the thief on the cross (Luke 23:39–42). A fourth emphasis of Luke/Acts is on those *marginalized* by society or religion. People who received little sympathy or who were kept to the sides of religious life repeatedly receive the direct help and care of Jesus.

Likewise, the early Christian community of Acts crossed social and religious boundaries. Welcomed into the community were Samaritans (Acts 8:4–7, 14–17), a violent persecutor of the community (Acts 9:1–18), and even a Roman **centurion** and his family (Acts 10:44–48). Christians crossed cultural boundaries at Antioch (Acts 11:19–26), cared for the hungry (Acts 11:27–30), sent workers into the Gentile world (Acts 13:1–14:28), and accorded equal status to all (Acts 15:1–29). As Luke envisions the community, the banquet is open to all, even "the poor, the crippled, the blind, and the lame" (Luke 14:21).

A corollary to Luke's interest in the marginalized is his collection of stories about *women*. From the beginning of Luke/Acts, women play a vital role in the story and are a particular focus of the care and respect of Jesus. The birth of Jesus is anticipated by a touching tale of two women, Elizabeth and Mary, both with exceptional pregnancies and an intimate interpersonal relationship. Elizabeth would give birth to the prophet, John, the forerunner of Jesus, and her cousin Mary would miraculously bear the Savior of all.

Other stories unique to Luke continue this emphasis. Jesus raises the only son of the widow of Nain out of compassion for her (Luke 7:11–16). Jesus accepts the tears and anointing of a sinful woman, even though the behavior was deemed offensive to his host (Luke 7:38–50). A group of women provide support for the ministry of Jesus, among whom Mary Magdalene is featured prominently (Luke 8:1–3). A different Mary, the sister of Martha, is commended for deciding to step out of her cultural role and sit at the feet of Jesus listening to his teaching like any male disciple (Luke 10:38–42). The parable of the persistent widow is recounted only by Luke (Luke 18:1–8). And women are important in the resurrection accounts. One of the two on the road to Emmaus may have been a woman, since the only one named is a man (Luke 24:13–34).

Although less prominent in Acts due to the focus on Paul's travels, women play important roles. Women, along with Mary the mother of Jesus, are counted with the disciples and the brothers of Jesus as part of the Jerusalem community (Acts 1:14). Care for widows was a critical task among the early Christians (Acts 6:1–6). The charity of Dorcas was renewed after Peter raised her (Acts 9:36–42). Mary from Jerusalem, the mother of John Mark, provided a gathering place for the community in her home (Acts 12:12). Lydia welcomed Paul and his companions to Philippi. The community that gathered in her home was the first church in Europe (Acts 16:11–15). At Thessalonica, leading women of the community were converted (Acts 17:4). From Paul's arrival at Corinth on, Priscilla and her husband Aquila would be vital co-workers (Acts 18:2), even providing theological instruction for Apollos (Acts 18:26). Women also fulfilled prophetic roles (Acts 21:9).

Implied by the inclusion of stories about women and the marginalized is Luke's major point. Christianity is for all people. It is not the religion of one people. It is a *universal* religion.

Inscribed capital from Ephesus

The universal theme is first annunciated in the song of Simeon. The child he held in his arms would be "a light for revelation to the Gentiles" (Luke 2:32). Luke affirms the theme by seeing in the work of John the Baptist the fulfillment of the prophecy of Isaiah: "All flesh shall see the salvation of God" (Luke 3:6). And when Luke gives a **genealogy** for Jesus (Luke 3:23–38), he traces Jesus back to Abraham, as did Matthew. Then Luke goes further, all the way back to Adam (Luke 3:38). Since Adam is the ancestor of all, this pedigree asserts that Jesus is for all.

In Acts, the universal reach of Christianity is inherent in the instruction to go to the "ends of the earth" (Acts 1:8). Many cultural and geographical boundaries later, the story ends with Paul in Rome—the capital of the empire and center of the world. Although the trial of Paul is unresolved, Paul's arrival in Rome is a symbolic completion of the instruction of Jesus. "This salvation of God has been sent to the Gentiles; they will listen" (Acts 28:28).

Key Texts

In our look at key texts from Luke/Acts we will focus on two types of material. For the gospel, we will look in detail at some of the stories that are unique to Luke. Although many have been mentioned above, we will treat a representative group at somewhat greater length to illustrate Luke's themes. The storyline of the book of Acts received significant treatment earlier in chapter 3, when we discussed the story of the earliest church. Here our focus will be on texts that illustrate Luke's theological themes. As with the gospels, the purpose of Acts has less to do with history and more to do with making theological assertions of import to the first readers (and us).

Key Texts Unique to Luke

1:46–56 Two annunciation and birth stories run in parallel in the opening chapters of the third gospel. The births of John (the Baptist) and then of Jesus are foretold. The births of John and then of Jesus are narrated. The stories are interspersed with hymns. The hymn in this section is the song of Mary, sometimes called the Magnificat (for the Latin translation of the first word of the song).

Mary, the mother of Jesus, is the most famous character in the New Testament except for Jesus himself. She was from Nazareth, a tiny village on the southern edge of the Galilean hill country and just four miles from its capital Sepphoris. Her family had arranged for her a marriage to a man named Joseph "of the house of David." In anticipation of the marriage (and to demonstrate her purity), she was secluded in her parental home. She was likely from a Levitical tribe, since she was a relative of Elizabeth, the wife of a priest. Luke focuses on Mary and her relative Elizabeth to demonstrate the significant role played by women in God's plan of salvation.

The song of Mary has striking similarities to the song of Hannah (1 Samuel 2:1–10). Both songs celebrate God's gift of a child given in unusual circumstances. Mary's song is also similar to other Jewish hymns because most lines reflect and reuse Old Testament language to create a new song of praise.

Of greater significance is the theology of the hymn. Elizabeth has just greeted Mary as the mother of her Lord. The child would be the "Son of the Most High" and would "reign over the house of Jacob forever" (1:32–33). Jesus would be the Messiah and the **Son of God**. Mary's song draws out the implications of this announcement—God's special favor for the poor and marginalized (a Lucan theme). God has looked on her "humble estate" and she is now "blessed." The birth of the child means that God "scatters the proud," "brings down the mighty," "exalts the humble," and "fills the hungry" (1:51–53). This reversal is quite similar to the language of the Sermon on the Plain from Luke's gospel, in which Jesus speaks blessings on the poor and hungry (6:20–21) and has words of woe to those who are rich and "full now" (6:24–25).

1:67–80 A second hymn in the opening chapters of Luke is the song of Zechariah, a blessing of God spoken at the birth of John the Baptist. Like Mary's song, almost every line uses language from different parts of the Old Testament. But the theological focus is different and reflects Luke's sense of time. Zechariah's song is cast as prophetic. He who had been silenced (1:20) when the coming birth of John was announced now prophesies under the influence of the Holy Spirit. Zechariah's prophecy gathers prophetic language and themes (the Messianic promise in 1:69, the oath to Abraham in 1:73) and even invokes the prophets themselves (1:70) to identify a prophetic mission for John. John would be the final prophet who prepares the way of the Lord. That theme returns when John the Baptist begins his work (3:4). By including the song of Zechariah, Luke stresses his sense of time. The Old Testament is the age of preparation. It culminates with the work of John who prepares for Jesus. The time of Jesus would be the center of history, followed by the age of the church (Acts).

2:1–2 As part of his sense of time, Luke connects the coming of Jesus at the center of history to a specific time in history. Augustus is emperor, and the movement of Joseph and Mary to Bethlehem in the south is brought about by a census "when Quirinius was governor of Syria" (2.2). Luke's sense of time is connected to a particular time. Unfortunately, the reference is problematic.

Josephus, a first-century Jewish historian, dates the governorship of Quirinius to A.D. 6–7 and mentions a census in Judea (*Antiquities* 18.1.1, 18.2.1). The discrepancy between the birth of Jesus and the census is some ten years.

No certain solution is at hand. A number of suggestions have been offered, such as one that translates the verse, "This was before the registration when Quirinius was governor of Syria." But such a translation is problematic grammatically. We simply do not have literary or material data that allows a complete reconciliation of Luke and Josephus. Nevertheless, the theological point is clear. The coming of Jesus at a particular time ushers in a new age, according to Luke's sense of time.

2:8–20 In the first gospel, Matthew chose to recount the visit of the magi. The story was a hint about the direction of the Christian mission to make disciples of all nations (Matt. 28:19). Luke chooses to narrate a different story of visitors in order to reaffirm his theme that Jesus is for the marginalized. The shepherds, who hear an angelic announcement that the Messiah has been born (2:11), visit the child and set an example for Luke's readers telling others (2:17) and praising God (2:20).

In the culture of Roman agrarian Palestine, shepherds came from the lowest class of people and could be representative of the poor to whom Jesus proclaimed good news (4:18). Later rabbinical sources speak of shepherds as disreputable, alluding to a marginalized state in society. On the other hand, in the Old Testament God is a shepherd who protects his flock (Genesis 48:15; 49:24; Deuteronomy 26:5–8; Jeremiah 13:17; Micah 7:14). Beloved are the words of the psalm, "The Lord is my shepherd" (Psalm 27:1). Especially after the time of David—the shepherd who became a king—the ruling class was referred to as shepherds and were judged for their failure to tend the flock of God's people (Ezekiel 34). As a result, the Messiah was expected to "shepherd" the people (Psalms of Solomon 17:23–46; 2 Esdras 2:34). There seems to be a split in the usage of the word shepherd. In the real world, shepherds were poor and marginalized, even though their work could be used as a metaphor for the acts of God and the Messiah. Perhaps to clarify this distinction, in John's gospel Jesus uses the adjective "good" to describe himself as a shepherd (John 10:11).

2:36–38 Because of the import Luke places on the role of women in the history of salvation, Luke tells the story of a certain Anna. In the tradition of pious widows (Judith 8:4–8), she had not remarried after the early death of her husband, but instead devoted herself to fasting and prayer (Luke 2:37). She is also called a prophetess (2:36) and in line with Zechariah speaks of the messianic hope. After seeing Jesus presented in the temple, Anna thanked God and spoke of Jesus to all who were waiting for the "redemption of Jerusalem" (2:38). This phrase parallels the "consolation of Israel" for which her prophetic compatriot Simeon watched (2:26). Three times Luke mentions the role of the Holy Spirit in his prophecy (2:25–27). Language from the prophet Isaiah features prominently in the description and speech of Anna and Simeon (Isaiah 42:6; 49:6; 52:9–10; 60:3)

3:23–38 After the baptism of Jesus that occurred while he was praying, Luke provides a genealogy of Jesus. As with Matthew's genealogy, the purpose is not to list every ancestor but to speak (theologically) of the honor of the individual. As a result, the genealogies are not identical. But in agreement with Matthew, Luke traces Jesus through Joseph (indirectly) to David. Jesus is the Messiah and the promise to David is fulfilled. In further agreement, Luke traces Jesus back to Abraham and thereby embraces the covenant with Abraham. Both are important to Luke, are mentioned in Zechariah's song, and fit with Luke's sense of time. Going further, Luke traces Jesus back to Adam, the son of God (3:38). Jesus is more than the consolation of Israel; his salvation has a universal embrace.

Shore of the Sea of Galilee

5:1–11 Comparison of gospels with each other helps to highlight the emphases of a particular writer. In the previous chapter, we noted how Matthew stressed the urgency of discipleship by describing the call Simon Peter and Andrew with a concisely written narrative. "Immediately they left their nets and followed him" (Matthew 4:20). Luke describes the call of Simon in much greater detail and at greater length. The call involves a daytime fishing excursion instigated by Jesus after a night of fruitless work. The result is a catch of fish so great that "their nets were breaking" and the boats "began to sink" (Luke 5:7–8). Fishermen eking out an existence on the lake were among the marginalized of society. The catch was an overwhelming sign of divine favor (if not intervention). Peter falls at Jesus' feet, "Depart from me for I am a sinful man, O Lord" (5:8). Peter thought he ought properly to be on the margins in the presence of such a divine character as Jesus. Jesus welcomes this marginalized one with comforting words and gives him a new commission (5:10). Peter left everything and followed Jesus (5:10). Luke's longer narrative stresses that the salvation brought by Jesus extends to those on the fringe economically and theologically.

6:17–49 A sermon opens that section of the gospel called the "lesser interpolation" where significant material unique to Luke departs from the outline in the other synoptic gospels. In what is sometimes called the Sermon on the Plain, Luke gathers sermonic material as did Matthew in the Sermon on the Mount. Comparative examination again reveals Luke's thematic emphases. Since Luke writes to a Gentile audience, he omits Jesus' variation on the rabbinic style

("You have heard it said … but I say to you."). Likewise, the acts of Jewish piety (fasting, prayer, and almsgiving) are not discussed. Luke takes up prayer in a different context, since it is one of his themes.

Most significant is Luke's collection of blessings and "woes." Matthew had included nine blessings (beatitudes) in his sermonic collection. Luke has only four and they are balanced with four "woes." Luke's four are more materialistic than those in Matthew. Jesus in Matthew blesses the "poor in spirit" and those who "hunger and thirst for righteousness" (Matt 5:3, 6). Jesus in Luke blesses those who are physically poor and hungry (Luke 6:20–21). In addition, Jesus harshly judges those who are rich and "full now" by speaking words of woe against them (6:24–25). The contrast of rich and poor and the reversal to come are part of Luke's theme through which Luke stresses Jesus' concern for the marginalized. This language will return in two stories recounted only by Luke: the parable of the Great Banquet, to which the poor and crippled are invited (14:21), and reversal of fortunes in the parable of the Rich Man and Lazarus (16:19–31).

7:11–17 Another story unique to Luke tells of a widow from the village of Nain whose only son had died. Luke would have interest in the story, because the protagonist is a woman whose circumstances would put her among the marginalized. Widows were in a vulnerable position in ancient societies, especially if their dowry had long been spent. Among the poor classes, dowries were meager at best. Ruth and Naomi, both widows, had to rely on gleanings from the fields to survive (Ruth 2:2). Mistreatment of widows could be a problem (Exodus 22:22, Deuteronomy 27:19). The loss of an only son made her misery even more bitter. It is as if she were under God's judgment (Amos 8:10).

According to Luke, the response of Jesus to her is one of compassion (7:13). The word for compassion shows up only two other times in Luke's gospel. Both are stories told uniquely by Luke. In one, a Samaritan is the one to show compassion on a wounded traveler (10:33). In the other, the word described the compassion of a father who welcomes home a wayward son (15:20). The salvation brought by Jesus extends to all—even a marginalized woman. Jesus raises her son and the crowd glorifies God (7:16).

7:36–50 All four gospels recount a story of a woman anointing Jesus either on the head or the feet. In the other traditions, the anointing anticipates the events of holy week. Luke's account is prior to his long narrative of Jesus' travel to Jerusalem. It is a different story and reflects Lucan themes.

The story concerns a woman who is also identified to the reader as a "sinner" (7:37). The **Pharisee** who invited Jesus to table uses the same word for her (7:39). In the Psalms of Solomon, which reflect Pharisaic teaching, the son of David will "drive out sinners from the inheritance" (Psalms of Solomon 17:23). In the view of the Pharisees, a woman such as this would have no place in the messianic kingdom. So, she ought to be marginalized.

Jesus refuses to do so. Instead, through the story of two debtors, Jesus makes the point that the woman shows such love because she has been forgiven so much (7:47). Jesus speaks words of forgiveness to her and commends her faith (7:48–50). Although those at table continue to question his actions, the message of the story is clear to the reader. The salvation and forgiveness brought by Jesus is for all, even those on the margins.

8:1–3 Luke closes the lesser interpolation with a note about Jesus' continued work in the cities and villages of Galilee. The Twelve are with him, as are a group of women. Mary Magdalene is prominent, and among the women is the wife of a Herodian official. Luke adds that the women provided for Jesus and the Twelve "out of their means" (8:3). The listing of the women at this point anticipates the important presence of women in Luke's telling of the crucifixion (23:49), the resurrection (24:10, 13) and in the early community in Jerusalem (Acts 1:14; 12:12). But these women were also behaving in a way atypical of the roles held by women in the agrarian communities and fishing villages of Galilee. Women are important characters in Luke's gospel because the good news is for them, too.

9:20–22 As we have already noted, the words of Peter's confession differ in each of the gospels. The individual gospel writers choose how much of Peter's speech they will recount and into what Greek phrases they will translate it. In so doing, each writer can make his point about who Jesus is.

In Luke's narrative, Peter says, "You are the Christ (Messiah) of God" (9:20). Even in English we must choose whether to translate "Christ" or "Messiah"! Although Luke writes to Gentiles, Luke introduces messianic terminology early. At the annunciation, Gabriel says that Jesus will be given "the throne of his father David" (1:32). Zechariah's song speaks of a "horn of salvation for us in the house of his servant David" (1:69). The angels announce, "Born this day in the city of David is a Savior, who is Christ the Lord" (2:11). And Simeon waits in the temple to see "the Lord's Christ" (2:26), a phrase almost the same as Peter's acclamation of "God's Christ." For Luke, Jesus is the Messiah expected by the prophets in the first era of Luke's sense of time. In the next verses, Jesus foretells his death (9:22). Jesus is a different kind of Messiah. He is not a political one, but one who serves and suffers. His coming marks the center of time.

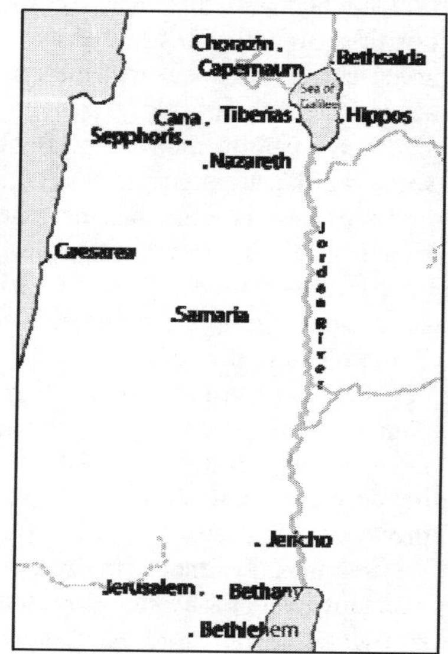

9:57–62 At Luke 9:51, "Jesus set his face to go to Jerusalem." For the next ten chapters Luke will loosely narrate the travels of Jesus from Galilee to Jerusalem. Mark covers the same material in one chapter. This greater interpolation in Luke's gospel is often called the "travel narrative." But in it, Luke narrates little traveling. Instead, Luke presents teachings, incidents, and parables, many of which are unique to Luke. Jesus is going to Jerusalem to die.

The accounts of the travel narrative start by noting the cost of following a suffering Messiah.

As in Matthew, so in Luke someone from the crowd promises to "follow you wherever you go" (9:57). In Luke the encounter has greater significance, for Luke tells of challenges issued by Jesus to three different people. Matthew's account is shorter and involves only two would-be disciples. In Luke account, discipleship involves a single-minded commitment overriding the important task of burying a father (Leviticus 21:1–3). A disciple of Jesus would not even be afforded the opportunity to say farewell to family—an opportunity Elijah gave Elisha (1 Kings 19:19–20).

Discipleship brooks no compromise, according to Jesus. As the Messiah who will suffer and calls others to follow, Jesus has set a standard different from contemporary expectations. In a series of two stories chosen by Luke, the most unexpected of people become exemplars of the way of Jesus.

10:25–37 In the first story, an expert in the **Torah**, wanting to follow a the way that leads to eternal life, proposes two Mosaic teachings as a summary: love of God (Deuteronomy 6:5) and love of neighbor (Leviticus 19:18). Jesus affirms his answer. But when the man then asks, "Who is my neighbor?" Jesus responds with a parable that also presents an ethical dilemma. While traveling from Jerusalem to Jericho, a man is robbed and left for dead. A priest and then a Levite come upon him. Since the victim might be dead, both risk incurring the impurity that comes from touching a corpse. Such impurity would mean that they could not fulfill their duties in the temple (Leviticus 22:4). In a sense, they pass by this nearly dead man in service of a higher law. But the text also notes that the priest is "going down" the road (Luke 10:31). He was leaving Jerusalem, likely because his time of service was over (1:8). Were the priest to come into contact with the man's corpse, he would have time to perform rituals of purification before his next duty cycle (Leviticus 22:6). By this point in the parable, it would be clear that the priest and Levite did not act with compassion for all as Jesus exemplified.

Surprising in the story is the one who does provide care. It is not a Pharisee, a **rabbi**, an expert in the Torah, or even a disciple of Jesus. The one who provides help is a Samaritan—one of those who were at best on the margins of Judaism. In the previous chapter, Samaritans had refused to receive Jesus; and the disciples called for divine retribution (9:51–54). Still, a Samaritan becomes an exemplar of the uncompromising discipleship for which Jesus calls. Only Luke tells this story.

10:38–42 Another surprising exemplar appears in the home of a woman named Martha. Martha is a person of note. The place where Jesus is welcomed is called "her house" (10:38). No husband is mentioned. The Greek word for her service (10:40) to Jesus is the same used for the action of those women who provided for Jesus and the Twelve (8:3). Martha's hospitality ought to be viewed as part of that extraordinary service that several women gave to Jesus.

However, in the story, another woman outshines Martha's service as an exemplar of discipleship—her sister Mary. Mary sits at the feet of Jesus and listens to his teaching (10:39). To sit at the feet of a renowned teacher was to assume the position of a disciple. Luke uses the same expression to describe Paul's studies as a disciple of the famous rabbi Gamaliel (Acts 22:3). But in the Second Temple and later rabbinic periods, rabbis did not have women disciples. By affirming that Mary "has chosen the good portion" (Luke 10:42), Jesus welcomes all as disciples.

In these two stories, characters of interest to Luke (a marginalized Samaritan and a woman) are upheld as people who do what is right and necessary as followers of the one headed resolutely to Jerusalem.

11:1–13 To this point in the gospel, Luke has included stories and editorial notes about people praying. Now Luke takes up the concept of prayer. Jesus taught about prayer on many occasions. In Matthew's gospel, prayer is dealt with along with other acts of Jewish piety in the Sermon on the Mount. As part of the materials collected to comprise the sermon, Matthew included the Lord's Prayer. Luke provides a different context for the Lord's Prayer. Jesus is praying and his disciples ask him to teach them how to pray (11:1).

Prayer at the Wailing Wall

The request needs explanation. In the Second Temple period, prayer was an individualized and even private practice (Matthew 6:6). **Synagogues** were a place for reading the Scriptures and expounding their meaning. Ritual or communal prayer was not practiced there. Even individual prayer was frowned upon (Matthew 6:5). At the temple, individual prayer was proper (Luke 18:9–13); but communal prayer following a common text was not practiced. Only after the destruction of the temple did the surviving rabbinic tradition develop a standard text for prayer. When the disciples ask Jesus to teach them how to pray, they are likely asking for a specific prayer text that they might use (individually or communally). Rabbis taught such standard prayer texts as a way of instructing their followers in their teachings. Apparently, John the Baptist did so (11:1).

The prayer forms a conclusion to a block of material in which Luke has laid out the ideals of discipleship. To care of neighbor and listening to Jesus, a pattern for prayer is added. Luke's version of the Lord's Prayer is shorter than the one in Matthew's gospel. Luke omits some language that might be more suitable for a Jewish audience.

To the prayer pattern Luke adds two stories that Jesus told about prayer. In the first, a neighbor looks for help from another neighbor due to the late arrival of a visitor. Persistence seems to be the theme of the story, for Jesus follows with exhortations to "ask," "seek," and "knock" (11:9). Parental care for children is the second example meant to motivate prayers to the heavenly Father. The consequence of prayer will be the gift of the Holy Spirit (11:13). In Lucan materials, prayer and the Holy Spirit are associated. While Jesus prays, the Holy Spirit comes upon him at his baptism (3:21–22). In Acts, the early community devote itself to prayer (Acts 1:14), and the Holy Spirit is poured out on that gathered community (2:1). Luke will take up the topic of prayer again toward the end of the travel narrative in chapter 28.

14:15–24 As Jesus progresses toward his end in Jerusalem, he increasingly uses parables to convey his message. In a cluster of parables in chapters 14 and 15, Luke makes clear the consequence of the events to occur in Jerusalem. Salvation will be offered to all, even those most marginalized.

The parable of the Great Banquet recalls texts from the Old Testament anticipating a banquet that God prepares for the people. The psalmist writes: "You prepare a table before me in the presence of my enemies" (Psalm 23:5). Isaiah prophecies: "On this mountain the Lord of hosts will make for all peoples a feast of rich food, a feast of well-aged wine, of rich food full of marrow, of aged wine well refined" (Isaiah 25:6). Luke would resonate with the second text with its stress on the universal welcome to the banquet.

By contrast, in the time of Jesus, expectation about the meal had changed. According to 1 Enoch, after the sinners and oppressors have been punished and driven off, only the righteous and elect will "eat and rest and rise with that Son of Man forever and ever" (1 Enoch 62:11–14). In a document from Qumran called "The Messianic Rule," the Messiah of Israel will sit at the head of the whole congregation of Israel. "They shall gather for the common table to eat and to drink new wine, when the common table shall be set for eating and the new wine poured for drinking." But "no man smitten in his flesh, or paralyzed in his feet and hands, or lame, or blind, or deaf, or dumb, or smitten in the flesh with a visible blemish, no old and tottery man … [will be allowed to] enter among the congregation" (1QSa 2:11–22, from the Vermes translation).

In the version of the parable recounted by Luke, there is no vengeance exacted on those who reject the initial invitation (Matthew 22:7). Instead, the invitation to others is much more explicit. In Matthew, there is only one sending of the servants to bring in "as many as you find" (Matthew 22:9). In Luke, the instructions are explicit and even expanded in a third invitation: "Go out quickly to the streets and lanes of the city, and bring in the poor and crippled and blind and lame … Go out to the highways and hedges and compel people to come in, that my house may be filled" (Luke 14:21, 23). Those now invited were already part of the community, although marginalized from participation in its social activities. But as Jesus approaches Jerusalem, they are welcomed explicitly. The messianic age to be ushered in by Jesus was markedly different from popular expectations.

15:11–31 Although Jesus was explicit (and Luke has selected stories to affirm) that the messianic banquet is for all, religious elites continued to complain,

"This man receives sinners and eats with them" (Luke 15:2). Luke counters with a collection of three parables. The first (told also by Matthew) recounts the joy of a shepherd who finds one lost sheep (15:7). In the second, similar joy is expressed by a woman who finds a lost coin. Two marginal characters in the social hierarchy of Roman Palestine exemplify the work of Jesus. The next parable, popularly called the parable of the Prodigal Son, is in fact two parables about two sons who each in his own way is lost.

The younger son demands of his father "the share of the property that is coming to me" (15:12). Property was normally divided among the heirs after the death of the father. To ask for his share and then to liquidate it (15:13), broke the relationship between this son and his father (and the rest of the family who were deprived of the livelihood to be gained from the property). The son could not wait for the father to die and had no concern for the rest of the family. By violating so many social conventions, the son proved that he was lost. By granting the request, the father imperils himself and his household for the sake of the son.

The son's actions in a far country are labeled "reckless" (15:13). He squandered his property. The issue is not one of sexual immorality (as his brother will charge), but of waste. The word for the son's behavior is used in another context to describe washing feet with spiced wine. When an inevitable famine strikes, the son "glues" himself to a local citizen, takes the job of a pig herder, and wants to supplement his meager rations with the wild carob pods that were being used to keep the pigs alive. This Jewish boy was far from home, dependent on a Gentile, in constant contact with unclean animals (making him ritually impure), and near starvation, not to mention what he had done to father and family at home. Socially, religiously, and economically he was imperiled. Although in the ancient world (and today), it was often assumed that people on the margins were in some way responsible for their precarious state (John 9:2), this boy was not someone marginalized by others; he had done it to himself.

In desperation the son decides to go home. He plans to earn his way back into the household as a slave by an act of repentance. The resources of the family may be diminished by half, but the life of a slave even in such circumstances was better than starvation. Still, when the father sees him a long way off, the father "runs" to him. The behavior is shocking, as a wise an honorable man never runs (Sirach 19:30). The father humiliates himself to protect the son from ridicule or mistreatment by neighbors and family. By dressing his son and adorning him with ring and sandals, the father completely restores him to his former place in the household. Killing a fatted calf would commence a feast for household and the neighboring community. The father left no doubt among all in his circle that the lost is found.

The older son, as he approaches the house, hears the music and dancing. Surprisingly, he does not join the party right away, as one would expect of the heir whose wealth was bringing joy to the family and community. He is immediately suspicious, keeps his distance, and asks a servant to tell him what is happening. His suspicion suggests that his relationship with father and family is ruptured, too. Upon hearing of his brother's return, he refuses to join the banquet. Just as the younger son cut himself off from family and community by leaving with half of the family's wealth, the older son marginalizes himself from the family. He cuts himself off; he, too, is lost. Also, the older son argues with his father in front of those assembled for the feast. He exaggerates the circumstance by accusing his father's son (he refuses to acknowledge blood relations) of consorting with prostitutes (15:30). The behavior of the elder son is as dishonorable as was the demand of the younger son for the inheritance.

As he did a few verses earlier, the father again humiliates himself. He goes out to his son rather than commanding him to enter. Just as the father had restored the younger son, he reassures his elder son of his place in the family, "You are always with me, and all that is mine is yours" (15:31). But unlike the case of the younger son, the story of the older son is left unresolved. The chapter began with the religious elite complaining about Jesus' association with sinners. The chapter ends with an open invitation to them to come to the celebration also. Since the parable does not end with the elder son joining the banquet, Luke implies that religious elites who would keep others at a distance are themselves lost.

16:19–31 Earlier in Luke's gospel, the coming of salvation to those on the margins hints at a reversal of fortune for those who seem to be recipients of God's favor. In response to the annunciation, Mary praises God because "he has filled the hungry with good things, and the rich he has sent empty away" (1:53). In the Sermon on the Plain, Jesus speaks words of blessing to the poor (6:20) and pronounces woe upon the rich (6:24). The parable of the Rich Man and Lazarus illustrates again that reversal and the offer of salvation to the marginalized.

The contrast could not be greater between the rich man and Lazarus. In mortal life, the rich man is dressed like Roman royalty (to enter the senate was "to take up the purple") and feasts sumptuously (16:19). Lazarus is a beggar covered with sores, relying on scraps, and licked by dogs. Those familiar with the Old Testament would recall the shameful death of King Ahab in battle. "The dogs licked up his blood and the prostitutes washed themselves in it" (1 Kings 22:38). The degradation of Lazarus is absolute. However, after death Lazarus is carried by the angels to Abraham's side (16:22). The scene is a luxurious banquet at which the guests recline side by side (John 13:23). The rich man is in Hades and is longing for a drop of water to cool his tongue. No meal is in his torment. The reversal is complete. At the messianic banquet, the marginalized will be honored, and those who would keep others at a distance will be on the outside. The barb against the religious elites is sharp, suggesting that the elites do not listen to Moses and the prophets (16:29), whose teaching they claim to uphold by keeping others at a distance.

18:1–18 Lucan emphases help to explain two more parables that are only recounted in his gospel. Both focus on prayer. In the first parable, the key character is a woman. She can attain justice from an "unjust" judge because she "kept coming to him" (18:3). Her persistence is an example for those who pray.

In the second parable, two are praying. The first is a Pharisee whose actions are the opposite of the piety Jesus promotes in the Sermon on the Mount (Matthew 6:1–18). The second is a tax collector "standing far off" (18:13). In Second Temple society and by virtue of the place where he stands, the tax collector is on the margins. He pleads for mercy because he is a sinner. The marginalized one is justified (18:14).

19:1–10 As Luke draws the travel narrative to a close, Jesus passes through Jericho. There a certain Zacchaeus tries to see him. Only Luke tells this story, likely because it fits his theme. Zacchaeus is a "chief tax collector" (19:2). As hated as tax collectors were, Zacchaeus would have been particularly reviled. As "chief," he had larger regional responsibilities and had enriched himself in the process. Jericho was a juncture on trade routes and at the border of the administrative regions of Judea and Perea, so collection of custom duties might also be involved. In the view of most first-century Jews, Zacchaeus would be the epitome of those unrighteous ones who would have no place in the messianic kingdom.

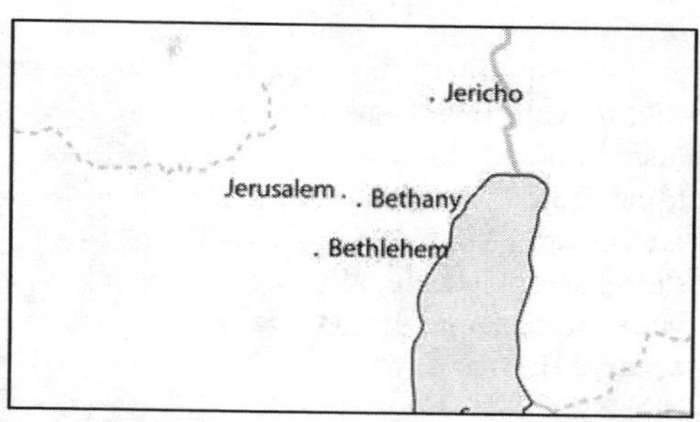

But Jesus invites himself to stay at Zacchaeus' home (19:5), an act offensive to those particular about purity. In response to Zacchaeus' pledge of restoration and charity for the poor, Jesus declares, "Today salvation has come to this house" (19:9). Jesus use of "today" fits with Luke's sense of time. For the salvation brought by Jesus marks the center of history. "Today a savior is born," said the angels (2:11). "Today this scripture has been fulfilled," Jesus announced in the synagogue in Nazareth (4:21). "Today you will deny me," Jesus would warn Peter (22:61). "Today you will be with me in paradise," Jesus would assure the thief on the cross (23:43). Jesus' words to Zacchaeus end with a statement that summarizes Luke's inclusion of so many stories about those on the margins of society and religion: "The son of man came to seek and to save the lost" (19:10). The verse serves as an adequate summation of the Gospel according to Luke.

23:1–25 The Passion Narrative in Luke follows the synoptic outline, although Luke does not stress the conflict as much as does Matthew. Also, since Luke's sense of time includes the age of the church, less stress is placed on teachings about the end of time. In Matthew and Mark, the focus is on the return of the Son of Man and the judgment that attends his coming. In Luke, the focus is on the period before the return.

In Luke's telling of the Roman trial there are two aspects of note: Pilate's judgment of Jesus and the appearance of Jesus before Herod. The religious authorities bring Jesus before Pilate and accuse him of political crimes: misleading the nation, forbidding Roman taxes, and claiming to be a king (23:2). Pilate quickly comes to a conclusion, "I find no guilt in this man" (23:4). He will repeat the judgment later (23:14). He even announces that he will release Jesus (23:22). But Pilate gives in to the demands of the religious leaders and the people. Pilate was known to be ruthless, but he could also back down in the face of pressure, as he did when he withdrew standards he had set up that the crowds considered offensive. The reader knows that Jesus is innocent under Roman law; instead politics (and survival) got the upper hand.

At a point in the trial when Pilate hears that Jesus is a Galilean, he sends him to Herod Antipas (23:7). Pilate ruled Judea. Herod was king of Galilee and Perea. Jesus was legally Herod's subject. Although glad to see Jesus, Herod soon resorts to mockery and returns Jesus to Pilate. Luke notes that Herod and Pilate became friends from that day (23:12). There is irony in this account. The Jesus, who reconciled so many marginalized people to the community of the faithful by welcoming or healing them, at his trial even reconciles two Roman officials to each other!

Pilate stayed at Herod's palace (model)

23:27–31 Luke's interest in stories about women surfaces again as Jesus is on the way to the cross. Some people, including many women, mourn for him. Jesus warns them of worse days to come.

23:43 Jesus was crucified between two bandits, according to all three synoptic gospels. As shameful as crucifixion was, placing Jesus between two such men was itself an act of mockery and shame. Luke alone tells that one of the thieves sought mercy from Jesus. Even a guilty criminal such as this could receive mercy and favor from Jesus. "Today you will be with me in paradise" (23:43) is further confirmation of Luke's theme. Jesus is savior of all, even the most marginalized.

23:46 All three Synoptic Gospels say that Jesus cried out at the moment of death. John summarized the cry in one word (in Greek), "It is finished" (John 19:30). Luke gives a fuller wording in the form of a prayer. Jesus addresses God as he taught his disciples (Luke 11:2), "Father" (23:46). To the prayer, Jesus adds, "Into your hands I commit my spirit." The language echoes Psalm 31:5, and may show that Jesus recited the entire Psalm, even as he had likely recited Psalm 22 earlier (Matthew 27:46; Mark 15:34). The prayer of Jesus would be revised on the lips of Stephen as he is being lynched. Stephen prays to Jesus rather than the Father: "Lord Jesus, receive my spirit" (Acts 7:59). Stephen also prays that the Lord "not hold this sin against them" (Acts 7:60). Stephen's prayer is again similar to a prayer of Jesus from the cross in Luke 23:34. But the best manuscripts indicate that the prayer, "Father, forgive them …," may not have been a part of the original text of the gospel. However the manuscript problem is resolved, because for Luke, prayer is an important act of piety and plays a significant role in the lives of the first Christians.

24:13–35 Luke's universal concern surfaces in the story about two confused disciples on the road to Emmaus. An abbreviation of the story may be seen in Mark 16:12–13. But the Marcan story exists only in later manuscripts and is likely influenced by the Lucan story.

Luke's story features two characters: a Cleopas and a second unnamed person. In John 19:25, a Mary present at the crucifixion is the "wife of Clopas." If these are variants of the same name and refer to the same person, the unnamed person may be that Mary. Since the second character in Luke's story is unnamed, many do speculate that she was Cleopas' wife. Should the character be a woman, another of Luke's emphases may be in play.

Luke's main point, however, is to show the confusion present in the community at the reports of the resurrection and to illustrate through the story means by which the confusion is overcome.

The story has its humorous side. Cleopas asks, "Are you the only visitor to Jerusalem who does not know the things that have happened there?" Jesus, who knew such things intimately, responds, "What things?" (24:18–19) Then, in response to Cleopas' confused summary, Jesus turns to "Moses and the prophets" (24:27) and is then recognized when "he took bread and blessed and broke it and gave it to them" (24:30). Confusion gives way to certainty based on the "Scriptures" (24:32) and leads to witness (24:35–35). Teaching, breaking bread, and prayer will characterize the life of the community in the age of the church (Acts 1:14, 2:42, 20:7).

24:50–53 Luke gospel ends with a brief account of the ascension. Jesus is carried up and the ongoing era of the church begins with the disciples "continually in the temple blessing God" (Luke 24:54). In Acts, Luke returns to the same story in the opening chapter. The story launches the second volume and gives a basic direction to it. In Luke's sense of time, the ascension marks the transition from the center of history to the age of the church.

Thematic Theological Texts from Acts

1:2–11 Many of the same theological themes that characterized the third gospel also appear in Acts. In Luke's opening words to Theophilus, the Holy Spirit is identified as the means through which Jesus would guide and direct his chosen apostles (1:2). As important as was the role of the Holy Spirit in the story of Jesus, the Spirit's role becomes predominant in Acts. John the Baptist had promised that the one to come would baptize with the Holy Spirit (Luke 3:16). His promise is the basis for Jesus' instruction to the disciples "not to depart from Jerusalem, but to wait for the promise of the Father" (Acts 1:4). And the final words of Jesus to the disciple before the ascension promised, "You will receive power when the Holy Spirit has come upon you" (1:8). The outpouring of the Holy Spirit on Jesus at his baptism anticipated the outpouring of that same Spirit on the disciples.

A second characteristic of Luke's presentation is his sense of time: the era of promise yields to the center of history in the story of Jesus, to be followed by the time of the church. This sense of time is also a theological factor in the opening story of Acts. The forty days that Jesus spent with his disciples after his resurrection (1:3) recalls the forty days in the desert that started his ministry (Luke 4:2). In the background is the story of the forty-year wandering in the desert of Sinai that forged a slave people into the people of promise. So forty years began the era of promise; forty days began the work of Jesus at the center of time; and forty days with the resurrected Jesus initiated the age of the church. But speculation is to be avoiding about the exact timing that "the Father has fixed by his own authority" (1:7). Instead, the tasks of the age of the church call for action. But even that age has its end: "This Jesus, who was taken up from you into heaven, will come in the same way as you saw him go into heaven" (1:11).

Commemorative site of the Ascension

Just before his ascension, Jesus details a program for his followers: "You will be my witnesses in Jerusalem and in all Judea and Samaria, and to the end of the earth" (1:8). These words serve as an outline for the book of Acts. For its opening chapters (1–7) recount the early work of the church in Jerusalem, then the church moves across geographical and cultural boundaries out into the region of Judea and Samaria (8–11), and finally, the book traces the work of Paul in the eastern Mediterranean as far as Rome (12–28). But this verse also affirms a theological theme of Luke: Christianity is a religion that reaches out to all with a universal appeal. As Rome symbolized the center of the political world, Paul's arrival at Rome affirmed "that this salvation of God has been sent to the Gentiles" (28:28).

1:15–26 The replacement of Judas by Matthias is a story rarely studied in Acts, perhaps because Matthias is never mentioned again in the New Testament. Still, this story about the first community echoes important Lucan theological themes. The stage for the story is set by a description of the early community. Along with the remaining eleven of the disciples, the women and Mary the mother of Jesus are specifically mentioned (1:14). Luke's interest in stories about women continues. The mention of Mary recalls her prominent place in the opening of the gospel. The community numbered "about 120" (1:15), significantly larger than the eleven and their companions. The community is growing.

As the number is approximate, it could have symbolic overtones, as a multiple of the number of tribes of Israel. The universal reach of the gospel may be implied. The community is characterized as continually "devoting themselves to prayer" (1:14). Prayer has featured prominently in the gospel narrative. In the description of the community alone, three Lucan themes are visible.

Peter is the first of the disciples to speak. Peter and, later, Paul will be the two prominent characters in Acts. Peter tackles the problem in the community caused by the betrayal and suicide of Judas. Significantly, Peter turns to "the Scripture" (1:16) for help in understanding their circumstance and for direction for the future. Psalm 69 is cited as an explanation for the behavior of Judas. Psalm 109 directs the community to replace Judas. This practice of turning to "the Scripture(s)" for understanding and guidance becomes a recurring pattern in the early community (2:16, 25; 4:25; 15:15).

Citation of the Scriptures of the Old Testament is part of Luke's emphasis on the role of the Holy Spirit. Luke makes that point clear in the words of Peter that Luke recounts, for the Scripture cited by Peter is that "which the Holy Spirit spoke" (1:16). This perspective was not unique to Peter, for the community together would pray using words "our father David said by the Holy Spirit" (4:25). It is fair to assume that any citation of Scripture by Luke or by a character in Luke's story is an indirect reference to the role of the Holy Spirit in the life and story of the community.

The selection of Matthias is done by casting lots (1:26). The names of the candidates were written on stones, placed in a jar and one was drawn or shaken out. As is suggested by the prayer of the community, the use of such a method was to assure that the choice was God's (1:24). The idea is mentioned in Proverbs, "The lot is cast into the lap, but its every decision is from the Lord" (Proverbs 16:33). As Luke places this story about Matthias immediately before the Pentecost narrative, Luke may imply that the Holy Spirit works through such means. However, after Pentecost the community uses prayer and Scripture in its decision making, but it never again casts lots.

2:1–13 The detail and length of the story of the outpouring of the Holy Spirit at the festival of Pentecost testifies to the import of the Holy Spirit in Luke's telling of the story of the earliest Christians. In Peter's sermon, he cites at length from Joel and from two Psalms of David to explain the unusual events. The addition of "three thousand souls" to the community on that day (2:41) affirms the significance of the gift of the Holy Spirit. These "were added." The passive voice points to the divine activity involved. Peter's concluding words announce the universal implications: "For the promise is for you and for your children and for all who are far off, everyone whom the Lord our God calls to himself" (2:39).

Pentecost, which means "the fiftieth day," marks a period after **Passover** when the people celebrated the Feast of Weeks. It corresponded with the conclusion of the grain harvest and was one of three pilgrimage festivals (Deuteronomy 16:16). There was a degree of variance in the exact date for Pentecost among Jews from the Second Temple period. Some even celebrated multiple pentecosts. Jerusalem would swell with pilgrims from Galilee and Judea, and from the larger Graeco-Roman world.

The outpouring of the Holy Spirit is attended by the symbols of wind and fire. The wind starts out as a sound from heaven, something heard before it is felt. In a similar way at Mount Sinai, loud sound warns of the coming of God (Exodus 19:16, 19). With a wind, God provided a miraculous rescue at the Red Sea, driving back the waters and creating a dry path (Exodus 14:21). Wind also attends the coming of the Lord to Elijah (1 Kings 19:11). And in Ezekiel's vision of the valley of dry bones, it is the wind or breath of God that gives life to the slain (Ezekiel 37:9). Likely involved as well is a play on the Hebrew and Greek words for "spirit," which can also mean "wind" or "breath." By invoking Old Testament imagery even as he plays with the meaning of the word "spirit," Luke creates a mystical scene to empower and authorize the community, just as Jesus was empowered at his baptism.

Fire can also be a symbol for the presence of God. The God of Israel appeared to Moses in a burning bush (Exodus 3:2). A pillar of fire guided the Israelites out of Egypt (Exodus 13:21). Fire and smoke shrouded the peak of Sinai when God met Moses and Israel there (Exodus 19:18; Deuteronomy 4:36). The dedication of the tabernacle/temple (Exodus 40:34; 1 Kings 8:10) and the throne of God (Isaiah 6:4) are filled with smoke. Destructive themes sometimes associated with God's judgment seem to be lacking in this story (Genesis 3:24; Exodus 9:23–24; Numbers 11:1; Job 1:16; Psalm 46:9; Isaiah 66:15; Luke 3:16). Instead, the divided tongues of fire resting on each person in the room symbolically empower their speech, as the burning coal gave the prophet Isaiah the ability to speak for God (Is. 6:6–7).

The outpouring of the Holy Spirit is summarized in a final verse that names the Spirit twice (Acts 2:4). The Spirit fills all, creating a unity, and speaks through the community in "other tongues." As implied by those present hearing in their own languages (2:6), the tongues to which the text refers are foreign languages, not the ecstatic speech with which Paul would deal in 1 Corinthians. Luke recounts this aspect of the Pentecost event, since it fits well with his presentation of Christianity as a religion with a universal appeal.

Those who reacted to the events of Pentecost are called "devout men from every nation under heaven" (2:5). Those present foreshadow the ultimate reach of the Gospel. For Luke's Roman readers, the universal reach of Christianity would be reinforced by the list of nations whose inhabitants were present at Jerusalem. In the Augustan age, Rome would assert its authority in the far reaches of the empire by the construction of imperial edifices, temples, and even inscribed proclamations. Commonly, the dedications on such structures would name the emperor and include a list of nations ruled or conquered by the individual. Such lists served as imperial propaganda for the universal rule of Rome. The list of names offered by Luke stretches in all four directions from Jerusalem and serves as counter propaganda for the **kingdom of God**. Romans might give Caesar the title of "Lord," but the Christian gospel would acclaim by contrast that Jesus is "Lord of all" (Acts 10:36; Philippians. 2:11).

2:42–47 The outpouring of the Holy Spirit has a marked affect on the community. Their numbers increased and the practices of the community matured. At first, they had "devoted themselves to prayer" (1:14). Infilling by the Spirit meant richer community practices: "teaching and fellowship … the breaking of bread and the prayers" (2:42). Wonders and signs were done by the apostles. And there was a unity to their communal life—sharing and distributing according to need—as they awaited the return of Jesus. The idealized life of the early community likely reflected their expectation of an imminent return by Jesus. The giving up of belongings for common use by a community is a religious practice known from the Qumran documents. They, too, were awaiting the imminent coming of God's day and rule. The earliest Christians simply did what others with similar expectations did. Their practice is not a model for contemporary Christian life. Soon both internal and external problems would impinge on their idealistic world. Nevertheless, Luke describes these first Christians as "praising God and having favor with all the people" (2:47). That favor suggests a universal appeal leading to numerical growth brought about by the action of "the Lord."

4:5–20 The community faced pressure from external forces. After Peter and John had healed a lame beggar while going into the temple (3:1–10) and then taught in Solomon's portico (3:11–26), religious authorities and the **Sadducees** arrested them for "proclaiming in Jesus the resurrection from the dead" (4:2). Luke describes Peter's response to interrogation by the authorities with language that reflects one of Luke's theological themes. Peter is "filled with the Holy Spirit" as he begins to speak (4:8) and his speech ends with a quotation from Psalm 118. In the age of the church, the Holy Spirit directly helps its leaders and also speaks through the Scriptures.

Having quoted the Psalm, Peter ends his speech with a conclusion: "There is salvation in no one else, for there is no other name under heaven given among men by which we must be saved" (4:12).The words may be spoken in the midst of controversy, but they also affirm another of Luke's themes. The universal appeal of the Gospel is an exclusive claim. If Jesus is for all and God raised him, there is no other name. This claim is the first clearly stated theological conclusion of the early followers of Jesus and is foundational for their work and witness. They would carry the Gospel to the ends of the earth because there is no other name.

After two millennia, many contemporary Christians, especially in Europe and America, are uncomfortable with exclusive claims. The challenges of modernity, comparative study of religions, the abhorrent violence of militant religious groups, and the privatization of religious expression put social pressure on exclusive claims, especially in pluralistic western societies. However, the Christianity of Luke/Acts has at its foundation an exclusive claim. To qualify or negate that claim is to challenge the core of Christianity. In Luke's telling, this claim is inspired by that Spirit poured out on the church. For this reason, Peter could respond to those authorities who would silence him, "We cannot but speak of what we have seen and heard" (4:20). When Peter later reports to the community, they lift their voices in prayer, quote what David said "by the Holy Spirit" (4:25), and as the place was shaken "they were all filled with the Holy Spirit and continued to speak the word of God with boldness" (4:31).

7:54–8:1 Internal pressures also weighed on the life of the community life. The dark story of Ananias and Sapphira (5:1–11) marks the coming end of the communal life in which everything was held in common (2:44; 4:32). The early idealism when there was "not a needy person among them" (4:34) quickly broke down into complaints among different Christian subgroups that some "were being neglected in the daily distribution" (6:1). Differences in language and culture contributed to the strife. This dissonance in the community is dealt with by the appointment of seven extra leaders with specific responsibility for the distribution. These men are "full of the Spirit," in keeping with Luke's theology (6:3). One is identified as "a man full of faith and the Holy Spirit" (6:5): Stephen.

Stephen comes into conflict with people from several synagogue communities for his preaching about Jesus and is brought before the **Sanhedrin**. In a long speech, Stephen sidesteps the charges against him. Instead he offers a broader defense of Christianity by tracing the sweep of Israelite history. The speech is about God's workings in history and concludes, "You always resist the Holy Spirit. As your fathers did, so do you" (7:51). Luke's theological project is to stress the important role of the Holy Spirit in the early community. When trouble came to the community internally, it was because people like Ananias "lied to the Holy Spirit" (5:3). External pressures result because people like the religious authorities resist the Holy Spirit. The culmination of these pressures is the lynching of Stephen, an event that drives the church and its mission outside of Jerusalem.

Luke's narration of the death of Stephen continues to assert Luke's theological themes. The final event is precipitated as Stephen, "full of the Holy Spirit" (7:54), gazes into heaven, sees Jesus standing at the right hand of God, and reports his vision to his accusers. As the stoning begins, Stephen prays. His prayer echoes the death prayer of Jesus. Luke reported Jesus as saying, "Into your hands I commit my spirit" (Luke 23:46). Stephen prays, "Receive my spirit" (Acts 7:59). Jesus' prayer was addressed to the Father, Stephen's to the Lord Jesus. Stephen also prays, "Lord, do not hold this sin against them" (Acts 7:60), even as Jesus had prayed, "Father, forgive them" (Luke 23:34). Stephen may have been a minor character and a sad victim of violence, but his story is rich in themes important to Luke, especially the Spirit and prayer.

8:4–25 Luke's focus on the marginalized and his stress on the guidance of the Holy Spirit both come to the fore as Luke tells how Philip proclaimed Christ in Samaria. Just as Luke narrated the stories of the Good Samaritan (Luke 10:30–37) and of the thankful Samaritan leper (Luke 17:16) to show how those on the edges could exemplify faithfulness, he portrays Philip's work as the crossing of the Christian mission beyond the boundaries of Judaism to those on its fringes. Philip's work of healing involved casting out unclean spirits (Acts 8:6) and was confirmed when Peter and John prayed and laid hands on the Samaritans, that they also might receive the Holy Spirit (8:15–17). So important is this "Samaritan Pentecost" that misunderstanding of the working of the Spirit by Simon the magician had to be corrected (8:18–24). Each time a new cultural group is embraced by Christianity, Luke narratives an outpouring of the Holy Spirit. For Luke, the movement of Christianity beyond the cultural limits of Judaism is the working of the Spirit.

8:26–40 Another character in the margins of Judaism is drawn to Christianity through the ministry of Philip. The eunuch from Ethiopia "has come to Jerusalem to worship" (8:27). Although rich and of high social status, his mutilation placed him in a state of ritual impurity (Lev. 21:20; 22:24). He was not allowed to enter the assembly of the Lord (Deuteronomy 23:1). Still, Philip is sent to him by an "angel of the Lord" (8:26) later identified as the "Spirit of the Lord" (8:39). For Luke, the Holy Spirit plays a role in this story as well. Scripture is quoted and interpreted. Baptism is the result. By this point in Luke's narrative, the reader associates both actions with the working of the Spirit of Jesus.

9:1–22 Pivotal in Luke's narrative concerning the early years of the age of the church is the transformation of the persecutor Saul into God's "chosen instrument" (9:15) to carry the gospel into the non-Jewish world (Saul will later be known by the Roman name Paul). It is best to label Saul's experience a transformation. Conversion describes rejection of another religion and embrace of Christianity, or turning away from immorality to the life of holiness. Saul was not converted from Judaism to Christianity, since Christianity was still a variant of Judaism. Instead, his Judaism underwent a transformation so that Saul began to proclaim Jesus as the Messiah (9:22). In addition, his experience has a similarity to the call of Old Testament prophets (Isaiah 6:1–10; Jeremiah 1:4–10) in that Saul is given a specific mission different from his earlier role as a persecutor. Saul has been transformed into a witness.

Saul's transformation is so important to Luke that he narrates it three times in Acts: 9:1–22; 22:1–16; and 26:9–18. Luke's concern is to prove the universal appeal of the Gospel. As the community has embraced those on the margins such as the Samaritans and the Ethiopian, the transformation of the one persecuting "the Way" (9:2) is the next logical step toward the Gentile mission. This transformation must be embraced within the church before it can be carried out externally. Ananias of Damascus must be persuaded that Saul is a "chosen instrument" before he goes to lay his hands on him (9:13–16). Also, Barnabas must convince the leaders in Jerusalem (9:26–27). The transformation of Saul prepares the church internally for the future work of the Gentile mission. Later accounts of the story in Acts are specifically linked to this universal mission (22:21; 26:20).

The story of Saul's transformation also continues to uphold the role of the Holy Spirit in the life the early communities. The voice of Jesus—addressing Saul and telling him what to do—functions in a way similar to the Holy Spirit or the "Spirit of Jesus" (16:17) in other parts of Luke's work. Later distinctions between the persons of the Trinity ought not be pressed too precisely on the text of Acts. Whether Luke speaks of the "Spirit," the "Holy Spirit," the "Spirit of the Lord," the "Spirit of Jesus," "Jesus," the "Lord," or "God," Luke is asserting divine guidance and action behind the growth and work of the early church. Ananias laid hands on Saul "that you may regain your sight and be filled with the Hoy Spirit" (9:17). Finally, Luke summarizes the narrative of the transformation of Saul: "So the church throughout all Judea and Galilee and Samaria had peace and was being built up [notice the passive voice]. And walking in the fear of the Lord and in the comfort of the Holy Spirit, it multiplied" (9:31). The next major step in that universal direction guided by the Holy Spirit would be the conversion of Gentiles.

10:34–48 The conversion of Cornelius marks an important event in Luke's theological program. As Christianity is a universal religion with appeal to all, the conversion of a Gentile who also is an officer of the Roman Empire calls for detailed treatment. Several of Luke's other theological themes surface in the story as well.

Cornelius is one of two key characters in the story. He lived with his family at Caesarea (10:1), implying a long service or perhaps that he retired there. He is a centurion, a professional soldier in the Roman army in charge of eighty to one hundred men (the same Latin word for "one hundred" is behind the English word "century"). He is a member of the Italian Cohort—the *Cohors II Italica voluntariorum civium Romanorum*—a Roman citizen with a family connection to Italy. He is described as "a devout man who feared God with all his household, gave alms generously to the people, and prayed continually to God" (10:2). Apparently, Cornelius had been attracted to Judaism and had attached himself to a local synagogue. He is not called a **proselyte**, so he had not converted to Judaism. But he was attracted to its piety of prayer and supported the community with alms. A close association with a synagogue by Cornelius and his family supports the theory that he was retired. Since Luke is interested in stories about prayer, Luke notes that Cornelius had a vision while praying (10:3). The prayers of Cornelius had been heard (10:4), and he was instructed to send to Joppa for Peter—the second major character in the story.

Peter is at Joppa because he was summoned there at the death of Tabitha—another of Luke's many stories about women. Like Cornelius, Peter has a vision while he is praying. His vision is symbolic. Three times he is challenged to break Jewish dietary laws, "What God has made clean, do not call common" (10:15). Such laws were one of the most public signs of the Jewish bifurcation of the world into Jews and Gentiles. While Peter thinks about the vision, the Spirit directs him to go with the men sent by Cornelius (10:19).

When Peter enters the home of Cornelius, Peter knows he is violating Jewish laws of purity (10:28), but in meeting Cornelius, Peter draws a second important theological conclusion. Previously Peter was led to assert that "there is no other name" (4:12)—a foundational theological premise for early Christianity. With Cornelius, Peter draws the logical conclusion from that first premise: "Truly I understand that God shows no partiality, but in every nation anyone who fears him and does what is right is acceptable to him" (10:34–35). Luke's universal theme has its ultimate expression on the lips of Peter. The dividing wall of hostility (Ephesians 2:14) has been broken down, at least in theory.

To confirm this conversion, "the Holy Spirit fell on all who heard the word" (Acts 10:44). As with the events of Pentecost and the conversion of the Samaritans, the outpouring of the Holy Spirit with accompanying signs marks the crossing of another cultural boundary. Cornelius and his household are baptized.

Peter's subsequent report of the event was criticized by some in Jerusalem. Many in the early Jesus movement believed that people had to become observant Jews to be true followers of Jesus the Messiah. Peter recounted the outpouring of the Holy Spirit "on them just as on us" (11:15) and reminded the community of the words of Jesus, "John baptized with water, but you will be baptized with the Holy Spirit" (11:16). Peter persuaded the Jerusalem community to accept what he had to learn to accept: "to the Gentiles also God has granted repentance that leads to life" (11:18). The conversion of Cornelius, echoing Lucan themes about prayer and the Holy Spirit, was also the story of the theological conversion of the first followers of Jesus from a sect within Judaism to a universal religion.

11:19–26 According to Acts, Jesus had given his followers a universal program: "You will be my witnesses in Jerusalem, in all Judea and Samaria, and to the end of the earth" (1:8). Luke traced that program outward across geographical and cultural boundaries. With the conversions of those on the margins of Judaism, such as the Samaritans and the eunuch, with the transformation of the persecutor Saul, and with conversion of the first Gentile, Luke shifts his focus to one narrow slice of the outward spread of Christianity—the mission centered in Antioch of Syria. Later written sources, as well as archaeology, confirm that Christianity spread in many directions—to the Galilee, Syria, Arabia, and Egypt. The story of the Antioch mission is merely illustrative of the larger program.

Luke's choice of the Antioch mission for his focus may have been personal, for some later traditions suggest that Antioch was his birthplace. But the mission at Antioch also reflects strongly Luke's theological program. At Antioch, Jewish Christians "spoke to the Hellenists also, preaching the Lord Jesus" (11:20). The outreach to non-Jews was intentional. Barnabas, a man "full of the Holy Spirit" (11:24), was sent to lead the work. He recruited the help of Saul, the former persecutor. In Antioch the name "Christian" was first applied to the disciples (11:26)—hinting at their universal program. The role of the Spirit even guided their provision of famine relief for the communities in Judea (11:28–29).

13:4–12 The mission to Cyprus continues the outward geographic and cultural spread of Christianity, even as it displays characteristics with which Luke is interested theologically. The leaders gathered for worship at Antioch are a diverse group (13:1). Barnabas and Saul are Jews. Simeon seems to come from northern Africa, since he has a nickname based on the Latin word for "black." Lucius (a Greek name) is from Cyrene. And Manaen was raised as the foster brother of Herod Antipas. Together, these five are symbolic of the universal reach of the Gospel stressed by Luke.

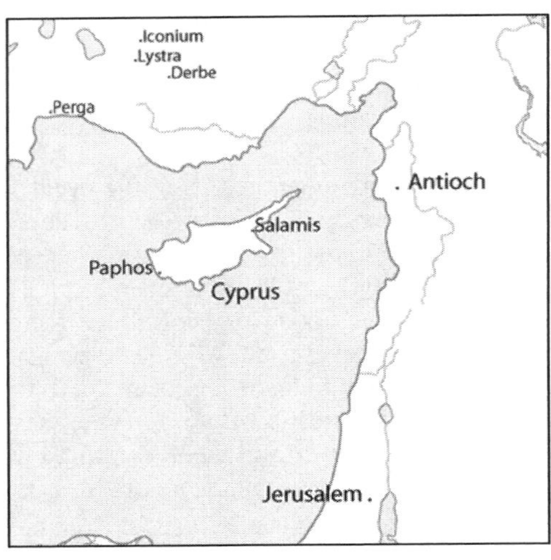

Guidance by the Holy Spirit, another Lucan theme, is the basis for sending Barnabas and Saul (13:2). Their mission on the island begins in the synagogues of the Jews but also includes a hearing by and conversion of the Roman proconsul, Sergius Paulus (13:7,12). Saul, full of the Holy Spirit, assumes a greater leadership role through a confrontation with Elymas bar-Jesus (13:9). The Roman name, Paul, is also given for the first time in this context. With the name of Paul, the former persecutor will be known as the missionary to the Gentile and will count as one of his valued assistants to the very end a man named Luke (2 Timothy 4:11).

13:26–42 After departing from Cyprus, Paul assumes leadership of the mission and takes the group (minus John Mark) inland as far as Antioch of Pisidia. Luke recounts a speech of Paul given at the synagogue in Antioch. This crucial speech and subsequent events establish the theology and practice for the Gentile mission as Paul would conduct it. The universal appeal to Jew and Gentile is asserted.

In response to readings from the Torah and the prophets, Paul opens his comments with the Exodus account and traces the messianic hope of Israel through David to the coming of John the Baptist (13:16–25). Paul next narrates the death and resurrection of Jesus as fulfillment of the Scripture (13:26–37). Paul's narrative yields a theological consequence cast in universal tones: "Let it be known to you therefore, brothers, that through this man forgiveness of sins is proclaimed to you, and by him everyone who believes is freed from everything from which you could not be freed by the law of Moses" (13:38–39). The phase "is freed" translates the first use of the Greek term that would become central to Paul's expression of the doctrine justification.

Paul's message is well received by "many Jews and devout converts" (13:43). But when opposition arises from others a week later, Paul turns to the Gentiles (13:46). The Gentiles rejoice "and the word of the Lord was spreading throughout the whole region" (13:49). Such would be Paul's future pattern. He would first approach Jews in the local synagogue and then, when opposition occurred, he would turn to the Gentiles. Doing so was commanded by the Lord (13:47).

15:1–29 Although Luke has methodically set the stage for the universal appeal of Christianity, Christianity had sprung from within Judaism. Many Jewish Christians struggled with the embrace of Gentiles into their community without requiring **circumcision** and Torah observance. After all, Jesus was a Jew, had come to fulfill the Torah (Matthew 5:17), as was himself the culmination of the Jewish messianic hope. When some teachers "came down from Judea" with the message that circumcision was a prerequisite for salvation (Acts 15:1), dissension broke out at Antioch of Syria. Luke is being diplomatic with his description. Paul would write bluntly, putting the blame on people from James and confronting Peter for giving in too easily to them (Galatians 2:11–14). A delegation was sent from Antioch to Jerusalem over the matter. As the delegation traveled and reported their work along the way, they "brought great joy to all the brothers" (Acts 15:3) according to Luke. The universal perspective would win the day.

At the meeting with the leaders in Jerusalem, the stakes were raised. Besides circumcision, keeping the whole Law of Moses was also at issue (15:5). Three speeches carry the day. Peter cites the outpouring of the Holy Spirit to show God makes no distinction (15:8–9). Barnabas and Paul (note the astute change in order of precedence) recount the signs and wonders done among the Gentiles (15:12). Then James, the leader of the church in Jerusalem whose people started the controversy, gives his personal pronouncement in favor of the Gentiles by citing material drawn from Amos 9:11–12. Both "signs and wonders" and the scriptural source would have been understood by the community as coming from the Holy Spirit. The letter sent back to Antioch makes its pronouncement because "it seemed good to the Holy Spirit and to us" (15:28). The universal mission is sanctioned by the Holy Spirit.

16:11–40 Paul's first work in Europe takes place at the Roman **colony** of Philippi. Luke attributes their arrival at Philippi to the guidance of the Holy Spirit and a vision (16:6–9). Luke's interest in the impact of the Gospel on women and the marginalized may also influence the choice of stories. After meeting Paul at a place of prayer, Lydia, a woman of commerce and means, opens her home to the new mission (16:14–15). A slave girl, whose spirit of divination is a source of profit for her owners, is exorcised by Paul (16:18). And a jailer and his family are baptized after hearing the good news from Paul and his companions (16:33–34).

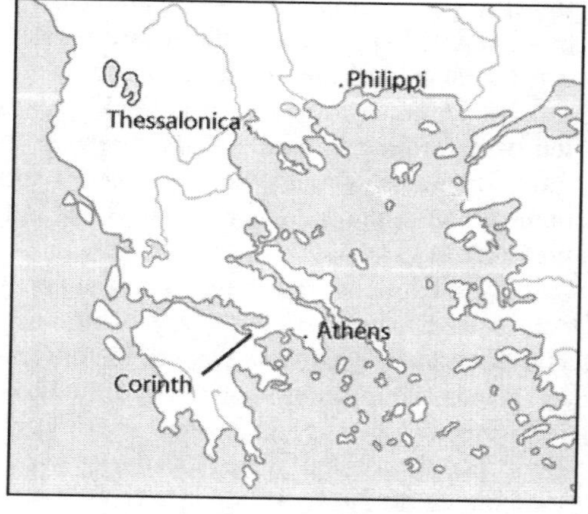

17:22–34 Paul's method and proclamation at Athens differ notably from his earlier efforts. He works both in the synagogue and in the marketplace, abandoning the sequence of going to the Jews first and then to the Gentiles. When given an opportunity to address the Areopagus, he begins with an inscription to an unknown god and quotes from the Stoic poets Epimedes and Arastus. Those theological emphases so prized by Luke are missing from the narrative. Notably, Paul's work has but minor success (17:32–34). Paul himself would speak of a change of tactics when he left Athens and came to Corinth (1 Corinthians 2:2).

18:1–11 Paul's long ministry at Corinth (one and half years) witnesses a return of Lucan themes. Paul connects up with two Jews who are refugees expelled from Rome, making a marginal existence through their common trade of tent making. The woman of the couple was Priscilla. She would also take a leading role in the work at Ephesus (Acts 18:18, 26) and would be warmly mentioned in three of Paul's letters (Romans 16:3; 1 Corinthians 16:19; 2 Timothy 4:19). And a vision from the Lord would inspire Paul's lengthy stay (Acts 18:9). The vision accords with other guidance that Paul got from the Holy Spirit in his work.

20:17–37 At the conclusion of Paul's travels and mission work around the Aegean, he was returning to Jerusalem, hoping to arrive by Pentecost (20:16). Although Pentecost was a Jewish festival, it was also the time when the Holy Spirit had first been poured out on the community. When he stopped at Miletus, he sent for the elders from Ephesus for a farewell.

Paul's speech recalls his work among them over the last four years and charges them to look after the church of God. Through his speech, Paul says that the Holy Spirit continues to guide their work. Paul is constrained by the Spirit to go to Jerusalem, even as the Holy Spirit testifies to him that imprisonment and afflictions await him (20:22–23). Paul makes his charge to the overseers to shepherd the church because the Holy Spirit has given them that task (20:28). Paul, who had been guided in his work by the Holy Spirit and now is led by the Spirit in a dangerous direction, passes on his leadership role to the next generation who also had been led by the Spirit to continue the work of the church. After the speech, they kneel and pray, and bid each other a tearful farewell (20:36–37)

22:1–22 Upon returning to Jerusalem, Paul agreed to pay for the vows of four Jewish Christians as a way of proving his respect for the Torah (21:24). Although many years had passed, the universal appeal of the Gospel at the heart of the Gentile mission was still troubling to Christians in Jerusalem. But while Paul purified himself and went with those keeping their vows to the temple, some people present stirred up the crowds in the temple with the charge that Paul had defiled it by bringing a Gentile into its sacred areas. A subsequent riot led to the arrest of Paul.

At issue in the unfolding events at Jerusalem was the clash between two religious perspectives. The Jewish religion of the Second Temple period believed God made a unique covenant with their race that would be consummated in the

Messianic age when pagans and sinners would be driven from the land. Ritual purity and Torah observance separated the Jews from the Gentile world and prepared them for this coming age. The Christianity represented by Paul (and Luke) by contrast, held that God shows no partiality, that non-Jews are saved by the same mercy God shows to the people of promise. Christianity is a religion with a universal appeal. So, when Paul is allowed to make a public defense before his people, two critical moments are of note in his story.

In recounting the blinding on the road to Damascus, Paul relates what Ananias said to him, "You will be a witness for him to everyone of what you have seen and heard" (22:15). This critical quote, which was not part of the original story in Acts 9, combines three elements. First, "You will be a witness for him" echoes the command of Jesus in Acts 1:8: "You will be my witnesses." Second, "What you have seen and heard" recalls Peter's confident words before the council in Acts 4:20: "We cannot but speak of what we have seen and heard." Third, the words "to everyone" summarize the Gentile mission. In response to those who would contest the universal reach of the good news, Paul's defense makes clear that, from the moment of his transformation, this was his project.

The second critical moment comes from the end of the speech. In Luke's earlier telling, Paul departed quickly from Jerusalem after his transformation because a plot against him had become know to the community (9:29–30). But in Paul's speech, other circumstances are revealed. Paul recalls that he was praying in the temple when he fell into a trance (22:17). He is warned to flee Jerusalem. But the vision also gives him a specific task: "Go, for I will send you far away to the Gentiles" (22:21). Paul's mission to the Gentiles is not only his mission; it is God's universal mission. The riotous response of the crowds to the defense made by Paul highlights the clash between the perspectives of those gathered in Jerusalem and the universal project about which Luke writes.

23:11 Although Paul's defense was rejected by the crowds and violence broke out at his appearance before the religious council (23:10), Paul was encouraged by a second vision. In the former vision at the beginning of his work, the threats against him had propelled him on a mission to the Gentiles (22:21). In the second vision at the end of his Gentile mission, the Lord tells him to take courage, for "you must testify also in Rome" (23:11). Both visions specifically name his universal mission. As visions, these experiences accord with Luke's theme that the church and its leaders are specifically guided by the Holy Spirit.

26:1–32 Paul was turned over to the prefect Felix, who held him in prison for two years at Caesarea awaiting a bribe (24:26–27). Felix was succeeded by Porcius Festus before whom Paul appealed his case to the emperor in Rome (25:11). Before Paul is shipped off, Luke devotes some forty-six verses to an appearance Paul made before Festus, King Herod Agrippa II, and Agrippa's younger sister Bernice.

Throughout Luke/Acts, the author has presented good news with a universal appeal. In Acts, Luke notes that Jesus specifically sent his disciples to the "end of the earth" (1:8). Paul is about to embark for Rome where his appearance before the emperor will carry out that "end." The appearance before Festus,

Agrippa, and Bernice supports the universal theme. Festus stands for the power of Nero, the world ruler at the time. Marcus Julius Agrippa, the only son of Agrippa I, was a favorite of Emperor Claudius, held the title of "great king" over Chalcis and the Galilee and Perea, and stayed loyal to Rome through the time of the Jewish revolt. Bernice, after the deaths of two husbands, lived with Agrippa for fifteen years. She would later become the lover of Titus, the Roman general who destroyed Jerusalem. In appearing before these three, Paul brings his story into the power circles of the empire.

The regal entrance of Agrippa and Bernice "with the military tribunes and prominent men of the city" (25:23) suggests the scope of the audience. Luke further notes that Festus intends this hearing to be the basis of his report to the emperor (25:26). Paul's defense is similar to earlier statements. He recounts his background as a Pharisee, the persecution of the followers of Jesus, and the vision he had on the road to Damascus. But in this version, it is Jesus himself who speaks of Paul's commission to the Gentiles (26:17). In Acts 9, the commission of Paul to the Gentiles is mentioned in a divine message to Ananias (9:15). In Acts 22, Ananias speaks a word to Paul that commissions him to a universal mission (22:15). But here in Acts 26, the commission comes through words of the risen Jesus spoken directly to Paul in that first vision on the road to Damascus.

Paul next details his own preaching, making specific mention twice of his mission to both Jews and Gentiles (26:20, 23). A polite exchange with Agrippa ends the speech. Agrippa says to Paul, "In a short time would you persuade me to be a Christian?" Paul responds, "Whether short or long, I would to God that not only you but also all who hear me this day might become such as I am—except for these chains" (26:28–29). Paul's final word is a universal appeal.

27:1–44 Paul's journey to the capital of the Roman Empire is a perilous one. Luke, who likely went with Paul, offers great detail of the trying experience. After departing Fair Havens in an attempt to reach Phoenix before the winter, a storm blows the boat far off course. For almost two weeks the damaged ship was adrift. Then the prisoner Paul stood up to encourage the crew. He had just had a vision in which an angel of God promised that Paul would indeed stand before Caesar (27:24). Further, Paul conveyed the divine assurance that "there would be no loss of life among you" (27:22). The subsequent shipwreck at Malta and safe travel to Rome symbolize Luke's universal theme. The gospel delivers all, even as Paul and all the people on the boat would survive the shipwreck and come to the end of their journey.

28:23–31 The final scenes in Acts place Paul at Rome. He is under house arrest, waiting two years for his trial. But even under those circumstances, Paul's mission to bring the Gospel to both Jews and Gentiles continues. Local leaders from the Jews come to hear him (28:17). When some disagree, Paul turns to a text from Isaiah. Paul claims the Holy Spirit is right in so speaking of their refusal to hear (28:25). Paul concludes: "Therefore let it be known to you that this salvation of God has been sent to the Gentiles; they will listen" (28:28). Luke's final paragraph punctuates the universal offer of the Gospel, for Paul

Temple of Vesta at Rome

"welcomed all who came to him, proclaiming the kingdom of God and teaching about the Lord Jesus Christ" (28:30–31).

Throughout the third gospel and Acts, Luke has "compiled a narrative of the things that have been accomplished among us" (Luke 1:1). But Luke/Acts is far more than a neutral narrative. Luke has selected material and focused his descriptions so that certain theological themes repeatedly surface. Luke's sense of time places Jesus at the center of history, the outpouring of whose Spirit inaugurates the age of the church. This community is led by the Holy Spirit and devoted to prayer even as Jesus was. The community has a universal commission to carry the good news to all people, a point reinforced by stories that show the impact of the good news in the lives of women and the marginalized. Together, these themes assert that Jesus is the savior of all.

Jesus in Luke/Acts

Of the various titles for Jesus used by the evangelists, one title is used almost exclusively by Luke: savior (Luke 1:47, 69; 2:11; Acts 5:31; 13:23; compare John 4:42). With other words from the same root, Luke answers the christological question about the identity of Jesus by presenting Jesus as savior of all. (The word "salvation" is used four times in Luke and five times in Acts. The word "save" is used fifteen times in Luke and thirteen times in Acts.) In Luke's day, the word "savior" was a title of honor for a deserving person. It could be applied to a divinity in one of the mystery religions. Of much greater import is its use to designate a (deified) ruler. For Luke to use such a term in a work addressed to "most excellent" Theophilus, is to use a term to which an official like Theophilus might relate, but to use it in a way that gave it new meaning. Jesus was not the savior of the Roman people and nation in a political sense. He was the savior of all, even the most marginalized, and in ways far beyond the pale of politics.

The savior-theme is announced in the birth narratives of Luke. Upon hearing the blessing of Elizabeth, Mary sings of "God my Savior" (Luke 1:47). In the same way, Zachariah blessed God since God "has raised up a horn of salvation for us" (1:68). To these songs the angels outside of Bethlehem give their announcement of the birth of "a Savior" (2:11). And when Jesus is presented in the temple, Simeon too blesses God, "for my eyes have seen your salvation … a light for revelation to the Gentiles and for glory to your people Israel" (2:30, 32). In these birth narratives, all unique to Luke, Jesus is savior of all.

The many and diverse people who experience the help of Jesus confirm the words of Isaiah quoted by Luke: "and all flesh shall see the salvation of God" (3:6). Luke is the only evangelist to quote this part of the prophecy. To a sinful woman who anointed his feet at the home of Simon, Jesus declared, "Your faith has saved you" (7:50). To a blind beggar outside of Jericho, Jesus said, "Receive your sight, your faith has saved you" (18:42). To the tax collector Zacchaeus, Jesus brought the good news, "Today salvation has come to this house…for the Son of Man came to seek and to save the lost" (29:9–10). To a dying criminal, Jesus gave assurance, "Today you will be with me in Paradise" (23:43). In Luke's gospel, Jesus is savior of all.

In Acts, the same Christology predominates. On a foundational level, the early followers of Jesus were convinced that "there is salvation in no one else" (Acts 4:12). In Paul's pivotal sermon at Antioch of Pisidia, Paul speaks of Jesus as the promised "Savior" (13:23). In this context Paul would be expected to use "Messiah" but instead he used "Savior." Paul goes on to speak of the "message of salvation" (13:26). He concludes the sermon by annunciating his commission to "bring salvation to the ends of the earth" (13:47). And in his final speech recorded by Luke, Paul declares: "Therefore let it be known to you that this salvation of God has been sent to the Gentiles; they will listen" (28:28).

In Acts, Jesus is the savior of all and offers salvation to all, both Jew and Gentile. The same word family is used repeatedly in the growth and spread of the church. "And the Lord added to their number day by day those who were being saved" (2:47). "There is no other name under heaven given among men by which we must be saved" (4:12). "But we believe that we will be saved through the grace of the Lord Jesus, just as … [the Gentiles] will" (15:11). "Believe in the Lord Jesus, and you will be saved, you and your household" (16:31). Luke's sense of time, his interest in stories about women and the marginalized, his stress on the guidance of the Spirit, and his insistence that Christianity is a universal religion all flow from a core christological belief. That belief is the distinct portrait of Jesus offered by Luke in the third gospel and Acts: Jesus is savior of all.

For Further Discussion

1. Luke and Matthew both have birth stories and the Lord's Prayer. When you compare their accounts and the subtle differences, what do you discover about the emphasis of each author?

2. Compare Lucan themes to the practice of contemporary Christianity in the west. What is similar? different? Do the same exercise, but this time look at the rapidly growing churches of the southern hemisphere.

3. How does the parable of the two sons (Luke 15) speak to contemporary families and churches? Can you see yourself in the parable? Where?

4. We have suggested that Luke addresses his works, at least initially, to a Roman official. Luke was arguing that Christianity had a place in the Roman world. In contemporary American culture, many argue for an interface between religion and politics. How might the Lucan writings address the issues of faith and politics?

5. In Luke's gospel Jesus, the savior of all, reaches out to the marginalized in Jewish society. What people live on the margins of society today? Why do you think is it so hard for Christians to reach out to these people?

For Further Reading

Bruce, F. F. *Commentary on the Book of Acts*. New International Commentary on the New Testament. Grand Rapids: Eerdmans, 1980.

Conzelmann, Hans. *The Theology of St. Luke*. Philadelphia: Fortress, 1961.

Fitzmyer, Joseph A. *The Acts of the Apostles.* The Anchor Bible 31. New York: Doubleday, 1997.

________. *The Gospel According to Luke.* The Anchor Bible 28-29. New York: Doubleday, 1981.

Jervell, Jacob. *The Theology of the Acts of the Apostles*. Cambridge: Cambridge University Press, 1996.

Just, Arthur. *Luke*. Concordia Commentary series. 2 volumes. St. Louis: Concordia Publishing House, 1996.

Marshall, I. Howard. *Luke: Historian and Theologian.* Grand Rapids: Zondervan, 1970.

Pelikan, Jaroslav. *Acts*. Brazos Theological Commentary. Grand Rapids: Brazos Press, 2005.

1 and 2 Peter

In the previous chapter, we examined the book of James, a letter attributed to James, the brother of Jesus. Following James in the New Testament are the letters of Peter and the letters of John. James, Cephas (the Aramaic name for Peter), and John are called "pillars" of the Jerusalem church in Galatians 2:9. That designation is likely behind the order of the books as they are listed in the New Testament. Since Jude was identified as a brother of Jesus by church tradition, that book comes at the end of this grouping.

Along with James, the Petrine letters, the three Johannine epistles, and Jude are sometimes titled the General Epistles, for they seem to address a more universal audience. In the fourth century, the church historian Eusebius called them **catholic** or "universal" letters (*Ecclesiastical History* 2.23.25). Of the Catholic Epistles, 1 Peter and 1 John were the most well known and frequently used in the early Christian centuries.

As a group, these letters encourage faithful practice of Christianity. Through correct belief and moral conduct Christians can address the challenges they face. In 1 Peter, the challenge is hostility from a larger public.

In the context of hostility

In the short book of 1 Peter, there are at least eight specific references to suffering. 1 Peter 4:12 warns of a "fiery trial" coming upon the community. What were the readers of this letter experiencing?

Claudius

Tales of persecutions faced by early Christians raise the possibility that Peter is addressing some sort of imperial persecution. Roman emperors could lash out at religious groups perceived as unruly. Acts 18 mentions an expulsion of Jews from Rome in A.D. 49 by Emperor Claudius, because the Jews were indulging in constant riots "at the instigation of Chrestus" (Suetonius, *Life of Claudius* 24.4). A letter from Pliny the Younger, governor of Bithynia, to Emperor Trajan in A.D. 112 sets the precedent of executing those who persevered in their Christian faith. Such executions would become empire wide in the second and third centuries. But during the lifetime of Peter, the only known persecution takes place at Rome after the great fire of 64, for which Emperor Nero blamed the Christians. Church tradition places the death of Peter in this persecution. Since Peter writes to the "exiles of the dispersion in Pontus, Galatia, Cappadocia, Asia, and Bithynia" (1 Peter 1:1), both the location (the north part of modern Turkey) and the timing (Peter is still alive) rule out the persecution by Nero as the context for 1 Peter. In addition, were the suffering caused by imperial persecution, the instruction to "honor the emperor" (1 Peter 2:17) would seem out of place.

Since direct imperial persecution is unlikely, some sort of local pressure or societal estrangement seems to be a more plausible circumstance. When members of Graeco-Roman society converted to Christianity, their neighbors noticed. Christians gathered regularly in homes for meals that were secretive. Christians were suspected of immoral practices. In addition, Christian converts no longer participated in the regular rituals and sacrifices of Roman public life. People wondered if Christians were atheists, no longer believing in the gods that upheld the state. Since the time of Augustus, the public worship of the Roman gods was expected patriotic behavior. Pliny makes that very point in his letter to Trajan about the Christians. The behavior of the first Christians would have been viewed negatively by loyal Roman citizens, even as acts such as flag burning, refusing to stand for the national anthem, or declining to speak the pledge of allegiance seem shocking to many Americans today—especially in a time of war. Such seemingly "irreligious" or "unpatriotic" behavior by the Christians to whom Peter writes would explain why some "speak against you as evildoers" (2:12), "revile your good behavior in Christ" (3:16), "are surprised when you do not join them … and they malign you" (4:4), and "you are insulted for the name of Christ" (4:14). An air of hostility pervades 1 Peter, a "fiery trial" is expected in the future (4:12). If this reconstruction is correct, then Peter is writing to encourage Christians in a time of hostility. They may feel like "sojourners and exiles" (2:11), but they are in fact a "people of God's own possession … called … out of darkness into his marvelous light" (2:9). Such encouragement continues to speak to us today, as we seek to live faithful lives in a context of secular and pluralistic hostility.

Authorship

Following the format of letters from antiquity, 1 Peter opens by naming the author: "Peter, an apostle of Jesus Christ" (1:1). Later in the letter, the author calls himself "a witness of the sufferings of Christ" (5:1). Silvanus, known as Silas in Acts, seems to have assisted in the writing of the letter (5:12). Such assistance may explain the high quality of the Greek text, considered beyond the abilities of a typical fisherman from Galilee.

These verses point to authorship by Peter, the leader of the twelve original disciples who was an active missionary and was directly though reluctantly involved in the outreach to Gentiles. His words helped sway the Jerusalem community that Gentiles need not observe the Jewish Law in order to be Christians

(Acts 15:6–11). Silas/Silvanus conveyed the decision of the Jerusalem church to the Gentile communities (15:22, 32).

Apparently 1 Peter was a popular and well-received letter among early Christians. Similar language and phraseology shows up in *1 Clement*, the *Epistle of Barnabas*, the *Shepherd of Hermas* and other early Christian writings. Likely, the authors of these works knew 1 Peter. By the time of Irenaeus, bishop of Lyon, (middle of the second century), the letter is quoted explicitly and considered authoritative. Second Peter is a different case entirely.

As you consider 2 Peter, you may wish to recall the distinction between ***homologoumena*** and ***antilegomena***. 1 Peter is firmly among the *homologoumena*. But 2 Peter is one of the seven *antilegomena*. Of those seven, no letter is as poorly attested in the early church as 2 Peter. As we turn to the letter itself, additional problems surface.

Following the format of letters from antiquity, 2 Peter opens by naming the author: "Simeon Peter, a servant and apostle of Jesus Christ" (2 Peter 1:1). Note that Peter is called by the unusual spelling *Simeon*, not Simon. *Simeon* is closer to the sound of Peter's name in Aramaic, the language Peter spoke in Galilee. But in Graeco-Roman contexts, the spelling is always *Simon*. The spelling *Simeon* never occurs in other early Christian writings. Second Peter seems to claim a more authentic name for the apostle.

Second Peter includes additional comments seeming to stress authentic Petrine authorship. Second Peter 1:14 references the story in John 21:18–19 where Jesus predicts the death of Peter. Second Peter 1:17–18 puts the author of the letter with Jesus at his transfiguration. The gospels (Matthew 17:1; Mark 9:2; Luke 9:28) place Peter, James, and John with Jesus on the mountain. Second Peter 3:1 references a previous letter—the well-received 1 Peter. And 2 Peter 3:16 specifically mentions all the letters of Paul. Second Peter goes to great lengths to claim Petrine authorship. In later church tradition that mentions 2 Peter, no other name is associated with the letter.

Despite such claims, the weak support for the position of 2 Peter in the canon of the New Testament hints at potential problems with the authorship of the letter (apostolicity was a key criterion for canonicity). Four points are worthy of consideration:

First, in 2 Peter, reference is made to "all his [Paul's] letters"; these letters are equated with "other Scriptures" (2 Peter 3:16). Assumed by such references is a circulating collection of Pauline letters already considered as authoritative as the Scriptures of the Old Testament. Colossians 4:16 does mention some trading of Pauline letters, and Ephesians may have been a circular letter. But a collection already considered as Scripture prior to the death of Peter in the mid-sixties seems inconsistent with the opposition Paul still faced in the early sixties (Acts 28:24). From the second century come references to collections of Paul's writings, but the existence of these collections would be too late for genuine Petrine authorship of 2 Peter.

Second, there seems to be a very close connection between 2 Peter and Jude. Nineteen of the twenty-five verses in Jude have parallels in 2 Peter. While both Jude and 2 Peter could be drawing from another source, 2 Peter has none of the specific quotations from **Pseudepigrapha** that are sometimes considered problematic in Jude. If 2 Peter is using Jude as a source, then 2 Peter would be later and is avoiding the problematic material. To maintain genuine Petrine authorship of 2 Peter would then require a very early date for Jude and raise many associated problems. We cannot state with certainty what, if any, relationship exists between 2 Peter and Jude. But the commonality of content is one more factor in the murky issue of the authorship of 2 Peter.

Third, 2 Peter writes as if the author were a second-generation Christian. 2 Peter calls on readers to remember the prediction spoken "though your holy apostles" (3:2). If sufficient time has passed for people to forget the predictions of the apostles, the author seems to be writing at a time when the apostles are no longer present. Second Peter 3:4 confirms this interpretation by addressing circumstances "since the fathers fell asleep." Because the topic is teaching about the second coming of Jesus, "the fathers" must be the first leaders of early Christianity. For Peter to make such statements before the mid-sixties seems odd, since the New Testament has only narrated the deaths of Stephen and James, the brother of John (Acts 7 and 12). Objections to apostolic teaching based on the delay in the return of Jesus make sense better in generations after the apostles are gone.

Fourth, none of the above factors rule out Petrine authorship of 2 Peter. The claims of the letter are possible, even if the letter itself suggests they may not be plausible. However, if we are to consider the possibility that 2 Peter is attributed to the apostle but not written by him, we are forced to ask, What would such a possibility say about the inspiration of the letter and about the truth of the letter's teachings? Would not a denial of Petrine authorship call into question the content of the letter?

As to the inspiration of 2 Peter, even if the letter were not written by the apostle, through the process of canonization the Holy Spirit led the church to recognize the rightful place of 2 Peter in the New Testament. The Letter to the Hebrews came to be recognized as canonical partly due to the mistaken notion that it was written by Paul. Authorship was a factor, but not a deciding one.

As to the truth of the teachings of 2 Peter, questions of authorship do not negate the content, for much of the same content is affirmed by another letter of the New Testament—Jude. Moreover, we ought to be careful not to apply modern understandings of authorship (implied by copyrights and policies against plagiarism) to works of antiquity. In antiquity, attribution of a work to a famous leader was a compliment and an assertion that the work accords with or builds on the teaching of the individual to whom the work is attributed. Peter was such a character with a number of works attributed to him: *Acts of Peter, Apocalypse of Peter, Kerygma Petrou*, and *Kerygmata Petrou*. Although none of these later works came to be recognized as Scripture and some display heretical teaching, attribution to Peter was not the critical issue. Content was the ultimate criterion of acceptance.

Based on the above discussion, we will speak of 2 Peter as a work attributed to Peter. The letter claims it was written by Peter, but the same letter also suggests a time of composition after Peter and the other fathers of the faith have fallen asleep. Not open for question is the place of 2 Peter among the *antilegomena* of the New Testament and the worthiness of its message for our consideration.

Audience

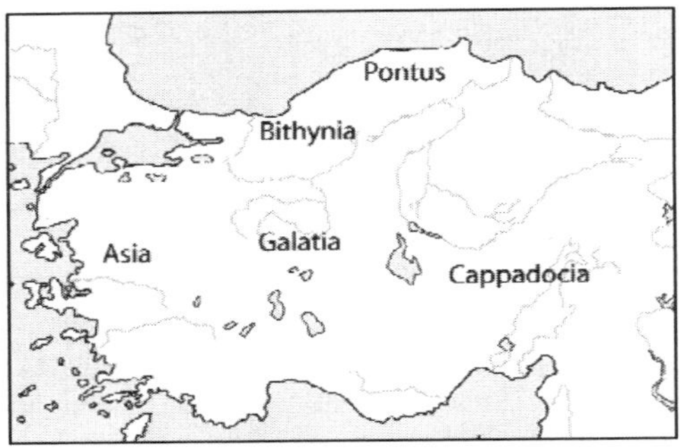

First Peter is addressed to "elect exiles of the dispersion in Pontus, Galatia, Cappadocia, Asia, and Bithynia" (1 Peter 1:1). These names likely refer to ethnic regions (see map). They are located in the northern sectors of modern Turkey in areas that Paul did not visit (Acts 16:6–8). Three of the regions are listed among those whose devout Jews heard Peter preach on Pentecost (Acts 2:9), so it is plausible that these communities had their origin in the Christianity of Jerusalem and the remembered preaching of Peter. But the communities seem to be Gentile by the time of Peter's writing (1 Peter 1:14, 18; 2:9; 4:3). In the community were slaves, people who had formerly been slaves, women who were married to non-Christians, men with Christian wives, elders, and recent converts (2:16, 18; 3:1, 7; 5:1, 5). Peter also describes them as "exiles" and "sojourners" (1:1, 17; 2:11). Peter may have had in a mind a figurative sense—Christians living in a hostile environment while awaiting their true home in heaven (compare Philippians 3:20). But social or economic ostracism may also have been involved. Many of them may have been aliens of sorts, people who have migrated among the provinces and thus had limited political rights. Christians may also have been few and far between, as Peter's letter addresses a large geographic area. Isolation could have compounded their sense of alienation.

The greeting of 2 Peter is more vague or general than 1 Peter. Second Peter 3:1 suggests that the audience is the same group addressed by 1 Peter. If we assume Petrine authorship, then we must assume the same group is addressed. But, as we will see, the contents of the letters are strikingly different. If the letters are addressed to the same communities, we must assume a significant change in local circumstances. If, on the other hand, the authorship of 2 Peter is left open, then the more general nature of the letter agrees with its classification by the church historian Eusebius (c. A.D. 260–c. 340) as a **Catholic Epistle**.

Structure and Themes

In its basic form, 1 Peter looks like an ancient letter. It has an opening greeting and blessing (1:1–2), followed by a body, and concluding with additional greetings (5:12–14). But its frequent references to baptism (1:3, 23; 3:18–22) have led some to suggest that the letter had its origins in a sermon given on the occasion of baptism or perhaps reflects the actual liturgy of baptism used at Rome in Peter's day. According to this latter theory, the baptism took place between verses twenty-one and twenty-two of chapter 1. The liturgy would look like this:

Ancient Baptistery

- The community celebrates (1 Peter 1:3–21): "Blessed be the God and Father of our Lord Jesus Christ! According to his great mercy, he has caused us to be born again to a living hope through the resurrection of Jesus Christ from the dead, … you were ransomed from the futile ways inherited from your forefathers, … who through [Jesus Christ] are believers in God, who raised him from the dead and gave him glory, so that your faith and hope are in God."
- Baptism of the Candidates
- Instruction of the Newly Baptized: (1 Peter 1:22–4:11): "Having purified your souls by your obedience to the truth for a sincere brotherly love, love one another earnestly from a pure heart,…whoever speaks, as one who speaks oracles of God; whoever serves, as one who serves by the strength that God supplies—in order that in everything God may be glorified through Jesus Christ. To him belong glory and dominion forever and ever. Amen."

The sermonic nature of the material is reinforced by repeated use of imperatives or commands. As many as forty-two imperatives are scattered throughout 1 Peter. Examples include: "set your hope" (1:13); "love one another" (1:22); "be subject" (2:13); "honor everyone" (2:17); "seek peace and pursue it" (3:11); "arm yourselves" (4:1); "be sober-minded" (4:7); "humble yourselves" (5:6); "be watchful" (5:8); and "greet one another" (5:14). Although 1 Peter is a letter in form, its sermonic content broadens its applicability beyond its first readers to all who have been baptized and consequently find themselves isolated or under pressure for their faith. Even in the deceptively safe confines of a free society such as the United States, we who are Christians can find ourselves at odds with our culture and country, even our neighbors and friends. Reminders of God's call in baptism and encouragement to live faithful and ethical lives can be a good message for us to hear even today.

The sermonic content of 1 Peter can be divided into three sections. 1:3–2:10 speak of the Christian calling. Christians have been born again to a living hope (2:3). That hope leads to the very salvation anticipated by the prophets of the Old Testament (1:10). That hope also calls for holiness "in all your conduct" (1:15). Those who have been baptized have a precious calling: "you are a chosen race, a royal priesthood, a holy nation, a people for his own possession, that you may proclaim the excellencies of him who called you out of darkness into his marvelous light" (2:9). In the second section of the letter (2:11–4:11), Peter advocates submission and righteous conduct as the appropriate response to hostility. Fighting back, retribution, and violence—so characteristic of our modern world—have no place. Authorities are worthy of honor; masters are to be obeyed, spouses treated reverently (even if not Christian), and suffering (even if unjustly) is better than doing evil. At the base of this ethic is a call to love: "Above all, keep loving one another earnestly, since love covers a multitude of sins" (4:8). The third section of the letter (4:12–5:11) explores suffering for the faith and offers specific guidance for leaders and members of the Christian community in such circumstances. Humility and watchfulness are made possible because "the God of all grace, who has called you to his eternal glory in Christ, will himself restore, confirm, strengthen, and establish you" (5:10).

Second Peter is set in the time just prior to the death of the apostle (1:14) and so functions as a final exhortation to readers. After an opening greeting (1:1–2), the first chapter offers a word of encouragement to readers to "become partakers of the divine nature, having escaped from the corruption of this world" (1:4, see below for a detailed discussion). Such participation is made possible by virtuous living (1:5–9) and by paying attention to the "prophetic word" (1:19–21).

Chapter 2 of 2 Peter is brutal. Opponents are attacked with language seemingly inconsistent with earlier calls to "brotherly affection with love" (1:7). False teachers are compared to "irrational animals, creatures of instinct, born to be caught and destroyed" (2:12). They are likened to "the dog [who] returns to its own vomit" (2:22). Much of the language in this chapter echoes that of Jude, if it is not drawn directly from it. When we read such language today, we need to recall that harsh invective was part of the cultural landscape in antiquity. Even Jesus could so condemn his enemies (Matthew 23). But after two thousands years of Christian history during which harsh language often overflowed into violence (the Crusades, the Inquisition, the Holocaust, Northern Ireland), we ought be cautious about employing similar invective today, especially in the highly nuanced world of inter-Christian relations. Christians who prefer vitriol to loving concern for other believers with whom they disagree may claim technical precedent from 2 Peter 2, but they lack support from the greater prophetic word that has guided the church through the millennia. To employ a linguistic Christian noose against others is simply wrong.

In the third chapter of this letter, the theological issue comes into focus. Although Jesus had promised to return (the technical term for his second coming is the **Parousia**), the fathers have fallen asleep, "all things are continuing as they were from the beginning of creation" (3:4), and Jesus has not come back. It is almost possible to hear opponents making fun of the Christians who wait for Jesus, even as our own culture caricatures the street preacher holding a placard, "The end is at hand." In response, 2 Peter claims that God's kindness is evident in the delay, for more people will have opportunity to repent prior to the end (3:9, 15). In addition, as God by definition is beyond time ("with the Lord one day is as a thousand years"), delay is a meaningless concept. What looks like a delay to us is God's patience, showing that God does not wish anyone to perish (3:9). An appropriate response on the part of the readers both ancient and modern is to live "lives of holiness and godliness, waiting for and hastening the coming day of the Lord" (3:11–12). The letter concludes by aligning its teaching with the letters of Paul and by calling for growth "in the grace and knowledge of our Lord and Savior Jesus Christ" (3:18).

1 PETER	
ADDRESS	1:1–2
CHRISTIAN HOPE	2:3–2:10
SUBMIT TO HOSTILE FORCES	2:11–4:11
SUFFERING AND FAITH	4:12–5:11
GREETINGS	5:12–14

2 PETER	
FAREWELL EXHORTATION	1:1–21
ATTACK ON OPPONENTS	2:1–22
PROMISED RETURN OF JESUS	3:1–18

Key Texts

1 Peter 1:3–5 With language similar to the baptismal reference in Titus 3:5–7, Peter speaks of Christians as "born again to a living hope" (1:3). But in place of the specific baptismal language of Titus, Peter uses a rare phrase in Greek stressing a "new begetting" rather than a "new birth." Certainly birth follows conception. But Peter's choice of language put the emphasis on God's work in baptism rather than on the experience or participation of the Christian in baptism.

A consequence of God's new begetting is hope. Considering the **astral fatalism** that dominated life in the Graeco-Roman world and the tough situation faced by Peter's readers, this hope is significant. "Hope" is modified by the concept "living." Hope is not vain or dead, a mere wish in the face of bleak reality. It is as certain as is the resurrection of Jesus. The core belief of Christianity is the basis for hope.

To reinforce his message, Peter compares this hope to an inheritance. Rights of inheritance were central to the family structure of antiquity. They were carefully protected. Cheating someone of a birthright was a grave offence (compare the story of Jacob and Esau in Genesis 27). By comparing hope to an inheritance Peter assures his readers that hope cannot be taken away.

To make his case even stronger, Peter uses three adjectives to qualify the inheritance. It is imperishable, undefiled, and unfading. Note that each of these characteristics of the inheritance/hope is also a characteristic of God. The inheritance does not perish, even as God and the new creation to be ushered in at the end will never perish. There is no defilement in the inheritance, even as the holy of holies in the temple is without defilement. Echoing the language of Jesus (Matthew 6:19–20), this inheritance will not erode away like some sort of "treasure on earth." It is as permanent as God.

Peter moves beyond metaphor with one more flourish. Not only is the inheritance like God in its characteristics, it is "kept in heaven for you" (1:4). By using the passive voice ("kept") and speaking of heaven, Peter assures his readers that God himself guarantees the inheritance.

On what basis could Peter's readers face the daunting challenges before them? The case is impressive in these few verses: God has begotten them anew, theirs is a living hope, its basis is the resurrection, and theirs is an inheritance with God-like characteristics guaranteed by God himself. With this certainty, they could face hostility. With this certainty, we can face the challenges that frighten us.

1 Peter 1:13–2:2 Given such hope, even those who face hostility and suffering can live with boldness and confidence. With five imperatives or commands, Peter describes just how much these bold Christian can do. They can "prepare their minds for action" (1:13) by setting all their hope on the grace Jesus will bring. They can "be holy" in all their conduct, because they have been called by a holy God (1:15). They can "conduct themselves" with godly fear, knowing they have been ransomed by the precious blood of Jesus. They can "love one another" (1:22) because of the living and abiding word of God. And they can "long for" (2:2) the pure spiritual milk because they have tasted that the Lord is good. Christians do not act this way to get or earn their hope. Rather, since they already have hope, they can face the future.

1 Peter 2:9–10 Together with verse five of chapter two, verses nine and ten served as the basis for Martin Luther's articulation of the **priesthood of all believers**. In Luther's day, the church's clergy controlled the means of grace in what Luther viewed as an abusive way. Luther was also troubled by beliefs asserting the clergy to be in some way superior to other Christians. By contrast, Luther taught that "all [people] are truly priests," citing 1 Peter 2 for support (*Luther's Works,* American edition, 44:129). This teaching of Luther, along with other theological and political factors, motivated the Protestant Reformation and gave rise to church structures with limited or no hierarchy of clergy.

Luther's assertion that each individual Christian is a priest before God may have been inspiring at the time of the Reformation and may fit well with American concepts of individuality. But 1 Peter 2:9, when read on its own terms, has a different focus. Rather than the individual, it is the community that is the focus.

The verse begins, "You are a chosen race" (2:9). Unfortunately, the English language does not distinguish between singular and plural forms of the word *you.* In 1 Peter 2:9, the *you* is plural, referring to the community. In American slang, this concept is captured with the phrase "y'all." In verse nine, Peter is saying that all of you together, all of you in the Christian community, make up a "chosen race." You the community are a "holy nation." You the community are a "people for his [God's] own possession." With each of these predicates the communal context is clear—race, nation, and people are collective terms. When Peter includes in the grouping a declaration that you are a "royal priesthood," he names Christians together a priestly community. Together, the community serves a priestly function. If Peter had wanted to call each member of the community a priest, he would have used a different term in Greek and would have done so in a context where the topic is the individual, nor the community.

Instead, Peter invokes images from Old Testament stories of the Exodus and the covenant at Sinai as a way of reassuring isolated and beleaguered Christians that they are not alone. They are part of a community chosen by God and redeemed by Jesus. They can face the challenges before them. To back up his assertion, Peter points directly to the assurance of God's faithfulness in difficult times offered by the prophet Hosea: "Once you were not a people, but now you are God's people; once you had not received mercy, but now you have received mercy" (1 Peter 2:10).

While 1 Peter 2:9 does not explicitly teach that each individual is a priest before God, the hope and encouragement Luther sought to convey does reflect the larger themes of 1 Peter. In Luther's eyes, common people were oppressed and in need of assurance that they, too, were elect and chosen of God. Peter's word of assurance to an earlier generation of Christians inspired Luther's work. Peter's assuring words still speak today when Christians are alone, isolated, and under pressure. We can be confident, for with other Christians around the world, we are a chosen people able to proclaim the excellencies of the one who called us out of darkness into his marvelous light (2:9).

2:13–3:7 In a central section of the letter, Peter instructs his readers on how they can live in a hostile environment. He addresses two realms of behavior: in the larger civil society and in domestic households. Peter's categories and descriptors are quite similar to those of ancient writers such as Plato, Aristotle, Xenephon, Seneca, Plutarch, and others. Paul writes similarly in Colossians 3 and Ephesians 5–6. In many ways, Christian civil and domestic behavior reflected the ideal standards of the day, including assertions that a woman is "the weaker vessel" (1 Peter 3:7; Aristotle, *Politics*, 1:1253b). The ideal Christian is submissive and deferential in civil and domestic relationships.

Tombstone for Husband and Wife

What marks Christians as distinct from their Graeco-Roman counterparts is not the particular behaviors and roles. Those were common in the society of the day. What marked Christians as different was their motivation for and means by which they conducted themselves in their culturally assigned roles. Where Aristotle would argue that roles and behaviors are inherent by nature, reflect physical and intellectual capabilities, and ought to support the state, Peter motivates his readers to honorable behavior in their roles in order to "glorify God" (2:12), "for the Lord's sake" (2:13), "because Christ suffered for you" (2:21), to win the other over (3:1), and because others "are also heirs of the gracious gift of life" (3:7). Likewise, in today's egalitarian world, Christian and non-Christians households may look quite similar in the roles that people perform and the behaviors in which they engage. What marks Christian homes as distinct are the motivations believers find in Christ and the means by which they give of themselves for each other to the glory of God.

1 Peter 3:19; 4:6 According to 3:19, Jesus "went and proclaimed to the spirits in prison." According to 4:6, "the gospel was preached even to those who are dead." Even though the second text does not specifically say that Jesus did the preaching, these two obscure passages in 1 Peter seem to be part of a larger tradition about the actions of Jesus between his death and resurrection. Both Romans 10:7 and Ephesians 4:9 allude to some sort of "descent." Matthew refers to the resurrection of many "saints" after the death of Jesus (Matthew 27:52). According to Colossians, Jesus triumphed over "rulers and authorities" (Colossians 2:15), perhaps a reference to some spiritual powers. These vague biblical texts get expanded in later writings. According to the *Ascension of Isaiah* 9:16, Jesus "made spoil of the angel of death" before he rose on the third day. The *Gospel of Nicodemus* narrates a descent of Jesus to rescue the faithful of the Old Testament. Some or all of these texts may have influenced the wording of the Apostolic Creed: "He descended into hell."

The ambiguity of the creedal statement does not explain the purpose of the descent, even as the Petrine verses are difficult to decipher. Did Jesus descend to rescue and save those who had gone before? Did Jesus descend to proclaim victory over demonic and unbelieving forces? Later traditions seem to imply the former. By themselves, the texts from 1 Peter seem to imply the latter. The texts remain a debated part of 1 Peter.

1 Peter 4:12–13 Above we discussed the various options for interpreting the "fiery trial" anticipated by 1 Peter. Of note is the consequent call to rejoice (4:13). When Paul was in prison, likely at Rome in the early 60s, he encouraged his readers to "rejoice in the Lord always; again I will say, Rejoice" (Philippians 4:4). To experience joy in times of oppression and persecution is a recurrent Christian theme. For Paul, that joy came from the presence of the Lord and the peace that the Lord provides (Philippians 4:5, 7). Peter points specifically to the suffering and resurrection of Jesus. As surely as Jesus died and rose, the Christian who "shares in Christ's sufferings" will also "rejoice and be glad when his glory is revealed" (1 Peter 4:13). The pattern witnessed in the passion of Jesus—suffering followed almost immediately by resurrection—is repeated in the lives of those who endure the fiery trial. Peter, writing from Rome, echoes a theme about which Paul wrote to Rome: "We were buried therefore with him by baptism into death…. For if we have been united with him in a death like his, we shall certainly be united with him in a resurrection like his" (Romans 6:4–5).

1 Peter 5:6–10 A theology of union between the believer and Christ in both suffering and glory is difficult in an abstract sense. So Peter concludes with simple advice: "Humble yourselves under the mighty hand of God … cast your anxieties on him … be watchful" (1 Peter 5:5–8). These words read like the personal reflections of one who has seen much, experienced much, failed often, and yet is full of hope. Those who have experienced the presence of Jesus as they have gone though the pain and losses that come in life are often those best equipped to support others in similar circumstances. It is a very experienced Peter who concludes: "And after you have suffered a little while, the God of all grace, who has called you to his eternal glory in Christ, will himself restore, confirm, strengthen, and establish you" (5:10)

2 Peter 1:4 In 1 Peter, the believer shares in Christ's suffering (4:13) and will be a "partaker in the glory that is going to be revealed" (5:1). Second Peter puts things quite differently. The goal of the believer is to "escape from the corruption that is in this world due to sinful desire" and to become a "partaker of the divine nature" (2 Peter 1:4). The language of 2 Peter sounds very similar to the dualism of many Greek philosophies. These systems, going back to the Greek philosopher Plato (427–347 B.C.), viewed the physical world and the body in particular as corrupt. Escape from the body and union with the divine nature are the goals of humanity. Plato wrote: "We ought to try to escape from here to there as quickly as possible; and to escape is to become like God so far as possible" (*Theaetetus* 176ab). **Mystery religions**, especially in their rituals, provided means for union with the divine. The imperial cult accorded emperors divine honors and status. The later Christian ascetic movements would follow this trend by subjugating the flesh and its desires in pursuit of union with God.

Two points are worthy of note. First, although earlier biblical writers employ familiar metaphors to describe the Christian as a child of God and part of a family of believers, in 2 Peter metaphysical language of the Hellenistic world is used instead. Second, as pointed out above, 1 Peter stresses the corporate nature of the Christian family. All believers together are a chosen race. But in 2 Peter, the focus shifts to the individual. Believers become partakers in the divine nature. The union is with God, not with each other. As Christianity moved beyond its first decades and generation, it became increasingly a Graeco-Roman phenomenon, employing the language of that dualistic culture. The unitary and communal language of the Jewish culture of Jesus and Peter had to be translated. Second Peter reflects that translation.

2 Peter 1:19–21 In contrast to "cleverly devised myths" about Graeco-Roman gods and goddesses, according to 2 Peter "we made known to you the power and coming of our Lord Jesus" (1:16). Not only are the stories of Jesus' mighty deeds important, at issue is his second coming at the end of time, the Parousia. Chapter three will offer a defense of this disputed teaching. In chapter one, the author is claiming authority as an eyewitness (see comments above), but more significantly points to an even greater authority—the prophetic word. Peter may have been an eyewitness. He may have experienced the majestic glory at the transfiguration (1:17). But according to 2 Peter, the prophetic word is more reliable, more abiding, more valid than such eyewitness testimony. As Luke quoted Peter, "All the prophets who have spoken, from Samuel to those who came after him, also proclaimed these days" (Acts 3:24). It is the witness of the Old Testament as a whole that affirms the apostolic message about the death and resurrection of Jesus and about his promised return (the key issue in dispute). The prophetic word is like a "lamp shining in a dark place, until the day dawns" (2 Peter 2:19). In this intermediate time, the prophetic word is the lamp until at the end of time "the morning star rises" (2:19).

Not only is the prophetic word of greater authority than an eyewitness account, it is also superior to "someone's own interpretation" (2:20), whether one is interpreting current circumstances or the prophetic word. The opponents in 2 Peter are people who looked at the world, noted the passing of the first generation of leaders, observed how unchanged the world was, and questioned the veracity of belief in the Parousia. But this was their human interpretation. Of far greater authority is that prophecy that comes through the working of the Holy Spirit and not from some human perspective or desire. Peter's teaching about the promised return of Jesus is based in part on his eyewitness testimony, but it is true only because it agrees with the prophetic word.

The contrast between that which comes from the Holy Spirit and that which comes from one's own interpretation remains important. The contrast points out the provisional nature of the interpretive task. We who work with the Bible, including those of us who write textbooks, need to be cautious and humble in our conclusions. We may think we understand the text, but our conclusions and our reconstructions ought not to be confused with the authority of the text itself. On critical matters of life and salvation, the Bible is clear. But in many other matters, the clarity is not so simple, and charity must prevail as we attempt to interpret and apply texts.

2 Peter 3:8–10 As has already been noted, the issue in dispute is the second coming of Jesus. Opponents say, "Where is the promise of his coming?" (3:4) The lively expectation of the first Christians had faded, as the return of Jesus apparently had been delayed. This delay caused some like Paul to adjust his advice (compare what Paul says about marriage in an early letter like 1 Corinthians to what he writes in the later letter to the Ephesians). For others, such as the opponents in 2 Peter, the delay was a cause to question the teaching itself.

Christian Tombstone

But there was a deeper issue—the problem of evil. In the words of the opponents, "For ever since the fathers fell asleep, all things are continuing as they were from the beginning of creation" (3:4). In other words, if the coming of Jesus, whom the fathers proclaim, is so significant, why is the world unchanged? Or more bluntly, if there is a loving God, why do bad things happen to good people? This question, raised by the persistent existence of evil in our world, is a challenging one. It is one we experience individually when tragedy or violence strikes. It is one we experienced as a community on days such as September 11, 2001. Why does the God who came in Jesus still allow such things to happen?

The technical term for an attempt to justify the ways of God is **theodicy**. The term comes from two Greek words: *theos* for "God" and *dikē* for "justice." A theodicy tries to resolve the problem of evil by showing that God is all-powerful and just, despite evil's existence. The theodicy of 2 Peter points to the eternal character of God and to God's desire to save. Since God is eternal, God does not count time as we count time. What seems like a delay to us is no delay to God, for "with the Lord one day is as a thousand years, and a thousand years as one day" (3:8). In addition, God does not desire "that any should perish" (3:9). If Jesus were to return immediately, many would not have opportunity to "reach repentance" (3:9). By showing "patience," even though it means people will still experience evil in this life, many more will be saved for eternal life. In the context of eternity, momentary experiences of evil, even from the beginning of creation, lose their significance.

A theodicy may offer an argument that seems to preserve the justice of God in the face of the existence of evil, but in the midst of tragic and painful circumstances, reasonable arguments provide little comfort. In verse ten 2 Peter reminds readers that "the day of the Lord will come like a thief." Evil will be defeated. Justice will prevail. In subsequent verses, very practical advice prevails. Holiness, godliness, watchfulness, diligence—these enable the faithful to "grow in the grace and knowledge of our Lord and Savior Jesus Christ" (3:18). That grace enables endurance and empowers the faithful to "overcome evil with good" (Romans 12:21).

Jesus in 1 and 2 Peter

Second Peter uses descriptions of Jesus that are quite similar to those in Paul. The death and resurrection of Jesus are central. Jesus is both *Lord* and *Christ*. *Christ*, by itself, is the primary designator for Jesus, although the title does not convey significant allusions to the Jewish Messiah and the reign of God over Israel.

The suffering of Jesus is a particular focus of 1 Peter. In the initial greeting, the readers are elected "for sprinkling with his blood" (1:2). Peter assured his readers that they have been ransomed "with the precious blood of Christ," which Peter likens to that of a "lamb without blemish or spot" used in sacrifice (1:19). Peter continues later, "He himself bore our sins in his body on the tree ... By his wounds you have been healed" (2:24). In language similar to Hebrews, "For Christ also suffered once for sins, ... being put to death in the flesh but made alive in the spirit" (3:18). The suffering of Jesus continues to be a focus in 4:1, 13 and 5:1, 9. For Peter, Jesus is the one who suffers, and his suffering rescues the faithful.

But the suffering of Jesus also functions as an exemplar. Because Jesus suffered, his followers can endure suffering. But Jesus is more than a model of suffering, an ideal to be imitated in order than one might receive a similar reward. The believer "shares in the suffering of Christ" (4:13). That is, the believer is so united with Christ that, even as Jesus was raised, so the believer will move from suffering to glory (4:13). The resurrection of Jesus is the guarantee that "the God of all grace ... will himself restore, confirm, strengthen, and establish you" (5:10). Jesus is more than an example, he is inspiration and salvation. God is the one who will "at the proper time exalt you, casting all your anxieties on him because he cares for you" (5:6–7).

In 2 Peter, the suffering and death of Jesus are not mentioned. Rather Jesus is spoken of with honorifics such as *Lord* and *Savior*. The title *Christ* is essentially part of his name, as in Jesus Christ. The word is never used alone, nor does it carry specific messianic overtones with the possible exception of a reference to his "eternal kingdom" (1:11)

As 2 Peter addresses doubt about the parousia, the Jesus of 2 Peter is the coming one. His arrival will be at an unexpected time (3:10) and at his coming he will function as judge, bringing about the justice of God (2:9; 3:7, 10). Knowledge of the Lord Jesus Christ is the goal of the believer (1:3, 8; 2:20; 3:18), for Jesus will rescue and save the believer at the end (1:1, 11; 2:9, 20; 3:2, 18).

For Further Discussion

1. Many Christians read 1 Peter 2:9 to suggest that "everyone is a minister" before God. But the "you" in the verse is plural, implying that the community as a whole functions like a priest. Since this verse addresses the community and not the individual, how can communities of Christians function in a priestly way?

2. First Peter tells its readers in their situation to "submit," even if they are being treated unjustly. Was this instruction specific to that situation alone, or does it apply to Christians today? Why? Under what circumstances may a Christian resist (the opposite of submit!) unjust actions? Should an abused wife submit? Should a victim of racial discrimination submit?

3. Christians say that Jesus is coming again. But it has been two thousand years. Christians take out mortgages and student loans! You expect to pay them back. What is the practical implication of the teaching that Jesus will return?

For Further Reading

Elliott, John. *I Peter*. The Anchor Bible. Volume 37B. New York: Doubleday, 2000.

__________. *A Home for the Homeless: A Social-Scientific Criticism of I Peter, Its Situation and Strategy*. Minneapolis: Fortress, 1990.

Goppelt, Leonhard. *A Commentary on I Peter*. Translated by John E. Alsup. Grand Rapids: Eerdmans, 1978.

Kelly, J. D. N. *The Epistles of Peter and of Jude*. London: Adam and Charles Black, 1969.

Mark

The second gospel is the shortest gospel, and until the nineteenth century, it was the most neglected gospel. As more than 90 percent of Mark has parallels in Matthew and/or Luke, as it lacks birth narratives, and as its ending is confused, the second gospel received little attention throughout most of the history of Christianity. With the rise of critical studies and the broad embrace of evolutionary paradigms, the second gospel as shortest was assumed to be the oldest. It thus became the starting point for most modern reconstructions of the life of Jesus. This textbook varies dramatically from contemporary works because it does not treat the second gospel first.

The second gospel, however, has its own unique portrait of Jesus. It was written in a time of conflict and upholds the cross as central for understanding Jesus. By telling the story with bold and dramatic narrative, Mark races to the cross, there to uncover the mystery of Jesus, discipleship, and hope in dark times.

Author

As with the other Synoptic Gospels, the author of the second gospel is unnamed. The tradition attribution to Mark is a later tradition. Although plausible (and assumed in this presentation), Marcan authorship is no certainty. As helpful as reconstructions based on Marcan authorship may be, they remain hypothetical.

Justin Martyr, a Christian author from the mid-second century, quotes a passage from "Peter's memoirs" (*Trypho* 106.3). The wording of that passage occurs only in Mark 3:16–17. If reference is to the second gospel, then Justin seems to attribute the gospel to Peter. Papias, a second-century church leader quoted by Eusebius, gives greater detail: "Mark, who had been Peter's interpreter, wrote down carefully, but not in order, all that he remembered of the Lords sayings and doings" (Eusebius, *Ecclesiastical History* 3.39). According to the tradition known to Papias, Mark was not a disciple of Jesus but a disciple of Peter. By the middle of the second century, a tradition was in circulation connecting the second gospel to Peter but attributing its actual authorship to a certain Mark.

The name "Mark" shows up in several interesting locales in the New Testament. The earliest references are from Colossians and Philemon, especially if these prison epistles are written from Ephesus during the third journey (55–58) rather than from Rome (61–62). In Colossians 4:10, a Mark is with Paul while the latter is in prison. He is called the "cousin of Barnabas." In the letter to Philemon, Mark is one of "my fellow workers" and sends greetings along with Paul and others (Philemon 24). In a different context, Peter includes greetings from a Mark, who is called "my son" (1 Peter 5:13). In Acts, reference is made to a "John whose other name is Mark" (Acts 12:12). His mother hosts the church of Jerusalem in her home. He goes with Barnabas and Saul (Paul) on the first mission journey (Acts 13:5) only to leave prematurely (Acts 13:13) and become a cause for division between Paul and Barnabas (Acts 15:37–39). But when Paul seems to be at the end of his career and life, he writes to Timothy, "Get Mark and bring him with you, for he is very useful for my ministry" (2 Timothy 4:11). Assuming these references speak of the same person, John Mark was known to Peter in Jerusalem, had a falling out with Paul, was later reconciled to him, and ended up in Rome as a helper both to Peter and Paul. Papias seems to refer to this person as the author of the second gospel. The reconstruction is plausible and is the basis for calling the second gospel the Gospel according to St. Mark.

Audience and Purpose

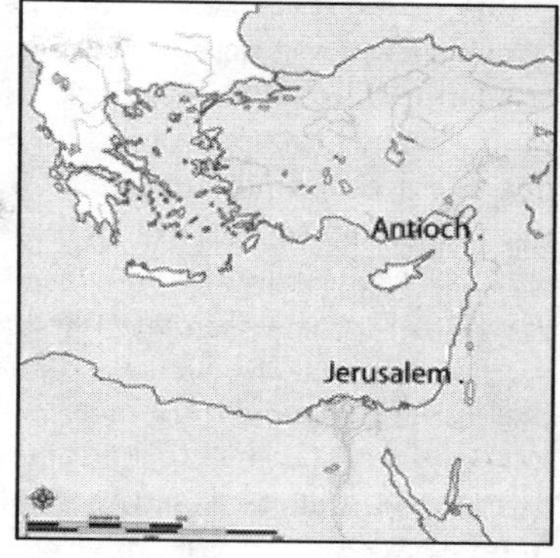

Some scholars place the composition of Mark in Palestine, Syria or Antioch—all in the eastern part of the Roman Empire. But Clement of Alexandria (late second century) claims that Mark wrote the gospel in Rome (Eusebius, *Ecclesiastical History* 6.14.6). This tradition accords with the biblical witness to Mark's last known location and fits the hypothesis derived from Papias that Mark wrote after the death of Peter in Nero's persecution.

There are in the second gospel Greek loan words derived from Latin as well as grammatical constructions seemingly influenced by Latin. These could show that the gospel was written in a place where Latin was spoken. If Mark, for whom both Greek and Latin would have been second languages, developed a writing competency during travels with Paul and at Rome, such imprecision with Greek is understandable.

Of greater significance is the content of the gospel. It was directed to a non-Jewish audience to whom Jewish practices had to be explained (Mark 7:3). The audience seems to be facing a severe persecution (13:9–13). Mark's choice of many stories in which the disciples are confused (4:13; 6:52; 7:18; 8:14–21) may suggest that his readers were likewise confused or afraid (16:8!). Christians may have been under pressure and even fallen victim to the violence surrounding the first revolt in Jerusalem (A.D. 68–72). But the only known persecution of Christians followed the fire at Rome, the blame for which Nero gave to the Christians (A.D. 65–66). In those persecutions, both Peter and Paul likely were executed. But Christian and secular sources both suggest that some Christians capitulated and betrayed other Christians (1 Clement 5:2–7; Tacitus *Annals* 15:44).

The gospel likely was written during or shortly after Nero's persecution and the deaths of Peter and Paul. It would have been a frightening, chaotic, and violent time among the survivors. Doubt, fear, confusion, and betrayal afflicted the survivors. The preaching of Peter was crafted by Mark into a gospel for such a time and place.

Structure

Before discussing the structure of Mark, the integrity of its text must be examined. The footnotes in modern translations of Mark 16 indicate problems with this chapter. How the gospel ends is uncertain.

Modern translations of the New Testament are based on a composite Greek text derived from the five thousand fragments or whole texts that have survived from antiquity. Since these ancient manuscripts display important verbal differences, scholars have reconstructed through a process of comparison and categorization what they believe to be a text close to the original. For most New Testament texts, scholars are sure of their reconstructions. But in some places, the evidence is less certain. Mark 16 is one such place.

The earliest and best manuscripts of Mark 16 end with verse 8. Many later manuscripts include verses 9–20. Some have extra material after verse 14. A few put in an extra verse between verses 8 and 9. These various additions are suspect because some content directly parallels other texts. Verses 12–13 are a shortened version of the two people on the road to Emmaus from Luke; verse 15 is a restatement of the Great Commission from Matthew. The additions also smooth out what would be a rough ending at verse 8. For, if verse 8 were the end of the work, the content of the gospel would end with an uncomfortable note of fear and doubt at the report of the resurrection. Also, the style of writing in the Greek of verse 8 is awkward for a sentence ending a work. The manuscript evidence indicates that the gospel ends at verse 8; but the content suggests otherwise. Later we will propose that the content of Mark as a whole supports an ending at verse 8.

Of all the gospels, Mark could best be described by Martin Kähler's adage. It is a "passion narrative with an extended introduction." Mark omits any reference to the origin and birth of Jesus. Instead, after briefly recounting the baptism and temptation, Mark's Jesus plunges into a ministry of mighty deeds (1:14–3:12). Jesus then chooses the twelve and continues his ministry with parables and more miracles (3:13–6:6). The sending of the twelve is followed by feedings, controversies and misunderstandings (6:7–8:26). The stories are told in rapid succession. Mark connects them with little more than the Greek word for "and."

In chapter 8, a distinct shift occurs. Having been repeatedly misconstrued or rejected, Jesus begins to "teach them that the Son of Man must suffer ... and be killed" (8:31). He further challenges his followers, "If anyone would come after me, let him deny himself and take up his cross and follow me" (8:34). The intensity of what Jesus and his followers will face surfaces in the subsequent narrative. In many ways, Mark's writing is similar to other apocalyptic materials from the Second Temple period. The small community faces severe trial, violence, darkness and death. In the conflict before the end, Satan will blind even the elect. But those who endure will be saved. Mark's narrative differs from other apocalyptic writers in one critical point. According to Mark, darkness descends on Jesus as well (15:33). Jesus dies violently (15:37). But his death is vindicated by resurrection that gives his followers hope in the middle of their fears (16:7–8).

Three passion predictions frame the next section of the gospel (8:27–10:52), the last chapter of which is a brief travel narrative to Jerusalem. Chapters 11–13 tell of Jesus entry into Jerusalem, his actions and teaching in the temple, and a speech about the end times. His arrest, trial and crucifixion are brutally told

(Mark 14–15). A brief announcement of the resurrection to three frightened women concludes the gospel (16:1–8).

MARK: JESUS IS THE SON OF GOD, KNOWN AT THE CROSS	
INTRODUCTION OF JOHN THE BAPTIST	1:1–13
JESUS, MIGHTY IN WORD AND DEED	1:14–3:12
MINISTRY OF PARABLES AND MIRACLES	3:13–6:6
CONTROVERSY AND MISUNDERSTANDING	6:7–8:28
PASSION PREDICTED	8:27–10:52
ENTRY AND END TIMES	11:1–13:37
A VIOLENT END	14:1–15:47
RESURRECTION	16:1–8

Themes

As the key verses below will show, the **cross** plays a pivotal role in Mark's portrait of Jesus. From the point in chapter eight when Jesus first predicts his suffering (8:31) and defines discipleship as cross bearing (8:34) through the violence at the "Place of the Skull," the cross looms large. To many the cross was "folly" (1 Corinthians 1:18). In many ways, Mark's Gospel is an apology for the cross (see Gundry's commentary). So central is the cross that the resurrection is told but briefly (assuming the gospel ends at 16:8).

In Mark, Jesus draws a direct connection between his coming suffering and a discipleship of "taking up the cross" (8:34). Suffering is the lot of a disciple—a reality to which Mark's readers could likely relate, especially if Mark wrote at Rome in the context of the persecution under Nero. "Persecutions" are to be expected (10:30). To some of his disciples, Jesus said, "The cup that I drink, you will drink" (10:39). "Drinking a cup" was an Old Testament euphemism for suffering because of divine wrath (Psalm 75:8; Isaiah 51:17, 22; Jeremiah 25:15, 28; 49:12). Jesus would use the same metaphor when he prayed that his Father might "remove this cup from me" (Mark 14:36). The horrors to be experienced at the close of the age anticipate suffering and betrayal among the community of disciples (13:9–13). The rather odd inclusion by Mark of the story of a young man seized at Gethsemane who ran away naked (14:51–52) may be part of this same theme. When Simon of Cyrene took up the cross and carried it for Jesus (15:21), he also functioned as a symbolic teacher for future disciples. The trembling and fear with which the gospel closes (16:8) is what would be expected of a persecuted community. Significantly, the same theme of suffering features prominently in 1 Peter, as we noted earlier. If Mark indeed records the preaching of Peter, a focus on suffering might be expected.

Mark's portrayal of the disciples is most unflattering. In this gospel, the disciples do *not understand* who Jesus is or what Jesus is about. Jesus chose the disciples to follow him (3:13–19) and gave them personal instruction (4:10–20). But they just did not get it. They do not understand a simple parable (4:13). They "did not understand" the feeding of the five thousand nor when Jesus walked on the sea (6:51). Although Jesus pleaded with them to "understand" (7:14), they were "without understanding" (7:18). The disciples think that Jesus' metaphoric warning about the "leaven of the Pharisees" (8:15) is a complaint about a lack of bread. With exasperation, Jesus twice retorts, "Do you not yet perceive or understand?" (8:17, 21). Twice the lack of understanding by the disciples is equated with hardness of heart (6:51; 8:17)—a serious charge first leveled against the pharaoh who enslaved the Israelites in Egypt (Exodus 7:13).

The *lack of understanding* by the disciples comes into sharpest relief when Jesus predicts his passion. After the first prediction (8:31), Peter takes Jesus aside and rebukes him (8:32). Peter is thinking only of earthly matters (8:33). After Jesus shows his glory to some of his disciples in a transfiguration, they are confused (9:10). When he again predicts his death, Mark observes, "They did not understand the saying, and were afraid to ask him" (9:32). Instead the disciples argue as to who is the greatest (9:33–34). When Jesus for a third time predicts his suffering (10:33–34) as the culmination and purpose of his coming into the world (10:45), James and John request to sit at the right and left of Jesus in his glory (10:37). The disciples do not understand. And when confronted with the terrible reality of Jesus' impending death, Peter denies every knowing Jesus. Significantly, Mark quotes Peter as saying, "I neither know *nor understand* what you mean" (14:68). The other gospel writers omitted the phrase, "nor understand" (Matt. 26:70; Luke 22:57). Mark's point, possibly derived from Peter himself, is that the disciples do *not understand*.

Another and perhaps related theme of Mark's Gospel is the so-called "**messianic secret**." Commentators use this term is describe the many times in Mark's Gospel that Jesus tries to keep his identity and abilities secret. After healing a leper, Jesus warned him, "See that you say nothing to anyone" (Mark 1:44). Jesus warned unclean spirits "not to make him known" (3:11). After resuscitating a girl, Jesus "strictly charged them that no one should know this" (5:43). After healing a deaf mute, Jesus "charged them to tell no one" (7:36). When Peter made his confession, Jesus "strictly charged them to tell no one about him" (8:30). As Jesus and the disciple came down from the mount of transfiguration, Jesus "charged them to tell no one what they had seen" (9:9). Even when the chief priests, scribes, and elders challenge the authority of Jesus in the temple, he shoots back, "Neither will I tell you by what authority I do these things" (11:33). Such warnings can be found in other gospels, but they occur much more often in Mark. Perhaps due to the prevalent misunderstanding narrated by Mark, the gospel writer stresses corresponding commands of Jesus to silence (see below for more on the messianic secret).

Misunderstanding and commands to silence suggest that the identity of Jesus is crucial to the second gospel. A distinct characteristic of Mark's Gospel is how often Jesus uses the phrase **Son of Man** to identify himself. No other character calls Jesus the Son of Man. In normal English usage, this self-identification would seem to refer to the human side of Jesus, that Jesus is a mortal human being. That is how the phrase is used in the book of Ezekiel, where it often refers to the prophet.

But in the Second Temple period, Son of Man could carry a different connotation. In the book of Daniel, "one like a son of man" comes to the Ancient of Days. "And there was given him dominion, and glory, and a kingdom, that all people, nations, and languages, should serve him: his dominion is an everlasting dominion, which shall not pass away, and his kingdom that which shall not be destroyed" (Daniel 7:14). The language of kingdom and rule is similar to the language used elsewhere in the Bible for the Messiah. In 1 Enoch, a book from the **Pseudepigrapha** quoted in the New Testament by Jude (13–14), the Son of Man comes at the end of time to judge humanity (1 Enoch 37–71). This Son of Man is an eschatological judge.

Some of these biblical themes show up in the material that Mark chooses to narrate about Jesus. Jesus uses Son of Man to refer to his prophetic ministry. The Son of Man has authority to forgive sins (Mark 2:10) and is Lord of the Sabbath (2:28). Secondly, Jesus uses Son of Man in an eschatological sense. The Son of Man comes in glory with the angels (8:38; 14:26) and sits at the right hand of power (14:62). But thirdly, Jesus uses Son of Man in a way different from popular expectations. Jesus is the Son of Man who must suffer (8:31; 9:12) and be delivered over for death (9:31; 10:33). "The Son of Man came not to be served but to serve, and to give his life as a ransom for many" (10:45). The messianic Son of Man rules by dying. The eschatological Son of Man exercises judgment in his death.

The death of Jesus, toward which the second gospel hurtles and by which the disciples were completely confused, unlocks the other key concept of Jesus' identity. Jesus is the **SON OF GOD**. The gospel opens, "The beginning of the gospel of Jesus Christ, the Son of God" (1:1). In some early manuscripts, the phrase, "the Son of God," is missing. If the phrase is from Mark, it clearly identifies who Jesus is for the gospel writer. If the phrase comes from a later copyist, the phrase reflects the common understanding of the Jesus in this gospel. He is the Son of God.

The Roman religious world had many stories of gods who consorted with mortals. Their offspring were more than mortal—sons of the gods. For example, Heracles had a god as one of his parents, being the son of Zeus and a mortal woman named Alcmene. The imperial cult could at times label the emperor as God's son. To name Jesus as Son of God uses terminology to which a Roman audience could relate better than to a Jewish concept like Messiah.

Son of God was also a designation used in the religious literature of the Old Testament. The king is called "my son" by the Lord (Psalm 2:7); the king is God's "firstborn" (Psalm 89:27). The people of Israel are called "my firstborn son" (Exodus 4:22), "my firstborn" (Jeremiah 31:9), or "my son" (Hosea 11:1). Returning exiles are "my sons" and "my daughters" (Isaiah 43:6). A person or people who have a close relationship to God could be called a "son" or "daughter" of God

But for Mark, Jesus is more than a son of God like Heracles. He is more than a member of the family of God with the right to address God as "our Father." He is the unique Son of God whose identity will be confirmed in a most unexpected way.

Key Texts

Each passage to be considered below deals with the identity of Jesus. In each passage a character or group of characters will say or do something that shows who they think Jesus is. This list of passages is comprehensive, including every instance in the gospel.

1:11 The baptism of Jesus starts his ministry in Mark's Gospel. Since Mark omits a birth story, Jesus first appears at the Jordan, where John the Baptist conducts a prophetic ministry. When Jesus comes up out of the water, he sees the heavens ripped open. The same verb used to describe the tearing of the heavens will appear again at the end of the gospel when the veil of the temple is ripped in two at the death of Jesus (15:38). Both the baptism and death of Jesus reveal his identity.

The baptism is also attended by the Spirit descending on Jesus like a dove and a voice speaking from the heaven. Many in the Second Temple period thought the working of the Spirit had stopped with the last of the prophets. Only an echo of the divine voice called a *bat qôl* ("daughter of the voice") could still be heard. So the signs and manner of speech gave impact to the words, "You are my beloved son." The voice from heaven identifies Jesus as the unique SON OF GOD. The identification is certain, as the Fourth Gospel affirms when it explains the same event, "I have seen and have borne witness that this is the Son of God" (John 1:34).

1:24 The urgent, end-times ministry of Jesus begins with a string of mighty deeds. "Immediately" (Mark 1:23) Jesus meets a man with an unclean spirit in the synagogue at Capernaum. The spirit identifies Jesus as the "Holy One of God" (1:24). In contrast to the unclean spirit, Jesus is holy. He is the one on whom the Holy Spirit descended. The demon recognizes it is up against a superior spiritual power. On its own, the title is not a divine attribution, for it is used of Aaron (Psalm 106:16) and Elisha (2 Kings 4:9). But in view of the preceding material in the gospel (Mark 1:1, 11), the story would affirm Jesus' divinity to Mark's readers. For the demon came out of the man (1:26).

1:27 The response of those present at the exorcism provides and interesting contrast. The crowds are impressed with Jesus' authority, recognize what he did, and spread his fame (1:27–28). But Mark describes their reaction as one of amazement (not faith!). They question among themselves, "What is this?" In contrast to the demon, those present at the exorcism at Capernaum did NOT UNDERSTAND who Jesus was.

2:7 Later, when Jesus returns to Capernaum, four people bring a paralytic to Jesus by lowering the paralytic through the roof. When Jesus speak a word of forgiveness, some religious leaders present (called "scribes") are convinced that Jesus has blasphemed (2:7). **Blasphemy** is to curse or slander the name of God. In the view of the scribes, when Jesus forgave the paralytic, Jesus was usurping an action that only God could rightly do. "Who can forgive sins but God alone?" His actions were an affront to the name of God. Although Jesus had done a divine act, he was certainly NOT GOD. Later the judgment of Leviticus (24:16) against blasphemy would be the basis for sending Jesus to Pilate (Mark 14:64).

Stairs to rooftop at Capernaum

In a gospel where the identity of Jesus in critical, three differing perspectives have surfaced. To certain characters (the voice and the demon), Jesus is "of God," even the Son of God. To other characters (the scribes), Jesus is a blasphemer. He may claim a divine prerogative, but he is "not God." A third group of characters is impressed by Jesus. They see the mighty deeds, but do not understand fully who he is. After the healing of the paralytic, they are again "amazed" and exclaim, "We never saw anything like this" (2:12). But they are unable to identify Jesus properly. As the following verses will show, the characters in Mark either believe Jesus is (THE SON) OF GOD or NOT OF GOD or they do NOT UNDERSTAND who he is.

3:6 After a controversy with Jesus over Sabbath rules, the Pharisees watch him closely when he meets a man with a withered hand in a synagogue on the Sabbath. When Jesus restores the hand, "the Pharisees went out and at once held counsel with the Herodians against him, how to destroy him" (3:6). To these religious and political leaders Jesus was a law breaker if not a threat. He was certainly NOT OF GOD.

3:11 In the subsequent story, Jesus "withdraws" in reaction to the threat (3:7). Crowds from a wide area continue to come to him with their sick. Mark further notes, "Whenever the unclean spirits saw him, they fell down before him and cried out, 'You are the Son of God'" (3:11). The demonic spirits are the one who clearly identify Jesus and are the first to use the title preferred by Mark—the SON OF GOD.

3:22 As if Mark were narrating an ancient tennis match, scribes from Jerusalem appear. Since they are from Jerusalem, their judgment would be of greater import than the words of village scribes. They take earlier scribal judgments to their logical extreme. Jesus is NOT OF GOD. Instead, "he is possessed by

Beelzebul," and "by the prince of demons he casts out the demons" (3:22). They kept saying, "He has an unclean spirit" (3:30).

4:41 After withdrawing, Jesus teaches his disciples in parables. The twelve ask about the parables because they do not understand (4:13). After Jesus explains everything to them and at his direction, they cross the sea in a boat. While Jesus sleeps, a windstorm and its wave threaten the boat. After the disciples awaken him, Jesus calms the storm. Mark says that Jesus "rebuked" the wind and said to the sea, "Be still" (4:39). Mark's description uses the language of exorcism. Earlier Jesus had "rebuked" the unclean spirit and said to it, "Be still" (1:25). That spirit has identified Jesus as the "holy one of God." With a divine display of power, Jesus calms the wind and wave. But the disciples do NOT UNDERSTAND. "And they were filled with great fear and said to one another, 'Who then is this, that even wind and sea obey him?'" (4:41).

Temple of Artemis at Jerash

5:7 Jesus and the disciples cross the sea into the country of the Gerasenes. Gerasa, known today as Jerash, was a Decapolis city some thirty miles east of the Sea of Galilee. Whether Jesus and his followers traveled that far or simply went into territory controlled by Gerasa, they were in an area of mixed religious and cultural practice. They met an individual who lived among the tombs and was possessed by an evil spirit. The spirit, called Legion, cries out, "What have you to do with me, Jesus, SON OF THE MOST HIGH GOD?" (5:11) The language shifts between singular and plural in describing the demon(s). This demon(s) knows who Jesus is. In an act of divine power, Jesus sends the unclean spirits into a herd of swine. The herd plunges down a bank into the sea. Both language and action clarify Jesus' identity. By contrast, people from the area ask Jesus to leave (5:17); they marvel (5:20), but they do *not understand.*

6:3 The identity of Jesus is at stake when he returns to his hometown of Nazareth. On the Sabbath, Jesus goes to the local synagogue assembly and begins to teach. In contrast to other contexts in which the crowds are "amazed" by Jesus (5:42) even if they do not understand, the people from his hometown question his words and works (6:2). This questioning is more than just confusion. The people "took offense" at him; that is, they rejected his words and works because they knew him and his family: "Is not this the carpenter, the son of Mary and brother of James and Joses and Judas and Simon? And are not his sisters here with us?" (6:3) Nazareth was of small village, probably of less than two hundred people. In their view, Jesus ought not speak and act the way he did because he was NOT OF GOD but of Nazareth (see what Nathanael said about Nazareth in John 1:46).

6:14–16 Mark interrupts the story of the mission of the twelve with an aside about Herod Antipas and the death of John the Baptist. Antipas, one of the three heirs of Herod the Great, still ruled Galilee in the north and Perea on the east side of the Jordan when Jesus was an adult. Mark's narration of the death of John is much more detailed than the other Synoptic Gospels, since Mark focuses on the suffering that comes on the faithful. In telling the story, Mark includes speculation about the identity of Jesus, for Antipas thought, "John, whom I beheaded, as been raised" (Mark 6:16). Other speculation is also presented, "He is Elijah . . . He is a prophet like one of the prophets of old" (6:15). Among those who heard of the words and deeds of Jesus, there was much misunderstanding and a variety of opinion. Herod's guilt raised the possibility that Jesus was John; the name of Elijah surfaced because of similarities between the actions of Jesus to the biblical stories about Elijah. No one had a clear answer, since they did NOT UNDERSTAND who Jesus actually was.

6:51–52 When Jesus comes walking on the sea, Mark uses the language of a **theophany**—an appearance of God. First, Jesus is walking on the sea. Such walking recalls the God who "hovered over the face of the waters" at creation (Genesis 1:2), who "makes a path in the mighty waters" (Isaiah 43:16), and who "trampled the waves of the sea" (Job 9:8). Second, Jesus "meant to pass by them" (Mark 6:48) even as God's glory "passed by" Moses (Exodus 33:22). Third, since the disciples thought he was a ghost, Jesus replied, "Do not be afraid" (Mark 6:50). From Genesis 15:1 on through the Old Testament, it is God or God's messenger who sends the greeting, "Do not be afraid." But most significantly, Jesus answers their cries with, "It is I," the same formula (in Greek) with which God revealed the divine name to Moses (Exodus 3:14). Jesus' words and actions identify him as divine. But the disciples "were utterly astounded, for they did NOT UNDERSTAND about the loaves, but their hearts were hardened" (Mark 6:51–52). The disciples stand with crowds in their confusion. They do not know who Jesus is.

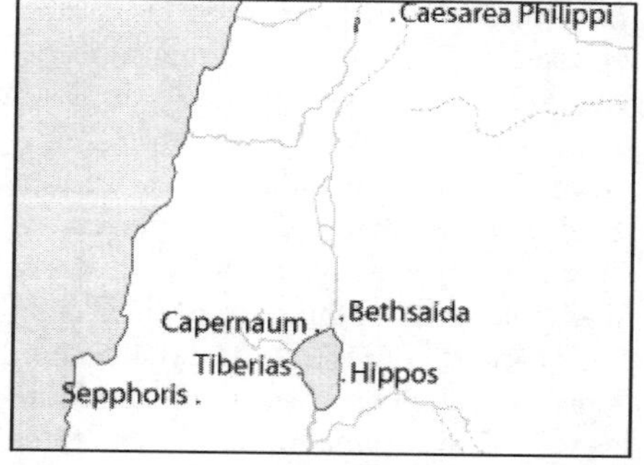

8:28–29 At Caesarea Philippi, the identity of Jesus is raised by a question from Jesus himself, "Who do people say that I am?" (8:27) The continuing confusion of the people is witnessed by a variety of answers, "John the Baptist; and others say, Elijah; and others, one of the prophets" (8:28). When Jesus asked the disciples directly, Peter answers, "You are the Christ" (8:29). In a sense, Peter is correct, for Mark begins the gospel by identifying Jesus as the Messiah (= Christ). But in the Second Temple period, most expected a Messiah whose rescue and deliverance would be political and national in scope. They did not expect a Messiah who would "suffer many things" (8:31). What is more, Mark has been stressing through his story selection that Jesus is the Son of God.

Why then would Mark only record part of Peter's words? For according to Matthew, Peter had said, "You are the Messiah, the Son of the Living God" (Matthew 16:16). Mark only gives part of the Petrine speech as a way of saying that Peter did NOT UNDERSTAND fully who Jesus was or what Jesus was about. Even in Matthew, Peter's understanding is faulty and he is condemned as a "Satan" (Matthew 16:23; Mark 8:33). To Mark, Jesus is more than a political Messiah, he is God's unique Son.

9:7 In all three Synoptic Gospels, the transfiguration helps to mark Jesus' turn toward Jerusalem even as it anticipates his resurrection. Mark's report continues to affirm the larger theme: "This is my beloved Son," says a voice from the cloud. Jesus is the SON OF GOD. As to the disciples present, their confusion remains (9:10). They do NOT UNDERSTAND his word about resurrection. Amazement and fear continue to characterize their reaction to Jesus, especially as he goes to Jerusalem (10:32).

11:28 The entry of Jesus into Jerusalem has connotations for his identity. The actions and words of the people who accompanied Jesus convey political and messianic overtones (see the discussion above in chapter three). When Jesus cleansed the temple, the religious leaders "sought a way to destroy him" while "all the crowd was astonished at his teaching" (11:18). The excitement and amazement of the public were not matched by the religious hierarchy. The "chief priests, scribes, and elders" confront Jesus in the temple, "By what authority are you doing these things. Or who gave you authority to do them?" (11:27–28) Their questions are rhetorical. Their manner and tone suggest they have prejudged that Jesus has no proper authority. His words and actions are NOT OF GOD. The testy exchange between Jesus and these authorities hints at what is to come. The authorities have made up their minds about Jesus. They plot "to arrest him by stealth and kill him" (14:1).

14:64 In a trial before the religious leaders, the identity of Jesus becomes the central issue. As witnesses could not agree in their testimony against Jesus (14:56), the high priest asks Jesus directly, "Are you the Christ, the Son of the Blessed?" (14:61) In Matthew's Gospel Jesus says, "You have said so" (26:64). In Luke, Jesus says, "If I tell you, you will not believe" (22:67). But in Mark, the answer is direct: "I am" (14:62). By using the self-revelatory name of God from Exodus to translate Jesus' response, Mark makes clear who Jesus is: the SON OF GOD. In subsequent verses, the high priest and those present condemn Jesus as a blasphemer worthy of death. To them Jesus' words are presumptive and a violation of the rules of the Torah. He is NOT OF GOD.

15:2, 9, 12, 18 In the trial before Pilate, the issue of Jesus' identity shifts from the religious to the political realm. "Are you the King of the Jews?" Pilate asks. Pilate seemed to identify the title with political insurrection, as he gave the people a choice between Jesus and Barabbas (Mark 15:7). In the exchanges, Pilate keeps calling Jesus "the King of the Jews" (15:9, 12). After the sentence of death is given, the soldiers gather in the governor's headquarters where they dress Jesus in a purple cloak and crown of thorns and hail him as the "King of the Jews" (15:18). Their mockery provides a stark contrast with the message suggested by so may of the stories in Mark's Gospel. For to Mark Jesus is more than a king or messiah; he is the Son of God.

15:32 Similar language continues in the short and violent telling of the crucifixion. An inscription of the charge read, "the King of the Jews" (15:26). The religious authorities mocked Jesus with similar tones, "Let the Christ, the King of Israel, come down now from the cross that we may see and believe" (15:32). Even those who were crucified with him reviled him. The shame and horror of death by crucifixion were meant to convey a message. This Jesus was not the King of the Jews, he was not the promised Messiah, he was not even a righteous man who Elijah might rescue (15:35). He was nothing but one forsaken by God.

Throughout the second gospel, three different answers have been given to the question, "Who is Jesus?" The author, the voice from above, and the demons affirm repeatedly that Jesus is of God, the unique SON OF GOD. By contrast, the religious authorities consistently view Jesus as demonic, as one worthy of death, a blasphemer, one who is NOT OF GOD. Between these two groups stand the crowds and the disciples. At times that are amazed, at other times they are frightened. They speculate about who Jesus might be, but they do NOT UNDERSTAND.

15:39 The death of Jesus in Mark is dramatic. It is set in darkness (15:33). Jesus cries out in abandonment (15:34). He is refused relief with twisted mockery, "Wait, let us see whether Elijah will come and take him down" (15:36). "And Jesus uttered a loud cry and breathed his last" (15:37). The staccato of Mark's narrative has come to its explanation.

When Jesus dies, the centurion says, "Truly this man was the Son of God!" (15:39) What the centurion meant by those words is open to debate. But in the flow of Mark's narrative, the reader would hear the centurion affirming what has been repeated by demons and the voices from above. Jesus is the unique SON OF GOD. To the religious authorities Jesus was a blasphemer. The crowds and disciples did not understand who Jesus was. The only human being to state correctly the identity of Jesus is the centurion, and he does so when Jesus dies.

Jesus in Mark

Matthew portrays Jesus as the Messiah and Son of God for a Jewish Christian community involved in the Gentile mission. Luke portrays Jesus as the Savior of all in the instruction he offers to "most excellent" Theophilus. For Mark, writing for the church in a time of violent opposition, Jesus is the unique Son of God, but only at the cross can that truth can be grasped fully by mortals. To a community tormented by violence at the hand of imperial power, Mark proclaims Jesus as the ultimate Son of God in opposition to the emperor's self-claim at the moment Jesus dies on an instrument of imperial violence.

The messianic secret that features so prominently in this gospel is now understandable. During his ministry Jesus pleaded with people not to speak of him since they did not and could not understand who he was until he was crucified. Peter could not state fully who Jesus was, since neither Peter nor any of the disciple could yet understand. The irony for Mark's readers rests in the one who utters the true confession. The faithful women stand at a distance when Jesus dies (15:40). Joseph of Arimathea provides burial in a rock-cut tomb (15:46). Those who hear the report of resurrection "said nothing to anyone" (16:8). Only a centurion—a representative of Roman power and violence—speaks the truth: "This man was the SON OF GOD."

The second gospel serves as a dramatic encouragement to a persecuted community. In the midst of violence, fear, confusion, betrayal and even death—there Jesus is. And there Jesus is identified as the unique SON OF GOD. A similar encouragement is penned by Peter whose preaching Mark recorded according to early tradition, "Beloved, do not be surprised at the fiery trial when it comes upon you to test you, as though something strange were happening to you. But rejoice insofar as you share Christ's sufferings, that you may also rejoice and be glad when his glory is revealed" (1 Peter 4:12–13). For Peter, suffering yields revelation: Jesus is the SON OF GOD—a truth revealed through his suffering.

For Further Discussion

1. The multiple endings of the second gospel indicate that early Christian readers had difficulty with a gospel which ends on an uncertain note. Happy endings are expected, and provided, if necessary. How comfortable are you with stories that tell of Christians who are not always faithful and bold? What is the value of a story in which the characters "said nothing to anyone, for they were afraid"?

2. Mark's telling of the death of Jesus is the most violent of the four gospels. Why the stress on violence (compare Mel Gibson's movie *The Passion of the Christ*)? What do you think of a religion that redeems through violence?

3. Look at other books discussed in this chapter. How is Mark's message similar to or different from these other confessions made in times of conflict? What role does conflict and opposition play in your expression of the faith?

4. Compare and contrast the "young man" in Mark 14:51 and 16:5? Although they are clearly different characters, Mark calls them by the same name. What might Mark be doing literarily?

5. Jesus often commands people, "Don't tell." What might those stories be teaching modern readers? When should someone "not tell"?

For Further Reading

Cranfield, C. E. B. *The Gospel according to St. Mark*. Cambridge: Cambridge University Press, 1959.

Gundry, Robert M. *Mark: A Commentary on His Apology for the Cross*. Grand Rapids: Eerdmans, 1992.

Lane, William. *The Gospel according to Mark.* New International Commentary of the New Testament. Grand Rapids: Eerdmans, 1973.

Mann, C. S. *Mark.* Anchor Bible Commentary, volume XX. New York: Doubleday, 1986.

Martin, R. P. *Mark: Evangelist and Theologian.* Grand Rapids: Zondervan, 1986.

Hebrews

Melchizedek and the Messiah, Texts and Temple

Hebrews strikes many in our day as one of the most difficult books in the New Testament to understand. This is partially due to its sermonic nature and a style of argumentation which seems both complex and unfamiliar. The majority of the problem, however, is the extent of Old Testament knowledge which the author assumes his hearers have. Constant references are made to the Old Testament. These focus on the priesthood, sacrificial system, and worship that took place at the tabernacle and, later, the Jerusalem temple. Without a rather high degree of familiarity with these Old Testament figures and the theology which accompanies them, much of Hebrews remains obscure.

Model of Jerusalem with temple in far center

Melchizedek is one example we will use to illustrate a small portion of what lies behind Hebrews. He is a shadowy character who shows up for three short verses in Genesis 14:18–20. Melchizedek appears without any introduction and then just as quickly disappears from view. Yet part of Hebrews 5 and all of chapter seven build on this character and associate him with Christ. What is there about such an esoteric Old Testament person that makes him so significant?

Melchizedek was both a king and a priest (Genesis 14:18). And he was king of "Salem," a term associated with Jerusalem. Abraham gave a tithe or tenth of the plunder he had won in battle to Melchizedek, who blessed Abraham in return (Genesis 14:19–20). This implies Melchizedek, who received the offering and pronounced the blessing, was greater than Abraham, a point explicitly made in Hebrews (see Hebrews 7:4, 6–7). Finally, Psalm 110 is the most commonly quoted chapter of the Old Testament in the New. It speaks of a coming ruler who would be David's lord and also "a priest forever after the order of Melchizedek" (Psalm 110:1, 4).

According to Hebrews, all of this comes together in Christ, who is literally without beginning and end. He is descended from the tribe of Judah; he is David's greater son and lord (Hebrews 7:14; compare Matthew 23:43–45). Jesus is both a king and a priest who was put in place permanently by the oath of God himself (Hebrews 7:20–21). Since Jesus is a priest in the order of Melchizedek, he is also greater than Abraham. He is, therefore, superior to any of the priests descended from Abraham through the tribe of Levi (7:9–10, 16). Indeed, Jesus Christ "holds his priesthood permanently, because he continues forever" (7:24).

This illustrates just one small portion of the Old Testament background that the author of Hebrews presumes his hearers have. The key point is that he uses Melchizedek, as well as many other Old Testament references, to make the Gospel more certain based upon the "once for all" sacrifice offered by Christ, the Messiah (7:27). He is "the guarantor of a better covenant.... [and] is able to save to the uttermost those who draw near to God through him, since he always lives to make intercession for them" (7:22, 25).

Hebrews also cites many Old Testament texts. At first glance, the author appears to be using some of them rather creatively; at other times, he draws conclusions from Scriptures which do not seem to be warranted. For example, Hebrews chapter 2 quotes Psalm 8, a psalm of praise to the Creator God. In the midst of the immensity of the universe, the psalmist asks, "What is man that you are mindful of him or the son of man that you care for him?" (Psalm 8:4). Based on Genesis 1:28, Psalm 8:5 responds that God gave Adam and Eve and those who follow after them dominion over his entire creation. The psalmist is speaking generally about God's care for all people and the exalted role he has given humanity over everything he made.

Hebrews 2, however, applies these verses specifically to "him who for a little while was made lower than the angels, namely Jesus" (Hebrews 2:9). He became human to suffer death for everyone (2:9, 29); he is now "crowned with glory and honor" (2:9), and God will one day place "everything in subjection" to him (2:8).

Here, as elsewhere, Christ is portrayed as the central point of God's Old Testament word. Picture the author of Hebrews on the right side of the bow-tie diagram introduced in chapter one of this textbook. He is gazing back toward the left or Old Testament side. But he now reads and understands those Scriptures by looking at them through the focal point of the diagram, the person and work of Jesus Christ.

In order to understand the significance of many of the passages used in Hebrews, one will have to engage in research into their Old Testament background.

Even then, the passages often require in-depth thinking to analyze and may still leave the reader wrestling with the truths presented. Yet the struggle is well worth it. Hebrews is one of the most valuable books in the entire Bible because it unites both testaments together. It demonstrates that the Bible is one story that culminates in the person and all-sufficient work of Jesus Christ.

Introduction

In a number of ways, Hebrews is unique among the letters in the New Testament. First, it is not really a letter in the usual sense of the term. It lacks any kind of opening and does not follow the outline of first-century letters. Hebrews is more like a sermon put down in writing. The author calls it a "word of exhortation" (13:22).

Second, the title is a word used nowhere within the sermon. "Hebrews" was attached to this document long after it was written. The term is another name for the Jewish people or the people of Israel. The argument of the sermon and its dominant Old Testament content have led scholars to conclude that Hebrews was addressed to Jews who had previously practiced the religion of the Old Testament. Now they have accepted Jesus as their promised Messiah. In the midst of trials, harassment, ostracism, persecution, and other difficulties, they are being tempted to return to their former beliefs and ways. This "word of exhortation" encourages them to be steadfast and to keep the eyes of their faith firmly fixed upon Jesus (13:22; 12:2).

Third, the text does not reveal its author; the identity of the highly gifted person who carefully crafted these words remains a mystery. The entire text refers to only one contemporary person by name. Hebrews 13:23 states, "You should know that our brother Timothy has been released, with whom I shall see you if he comes soon." Timothy had a long and close association with Paul. This factor has led many to conclude Hebrews is the fourteenth book of the New Testament written by the Apostle Paul. In fact, the King James Version of the Bible calls it "the Epistle of St. Paul to the Hebrews."

The attestation to Paul has a long history dating back to A. D. 400, but it is generally not accepted in modern times. The Greek vocabulary and style are quite different from that of Paul's letters. Although this is a fairly subjective conclusion, there are other anomalies that deviate from Paul's regular practice. Elsewhere Paul always identifies himself as the author. He usually fills his letters with personal references and sends greetings to others by name. Furthermore, the author of Hebrews states that he did not receive the message "as it was declared at first by the Lord, … [rather] it was attested to us by those who heard" (2:3). Paul vehemently insists that he received the gospel message directly from Christ (for example, Galatians 1:12; Ephesians 3:3).

The identification of the author was a mystery as far back as the third century when the Christian theologian Origen (A.D. c. 185-254) made this famous statement: "Only God knows who wrote Hebrews" (cited in Eusebius' *Ecclesiastical History*, VI.25.14). As a result, theories regarding the author's identity have abounded. Some suggestions include Barnabus, Luke, Silas/Silvanus, Philip, Priscilla and/or Aquila and Apollos (Luther's favorite). Good cases can be made for a number of these people, but without further evidence all we have are theories. One could conclude the author was male, based on the masculine form he uses for himself in Hebrews 11:32.

Fourth, the text gives no indication of the author's location or that of the recipients. One clue does enable us to speculate about its destination. As Hebrews draws to a close, its author states, "Those who come from Italy send you greetings" (Hebrews 13:24). This seems to indicate that the addressees are in or near Rome, and that greetings are being sent back to them from others who have left Italy (compare Acts 18:2). In A.D. 96 Bishop Clement of Rome, cites Hebrews, attesting to the presence of the letter in the city by that time.

Fifth, the date when Hebrews was written is also a matter of speculation. Due to the content of the sermon, it seems very likely that the Jerusalem temple, along with its priesthood and sacrifices, is still functioning. Indeed, much of the argument of the letter is nonsensical if the temple is no longer in place. The temple was destroyed by the Roman army in A. D. 70. As a result, it is quite sound to date Hebrews prior to that date. In times of war and tragedy, Americans tend to rally around the flag and unite patriotically. The Jewish revolt which led to the destruction of Jerusalem began in A.D. 67. It is possible that this revolt against Rome also enticed Jewish Christians to rally back to Judaism. Hebrews may well have been written between A.D. 67 and 70.

Site of the temple in Jerusalem

Structure and Theme

As mentioned previously, Hebrews is not really a letter and does not follow the typical letter outline. The only exception is the closing greetings (Hebrews 13:22–25). At the beginning the author immediately launches into the subject matter without any opening or thanksgiving, reinforcing its sermonic tone.

On the other hand, it would be wrong to conclude that Hebrews has no definitive structure. The author skillfully alternates blocks of teaching material with smaller sections of exhortation or encouragement based on the doctrine just presented. Hebrews 3 will serve as an example. According to verses 1–6, Moses was a faithful servant in God's house, but Christ is greater as a Son over God's house. The rest of the chapter then urges the hearers to respond in faith, rather than with the unbelief of many who were freed from Egypt through Moses (3:7–19).

The overall theme of Hebrews is twofold. First, in the doctrinal sections, the author argues, "Jesus is greater than, fulfills, or completes ________." Throughout the first ten chapters of the sermon, the blank is filled in with various Old Testament figures, events, and institutions (see the outline below). The main sections of doctrine, therefore, all focus on the centrality and superiority of Christ.

However, Hebrews is much more than a doctrinal treatise. Interspersed among the doctrinal sections of Hebrews 1–10 are exhortations to the hearers. The bracketed sections below contain the second thematic focus of the letter, the words of exhortation and encouragement.

Hebrews	
Jesus is greater than the angels	1:1–2:18
Jesus is greater than Moses	3:1–6
Jesus gives a superior Sabbath rest	3:7–4:13
Jesus is the great High Priest	4:14–6:12
Jesus is of the order of Melchizedek	6:13–7:28
Jesus is the high priest of a new covenant	8:1–13
Jesus fulfills the earthly tabernacle/temple	9:1–10
The sacrifice of Jesus is "once for all"	9:11–10:18
Exhortation to approach	10:19–39
Roll call of the faithful	11:1–40
"Run the race"	12:1-13:25

As a result of the interplay between these two parts, it is no surprise that words and phrases translated "therefore" or "then" occur frequently in Hebrews (for example, 2:1; 3:1; 4:1, 6, 11, 14, 16; 6:1; 7:11).

Chapters eleven through thirteen take a different tack. Chapter eleven contains a list of Old Testament believers who kept the faith. This "great cloud of witnesses," culminating in Jesus himself (12:2–3), provides the basis for the author's encouragement in the remainder of chapter twelve. Hebrews 13 contains ethical instructions and concludes the sermon with a blessing and final greetings.

Key Texts

1:1–4 Hebrews begins by affirming the divine source of the prophetic writings we call the Old Testament. "God spoke" through those prophets (1:4). The point is not to disparage them in any way, but to hold up Jesus, the Son, as an even greater spokesperson. He is the ultimate revelation through whom God "in these last days … has spoken to us" (1:2). According to the New Testament, the coming of the Messiah marked the beginning of the last days and the start of the new messianic era.

Who is Jesus? The description of God's Son here is most impressive. He is the radiant brightness of God's glory and "the exact imprint of his nature" (1:3). He and "the name he has inherited" are superior to the angels, a topic that occupies the rest of Hebrews 1 (1:4; see 1:5–14). What has Jesus done? He is the one through whom the world was made, and he continues to uphold it by his word (1:2–3; compare 2:10). Indeed, he is the appointed heir of all (1:2). Yet, in the midst of this majestic description, the author also hints at the Gospel message, which will be expounded more fully later. Before Jesus ascended to sit at God's right hand, he made purification for sins (1:3).

2:17–18 The hymn "Beautiful Savior" wonderfully expresses how Jesus is both "Son of God and Son of Man." That hymn and the opening verses of Hebrews emphasize Jesus' divine nature. Hebrews 2:17–18 clearly assert his full humanity. It is a doctrinal truth of great comfort to know Jesus was made like us in every way and was even tempted as we are. Later, chapter five similarly describes how, "in the days of his flesh, Jesus offered up prayers and supplications with loud cries and tears" (5:7); he was a son who "learned obedience through what he suffered" (5:8). As a result, Jesus can relate to and help us in our times of temptation (2:18). He was also able to serve God as a merciful and faithful high priest who made atonement for the sins of all people.

5:11–6:6 We began our introduction to Hebrews by pointing out the difficulty many readers have in understanding its in-depth argument. The original hearers were also having some trouble. The author claims that some of what he has to say is "hard to explain, since you have become dull of hearing" (5:11). The initial recipients have also failed to grow spiritually beyond the basic principles. All they can handle is milk, when they ought to be ready for solid food (5:12–14). Perhaps this "milk" can be compared to the content of a confirmation class, a basic adult instruction course, or even the Apostles' Creed. Hebrews 6:1–3 lists the following as examples of the "elementary doctrine" of Christ: repentance, faith, washings (literally "baptisms"), the laying on of hands, the resurrection, and eternal judgment. These are the essentials of the faith, but God wants his people to move beyond the basics so that their "powers of discernment" might be trained to "distinguish good from evil" (5:14).

The most controversial section in Hebrews is 6:4–6. These verses seem to say that if a believer "falls away" from the faith (6:6), "it is impossible" for him to be restored again to repentance (6:4). How does this fit with the experience of Peter? He openly denied Christ, but was then restored by him after the resurrection (see Luke 22:31–34, especially verse 32; see also John 13:36–38; 18:15–18; 21:15–19).

Some assert that genuine, predestined believers cannot actually fall away from faith (**once saved, always saved**). The words of Hebrews 6, therefore, apply to those who were not really "true believers" in the first place; they will fall away and be lost eternally. Nothing in the text indicates that this is the sense of the passage. On the contrary, the extensive list in verses four and five emphasizes that the situation involves a genuine Christian.

Others suggest these verses refer to any willful "falling away" into sin after baptism. That interpretation contends believers should and can live completely sanctified lives here in this world (**sinless perfectionism**). The witness of the New Testament and the experience of many believers, including the Apostle Paul, challenge this view (James 3:2; Romans 7:14–25; 1 John 1:8, 10; 2:1).

Another interpretation is preferable. The "falling away" here is not simply a falling into sin due to fear or the weakness of our human nature. Instead, it describes outright apostasy and a complete renunciation of the faith by one who once believed. It is the repeated hardening of one's own heart against God and God's will, in other words, obstinate unbelief, the "unforgivable sin" against the Holy Spirit spoken of by Jesus (Mark 3:28–29). Is someone in this situation gone for good?

The Greek word translated "impossible" in 6:4 more accurately asserts that such a person is "unable" or "powerless" to return to God. According to Jesus, people are "unable" or "powerless" in terms of their own ability to be among the saved in the first place (Luke 18:24–27). Indeed, apart from God's intervention, it is impossible for any of us to repent and be saved. And so, the book of Acts speaks of repentance as God's gracious action in our lives (Acts 5:31; 11:18). This passage in Hebrews reinforces the point that such turning or, in this case, returning to God is something we are powerless to do; it happens only and always by the work of God's Spirit. Whether God the Holy Spirit is still attempting to work repentance in someone's heart or not is something only God knows. Other Scripture passages do indicate there is an ominous point at which even God gives up on people, such as Pharaoh (Exodus 9:12; 10:20, 27; 11:10; compare Romans 9:14–18).

9:22–10:10 Hebrews spends a great deal of time demonstrating how Jesus fulfilled the former covenant along with its tabernacle and temple, priesthood and sacrifices. These verses are the culmination of that argument. As with the Old Testament prophets in the opening verses of Hebrews (1:1–2), the author's main point is not to disparage what preceded. The former covenant was established by God (for example, 9:19–20). However, it was deficient and limited by the following:

- Priests who were subject to human weakness, sin, and death (7:16, 23, 27–28; 9:27);
- The inability of repeatedly offered animal sacrifices to actually remove sin (9:9, 25; 10:4, 11);

- The earthly tabernacle or temple in which it was practiced (8:2, 5; 9:23);
- The fact that it was intended to be temporary all along (7:18–19; 8:7, 13; 9:10).

Hebrews 8:8–12 quotes the prophet Jeremiah's promise of a "new covenant" which "is enacted on better promises" (9:6; Jeremiah 31:31–34). In it "a better hope is introduced, through which we draw near to God" (Hebrews 9:19). Yet, as we will see, this new covenant has many commonalities with the previous covenant. In fact, the Hebrew term used by Jeremiah to refer to the "new" covenant or testament (*chadash*) does not convey the idea of something totally new and different. For example, it is used to refer to a "new" moon. However, each month does not welcome a different moon. Instead, the same moon is renewed once again. Jeremiah's description of the "new" covenant cited here restates elements of the former covenant made at Sinai. According to Deuteronomy 6:7 God had already placed his words upon Israel's heart; in Leviticus 26:12 he declared, "And I will walk among you and be your God, and you shall be my people" (compare Jeremiah 31:33, cited in Hebrews 8:10). Rather than a totally "new" covenant, Hebrews announces that the former covenant is now renewed, restored and fulfilled just as Jeremiah predicted. Our great high priest, Jesus Christ, and his once-for-all sacrifice are what render the former covenant "obsolete" (8:13).

What are some of the ways in which the "former" and the "renewed" covenants are alike? First, both hold to this theological principle: "without the shedding of blood there is no forgiveness of sins" (9:22; see 9:18–21; Exodus 24:8; Matthew 26:28). Many in our day might ask, "Why?" Scripture responds, "The wages of sin is death" and "the soul that sins will surely die" (Romans 6:23; Ezekiel 18:20). In the Old Testament Leviticus explains that the life of flesh is in the blood (Leviticus 17:11). When enough blood is shed, the person or animal dies; the death penalty for sin is paid. Since all have sinned, Hebrews concludes, "It is appointed for man to die once, and after that comes judgment" (9:27). Note that the "once" of this verse rejects any kind of reincarnation. It also places a person's individual judgment at the time of his or her death. After that, there is no opportunity to make up for or work off sins in some place like purgatory. The public affirmation of one's personal judgment will occur at Jesus' second coming.

Second, in both old and new covenants or testaments, God provides a substitute to shed blood in the place of the sinner. In Old Testament times animal sacrifices occurred repeatedly at the tabernacle and temple. Yet Hebrews 10:3–4 asserts that those repeated sacrifices were actually "a reminder of sin … for it is impossible for the blood of bulls and goats to take away sins." Yes, when those sacrifices were offered, God forgave sins (Leviticus 4:20, 26, 31, 35; 5:10, 13, 16, 18). But the price paid for the sins committed by God's Old Testament people was actually the blood of Christ. His death "redeems them from the transgressions committed under the first covenant" (9:15; Paul similarly states that before Christ's blood was shed, God "passed over" the sins of Old Testament believers and, in the meantime, credited them as righteous by faith; Romans 3:25; 4:4, 6).

Hebrews, however, concludes that Christ's priestly sacrifice transcends and brings to an end all the sacrificial laws of the former covenant (Hebrews 8:7, 13), because it was not offered in some earthly tabernacle or temple, but in "heaven itself" where he now appears in the presence of God on our behalf (8:2; 9:24). Furthermore, his offering was not the blood of an animal. Instead, "Christ came into the world" and offered himself to be "sacrificed once to take away the sins of many people" (10:5; 9:28). As a result of his first coming, "we have been sanctified through the offering of the body of Jesus Christ once for all" (10:10). This means no additional offering *for sin* can or should be made (10:18). Now believers look ahead to the day when he "will appear a second time, not to deal with sin but to save those who are eagerly waiting for him" (9:28).

10:35–11:3 Based on Christ's fulfillment of the Old Testament covenant, Hebrews begins an extensive section of exhortation (10:19–39). Its essence is that these believers need to endure and persevere (10:36; 12:2, 7). The suggestion that believers are not actually able to fall away would makes this entire appeal absurd. The end of Hebrews 10 quotes Habakkuk 2:3–4, but in a sense quite different from the appeal Paul makes based upon that text (Romans 1:17; Galatians 3:11). Here "my righteous one" applies to a believer who is being warned against shrinking back or throwing away what is already theirs by faith (Hebrews 10:35, 39). Instead, he or she is to live by that faith or, even more literally, to live "out" the faith.

This exhortation leads to a definition of faith—"the assurance of things hoped for, the conviction of things not seen" (11:1). One affirmation of faith is stated in verse three: "by faith we understand that the universe was created by the word of God, so that what is seen was not made out of things that are visible." The ramifications of this assertion in an era when evolutionary science is so dominant are significant. At the same time, it is important to note that creation by the word of God is an article of faith accepted on that basis, not on scientific explanation.

The "by faith" section to follow refers to "the people of old" who were commended for their faith and who lived it out nobly (11:2; 4–38). This rehearsal of heroes and heroines of faith provides a wonderful overview of the Old Testament. It also emphasizes the unity of God's relationship with his people throughout the Scriptures. Hebrews 11:6 sounds a lot like St. Paul in asserting, "Without faith it is impossible to please" God (compare Romans 14:23). The basis of any righteous person's relationship with God has always been faith (Hebrews 10:38, citing Habakkuk 2:4; compare Genesis 15:6; Galatians 3:6; Romans 4:3). That was as true for Noah, Abraham, and Joseph as it was for the author of Hebrews and his hearers; it remains so for us today.

11:39–12:3 What point is to be drawn from these Old Testament heroes? The author of Hebrews stresses the faithful example they provide for those who follow after them. All these heroes "were commended through their faith" (39).

Yet they "did not receive what was promised" and will not receive it "apart from us" (11:39–40). Instead, they now form a great "cloud of witnesses" who encourage contemporary believers in their own faith. The testimony of their lives urges us to get rid of sin and whatever else hinders our faith, and to "run with endurance the race that is set before us" (12:1). But the focus of faith is neither on self nor on the cloud of witnesses. Rather, it is fixed on "Jesus, the founder and perfecter of our faith" (12:2). Jesus is the beginning or source of faith; he is also its completion and fulfillment. He is both source and fulfillment because he "endured the cross, despising its shame, and is seated at the right hand of the throne of God" (12:2).

Jesus' perseverance, and that of these Old Testament saints, is a motivator and model for us (compare Philippians 2:1–12). Since Jesus endured such derision, we should not grow weary. Instead, we are encouraged to keep the faith even in difficult times (13:3). The original recipients of Hebrews had not yet suffered death for their faith in Christ (12:4), but they were experiencing hardships. They should view them as evidence that God was at work, disciplining those whom he loves (12:6; citing Proverbs 3; 12).

13:7–21 Hebrews concludes with a list of specific instructions. It contains a number of significant statements about Christ and Christian leaders. Those who speak the word of God to others are to be imitated. Hebrews 13:7 speaks of leaders who have apparently died. After viewing the outcome of their way of life, Hebrews calls us to "imitate their faith" for they were faithful unto death (13:7). Later, verses 17–18 speak of current leaders who "are keeping watch over your souls" (Hebrews 13:17). They are to be obeyed so that when they give an account of their oversight to God, it will be filled with joy.

Jesus is spoken of in eternal and unchanging terms. He "is the same yesterday and today and forever" (13:8). Yet he, like the burned bodies of sacrificed animals in the Old Testament, "also suffered outside the gate in order to sanctify the people through his blood" (13:12; see Exodus 29:14; Leviticus 4:12, 21). Jesus died just outside the walls of Jerusalem. A final appeal is made for the hearers to "go to him outside the camp and bear the reproach he endured" (Hebrews 13:13). This summarizes Hebrews' "word of exhortation" to first-century Jews (13:22). They are to move to Jesus "outside the camp," that is, beyond the temple, priesthood, animal sacrifices, and other elements of the former covenant. Why? After citing the promise of a "new covenant" from Jeremiah 31, Hebrews 8:13 concludes: "In speaking of a new covenant, he makes the first one obsolete. And what is becoming obsolete and growing old is ready to vanish."

Yet these verses also reveal that many things remain the same. The example of faith for which Old Testament believers and leaders were commended is still relevant (Hebrews 11; 13:7). Additionally, for forgiveness to be granted, the new covenant also requires the shedding of sacrificial blood offered by a priest (9:23–26). However, these and many other aspects of God's covenant have been transformed in and through Christ. His blood was sacrificed once for all (13:20; 10:10, 14). His followers are still called to offer sacrifices, but they are now "a sacrifice of praise," of good works, and of sharing with others—"such sacrifices are pleasing to God" (13:15, 16).

Finally, Hebrews offers a blessing (13:20–21). It identifies the source of all blessings as "the God of peace" (13:20). The Hebrew concept of peace (*shalom*) denotes wholeness, health, and completeness within one's self, as well as in relationship with God and others. God's decisive action to enact this *shalom* was raising Jesus from the dead. The living Jesus, whose blood was shed to establish an everlasting covenant, now shepherds his flock (13:20). And through him God works within his people and equips us to do what is pleasing in his sight. The sermon ends appropriately by referring to this God of peace as the one to whom all glory is due "forever and ever. Amen" (13:21).

Jesus in Hebrews

The person and work of Christ so permeate this "letter of exhortation" (13:22) that it is almost impossible to summarize them adequately. The material already presented has attempted to point out the centrality of Jesus as the fulfillment and completion. In conclusion, it may be helpful to review the many titles and characteristics which Hebrews applies to him. Jesus is

- the one through whom God created and preserves all that exists (1:2; 2:10);
- the exalted Son of God who, as son and heir, "is faithful over God's house" (1:2, 5; 3:6; 4:14; 5:5; 7:28; 10:29);
- the apostle who was "sent forth" from God (3:1);
- the climactic revelation of God speaking to his people (1:1–2);
- a merciful, faithful, great and exalted high priest in the order of Melchizedek (2:17; 3:1; 4:14; 5:5–6,10; 6:20; 7:15–17, 26; 8:1; 9:11);
- the "once for all" sacrifice for sin by the offering of his own body (7:27; 9:14, 28; 10:10, 12, 14);
- the guarantor and mediator of a "better" and "eternal" covenant" (7:22; 8:6; 9:15; 13:20);
- the founder of salvation (2:10), as well as "the founder and perfecter of our faith" (12:2; compare 5:9; 10:14);
- "the great shepherd of the sheep" (13:20);
- crowned with glory and honor at God's right hand, where he intercedes for his people (1:3, 13; 2:9; 7:25; 8:1; 9:24; 10:12); and
- "the same yesterday and today and forever" (13:8).

For Further Discussion

1. List three unique characteristics of Hebrews compared with the other New Testament books we have studied.

2. Who do you think wrote Hebrews? Does authorship matter for how we read and understand Hebrews? Why or why not?

3. Chapter one of this textbook asked whether the Bible was one book or two. How does Hebrews answer? Explain your response.

4. Was your knowledge of the Old Testament sufficient for you to grasp the content of Hebrews? To what degree? How can your understanding be improved or does the author of Hebrews assume too much Old Testament knowledge? Explain.

5. What does Hebrews say about those who "fall away" from the faith?

6. Does our focus on God's faithful cloud of witnesses distract us from fixing the eyes of our faith on Jesus alone (Hebrews 12:3; see chapters 11–12)? Is it proper for us to look to contemporary church leaders and church leaders throughout history as models of faith? Why or why not?

7. List six characteristics or titles Hebrews attributes to Jesus. Explain each of them.

For Further Reading

Barclay, William. *Hebrews*. The New Daily Study Bible. rev. ed. Nashville: Westminster John Knox, 1976.

Brown, Raymond. *The Message of Hebrews*. The Bible Speaks Today. Downers Grove, IL: InterVarsity, 1988.

Guthrie, George. *Hebrews*. The Tyndale New Testament Commentaries. Grand Rapids: Eerdmans, 1983.

Hughes, Philip. *A Commentary on the Epistle to the Hebrews*. Grand Rapids: Eerdmans, 1977.

Hughes, R. Kent. *Hebrews: An Anchor for the Soul*. 2 vols. Wheaton, IL: Crossway, 1993.

Lane, William. *Hebrews*. Word Biblical Commentary. 2 vols. Waco, TX: Word, 1991.

________. *Call to Commitment: Responding to the Message of Hebrews*. Peabody, MA: Hendrickson, 1985.

Lauersdorf, Richard. *Hebrews*. People's Bible Commentary. St. Louis: Concordia, 1992.

Murray, Andrew. *The Holiest of All*. New Kensington, PA: Whitaker House, 1996.

Revelation

Revelation is the most fascinating and frightening book in the New Testament. It permeates our culture and is widely read as a predictor of how the world will end. From Michelangelo's "Last Judgment" in the Sistine Chapel to Handel's "Messiah," from the death star in the *Star Wars Episode IV* to *The Matrix Series*, from the Shakers and Owenites to the Branch Davidians, the themes of Revelation recur and inspire. The threat of judgment day and the fear of annihilation by cosmic demonic powers have motivated missionaries, fostered visions and predictions of the end, provided grist for political speeches in times of war or tragedy (especially after 9/11), generated an industry of publications about the last days (*The Left Behind Series*, *The Late Great Planet Earth*) and even moved people to uproot themselves in search of a utopia, a new heaven on earth (Revelation 21). Many Germans migrated to the wilderness of the middle parts of America in the nineteenth century due to then popular interpretations of their plight based on the story of the "sun woman" in Revelation 12:6.

Although Revelation is often read for the wrong reasons, as if it were a book of secret codes that unlock the future, the book has inspired the words of songs and faith of many in the darkest moments of life. When read on its own terms, as an apocalyptic work with a particular structure, its message accords with the encouragement Jesus offered his followers before he faced his end. A message of hope in the final victory of God through the sacrifice of Jesus is a fitting conclusion to the New Testament.

Apocalyptic as a Literary Form

In our studies so far, we have discovered that the New Testament has works that are of different literary forms. The most basic distinction has been between narratives such as the gospels, and Acts and letters, such as the writings of Paul. Within these larger forms, we have discovered other genres: hymns, prayers, parables, sermons, dialogues, and so on. We have paid attention to literary forms, because each form is read differently. Each work is read according to its form, according to what it claims to be. We make such decisions as we read written material today, too. We treat a love letter in a different way from an article in the *Encyclopedia Britannica*. If we don't, our romantic relationships will soon be on the rocks!

In the book of Revelation, we meet a different literary form we have met only briefly before (Matthew 24–25, Mark 13, Luke 21). Revelation is an **apo-**

calyptic work. Just as it would be a grave error to treat a valentine as if it were a letter from the IRS, so we must read an apocalyptic work on its own terms, as an apocalyptic work and not as a narrative or a letter. So, we need to ask, what is apocalyptic and how do we read it?

The Greek word *apocalypsis* conveys the idea of making something fully known, revealing it, stripping away so that what was covered is now clearly visible. An apocalypse is a revelation, thus the title of the twenty-seventh book of the New Testament. In many ways, Revelation is the prime example of apocalyptic literature. Apocalyptic writers are transported (note the *Star Trek* language!) in a dream or vision to a celestial locale where they view supernatural beings and hideous monsters in violent combat. These otherworldly events give perspective on current crises and on the end of all things.

Revelation is not the only apocalyptic text. Recent work on apocalyptic material in Jewish and Christian sources has identified many literary features that this material has in common. We will name some of those features and provide examples from Revelation.

Apocalyptic Characteristics

- Cryptic symbols and code words
- Graphic violence
- Dualisms
- Pre-determined end
- Exclusivism
- Universality

Cryptic symbols and code words: Well known from the pages of Revelation is its use of symbolic language. A symbol is a word that stands for something other than its normal meaning. People often ask about the arcane references in Revelation. Who or what is the "lamb" (6:1)? Who are the 144,000 (7:4)? Who is the "dragon" (12:3) or the woman "clothed with the sun" (12:1)? What does "666" stand for (13:18)? Where is "Babylon" (14:8)? Such arcane language, drawn from biblical and pagan sources, would communicate with the original readers and would befuddle outsiders (including us, sometimes). It served to hide the true meaning of the text from opponents.

Graphic violence: A second easily recognized characteristic of apocalyptic literature is its portrayal of violence and death. Stars from the sky fall to earth (6:13). Hail and fire mixed with blood are hurled to the earth and a third of the earth is burned up (8:7). A beast comes from a bottomless pit to make war and kill (11:7). War breaks out in heaven (12:7). Seven angels pour out seven plagues (chapter 16). To apocalyptic writers, the present age is so evil and its leaders so corrupt that only through violence could a new age dawn. Opponents might oppress the faithful, but in the end God will destroy them.

Dualisms: Earlier we have met up with the dualism of some Hellenistic philosophic thought. In apocalyptic literature, there are several dualisms. Ethical dualism reflects the apocalyptic division of humanity into two camps—the large majority that is in the dark and doomed and the small minority of the faithful who will be saved. The letters to the seven churches (Revelation 2–3) show this duality. There is no middle ground (3:16). *Cosmic dualism* takes the astral fatalism of Graeco-Roman antiquity a step further. Not only are heaven and earth in some way linked (the assumption of astrology), but cosmic struggles between good and evil forces in the heavens directly affect events on earth. The war between Michael and the dragon (12:7) leads to a consequent persecution of the faithful (12:13). Chronological dualism applies the same principle to time as has been applied to people and the cosmos. Although Revelation does look back to the Old Testament, quoting and alluding it more than any other book, the key contrast is between the present evil age and the future of a new heaven and a new earth (chapter 21).

Pre-determined end: Flowing from these dualistic perspectives is the apocalyptic concern about the end of all things. Judgment will come and with violent results. But for the faithful few, the end is predetermined. History will culminate according to God's plan. The Lamb is on the throne (7:17), Babylon is fallen (18:2), Death and Hades are cast into the lake of fire (20:14); the 144,000 are sealed (7:4). The vision of the apocalypticist is a certain reality.

Exclusivism: Revelation, like other apocalyptic literature, was written to encourage the faithful during a time of testing. Believers are to separate themselves from all that is evil or worldly, reject the pursuits of unbelieving society, and isolate themselves from corrupting influences. The letters to the churches (chapter 2 and 3) are full of calls for "love and faith and service and patient endurance" (2:19); but the letters also demand repentance (2:16), complain about tolerance (2:20), call on the community to "wake up" (3:3), and seek to "reprove and discipline" (3:19).

Universality: The book of Revelation, along with other apocalyptic writings, holds to a vision far broader than that of the Old Testament. The concern is no longer just one people (Israel) and those nations with whom that people has contact. In apocalyptic, the whole world is the stage. All nations and peoples, all beings and realms, all heaven and earth take part in a great conflict between good and evil, the end of which is certain—the victory of God and the arrival of a new heaven and earth. But the end of the New Testament, the story of a particular people (Israel) and a particular person (Jesus) has become a story impacting all people, nations, and more!

In a sense, apocalyptic writers are heirs of the Old Testament prophets. Revelation calls itself a prophecy (1:3). Active during the monarchy (1000–587 B.C.) and the Babylonian captivity (587–538), the prophets warned of coming judgment but also held out hope for a new future. They used visionary language of the coming conflict (Joel 1) but also looked for a new and majestic city of the Lord (Isaiah 60). Symbolism and allegory were richly employed by some (Ezekiel and Daniel). But the prophetic movement faded in the post-exilic period. Many Jews were scattered among the nations and the spread of Hellenism brought new cultural challenges. Unlike the prophets who spoke to Israel words of warning when times were good and words of hope when times were bad, apocalyptic writers faced new challenges in a larger world.

Apocalyptic writers first appear among the Jews in the three centuries before Christ. These pseudonymous works are attributed to long-dead heroes such as Moses, Enoch, or Ezra and take their stylistic cue from prophets like Ezekiel and Daniel, who wrote during Israel's darkest times. During the persecution of Jewish religion by Antiochus IV (176–164 B.C.), *I Enoch* uses apocalyptic symbolism to portray final judgment and a predetermined history according to a pattern of weeks. Turmoil among Jewish sects during the Hasmonean period (142–37 B.C.) caused the Dead Sea community to withdraw. Their War Scroll, dated to the last decades of the first century B.C., expects an end time battle between the sons of light and the sons of darkness. During the revolts against Rome at the end of the first Christian century, *IV Ezra* and *II Baruch* portray Rome as the embodiment of evil. As many as seventeen apocalypses have survived from Jewish sources. Later, Christian writers would attribute apocalypses to Peter, John, James, Thomas, and Paul.

This overview of apocalyptic characteristics and brief survey of Jewish and Christian apocalyptic literature suggests that the book of Revelation is written in a literary form as unique as a narrative or a letter, but different from both. We may detect in the text of Revelation references to historical realities, but the use of symbolism opens the possibility of applying these same referents to other places and times. What spoke to the first readers of Revelation could speak as well during later times of Christian martyrdom, to monks struggling with their evil thoughts in the deserts of Egypt, to artists and composers of the Baroque period, to Christians fleeing religious intolerance in Europe, to those today struggling with the demon of AIDS. The use of symbolism makes possible such readings.

There is also the reality that such visionary works capture the imagination like a work of art. The words appeal to the emotions, even the senses. They are not abstract concepts, nor are they mere narratives. Just as I cannot describe the ceiling of the Sistine Chapel (Michelangelo's *Last Judgment*), so attempts to find in Revelation a forecast of specific events in the millennia to follow are problematic. To do so is to read Revelation as if it were a narrative. Instead, Revelation is a work that ought to be experienced, sung (as many do in the liturgy), and cherished for the hope it offers.

Author, Audience, and Date

John, who identifies himself as a "servant" of Jesus Christ (1:1), mentions his name four times in the work (1:1, 4, 9; 22:8). But which John is he? The first John we met in the New Testament was John the Baptist. The book of Revelation has themes we heard in the preaching of John—Jesus as the Lamb, the coming in judgment, the baptism of fire. But the developed Christianity suggested by the work comes decades after the execution of John the Baptist.

A second candidate would be John the son of Zebedee, one of the twelve disciples. Some church traditions from the late second century make that identification. But the author calls himself a servant, not an apostle. In the vision of the new Jerusalem, the names of the twelve apostles are on the foundation walls

(21:14). By so wording the description, John seems to speak of them as a group distinct from himself.

A third candidate might be the "the disciple whom Jesus loved," the author of the Fourth Gospel (John 21:24). Already in the third century Dionysius of Alexander concluded that the John of Revelation was not the author of the Fourth Gospel. The language, style, and thought patterns are too different. There are points of contact between the two works—the Lamb, living water, light, "I am" statements, conflict with Satan, and so forth. But these parallels better suggest that the author of Revelation was familiar with Johannine traditions.

Church historian Eusebius (c. 260–c. 340) gives us a fourth candidate. In his *Ecclesiastical History*, Eusebius attributes Revelation to John the Elder, an official of the church at Ephesus in the late first century (3.39.1–11). But nothing else is known of this "elder." Interestingly, the author of 2 and 3 John calls himself "the elder."

These are the known possibilities. The John of Revelation could be an unknown John, or it is even possible that "John" is a codename, as Revelation often uses symbols and codes. Apocalyptic writings were often pseudonymous.

From the book of Revelation, we do know that John was exiled on the island of Patmos (Revelation 1:9); he was a seer of visions (1:10–11); he situated his work in the prophetic tradition (1:3; 22:18); and he was familiar with the community life of churches in cities surrounding Ephesus (chapters 2–3). The Greek of Revelation is of poor quality, confusing—even confounding—in its grammar. By contrast, the Greek of the Fourth Gospel is simple, but grammatically correct. For the John of Revelation, Greek was a second language.

The John of Revelation wrote at a time of significant pressure on the Christian community. Placing a date on that time of writing may bring us closer to the author and his life situation.

In the earlier discussion of 1 Peter, we mentioned the letter of Pliny the Younger, a Roman governor, to Emperor Trajan. In it, Pliny detailed his punishment of accused Christians in the province of Bithynia, north and west of the region addressed by John of Revelation. Pliny's letter comes from A.D.112. Revelation likely comes from an earlier time, for when Ignatius wrote to the same churches around A.D. 110, they had bishops. But John of Revelation only mentions elders (4:4). Other internal hints may bring us closer.

Domitian

Revelation 17:9–10 mentions five dead kings. If the count begins with Julius Caesar, then Claudius would be the fifth, and Revelation would come from the time of Nero, especially the years after the fire leading up to his death in A.D. 68. However, if the number of the mortally-wounded beast (666) is the total of the Hebrew consonants transliterating the Greek form of Nero Caesar (13:18), then the timeframe is later. If we count the emperors from Augustus, Nero is the fifth. If we skip the minor emperors in A.D. 68–69, the eighth king would be Domitian, whom Revelation suggests is still alive (17:11). Admittedly, either reconstruction pushes the symbolism to an exactitude that we have earlier suggested is problematic. But the internal hints do allow plausible dates for Revelation in the late sixties or the eighties and nineties of the first century.

Of the two possibilities, the time of Domitian (ruled 81–96) seems more plausible. Ancient sources depict Domitian as a severe ruler. He accepted the divine honors of the imperial cult and was suspicious of new sects. In such a context, Christians who refused to honor the Graeco-Roman gods or the deified emperor were considered unpatriotic. Some Romans feared the refusal of the Christians would bring down the wrath of the gods on the local community. Outbreaks against Christians and in support of Domitian could provide the context for Revelation. However, we have little objective data of actual persecution in his time.

John of Revelation seems to be writing in the last decades of the first century to Christians under local pressure or persecution. The seven churches named in chapters two and three are in the Roman province of Asia, the capital of which was Ephesus. The origin of these churches is unclear, although the lengthy work of Paul at Ephesus likely had a regional impact. The churches reflect a range of consistency in the practice of the faith. It is to encourage them that John of Revelation writes.

Theme and Structure

Early in the work, John of Revelation reports the instruction to "write therefore the things you have seen" (1:19). John sees himself as a conduit for a heavenly message; he is a prophet. As with those whose tradition he claims, John addresses the people of God with a call to persistent faithfulness. The letters to the churches are revealing. Some, such as Laodicea and Sardis, are warned harshly. Others, such as Ephesus and Thyatira, are praised but also charged to be more consistent. But the goal of the work seems to be crystallized in the letter to the church at Smyrna, "Be faithful unto death and I will give you the crown of life" (2:10).

The letters, the visions, the symbolic portrayals, even the apocalyptic literary form work together to one end. John of Revelation is concerned about the present crisis—the threatened and real affliction faced by the Christian communities. His visions call for faithfulness in these times of trial because one reality is certain. The outcome is predetermined. God will give to the faithful the victory, the crown of life. Persistent faithfulness is not only the best response to the present uncertainty but is also empowered by a clear vision of the future reality. At this basic thematic level the message of Revelation holds out hope for Christians in all sorts of circumstances. The significance of the mark of the beast may pass us by, but the certain defeat of the dragon and all its beastly cohorts can be a word of assurance in contemporary circumstances that seem to overmaster us. When life spins out of control—a problematic experience for most of us, when the demons and beasts of whatever sort seem to run wild, we, too, can hear and respond to the call for greater faithfulness, for we have that same certain promise, "I will give you the crown of life."

As a writing having more in common with a work of art than a logical treatise, we best be careful as we approach descriptions of the structure of the work. Revelation does not always proceed in a logical order, nor does it offer a symmetrical presentation. Instead, sections flow from one to another, sometimes after completing a sequence, sometimes after transforming one sequence into another. As a result, there are several ways Revelation can be outlined. One outline focuses on transitions in the visions. The seven letters to the churches are the result of the vision of the Son of Man (1:9–3:22). A second vision begins with an open door leading to the throne of heaven and the opening of seven seals (4:1–7:17). The opening of the seventh seal starts the sequence of the seven trumpets (8:1–11:19). Following the seventh trumpet the temple in heaven is opened and a sign appears: a woman clothed with the sun and pursued by the dragon. The escape of the woman and her child is the occasion for two other beasts to arise, the dragon and the beasts forming an unholy trinity (12:1–14:20). Another sign of seven angels with seven bowls announces the outpouring of God's wrath (15:1–16:21). Because of that outpouring, the fate of Babylon is revealed (17:1–19:10). Lastly, heaven opens to judgment and renewal (19:11–22:5).

We who have been brought up in the west have been taught by our culture to think in linear fashion. For example, throughout this textbook each chapter has followed a logical sequence. When we treat a book from the New Testament, we first talk about authorship and form, then representative content, and finally the book's presentation of Jesus. Point one leads to point two; point two leads to point three. Those of you who write papers will often outline the argument first: introduction, thesis, supporting arguments, and conclusion. We are so conditioned to think in this fashion that we logically read the sections of Revelation presented above as if they follow each other sequentially if not chronologically. Many readers therefore assume that the events of the seven seals (chapter 6) precede in time the events of the seven bowls (chapter 16).

A different way of reading Revelation is explained by the following story. If I were to buy a shirt in a department story in America, I would enter the store, rifle through the shelves, find a suitable item, try it on, check the price ($25), and then pay for it at the counter—a linear transaction. But if I were to shop for the same shirt in the markets of the old city of Jerusalem, I would enter a shop and choose a shirt as before. But, the shirt would have no price on it. I would have to ask the shopkeeper its cost. Then the process of bargaining would start. He would offer me a "very special deal" on the shirt for $45. I would protest that the price is way too high and offer $15. We would go back and forth for several minutes. I might even leave the stall because the price is too high, and he would follow after me with another offer. After we had gone round and round, we would probably settle on $25—the same price I would pay in an American store! The difference in method is important. The transaction in America is linear. The transaction in Jerusalem is spiral in form.

In the same way, Revelation presents its argument is a spiral form. The second vision (chapters 4–7) starts before the throne of God, seven seals are opened portraying the horrors to come, and then the vision ends with the faithful robed in white standing before the Lamb in heaven. In the same way, the third vision (chapters 8–11) begins before the throne of God, seven trumpets herald the horrors to come, and when the second woe has passed the vision ends with the elders before the throne of God. In Revelation, each of the first four visions recapitulates the previous one, and the final three vision work together as a larger recapitulation of what has been presented before. Just like a shopper and a shopkeeper bargaining over a price, Revelation goes round and round its basic message to restate its point: the present circumstances are bad and will get much worse, but in the end the faithful will see for themselves the victorious Lamb on the throne. Revelation spirals between the glory of heaven and the trouble on earth, ending with a new heaven and earth. Or to put it another way, "Be faithful until death, and I will give you a crown of life" (2:10).

REVELATION	
PROLOGUE AND SALUTATION	1:1–8
SEVEN LETTERS	1:9–3:22

SEVEN SEALS	4:1–7:17
SEVEN TRUMPETS	8:1–11:19
ANTI-TRINITY AND CHRIST	12:1–14:20
SEVEN BOWLS	15:1–16:21
FATE OF BABYLON	17:1–19:10
JUDGMENT AND RENEWAL	19:11-22:5
EPILOGUE	22:6–21

Key Texts

1:7–8 After a greeting with Trinitarian and baptismal overtones (1:4–5), John of Revelation asserts the fundamental thesis on the basis of which his readers can have hope and persevere in the present trying circumstances: "Behold, he is coming with the clouds" (1:7). The joyful expectation of the first Christians (1 Thessalonians 4:13–18; Acts 1:11) becomes the critical point of reversal. Those who pierced Jesus (John 19:31–37) and all the tribes of the earth who oppress Christian communities will lament. Their present position of seeming power over the Christian community will become one of a people conquered and carried off. The reversal will be complete.

To affirm this future reality, the voice of the Lord God breaks into the account. In keeping with verse four, the one speaking is the Father. He authenticates the Son who comes to judge (John 5:37). The language is reminiscent of God's self revelation to Moses at Sinai, "I am the One who is" (Exodus 3:14). To these familiar words, references to God's eternity and power are added. "I am the Alpha and the Omega" (Revelation 1:8) invokes the first and last letters of the Greek alphabet, even as rabbis would later use the first and last letters of the Hebrew alphabet to stand for God's visible presence with the people. The pair of letters appear again in Revelation 21:6 in speaking of the Father and in 22:13 where they are applied to Jesus. The adjective "almighty" is used nine times in Revelation and only once elsewhere in the New Testament (2 Corinthians 6:18). In the Byzantine centuries (fourth through seventh), Christians would often mark their graves with the alpha and omega and in their churches would depict Jesus as the enthroned and almighty emperor of heaven.

1:12–16 While in the spirit on the Lord's day (Sunday was already the day of worship for Christians, Acts 20:7), John of Revelation is instructed by a voice to write (Revelation 1:10). The voice comes from "one like a son of man" (1:13). Although Jesus had often talked about himself as the Son of Man, the text here seems to invoke the son of man of Daniel 7:13 and well as the Ancient of Days in Daniel 7:9. As it is a visionary scene using metaphorical language ("like"), we should not be surprised that descriptions and symbols blend and flow together, just as they do in our own dreams. The golden lamp stands recall a description of the temple (Exodus 25:37) even as the robe worn by the "one like a son of man" is that of a priest. The seven stars held in his hand (Revelation 1:16) may allude to the seven churches to whom John writes, but they may also be a regal symbolism, like the golden sash. Both Biblical and imperial imagery merge in the description of the one who speaks. In subsequent verses the speaker identifies himself as Jesus (1:18), but his appearance is that of the mighty judge of all, superior to any heavenly or earthly power. For desperate Christians to get a message from such a figure is to assure them of their final victory, even if the present times are horrible.

2:8–11 In the subsequent letters to the churches, the theme of Revelation is annunciated: a call to faithful perseverance even in the face of demonic opposition. The letter to the church at Smyrna is typical. The words of the letter come from the one who is "the first and the last" (2:8), recalling the earlier use of Alpha and Omega. But the one who speaks is also the "one who died and came to life" (2:8). It is a message from the one who is Father, Son, and Spirit (2:11). The message recognizes present challenges: "tribulation," "poverty," and "slander" (2:9). But the message also warns that matters will get worse—imprisonment and tribulation. Opponents seem to be Jews, but the message claims that Satan is in reality the one at work. As bad as matters seem, they are limited (only "ten days," although the number is probably symbolic).

Since the troubles are limited by God and since a "crown of life is promised," those facing difficulties at Smyrna can be "faithful unto death" (2:10). Whether the endurance is through the course of a long life or in the midst of horrors that lead to violent death, the crown is assured. Faithful endurance is possible because of the promise that limits are set on what might happen and because the victory is sure. This basic theme is treated repeatedly in Revelation. The elders around the throne have crowns on their heads (4:4), having persevered to the end. The woman clothed with the sun has a crown of twelve stars on her head (12:1), and will be given wings to escape the dragon forever (12:14). Even the one like the son of man wore a golden crown (14:14), for he had died and came to life.

2:12–17 The letters to the churches are a first-level attempt to address a call to faithfulness. The letters seems to allude to actual circumstances as part of their appeal, even as Revelation becomes more symbolic, as it recapitulates its theme through the cycle of visions. But even at this first level, many allusions are obscure. In the letter to Pergamum, reference is made to two groups: those who hold the teaching of Balaam and those who hold the teaching of the Nicolaitans. To the first reader, mention of such group applied the message to their specific circumstance. We, however,

Altar of Zeus at Pergamum (model)

are in the dark about either of these references. The reference to Pergamum as the place "where Satan's throne is" may sound obscure, but archaeology gives us two possibilities. There was a magnificent altar to Zeus on the acropolis, a hill eight hundred feet above the city. The frieze depicts the battle between the gods and giants. A second possibility is a temple to the godhead of Caesar built in 29 B.C in honor of Augustus. Revelation's identification of Rome with the working of Satan makes the second plausible.

4:6b–8 Following the letters to the churches, John of Revelation leaves behind the particular circumstances in the Roman province of Asia. Through a "door standing open in heaven" he is shown "what must take place after this" (4:1). John is ushered into the throne room of heaven and attempts to describe the one seated on the throne. Following the example of Ezekiel 1:26–28, John uses descriptions of precious gems to depict God rather than human features (Revelation 4:3). The throne is surrounded by twenty-four elders, seven torches of fire, and four living (literally "composite") creatures. Their six wings bring to mind the vision of heavenly seraphim by Isaiah (6:2) and cherubim by Ezekiel (1:15–21; 10:9–22). Isaiah's vision mentions no faces; in John's vision each has one face; in Ezekiel each has four faces. The heavenly scene had is counterpart in the Mosaic tabernacle where two cherubim faced each other on the lid of the ark (Exodus 25:17–22). We ought not be distracted by the chubby cherubs of European art or the movie portrayal in *Raiders of the Lost Ark*. The living creatures of Revelation are bizarre and frightening, all-seeing (covered with eyes), meant to inspire the fear of God. The heavenly court is a world far different from Roman Asia, and yet the two are linked in "what must take place after this."

The four creatures lead the heavenly praise of God with a threefold "holy" (as in Isaiah 6:3) and recall language used for God in the opening verses of the book ("who was and is and is to come"; 1:4; 4:8). Most of the heavenly scenes in Revelation involve the worship of God and the Lamb. Much of the imagery is drawn from the temple in Jerusalem. The altar, the gold lamp stand, the ark, the smoke, the incense, and the use of psalmody would be familiar to those who had been in Jerusalem or were versed in the texts of the Old Testament. But it is also possible that Revelation invokes practices of the early Christian community. John sees his vision on the Lord's day (1:10), on the day when Christians assembled to worship. Frequent references to the faithful clothed in white (3:5, 18; 4:4; 6:11; 7:13; 19:14) might recall the Christian practice documented from later times of clothing the newly baptized in white. The "marriage supper of the Lamb" (19:9) may be called to mind by early Christian communal meals (Acts 2:42) that included what we now call Holy Communion. The many hymns of Revelation are not surprising, in view of early practice of hymn singing (Acts 16:25; Ephesians 5:19; Colossians 3:16). And *1 Clement* 34:6–7 urges Christians to praise God even as the hosts of heaven sing the threefold "holy." If events in heaven and on earth are linked, then the worship of Christians on earth is joined with all around the heavenly throne. In describing the heavenly throne, John portrays what happened with ritual actions with which the community would be familiar from their own worship. The linkage of earthly and heavenly praise is at the center of Christian liturgical worship even today ("Therefore with angels and archangels and all the company of heaven, we laud and magnify your glorious name, evermore praising you …"; *Lutheran Worship*, pp. 146–148).

5:1–14 In a second scene of the vision, the one seated on the throne has a scroll with seven seals. The scroll is most important for the readers who with John want to see "what must take place after this." But none was worthy to open the scroll and break its seals. John of Revelation begins to weep, for the purpose of the vision (and the writing of the book) seems thwarted. How could John now bring comfort readers in trying times? But first an elder and then John himself behold the one who can open the scroll: the Lion of the tribe of Judah, the root of David, the Lamb standing as though it had been slain (5:5–6). Metaphors mix in paradoxical fashion—a reminder of how meager are human words when it comes to the mystery, majesty, and mercy of God. As God was "worthy" (4:11), so the Lamb is "worthy" (5:9)—the former because he created all things (4:11) and the latter because he "ransomed a people for God from every tribe and language and people and nation" (5:9). Such praise would come to find expression in the creeds and hymnody of the church. The repeated "worthy" and "amen" (5:12, 14) would inspire one of the final choruses of Handel's *Messiah* and well as the contemporary Christian artists such as Cindy Diane, Richard Smallwood, Michael W. Smith, and James Ingram.

6:1–8 As the first four seals are opened, John sees the coming of four riders on white, red, black, and pale horses. These horsemen are featured in the woodcuts of German artist Albrecht Dürer (1472–1528), have been equated with political leaders from Hitler to Napoleon to Washington, have been identified with economic disasters, and have even been seen in modern diseases such as AIDS, influenza, SARS, and Ebola. Against such speculations, John of Revelation calls on the standard apocalyptic used even by Jesus (Matthew 24–25; Mark 13).

At the opening of the first seal, the rider on the white horse receives a crown and comes out conquering. To our culture, this description sounds like a hero. In Israel, the crown was a designation of a king in the line of David; the rider on the white horse is a messianic figure. But in Jesus' apocalyptic speech, he warns against false messiahs (they look like good guys), but they lead people astray (Matthew 24:5). Therefore, the rider on the white horse is an anti-hero and one to be feared as much as the other three riders.

The parallelism continues with the opening of the second seal. The rider of the red horse takes peace from the earth; people slay each other. The speech of Jesus continues: " And you will hear of wars and rumors of wars. See that you are not alarmed, for this must take place, but the end is not yet. For nation will rise against nation, and kingdom against kingdom" (Matthew 24:6–7).

When the third seal is opened, the rider on the black horse comes with scales. From the middle of the living creatures, someone cries out, "A quart of wheat for a **denarius**, and three quarts of barley for a denarius, and do not harm the oil and wine" (Revelation 6:6). Apparently, the price is being fixed to prevent the price gouging that occurs when supplies are suddenly short, as after a natural disaster or earthquake. In the next phrase of his speech in Matthew, Jesus warns, "And there will be famines and earthquakes in various places" (Matthew 24:7).

The fourth seal marks the arrival of the pale horse. "Its rider's name is Death and Hades followed him" (Revelation 6:8). Jesus continues in Matthew, "Then they will deliver you up to tribulation and put you to death" (Matthew 24:9). A few verses later, Jesus adds, "But the one who endures to the end will be saved" (Matthew 24:13).

The four horsemen of the apocalypse are characters used by John to speak a warning about the end which is identical in sequence and tone to the warning Jesus gave his disciples just before his passion. But Jesus and John did so with a common intent—to encourage faithfulness to the end, for that is when salvation is revealed.

7:4–17 Chapter 7 interrupts the opening of the seals. Disaster is held back until the "servants of our God" are sealed (7:3). The message of the book repeats to the reader that the horrors they face are limited by God. The faithful will be sealed. Two descriptions are given of the faithful. In the first they are the 144,000 from the tribes of Israel (7:4–8). In the second, they are a great multitude from every nation that has come out of the great tribulation (7:9, 14). Since apocalyptic uses numerical symbolism, the number 144,000 is likely another way of saying a great multitude, for it involves multiples of twelve (the number of the tribes of Israel and of the first apostles) and numbers suggesting perfection such as three, seven (creation), and ten. The descriptions are of the same group—the faithful in heaven. It is a continuation of the historic Israel (144,000) and yet embraces the whole world. A great multitude is on earth waiting to be sealed even as a great multitude stands before the Lamb in heaven. The community of the faithful is earthly and heavenly, militant and triumphant.

While most heavenly scenes in Revelation focus on God and the Lamb, this scene concludes with language detailing the future state of the oppressed faithful. In hymnic language the full reversal of their present state announced. "He who sits upon the throne will shelter them with his presence" (7:15). Literally, he will "pitch his tent" among them. It is an intimate picture of family life together, recalling the lifestyle of the patriarch Abraham. But it also remembers and is made possible by the incarnation of Jesus, the one who "pitched his tent among us" (John 1:14).

"They shall hunger no more, neither thirst anymore; the sun shall not strike them, nor any scorching heat" (Revelation 7:16). Persecution experienced by the Christian communities is compared to the oppression of the children of Israel in Egypt and their difficult wandering in the wilderness. Just as God provided for the people then, so the faithful would be rescued and saved.

"For the Lamb … will be their shepherd, and he will guide them to springs of living water" (7:17). Echoing the famous psalm of David (Psalm 23), the scene culminates with the Lamb as Shepherd (visions do mix metaphors!). The Jesus who spoke of himself as the Good Shepherd (John 10:11–14) would fulfill the prophecy of Ezekiel (34:11–16). The faithful would be led to waters of life

(Genesis 2:10; Revelation 22:1). Weeping would be turned to joy (Psalm 126:5; Isaiah 25:8).

The heavenly interlude of chapter seven, prepares the readers for whatever may come when the seventh seal is opened. It continues to be a Christian practice to recall the sweet promises of God, the depictions of heaven, and the comforting presence of Jesus at those times when we Christians face crisis or loss.

8:1–9:10 With the opening of the seventh seal, the vision again spirals around its topic as seven angels blow seven trumpets. At each trumpet blast, disaster strikes. The first five blasts are called the first woe, with two woes to follow (9:12). Each disaster in this sequence we would classify as natural. But in the visionary world of John of Revelation, heaven and earth are one. The natural, the supernatural, and that caused by people are also one. But how could these horrid descriptions encourage readers who are facing violent political pressure?

In each case of natural calamity the results, bad as they are, have distinct limits. Only a third of the land is destroyed when the first trumpet blows. Only a third of the sea, a third of the waters, and a third of the heavenly lights are struck. Even the locusts, feared from ancient times (Joel 1), have limits placed on them (Revelation 9:4–5).

For the first readers in their difficult straights, John of Revelation uncovers what must take place. Yes, circumstances are bad and will get worse. Even more is involved than local political and religious opposition. Heaven and earth are joined in a cosmic struggle. But clear limits have been placed on destructive and demonic forces. Not all will be lost, and in the end the faithful will stand in the presence of the one seated on the throne and of the Lamb. So, believers can be faithful until death, knowing what must take place.

12:1–12 With the blowing of the seventh trumpet and the opening of God's temple in heaven, the vision of John of Revelation begins another cycle, another recapitulation of what must take place. In place of metaphors drawn from the natural world, this vision brings into play cosmic entities—dragons, angels, and a woman clothed with the sun.

In Genesis 3:15, God speaks a curse on the serpent for leading Eve into rebellion. That curse involves not on the serpent, but also the woman and her offspring. The curse on the woman would bring agony in childbirth (Genesis 3:16). These themes that mark the beginning of the struggle between good and evil recur in Revelation 12.

The woman is clothed with the sun, with the moon under her feet and a crown of twelve stars. The same celestial references appear in Joseph's dream as symbols for Jacob and his family. This woman is symbolic for the people of God (Israel and the church), for it is from the people of God that the Messiah was born. Memories of Mary the mother of Jesus may also be part of the metaphor. The pains of birth are a symbol Jesus uses when discussing his upcoming death with his disciples (John 16:20–22).

Opposing the woman and her child are a great red dragon with seven heads and ten horns. In Revelation 5, the Lamb has seven horns and seven eyes, symbolic of his power and authority. A multi-headed dragon wearing crowns and having ten horns would seem to be a most powerful opponent, even as John's readers likely trembled before those who opposed them. But in the vision, when this powerful dragon attacks, the child is caught up to God, the woman escapes to the wilderness, and the angel Michael defeats the dragon—called the devil and Satan—and casts it down to the earth. There the dragon will lash out, but "his time is short" (12:12). As with earlier cycles, John's vision repeats its encouraging word: "Now the salvation and the power and the kingdom of our God and the authority of his Christ have come, for the accuser of our brothers has been thrown down … And they have conquered him by the blood of the Lamb and by the word of their testimony, for they loved not their lives even unto death" (12:10–11).

14:6–7 Throughout this reading of Revelation, we have been suggesting that the work cycles repeatedly around the same topic. The key to Revelation is to recognize this cyclic form. Often, however, Revelation is read as a linear map to the future. Interpreters overlay its visions onto the history of the church or world and try to equate its scenes with moments in that history. One example is the identification of Martin Luther with the angel "with an eternal gospel to proclaim" (14:6). In some Lutheran lectionaries, Revelation 14 is read on the Festival of the Reformation. If we read Revelation on its own terms as an apocalyptic work that spirals again and again around its topic, such a direct identification is problematic. On the other hand, Luther's articulation of the gospel in the face of strong opposition and the threat of death is consistent with the message of Revelation. Luther was attempting to proclaim in his age the same message John of Revelation brought to his readers. In this way, Luther and the angel "with an eternal gospel to proclaim" share a common voice: "Fear God and give him glory, because the hour of his judgment has come" (14:7).

15:5–16:1 At the beginning of chapter 15, John sees "another sign in the heaven, great and amazing" (15:1). The message through which the book has cycled in the four previous visions is repeated one last time, but this time it is stretched over three visions: the pouring out of the seven bowls, the judgment of Babylon, and the new Jerusalem.

In the opening vision of this cycle, seven angels are given seven golden bowls full of the wrath of God. It is part of the holiness and justice of God to execute wrath (16:5–7), a concepts with which many contemporary Christian are uncomfortable. We prefer a Precious Moments™ God to a God who will pour out his wrath. But according to John's vision, this too must take place. The plagues poured out from the bowls of God's wrath (chapter 16) have marked similarities to the plagues poured out on Egypt before the Exodus (Exodus 7:14–12:32).

17:1–18 The judgment of the great prostitute and the beast flow from the outpouring of God's wrath. The Harlot, the beast, and Babylon are multiple symbolic representations of the opponents of the Christian community. In chapters seventeen and eighteen, they are identified with Rome and its power, although some specific allusions are difficult to pin down. In 17:9–11, the angel provides some clarity. "The seven heads are seven mountains" (17:9). The city of Rome sits on seven hills. The kings (17:10) are likely the major emperors from Augustus through Domitian.

Imperial Rome is characterized by sexual immorality (17:2–4; compare Romans 1:24–27). Presenting Rome as a prostitute has prophetic parallels in the treatment of Mesopotamian Babylon in Isaiah (47) and Jeremiah (50–51). Ezekiel, too, employed the language of harlotry in his condemnations (Ezekiel 16; 23; 26–27). But Rome has committed a greater crime: "And I saw the woman, drunk with the blood of the saints, the blood of the martyrs of Jesus" (Revelation 17:6). The vision of John of Revelation stands in stark contrast to that of Paul in Romans. Although both writers condemned the immorality of the Roman imperial court, Paul writes that "there is no authority except from God, and those that exist have been instituted by God" (Romans 13:1). In Paul's view the Christian ought submit to Roman authority for "he is the servant of God" (13:4). For John of Revelation, the fall of this Babylon (Revelation 18:2) is worthy of shouts of "Hallelujah" (19:1). This diversity of perspective on governing powers presented by these two New Testament books suggests to us contemporary readers that blind obedience to government is as problematic as open rebellion. Government can serve God and the devil. When it strikes out against the faithful, it is clearly doing the latter and stands under the judgment of God.

18:1–5 The fall of Rome, symbolically called Babylon, is announced as an already accomplished fact. To those under the heel of that oppressive government, these words announce the predetermined future. The time of oppression is short. It is as if Babylon has already fallen.

As a consequence of this certain future, the faithful are exhorted to "come out of her, my people" (18:5). The call to faithful perseverance, repeated in each cycle of Revelation, is a call to separate, to withdraw from, and not to take part in the practices of the corrupt society. For John of Revelation, the threat to the community is so great that such separation is a necessary part of faithfulness. Of greater challenge is the application of this instruction in other contexts. Throughout the history of Christianity, some have withdrawn from the world while others have attempted to set up utopian societies apart from the world. Some seek to transform the larger society; others compartmentalize their religious life from their daily life. This challenge is particularly difficult in a contemporary context such as America, which provides a relatively safe environment for the practice of Christianity. At the same time, this society moves in a more secular direction and imposes societal pressures counter to basic tenets of Christianity. When opposition is violent, withdrawal is a clear path to pursue. When opposition is subtle, the challenge is in some ways greater.

19:6–8 While reading through these concluding sections of Revelation, it is helpful to recall that three visions (15:1 to the end of the work) recapitulate earlier material: difficult days will come, but there will be an end, and the faithful will live in God's eternal kingdom. Through repeated use of metaphor and symbolism, John of Revelation makes this point. One of the metaphors to which John turns is marriage. Shouts of "Hallelujah" peal across the heavens because, "the marriage of the Lamb has come, and his bride has made herself ready" (19:7). Again, mixed metaphors (other than in farces such as *A Midsummer Night's Dream*, animals do not marry human beings) attempt to put into words the inexpressible. By speaking of marriage, John of Revelation calls to the minds of his readers an ancient biblical tradition.

Best known is the prophetic work of Hosea. God is a faithful husband to his people. Israel is an unfaithful wife. But as Hosea welcomed home his unfaithful wife, God will betroth himself to his people forever (Hosea 2:19–20). Isaiah speaks of the Lord as the "husband" of his people (Isaiah 54:5), and in Ezekiel God marries the people (Ezekiel 16:8). Paul would speak of the church as a woman set aside for her one husband (2 Corinthians 11:2) and would point to the marriage of Christ and the church as the exemplar for Christian marriage (Ephesians 5:21–33). Even Jesus talked about himself as the "bridegroom" (Mark 2:19).

To comfort his readers when pressure and persecution seemed to isolate them, John of Revelation uses the metaphor of marriage. It is a metaphor to which John would return, as he paints the final heavenly scene (Revelation 21:2, 9). In our contemporary culture, faithfulness is no longer a characteristic of most marriages, and so the impact of this metaphor might escape us. But in ancient cultures, the responsibilities of marriage were so important that extended families were involved. Marriage was not a mere contract between two people. Faithfulness was acculturated and supported by society. The faithfulness of marriage would be a reassuring metaphor.

20:1–10 As one more way of depicting the ultimate victory of God and the Lamb, John of Revelation sees a final battle scene. Many earthly and cosmic conflicts have already been described in earlier visions, so we ought expect in this occurrence similar themes. This vision has two stages. In the first stage, Satan is bound for a thousand years while the faithful are raised and reign with Christ. In the second stage, Satan is released and gathers all the nations (called God and Magog) for a final battle against the saints and the beloved city. But fire comes down from heaven to defeat the devil and its minions. By presenting the conflict in two stages—a peaceful period followed by a horrid battle—John's vision intensifies the call to faithfulness until death in view of the certain crown of life. The point made repeatedly before is restated with greater intensity here.

In the midst of this final battle scene, John says of the faithful, "They came to life and reigned with Christ for a thousand years" (20:4). From a literal reading of this one obscure reference, many in the history of the church and even today predict and speculate about a thousand year reign of Christ on earth. This teaching is called millenarianism. But, when apocalyptic writings speculate about the reign of the Messiah, the time span of Revelation is but one of many. *I Enoch* 91:12–17 divides history up into ten periods (weeks of years). The eighth period is one of righteousness (parallel to the thousand-year reign of Christ); the ninth is a period of destruction (like the final battle with God and Magog in Revelation); and the tenth is the period of judgment and renewal (comparable to Revelation 20:11–22:5). According to *IV Ezra* 7:28, after a period of evil, the Messiah and the faithful will reign on earth for four hundred years before the resurrection. In the reckoning of the Christian *Ascension of Isaiah*, after Beliar (an antichrist) has ruled for 1,332 days, the Lord and his saint and angels will come. They will cast Beliar into Gehenna (another name for hell). Then there will be a period of rest on earth. Later will come the resurrection.

Such variety in detail strongly suggests that any literal reading of the dates is not the intent of the material. Instead, affirming the reign of the Messiah (be it for a period of weeks, four hundred years, or a thousand years) is one of many ways of symbolizing the final victory of God over those forces of evil so seeming strong in the present moment. By going at his topic again and again with different cycles and symbols, John of Revelation works like an artist piling up textures and colors to make a powerful impression. As he has said so often before, horrors are yet to come, but God's victory is certain.

21:1–8 To symbolize the end of this evil world where so much opposes the faithful, John envisions "a new heaven and a new earth, for the first heaven and the first earth had passed away, and the sea was no more" (21:1). This first symbol recalls the stories of creation from Genesis, the marvelous provision for our first parents. With a second symbol, John envisions "the holy city, new Jerusalem, coming down out of heaven from God" (21:2). All the prophetic hope centered in Jerusalem (see especially Isaiah 65–66) comes to fruition. In a third symbol, John sees the church "as a bride adorned for her husband" (21:2). The piling up of metaphors is complete—creation, nation, family. In every way, the new and ideal is announced.

A voice makes the good news most personal. God dwells with his people ("pitches his tent"; compare 7:15). God is their God; they are God's people. With similar language, Peter comforted his readers at a time of social stress (1 Peter 2:9–10). And to deal with the terrors faced by the communities, the voice from Revelation adds, "He will wipe away every tear from their eyes, and death shall be no more, neither shall there be mourning nor crying nor pain anymore, for the former things have passed away" (Revelation 21:4). If people in the community are facing imprisonment or death, if they have lost loved ones, if some have surrendered their faith to save their skins, all these and more will be passed and gone—for God makes all things new (Revelation 21:5; 2 Corinthians 5:17).

The identity of the speaking voice comes into focus, "I am the **Alpha and the Omega**" (Revelation 21:6). It is the same personal voice that broke in to John's inaugural vision (1:8). The words become metaphorical again. The tribulation experienced by the community is compared to thirst. The voice promises to "give the spring of the water of life without payment" (21:6). Water is a frequent biblical symbol of salvation (flood, Red Sea, baptism). The metaphor then shifts from nature to the family, "I will be his God and he will be my son" (21:7). The inheritance of those who are faithful is certain.

In subsequent verses, the vision continues—the bride, the new Jerusalem, and the river of life are depicted with metaphor upon symbol. It is almost as if John were driven beyond words as he attempts to capture the vision and convey its hope to his readers. Pervious chapters of horror and violence are forgotten. God's future reign and God's promise to the faithful transcend expression.

22:12–17 A final epilogue asserts the truth of what has been written. It must be kept (22:6, 8). No one dare add to or subtract from it (22:18–19). The Lord is coming soon. There will be judgment (22:12). Mixing metaphors again, John declares that those who wash their robes have the right to the tree of life (cut off from Adam after the first sin; Genesis 3:24) and the right to enter the city (Revelation 22:14). Others remain outside (22:15). To this the church adds one of its ancient prayers, "Come, Lord Jesus" (22:17; 22:20; 1 Corinthians 16:22). Words of the Coming One and prayers of those who wait echo antiphonally.

I recall the first time I visited the Sistine Chapel in the Vatican. I stood in a long line early in the morning to gain entrance to the Vatican museums. Following the advice of a friend, I by-passed every other exhibit in order to get to the chapel before the crowds. I was not disappointed. To stand in the Sistine Chapel almost alone with the breath-taking work by Michelangelo soaring above is more than words, and is itself a metaphor for the work that is its basis.

Jesus in Revelation

Since the visions of Revelation focus on "those [things] that are and those that are to take place after this" (1:19), the work describes Jesus in a different way than the rest of the New Testament. The gospels and Paul looked back on Jesus, especially his death and resurrection, and then used christological terms to describe who Jesus is and what his death and resurrection mean. We have met such terms before—Messiah, Son of God, Savior, Son of Man, Lord.

On occasion Revelation uses many these titles. *Son of God* occurs only once, where the message to the church at Thyatira conveys "the words of the Son of God" (2:18). The phrase "son of man" occurs, but not as a title. Revelation does not seem to draw on the use of the title by Jesus, but instead patterns its usage on Daniel 7 (Revelation 1:13; 14:14). *Messiah/Christ* as a title turns up seven times in the work (1:1, 2, 5; 11:15; 12:10; 20:4–6). The first three are specifically connected to Jesus. In the others, Jesus is the assumed referent. Especially in the examples from chapter twenty, the messianic role blends with the role as final judge. A messianic variant *Root of David* is used twice (5:5; 22:6). *Savior* does not occur, although three times God and the Lamb are praised for salvation "belongs" to them (7:10; 12:10; 19:1).

Besides the above scattered references, two titles occur with some frequency: *Lord* and *Lamb*. *Lord* appears twenty-two times, mostly in hymns and songs of praise. Generally *Lord* is a title for God, as in the phrase "Lord God" (1:8,

16:7; 18:8; 22:5) or "Lord God Almighty" (4:8; 11:17; 15:3; 16:7) or "Lord of lords" (17:14; 19:16). In the last two examples, the appellation is given to the Lamb. A statement that "their Lord was crucified" (11:8) gives the title *Lord* to Jesus. The placement of the vision "on the Lord's day" (1:10) likely also is an ascription of the title to Jesus.

But the title used most often for Jesus is *Lamb*. The Lamb appears among the elders "standing as if it had been slaughtered" (5:6). For this reference, Isaiah's prophecy (Isaiah 53:7) and the announcement of John the Baptist (John 1:29) provide background. Along with the "one seated on the throne," the Lamb receives the praise of the heavenly host (Revelation 5:13; 7:10; 14:4; 21:22–23; 22:3). References to the passion of Jesus surface in references to the redemptive work of the Lamb. "You were slain, and by your blood you ransomed people for God from every tribe and language and people and nation," sing those around the throne (5:9; compare 7:14; 12:11). The redemptive work of the Lamb is mentioned twice is the account of the 144,000 (14:3–4). But the primary work of the Lamb, to be expected in a work looking to the future, is to usher in the new age through judgment and renewal. The Lamb is the one worthy to break the seals (6:1). The "wrath of the Lamb" will be poured out on the last day (6:16–17). The Lamb has the book of life (13:8; 21:27). The new creation is likened to the marriage supper of the Lamb (19:7–9). The Lamb is the lamp of the new Jerusalem (21:23). God and the Lamb are viewed as one, for "the throne of God and of the Lamb will be in it, and his servants will worship him. They will see his face, and his name will be on their foreheads" (22:3–4).

Through the metaphor of the *Lamb*, prophetic anticipation and eschatological hope merge. The Jesus spoken of so eloquently by other New Testament writers is in Revelation the coming Lamb. Of this Jesus presented by Revelation "the Spirit and the Bride say, 'Come'" (22:17).

For Further Discussion

1. What new significance do you find in the Revelation for a time marked by terrorism and violence? How does Revelation offer specific hope for such a time?

2. Revelation teaches that evil (and evil people) will be destroyed. Is violence the best response to evil? Is violence a practical response? Why? Why not?

3. As strange as Revelation may seem, it has inspired much of the song of the church. Identify and discuss the use of the language of Revelation in the liturgy, hymnody, and songs of the church.

4. It is easy to understand Revelation's identification of imperial Rome with the devil. The absolute power of a dictatorship tends to corrupt leaders.

What about freely elected democratic governments? Under what circumstances might such governments be of the devil? Of God?

5. If Christians are waiting for God to intervene against evil, when should Christians themselves stand up to evil? Under what circumstances?

For Further Reading

Brighton, Lewis. *Revelation*. Concordia Commentary. St. Louis: Concordia, 1999.

Collins, John J., ed. *The Encyclopedia of Apocalypticism*. Volume 1: The Origins of Apocalypticism in Judaism and Christianity. New York: Continuum, 2000.

Hemer, Colin J. *The Letters to the Seven Churches of Asia in Their Local Setting*. Grand Rapids: Eerdmans, 1986.

Thompson, Leonard L. *The Book of Revelation: Apocalypse and Empire*. Oxford: Oxford University Press, 1990.

Jude

Antilegomena

Jude is one of seven books in the New Testament about which people have asked the question, "Does it properly belong among the canonical books?" In our discussion of the canon in chapter one, we presented the issue in some detail. Jude, along with the other six disputed books (Hebrews, James, 2 Peter, 2 John, 3 John, and Revelation), was eventually recognized as the word of God to his people and included in the New Testament. However, due to the element of uncertainty, the Orthodox Church categorized them as ***antilegomena*** (literally, "being spoken against"). This understanding agreed that no doctrine could be drawn from one of these books alone.

Jude is a good test case to examine some of the issues surrounding the antilegomena. Why would certain people have objected to including Jude in the New Testament?

- One might think it is because Jude is so short. Since it contains only twenty-five verses, Jude may have been deemed insignificant. Yet Philemon is the same length and it was accepted without question (***homolegoumena*** refers to the unchallenged books). Brevity is one reason a number of New Testament books are often neglected, but it was not and is not a legitimate reason for their exclusion.

- Questions regarding authorship might be another consideration. However, in contrast with the anonymity of Hebrews, the author of Jude clearly identifies himself in verse 1.
- The fact we do not think this Jude was one of the apostles may also be a factor (see below). Yet the lack of apostolic authorship is not a criterion that has been raised against other books; Mark, Luke, and Acts were not challenged on this basis.
- Another factor may be the manner in which the book was evaluated by various leaders in the early church. Here again, Jude is attested to quite well. The letter is referred to or quoted favorably by a number of church fathers prior to A.D. 250 (for example, Clement of Rome in A.D. 96, Clement of Alexandria, Tertullian, and Origen).

These are some of the factors involved in debating and evaluating the antilegomena. By each of these criteria, Jude ought not to have been challenged.

The main reason Jude was called into question is that the letter contains quotes from two documents which are not part of the Scriptures. Verse nine states, "But when the archangel Michael, contending with the devil, was disputing about the body of Moses, he did not presume to pronounce a blasphemous judgment, but said, 'The Lord rebuke you.'" We do know of the angel named Michael from the Old Testament book of Daniel (Daniel 10:13, 21; 12:1). The Old Testament also records the death of Moses in Deuteronomy 34. However, no record of a dispute over his body is found in the Scriptures. In all likelihood, Jude is quoting from a non-canonical document called the *Assumption of Moses*.

Later, in verses 14–15 Jude says, "It was about these that Enoch, the seventh from Adam, prophesied, saying, 'Behold, the Lord came with ten thousand of his holy ones…." This quotation is also not present in the Old Testament. Enoch is the one who "walked with God, and he was not, for God took him" (Genesis 5:24). The experiences of a person who did not die, but was taken to heaven directly by God, quite naturally produced a great deal of speculation. During the intertestamental years, a number of works were composed and attributed to Enoch (pseudepigraphy is the name for this practice). They purport to record many details of what he saw in heaven and contain his prophecies about the future.

Both of the documents quoted by Jude are grouped together with a body of other writings related to the Old Testament. They are categorized as **Pseudepigrapha**, and most date from the intertestamental period. We should view much of this literature as devotional expansions based upon the biblical texts. A similar practice has been adopted by many Christian authors whose methodology is similar to this apocryphal literature. Such works do not rise to the level of inspired Scripture. Instead, they contain a mixture of biblical truth, biblically-based conjecture, additional historical accounts, and fiction. In this case, Jude may well be using the very literature used by the false teachers he is combating as ammunition against them.

Is there a problem with Jude quoting from these non-canonical sources? Some suggest this means he mistakenly regarded them as Scripture. However, Paul quotes unbelieving, pagan poets a number of times both orally (Acts 17:28) and within his letters (1 Corinthians 15:33; Titus 1:12). His quotations from extra-biblical sources have not led people to challenge the canonicity of those other books based on the assumption that Paul regarded those poets as inspired. The same should apply to Jude.

Introduction

The author of the letter identifies himself as "Jude, a servant of Jesus Christ and the brother of James" (Jude 1). Jude is the name of one of the more obscure of the twelve disciples (Luke 6:16; Acts 1:13; not Judas Iscariot). Yet the author of this letter does not claim to be an apostle; he speaks of the apostles in the third person ("they" in verses 17–18). This Jude is apparently the half brother of Jesus mentioned, along with James (also not the disciple James), in Matthew 13:55 and Mark 6:3. Here he refers to himself as a servant of Jesus rather than his brother. This is similar to the practice of James in his letter (James 1:1) and may reflect an appropriate degree of humility. James became the leader of the Jerusalem church. Perhaps this explains why Jude identifies himself as his brother. However, we know little else about Jude.

To whom was this letter written, when, and from where? The text of the letter is silent in regard to these matters. The false teachers it attacks seem to be similar to those opposed in 2 Peter 2. There may even be a literary relationship between the two letters. Some suggest Jude borrowed from 2 Peter; others assert the borrowing went in the other direction. The former is supported by the fact that Peter speaks of the false teachers in the future tense while Jude refers to them as already present. In any event, if Peter is accepted as the author of 2 Peter, he had to have written it prior to his death around A.D. 65. This would place Jude within a similar time frame in the early to mid-60's.

If the connection with 2 Peter holds, we may have a clue regarding the recipients. 1 Peter is written to Christians in the area we know of as northern Turkey (1 Peter 1:1). 2 Peter appears to be a second letter to the same group (2 Peter 3:1). Jude's addressees could be in the same, or a similar, setting.

Structure and Theme

Jude utilizes the typical opening of New Testament letters. However, as in Galatians, the author is unwilling to proceed with a thanksgiving. Although Jude intended to write a positive letter "about our common salvation" (Jude 3), he is compelled to spend most of the body of the letter countering false teachers (4–19). His words are full of Old Testament imagery and are quite blunt. Toward the end of the letter, the author turns to exhortation. He encourages the believers to avoid false teachers, to build themselves up in the true faith, and to do good works (20–23). Instead of any closing greetings, the letter ends with a powerful doxology of praise (24–25).

Key Texts

3–4 These early verses set the tone for the letter. Instead of writing about the wondrous salvation they share, Jude must urge his readers to "contend for the faith" (3). This is because godless, false teachers have snuck in among them. This is reminiscent of Jesus who described such teachers as wolves in sheep's clothing (Matthew 7:15). The key tenets of their false doctrine are identified in verse 4. First, they assert that God's grace provides a license to indulge in immoral sensuality. Advocating such a cheap view of grace is certainly an inappropriate response. Second, whether by this type of conduct and/or through other teachings, they deny Jesus Christ.

The prominence of the Old Testament is evident from the outset. "The faith that was once for all delivered to the saints" may encompass the steadfast believers of old (Jude 3; compare Hebrews 11). In addition, the condemnation of these false teachers had also literally "been written about long before" (4). As the letter continues, more explicit Old Testament references abound. The author refers to the deliverance from Egypt (5), to Sodom and Gomorrah (7), Moses (9), Cain, Balaam, and Korah (11). The author assumes his hearers already know the events and persons, and that they are able to connect the Old Testament story with the point being made about contemporary false teachers (compare Hebrews). Along with the scriptural parallels, Jude's opponents are also described with numerous, vivid metaphors (for example, waterless clouds, fruitless trees, and wandering stars; verses 12–13).

Two items should be mentioned which are outside the specific verses considered here. First, Jude mentions the angels who "left their proper dwelling" (6; compare Revelation 12:4). These "fallen" angels are now "kept in eternal chains" until judgment day (Jude 6). This need not mean these demonic beings are completely absent from or inactive within our world; rather, it stresses that their eternal fate is sealed. This paradox is comparable to the current "place" of Satan himself who is both bound, locked, and sealed in the Abyss (Revelation 20:2–3) and also prowling "around like a roaring lion, seeking someone to devour" (1 Peter 5:8).

Second, the reference to "love feasts" in verse 12 is probably a reference to communal meals within which the Lord's Supper was shared. This was a logical practice flowing from Jesus' institution of that sacred meal during a Passover celebration (see Matthew 26:17–29; compare 1 Corinthians 11:17–34). Even there, these ungodly people are blemishes.

17–25 Jude reminds his hearers of words which were literally "spoken beforehand" by Jesus' apostles (Jude 17). The quotation which follows may be drawn from the oral proclamation of the apostles, but it may also refer to written words from 2 Peter (compare 2 Peter 2:1; 3:3). In either case, Jude reminds his hearers that false, mocking teachers who lack the Spirit and indulge their own ungodly desires are to be expected. By way of contrast, however, believers are focused upon the Triune God. They keep themselves in God's love, they await the mercy of Jesus Christ, and they pray in the Spirit (Jude 20–21). In these ways, God's people build themselves up in their most holy faith (20).

False teachers are harshly denounced and to be vigorously opposed. Yet Jude asserts that their intended victims should be treated quite differently. "Doubters" are to receive mercy (22–23); if they fall into danger, God's people are to "snatch them out of the fire" (23).

Lest the more mature believers become self-sufficient or haughty regarding their own standing in the faith, Jude's closing doxology of praise refocuses their thinking as well. It is God alone who is able to keep them from stumbling and who will present them "blameless before the presence of his glory with great joy" (24). As a result, Jude concludes most appropriately by giving God all and eternal "glory, majesty, dominion and authority" (25).

Jesus in Jude

Despite the dominant theme of rebuking false teachers, Jesus is prominent in Jude's letter. He is mentioned at least five times in twenty-five verses. Verse four describes him as "our only Master and Lord." In the next verse some manuscripts state that "the Lord" delivered his people out of Egypt. This may mean the author is pointing to the Lord Jesus as the one who acted in the Exodus. Other manuscripts more definitively declare that it was "Jesus, who saved a people out of the land of Egypt" (5). The claim that Jesus was active as "Lord" in the Old Testament, and even in the act of creation itself, is made repeatedly in the New Testament and by Jesus himself (for example, John 1:1–3; 8:58; 1 Corinthians 10:1–4; Colossians 1:16–17).

Jude also identifies Jesus as one who called and sent his apostles (Jude 17). He will also return with the mercy "that leads to eternal life" (21). Finally, God keeps his people from stumbling and presents them blameless before his throne "through Jesus Christ our Lord" (25).

For Further Discussion

1. If you had to decide, would you have included Jude in the New Testament? Why or why not? On what basis would you have made your decision? Are there other books in the New Testament which you may have excluded? Why? Is the New Testament canon still open? If so, do you think other books could or should be added to the New Testament? Why?

2. When Jude quotes from documents that are not part of the Bible, what is he saying about those documents?

For Further Reading

Bauckham, Richard. *2 Peter and Jude*. Word Biblical Commentary. Waco, TX: Word, 1983.

Green, Michael. *2 Peter and Jude*. Tyndale New Testament Commentaries. Grand Rapids: Eerdmans, 1987.

Moo, Douglas. *2 Peter and Jude*. The NIV Application Commentary. Grand Rapids: Zondervan, 1996.

6

The Writings of the New Testament: Maturing Confession

Introduction

This chapter discusses the books of the New Testament that most scholars considered to be written last. But they are not gathered here simply because of the dates when they were composed. Their placement under the theme "Maturing Confession" is due primarily to their content. Paul's letter titled "Ephesians" is an excellent summary of his teachings presented in a general and overarching manner. His letters to Timothy and Titus fit at the end of his New Testament correspondence in terms of their date. They are written to colleagues who are continuing Paul's ministry within their particular setting. In modern terms we would call Timothy and Titus ministers or pastors, which is why the letters to Timothy and Titus are called **Pastoral Epistles**. They provide a good overview of the evolving life of the church in the mid-first century that anticipates a time after the direct involvement of Paul and the other apostles. Second Timothy is especially significant in this regard because it is written by Paul as he faces his imminent death.

John's letters and his gospel are also appropriately studied here. It is generally agreed that they were written very late in the first century. More importantly, they provide an articulation of the Christian faith that is both lofty and down to earth, abstract and intensely practical, deep and yet profoundly simple all at the same time.

Chapter Outline

Ephesians
1 Timothy and Titus
2 Timothy
John
1–3 John

Ephesians

Place in the Story of the New Testament

The document we call "Ephesians" was written by Paul while he was in prison (see Ephesians 3:1; 4:1; 6:20). As with the other Prison Epistles, its setting remains a mystery. The four Captivity Letters may or may not belong together. In chapter four, we placed Colossians and Philemon within a plausible imprisonment Paul endured during his extensive stay in Ephesus on his third missionary journey. The letter to the Philippians was located during Paul's two-year house arrest in Rome recorded at the end of Acts (Acts 28:30). Paul may have written Ephesians during either of those two points in his ministry or at another time.

The content of Ephesians parallels that of Colossians, leading many scholars to suggest the two were written together (compare Ephesians 1:3–14; 3:1–6; 4:17–6:9 with Colossians 1:3–14; 1:24–2:5 and 3:1–4:1, respectively). The mention of Tychicus in Ephesians 6:12 and Colossians 4:7 is another link between the two letters. In both places Tychicus is accompanying the delivery of the letter and, as Paul's personal representative, is to inform the recipients of his current situation.

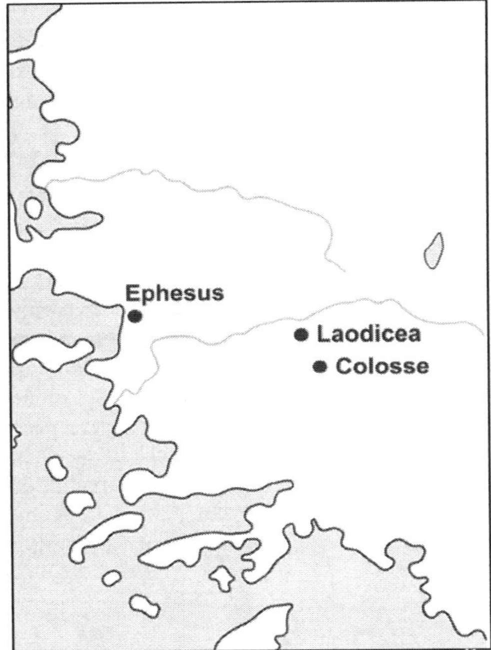

But Ephesians does not address the specific false teachings opposed in Colossians. Furthermore, Tychicus shows up in other places later in Paul's life. In Titus 3:12 Paul is contemplating sending him to Titus in Crete. He is even Paul's personal representative to Ephesus at the end of 2 Timothy (4:12). Finally, if Colossians were written from Ephesus, it is difficult to comprehend why Paul wrote a companion letter to the Ephesians from Ephesus! Ephesians 1:15 indicates Paul has (merely) heard of their faith and love. This also sounds odd in view of Paul three-year stay there. It should be noted that the address to those "in Ephesus" (1:1) is not present in some early manuscripts. If that phrase was not originally part of the letter, such problems are readily resolved. But then the destination of "Ephesians" also becomes an open question.

It is unusual that, aside from Paul himself, Tychicus is the only person mentioned by name in the entire letter (6:21). The lack of personal references in Ephesians is one reason it is so difficult to locate the place of this letter within the New Testament story. Rather than addressing a specific group of people in a particular setting, it seems to be directed toward a more widespread audience. The whole tone of the letter is also quite general. In fact, a number of scholars suggest it was a circular letter. If so, it was addressed to and intended to circulate among a number of different churches, one of which may have been the community in Ephesus (compare Revelation 1:11). As noted previously, there is textual evidence to support this theory since a number of manuscripts lack the words “in Ephesus” in 1:1. Perhaps no specific recipient was originally inserted or a number of different locations were intended. What we call “Ephesians” may even be “the letter from Laodicea” which Paul refers to in Colossians 4:16. There he asks the Colossians to obtain and read a letter he sent to the Laodiceans. They are also to share their own letter from Paul (that is, Colossians) with the believers in that neighboring town.

Many unresolved questions remain concerning the setting of “Ephesians.” It almost seems to transcend a specific set of circumstances. Yet this wider scope enables the letter to serve well as a summary of Paul’s teaching. Although Romans is usually viewed as Paul’s most general letter, Ephesians is even more adept at making broad statements with almost universal application.

Introduction

Ephesus was a great seaport city that excelled in commerce, learning, and religion. It was home to the Temple of Artemis, one of the Seven Wonders of the ancient world. For a time Ephesus was the second largest city in the Empire. However, its harbor on the Cayster River silted up to that point where Ephesus no longer had access to the Aegean Sea. That occurrence, together with earthquake damage, caused the city to be abandoned. Today its ruins are magnificently preserved.

Road to harbor from theatre at Ephesus

If Ephesians is addressed specifically to the believers in that city, an extensive amount of interaction has taken place between Paul and the recipients. His three-year stay in the city on his third missionary journey is partially described in Acts 19 and noted in Acts 20:31. Later on that same journey Paul stopped in Miletus on his way to Jerusalem. He delivered a warm farewell speech to the elders from Ephesus who met him there (Acts 20:17–38). Yet nothing specifically related to Paul’s extensive activity in Ephesus and among the Ephesians is present in this letter.

Structure and Theme

Ephesians was used in chapter four of this textbook to illustrate the basic structure of letters in the New Testament. Although chapter divisions were placed into the letter long after Paul wrote it, they divide the various sections quite well.

EPHESIANS	
OPENING	1:1–2
THANKSGIVING	1:3–22
BODY	2:1–3:21
EXHORTATION	4:1–6:20
CLOSING	6:21–24

The theme of the letter is the church, the community of God's people in Christ Jesus that is comprised of both Jews and Gentiles. Paul describes how the church came into being, what its nature is, and how it should function. Although the metaphor of "light" does not permeate the letter, Paul used it chapter five (5:8–14; compare 4:17–18). Ephesians 5:8 serves as an excellent summary of the letter's contents and also expresses the essence of Paul's theology of Law, Gospel, and response: "For at one time you were darkness, but now you are light in the Lord. Walk as children of light." In Ephesians Paul often describes what people are apart from God's action in Christ (2:1–3, 11–12; 4:17–19); "darkness" is an apt description. But then the light of Christ shines on, enlivens, and transforms them (5:14; see also 1:3–14; 2:4–9, 13–22; 4:20–24). Paul's appeal is simply for those who are "light in the Lord" to live like it; a good portion of the letter illustrates what it means to live as children of light (4:1–3; 4:25–6:9).

Imagine people lying out on a beach in complete darkness. Apart from anything they do, the sun comes out and simply shines its light upon them. Although the tendency of the sinful nature is to run off into the darkness (compare John 3:19–20), Paul urges Christ's enlightened people to stay and bask and live in the light of his love.

Key Texts

1:3–14 After his standard introduction in 1:1–2, Paul inserts a section of blessing or praise to God. This blessing leads Paul to conclude the chapter by thanking God for the work he has done within those to whom Paul writes (1:15–23). The middle section of Ephesians 1, verses 3–14, uses the word translated "predestined" twice (1:5, 11). Therefore, this is an appropriate place to comment on Paul's use of the term.

The topic of **predestination** has been and remains a controversial one in the Christian church. The key point in Ephesians 1 and throughout the New Testament is the use of the word only in relation to believers in Christ (see also Romans 8:29–30). Here Paul speaks of them in this way: "In [Christ] you also, when you heard the word of truth, the gospel of your salvation, and believed in him, were sealed with the promised Holy Spirit" (Ephesians 1:13). Believers are comforted with the knowledge that we were chosen and predestined "before the foundation of the world" (1:4). It is truly mysterious to ponder how this happened even before time began as we know it. Yet our relationship with God, even then, was not apart from Christ. God has now made "known to us the mystery of his will, according to his purpose, which he set forth in Christ as a plan for the fullness of time" (1:9). Whenever the New Testament speaks about the mystery of God's plan of salvation, it always announces that *the mystery has been revealed* in Jesus Christ. He entered our time and our world to shed his blood so that we might receive the forgiveness of sins and adoption into God's family (1:5, 7). Paul assures all those who hear and believe this good news that God predestined them to be his own even before creation; literally, God "marked us out ahead of time." In fact, "the riches of his grace which he lavished upon us" are even more bountiful; they also extend eternally into the future. The Holy Spirit, whose presence seals God's promises to us, is also "the guarantee of our inheritance until we acquire possession of it" (1:14; see also 1:11).

Affirming this profound teaching brings comfort, yet one must resist the temptation to go beyond what the New Testament says about predestination. For example, some agree that God predestined believers for salvation; however, since all people will not be saved, they conclude God must also have predestined others not to believe and, therefore, to be condemned. Double predestination is the phrase normally used to contend that God predestines some to salvation and others to damnation. Although this conclusion may seem logical and even inescapable to some, the New Testament nowhere teaches that God predestines anyone to unbelief or damnation. On the contrary, the Bible insists that God "desires all people to be saved and to come to the knowledge of the truth" (1 Timothy 2:4). In Ephesians 1 Paul describes this "word of truth, the gospel of your salvation" as the redemption we have through Christ's blood (Ephesians 1:13, 7). Elsewhere Paul declares that Jesus Christ shed his blood for all; "in Christ God was reconciling the world to himself" (2 Corinthians 5:15, 19; see also 1 John 2:2). While the New Testament does teach that not all people will be saved, this is not because God does not desire their salvation or because Jesus did not die and rise for them as well. Questions may still surround the topic of predestination, but it certainly provides another reason for all who hear and believe the gospel to bless "the God and Father of our Lord Jesus Christ, who has blessed us in Christ with every spiritual blessing" (Ephesians 1:3).

2:1–10 Chapter two is a well-known summary of Law and Gospel. Verses 1–3 describe the darkness of those who are apart from Christ with devastating words of Law. They are dead in transgressions and sins, disobedient, gratifying the cravings of the sinful nature, and following its desires. Yet this is not simply a description of others; Paul says it applies to how "we all once lived" (2:3; compare Romans 2:1). All of us are "by nature children of wrath" (Ephesians 2:3; compare Romans 1:18–3:20; 5:15–19). This statement implies that we are not under God's judgment merely because of what we do (for example, "the trespasses and sins"; 2:1) but also because of who we are by nature and from birth. As Paul goes on to describe how salvation is accomplished, he also makes clear how it does not come about. It "is not your own doing; it is ... not a result of works" (2:8–9). These "Law" phrases exclude all attempts to work for, earn, or boast about anything we are or do in our relationship with God.

The good news of the Gospel announces how God's plan of salvation does work. Because of his great love and mercy in Christ, he saves us by grace through faith as a gift (2:4–5, 7–8). In other words, God does all the work. We are God's "workmanship, created in Christ Jesus" (2:10). Paul even declares that God has already "raised us up with [Christ] and seated us with him in the heavenly places" (2:6). The phrase "raised us up with Christ" recalls the language of baptism (compare Romans 6:4; Colossians 2:12). But how are we already seated with him in heaven? There is certainly a *now/not yet* aspect to this verse that also reveals the fundamental reality of those who even now "walk by faith, not by sight" (2 Corinthians 5:7).

Ephesians 2:1–10 is Law and Gospel stated with great clarity and universal application. It reflects the consistent *either/or* argument which runs throughout Paul's letters, stretching all the way back to Galatians. One can *either* attempt to earn salvation by works *or* receive it as God's gift through faith. It is not a combination of both. However, even these verses call for a response from those of us who have been gifted with the riches of God's grace in Christ. He has prepared good works in advance and laid them out for us to do. Those who have been recreated in Christ Jesus "should walk in them" (2:10).

2:11–22 Many people love a good mystery story as long as the unknowns are brought to a satisfactory resolution. In Romans 11:25 Paul unveiled an important mystery. Ephesians 3 similarly refers to "the mystery of Christ" now made known to Paul by revelation (3:3–4). "The mystery is that the Gentiles are fellow heirs, members of the same body, and partakers of the promise in Christ Jesus through the gospel" (3:6). Here is something largely unforeseen in Old Testament times: the community of God's people in Christ now includes Gentiles as fellow members and co-heirs together with Israel.

The latter half of Ephesians 2 spells out how this occurred in another Law/Gospel section that can be pictured something like those "before" and "after" diet advertisements. "Before," uncircumcised Gentiles were separated from Christ and alienated from membership in Israel; they were strangers to God's covenant promises, without hope and without God in the world; they were far off and aliens (2:12,17,19).

But Christ, who "is our peace" (2:14), has reconciled both Israel and Gentiles to God through the cross. Paul's emphasis here is on the "after" status of Gentiles. They are fellow citizens with God's people and members of his household (2:19). Through Christ Israel and Gentiles "both have access in one Spirit to the Father" (5:18). Even Israel's access to the Father is in Christ and not apart from him. Note also that Gentiles do not displace Israel as God's people. Rather, they are joined together with Israel in Christ.

In Paul's effort to describe further this glorious "before" and "after," metaphors abound! The language of the theme verse for Ephesians asserts that Gentiles are now also "light in the Lord" (5:8). In chapters two and three Paul uses his characteristic image of a human body to describe God's people in Christ; both Israel and Gentiles have been joined together "as members of the same body" (3:6; see also 2:16; 4:16; 1 Corinthians 12:12–27; Romans 12:4–8). At the end of Ephesians 2, he turns to the metaphor of a building, describing a holy temple built together to become a dwelling in which God lives by his Spirit (2:21–22; compare 1 Corinthians 3:9–17). Christ is its only cornerstone. Upon him God laid the foundation of apostles and prophets. This could refer to the apostles and prophets who were active in the early church (as in Ephesians 4:11; see also 1 Corinthians 12:28; Acts 1:26; 21:9–11). Paul could also be describing those prophets who spoke God's Old Testament word and, then, the apostles through whom he gave the New Testament Scriptures.

Before we move on to the application section of Ephesians 4–6, the following analogy illustrates the significance of the transition.

> Songs from the 1950s and 1960s often have background vocalists singing apparently nonsensical syllables and phrases. One example is, "Do-Be-Do-Be-Do." Those little words express the American work ethic all too well. First we do; then we become. Our work makes us who we are. To illustrate this, simply ask people, "Who are you?" Most will respond with their occupation. Christianity asserts just the opposite and this is a fundamental difference. Who we are in Christ is of first importance; that is our essence or "be-ing" (Ephesians 1–3). Who we are then determines what we do (Ephesians 4–6). So, "Be-Do" is a much more appropriate lyric for the believer.

Some scholars make the same point about Paul's theology by speaking of the *indicative* and the *imperative*. First come indicatives—statements of fact—about what God has done for us in Christ; they "indicate" true reality and give us our identity. Paul then follows with imperatives. They exhort and urge believers toward particular godly behaviors in response to those indicatives.

4:1–6 A theme of oneness permeates Ephesians. The Gospel affirms all these ones: one body, one Spirit, one hope, one Lord, one faith, one baptism, one God and Father of all (4:4–6). However, Ephesians 4 marks a transition in the letter from doctrine to application. Paul affirms this unity at the beginning of his exhortations, then pleads for those who have been made one to live a life "worthy of the calling" (4:1). In other words, God first makes his people one in

Christ. They are then called to maintain that unity (4:3). Unity is kept when God's people "walk in humility and gentleness, with patience, bearing with one another in love" (4:2).

Later in the chapter Paul declares that God's people must get rid of things that would disrupt their oneness: "bitterness and wrath and anger and clamor and malice" (4:13; compare Colossians 3:5–9). Then, in the next two verses, he urges those who are God's dearly loved children to respond by imitating him ("Be-Do"; Ephesians 5:1) by being kind and tenderhearted and by "forgiving one another, as God in Christ forgave you" (4:32). In so doing, those who are light in the Lord live as children of light (5:8; compare Colossians 3:12–15).

5:21–6:4 (compare Colossians 3:18–21) Paul has been criticized harshly for being an old-fashioned chauvinist who oppresses women. These charges are often based on sections such as Ephesians 5:22–24. However, a closer look at those words in context reveals quite the opposite. Ephesians 5:21 serves as a theme verse which permeates the specific applications Paul makes in the verses to follow. Some scholars dispute this based upon the Greek verb forms and attach verse 21 with what precedes (for example, note the paragraph and section divisions in the *ESV*). Perhaps it functions as a transitional verse, but the "submit" language clearly points ahead toward what is to follow.

Living as children of light involves "submitting to one another" (5:21), a most unnatural state for those who are dead in the darkness of trespasses and sin (2:1–3; 4:17–19). Indeed, such a lifestyle is supernatural. It springs "out of reverence for Christ" (5:21). In other words, believers adhere to this lifestyle as a response to the gracious gift of the Gospel. We put others first because Christ first did that for us (2:13–14; 4:32; compare Philippians 2:1–11).

The thematic word translated "submit" conveys the idea of soldiers marching in their proper order. In verse twenty-two "submitting to one another" is applied to wives in relationship to their husbands. It would certainly seem odd if Paul called all believers to submit to one another (5:21), but omitted wives from doing so to their husbands! Note that Paul never tells husbands to make their wives submit. These words are addressed to wives, and Paul uses a verb in the Greek middle voice to indicate that wives are to submit themselves freely and willingly to others, including their husbands. They do so not out of force or compulsion, but because of their reverence for Christ.

To the question "Why?" Paul answers, "The husband is the head of the wife" (5:23). What does this mean? Is the husband her boss or master? There is a Greek word often translated "head" that implies origin and authority (*arche*). However, Paul never uses that to describe husbands. The word he uses (*kephale*) has a military background. As the Greek army attacked in battle, they often used a triangular formation called a phalanx. *Kephale* referred to the person at the point or "head" of the triangle. He went out first and, almost certainly, lost his life. That is the type of headship Paul is depicting here. He makes this clear in verse twenty-five when he begins to describe the husband's role. He is to love his wife "as Christ loved the church and gave himself up for her." Yes, wives are to submit to others, including husbands, out of their reverence for Christ; but husbands are called to do more, to follow Christ's example of headship, to go out first and lay down their entire lives for their wives.

Permeating this entire discussion is the believer's relationship to Christ. In fact, Paul himself mysteriously concludes that the ultimate subject matter here is not really husbands and wives at all, but Christ and the church (5:32)! In fulfillment of the Genesis 2 passage Paul quotes, Christ left his Father in heaven and came to this earth in order to be united to us, his bride, the church; we are now one with him (5:22; citing Genesis 2:23). Christ also cleanses the church by the baptismal "washing of water with the word" (5:26). He then presents us to his, and our, Father as a bride in a spotless and radiant white garment. When we mess up, we are cleaned up by the ultimate Bridegroom, Christ himself. This is an important message when husbands and wives fail to live up to God's ideal for marriage as described here.

Recent studies of wives and husbands have asked them to rank some of their most important needs in marriage. Wives generally rank first the need to know they are loved. Husbands, however, often say their number one need is to know they are respected. In Ephesians 5:33 Paul ends his discussion with advice that is very up to date and relevant. Husbands are to love their wives; wives are to respect their husbands.

Ephesians 6 marks an unfortunate chapter division. Right on the heels of a discussion about the roles of husbands and wives follow words to parents and children (6:1–4). Once again, Paul roots his teaching in the Old Testament, citing the commandment to honor father and mother (Deuteronomy 5:16). Obedience to this commandment has no time limit (for example, until the age of eighteen or when I leave the house).

It may strike us as odd that Paul only addresses fathers with words about how to raise their children (6:4). But in light of the previous discussion of headship and submission, the role of the wife is clearly encompassed here as well. Instead of being harsh and overbearing, fathers are given the privilege of raising their children "in the discipline and instruction of the Lord" (6:4). Too often, fathers abdicate this responsibility to mothers or, more often, the church. According to Scripture, however, training in God's word is primarily the role of the father as *kephale* head of the household (see Deuteronomy 6:7; Colossians 3:21).

Continuing under the thematic statement of 5:21, Paul proceeds to discuss the roles of slaves and masters in 6:5–9 (compare Colossians 3:22–4:1). Paul then concludes his section of exhortation by depicting believers as soldiers.

This does not mean the church is literally to take up arms as in the Crusades. Rather, the image or metaphor is more appropriately depicted by the mission of the Salvation Army and in the hymn, "Onward, Christians Soldiers." This is clear from Paul's description of the enemy at hand. It is no earthly foe, but "the cosmic powers of this present darkness" and "the spiritual forces of evil in the heavenly places" (6:12). Paul utilizes the common equipment of a Roman soldier to describe the God-given apparatus which enables the Christian to stay standing in battle against such ominous opponents (6:14–17). All the armor described is defensive except for "the sword of the Spirit, which is the word of God" (6:17). If God's people are to reach out on the offensive, their weapon is to be God's own words of Scripture.

Jesus in Ephesians

Ephesians speaks in lofty terms of God's "eternal purpose" (3:11). It is to make "known to us the mystery of his will … which he set forth in Christ as a plan for the fullness of time, to unite all things in him, things in heaven and things on earth" (1:9–10). The dominant description of Jesus in Ephesians is as head. While he is depicted as head over all things (1:10, 22), Paul emphasizes Jesus' *kephale* headship over his body, the church (3:6; 4:12, 15). There Jesus Christ has reconciled both Jews and Gentiles to God and to one another. Paul simply declares, "He himself is our peace" (2:14).

Jesus is also the chief cornerstone on whom the fellowship of God's people is founded. We are joined together as one in his body in order to grow and mature (2:20–21; 4:15). As head of the church, Jesus dwells within, sustains, equips, and nourishes us as his own body (3:17; 4:12; 5:29), because he loves his people with an immeasurable, all-surpassing love (3:18). Indeed, "Christ loved the Church and gave himself up for her" (5:25).

For Further Discussion

1. Why does Ephesians begin the chapter of this textbook titled "Maturing Confession?" Is Ephesians a generic summary of the Christian faith or a contextual letter? Explain.

2. Define predestination and double predestination. What do you believe about each of them?

3. Using specific words or phrases from Ephesians 2, illustrate the differences between Law and Gospel. Then use words or phrases from that same chapter to explain the terms "before" and "after" as they apply to Gentile believers.

4. Who are you? Does your identify come from what you do or who(se) you are? What does our culture say about issues of identity? What does Paul say? How, then, do you live a life worthy of your calling (Ephesians 4:1)?

5. Define what Paul means by the terms "submit," "headship," "love," and "respect" as they are lived out in Christian marriage (Ephesians 5:21–33). How does our society today view these words? Do you think what Paul wrote about marriage makes him a chauvinist or did he have an appropriate view of women and marriage? Explain your answer. Describe in your own words God's plan for the relationship between husband and wife.

6. Illustrate how Ephesians 5:8 is a summary of Paul's theology by using verses from Ephesians and some of his other letters. How does Paul use the metaphor of light? List five other metaphors used by Paul and explain their significance.

Ruins of ancient Ephesus

7. Does it matter if the letter we call Ephesians was not actually written "to the saints who are in Ephesus" (Ephesians 1:1)? Why or why not? In your answer, describe what a circular letter is.

For Further Reading

Bristow, John Temple. *What Paul Really Said about Women.* San Francisco: Harper and Row, 1988.

Hendrickson, William. *Ephesians*. New Testament Commentary. Grand Rapids: Baker, 1967.

Hughes, R. Kent. *Ephesians*. Preaching the Word. Wheaton, IL: Crossways, 1990.

Mitton, C. Leslie. *Ephesians*. The New Century Bible Commentary. Grand Rapids: Eerdmans, 1973.

O'Brien, Peter. *Ephesians*. The Pillar New Testament Commentary. Grand Rapids: Eerdmans, 1999.

Panning, Armin. *Galatians/Ephesians*. People's Bible Commentary. St. Louis: Concordia, 1997.

1 Timothy and Titus

Pastoral Epistles and the Chronology of the New Testament

The Pastoral Epistles (1 and 2 Timothy and Titus) do not seem to fit within the narrative provided by the books of Acts. They were probably written after Acts concludes. As a result, the New Testament does not provide us with a narrative framework within which to place these letters. However, the following scenario is one possible reconstruction:

- Acts ends with Paul in Rome for two years under house arrest (Acts 28:30).
- Early church tradition says Paul was released after his hearing before Nero's court. He then realized the dream he envisioned in Romans, carrying the Gospel further west toward Spain (Romans 15:28; Clement of Rome's *Letter to the Corinthians* 1:5–7, written in A.D. 96; the Muratorian Canon 40).
- Evidence from the Pastorals helps us to piece together what may have happened next. Paul returned to the east, perhaps by way of Crete, where he left Titus to continue the mission work there (Titus 1:5).
- Paul spent some time in Ephesus. Upon his departure Timothy was entrusted with the task of overseeing the believers in that city.
- Paul journeyed to Macedonia where he wrote 1 Timothy (1 Timothy 1:3).
- Paul then headed toward the city of Nicopolis in western Greece where he planned to spend the winter. He sent instructions back to "Pastor Titus" on Crete. He also asked Titus to join him once Titus was relieved by Artemis and Tychicus (Titus 3:12).

1 Timothy and Titus are, therefore, quite similar in terms of their addressees, context, and content. It is appropriate to study them together.

Authorship of the Pauline Epistles

Many scholars dispute whether all thirteen of the letters attributed to St. Paul in the New Testament were actually authored by him. In response, it is important to acknowledge that, at times, others were involved in shaping the content. For example, both letters to the Thessalonians are identified as being from "Paul, Silvanus [or Silas] and Timothy" (1 Thessalonians 1:1; 2 Thessalonians 1:1). Furthermore, the majority of these letters did not actually come from the pen of Paul himself. An amanuensis usually did the writing under the author's supervision (see, for example, Romans 16:22). Traditionally, however, the church has accepted Paul as the primary source of the thirteen letters which identify him as their author. Some even suggest that a fourteenth, Hebrews, was also composed by Paul (see the title page of Hebrews in a King James Version of the Bible).

On the other extreme, a number of modern scholars limit Paul's direct authorship to all or part of only seven or fewer of the letters attributed to him. The letters most commonly accepted as genuine are Galatians, 1 Thessalonians, 1 and 2 Corinthians, Romans, Philippians, and Philemon. Various scholars contend that some or all of the rest were written by other authors sometime after Paul died and attributed to him through a practice called ***pseudonymity****.*

The majority of New Testament scholars are probably somewhere in between those two positions. That is, they attribute between seven and fourteen of those epistles to Paul. The position taken here is that the inspired text of God's word is trustworthy and not deceptive. All thirteen of the letters which indicate that they are from Paul were authored by him.

It may be helpful to examine this issue more specifically. Among the letters most often singled out as coming from someone other than Paul are the Pastoral Epistles. Their authorship is questioned for the following reasons: 1) They do not fit into the narrative chronology provided by Acts; 2) when compared with Paul's other letters, scholars often note a change in Greek vocabulary and style; 3) it is argued that the content or teaching of the Pastorals is different from Paul's other letters; and 4) finally, the presence of various church offices or positions within the Pastoral Epistles is said to be developed beyond the time of Paul; the authentic Pauline letters lack a definite set of roles and do not reflect the ecclesiastical order or hierarchy present within these "later" letters.

In response, the differences in vocabulary are not as pronounced as often suggested. Similarly, while Paul may address issues differently, it is an exaggeration to assert there are contradictions between the doctrine of the Pastorals and his other letters. Additionally, the matters of different vocabulary and articulation can also be explained, at least to some degree, by two factors: First, according to the chronology presented here, the Pastorals were written years after Paul's other letters. His vocabulary and style logically would have changed since the time he wrote Galatians, for example, more than a decade earlier. Second, Paul is writing these three letters to a different audience. Instead of speaking to a congregation or a group, he is addressing specific individuals whom he knows well (compare Philemon). The recipients of these letters also occupy positions of leadership within the Christian community. It is only natural, then, that Paul would address issues in a different manner and deal with topics of specific relevance to Timothy and Titus. As far as the assertion that the Pastorals exhibit an ecclesiastical structure which did not yet exist in Paul's day, this reads more into the letters than is actually there. The discussion of 1 Timothy 3 below will illustrate this point.

Structure and Theme

The content and structure of 1 Timothy and Titus are similar. However, aside from the typical opening, they do not follow the normal letter outline. This deviation is understandable, since they are not addressed to a congregation of believers or a wider, public audience. At least initially, these letters are intended to be more private and personal (compare Philemon). After the opening, the letters both delve straight into the business at hand, the oversight Timothy and Titus are to provide for the Christian communities in Ephesus and Crete, respectively.

The ruins of Ephesus

First Timothy is longer than Titus, but both letters deal with the same two subjects. First, there are continued warnings about false teachers. They, along with their heretical teachings, must be effectively opposed by Timothy and Titus (for example, 1 Timothy 1:3–11, 18–20; 4:1–16; 6:3–5; Titus 1:10–16; 3:9–11). Second, Paul gives positive guidelines for how Timothy, Titus, and other church leaders are to oversee a community of believers (for example, 1 Timothy 2:1–3:13; 5:1–6:2; Titus 1:5–9; 2:1–3:8).

Because these letters address both areas, the title "pastoral" is most appropriate. The word "pastor" comes from the Latin word for a shepherd. The picture of a shepherd and his flock is a common biblical metaphor for the relationship between God and his people (Psalm 23; 95:7; Luke 15:1–7; John 10:11–18). But it also serves as a model for how various earthly leaders are to "tend" God's people (for example, Ezekiel 34; Acts 20:28–30; 1 Peter 5:1–4). Paul describes how "Pastors" Timothy and Titus are to care for, feed, nurture, heal, lead, and guide their "flock." They should also defend the "sheep" from harm and danger as well as seek the lost and straying.

Shepherd and a sheep

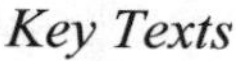

Key Texts

1 Timothy 1:12–17 Paul reflects on his life and, more importantly, the radical change Jesus brought about in it. As a Pharisee of Pharisees, Paul had endeavored to serve the God of the Scriptures with great zeal (Acts 22:3; 23:6). He now recognizes he was, in fact, a blasphemer of God, one of the most heinous sins (1 Timothy 1:13; see Leviticus 24:15–16; Mark 3:29). Even worse, he persecuted Christ's people. It is no wonder, then, that Paul describes himself as "the foremost" of sinners (1:15). In Paul's diagnosis of the problem, he acted in ignorance and unbelief (1:13). It is surprising that this great student of the Scriptures who "was advancing in Judaism beyond many of my own age" (Galatians 1:14) now admits that he had acted ignorantly. Even more insightful is the observation that as Paul was meticulously striving to serve God by keeping the Law and "the traditions of my fathers" (Philippians 3:6; Galatians 1:14), he was actually in a state of unbelief.

The Pastorals often describe or introduce key tenets of the faith with an expression such as, "The saying is trustworthy and deserving of full acceptance" (1:15; compare 2 Timothy 2:11; Titus 3:8). Significant here is that Christ Jesus came into the world to save sinners—echoing the words of Jesus himself (Luke 5:27–32). Among all those sinners, Paul asserts that he is the worst (1 Timothy 1:15). It may be hard to imagine a sinner much worse than Paul prior to his conversion. But this makes the intervention of Christ in his life all the more glorious. In spite of who Paul was and what he did, God's grace, faith and love were all showered upon him (1:14). In addition, Christ even appointed a man with Paul's history into the service of advancing the Gospel (1:12). As a result, Paul's story serves as a profound example for all believers; it shows the extent of Christ's mercy and perfect patience (1:16). What response could be more appropriate than a doxology of praise: "To the King of ages, immortal, invisible, the only God, be honor and glory forever and ever. Amen" (1:17).

2:1–15 This chapter addresses a wide variety of topics and contains a number of controversial words. Paul begins by urging prayer, specifically for those in positions of governmental authority (2:1–2; compare Romans 13:1–7). His petition asks that the authorities leave the church alone, so that God's people may live in peace and serve him in holiness. It is also God's good pleasure that all people be saved (2:4). God does not want to save only certain elect or chosen people. God desires to save all and aims to do so through one mediator, Jesus Christ (2:5). This is the message Paul was called to proclaim, especially to the Gentiles (2:7). This message excludes attempting to appeal to God through any other so-called mediators (for example, angels, saints, priests, our own efforts, Mohammed, or Buddha). In verse eight, Paul returns to prayer and commends the practice of "lifting holy hands" while doing so.

The rest of the chapter deals with the dress and conduct of women, perhaps during times of prayer, but not exclusively so. Verses 9–10 suggest that their dress be fitting for those who "profess godliness." This would certainly apply to what they wear outside of worship as well. Instead of expensive clothing, fancy hairstyles, or ornate jewelry, their entire lives are to be adorned with good works.

Verses 11–12 strike a note of discord to many in our day. They seem sexist and old fashioned. The phrases "quietly and with all submissiveness," "I do not permit a woman to teach," and "she is to remain quiet" are all controversial. However, in a society that did not normally educate women on equal terms with men, other words probably stood out more radically to those who first heard them: "Let a woman learn" (2:11). Paul breaks out of a cultural norm and asserts women should be taught the faith within the community of God's people.

A number of explanations for the restrictions Paul places upon women have been suggested. Here, as with 1 Corinthians 11 and 14, few press the absolute literal sense of the words. "I do not permit a woman to teach . . . ; she is to remain quiet" (2:12). Some believe Paul is limiting the teaching of women because they were not educated in that day and, therefore, were not properly equipped to teach. This position contends that once women have been taught on an equal footing with men, the restrictions would no longer be necessary or appropriate. Others suggest that there was a woman or a group of women in Ephesus who were engaged in deceptive teaching. Such teachers have been deceived like Eve and must be avoided. The force of Paul's words, then, is that the believers should not allow these misguided women to give false instruction. Along these lines, it is intriguing that Paul here refers to Eve being deceived first (2:14). Normally he identifies Adam as the one who brought sin and its resulting consequences into the world (Romans 5:12, 15–19; 1 Corinthians 15:22).

The more traditional interpretation focuses upon the phrase "or to exercise authority over a man" in 2:12. Paul attaches ongoing significance to the chronology of creation. Adam was created first as "head," followed by Eve (1 Timothy 2:13). Here Paul also introduces the sequence of the Fall into sin (1 Timothy

2:14). As a result, this line of interpretation concludes that women are not to be placed in teaching positions which set them in authority over men. The authoritative teaching position in the Christian congregation is identified with the role of overseer, elder, or pastor. It is interesting that Paul turns to this topic in the verses which immediately follow (3:1–7; see also 5:17). His words would then exclude a woman from occupying that position in a congregation.

A final comment concerns the seemingly outrageous statement that women "will be saved through childbearing" (2:15). Does this suggest women are saved by their own works or "labor" (compare Ephesians 2:8–9)? What about women who have no children? A better translation and understanding of the verse is that "women will be saved through *the* child-beared" (1 Timothy 2:15). This fits in with the reference to Eve in 2:13. After being deceived, she received the first promise that her offspring would crush Satan's head (Genesis 3:15). Ultimately, *the* child-beared is Christ. He was born of Mary to save women and all people who remain in him.

3:1–13 (and Titus 1:5–9) In both 1 Timothy and Titus, Paul spends a substantial amount of time addressing the character and lifestyle of those who occupy positions of leadership among God's people. One confusing thing is the matter of titles. What position(s) is Paul speaking about and to whom do his words apply today? In 1 Timothy 3:1 Paul refers to an *episkopos*. This word has been translated "bishop," which can be misleading because of the development of the term into a hierarchical role in subsequent church history. The term is better and more literally translated as "overseer." In 3:8–13 Paul goes on to discuss the role of a *diakonos*. This term is normally transliterated into English as "deacon." Titus 1:5 speaks of *presbyteroi* or elders. In verse seven Paul refers to a person who occupies that position as an overseer. In other words, a *presbyteros* is an *episkopos*. It seems best to conclude that those two terms refer respectively to a person's character and task. Paul speaks of elders who oversee.

In 1 Timothy 3:1–7 and Titus 1:5–9, Paul lists a number of *characteristics of elders/overseers*. For elders/overseers, the ability to teach the faith is critical and listed three times (1 Timothy 3:2; 5:17; Titus 1:9). Other positive qualities are mentioned (for example, hospitable and self-controlled); a good number of negatives are excluded as well (for example, not violent, not quarrelsome, not a drunkard, not a recent convert). Qualifications related to family life are also noted (for example, managing one's own household well, having children who are believers and submissive). One particular criterion is interesting here: "the husband of one wife" (1 Timothy 3:2; Titus 1:6). Whom or what does Paul aim to exclude? Those who are single or who are divorced or who have multiple wives? Does this criterion eliminate women from consideration? It seems most likely Paul is speaking against polygamous elders. Not only is having multiple wives morally questionable, it would also improperly burden the congregation which is directed to pay an appropriate wage to their elders (5:17–18).

There are two unwarranted conclusions to draw from these criteria. First, their cumulative effect might lead one to think overseers/elders need to be perfect. In fact, the characterization of "above reproach" or "blameless" (1 Timothy

3:2; Titus 1:6), if taken to its extreme, would eliminate everyone from consideration! On the other hand, there are those who would dispense with the list entirely. In contemporary times, some have asserted that spiritual leaders need to be experienced with the problems (or sins) confronted by those under their care. This enables them to understand those issues better and to work more effectively with people who are dealing with them.

Paul avoids both of those positions. He requires those who are placed in the position of elder/overseer to exhibit a godly and respectable lifestyle in public. They are held to a higher standard of conduct for two important reasons. First, sheep follow where their shepherd leads; similarly, God's people are called to follow the example of those who oversee them. Church leaders, therefore, are to serve as positive role models for the community of believers. Second, for better or worse, unbelievers derive a significant number of their perceptions about Christianity from the teachings and lifestyle of church leaders. Paul insists that overseers "be well thought of by outsiders" in order to give a positive witness to the world (1 Timothy 3:7).

Paul proceeds to lay out qualifications for *deacons* in 1 Timothy 3:8–13. It is noteworthy that he lists a number of traits identical to those he has just given for elders/overseers (for example, sober-minded, respectable, not a drunkard, holds to the mystery of the faith). In fact, as Paul addresses the conduct of other groups of believers (widows, slaves, older and younger men and women), they are also called to exhibit some of the same qualities which are "pleasing in the sight of God" (1 Timothy 5:4; see 5:1–6:2; Titus 2:1–10).

As discussed earlier, many scholars date the composition of the Pastoral Epistles some time after Paul's death, because these letters are said to exhibit regimented offices and a level of church organization and hierarchy that did not yet exist in the church of the mid-first century. However, there is some ambiguity present among the positions depicted by these letters. Things are not yet as developed or standardized as they were decades later. For example, the overlap in qualifications for overseers and deacons was noted above. Furthermore, 1 Timothy 5 Paul speaks of elders who "rule well" or "direct the affairs of the church" (NIV) and then narrows the field to speak especially of those elders "who labor in preaching and teaching" (5:17). Paul envisions that some elders/overseers preach and teach; others, who are also engaged in oversight, do not. Precise distinctions among these various elders, as well as between elders and deacons, are not yet present.

With this in mind, it seems reasonable to apply what Paul says of elders/overseers to pastors and ministers today, as well as to priests in Roman Catholic and Orthodox churches. They, at the very least, are to have the character and meet the qualifications Paul lays out for those who watch over God's people. What Paul says of deacons in 1 Timothy 3:8–13 may then be applied to other roles or positions of leadership in the church. But it is difficult to apply this distinction too narrowly in light of the broader scope of overseeing evidenced by 5:17 and the amount of overlap in qualifications between elders/overseers and deacons. One should also be cautious about directly equating too much of what Paul says to specific positions today. During the two thousand years since he wrote to Timothy and Titus, various churches have given a wide variety of different titles to those occupy any number of leadership positions within the Christian community.

4:1–4 The believers in Ephesus are plagued by false teachings similar to those that afflicted the Colossians when Paul wrote to them. These false teachings may have been an emerging form of what came to be called Gnosticism. In Gnosticism physical matter was viewed as lower, base, and evil. Salvation, attainable through knowledge (*gnosis* in Greek) passed on secretly, meant freedom from this worldly existence and ascent into the spiritual realm. The impact of these teachings on everyday behavior went in two divergent directions. Some Gnostics insisted upon abstaining from food, sexual relations, and the other things of this world (**asceticism**); others overindulged in them since those physical things no longer mattered (libertinism).

Paul vigorously opposes such deceitful and even demonic beliefs. He views the presence of these teachers as a sign from the Spirit that it is the "later times" (4:1). Those who insist on avoiding marriage and certain foods are wrong. A children's song by Maltbie Babcock is titled, "This is my Father's World." Each verse begins with those words that echo the sentiments expressed by Paul here. God is the Creator. Everything he made is good and intended to benefit his people (compare Psalm 24:1). As a result, nothing of this world is to be rejected; everything is to be received as a blessing from God's hand so long as "it is made holy by the word of God and prayer" (1 Timothy 4:4).

6:3–10 Throughout this letter, Paul has given Timothy sound words of instruction to teach the believers in Ephesus. Toward the end, he once again warns this young pastor about the evil results that follow those who have departed from the true teachings of Christ. Those who advocate false doctrines are conceited; they are mainly interested in promoting quarrels about words, dissension, slander, and constant friction (6:4–5).

A driving force which motivates such teachers, then as now, is the belief that "godliness is a means of gain" (6:5). In the section from 1 Timothy 4 just discussed, Paul asserted everything God created was good and was to be received as a blessing from him. At the same time, God's people are not to become too focused on the material things of this world. They also need to realize God does not guarantee earthly riches to those who dedicate themselves to his service or who endeavor to lead a godly lifestyle. The truth is "we brought nothing into the world, and we cannot take anything out of the world. But if we have food and clothing, with these we will be content" (6:7–8). If the primary motivation in someone's life is the love of money and a desire for earthly riches, they are in grave danger of falling into many temptations and even wandering from the faith (6:9–10). Such a materialistic outlook is idolatrous. Instead of loving God above all, it puts our selfish desire for things first (Deuteronomy 5:7; 6:5).

Titus 1:5–9 See the discussion of 1 Timothy 3:1–13, above.

2:11–14 Paul's brief letter to Titus contains a number of theological gems. These verses speak comprehensively of what is significant for believers in the past, present, and future. In the *past*, God's grace appeared bringing salvation for all in Jesus Christ; he died to redeem us from sinful lawlessness and to make us pure (Titus 2:11, 14). In the *present*, God's people are to "renounce ungodliness and worldly passions, and to live self-controlled, upright and godly lives" (2:12). What does the *future* hold? We look ahead to "our blessed hope, the appearing of the glory of our great God and Savior Jesus Christ" (2:13). Those two titles encompass who Jesus is ("our great God") and what he has done ("Savior"; also in 3:6). These four verses encapsulate the believer's entire existence. God acted in Christ to save us in the past; as a result, when he returns, our eternal future is secure. Those two truths are firm anchors on which the believer rests and lives boldly within the present.

The ruins of Knossos on Crete

3:3–8 This is an excellent statement of Law, Gospel, and response. First, the Law of 3:3 describes an existence which is utterly dismal and all inclusive ("we ourselves"). Any change in status occurs "not because of works done by us in righteousness" (3:5). Instead, the Gospel is all God's doing. Because of his goodness, loving kindness, and mercy, he saved us. How did God accomplish this? Paul says it is "by the washing of regeneration and renewal of the Holy Spirit whom he poured out on us richly through Jesus Christ our Savior" (3:5–6). The references to "washing" and "poured out" point to baptism. They describe the new birth which occurs there. Through the activity of Christ and the Spirit, we are put into a right relationship with God; already God's grace makes us heirs of eternal life (3:7). Paul refers back to this entire section with the initial words of verse eight: "The saying is trustworthy." The same verse proceeds to spell out the believers' response: "that those who believe in God may be careful to devote themselves to good works" (3:8).

Jesus in 1 Timothy and Titus

Jesus said, "I am the way, and the truth, and the life. No one comes to the Father except through me" (John 14:6). Paul similarly identifies Jesus as the "one mediator between God and men" (1 Timothy 2:5). He is this one and only go-between because "he gave himself as a ransom for all" (2:6; compare Mark 10:45). Whether the picture is drawn from the price paid to free a slave or the money offered as ransom in a kidnapping, the point is the same. Jesus paid the price once and for all.

1 Timothy 3:16 is a poem or song which beautifully rehearses God's plan of salvation in Jesus Christ. Each of its six lines makes an important assertion about Jesus that is supported elsewhere in the New Testament.

- He became a human being through Mary in the incarnation (Matthew 1:18–20; Luke 1:35–37).
- The Holy Spirit vindicated his life from conception on through his baptism (Matthew 3:16), public ministry (Acts 10:38), suffering, death (Hebrews 9:14), and resurrection (Romans 8:11).
- Angels "saw" him and were present throughout his earthly ministry (Mark 1:13; Luke 22:43). He has also now ascended to the throne of God where he is praised by all the angels of heaven (Revelation 5:11–14).
- The good news of salvation in Jesus has been proclaimed throughout the world as he mandated (Matthew 24:14; 28:18–20; Mark 16:16; Luke 24:47; Acts 1:8).
- Many of those who heard this message have believed in him (Romans 10:13–17).
- Finally, there is a reference back to his ascension which marked the culmination of all he accomplished "for us and for our salvation" (Nicene Creed; see Luke 24:51; Acts 1:9).

The quotation from the Nicene Creed, a fourth-century confession of faith, functions in the a way similar to this poem recorded in 1 Timothy. The earliest confession of Christians was, "Jesus is Lord" (Romans 10:9; Philippians 2:11). From it, further confessions like 1 Timothy 3:16 sprung forth from God's word. These statements of faith elaborated more and more fully upon the person and work of Jesus Christ. This practice follows the tradition of Jesus himself, who "in his testimony before Pontius Pilate made the good confession" (1 Timothy 6:13).

If one wanted to identify Jesus with the most essential attribute of God, what would that be? In his letter to Titus, Paul identifies Jesus this way: "For the grace of God has appeared, bringing salvation to all people" (2:11). Paul begins and ends every one of his letters with references to grace. Paul views grace as God's most fundamental characteristic. Here he asserts that God's grace is made visible in the person of Jesus Christ. Grace is unmerited or undeserved favor. A number of acronyms spell this out further:

- [We receive] **G**od's **R**iches **A**t **C**hrist's **E**xpense
- **G**od **R**eally **AC**complishes **E**verything [for our salvation]

Titus also refers to Jesus as our Savior (2:13; 3:6). The connection between the two is vital. God's grace is the source, content, and active force of our salvation. Jesus, therefore, is God's grace both incarnate and in action.

For Further Discussion

1. Do you think Paul wrote all thirteen of the letters attributed to him by the New Testament? If they are God's word, does it really matter who wrote them (compare Hebrews)? Why or why not?

2. Paul writes, "For there is one God, and there is one mediator between God and men, the man Jesus Christ" (1 Timothy 2:5). How does our modern world react to a statement like this? What does it say about other religions? Then consider this: since we do not have direct contact with Jesus today, are there mediators between us and Jesus? If so, who or what are they? If not, explain why we do not need them.

3. What titles are used for church leaders in the New Testament? What titles do we use for Christian leaders today? Are these titles appropriate? What kind of lifestyle should our church leaders have today? Why?

4. Is this world good or evil or some of both? How does 1 Timothy answer? What does this mean for how a believer lives out his or her life in this world?

5. What is grace? Define it. How does one deserve or receive it from God? Can we receive grace from other people? If so, how? If not, why not?

6. Review the sidebar on "Women/Wives in Worship" provided at the end of our discussion of 1 Corinthians 14. Compare it with the material on 1 Timothy 2 and 3 in this chapter. What role(s) do you think women should have in the church today? Give specific examples. Do you think women should be pastors or priests? List two or three points which support each side of the issue. Then provide your own conclusion.

7. What does Titus say is significant for believers in the past, present and future?

For Further Reading

Guthrie, Donald. *Pastoral Epistles*. Tyndale New Testament Commentaries. 1990.

Kelly, J. N. D. *A Commentary on the Pastoral Epistles*. Harper's New Testament Commentaries. New York: Harper and Row, 1993.

Moellering, H. Armin. *1 Timothy, 2 Timothy, Titus*. Concordia Commentary. St. Louis: Concordia, 1970.

Mounce, William D. *1 and 2 Timothy, Titus*. Word Biblical Commentary. Waco, TX: Word, 1997.

Keener, Craig. *Paul, Women and Wives*. Peabody, MA: Hendrickson, 1992.

Stott, John. *Guard the Truth*. The Bible Speaks Today. Downers Grove, IL: InterVarsity, 1996.

Towner, Philip. *1–2 Timothy and Titus*. Downers Grove, IL: InterVarsity, 1994.

2 Timothy

Place in the Story of the New Testament

After the sequence of events described above in the introduction to 1 Timothy and Titus, Paul probably traveled to Troas, Corinth, and Miletus (2 Timothy 4:13, 20). Somewhere in Greece he was once again arrested and taken to Rome. The reason for his arrest and the events of his trial, if there was one, remain a mystery. We know Luke was present with Paul during both of his Roman imprisonments (Acts 28:16; 2 Timothy 4:11). Otherwise, the circumstances of Paul's second Roman imprisonment seem far different from his house arrest at the end of Acts (Acts 28:30).

Emperor Nero

As Paul writes to Timothy, he has endured one hearing, his imprisonment seems harsh, and no end is in sight (2 Timothy 2:9; 4:16). Paul laments, "At my first defense no one came to stand by me, but all deserted me" (4:16). Paul was deserted by Demas and suffered the departure of Crescans, Titus, and Tychicus (1:15; 4:10–12). Paul is also fully aware of his impending execution (4:6). As a Roman citizen, Paul would face that fate only with the approval of Caesar's court and, perhaps, the emperor himself. All of this points toward a time of persecution.

In the mid 60's the Roman emperor was Nero. Paul's letter to Timothy has often been associated with Nero's brutal persecution of Christians after the fire that devastated Rome in A.D. 64. It is certainly plausible that a Christian leader like Paul would be arrested and executed under such circumstances. If this is what happened, we are able to identify the date and circumstances of his death with some certainty (and Peter's as well).

On the other hand, 2 Timothy 4:9–11 summons Timothy to join Paul in Rome and to bring Mark along as well (4:9–11). Such a request seems unusual if widespread persecutions were occurring throughout the city. In any event, according to church tradition, Paul was executed under Nero's reign by decapitation on a mile-marker post just outside of Rome (Eusebius, *Ecclesiastical History*, II.22).

Introduction

Second Timothy is usually grouped together with 1 Timothy and Titus as one of the Pastorals. However, its tone and content are markedly different from the other two. Second Timothy is really more of a personal letter than a pastoral one. Some time after writing 1 Timothy and Titus, Paul senses his execution is near. He sends a farewell letter from Rome to his dear friend, Timothy. The letter is both sad and glorious. It reveals that believers will suffer in this world, but it holds forth a great future with Christ even beyond death. When the letters of Paul were arranged in a particular order in the New Testament, it would have been most fitting to put 2 Timothy last. In essence, it serves as Paul's last will and testament.

Structure and Theme

The introduction to 1 Timothy and Titus noted they did not follow the typical letter outline, in part because those letters were written to individual church leaders rather than to congregations. Second Timothy becomes even more personal. Nevertheless, Paul begins with his typical opening (1:1–2). Then, even in the midst of the most difficult circumstances, he offers a thanksgiving to God (1:3).

The body of the letter is partially devoted to Paul's situation (for example, 1:15–18; 4:6–8). His attitude toward his impending martyrdom is most inspirational. Yet Paul also spends a great deal of time focusing on Timothy and his circumstances. Paul encourages Timothy to endure hardships in the midst of his own difficult times (2:13; 3:1–9). In the face of opposition, Timothy is to proclaim God's word and to defend the faith (2:14–26; 3:10–4:5). The end of the letter contains a number of personal remarks concerning those with whom Paul has had contact (4:9–18) and his final greetings (4:19–22).

Key Texts

1:8–11 Paul is encouraging Timothy in the midst of his own sufferings which are certainly not as severe as Paul's. Yet Paul's focus is not really on himself or Timothy, but on God and the power of the Gospel. Yes, God calls us to live a holy life, but before that he saved us apart from anything we had done (1:9), because of his transcendent purpose and the grace now revealed to us in Christ. As the apostle faces death, he boldly announces that "our Savior Christ Jesus ... abolished death and brought life and immortality to light through the gospel" (1:10). Paul views it as a great privilege to be a preacher, apostle, and teacher of that good news, whatever the consequences may be.

2:8–13 As Timothy endures hardships, Paul directs him once again to the Gospel in all its simplicity: "Remember Jesus Christ, risen from the dead, the offspring of David" (2:8). This good news proclaims the heart of the faith of the Scriptures and it unites both Old and New Testaments in Christ (compare the bow-tie diagram). As promised, he is descended from King David of old (2 Samuel 7:12–13); the essence of what is now fulfilled and new is his resurrection. Unlike prisoner Paul, the message of God's word cannot be bound (2 Timothy 2:9).

The Pastorals contain a number of trustworthy sayings which Paul is passing on to Timothy and Titus. Second Timothy 2:11–13 contains a memorable poem focusing on the believer's life in Christ. The first two lines assure us that our death with Christ in baptism guarantees our eternal life and reign with him so long as we endure in faith (compare Romans 6:3–4). The third line recalls the words of Jesus when he spoke of the severe consequences of denying or disowning him publicly (Matthew 10:33). Finally, Paul's words in verse 13 do not deny the truth that we can only be saved through faith in God's grace (see 2 Timothy 1:9; Ephesians 2:8). Rather, he here speaks of our faithfulness, or lack thereof, in living properly in response. Jesus Christ is faithful to his promise to save us apart from anything we do or fail to do. Our salvation is secure, therefore, even if we are not faithful in living the life to which God has called us (2 Timothy 1:9).

3:14–17 It is fitting that toward the end of Paul's final letter he describes the nature and purpose of God's word to his people. The immediate focus is on Timothy. From infancy his mother Eunice and his grandmother Lois had taught him the Scriptures we now call the Old Testament (1:5). Paul describes their primary purpose. Those sacred writings "are able to make you wise for salvation through faith in Christ Jesus" (3:15). In addition, the Scriptures have other vital functions: to teach, reprove, correct and train in righteousness. To say it very briefly, those Old Testament Scriptures were given to save us through faith in Christ and to equip us to do good works (3:15, 17). How can the Old Testament word accomplish such great things? "All Scripture is breathed out by God" (3:16).

God's word is not bound or limited to those Old Testament texts. God is free to speak further. The words of those appointed by Christ to write the New

Entrance to the stadium at Olympia, Greece

Testament can properly be characterized in the same way. Paul's letters, therefore, have the same character. They were also "breathed out" by God in order to accomplish those very same purposes, to announce the message of salvation by grace through faith in Christ and to equip those who believe it to do good works (see, for example, Ephesians 2:8–10).

4:6–8 Paul's death appears imminent. But just as his earthly existence was a "living sacrifice" (Romans 12:1), so his death is dedicated as an offering to God (2 Timothy 4:6). Paul boldly announces that he has kept the faith entrusted to him (4:7). As he lives and now dies in that relationship of faith, he is certain how his own personal race will turn out. The Lord Jesus has already won the crown of righteousness that Paul will receive, not when he dies, but on the day Christ returns (4:8).

Although Paul's life is coming to an end, he is aware that the over-arching struggle of God's people on earth continues. While Paul uses the metaphor of finishing his own race (4:7), it is best to view that contest as more of a relay than an individual competition. Therefore, he is writing this final letter to Timothy. As Paul's segment of the race comes to an end, he uses this letter to pass the baton of God's word on to Timothy who is then to pass it on to those who will follow in his footsteps. Paul is fully cognizant that this race does not simply involve his own life and death. The race will finally be over for all of God's people when the Lord Jesus returns. He is the righteous judge who, Paul says, will award the crown of righteousness "to me on that Day, and not only to me but to all who have loved his appearing" (4:8).

Jesus in 2 Timothy

As Paul faces his own death, he identifies "our Savior Christ Jesus [as the one] who abolished death and brought life and immortality to light through the gospel" (1:10). The now/not yet aspect of this verse is reflected in Jesus' words, "I am the resurrection and the life. Whoever believes in me, though he die, yet shall he live" (John 11:25). Paul is about to experience physical death, but, even in the midst of that experience, his life with Christ continues (see Philippians 1:23)

Two essential points in reference to who Jesus is and what he has done are reaffirmed in reverse order in 2 Timothy 2:8: "Remember Jesus Christ, risen from the dead, the offspring of David" (compare Romans 1:3–5). This does not mean Paul's appraisal of Jesus is based only in the historical past. Certainly it is rooted there, but it is also looks ahead to the future. Christ Jesus is the one who will return "to judge the living and the dead" (2 Timothy 4:1).

For Further Discussion

1. We often become preoccupied with our own struggles and problems. What lessons did Paul draw from his hardships? How did he respond to them? Is this a good example for us?

2. Imagine you are writing your last will and testament to a dear friend. What would you include? What message would you want to leave behind?

3. What have you learned about Paul's life and ministry that can be applied to your own "race of faith"?

4. One study ranked St. Paul the second most influential person in world history. In other words, out of all the people who have ever lived, Paul was said to have had the second greatest impact on this world. What do you think was the basis for such a conclusion? Do you think it was accurate? Who would you rank as the top three most influential people in the history of the human race? What about in your own life?

For Further Reading (see also 1 Timothy and Titus, above)

Stott, John. *Guard the Gospel.* The Bible Speaks Today. Downers Grove, IL: InterVarsity, 1984.

John

The Fourth Gospel is a favorite of many Christians. As we flip the pages of this gospel, Jesus claims, "I am the bread of life … the Good Shepherd … the way, the truth, and the life" (John 6:35; 10:11; 14:6). Jesus speaks in almost a mystical way of his relationship to the Father. Jesus rescues an adulterous woman, "Neither do I condemn you … Go and sin no more" (John 8:11). And he dies, only when all things have been "accomplished" (John 19:30). At the same time, John's Gospel inhabits a very different world from the three **Synoptic** Gospels, as a basic comparison demonstrates.

The Synoptic Gospels and the Fourth Gospel

Let's begin by noting a number of stories in the Fourth Gospel that are similar to those in the Synoptic Gospels. John the Baptist plays a similar role as forerunner. Jesus chooses personal disciples. He cleanses the temple (although the Fourth Gospel places this story early in its narrative). Miracles such as the healing of the official's son, the multiplication of the loaves, and the walking on the sea are reported by both traditions. Peter's confession and an anointing of Jesus lead to the last days in Jerusalem with a meal, arrest, trials before religious and political authorities, crucifixion, and resurrection appearances at the tomb and in the city. The stories share a common base.

However, roughly ninety percent of this gospel is without parallel in the Synoptic Gospels. In place of birth stories with magi and shepherds, the Gospel of John opens with a philosophic prologue identifying Jesus with the creative Word. Although the Synoptic Gospels place the ministry of Jesus primarily in Galilee, many of the stories in the Fourth Gospel are set in Jerusalem to which Jesus travels for a number of festivals. The Jesus of this gospel is conscious of pre-existence with God (John 17:5) and identifies himself explicitly with the Father (John 5:17–24; 8:19). Except in the conversation with Nicodemus, Jesus never speaks of the **kingdom of God** in the Fourth Gospel, nor does he tell **parables**. In sharp contrast to Mark, the Fourth Gospel never mentions demonic cleansing. Instead, Jesus seven times invokes a metaphor as he declares, "I am ..." And seven times Jesus works a mighty deed called a **sign**. When we turn to the passion narrative, although there is some similarity in outline, again the tone is strikingly different.

Some scholars have suggested that the author of John knew and used Mark or that the Fourth Gospel was written to "fill in" what was left out by the synoptic gospel tradition. More likely, this gospel and the Synoptic Gospels share a common awareness of the oral preaching of the disciples and early Christianity. As in previous cases, the particularity of the gospel is a product of the author's (inspired) choices to address the needs of a community for which the gospel was first written. To get at this point, we need to explore more about the author and audience.

The Beloved Disciple

As with the other gospels, no author is specifically named for the Fourth Gospel. However, John 21:24 offers an intriguing reference: "This is the disciple who is bearing witness about these things, and who has written these things, and we know that his testimony is true." The referenced disciple is to "one whom Jesus loved" (John 21:20). The text claims the beloved disciple bears witness about these things and "has written" these things, but the text does not explicitly claim authorship of the gospel by the beloved disciple. For example, the text could be read as claiming that the beloved disciple is a source for or authority behind the written gospel. Nevertheless, we are much closer to an identified author in this case than we are with the other gospels.

Who was the beloved disciple? Irenaeus, an early Christian bishop writing around A.D. 180, identified the beloved disciple with John, the son of Zebedee, who had moved to Ephesus and lived there until the time of Trajan (*Against Heresies* 3.1.2, 3.3.4). This identification was accepted by the early church, and so to this day the Fourth Gospel carries the title "the Gospel according to Saint John." In this chapter, we will continue to use that popular title, while at the same time recognizing that the identification is hardly certain.

"Grave" of John

The first major problem with the identification is the absence of direct reference to John the son of Zebedee in the gospel that now bears his name. In the fishing scene from John 21, those present include "the sons of Zebedee" (John 21:2) and later, one of the group is called "the disciple whom Jesus loved" (John 21:7), but the text does not connect the two. Hypothetically, any in the party (assuming the whole party named in John 21:2) could be the beloved disciple. Secondly, the gospel does specifically name one person, Lazarus, as "loved" by Jesus (John 11:5, 36). But he does not seem to be present in John 21. The question remains—who is the beloved disciple?

The beloved disciple first appears in John 13:23, reclining next to Jesus in the upper room. As many assume only the Twelve were present in the upper room, the identity of this disciple is sought among the Twelve. Around A.D. 190, Polycrates, a second-century bishop of Ephesus, identified John, who is buried at Ephesus, as the beloved disciple in John 13:23 (Eusebius, *Ecclesiastical History.* 3.31). However, no text limits the group to the Twelve. Others could have been in the upper room. Luke implies that women were among those in Jesus' close circle (Luke 23:49, 55; 24:22; Acts 1:14; 12:12).

In John 18:15–16, a character identified as "the other disciple" accompanies Simon Peter following the arrested Jesus. But this disciple gets into the courtyard because he "was known" to the high priest. Assuming this disciple is the beloved disciple (the text does not say so at this point) and assuming the beloved disciple is John the son of Zebedee (according to later tradition), a problem arises. Such renown and the attendant connections would be unlikely for a Galilean fisherman. As a result, later legends would claim that the house of Zebedee exported fish to Jerusalem or that John bought property in Jerusalem after Zebedee's death.

The beloved disciple next appears in a poignant scene with Mary the mother of Jesus at the cross. In John 19:26–27, Jesus gives the beloved disciple as a son to his mother and commends his mother into the care of that disciple. By this act, Jesus has created a new family. Subsequent followers of this disciple would be part of that family and family metaphors would become a prominent part of Christian identity.

The aside in John 19:35 implies that the beloved disciple was also an eyewitness to the death of Jesus. The language is quite similar to John 21:24. The beloved disciple "saw" how Jesus died. As we will learn later, "seeing" is one of the steps on the way to believing (John 20:8, 24–29).

The beloved disciple witnessed the crucifixion and also was a witness to the empty tomb. At the report of Mary Magdalene, Peter and "the other disciple, the one whom Jesus loved" (John 20:2) raced to the tomb (compare Luke 24:12 which mentions Peter only). In the Johannine version, the beloved disciple is the first to arrive, to see the evidence, and to "believe" (John 20:4–8). When the disciples later encounter the risen Jesus while fishing on the Sea of Galilee, the beloved disciple is the one who says to Peter, "It is the Lord" (John 21:7). The Lord may have appeared to Simon (Luke 24:34), but it is the beloved disciple who can first identify him. The beloved disciple is a distinct witness to the passion, death and resurrection of Jesus. As such, his testimony gives authority to the Fourth Gospel (John 21:24).

No definitive answer can be given to the identity of the beloved disciple. Whether this disciple is John the son of Zebedee, Lazarus, John Mark, Matthias, the rich young ruler ("loved" by Jesus in Mark 10:21), or someone else, only God knows. Although the gospel bears the name of John, the authority behind it is the beloved (and mysterious) disciple.

Audience and Purpose

Unlike many of the epistles of the New Testament that are directed to particular audiences, we have to read between the lines in a gospel to get hints about the first readers for whom the gospel was written. In the case of the Fourth Gospel, we have subtle clues from the material selected by the gospel writer and we have substantial help from a verse that seems to summarize the gospel. Unfortunately, there is a textual problem with the verse.

John 20:31 states the purpose of the gospel. After noting the selective nature of the signs reported in the gospel, the author continues, "but these are written so that you may believe that Jesus is the Christ, the Son of God, and that by believing you may have life in his name." The purpose of the gospel is to foster belief. But what kind of belief? And by whom?

Making the question even more challenging is a textual problem. The problem involves one letter in one word in the Greek text: a sigma. Our English Bibles attempt to translate the original Greek; but when the original Greek is unclear, then the act of translation (and interpretation) is even more difficult. The word in question is a form of the verb "to believe." If the sigma is present, the verb is translated “that you may come to believe.” But if the sigma is absent, then the verb is translated “that you may continue to believe.” One letter makes all the difference in determining whether the gospel was written as an evangelistic text (“that you may come to believe”) or as a text for a Christian community (“that you may continue to believe”). Both readings have significant ancient support and scholars are divided as to which is correct. For this reason, many translations employ the ambiguous “that you may believe” which can be understood either way.

However, if the selection of material by the gospel writer was made in view of the needs and concerns of the community for whom the gospel was written, then this material provides hints about the community and seems to tip the balance in favor of a gospel written to encourage people who were already believers. What we offer here is a hypothesis that many scholars have adopted. As with any hypothesis, the best we can say is “perhaps.”

Synagogue at Gamla

The first readers of the Fourth Gospel were likely Jewish Christians. They may have been followers of John the Baptist and had accepted his identification of Jesus as the promised prophet (John 1:19–36). Stories are told that stress the Jewishness of Jesus, and Jesus frequently goes to Jerusalem for Jewish festivals. But the Jesus of the Fourth Gospel is also divine. At some point these Jewish Christians likely came into conflict with other Jews. Perhaps the conflict arose because Jesus was not the kind of Messiah people were expecting who would drive out the hated Romans. Perhaps Christian claims about the divinity of Jesus conflicted with strict monotheism and seemed to make Jesus into another god (John 5:18). Apparently these Jewish Christians were driven out of the **synagogues** (John 9:22; 12:42–43; 16:2), an issue taken up only in the Fourth Gospel. As a result, their opponents, called the “Jews,” are considered blind and unbelieving (John 12:37–40) even children of the devil (8:44). This beleaguered group of Jewish Christians found reason to continue to believe. They found it in a writing that had the authority of the beloved disciple, an eyewitness of the passion, death, and resurrection of Jesus. Even in the midst of their troubles, they had life in the name of Jesus.

The Jews

The harsh portrayal of "the Jews" in the Fourth Gospel has been used frequently in history to justify untold violence against Jewish people—from murder to pogroms to the Holocaust. Jews have been abused as "Christ-killers," even though our theology teaches that we and our sins are the cause of the death of Jesus. Therefore, Christians must always stand against such anti-Semitism, even as they reckon with the misuse of their sacred writings to justify such horrors. Careful examination notes that the term "the Jews" is used in the gospel not for the Jewish people as a whole but for the religious and political elite of Jerusalem and their representatives, who were so often opposed to Jesus. "Israelite" seems to be the more inclusive term for the Jewish people (John 1:47). Jesus and his disciples still followed the laws of Moses and observed Jewish festivals. If all Jews are enemies of God, why would the author portray Jesus as a good Jew? So in recent years, some have translated the frequent Johannine reference as "Judeans." This translation has the advantage of identifying more precisely the opposition to Jesus without seeming to smear an entire people group. But the translation hides the sharp conflict experienced by the Jewish Christian community expelled from the synagogue(s) for their belief in Jesus as the Messiah and Son of God.

Structure

Although in bold form the gospel adheres to the story of Jesus as a teacher with a public ministry prior to this passion and death, the material in the Fourth Gospel is arranged more thematically and is clustered into two major blocks. After a philosophic prologue, the public ministry of Jesus is portrayed by a collection of seven signs. Each sign is attended by a poetic discourse. The Passion Narrative is the second major block in the gospel. Unlike the Synoptic Gospels, the Fourth Gospel portrays the death of Jesus as his glorification. Central to this story is the extensive upper room discourse and prayer (John 13–17). Chapter twenty draws the gospel to a seeming conclusion with a summary and purpose statement. Chapter 21 has all the earmarks of an epilogue, perhaps added shortly after the original composition. The following is a simple outline of John's Gospel:

JOHN: THE WORD MADE FLESH IS THE SON OF GOD,
GLORIFIED AT THE CROSS

PROLOGUE	1:1–18

BOOK OF SIGNS	1:19–12:50
BOOK OF GLORY	13:1–20:31
EPILOGUE	21:1–25

Style

When Jesus speaks in John, his speeches are more solemn than what we meet in the Synoptic Gospels. The discourses have a formal sense not unlike the poetic language used in sacred texts to distinguish the speech of God(s) from that of mortals. When we see lines of approximately the same length, we might even be reminded of poetry:

> Let not your hearts be troubled.
> Believe in God; believe also in me (John 14:1).

As Jesus is the one who makes the Father known (John 8:19), it is appropriate that the words of Jesus have a sacral overtone.

The appearance of various levels of meaning is a second characteristic of the writing of the Fourth Gospel. For example, the "Lamb of God" (John 1:29, 36) could be the **Passover** lamb, as Jesus dies on the Passover (John 18:28). The Lamb metaphor could invoke the Isaiah prophecy of the suffering servant going like a lamb to the slaughter (Isaiah 53:7). Or the Lamb could be the one who is worthy to judge at the end of time (Revelation 5:6). As a second example, reference to being "lifted up" (John 3:14; 8:28; 12:34) could refer either to crucifixion or to Jesus returning to the Father (see commend below on "glorification"). Perhaps a corollary of such usages is the appearance of instances of irony where a statement carries a sense that the speaker does not recognize (John 3:2; 4:12; 6:42; 7:35; 9:40–42; 11:50). The solemn tone of the Fourth Gospel is made more mysterious by various levels of meaning.

A third literary characteristic of the Fourth Gospel is the frequent use of abstractions. Twenty-six times, Jesus or another character takes up the topic of truth. Even Pilate asks, "What is truth?" (John 18:38). Twenty-three times the topic is light, often in contrast with darkness (John 1:5)—a basic dualism of the gospel that was characteristic of other Jewish groups, such as the sectarians of the Dead Sea Scrolls. Most significant and frequent is the abstraction "love" and the new commandment to love one another (John 13:34), the Greek using two different terms almost synonymously. Many of these abstractions appear in very similar contexts in the Johannine epistles.

A fourth characteristic of the gospel is the usage of a cyclical writing pattern. In contrast to western, linear forms of reasoning and address, the discourses and even the narratives seem to spiral around topics. The placement of the temple cleansing "early" is the gospel may be an indicator that chronological sequence is of lesser importance. In the upper room discourse, promise and discussion of the coming Paraclete comes up repetitively (John 14:15–27; 15:26; 16:7–11; 16:13–14). Such cyclical writing appears in the repetition of the three major themes in 1 John and in the seven visions of Revelation.

Parenthetic comments are a fifth literary device visible in the text. Explaining the meaning of the word Siloam is the simplest example (John 9:7). At other times, obscure comments are made clear. When Jesus calls one of the Twelve a devil, the author inserts the explanation that Judas would betray Jesus (John 6:71). A third type of parenthesis provides a theological explanation to an action or instance. When the high priest declares, "It is better for you that one man should die for the people, not that the whole nation should perish" (John 11:50), a significant theological interpretation is placed on the speech, "He did not say this of his own accord, but being high priest that year he prophesied that Jesus would die for the nation, and not for the nation only, but also to gather into one the children of God who are scattered abroad" (John 11:51–52).

At times such parentheses are hard to detect and their identification is uncertain. The well-known passage, "For God so loved the world, that he gave his only Son, that whoever believes in him should not perish but have eternal life" (John 3:16), may itself be a theological parenthesis drawing out the full implications of the discourse with Nicodemus. The first- and second-person discourse of chapter three changes abruptly to the third person at verse fourteen. Perhaps here the author of the gospel is making a point about Jesus. Whether the words were spoken by Jesus or were inserted as an explanation by the author, their point is true in either case. As an aside, the red letters used by many Bibles to identify the words of Jesus are the interpretation of those who publish that version of the Bible. Other interpretations, such as the one offered here, are possible.

The characteristics listed here are some of the more significant examples of the writing style used by the Fourth Gospel. Literary devices merge with theology to provide a lofty portrayal of Jesus, as the following major themes of the Fourth Gospel will affirm.

Themes

The Word—In his discourses, Jesus often speaks of "my word" (John 8:31, 37, 43). But in the prologue to the gospel, Jesus himself is identified with the "the Word" (in Greek: the ***logos***). The Word is preexistent (John 1:1–2), worked creation (John 1:3), and is life and light (John 1:4). This Word also comes into the world (John 1:10) in the flesh (John 1:14).

The language of the prologue is reminiscent of the speculation of **Hellenistic Judaism** about the Word. The Word is the mind of God, but becomes an independent person (the Son) who completes the work of creation and enables those who accept him to become children of God (John 1:12). Background for such language is in the portrayal of a personified wisdom (Proverbs 8). Later intertestamental works (see Wisdom 9 and Sirach 24) spoke of wisdom being with God at creation and coming to be with humanity when the Law was given through Moses.

The lofty identification of Jesus as the Word in the prologue sets the stage for the identification of Jesus with the Father so prevalent in the discourses of the Fourth Gospel. However, the language of the prologue does not reappear in the gospel. Once incarnate, Jesus is known as the divine Son.

Signs—Seven times in the Fourth Gospel, Jesus "does" a "sign." The Gospel of John, like the other gospels, avoids the typical Greek language for a miracle and gives to these selected accounts a theological interpretation. In the Old Testament, a sign could be a miraculous event, but more often was a prophetic activity pointing to a greater reality. Even as a stop sign warns of a coming intersection, a sign called the attention of the people of God to the fulfillment of God's purposes (Isaiah 66.19). A sign is a marker of that which is to come. In the Synoptic Gospels, signs anticipant the end of all things and the final judgment (Matthew 24). They announce that the end is near. In the Fourth Gospel, the signs are present events that feed the faith for those who believe. The signs are about the end and so they point ahead. Wine for a wedding anticipates the heavenly banquet (John 2.9; Isaiah 25:6). The healing of a blind man anticipates the messianic age (John 9:1–2; Isaiah 29:18). But signs are also the end-time reign of God crashing into the present. In the Fourth Gospel, the signs are grouped together in the first major block of material, often designed the Book of Signs.

"I am"—The prologue presented Jesus the Word as God. When Jesus seven times uses "I am" statement, his divine nature is reinforced. Behind such usage is God's call of Moses to be the agent of deliverance. When Moses offers an objection based on his ignorance of the name of God, "God said to Moses, 'I AM WHO I AM.'" God added, "Say this to the people of Israel, 'I am has sent me to you.'" (Exodus 3:14). The Jewish Christians for whom the Fourth Gospel was written would have immediately recognized the connection. Jesus is (self)identified with the I AM. Similarly such an identification would have offended more traditional Jews (John 8:56). The author of the gospel extends the allusion by making Jesus clearly superior to Moses (John 1:17; 5:45).

Each "I am" statement invokes a metaphor, most of which are drawn from the daily life of Roman agrarian Palestine. "I am the bread of life" (John 6:35). "I am the light of the world" (John 8:12). "I am the good shepherd" (John 10:11). In a way these "I am" statements function in the Fourth Gospel like the parables in the synoptic tradition. Since there are no parables in the Fourth Gospel, "I am" statements hold a middle ground between the lofty discourses and the signs done by Jesus. They give insight into the divinity of Jesus through more concrete examples. The statements, "I am the resurrection and the life" (John 11:25) and "I am the way, the truth, and the life" (John 14:6) operate on a higher and more abstract level.

The "I am" statements also serve a literary function. As they appear in both the Book of Signs and the Book of Glory, they serve to link and unify both major blocks of material in the gospel. The signs and the glorification of Jesus have their center in "I am."

Glorification—the second half of the Fourth Gospel is often called the Book of Glory, for it presents the passion and resurrection of Jesus as one act of glorification. This glorification is asserted by the vocabulary used by the author and by comparison of Johannine scenes to ones drawn from the synoptic tradition.

The Book of Glory is set up by Jesus' arrival in Jerusalem. Some Greeks come wishing to see Jesus, to which he responds, "The hour has come for the Son of Man to be *glorified*" (John 12:23). After alluding to his impending death, Jesus continues, "Now is my soul troubled. And what shall I say? 'Father, save me from this hour'? But for this purpose I have come to this hour. Father, *glorify* your name" (John 12:27–28). Then a voice comes from heaven: "I have *glorified* it, and I will *glorify* it again" (John 12:28. By repeatedly selecting sayings that use the root "glorify," the Fourth Gospel sets the tone for the passion as one of glorification. Throughout the upper room discourse, words based on this root are repeated (John 13:31; 14:13; 15:8; and 16:14). The discourse culminates with a prayer that begins, "Father, the hour has come; *glorify* your Son that the Son may *glorify* you.... I *glorified* you on earth, having accomplished the work that you gave me to do. And now, Father, *glorify* me in your own presence with the *glory* that I had with you before the world existed" (John 17:1, 4–5; compare 17:10, 22, 24). The drumbeat of this set of vocables is one piece of evidence in support of reading the passion in the Fourth Gospel as the glorification of Jesus, the Son of God.

The events at Gethsemane and at the cross further illustrate the glorification of Jesus in the Fourth Gospel. For example, Mark's telling of the happenings at Gethsemane is dark and violent. Jesus in anguish prays that the Father remove the cup from him. He is set upon by the betrayer and a "crowd with swords and clubs" (Mark 14:43). A sword strikes a slave, cutting off his ear. Jesus protests that they are handling him like a "bandit" (Mark 14:48). The disciples desert him, and a young follower slips from the clutches of his captors to run off naked. In the Fourth Gospel there is no anguished prayer (compare John 12:27–28). Jesus goes out to the "detachment of the soldiers and police" accompanying Judas (John 18:3). Twice Jesus asks for whom they are looking and identifies himself. They step back and fall to the ground when Jesus says, "I am he" (John 18:5). Jesus even protests Peter's violent act of defense when Peter drew a sword and cut off the ear of the slave Malchus. If Mark portrays the violent and human side of Gethsemane, the Fourth Gospel stresses a divine Jesus who is glorified by accomplishing the purpose for which he was sent.

Similarly, the violent death of Jesus in Mark is juxtaposed by the accomplishment of God's purpose in John. It is almost as if Mark were narrating the human element of the death of Jesus while John portrays the acts of the divine Son on behalf of all humanity. In Mark, the death scene commences with darkness over the whole land (Mark 15:33). At about three o'clock, Jesus cries, "My God, my God, why have you forsaken me?" (Mark 15:34) These are the only words of Jesus reported by Mark during the crucifixion. The taunting of bystanders then continues. "And Jesus uttered a loud cry and breathed his last" (Mark 15:37). In John, Jesus speaks several times from the cross. He commends his mother to the beloved disciple. Then Jesus, "knowing that all was now finished," said, "I thirst" (John 19:28). Death comes solemnly, "When Jesus had received the sour wine, he said, 'It is finished,' and he bowed his head and gave up his spirit" (John 19:30). The Fourth Gospel mentions none of the violent events the followed the death. In this Gospel, Jesus is very much in control, "finishing" the work for which he was sent. The death of Jesus is his glorification.

The author of the Fourth Gospel, through repeated use of the language of glorification and through careful selection of particular elements of the passion story, portrays Jesus as the divine Son accomplishing the task given to him by the Father. Jesus glorifies the Father in his passion, and the Father glorifies Jesus in the resurrection.

Life—"Life in his name" is a stated purpose of this gospel. When we think about the life that Jesus offers, most of us envision life on the other side of the resurrection, an eternal life in heaven. This conception of a future life in the age to come is central to the stories of the Synoptic Gospels. Jesus ascends to heaven from which he will return (Luke 24). Jesus teaches of the signs of the end (Matthew 24; Mark 13) and tells parables about the coming judgment (Matthew 25).

By contrast, John's Gospel has what many call a **realized eschatology**. "Eschatology," you may recall, is the teaching about the last things. A "realized" eschatology would suggest that the promised future is also experienced in a way in the present. It is "now" and "not yet." According to John, eternal life is not just something to be anticipated in the future. It is also a present reality. At the raising of Lazarus, Jesus declared, "I am the resurrection and the life. Whoever believes in me, though he die, yet shall he live, and everyone who lives and believes in me shall never die" (John 11:25–26). The present sense is captured well when Jesus declares, "Truly, truly, I say to you, whoever hears my word and believes him who sent me has eternal life. He does not come into judgment, but has passed from death to life" (John 5:24). But in the very next verse Jesus speaks of the "not yet": "Truly, truly, I say to you, an hour is coming, and is now here, when the dead will hear the voice of the Son of God, and those who hear will live" (John 5:25). Eternal life begins now and continues through the resurrection forever. "For as the Father has life in himself, so he has granted the Son also to have life in himself" (John 5:26).

Belief—"That you may [come to/continue to] believe" is also a key purpose of the gospel (John 20:31). This belief is always expressed through a verbal form. The noun for "faith" is not used in the Fourth Gospel. Put simply, to believe is to accept the message about Jesus. To believe Jesus and his words (John 2:22; 5:47) is to believe in Jesus and in the one who sent him (John 5:24).

In John, belief is connected to seeing and to knowing. In the scene of Peter and the beloved disciple racing to the tomb, the sequence seems to be "see," "believe," and then "know": "Then the other disciple … *saw* and *believed*; for as yet they did not *understand* the Scripture, that he must rise from the dead" (John 20:8–9). At other times "believing" and "knowing" are interchangeable (note the pairing of the terms in John 8:32, 45 and in John 14:7, 10).

Belief in the Fourth Gospel seems to involve a movement from doubt to faith, especially in terms of the resurrection. Mary Magdalene is convinced the body was stolen from the tomb (John 20: 2, 13). Only in a later scene does she recognize the risen Jesus (John 20:16). Similarly, the disciples who first come to the tomb do not understand (John 20:9). Only later do they rejoice when they see the Lord (John 20:20). Most obvious is the case of Thomas who doubts the report and only a week later sees for himself and believes (John 20:24–29). Belief comes after doubt.

Key Texts—Introducing Jesus

1:14 Foundational to the theology of the Fourth Gospel is the declaration of John 1:14: "And the Word became flesh and dwelt among us." A few verses earlier the gospel opened in a philosophic way by discussing the Word in language drawn from Hellenistic Judaism—quite understandable from the dualistic perspectives of Greek philosophy. But here the Word becomes "flesh," a jarring acclamation! Romans could picture gods who came among mortals in disguise or who seemed to be human. But the gods actually dwelt in another reality devoid of physicality. To claim that a god became human would be nonsense, as silly as a robot with actual feelings.

Nevertheless, Christianity affirms the **incarnation**, that God came in the flesh—a claim echoed by Paul in his letter to the Colossians (2:9) and by 1 John (1:1–4; 2:18–28; 3:24b–4:6). In subsequent church history, the Docetist heresy would assert that Jesus only "seems" to be human. **Gnosticism** would put forward a Jesus who came to convey secret knowledge to a select few. Such a Jesus did not need the flesh and the actuality of his death was questioned by this variant of Christianity. Johannine insistence on the incarnation would be critical to the expression of the faith of the church in a Jesus who is fully divine and fully human.

To believe the incarnation is one of the greatest challenges for Christianity, for most of us are more comfortable with a superhuman Jesus (read "not really human"). We sing of a "little Lord Jesus, no crying he makes" but never of a baby Jesus with diaper rash. Our religious art tends to picture Jesus as an ideal prom date—warm and caring. And in our generation, Gnosticism is increasingly popular. But for the Fourth Gospel, the incarnation is fundamental. Through the Word become flesh "we have seen his glory, glory as of the only Son from the Father, full of grace and truth" (John 1:14). We cannot believe in Jesus as the Son of God unless we also confess that he is God in our flesh.

1:29–34 As with the synoptic tradition, the Gospel of John places the inauguration of the ministry of Jesus in the context of the work of John the Baptist. In the Synoptic Gospels, the ministry of Jesus begins with two acts: baptism by

John and a forty-day period of testing in the wilderness. The wilderness of Judea was the place of John's work and recalled the forty-year testing of the children of Israel after the Exodus from Egypt.

In the Fourth Gospel, the words of the Baptist take precedence over action. He declares that Jesus is "the Lamb of God, who takes away the sin of the world!" (John 1:29; compare 1:36) As the function of the Lamb is to take away sin, John probably has in mind the sacrificial system of the temple. However, the Passover lamb was a celebratory sacrifice recalling the Exodus, and the lamb sacrificed on the Day of Atonement only covered the sins of the Israelite people (Leviticus 16:34). The sacrifice of the Lamb to whom John the Baptist pointed would take away the sin of the whole world. This singular Lamb is worthy (Revelation 5:6).

Second, John the Baptist recounts, "I saw the Spirit descend from heaven like a dove, and it remained on him" (John 1:32). In the Synoptic Gospels similar language attends the act of baptism (Matthew 3:16; Mark 1:10; Luke 3:22). In the Fourth Gospel, the announcement is key, not the act of baptism; for the Spirit not only descends, it also "remains" on Jesus—a point made only by this gospel. This durative character of the presence of the Spirit would also be a part of the promised Spirit who would come when Jesus returns to the Father (John 14:17).

The third announcement of the Baptist restates a theme of the gospel: "And I have seen and have borne witness that this is the Son of God" (John 1:34). The divine sonship of Jesus is seen in the incarnation (John 1:14), affirmed as Jesus makes the Father known (John 1:18), and proclaimed first by John the Baptist (1:34).

1:43–51 In the Synoptic Gospels, Jesus had summoned his first disciples with the words, "Follow me." Philip responds to the same word in the Fourth Gospel (John 1:43). When Philip seeks Nathaniel and identifies Jesus as the one of whom Moses and the prophets wrote, Nathaniel jeers, "Can anything good come out of Nazareth?" (John 1:46). Regional rivalry and economic status are probably behind the remark, for Nazareth was a very small community of some twenty families on the edge of the Bet Netofa valley and in the shadow of the former Galilean capital. Bethsaida was enjoying an increase of status, and would be christened a Greek city in 30 A.D., renamed Julias in honor of Julia-Livia, wife of Emperor Augustus and mother of Emperor Tiberius. A temple in her honor was built at about this time.

When Nathaniel subsequently meets Jesus, he is impressed by Jesus' knowledge of Nathaniel's past. More important is the confession of Nathaniel, for it reiterates the Johannine theme: "**Rabbi**, you are the Son of God! You are the King of Israel!" (John 1:49)

Key Texts—Promise of Life

The Book of Signs opens with two miracles set in Cana. The first occurs at the wedding of Cana (John 2:1–11). The second is the healing of a royal official's son (John 4:43–54). Together with the intervening dialogues, the theme of this subsection is the giving of life.

2:1–11 A wedding is a celebration of life. Unlike modern weddings with their emphasis on romantic love, weddings in antiquity were formal arrangements between two families with the purpose of producing life. At such a festival the wine gave out, and Jesus turned water into wine of significantly higher quality than that which had been already served (John 2:10). The quantity of wine produced (some 150 gallons!) attests to Jesus' qualification to host the messianic banquet (Genesis 29:11–12; Isaiah 25:6; Amos 9:14) and to inaugurate that abundant life he promises (John 10:10). As a result of this "sign," God's glory is revealed and the disciples believed in him (John 2:11). Present at this event is the mother of Jesus, who will also witness the crucifixion at which water and wine-colored blood flow to the glory of the Father (John 19:34).

Somewhat confusing in the Fourth Gospel is the placement of the cleansing of the temple (John 2:13–25) as the next story following the wedding at Cana. Seemingly, in John the cleansing happens early in the ministry of Jesus in contrast to the placement of the event during Jesus' final week according to the synoptic tradition. As a result, some see the gospel accounts in conflict while others suggest two distinct cleansings. In contrast, we suggest that the writer placed the story at this point because of a thematic connection to the story of the wedding at Cana. Jesus drove out the merchants and money changers because they made "my Father's house a house of trade" (John 2:16). Transforming the usage of the temple precincts parallels a similar reversal in the sign at Cana where stone water jars for the Jewish rites of purification become reservoirs of good wine. Both transformations anticipate coming chapters in the Book of Signs (John 5–10), where the signs and discourses of Jesus transform the meaning of the Sabbath and major religious festivals. The evangelist selects and presents material thematically (not chronologically) so that "you may have life in his name" (John 20:31).

3:1–16 The topic of a dialogue between Jesus and Nicodemus, a member of the **Sanhedrin**, is the source of that life which comes from Jesus. Notably, Nicodemus approaches Jesus at night. As the Fourth Gospel makes much of light and darkness and directly connects light and life (John 1:3b–8), Nicodemus is in the dark religiously as well as physically. Jesus teaches Nicodemus, "Truly, truly, I say to you, unless one is born again he cannot see the kingdom of God" (John 3:3; the words translated "born again" could also be translated "born from above"). Nicodemus misunderstands Jesus and thinks Jesus is talking about a second physical birth from a human mother. Perhaps the misunderstanding of Nicodemus is a consequence of the belief that birth from a Jewish mother makes a person God's child (Exodus 4:22; Deuteronomy 32:6; Hosea 11:1). But Jesus refers to a birth of water and the Spirit (Christian baptism) that births the Christian life (John 3:5). The gospel writer goes on to connect this baptismal allusion to the death and resurrection of Jesus (compare Romans 6:3–11): "And as Moses lifted up the serpent in the wilderness, so must the Son of Man be lifted up" (John 3:14). As a result, those who believe in Jesus have "eternal life" (John 3:15). New birth of water and the Spirit leads to eternal life because "God so loved the world, that he gave his only Son, that whoever believes in him should not perish but have eternal life" (John 3:16). The wedding of Cana celebrated anticipated life; the discourse with Nicodemus point to a rebirth that leads to life.

In the dialogue with Nicodemus, as with many other dialogues in the Gospel of John, Jesus uses a metaphor, a figure of speech in which a word or phrase that ordinarily designates one thing is used to designate another and makes an implicit comparison. Frequently, the hearer will make the mistake of taking Jesus literally, as did Nicodemus. Jesus will then launch into an extensive explanation or discussion to correct the confusion. The topic almost inevitably will come to focus on Jesus' relationship with the Father (John 3:16–18). The pattern can be seen again at the end of the chapter, but this time on the lips of John the Baptist. The Baptist invokes the metaphor of a wedding (bridegroom, bride, and friend of the bridegroom) and the segment ends with an affirmation about the Father, the Son, and life: "The Father loves the Son and has given all things into his hand. Whoever believes in the Son has eternal life" (John 3:35–36). Watch for this pattern in the rest of the Book of Signs!

4:7–26 At midday Jesus meets a **Samaritan** woman at a well (John 4:6–7). Nicodemus came at night and was theologically in the dark. In keeping with Johannine themes, we rightly expect that the Samaritan will understand, for she comes in the light. However, the contrast between Nicodemus and the Samaritan woman is even greater. He was a high standing member of the Sanhedrin; she has "had five husbands, and the one you now have is not your husband" (John 4:18). This woman had been abused and passed around from husband to husband so much that her current "man" would not even marry her. Further, she had been ostracized by the other women of the community. She could not come with them in the morning to fetch water, but had to endanger herself and come at midday by herself. Her place in life was at the far opposite end of the social ladder from Nicodemus. Her future behavior would differ dramatically from Nicodemus as well. After her encounter with Jesus, she would leave her water jar and race back to the city with the news, "Come and see" (John 4:28–29), even as Mary of Magdala would serve as the apostle to the apostles with the news, "I have seen the Lord" (John 20:18). Nicodemus would merely assist with the burial of Jesus (John 19:39).

When Jesus meets the woman, we see the pattern repeated of a misunderstood metaphor leading through discussion to a revelation of the nature of Jesus. In view of the difficult relationship between Jews and Samaritans, the Samaritan woman is surprised that Jesus would ask for a drink from her. Jesus responds with a metaphor: "If you knew the gift of God, and who it is that is saying to you, 'Give me a drink,' you would have asked him, and he would have given you living water" (John 4:10). The woman misunderstands the metaphor and takes Jesus literally. The only water source in the area is this deep well. She wonders where Jesus would get running water (John 4:11). Jesus explains the metaphor, "The water that I will give him will become in him a spring of water welling up to eternal life" (John 4:14). Their subsequent discussion leads the women to mention the coming Messiah. In response, Jesus said to her, "I who speak to you am he" (John 4:26). From a misunderstood metaphor comes a revelation about Jesus.

In the stories of Nicodemus and the Samaritan women a misunderstood metaphor leads to a promise of life and a disclosure of the unique nature of Jesus. For Nicodemus, new birth brings one into the kingdom and discloses Jesus as the only Son of God, "that whoever believes in him should not perish but have eternal life" (John 3:16). For the Samaritan woman, living water is a "spring of water welling up to eternal life" (John 4:14) and discloses Jesus as the Messiah. Unfortunately, Nicodemus remains in the dark; the Samaritan woman is in the light.

4:46–54 As a sign of the promise of life made to Nicodemus and the Samaritan woman, Jesus raises to life the son of a regional official. Jesus is in Cana and the official comes to him from Capernaum with his request for help. As with Nicodemus and the Samaritan woman, Jesus promises life: "Go; your son will live" (John 4:50). The official believes the word that Jesus speaks to him and departs. On his way home he receives a report that corresponds with the promise of Jesus. "And he himself believed, and all his household" (John 4:53). Although the story lacks any exposition of the divine sonship of Jesus, the word "son" is part of the promise of life to the official. Readers ancient and modern might make the connection, for in giving life the Son is revealed (John 5:21).

Key Texts—Jesus is Light and Life

Themes of life and light continue through chapters 5–9. But in this section signs by Jesus and the subsequent discourses are reported in the context of Jewish festivals. The actions and words of Jesus bring life and light to these Jewish holy days by replacing the significance of the festivals with aspects of Jesus' self-disclosure. For a community of Jewish Christians who have been expelled from their synagogues (see above), these texts help to form a new religious identity supplanting their former identities. In the place of the **Torah** and its rituals, these stories are written that they (and we) might "believe that Jesus is the Christ, the Son of God, and that by believing … have life in his name" (John 20:31).

5:1–29 Jesus works another sign by healing a paralyzed man at a pool "called Bethesda, which has five roofed colonnades" (John 5:2). Excavations at the church of St. Anna in northeast Jerusalem have revealed just such a pool. Jesus works the sign by instructing the man, "Get up, take up your bed, and walk" (John 5:8). Significantly, the healing takes place on a **Sabbath**. As a result, some of the religious elites of Jerusalem start to persecute Jesus because he did such things on the Sabbath.

Carrying a mat, or, for that matter, healing were considered violations of the Sabbath prohibition against work (Exodus 20:10). The prohibition is traced theologically to the creation narrative where God rested on the seventh day

(Exodus 20:11; Genesis 2:2). Jesus counters his critics by saying, "My Father is working until now, and I am working" (John 5:17). If God could work on the seventh day (by healing), so could Jesus as the Son of God. His opponents recognized the divine claim and sought to kill him for "making himself equal with God" (John 5:18). With this sign Jesus replaces the Sabbath by pointing beyond it to a time when there will be no more sorrow, sickness, pain or death (Isaiah 35:5–4). In his subsequent discourse, Jesus connects his divine sonship with the gift of eternal life:

> Truly, truly, I say to you, whoever hears my word and believes him who sent me has eternal life. He does not come into judgment, but has passed from death to life. Truly, truly, I say to you, an hour is coming, and is now here, when the dead will hear the voice of the Son of God, and those who hear will live. For as the Father has life in himself, so he has granted the Son also to have life in himself (John 5:24–26).

6:1–51 The signs of the feeding of the five thousand and the walking on the sea along with the first of the major "I am" discourses are set at the time of the **Passover** (John 6:4). This annual festival commemorates the rescue of the Israelites from slavery in Egypt. Its meal recalls rescue through the parting of the sea and through miraculous provision of manna in the wilderness. In a way, Jesus' signs of feeding and sea walking recapitulate the Passover events in reverse order and replace them. Now belief centers not in an ancient rescue but in the one whom God has sent (John 6:29). The ancient bread from heaven is supplanted by the one who says, "I am the bread of life; whoever comes to me shall not hunger, and whoever believes in me shall never thirst.... If anyone eats of this bread, he will live forever. And the bread that I will give for the life of the world is my flesh" (John 6:35, 51). In the synoptic and Pauline traditions, Jesus reinterprets the Passover meal by saying of the bread and wine, "This is my body.... This is my blood.... Do this in remembrance of me." The Johannine tradition omits the Lord's Supper, perhaps because the Passover has already been reinterpreted with an "I am" statement that is also linked to the death of Jesus. At this point in the Fourth Gospel, Jesus is not specifically speaking of the Eucharist. He speaks only metaphorically. But that metaphor will become real on the night when he was betrayed.

7:37–39 The next feast in the narrative is the **Feast of Booths** (John 7:2), which marked the end of the grape and olive harvests. The festival gets its name from the temporary shelters or booths that the people constructed and in which they lived during the festival (Nehemiah 8:14–17) as a reminder of God's protection during their wilderness wanderings (Leviticus 23:42–43). During the **Second Temple period**, according to the **Mishnah**, giant menorahs (candelabras) were lit in the temple and the festivities included dancing to flutes by torchlight. Libations of water were poured out at the bronze altar as part of the prayers for rains to renew the agricultural cycle. Both light and water were themes of the Feast of Booths.

Recalling words to the Samaritan woman, Jesus exclaims on the last day of the festival, "If anyone thirsts, let him come to me and drink. Whoever believes in me, as the Scripture has said, 'Out of his heart will flow rivers of living water'" (John 7:37–38). The Feast of Booths may pray to God for that water which restarts the agricultural cycle on which this life depends. But Jesus offers the living water of eternal life.

7:53–8:11 The story of the adulterous woman does not appear in some of the oldest manuscripts of John. In some manuscripts it shows up in Luke. Although set in the temple, it seems to have no connection to the Feast of Booths, which is the concern of the author at this point in the narrative. Nevertheless the story is characteristic of Jesus' concern for the marginalized and his abhorrence for the use of Torah regulations to cut off people from God. Although the Torah calls for the stoning of adulterers, Jesus put the responsibility on the accusers. Only those who are faultless may enforce legal penalties. When no one remains but Jesus, he does not condemn the woman. He simply instructs her: "Go, and from now on sin no more" (John 8:11). Even if the story is not original to the gospel, its conforms with the character and teaching of Jesus witnessed by all four gospels.

8:12–59 Even as the living water offered by Jesus had supplanted the libation themes of the Feast of Booths, so in contrast to the light of the temple menorah, Jesus declared, "I am the light of the world. Whoever follows me will not walk in darkness, but will have the light of life" (John 8:12). According to the pattern we saw earlier, the metaphor is misunderstood, leading to a series of discussions that reveal more about Jesus. In the first we learn, "The Father who sent me bears witness about me" (John 8:18). In a second scene, "I am from above …; I am not of this world" (John 8:23). But in a third scene, Jesus makes his greatest claim. Jesus opens by asserting, "If you abide in my word, you are truly my disciples, and you will know the truth, and the truth will set you free" (John 8:32). His opponents counter by pointing to their heritage as children of Abraham, to which Jesus retorts, after a number of exchanges, "Truly, truly, I say to you, before Abraham was, I am" (John 8:58). Here we see the full implication of the metaphorical "I am the light of the world." It is a divine claim making Jesus superior to all those characters and stories that provide Jewish identity. The Fourth Gospel is making an argument that the writer of the letter to the Hebrews echoes, "Long ago, at many times and in many ways, God spoke to our fathers by the prophets, but in these last days he has spoken to us by his Son, whom he appointed the heir of all things, through whom also he created the world" (Hebrews 1:1–2). The Fourth Gospel and the letter to the Hebrews are written to similar audiences and are making similar points.

9:1–41 The verbal claim to be "light of the world" with all of its implications for Jesus' divine identity is confirmed by a sign. In response to those who

"Wheel" lamps

suggest that sin is behind the misfortune of a man born blind, Jesus heals the man, saying, "As long as I am in the world, I am the light of the world" (John 9:5). Jesus mixes mud, places it on the man's eyes, and sends him to the Pool of Siloam to wash. The pool was located in the southern tip of the city and has recently been discovered by archaeologists. The man came back able to see.

The rest of the chapter details a number of exchanges between the man who could now see and the religious authorities. The end result is that they drove him out (John 9:34). He then meets Jesus again and become one who not only sees but also believes (John 9:37–38).

This sign seems to operate on two levels at least. In a physical sense, a blind man is given sight—a sure sign of the messianic age (Matthew 11:4–5) and a demonstration of Jesus as the light of the world. But in a spiritual sense, the sign also has import. For seeing is part of believing, as the three resurrection stories in the gospel make clear (Mary Magdalene, Peter and the beloved disciple, and Thomas). The readers of this gospel are thus led well beyond the symbols of the Feast of Booths. They are ready to see and believe in the Son of God who is glorified in suffering.

Key Texts—Jesus the Good Shepherd and the Resurrection

The best-known words of Jesus from the Gospel of John are two "I am" statements: "I am the Good Shepherd" (John 10:11) and "I am the resurrection and the life" (John 11:25). Jesus links the former to his death (John 10:15), and the raising of Lazarus is the final sign before the Book of Glory, which culminates with the resurrection of Jesus. That eternal life promised by the Book of Signs will be brought about by the death and resurrection of Jesus. These two chapters therefore function as a transition between the Book of Signs and the Book of Glory.

10:1–18 The "Good Shepherd" is one of the more concrete metaphors used by Jesus in his "I am" statements. The shepherding of sheep and goats was (and still is) a common practice in Palestine. Details about hirelings and wolves would be easily understood. The metaphor may be understandable, but Jesus seems to mix it with a related metaphor, when he says, "Truly, truly, I say to you, I am the door of the sheep" (John 10:7). Likely, Jesus refers to the practice of a shepherd sleeping across the entrance to a wilderness sheepfold at night. Neither wire nor wood (used in modern agricultural gates) were available in antiquity. The walls of the fold were piled stones, so the shepherd often served as the gate.

Sheepfold in Judean wilderness

Shepherds in antiquity were often considered disreputable and dishonest. Luke plays on this social status by telling of shepherds as the first visitors after the birth of Jesus. For this reason, Jesus always speaks of the "good" shepherd. A second reason for the use of the adjective is the prophetic tradition of referring to the kings as the shepherds of the people of Israel. The tradition may go back to David who was first a shepherd. But when the prophets label kings as shepherds, the metaphor is always used negatively. The kings were faithless shepherds (Jeremiah 10:21; 22:22; 23:1–4; 25:34–38; Ezekiel 34:1–10; Zechariah 10:3; 11:4–17). Therefore the prophets promised that God would shepherd the people (Ezekiel 34:11–16) and the psalms made that shepherding personal (Psalm 23). When Jesus says, "I am the good shepherd" (John 10:11), he is claiming this tradition. It is a divine claim.

The metaphor may work in another direction as well. Not only were sheep and goats important to the livelihood and economy of the land, they were central to the sacrificial system of the temple. When the good shepherd lays down his life for the sheep (John 10:11), the shepherd become the sacrificial lamb—a symbol central to Revelation. When Jesus lays down his life for the sheep, he does so not as a victim but of his own power, in accord with the directive of his Father (John 10:18). The result will be "one flock, one shepherd" (John 10:16).

10:22–30 The transitional metaphor of the good shepherd resurfaces during the Feast of Dedication in Jerusalem. Dedication (we know it as Hanukah) was a festival of lights that celebrated the reconsecrating of the altar and temple by the Maccabees after its desecration by the Seleucids (164 B.C.). The work of this ruling family is supplanted by the good shepherd/king who promises eternal life (John 10:28), is one with the Father (John 10:30), and rightly calls himself the Son of God (John 10:36). Many themes from earlier sections of the Fourth Gospel come together here and as a result "many believed in him" (John 10:42). A final sign and word are yet to be spoken before the hour of his glorification comes.

11:1–53 The raising of Lazarus provides the final transition from signs to glory in the Fourth Gospel. The author's literary skill is evident, for he includes a reference back to the light of the world (John 11:10) and well as an anticipation of the theme of glorification (John 11:4). As the story opens, a report comes to Jesus, "Lord, he whom you love is ill" (John 11:3). Later in the Book of Glory we will meet the beloved disciple, but nothing specifically ties that character to this tantalizing reference.

When Jesus does arrive at the town of Martha and Mary, Lazarus has been dead for four days. According to later Jewish traditions, the soul hovered near the body for three days and then departed. Lazarus was truly dead. In the Fourth Gospel at two key milestones of life—wedding and death—Jesus brings life.

In the raising of Lazarus, Jesus demonstrates that he is Lord of the living and the dead (Acts 10:42) and can effect those events normally associated with the end of times (such as the raising of the dead; Ezekiel 37:1–14; John 5:28). Eternal life is a present reality for believers for they have already "passed from death to life" (John 5:24). As Jesus said to Martha, "I am the resurrection and the life. Whoever believes in me, though he die, yet shall he live, and everyone who lives and believes in me shall never die" (John 11:25–26). In response, Martha confesses that Jesus is the Son of God, a recurrent theme of the gospel (John 11:27).

As a transitional story, the raising of Lazarus anticipates the coming Passion Narrative and Jesus' own resurrection. In this sense it functions as a sign, pointing beyond itself to something greater. And as with all signs, the greater event is not just a replication of the sign. Lazarus was resuscitated to this life. Jesus would be raised gloriously, never to die again. In terms of the narrative, the story is also pivotal. Jesus' divine claims had aroused opposition previously (John 5:16; 6:41, 52; 7:1, 45; 8:59; 10:31). But after Lazarus, the religious authorities begin to plot against Jesus and plan to put him to death (John 11:46–53).

Key Texts—Book of Glory

In broad strokes, the Book of Glory follows the familiar outline of the Passion Narrative. Jesus enters Jerusalem and teaches (John 12). Jesus shares a meal with his disciples and predicts the betrayal (John 13). Jesus is arrested at Gethsemane and is tried by religious and political leaders (John 18). He is condemned by Pilate and crucified (John 19). He is raised and appears to his followers (John 20). An epilogue continues the appearances.

But in a number of ways, the story is told from a distinct perspective. First of all, there are chronological issues. In John 19:14, Jesus appears before Pilate at the sixth hour; but Matthew reports darkness over the land from the sixth to the ninth hour as Jesus dies (Matthew 27:45). The seeming difference is easily resolved when we realize that Romans counted their hours from midnight, while Jews counted them from sundown. The sixth hour in John is 6:00 am; the sixth hour in Matthew is noon. More significantly, John places the death of Jesus on the Passover (John 12:1; 13:1; 19:14, 31); the Synoptic Gospels place it on the day after the Passover. A possible explanation for the difference may be that different communities celebrated the meal according to different calendars. In the New Testament the word "Passover" may refer to the day or to the whole week of festivities. More likely, John is making a theological point about the sacrifice of Jesus. We have noted earlier the interplay between the shepherd and lamb motifs. The sacrifice of Jesus supplants any Passover sacrifice. What better way to make that point than to call the day of Jesus' crucifixion the Passover (compare Luke 9:31 which calls the passion of Jesus his Exodus)!

13:1–15 A meal opens with Jesus knowing that the hour of his departure and glorification has come (John 13:1; compare John 12:23, 27–28). All Passover implications are missing (John 13:1). In place of bread, wine, and the institution of the Lord's Supper, John narrates the washing of the disciples' feet. This act of humility on Jesus' part is an example to his followers (John 13:15) and a paradigm of all that is about to take place. Subsequently Jesus predicts the betrayal by Judas, a story set in the upper room by the synoptic tradition.

13:31–35; 15:12–17 The dialogue of Jesus with the disciples about betrayal gradually shifts to a monologue. The form is similar to a farewell discourse and Jesus concludes it with a prayer (John 17). Although sometimes called the upper room discourse, no mention is made in the Fourth Gospel of such a room.

Two important themes open the discourse. The first is a repeated refrain of glorification. The departure of Jesus in a very short time will be for his glorification and for the glorification of his Father. As a consequence of his departure, he calls on his followers to "love one another" (John 13:34). It is the new commandment of Jesus. In Latin the word for "commandment" is *mandatum*. From this Latin term comes the popular name for Holy Thursday: Maundy Thursday. This commandment, and not the Torah, will provide an identity for the community of followers of Jesus: "By this all people will know that you are my disciples, if you have love for one another" (John 13:35). In the typical style of cyclical writing, the new commandment comes up again later in the discourse. This time such love is characterized by laying down one's life for one's friends (John 15:13). Jesus' glorification calls for the mandate to love, a love characterized by self-sacrifice.

14:1–7 The imminent departure of Jesus call for reassurance: "Let not your hearts be troubled. Believe in God; believe also in me" (John 14:1). Interestingly, both uses of the verb "believe" can be indicative or imperative. "You are believing in God and you are believing in me"; or "Keep believing in God and keep believing in me"; or any combination of the two is possible. Equally possible is the use of deliberate ambiguity. The gospel writer translates the words of Jesus to both commend current practice and to encourage future faithfulness. The writer can so translate the word of Jesus because of the promise Jesus gives, "And if I go and prepare a place for you, I will come again and will take you to myself, that where I am you may be also" (John 14:3). To the promise Jesus appends another "I am" statement that merges several recurring Johannine themes: "I am the way, and the truth, and the life. No one comes to the Father except through me" (John 14:6).

14:15–17, 25–26; 15:26; 16:7–14 Repeatedly in the discourse, Jesus connects his departure to the coming of the Holy Spirit. In the Fourth Gospel, this one who comes at the departure of Jesus is the **Paraclete**, sometimes translated Counselor or Advocate (John 14:16). The one who comes is the "Spirit of truth" who will abide with and in the followers of Jesus (John 14:17). This one "will teach you all things and bring to your remembrance all that I have said to you" (John 14:26). The coming of the Paraclete is part of the glorification of Jesus (John 16:14). Jesus bestows the Spirit when, after the resurrection, he breathes on his disciples (John 20:22), even as God breathed the breath of life into Adam (Genesis 2:7). Significantly, in the Johannine epistles the term "Paraclete" is used for Jesus (1 John 2:1).

15:1–7 An interesting seam in the farewell discourse occurs at chapter 15. At the end of chapter 14, Jesus seems to conclude the discourse, "Rise, let us go from here" (John 14:31). But the discourse immediately resumes (and continues for three more chapters!) with an "I am" statement. Two metaphors are used.

Jesus is the true vine and his Father is the vine grower (John 15:1). The focus of this metaphor is on Jesus' relationship with his followers and not on Jesus' relationship with the Father. As with parables, so with the Johannine metaphors, one primary point is in view. Metaphors are not meant to explain matters comprehensively.

The focus on the relationship between Jesus and his followers is further emphasized by the repetitive use of the term "abide" (John 15:4–7). This same term in Greek first surfaced when Jesus began to gather followers in John 1:38. It would also characterize the relationship between Jesus and his followers in the Johannine epistles (1 John 2:24–25; 3:24; 4:13, 15; 2 John 2, 9). The relationship is further characterized by love: "As the Father has loved me, so have I loved you. Abide in my love" (John 15:9). The new commandment to love one another flows from this abiding in the gospel (John 15:12) and in the epistles (1 John 4:7–16). Love is the fruit that comes from branches connected to the vine (John 15:5, 16).

The reappearance of the glorification theme in the midst of this section (John 15:8) connects the nourishing metaphor to the larger narrative—Jesus' impending passion. Abiding in the vine and the fruit of love for others are not possible without the glorification of Jesus in his death and resurrection. By itself, the metaphor of vine and branches has a pleasant and almost bucolic feel. However, without the sacrifice of Jesus such pleasantries would be mere trivialities.

17:1–26 The farewell discourse concludes with an extended prayer offered by Jesus on behalf of his followers and also for "those who will believe in me through their word" (John 17:20). The prayer is sometimes called a high priestly prayer, because Jesus stands between the world and God and offers prayers on behalf of his followers.

In the opening section (John 17:1–8), Jesus prays for glorification, that the Son may glorify the Father and the Father glorify the Son. This theme, from which the name Book of Glory is drawn, is repeated several times here and in the other two sections of the prayer (John 17:10 and John 17: 22, 24). The glory theme will then disappear from the gospel, with the exception of its usage to describe the predicted death of Peter (John 19:31). In terms of his public ministry, Jesus has done all that was asked of him. The hour has now come for the final act to commence (John 17:1).

In the second section (John 17:9–19), Jesus prays for his followers—"those you gave me" (John 17:9). These followers are distinguished from the "world" that from the beginning of the gospel did not know or accept Jesus (John 1:10–11). To these followers, Jesus has given "your word" (John 17:14). Jesus prays that they might be protected from the evil one or evil itself (the Greek is ambiguous here even as it is in the Lord's Prayer); and Jesus asks that God would "sanctify them in the truth; your word is truth" (John 17:17). The purpose of these two petitions is to assure successful mission work, for Jesus has sent them into the world (John 17:18). The first readers of the Fourth Gospel—Jewish Christians who had been expelled from their synagogues—would be relying on the word of Jesus, requiring support in the midst of hostility, and working at their mission in the world. They would hear the prayer of Jesus as specifically addressing their circumstance, and not just that of the first disciples.

The third section of the prayer (John 17:20–26) looks beyond the first generations of Christians to "those who will believe in me through their word, that they may all be one" (John 17:20–21). This unity has its origin and paradigm in the unity of the Father and the Son and has a purpose "that the world may know that you sent me and loved them even as you loved me" (John 17:23). Jesus comes from the Father and his salvific work is for the whole world, not just the community of initial followers. The result of it all is the final plea of the prayer, "that the love with which you have loved me may be in them, and I in them" (John 17:26). The prayer and farewell discourse thus concluded, Jesus goes out to those precipitous events that are his glorification.

Key Texts—The Passion

Throughout the Fourth Gospel, Jesus has been presented as the Word made flesh, as the one who makes the Father known, as the divine Son of God. For someone who works such signs and whose words are so persuasive, how is it possible that he was crucified? John's answer is simple: the death of Jesus is his glorification. Jesus retains control of the situation but declines to use his power in order to fulfill his purpose. The Son of God must lay down his life for the world. Three scenes in particular illustrate the crucifixion as glorification.

18:1–10 After the farewell discourse, Jesus crosses the Kidron Valley to a place where there was a "garden" (John 18:1). The Synoptic Gospels call the place Gethsemane. The term is the Fourth Gospel is more generic and may denote almost any sort of agricultural plot. "Garden of Gethsemane" is a pious description concocted by merging these two designations.

We already discussed above some of the differences between the violent account of the arrest in the Synoptic Gospels when compared with the Fourth Gospel. There is no agony in John's account of the events in the garden. Instead, Jesus identifies himself to those who come to arrest him with the words "I am" (John 18:5, 8). When Jesus utters these words, "they drew back and fell to the ground" (John 18:6). Their behavior is reminiscent of the initial fear of Moses when he encounters the "I AM" in the burning bush (Exodus 3:6). The words of Jesus recall his own claim to be the divine "I am" (John 8:58). Judas and the detachment from the chief priests and **Pharisees** only seem to be in control. In fact, Jesus is the one who has the power to lay down his life of his own accord (John 10:18).

18:28–19:16 The second scene illustrating Jesus' control of matters is the trial before Pilate. The Luke's Gospel, Pilate declared Jesus innocent three times. In the Fourth Gospel, Pilate, the powerful and bloody prefect from Rome, seems to have lost all control. Pilate has to go out to the religious authorities, because they wish to avoid defilement (John 18:28). Then he goes inside to interrogate Jesus (John 18:33). He goes out to declare there is no case against

Jesus (John 18:38) and then goes back in to have Jesus flogged (John 19:1). He goes out to present Jesus to the crowd (John 19:5) and then takes Jesus back in for more interrogation (John 19:9). Again he goes out to sit in judgment (John 19:13) and finally capitulates to the wishes of the crowd (John 19:16). In almost comical fashion, Pilate is run ragged by the trial. He is clearly not in control.

The two dialogues between Pilate and Jesus also reinforce the Johannine theme that Jesus is in control, acting of his own accord. In the first, Jesus declares, "My kingdom is not of this world. If my kingdom were of this world, my servants would have been fighting, that I might not be delivered over to the Jews. But my kingdom is not from the world" (John 18:36). Jesus firmly places himself outside the dominion of Pilate. In the second dialogue, Jesus is even blunter: Pilate is irrelevant. In response to Pilate's claim of power, Jesus asserts, "You would have no authority over me at all unless it had been given you from above" (John 19:11). Pilate may issue the decree for Jesus' death, but "I lay down my life for the sheep" (John 10:15). At the trial, Jesus is glorified; Pilate is a prop.

19:17–36 As we noted above, the Fourth Gospel has a very different focus in describing the death of Jesus. The agony and abandonment so prevalent in the synoptic tradition is supplemented by a portrayal of Jesus fulfilling his divine mission with confidence and serenity. He is not alone but in the company of his mother and the disciple whom he loved. In the Fourth Gospel, Jesus carries the cross "by himself" (John 19:17). He provides for his mother and symbolically adopts the beloved disciple as his brother (John 19:26). Only when he knows "that all was now finished" (John 19:28) does he ask for something to drink. He does so not because of the agony of suffering but "to fulfill the Scripture" (John 19:28). And when he "gave up his spirit," he did so declaring, "It is finished" (John 19:30). Even in death there is glorification, for when the soldier pierces Jesus' side, "at once there came out blood and water" (John 19:34). Both blood and water were symbolic themes in the Book of Signs—the flesh and blood of Jesus providing a replacement meal for the Passover and the living water of Jesus replacing the libations of the Feast of Booths. Jesus has accomplished his divine purpose, and God is glorified in him.

Key Texts—The Resurrection

The final and supreme sign, anticipated by the seven others, is the resurrection. Jesus glorified the Father by accomplishing the purpose for which he was sent. The Father now glorifies him by raising Jesus from the dead. The moment of resurrection is not, however, the focus of the narrative. Instead stories are told of followers moved from initial doubt, fear, or disbelief to faith. In the Fourth Gospel, this movement is always a two-step process.

20:11–18 The empty tomb is initially a cause of confusion. The report of Mary of Magdala led Peter and the beloved disciple to race to the tomb. But "they did not understand the Scripture, that he must rise from the dead" (John

20:9). When Mary hears Jesus call her by name, she then recognizes him. The personal encounter moves the first followers from doubt to belief.

The scene with Mary is quite tender, suggesting an especially close relationship between Jesus and Mary. The scene also has a humorous element, for Jesus says to Mary, "Do not cling to me, for I have not yet ascended to the Father" (John 20:17). The King James Version translated these words, "Touch me not." And so, religious art depicts Mary bowing at the feet of Jesus. The Greek would better be translated, "Stop holding on to me." The text implies that Mary, who had once lost Jesus and in horrid grief had been searching for his body, now was not going to lose him again! She clung to him with joy and belief. As Jesus extricated himself from her emotional embrace, he gave to Mary a particular commission, "Go to my brothers and say to them, 'I am ascending to my Father and your Father, to my God and your God'" (John 20:17). Mary became the apostle to the apostles: "I have seen the Lord" (John 20:18).

20:19–29 The disciples come to believe when they, too, "see" the Lord (John 19:20). As Mary had been sent, they are now sent with the gift of the Holy Spirit and the charge to forgive sins (John 20:21–23). Although they did not initially understand that he must rise from the dead, they are now charged to continue the work of Jesus. That same process of movement from disbelief to belief occurs with Thomas, when he sees the Lord. However, that process of moving people from disbelief to belief must now continue in the community without actually seeing Jesus. For this reason Jesus says to Thomas, "Blessed are those who have not seen and yet have believed" (John 20:29). And for this same reason, the gospel was composed, "These are written so that you may believe that Jesus is the Christ, the Son of God, and that by believing you may have life in his name" (John 20:31).

Key Texts—Epilogue

The scene in the epilogue shifts north to Galilee. Although the focus of the epilogue is on Peter, the beloved disciple plays a role. He is the one who first recognizes Jesus (John 21:7) and who testifies to the truth of the gospel (John 21:24–25). Both Peter and the beloved disciple are accorded significant roles in the early Christians communities. Perhaps these stories had a secondary function to downplay rivalry between followers of these leaders, since rivalry based on loyalty to a certain leader was a problem in

A boat by the Sea of Galilee

the church (1 Corinthians 1–3).

21:15–29 The scene in Galilee had opened with a miraculous catch of fish that Peter had hauled ashore. Much speculation surrounds the specific number of fish (153) and what the number might symbolize. Although any symbolism in the number is lost, the catch does seem to point to the role of Peter (and the others) as missionaries, for in the synoptic tradition the disciples had been called to catch people (Luke 5:10).

In a private scene involving Jesus and Peter, the premier Johannine theme of love is raised and the metaphor shifts from fish to sheep. Using three different Greek verbs for love, Jesus redirects Peter's love for him into care for his flock. Peter was troubled that Jesus questioned him about his love three times (John 21:17). Many seen the triple question as reminiscent of Peter's triple denial (John 18:17, 25–27). But the gospel does not make the connection specific.

If the fishing scene was a metaphor for missionary work, this scene commissioned Peter for pastoral work. The two are intimately connected for Jesus spoke earlier of "other sheep that are not of this fold. I must bring them also, and they will listen to my voice. So there will be one flock, one shepherd" (John 10:16). Peter would play a significant role in mission and care.

Together, the resurrection appearances and the epilogue shift the focus of the community outward. The Father has glorified the Son. Those who have seen came to believe and now have the commission to carry the good news to others that they, too, might believe. This task occurs as the community with its testimony and its love engages in mission work and care for the flock.

Jesus in the Fourth Gospel

The Synoptic Gospels have presented Jesus as the Messiah, the Son of God, and the Savior of all. In the Fourth Gospel, Jesus is the Word who assisted in creation, came in the flesh, and is the Father's only Son (John 1:14). Although other titles such as Messiah and Son of Man do occur, the high Christology of the Fourth Gospel centers in the title Son of God. The relationship of Jesus to the Father seems to be the end point of most dialogues. Jesus speaks of the Father at least 120 times. The writer of this gospel selected so many such instances as a way of expressing his perspective on Jesus.

Jesus' role as the Son of God is evident in a number of aspects. As the Son, Jesus is the agent of the Father. "Truly, truly, I say to you, the Son can do nothing of his own accord, but only what he sees the Father doing. For whatever the Father does, that the Son does likewise" (John 5:19). "For the works that the Father has given me to accomplish, the very works that I am doing, bear witness about me that the Father has sent me" (John 5:36). As the Son, Jesus depends on the Father and his love. "Truly, truly, I say to you, the Son can do nothing of his own accord, but only what he sees the Father doing" (John 5:19). "The Father loves the Son and has given all things into his hand" (John 3:35). As the Son, Jesus reveals the Father and speaks the words of the Father. "Whoever has seen me has seen the Father" (John 14:9). "For all that I have heard from my Father I have made known to you" (John 15:15). Finally, the Son in his act of glorification returns to the Father. "If you loved me, you would have rejoiced, because I am going to the Father" (John 14:28). It is the purpose of the Fourth Gospel to call forth belief in Jesus as the Son of God (John 20:31).

For Further Discussion

1. Compare and contrast particular miracles stories in the Synoptic Gospels and in the Fourth Gospel. What do the differences suggest?

2. The Fourth Gospel is often called the most theological. Do you agree or disagree? Why or why not?

3. Explore some of the minor characters in the gospel. To whom do you relate? Why? Why might the author have selected these stories to tell?

4. How does the humanity of Jesus show in the Fourth Gospel? Beyond the fact of the incarnation, what "human" characteristics are present? Why is it important that the Son of God also be fully human?

5. How can suffering be glorification? What words or actions of Jesus might help you in a time of suffering?

For Further Reading

Barrett, C. K. *The Gospel According to St. John*. 2nd ed. Philadelphia: Westminster, 1978.

Brown, Raymond E. *The Gospel According to John*. Anchor Bible 29 and 29A. Garden City, NY: Doubleday, 1966, 1970.

Culpepper, R. Alan. *John: The Son of Zebedee, the Life of a Legend*. Minneapolis, Fortress, 2000.

Keener, Craig. *The Gospel of John*. 2 volumes. Peabody, MA: Hendrickson, 2003.

Morris, Leon. *The Gospel According to John*. New International Commentaries on the New Testament. Grand Rapids: Eerdmans, 1971.

Smith, D. Moody. *John*. 2nd ed. Minneapolis: Fortress, 1986.

1–3 John

"John" and the Johannine community

Although these three letters bear the name of John and were associated with the son of Zebedee since the fourth century, the name of John is not mentioned in any of them. And 1 John seems to be more of a treatise than a letter. Explanation is in order as we look at the Johannine epistles.

Second John and 3 John, because they follow the form of ancient letters, mention an author—"the elder" (2 John 1; 3 John 1). It is a title, not a name. In Greek, a *presbyteros* was a person of advanced years. In Jewish communities, the term could be applied leaders of local councils or of the Sanhedrin. Among early Christians, elders are named along with apostles as leaders (Acts 11:30; 14:23; 15:2, 4, 6, 22; 16:4; 20:17; 21:18; 1 Timothy 5:17, 19; Titus 1:5; James 5:14; 1 Peter 5:1, 5). Later in Christian history, elders would rank between bishops and deacons. We see this ranking already in Ignatius (died A.D. 107), suggesting that the Johannine epistles were written before his time. Still, the authorship of the Johannine epistles is hardly clarified by the author's designation of himself as "the elder."

The early church historian Eusebius (c. 260–c.340) in his *Ecclesiastical History* (3:39), quotes a fragment from Papias (bishop from Asia Minor; c. 60–130) that suggests to Eusebius the existence of a "John the elder" who was a different person from John the apostle, the tombs of both being at Ephesus in Eusebius' day. Some suggest this John the Elder is "the elder" of 2 and 3 John. Perhaps it is better simply to note that fragmentary traditions associate the common name John with the title *elder*, and much later "the elder" of 2 and 3 John was identified with the John who was an apostle. In other words, historical references are of little help in identifying the author or authors of these writings.

Church holding "tomb" of John

The content of the writings may give us more help. Although 1 John does not mention "the elder," most think it was written by the same person. Similar concerns are brought up, and 1 John is addressed to "little children" (1 John 2:1, 12, 14, 18, 28; 3:7, 18; 4:4; 5:21). Internally, the writings seem to come from a common source.

When compared to the Fourth Gospel many similarities in content surface, especially in the use of such terms as light, life, love, abide, flesh, Spirit, and truth. But there is a marked difference. In the Fourth Gospel, the enemies are "the Jews"—a technical term for the elites from the Jerusalem area. Some early Christian communities struggled with their relationships to other Jews (see many stories in Acts and Paul's own struggle in Romans 9–11). But in the Johannine epistles, the opposition is from within their own community. Certain "antichrists" are causing splits in the community over their understanding of Jesus, their moral practices, and their claim to leadership by the Spirit. This change in focus between the Fourth Gospel and the epistles—from external opponents to internal troublemakers—may suggest that the epistles come from a later period. Written later, the epistles came from an author and were addressed to a community that knew well the Fourth Gospel. Their common understanding as a community shows up in the use of first personal plural discourse in the introductory verses of 1 John (1:1–4).

So these epistles, although popularly called Johannine, probably reflect the beliefs of a community well-versed in the Fourth Gospel but struggling with issues caused by internal divisions. Ironically, a community so identified with Jesus' new commandment to love one another (John 13) is torn apart. Tradition assigns to them the name of John, even if the texts do not.

Audience

In 1 John, the author directs his words with authority and affection to his "little children." As befits a sermon or treatise, specific references are lacking. All we know about the readers is that some have left their community (1 John 2:19–20), leaving a situation of confusion and hostility. Those who remain are devoted to the Son of God (1 John 5:13), suggesting that the division had doctrinal overtones. Tradition places the readers in the Roman province of Asia, with some suggesting one or more of the cities to which Revelation was directed (Revelation 2:1–3:22). First John is not specific.

Second John in tantalizing fashion identifies the recipients of the letter as "the elect lady and her children" (2 John 1). She is the one "whom I love in the truth" (2 John 1) and is also called "dear lady" (2 John 5). "The elder" has much to write her, but would rather not use paper and ink. Instead he hopes "to come to you and talk face to face so our joy may be complete" (2 John 12). "The elder" concludes with greetings from the "children of your elect sister" (2 John 13).

The identity of the "lady" depends on whether the term is read literally or metaphorically. If the lady is a person, she would likely be someone such as Lydia at Philippi or Mary of Jerusalem, who hosted Christian communities in their homes. Until the fourth century most Christians gathered in homes rather than separate buildings or churches. As the owner of the gathering place, she likely had a leadership role in the community. If the "lady" is to be understood metaphorically, the word probably talks about a Christian community the members of which are the "children." In Revelation, the new Jerusalem is like a "bride adorned for her husband" (Revelation 21:2). A metaphorical reading seems more likely, but nothing in the letter itself rules out an actual woman as the recipient.

Third John is addressed to Gaius. But even such a reference to a specific person leaves many questions unanswered. There are four other references to a Gaius in the New Testament: a Gaius from Derbe traveled with Paul (Acts 20:4); Paul baptized a Gaius at Corinth (1 Corinthians 1:14); a Gaius helped Paul when he wrote to the Romans (Romans 16:23); and a Gaius from Macedonia was dragged before the crowds at Ephesus (Acts 19:29). Of these four, the Gaius at Ephesus would be from the general area associated with the Johannine writings. But even the complaints about Diotrephes and the introduction of Demetrius bring us no closer to identifying Gaius. (Demetrius is also the name of the complaining silversmith from Ephesus, but a connection to him is tenuous, at best.)

Possibly contributing to our confusion is the church's designation of these writings as 1 John, 2 John, and 3 John. Based on these names, it is natural to assume that the books were written in the order we now find them in the Bible. But, the writings could be in this sequence based on their size. Recall that the Pauline writings are arranged in their New Testament order essentially from longest to shortest.

If we assume a different sequence of writing, then other possibilities arise. Since 3 John 11–12 introduces and commends Demetrius to Gaius, Demetrius was likely the courier of the letter, even as Phoebe was for Romans (Romans 16:1–2). Luke Timothy Johnson builds on this reference to suggest that the three works were written and sent at the same time. 3 John was a cover letter introducing Demetrius to Gaius. Along with 3 John, Demetrius carried 2 John, a personal letter to the community that in turn introduced the themes to be addressed more fully in the sermon/treatise we know as 1 John, which Demetrius also carried. Although Johnson's proposal makes sense of the writings as we have them and explains the lack of import given to 2 and 3 John in the early Christian centuries, it remains a hypothesis. "My little children," "the elect lady," Gaius, and Demetrius remain the fascinating focus of speculation, but fade before the greater significance of the writings themselves.

Structure and theme

Several topics seem to be on the mind of the author of 1 John. Fostering fellowship and joy are one reason for writing (1 John 1:3–4). Discouraging sin and encouraging love are also objectives (1 John 2:1, 8–11). The tract tries to correct misconceptions about Christianity (1 John 2:26) and to assure readers of eternal life (1 John 5:13). But most on the mind of the author is the split in the community (1 John 2:19–20). Recriminations and slander have made the rift worse. Members of the community need help distinguishing "the Spirit of truth and the spirit of error" (1 John 4:6).

With the first generation of Christians gone, with no developed church authority, and with no clearly defined Scripture except the **Septuagint**, the author of 1 John is one of the first writers to provide standards by which Christians can "test the spirits" (1 John 4:1). In an early letter dealing with controversy, Paul had encouraged such testing (1 Thessalonians 5:21), but he gave no criteria for such tests. In a situation that split the community, 1 John provides three criteria which are reinforced by the literary structure of the work.

Two of the criteria are ethical; one is doctrinal. In an opening section that echoes the prologue of the Fourth Gospel, 1 John asserts an **incarnational** Christology; that is, the word of God has come in the flesh. Jesus of Nazareth is the Son of God. Apparently, those who broke from the community denied the full humanity of Jesus. "By this you know the Spirit of God: every spirit that confesses that Jesus Christ has come in the flesh is from God, and every spirit that does not confess Jesus is not from God. This is the spirit of the antichrist" (1 John 4:2–3). Later second-century **Gnosticism** and Docetism would claim that Jesus only seemed to be human. The first criterion for distinguishing truth from error is incarnational Christology.

The second criterion is righteous conduct. Sin ought be confessed (1 John 1:9), and his commandments kept (1 John 2:3). The faithful ought "walk in the same way as he walked" (1 John 2:6). "Whoever makes a practice of sinning is of the devil" (1 John 3:8). "Everyone who is born of God does not keep on sinning" (1 John 5:18). Related is the third criterion, the central rule of the community: "we should love one another" (1 John 3:11). True members of the community "love one another, for love is from God, and whoever loves has been born of God and knows God" (1 John 4:7). The triple themes—righteous conduct, mutual love, and incarnational Christology—provide a means of discernment for the community, even as they reinforce core beliefs and practices of the community.

The literary structure of 1 John also reinforces these themes. Even as the book of Revelation cycles around its themes through a series of visions, 1 John presents its three themes repeatedly through three cycles, varying the order of the third cycle slightly.

1 JOHN	
INCARNATIONAL CHRISTOLOGY	1:1–4
RIGHTEOUS CONDUCT	1:5–2:6
MUTUAL LOVE	2:7–17
INCARNATIONAL CHRISTOLOGY	2:8–18
RIGHTEOUS CONDUCT	2:29–3:10a
MUTUAL LOVE	3:10b–24a
INCARNATIONAL CHRISTOLOGY	3:24b–4:6

MUTUAL LOVE	4:7–5:3
RIGHTEOUS CONDUCT	5:4–21

All three of these criteria are introduced when the elder writers a brief note to the elect lady. Anyone who denies the "coming of Jesus Christ in the flesh" is a deceiver and antichrist (2 John 7). The commandment "that we love one another" (2 John 5) is explained by a definition of love, "that we walk according to his commandments" (2 John 6). The themes of love and righteous conduct also surface in the practical encouragement of 3 John (3 John 5, 11), even as the Elder contrasts Gaius with Diotrephes and introduces Demetrius. But the fullest treatment of these themes is 1 John.

Key Texts

1:5–9 A contrast between light and darkness serves as a metaphor for the dualistic perspective of 1 John. We see the same description of a world divided into light and darkness in the Fourth Gospel (John 3:19–21). Darkness is symbolic for troubled times in Revelation (Revelation 8:12; 9:2;16:10). Light bathes the images of the new creation (Revelation 21:23–24; 22:5). Although in the natural world shade and twilight suggest a spectrum between light and darkness, the contrast is absolute in Johannine literature. Because the community has been divided, there is no middle ground in 1 John. Contrasts abound: children of the devil versus children of God, evil versus good, hate versus love, lies versus truth, lawlessness versus righteousness, murderers versus those who lay down their lives for each other, no life versus eternal life, and so on. The contrast is drawn most sharply in the realm of ethics. Sin is walking in the darkness (1 John 1:6). Those who have been born of God do not keep on sinning (1 John 5:18, see below).

"Virtue" at Ephesus

As sharply as the ethical contrast is drawn, it is tempered by reality in the community: "If we say we have no sin, we deceive ourselves, and the truth is not in us" (1 John 1:8). Sin had shown itself in the division of the community. Sin continues to be a reality in the lives of Christians. But sin need not dominate. The world may lie under the power of the evil one but the evil one does not touch the Christian (1 John 5:18–19). As a comfort to the community, 1 John says, "If we confess our sins, he is faithful and just to forgive us our sins and to cleanse us from all unrighteousness" (1 John 1:9). These words from 1 John have been incorporated into the Sunday liturgies of some Christian communities, where they serve a similar role for us today—recognizing the divisive reality of sin and offering the forgiveness and cleansing that make possible walking in the light.

2:1–2 As the author of 1 John continues to help the community deal with sin and its fractious results, he points the community to "Jesus Christ the righteous." This Jesus is an "advocate" and "the propitiation for our sins." Both terms are noteworthy in this document and in comparison with the Fourth Gospel.

The English word "advocate" translates the Greek word *parakletos*. In the Fourth Gospel, same Greek word refers to the advocate whom Jesus promises that the Father will send after glorification of Jesus (John 14:16, 25; 15:26; 16:7, 13). Jesus and subsequent Christian theology identify the advocate with the Holy Spirit. 1 John uses the term for Jesus. The seeming contradiction is clarified when we notice that the Holy Spirit does the work of advocacy in the community on earth, coming after Jesus departs. Jesus does his work of advocacy in the presence of the Father in heaven, ascending to fulfill that role. The work of Jesus and the Holy Spirit are complementary, a point Christian theology would assert as it developed its articulation of Trinitarian doctrine.

The saving value of the death of Jesus is stressed by the term **propitiation**. In the Fourth Gospel, the death and resurrection (and ascension) are one act that serves as his glorification (see discussion above). Only rarely does the Fourth Gospel speak of the import of the death alone (John 10:11). But in 1 John, "propitiation" is used twice (see also 4:10). The idea is somewhat foreign to our culture. A propitiation is an appeasement, here not only for the sins of the community, but for the sins of the whole world. For the readers of 1 John, this way of speaking was unusual as well. In the pagan literature of the time, the root concept spoke of an instrument someone might use to regain the goodwill of a deity. It might be an offering, a pledge, or an act of heroism. But such appeasement only benefited the person(s) involved. Likewise, those of Jewish background would know of the sacrificial system that benefited the individual or the nation (compare Ezekiel 44:27; note that by the writing of 1 John, the temple in Jerusalem had been destroyed and with it all sacrifices had come to an end). But for 1 John, the death of Jesus appeases for the sins of all! It does far more than anything in the sacrificial systems with which the readers might have been familiar. The death of Jesus rights the relationship with God and overflows in the love and righteous conduct of the community.

It is a radical religious notion that God acts for all, rather than just for those inside the community. We who believe and benefit from the propitiation brought about by the death of Jesus can serve others in love (1 John 2:3–6), both those within our Christian communities and those outside our communities. For the death of Jesus offers to all the same benefits offered to us. Recognizing every person as one for whom Jesus died is the opportunity of the Christian life.

2:7–11 When 1 John turns to ethics, the focus is on two specific aspects: the "old and new" and the "love of the brother." 1 John invokes an "old commandment that you have heard from the beginning" as well as a "new commandment that I am writing to you" (1 John 2:7–8). To our ears, it sounds like 1 John is speaking about two different commandments. But the author is speaking of only one: the commandment to "love one another." This commandment was a central teaching of the community from the beginning and played a prominent role in the Fourth Gospel (John 13:34). But it is a commandment hard to keep. Divisions in the community prove its difficulty. So there is newness to the commandment as well. There is room for the readers to grow in love, as they go from darkness to light.

As with other theological concepts, such as salvation and eternal life, love is "now" and "not yet." Christians are joined in a community motivated by the love of God and are charged to love one another. Love is *now* their way of life. But love is not always fully (or even partly) expressed. Anger, hatred, and division come to the surface. The life of love is *not yet* fully formed. In the same way, the Christian already has *now* the gift of eternal life. That life enriches daily life. But the Christian does *not yet* fully experience the joy and bliss of the resurrected life. That will be given at the end. So both salvation and love are lived between *now* and *not yet*.

In 1 John, love is directed to "the brother." We noted above that the death of Jesus appeases the sins of all people. But this text speaks only of love of people in the community—the "brother." By addressing the readers as "my little children" (1 John 2:1), the community is compared to a family. Members would be brothers and sisters in a spiritual sense. It is common for New Testament writers to refer to members of the Christian community as *adelphoi*, that is, "brothers." Jesus taught his followers to call God "our Father." Culturally the term would include women as well as men, so we might translate the term with "brothers and sisters." More importantly, 1 John focuses his comments about love internally, that is on the love of members of the community for one another. "Brother" here is not equal to "neighbor" (Luke 10:25–37). The problem faced by the community is internal. People may claim to "know him" (1 John 2:4), to "abide in him" (1 John 2:6), and to be "in the light" (1 John 2:9). But the community has divided; some have left; hate has led to darkness. So 1 John pleads, "love the brother."

"Brothers"

Even today Christianity is known by its teaching, "love one another." So Christianity bears legitimate criticism when its internal squabbles and struggles become obvious to the world. When Christians fail to love "the brother" in the community, any love toward fellow human beings outside the community is compromised. So love of the brother or sister in the community is a prerequisite for love of the neighbor outside the community. As we love one another in the Christian community, we learn how to love others outside our particular community. Our love may start with "the brother," but it does not end there. Sadly, we often do not make it to the start.

2:18 Recall from earlier reading the discussion of **eschatology**—a concern about those events at the end of time and the final fate of humanity. For those to whom 1 John is addressed, it is the "last hour," because there has been a split in the community. The warning of Jesus about coming opposition in the persons of "false christs and false prophets" (Matthew 24:24) is applied to those who have gone out from the community. As they oppose a true understanding of Jesus as God come in the flesh, they are against the Christ. They are antichrists. The term **antichrist** is unique to Christian circles. Jewish messianic expectation did not envision such opposition. *Antichrist* refers to an opponent to the Messiah who would appear at the end of time. In the New Testament, the term only occurs in the Johannine epistles, but the concept is inferred in 2 Thessalonians 2 and Revelation 12–14.

The community identified by their love for one another had split. For 1 John, the fracture was so serious that it is likened to the final struggle between good and evil, light and darkness. In contemporary culture, with its stress on individualism, its splintering into interest groups, the easy break-up of families, and Christians of diverse stripes on every corner, such concern over a break in the community seems overstated. Perhaps that is the problem. For us, going separate ways is the standard way out of conflict. But for 1 John, the community is critical. In the community, love for each other is the first step toward the ultimate embrace of all people through the atoning death of Jesus. If we cannot love each other, how can we love our neighbor? For 1 John, and for contemporary Christians, that question is of ultimate if not eschatological import.

2:24–25 As noted before, the Johannine epistles echo many of the same themes as the Fourth Gospel. These two verses are a good example. Notice the recurring use of the word *abide*. The teachings of Jesus ought "abide in you" (1 John 2:24). And if they do, "you too will abide in the Son and in the Father" (1 John 2:24). The concept occurs forty times in the Fourth Gospel, from the Spirit abiding on Jesus at his baptism (John 1:32) to the beloved disciple "abiding" until Jesus comes (John 21:23), including the well-know repetition in the teaching about the vine and the branches (John 15:1–11). While Johannine material commonly presents the Christian abiding in Jesus or in God, this passage is unique, for the Father and the Son are mentioned together. The verse makes explicit what is implicit in the gospel—a connection between abiding in the Son and abiding in God.

That teaching of Jesus dear to the community contains a promise of eternal life (1 John 2:25). Those who abide have life. Again, echoes of the Fourth Gospel are present. Jesus often offers eternal life to those who believe (John 3:16, 36; 5:24; 6:40, 47, 54; 6:69; 10:28; 12:25; 17:2–3). Such life is the purpose for which the gospel was written (John 20:31). In the same way, 1 John opens with a reminder of eternal life (1 John 1:2) and three times in its final chapter recalls the promise of eternal life (1 John 5:11, 13, 20). The community that received 1–3 John was well versed in the particular language of the Fourth Gospel.

3:11–24 Jesus had taught, "Love one another" (John 15:12). As we have seen above, 1 John interprets the commandment primarily with reference to the members of the community, since it had been ruptured by a lack of love. 1 John cites Cain as an example of one who did wrong to his brother. Murder by Cain is equated with hatred, and the converse is also true. "Everyone who hates his brother is a murderer" (1 John 3:15). Apparently the fracture was so serious in the community that hatred (and perhaps violence) resulted. Brothers in need were also victimized (1 John 3:17).

In contrast to Cain, 1 John points to Jesus, who "laid down his life for us" (1 John 3:16). His act of love motivates the community to "lay down our lives for the brothers" (1 John 3:16). Love is "deed and truth," not just words or talk (1 John 3:18). Failures to love are overcome by God "who is greater than our hearts" (1 John 3:20). God gives confidence to believe and to love (1 John 3:23).

When we look back on the history of early Christianity, especially its struggles with outside pressure and internal divisions, it is worthy of note that 1 John was known and quoted by Polycarp (c.69–c. 155; bishop of Smyrna) and Justin (c. 100–c. 165; early Christian apologist) and often by later writers. From the middle of the second century, in the midst of such troubles, a persistent voice called upon the community to show love to "the brother" as the first step to love of neighbor and the world. That persistent and repeated message of 1 John is as necessary in Christian communities today.

4:7–19 After proposing that the readers test the spirits to decide which is from God, 1 John returns to plead, "Let us love one another" (1 John 4:7). The sacrificial death of Jesus "for our sins" (1 John 4:10) is again the example and means to do so. But this time, the tract adds a second factor: "God is love" (1 John 4:7). The essence as well as the action of God in Christ is behind the love that characterizes the community of Christians. The initiative resides with God: "not that we have love God but that he loved us and sent his Son" (1 John 4:10). Those who love have been born of God, know God, and God abides in them. The evidence or fruit is their love of one another. "We love because he first loved us" (1 John 4:19).

Since there are several words in the Greek language all translated by the English word *love*, the persistent point of 1 John becomes clearer by noting the particular Greek used. In 1 John, the term is *agape*. Absent from this concept are casual notions of friendship or the passion of romance. The word *agape* conveys genuine regard for and interest in another. The term is used often in the New Testament for the love one Christian shows another. The author of 1 John does this. But this authentic interest is even more a quality shown by God and Jesus, especially in his death for humanity. God's love sets the example for and even makes possible the love of Christians for one another. As a sign and expression of this love, the term *agape* is applied to a common meal shared by Christians (1 Corinthians 11:17; 2 Peter 2:13; Jude 12). There the death of Jesus is remembered and love is expressed. Failure to care for the brother or dishonoring of the table strike at the heart of the Christian concept of love. Or in the words of the text, "No one has ever seen God; if we love one another, God abides in us and his love is perfected in us" (1 John 4:12).

A second sign that Christians "abide in him" is the gift of his Spirit (1 John 4:13). The Spirit's gift is not a charismatic sign (as sometimes in Paul) but the testimony of the community to the incarnation. "Whoever confesses that Jesus is the Son of God, God abides in him, and he in God" (1 John 4:15). That testimony gives confidence for the Day of Judgment and is linked to love. "Perfect love casts out fear" (1 John 4:18). The various criteria set out by 1 John as a response to the fracture in the community merge at this point. Incarnational Christology and the commandment to love go together, even as the death of Jesus makes it possible for Christians to abide in God.

5:6–8 When 1 John says that the Spirit and the water and the blood testify together and agree, the author offers a powerful but obscure image. The Spirit likely refers to the descent of the Spirit like a dove at Jesus' baptism (John 1:32). Earlier in the work, 1 John writes of the blood of Jesus Christ cleansing from all sin (1 John 1:7). The water that testifies may be the water of baptism, but from the Fourth Gospel the community would know well of the living water of which Jesus spoke to the Samaritan woman (John 4:10), the metaphor of living water flowing from the believer's heart and a sign of the Spirit (John 7:38), and the flow of water and blood when the side of Jesus was pierced (John 19:34). Later Christian writers would find sacramental overtones in this text. While not directly intended by the author, 1 John would have little understanding of a Christianity without flesh and blood, as later Gnosticism would.

5:18 Two concepts are held in tension as 1 John deals with the aftermath of painful division in the community. On the one hand, the faithful do "not keep on sinning" (1 John 5:18). The Greek could also be translated, "do not sin." On the other hand, "If we say we have no sin, we deceive ourselves, and the truth is not in us" (1 John 1:8). In such a tension, problems arise whenever one side dominates the other. Either sin runs so free that immorality is tolerated (the community is torn apart) or the requirements of perfection lead to despair (no one is worthy of being part of the community). The writings of Martin Luther would probe this tension and cause Luther to assert that the Christian is at the same time sinner and saint. 1 John pleads for greater love in a community where sin has gotten the upper hand and has broken relationships among the members.

We Christians today struggle with the tension of being at the same time sinner and saint. We can all point to broken relationships that are a sign of sin. Still, we can all seek to show love to one another, especially those close to us, "because he first loved us." We do not have to keep on sinning. The treatise we know as 1 John, valued as it was in the early church, speaks powerfully and practically today.

Jesus in the Johannine Epistles

Apparently those who left the community, whose departure so troubled our author, held a differing view of Jesus. For them Jesus was a spiritual creature seemingly human in form. Salvation came through embrace of his teachings. In contrast, as we noted above, 1 John repeatedly asserts an incarnational Christology.

The name *Jesus* and the title *Christ* appear in combination often in the Johannine epistles (1 John 1:3; 2:1; 3:23; 4:2; 5:6; 5:20; 2 John 7). It is a core Christian belief that "Jesus is the Christ" (1 John 5:1). Opponents are "liars" when they "deny that Jesus is the Christ" (1 John 2:22). Those who do not so confess Jesus display the "spirit of the antichrist" (1 John 4:3). They are "deceivers" if they do not "confess the coming of Jesus Christ in the flesh" (2 John 7). For 1 John, Jesus is the incarnate Messiah.

In parallel, the Johannine epistles stress with vigor that Jesus is the Son of God. More that twenty times in the short work of 1 John, sonship is alluded to or stated. The Christian has "fellowship with the Father and with his Son Jesus Christ" (1 John 1:3). It is the spirit of the antichrist to deny "the Father and the Son" (1 John 2:22). Those who "confess the Son" have the Father also and "abide in the Father and the Son" (1 John 2:23–24). God's commandment involves belief "in the name of his Son Jesus" along with love for one another (1 John 3:23). "Whoever confesses that Jesus is the Son of God, God abides in him, and he in God" (1 John 4:15). Those who believe that Jesus is the Son of God overcome the world (1 John 5:5). "Whoever has the Son has life" (1 John 5:12). "He is the true God and eternal life" (1 John 5:20). From beginning to end, 1 John identifies Jesus and the Son of God.

Along with such clarity in identifying the person of Jesus, 1 John speaks of the work of the Son Jesus Christ. That work is inseparable from the reality of the incarnation and the import of the death of Jesus. Put simply, "the blood of Jesus his Son cleanses us from all sin" (1 John 1:7). Invoking but going beyond sacrificial systems, 1 John says that Jesus is the "propitiation for our sins" (1 John 2:2; 4:10). Those within the Christian community are not the only beneficiaries. The work of Jesus was "also for the sins of the whole world" (1 John 2:2). The Son sent by the Father is "the Savior of the world" (1 John 4:14). He destroys "the works of the devil" (1 John 3:8).

Lest the sacrifice of Jesus on the cross be viewed in a symbolic or metaphoric way, the Johannine epistles stress its reality by asserting the reality of the incarnation. Jesus Christ "has come in the flesh (1 John 4:2; 2 John 1:7). Such an incarnational perspective has indirect support by the repeated portrayal of Christians as people "born of God" (1 John 2:29; 3:9; 4:7; 5:4, 18). Were the birth of Jesus not a real event, the use of the metaphor of birth to express the state of Christians would be out of place. Interestingly, the author may be making this very point by using a subtle capability of Greek grammar that is a bit hard to convey in English. With our English verbs, we can describe an action that takes place in the past, present, or future. In Greek there is another form of the verb that describes an event in the past that has ongoing import and effect in the present. This so-called "perfect tense" of the Greek verb is used every time Christians are spoken of as "born of God." Christians now benefit as ones born of God because of a birth event in the past. Theology would point to baptism as the birth, but without the real incarnation and death of Jesus such birth would be symbolism at best.

1 John sets forth an incarnational Christology. It is one criterion by which Christians may test the spirits, but it is also one that identifies the community of those who know the love of God and show love for one another. "And we know that the Son of God has come and has given us understanding, so that we may know him who is true; and we are in him who is true, in his Son Jesus Christ. He is the true God and eternal life" (1 John 5:20).

For Further Discussion

1. The Johannine epistles use much "family" language. What are the positive and negative elements in such an approach with modern audiences? How well does the concept of family in the letters align with contemporary concepts of family?

2. A direct connection is drawn between belief in Jesus and ethical conduct. How does this connection work? Are these letters similar to or different from Paul? Why?

3. In the later writings of the New Testament, false teachers are becoming a concern. Yet contemporary Christianity stresses inclusivity. When are Christians too narrow or too loose in their teachings and practices? How do you know?

4. How does "love one another" work in an age of terrorism?

For Further Reading

Brown, Raymond E. *The Epistles of John*. The Anchor Bible 30. New York: Doubleday 1982.

Westcott, B. F. *The Epistles of St. John*. Grand Rapids: Eerdmans, 1966.

7

Jesus in the New Testament: Christology and Christologies

Many people in our day describe themselves as visual learners. By this, they mean they are best able to learn and remember material by absorbing it through their eyes. These visual images are seen on movie, television and computer screens, but they also come from looking at pictures, charts, or graphs in books, journals and magazines.

For better or worse, much of what we believe about Jesus and Christianity is also embedded in us from visual images we have seen. Actually, this is a very ancient phenomenon. Before the printing press was invented in the fifteenth century, books were expensive and rare. The vast majority of Christian people prior to that time did not have a Bible of their own and most were not able to read. As a result, their images of Jesus were formed less by reading words of Jesus from the Bible than from hearing his words read orally and, more importantly, by seeing images of him on paintings, mosaics, stained glass, and statutes placed in and around churches and other holy places. They learned about Jesus and the events of his life by seeing them portrayed visually. The Orthodox Church calls some of these images icons. According to John of Damascus, "What the word is for hearing, the icon is for sight" (*Defense of Icons* 1.17). Having our contemporary images of Jesus formed by visual portrayals of him is not something new at all; learning about Jesus through our eyes actually returns us to something quite ancient.

Different, of course, is the technology of television and motion pictures, as well as the plethora of pictures being printed and placed on the internet today. Contemporary images of Jesus are drawn from movies and television shows. They also come from diverse artistic renderings of him found in many and various other places including instructional materials, Bibles, paintings, jewelry, and so forth.

A problem develops when we consider one visual depiction of Jesus as the "real" or authoritative one. Did Jim Caviezel, the actor who played Jesus in Mel Gibson's *The Passion of the Christ*, convey the definitive image of Jesus or was it Robert Powell who performed the role in Franco Zeffirelli's *Jesus of Nazareth*? What about the actors who have played him in many other "Jesus movies"? The reality is that none of them adequately or authoritatively captures the image of Christ. They are simply actors portraying him.

The same question could be asked in regard to all paintings, sculptures, and pictures of Jesus, whether ancient or modern. To what degree do the artists or those who served as models for them communicate the "real" Jesus? The fact is we simply do not have any reliable visual depictions of Jesus, nor do we have any early written description of his physical characteristics. Certainly he was a first-century Jewish male. But, other than that, all we have are mental images of what we, an artist, or a director thinks Jesus may have looked like. Some of these depictions may strike us personally as more or less accurate; they might connect with us in a certain way. But, due to our lack of knowledge, they are all based largely upon conjecture, and many people judge them based on a stereotypical image they have developed in their own mind.

Imagine that a number of sculptors or painters had gathered in Jesus' day to make his official portrait, much as we do with presidents of the United States today. Those paintings or statues of Jesus would have been made of the actual living Jesus who had been physically present in front of the artists. Yet would their representations of him have been identical? No. Each artist would have made a different interpretation of the same figure. In addition, their works of art would have varied depending on their skills, interests and perceptions. Although their visual productions would have all been based upon the same identical person, they would all be different and none would fully convey or embody Jesus himself.

Aside from the fact that the New Testament provides us with literary, rather than visual, portraits of Jesus, the situation is much the same. Each New Testament author focused his literary work on the same person, Jesus Christ. This is exemplified by the *christological* focal point with which our textbook began. Yet, as each New Testament writer painted his literary portrait, he portrayed the same Jesus in a different manner. We have illustrated this point with the "Jesus in …" section that concludes the discussion of each New Testament book. But when we survey the results, we might ask, Does the New Testament have a consistent **Christology** or are there many and varied Christologies?

In response to this situation, there are two extremes to be avoided. One is the overly simplistic assumption that the New Testament authors all portray Jesus in a uniform, flat, or standard manner—as if Jesus is portrayed in exactly the same way throughout. The "Jesus in" sections of this book have shown that such an understanding is inadequate. On the other hand, many contemporary scholars contend that the various literary portraits of Jesus drawn throughout the New Testament are so varied as to be contradictory and, in many cases, mutually exclusive. As a result, by the time one gets to the end of the New Testament, there is no coherent Jesus left at all.

A similar situation exists in regard to the first five books of the Old Testament which are called the **Torah** or **Pentateuch** (Genesis, Exodus, Leviticus, Numbers and Deuteronomy). Are they all uniform in their teachings about God and his activity in this world? Perhaps not. But to inject wordplay, there remains a "Mosaic" unity among them—because these five books are traditionally all attributed to Moses as their author or editor. A similar view should be maintained in regard to the Jesus of the New Testament. The Jesus of the New Testament is a coherent unity; that is to say, the literary artists are all painting a portrait of one and the same person. But, these various authors do not choose to "paint" the same features in all their portraits. Rather, each author selects those aspects of the story that enable the author to make a point about who Jesus is or meaning of his death and resurrection. Often these selections may be attributable in part to the situation or audience addressed by the author. And so, each author paints Jesus in a slightly—at times, even starkly—distinct manner.

As a result, the situation is more like an artist making a mosaic. A mosaic, like a jig-saw puzzle, has many different pieces, and one needs each piece to make the picture whole. When the work of art is complete, many different elements have been combined in order to form a unity.

The "Jesus in …" sections throughout this book have endeavored to make that point. The partial summary below illustrates the particular emphases of various books:

- Matthew portrays Jesus as the Messiah, the Son of God.
- Mark depicts Jesus as the unique Son of God, a truth grasped only at the cross.
- Luke describes Jesus as the Savior of all; in Acts this is specifically applied to both Jews and Gentiles.
- In Romans Jesus is the one whose shed blood justifies people before God through faith.
- Philippians proclaims Jesus the eternal God who became human in order to suffer death on a cross. In response, God the Father has now given him the name above every name.
- Colossians asserts that all the fulness of God dwells in Jesus Christ. He is the firstborn, both over all creation and from the dead, as well as the head of all rule and authority.
- 1 and 2 Thessalonians portray him as the returning king.
- Hebrews views him as the "greater than" fulfillment of the temple, priests, sacrifices and covenant of the Old Testament.
- Peter describes Jesus as the Lord and Christ who came once to suffer and who will come again in glory.
- John's letters insist that Jesus be portrayed as the Christ, the Son of God who came in the flesh.
- Revelation reveals Jesus as the slaughtered Lamb who is worthy to receive the praise of heaven.

The Christologies of the New Testament are all these and so much more. Together, they combine like the pieces of a mosaic to form a Christology that is rich and diverse but also unified by and focused on a single person, Jesus Christ. Here the old adage is true—the whole is more than the sum of the parts.

Yet the mosaic analogy, like all analogies, falls short of expressing the entire picture. The problem is that one piece of a mosaic, or a jigsaw puzzle, actually tells you very little in and of itself. It usually needs to be put into combination with any number of other pieces before its place, as well as the entire picture, can be deciphered. That is not the case with the Christologies of the New

Testament. It is not as though the Jesus depicted in one book of the New Testament is incoherent or indecipherable in and of itself, like a single, unidentifiable piece of a mosaic or puzzle. On the contrary, the Jesus conveyed in and by each book of the New Testament is the whole Jesus, not merely a piece of him.

Another analogy might be helpful. When one looks at a large diamond, one sees the whole diamond. Yet at any moment in time a person can only view it from a particular perspective; in so doing, one see distinct facets of it. If one turns the diamond or moves to look at it from a different angle, the person still sees the same whole diamond, but different aspects of the diamond are now visible.

To illustrate, let us look closer at the portrayals of Jesus in the Synoptic Gospels. Recall that the first three gospels tell the story of Jesus' life in much the same way. If one reads of Jesus *only* in Matthew's Gospel, for example, the Jesus displayed there is not incomplete or insufficient. Rather, the reader is confronted with the whole and complete person of Jesus Christ. Certainly, particular facets of Jesus' person and work are highlighted when viewed from Matthew's perspective. Jesus is the Messiah, the promised anointed one of the Old Testament, illustrated by the genealogy that opens the gospel, as well as by the many Old Testament prophecies fulfilled by Jesus. Matthew also portrays Jesus as the Son of God. Looking at Jesus from Mark's perspective, one does not see as much of the Old Testament roots of Jesus' life and ministry. Yet Mark debates whether Jesus is the Son of God and emphatically asserts, along with Matthew, that he is. For Mark this conclusion is grasped only through the event of the cross. From Luke's perspective, the most distinctive facet of Jesus' ministry is that he is seen as the Savior of all.

The various descriptions of Jesus throughout the New Testament combine to tell us a great deal about who he is and what he has done. Yet the person and work of Christ involve even more than we can fathom or fully understand now. In recognition of this, St. Paul states: "For now we see in a mirror dimly, but then face to face. Now I know in part; then I shall know fully" (1 Corinthians 13:12). For example, many questions may remain about Jesus' nature as God, his role in creation, his earthly life between the ages of twelve and thirty, his present activity, his precise will for our lives, and the events of his return.

However, together the Scriptures do reveal a multifaceted portrait of one and the same Jesus. The many verbal images of him in the New Testament provide us with Christologies and a Christology. But that Christology and those Christologies, while not complete in every way, all combine to focus our attention on the other main point of the New Testament emphasized at the very beginning of this textbook. The New Testament's other overarching interest is *soteriological*. Its twenty-seven documents are clearly unified in proclaiming the message of salvation to us. Their focal point is the Jesus who has saved us by his birth, life, suffering, death, and resurrection. Together they answer those simple questions we asked in chapter one: "Who is Jesus?" and "What has he done?"

But the story of Jesus does not end with the New Testament. "So Christ, having been offered once to bear the sins of many, will appear a second time, not to deal with sin but to save those who are eagerly waiting for him" (Hebrews 9:28). Whatever we have learned about Jesus from reading the words of the New Testament will finally give way to visual learning. All our questions about Jesus Christ and the salvation he has won for us will ultimately be answered when these words from Revelation are fulfilled: "Behold, he is coming with the clouds, and every eye will see him" (Revelation 1:7). "When he appears," 1 John declares, "we shall see him as he is" (3:2). When we do see Jesus "face to face" (1 Corinthians 13:12), every knee will bow and "every tongue confess that Jesus Christ is Lord, to the glory of God the Father" (Philippians 2:11).

For Further Discussion

1. Describe your visual image of Jesus. Identify the sources(s) of it.

2. Discuss the point(s) made in this chapter by the following analogies:

- a hypothetical collection of portraits or sculptures of Jesus from the first century
- the pieces of a mosaic or jig-saw puzzle
- a multi-faceted diamond

3. Does the New Testament present you with a Christology, Christologies, or both? Explain your answer.

Glossary

Agape feast — a gathering for a common meal in which the Lord's Supper was shared.

Agape — one of several Greek words for "love"; emphasizes the self-sacrificial giving of God and God's people. Other Greek words for love are *eros* (sensual love), *philos* (love of friends), and *storge* (familial love); agape is able to permeate and influence all other loves.

Alpha and Omega — first and last letters of the Greek alphabet used as title for Jesus Christ in Revelation.

Amanuensis — the occupation of one who wrote documents.

Antichrist — "opposed to" or "in place of Christ"; used only by 1 John and in the plural in the New Testament; some equate this term with the "man of lawlessness" in 2 Thessalonians.

Antilegomena — "being spoken against"; refers to seven New Testament books whose place in the canon of the New Testament was questioned by some in the early church.

Antinomianism —"against the Law"; asserts that the Law is no longer valid or to be applied and obeyed in New Testament times.

Apocalyptic — a distinct literary genre using visions, symbolism, cosmic struggles and violent imagery to disclose what will happen at the end of time.

Apocrypha — "hidden"; fourteen book in the Septuagint but not in the Hebrew Bible; accepted as authoritative by most Christians except Protestants.

Apostles' Creed — Christian statement of faith developed from early third-century Roman creed used in baptismal rite; present form not set until centuries later.

Aramaic — the native language of most people in the Jesus' time in the Jewish homelands, derived from Hebrew.

Aretology — popular Roman stories if individuals born of divine and human parents who were known for their ability to perform miracles.

Ark of the Covenant — the gold-covered box which the Israelites made at Mount Sinai containing the tablets with 10 Commandments, jar of manna, and Aaron's staff; Ark led Israel through the wilderness and into the promised land; later placed in the Holy of Holies of Solomon's temple; lost prior to or during the destruction of Solomon's temple by the Babylonians in 586 B.C.

Asceticism — adoption of a rigorous way of life characterized by self denial as part of a spiritual discipline.

Astral fatalism — the belief that one's future is set by fate and that fate may be discerned at least partially by studying the stars (astrology).

Baptism — a ritual washing of purification in Jewish circles; in Christianity, a rite by which a person is joined with Jesus Christ and enters the Christian community.

Biblical theology — field of study identifying themes and a consistent theology that run throughout the Old and New Testaments.

Blasphemy — the charge leveled against Jesus by the religious authorities; technically, involves cursing or slandering the divine name or acting in such a way as to imply such defamation.

Book of Concord — the official statement of Lutheran doctrine, also known as the Lutheran Confessions; assembled into a book in 1580; includes the Augsburg Confession and Luther's Small and Large Catechisms; "concord" means harmony or agreement.

Catholic — as in "Catholic Epistles" refers to a subset of New Testament books a having a more universal address; also called the General Epistles; includes James, the Petrine and Johannine letters, and Jude.

Canon — from the Greek work for a reed used as a measuring stick; refers to the authoritative collection of texts in the Old and/or New Testament.

Christ — Greek word for an "anointed one"; translates the Hebrew "Messiah."

Christocentric — "Christ-centered"; Christ is the focal point or center of Scripture.

Christology — subset of Christian theology that attempt to answer the question, "Who is Jesus?"

Circular letter — a letter written to groups in different locations that was carried from place to place and read in those various locations (see Revelation 1:11).

Circumcision — cutting off the foreskin of the penis as a sign of God's covenant with Abraham in Genesis 17 and the promise given to Abraham and his seed/offspring.

Centurion — a Roman military officer in command of 100 men; the term could be used more generically for any lower level military officer.

Colony — a city in the Roman Empire established to exert Roman control in a region; sometimes populated by veteran legionnaires; considered a part of Rome itself.

Contextual — emphasizes the setting in which the New Testament documents were written and/or the setting to which they were addressed; includes such things as personal interaction, cultural factors, and geographical issues.

Covenantal nomism — term coined by E. P. Sanders asserting that first-century Judaism was dominated by the belief that Israelites got into God's covenant by his election and mercy; obedience to the Law was the required response for staying in the covenant; atonement was available for those who sinned through repentance and sacrifice.

Cross — the instrument of crucifixion used by the Romans again non-Roman insurrectionists; an instrument of humiliation and intimidation as well as execution, the cross came to be a symbol of Christian identification.

Curse — penalty God placed upon those who sin beginning in Genesis 3.

Deacon — from Greek *diakonos,* translated "minister" or "servant"; term later referred to a specific church official, but the role and functions are fairly undefined in New Testament times.

Defilement — a temporary state ritual impurity, making one ineligible to participate in temple or synagogue practices; examples that made on ritual impure include contact with blood, corpses, and unclean animals.

Decapolis — ten Graeco-Roman cites generally east and south of the Sea of Galilee that functioned as quasi-independent cultural outposts on the eastern fringe of the Roman Empire.

Decalogue — the "ten words" known popularly as the Ten Commandments.

Denarius — the standard coin of the Roman Empire; the wage paid to a common laborer for a day's work.

Diasopora — Greek word that means "scattering"; refers to the Jews who were scattered through the Roman Empire prior to and during the time of the New Testament.

***Didache* (or Teaching of the Twelve Apostles)** — a late first-century or early second-century Christian document; first part describes "the two ways" of life or death and serves as catechetical manual; part two includes instructions on baptism, the Lord's Supper, worship, and church leadership.

Discipleship — following Jesus; the lifestyle, actions, and words of a disciple.

Epiphany — "appearance" or "manifestation"; used for an even when God or God-like characteristics are visible; designation for the Christian festival commemorating the Magi who follow the star to Bethlehem.

Epistle — related to the Latin word for "letter"; a term used for New Testament letters.

Eschatology — "study of last things"; deals with events surrounding the return of Christ, the final judgment, and the end of this world.

Essene — holiness sect of Judaism who withdrew from social life during the Second Temple period out of frustration with Hasmonean squabbles over the priesthood; teachings are represented in the Dead Sea Scrolls.

Faith[fulness] — based on a Hebrew word which conveys steadfastness, loyalty, and fidelity; but also came to be used as the passive receiving of God's grace in Christ.

Fate — belief in antiquity that the course of one's life was set; fates were often considered cruel.

Feast of Booths — Jewish pilgrimage festival commemorating the wandering in the wilderness.

Fellowship — translation of Greek word *koinonia*; refers to the oneness of believers and the things which they share in common.

Firstfruits — term used in the Old Testament for the first part of a crop or fruit which was given to God as an offering; implies that much more is to follow.

Formal principle — the Bible is the form in which God reveals himself to us; Scripture is the sure and certain revelation of God.

Four Document Hypothesis — prominent critical reconstruction of the genesis of the Synoptic Gospels Matthew and Luke from Mark, Q, and M-source, and an L-source.

Fulfillment prophecy — a Matthean practice of citing Old Testament precedent for an event in the story of Jesus.

Genealogy — A selective list of ancestors meant to establish the honor of an individual.

Gentile — a non-Israelite or non-Jew; refers to all people not descended from the twelve tribes of Jacob/Israel.

Gnosticism — heretical view of God which came to full flowering in the second and third centuries A.D.; taught that salvation came by acquiring a secret knowledge (*gnosis* in Greek); viewed physical matter as evil; resulted either in ascetic withdrawal from the world or an overindulgence in it.

God-fearer — a Gentile or non-Jew drawn to the monotheism and/or ethical teaching of Judaism but who did not convert to Judaism.

Golgotha — the place of the skull where Jesus was crucified.

Gospel — from the Greek word for good news (*euangellion*); as a teaching, it speaks of God's grace, mercy and forgiveness which are ours in Jesus Christ; also used to refer to the first four books of the New Testament which are narrative accounts of Jesus' earthly life and ministry (lower case in this textbook).

Hellenistic — a word which refers to Greek culture including language, law, art, religion, games, and drama; spread around the Mediterranean world by the conquests of Alexander the Great in the fourth century B.C.; by and large adopted throughout the Roman Empire.

Hellenistic Judaism — a merging of Greek thought with Old Testament/Jewish beliefs; Philo of Alexandria (c. 20 B.C.–A.D. 50) is a prominent example.

Hellenization — the process of accommodation to Hellenistic culture; generally yielded a hybrid of native and Hellenic ways.

Hermeneutics — a Greek work for interpretation and translation; functions as a technical term for principles used to understand and apply a text.

Homologoumena — twenty New Testament writings consistently affirmed as biblical through the processes of canonization.

Hosanna — Hebrew for "Pray, Save (us)!"

Incarnation — "enfleshment"; term to describe God becoming human in the person of Jesus.

Immanuel — a name for Jesus from the birth narrative in Matthew (1:23) meaning "God is with us"; may also come into English as "Emmanuel."

Inspiration — describes how the Holy Spirit breathed out the Scriptures so that words written by humans are the Word of God (2 Timothy 3:16).

Judaizers — term for those who impose the Old Testament or Jewish laws on New Testament believers; term is pejorative and unfortunate, since the majority of New Testament Christians were Jewish.

Justification — a legal or forensic term for being declared righteous; being put in a right relationship with God; a favorite metaphor of St. Paul.

Kingdom of heaven/God — the imminent reign of God announced by the preaching of John the Baptist and Jesus of Nazareth; "heaven" is sometimes used for Jewish readers in place of "God" so as not to offend Jewish sensibilities about speaking the name of God.

***Koine* —** the Greek word for common; refers to the style of Greek that was used throughout the Roman Empire in the first century; New Testament is written in this form of Greek.

Law and Gospel — distinctive Lutheran terminology for an understanding of what God speaks in the Bible. The Law is good and holy; it reveals God"s will for how one should live. It commands and makes demands and, as a result, provokes, identifies, and condemns sin. "Gospel" comes from the Greek word for good news (*euangelion*). It speaks of God's grace, mercy, and forgiveness given through faith in Jesus Christ.

Legalism — asserts that the law must still be imposed and obeyed; normally in relation to one's salvation.

Legion — major component of the Roman army; recruited from Roman citizenry; raised and disbanded as needed; consisted for four to six thousand men plus auxiliaries; twenty-five to thirty-five legions served the empire at one time.

Libertinism — the belief that New Testament believers are liberated from the Law and, therefore, free to live however they want.

Logos — the "word," key term in the prologue of the Fourth Gospel.

Lutheran Confessions — see Book of Concord

Man of lawlessness — a figure Paul says will arise along with an apostasy or turning away from God before the return of Christ.

Material remains — remains of ancient cultures and life exposed by the science of archaeology.

Messiah — derives from Hebrew for "anointed one," a designation for a king in the line of David; used for the kingly deliverer expected by the Jewish people; equivalent to the Greek *christos*.

Messianic secret — a theme in Mark's Gospel, particularly Jesus' repeated injunctions to those he heals to keep quiet about his mighty deeds.

Mikveh (pl. mikva'ot) — a stepped pool for Jewish ritual purification rites.

Mishnah — the oral Law commenting on the Torah that was put into writing around A.D. 200.

Mystery religion — secretive religious practice in the Roman period by which practitioners were joined to the life of the god and in some way reborn.

Narrative Christology — Answers the Christological question through a selective presentation of stories about Jesus.

Natural knowledge of God — doctrinal term for those things about God revealed in creation; also applied to the sense of right and wrong which God has placed in all people's hearts.

Norm — a rule or standard by which other things are judged; Scripture norms what we believe and teach about God.

Now/not yet — phrase used to describe elements of New Testament theology which are now already present and experienced by believers but which are yet to be fully realized. For example, Christ has come and ushered in the kingdom. Yet Christ will come again and bring it to complete fulfillment.

Offspring/seed — related to the promise to Abraham and his offspring.

Once saved, always saved — the teaching that if people are true believers, they will not and cannot fall away from the faith.

Paraclete — the "comforter"; name for the Holy Spirit in the Fourth Gospel; also used for Jesus in the Johannine epistles.

Parable — stories told by Jesus using common metaphors to describe what "the kingdom of God is like."

Parousia — means "presence" or "appearing"; drawn from its use of the arrival of a Roman emperor or other dignitary, it came to be a technical term for the second coming of Christ.

Passover — Jewish pilgrimage festival at the beginning of the wheat harvest commemorating the Exodus from Egypt.

Pastoral Epistles — 1 Timothy, Titus, and 2 Timothy.

Pax Romana — "the peace of Rome"; used to describe the stability, law, and order of the Roman Empire from the time when Augustus (Octavian) secured control of the empire in 31 B.C.

Pentateuch — the first five book of the Hebrew Bible (Genesis, Exodus, Leviticus, Number, Deuteronomy); see Torah.

Pharisee — a Jewish sect that emphasized strict observance of the Torah, especially its purity regulations.

Plenary (inspiration) — all of the Scriptures are from God, not just certain sections or teachings.

Predestination — term the New Testament uses to assure believers that God had chosen them before time began.

Priesthood of all believers — derived from 1 Peter to counter the belief that some Christians hold superior standing before God by virtue of their service as priests or as people dedicated a religious life apart from society and family; affirms that all Christians function in a priestly way in whatever service they offer.

Prison Epistles — the four letters of Paul in which he identifies himself as a prisoner (Ephesians, Philippians, Colossians and Philemon).

Prophecy — normally misunderstood simply in terms of predicting the future, the biblical term means to speak God's word and will about the past, present, or the future; emphasis is on God's work in the past and on applying his will to the present situation.

Propitiation — the gift of and place where Jesus by his death on the cross appeases the wrath of God.

Proselyte — a Gentile who has undergone ritual of conversion to become a Jew, including circumcision.

Pseudepigrapha — works ascribed to important biblical figures of the past, such as Enoch, Noah, Moses, or Isaiah, but not written by them; writings were composed during a period from 200 B.C to A.D. 200, but not part of the Bible or the Apocrypha.

Pseudonymity — an ancient practice where an author adopts the figure of some famous person of the past (e.g. Enoch, Noah) and writes an account of events which happened to that person.

Q source — a supposed document containing sayings of Jesus that was used as a source by the writers of Matthew and Luke. The Q refers to the German word *Quelle* meaning "source."

Rabbi — a "teacher" in the Jewish religious tradition, at times itinerant, not associated in antiquity with a synagogue.

Rapture — to "grasp" or "seize"; a technical term which some Christians use to assert that Jesus will secretly return and rapture up believers.

Realized eschatology — Johannine emphasis on the present experience of the promises of God to be fulfilled at the end of time.

Redeem — to "purchase" or "buy back"; a metaphor from the language of commerce and, particularly, slavery.

Religio licita — literally, "legal religion"; denotes religions officially recognized by the Roman Empire that could be openly practiced; Julius Caesar made Judaism a *religio licita*.

Roman citizen — a special status in the Empire enjoyed by citizens of Rome and others to whom it was granted or by whom it was purchased.

Sabbath — the sixth day; from sundown on Friday to sundown on Saturday.

Sadducee — Jewish sect controlling the priesthood and accepting only the Torah as authoritative.

Samaritan — from the central hill country between Judea and Galilee; on the margins of Judaism with its own temple and version of the Pentateuch.

Sanctification — related to the word for "holiness"; in a narrow sense describes what God does to make us holy in Christ; in a broader sense describes the ways in which believers are called to live in response to God's action.

Sanhedrin — a occasional gathering of Judean elites affirming decisions in capital cases.

Second Temple period — broadly from the dedication of the second temple (514 B.C.) to its destruction (A.D. 70); often the focus is on the later portion of time from Hasmonean independence (142 B.C.) to the temple's destruction.

Septuagint — the Greek translation of the Hebrew Bible done in Egypt c. 200 B.C. supposedly by seventy scholars; it was the Bible of early Gentile Christianity.

Sermon on the Mount — a Matthean collection of the teachings of Jesus.

Shema — "Listen!"; first Hebrew word in Deuteronomy 6:4, "Hear, O Israel: The LORD our God, the LORD is one"; eventually became a title for that foundational statement of the Old Testament faith.

Sign — seven mighty deeds of Jesus in the Fourth Gospel, written that "you might believe."

Sinless perfectionism — the teaching that believers, by indwelling and power of the Holy Spirit, are able to achieve moral perfection or holiness here in this life.

Son of God — the central identification of Jesus in Mark's Gospel; however, no human character so recognizes Jesus until he has been crucified; other writers also employ this phrase to speak of the divine nature of Jesus.

Son of Man — euphemism for a human being in the Old Testament, especially the book of Ezekiel; in Daniel, one "like a son of man" is a divinely appointed future ruler of Israel; in the Pseudepigrapha, the title is used for one who serves as the agent of God at the time of judgment; Jesus uses the title as a self-designation.

Soteriological — related to salvation; the study or teachings about salvation.

Suffering Servant — "servant" is used as a technical term in parts Isaiah called "the Servant Songs"; at times "Servant" refers to the whole nation of Israel, but the Suffering Servant more narrowly describes an individual who suffers to atone for the sins of the nations.

Synagogue — an assembly of at least ten men; dedicated buildings for such assemblies came into prominence after the destruction of the temple.

Synoptic — literally "with one perspective"; used to describe the common story line and oft-times verbal agreement in the first three gospels.

Talmud — a record of rabbinic teaching comprised of the Mishnah and the Gemara.

Ten Commandments — the "Ten Words" given on Mount Sinai in Exodus 20:1-17; Decalogue; various traditions number the ten in different ways.

Textual criticism — the study that deals with discrepancies between copies of New Testament texts.

Theodicy — resolving the problem of evil by showing that God is all-powerful and just, despite evil's existence.

Theophany — an appearance of God to a person in a form clearly recognized as divine.

Tongues — the Greek term *glossa* can refer to the body part, but also came to describe languages (*glossolalia*); normally in another human language, but 1 Corinthians 14 uses the term to describe a spirit or prayer language.

Torah — Hebrew word for the five books of Moses, Genesis through Deuteronomy at the beginning of the Old Testament or Hebrew Bible; from the Hebrew word for "instruction" or "revelation" and often mistranslated as "Law."

Tradition of the elders — an oral tradition meant to help people apply the teachings of the Torah to their daily lives.

Transfiguration — the story of a temporary change in Jesus' appearance to convey his heavenly glory, witnessed by Peter, James, and John; Moses and Elijah appear talking with Jesus; a heavenly voice affirmed Jesus as "my Son."

Transmission — the process by which the texts of the New Testament were copied and handed down from generation to generation.

Two covenant theory — a position that there are two different covenants or paths established by God for access into a relationship with him as his people; asserts that Israel is God's chosen people by virtue of physical descent from Abraham; Jesus opens up a separate way for Gentiles to be included.

Type — an Old Testament person, office, practice, or event which foreshadows a fulfillment in Jesus; fulfillment is called an Anti-type.

Variant reading — a reading which differs from another copy of the same text.

Verbal inspiration — the actual "words" (*verba* in Latin) are from the Holy Spirit, not merely the thoughts or ideas.

Via Egnatia — major Roman highway running from the Adriatic to the Bosporus across the Roman provinces of Illyria, Macedonia, and Thrace.

Wisdom — Hebrew term for practical insights into living a godly, day-to-day life; became more of an abstract, philosophical concept about the deeper meaning of life in the Greek world.

Yahweh — the personal name by which the God of the Old Testament identifies himself; explicitly revealed to Moses at the burning bush.

Zealots — political revolutionaries opposed to Hellenization and Roman occupation; led the revolt against Rome.